V. Lyle Hoffman

AROUND THEATRES

From a Portrait by Will Rothenstein, 1897

AROUND
THEATRES

MAX
BEERBOHM

RUPERT HART-DAVIS
36 Soho Square, London, W1
1953

This book was first published in two volumes as part of a limited edition of Max Beerbohm's works in 1924. A two-volume edition was published in New York in 1930. The book has not since been reprinted.

MADE AND PRINTED IN GREAT BRITAIN BY
WILLIAM CLOWES AND SONS, LIMITED, LONDON AND BECCLES

A NOTE TO THE READER

It might seem that in a new edition of a book published so very many years ago some sort of preface by the author would not be amiss. But if you will read my Epistle Dedicatory to Edward Gordon Craig (1924), and my initial article (1898), and my valedictory one (1910), you will not wonder at my feeling that I have left nothing to be said—by *me*—about myself as dramatic critic. You, on the other hand, may find quite a lot to say about me in that rôle, and if you find little or nothing to say in favour of me I shall not blame you (except perhaps in my own heart) so long as you give me credit for having done, as I do claim to have, my best.

M. B.

1953

EPISTLE DEDICATORY

to

Edward Gordon Craig

My dear Ted,—

Will you accept the dedication of a book of mine? Don't bother to write. Just give a verbal answer, Yes or No, to the bearer of this.

As your house is within a stone's throw of mine, you may wonder, "Why does he write?—why doesn't he come round and ask me by word of mouth?" My reason is that it is difficult for so good-natured a fellow as you to refuse anything to a friend pleading *in propria persona*. My faltering voice, my appealing gaze, would move you to say Yes, and have done with it. "Perhaps," you rejoin; "but why such a huge *long* letter? My time is precious. Must I read it *all*?" No; you need not do that. You need only skim through it. I merely want you to know what manner of book it is, before you make your decision. And I can't describe it in two words.

The very fact that a book needs a description by its author is a bad sign. I agree with you there. A book ought to be able to stand by itself. I think my other books do so. But I have my doubts about this one.

No doubt I have mentioned to you more than once, in the vein of maudlin reminiscence, that I was at one time a dramatic critic; but I don't think you have ever said that you had read any of my articles. There the articles were, nevertheless, in "The Saturday Review," week by week. And there were a great many of them. I went on for twelve whole years. On and on I went, doggedly, from the age of twenty-five to the age of thirty-seven. It seems incredible; but it is a fact. And it is also a fact that in the fourteen years that have elapsed since I turned aside from that hard straight stony path, many people have told me that I ought to make a selection from those old articles—make a book of them. I used to say I would think of it; but I didn't really mean to think of it: the idea seemed to me a trifle ghastly. I have a reverence for literature. For journalism I have merely a kind regard. I had never scamped my job on "The Saturday"; but I shrank from the notion of burrowing down among those conscientious old efforts and bringing up some of them to be read in broad daylight, by the present generation, between the covers of a book. However, when it was arranged that there should be a limited edition of my "works," I agreed that a volume or two of my dramatic criticism might be slipped into it. One *might* offer to just a few well-disposed people what one would tenderly withhold from the judgment of the vast cold world.

Should there be one volume or two? That was among the many questions that I asked myself while I groped through the purlieus of my hideous past. In course of time I decided (let me break the news to you gently) on the double measure. It isn't merely one volume that I wish to gild by connexion with your name; it's two. But you need only say No once.

Had my form been very uneven in those old weekly screeds, the favour that I now ask of you would be half its actual size. Had I sometimes written trash, and at other times deserved favourable comparison with Lessing, I could have made one chaste volume of my best things. "Behold," I could have said, "in this small compass, the fine fruit of twelve years' work!" But, as it is, if I were to offer only a little of my best, any one reading it would exclaim, "Is *this* all he has to show for all that labour?" Which would be rather unfair to me. For among what I had suppressed there would be quite as much of my best as in what I had revealed.

The general evenness of my work for "The Saturday"—my seldom-sinking and alas-never-soaring way—has made the task of selection a hard one. The comparative importance or unimportance of the theme of this and that article was no guide to me. I had decided that I must choose the articles as in themselves (such as they were) they were. Whether the play I had criticised were by Shakespeare or by Mr. Tomkins must not matter to me. *I* was what I must bear in mind. And I fear I had always preferred Mr. Tomkins, as a theme, to Shakespeare. I felt more at home with him, and wrote better about him. That is a drawback of the satiric temperament; and I deplore it. But I have had to take my articles as I found them. And if in the two forthcoming volumes the name of Tomkins is mentioned overmuch, I can't help it. The defect is inherent in me. My readers (among whom you will not be one) must take me as I am, at what I suppose to be my best—or my least bad; and I even crave their sympathy for me in all the pains I have taken to judge, among five hundred articles or so, where my least bad came in.

What is in these volumes is just as it was aforetime in "The Saturday," save that here and there I have corrected a slip in grammar or a misprint, and have often deleted at the end of an article some rather perfunctory compliments or reproofs to the performers of the play I had written about—or, as mostly happened, the play I had taken as a peg to hang some general disquisition on. Needless to say that with many of the things I said about life and art and manners and morals and what-not I entirely disagree now. I should feel sad if my mind hadn't developed at all in later years. It certainly was developing in the course of my twelve years' bondage to dramatic criticism. If ever you do dip into the books, I advise you to start at about the year 1901. So as not to offend my earlier self by leaving it unrepresented, I have begun at the year 1898. But I do think I improved as I went on.

One thing I never could, from first to last, make up my mind about; and that thing was the most salient phenomenon "around theatres" in my day: "G. B. S." Did I love his genius or hate it? You, of course, survey it from the firm rock of your ideals. I wish I had had a rock of some sort. I went wavering hither and thither in the strangest fashion, now frankly indignant, now full of enthusiasm, now piling reservation on reservation, and then again frankly indignant. My vicissitudes in the matter of G. B. S. were lamentable. But they amuse me very much. The satiric temperament again.

As for *your* genius, I've never had any misgivings about that. Would that I could have expressed my admiration worthily! I've found only one article of mine about you that isn't far below the mark. That is one of the reasons why I should like to dedicate these two volumes to you. May I? Don't be influenced by my wish. Make your decision according to your own feelings. But for Heaven's sake *make* it, my dear Ted. The bearer waits.

Your affectionate old friend and neighbour,

Max Beerbohm.

Villino Chiaro, Rapallo.   *1924.*

CONTENTS

CONTENTS

CONTENTS

CONTENTS

CONTENTS

CONTENTS

WHY I OUGHT NOT TO HAVE BECOME A DRAMATIC CRITIC

May 28, 1898

Every one delighted in G. B. S. Even they who were his targets snatched an awful joy in the illicit study of his writings, and will have heaved a sigh, not wholly of relief, at the news of his resignation. I am disappointed by that stroke of fate which has eclipsed the gaiety of green-rooms. Of all his readers none mourns G. B. S. more inconsolably than I, his pious successor. For, with all his faults—grave though they are and not to be counted on the fingers of one hand—he is, I think, by far the most brilliant and remarkable journalist in London, and, in succeeding him, I labour not merely under my own modesty, but also under the impatience of the public before me. I am in the predicament of the minor music-hall artist sent on as an "extra-turn," tremulously facing the prolonged thunder of calls for the "star" who has just sung. A pathetic smile, a little gesture of appeal—and the thunder, still rumbling round the distant gallery, gradually subsides. My voice is audible at length. But it is not much of a voice. My song, also, is not much of a song.

I will not raise in my readers hopes which I cannot realise for them. It is best to be quite frank. Frankly, I have none of that instinctive love for the theatre which is the first step towards good criticism of drama. I am not fond of the theatre. Dramatic art interests and moves me less than any of the other arts. I am happy among pictures, and, being a constant intruder into studios, have learnt enough to know that I know nothing whatever about painting—knowledge which, had I taken to what is called "art-criticism," would have set me head-and-shoulders above the great majority of my colleagues. Of music I have a genuine, though quite unenlightened, love. Literature I love best of all, and I have some knowledge of its technicalities. I can talk intelligently about it. I have my little theories about it. But in drama I take, unfortunately, neither emotional nor intellectual pleasure. I am innocent of any theories on the subject. I shall have to vamp up my first principles as I go along, and they will probably be all wrong and all dull. For I have never even acquired any lore in this kind of criticism. I could not test a theory nor quote a line of Hazlitt, Lamb, Lewes and the rest, whose essays in dramatic criticism I have never read. I have, however, a fragmentary recollection of Aristotle's fragment on the drama, which I read for "Mods." The examiners, if I remember rightly, marked my paper "gamma-minus-query"—a clear proof that even in my adolescence I was not stage-struck. Ignorance of the ideas expressed by previous critics is not, I admit, in itself a grave defect. It may even be an advantage, as making cerebration compulsory, and so giving freshness to one's style. Likewise, I can imagine that a man who had never been in a theatre might, were he suddenly sent forth as a dramatic critic, be able to write really charming and surprising and instructive things about the stage. But my readers must not look for any freshness or cerebration from me. I could find my way blindfold about every theatre in the metropolis, and could recite backwards most of the successful plays that have been produced in the last ten years. Though I have no theoretic knowledge of the drama, I am a rich mine of theatrical gossip, and I know (and do not dispute) all the current judgments on actor Tom, playwright Dick, and stage-manager Harry. Out of my very cradle I stepped upon the fringe of the theatrical world, and my familiarity with the theatre has been a matter of circumstance rather than of choice. I remember being really bored by a play on the evening of my tenth birthday. That a visit to the theatre can be regarded, as it is regarded by some men to their dying day, as a treat, has always bewildered and baffled my imagination. In the whole world, no phenomenon is so inexplicable to me as a queue of men and women at a pit-door. I am not, fortunately, a person of expensive habits, but I confess that I have never regarded any theatre as much more than the conclusion to a dinner or the prelude to a supper. It appals me to think that in future I shall be obliged to keep my attention fixed, never taking my eyes from the stage except to make a note upon my cuff. I, who have never left a theatre with any definite impression of pleasure or displeasure, am curious to know how on earth I am going to fill so much as half a column of this paper, week by

2

week, with my impressions. My self-respect and my ignorance
of bygone formulæ of drama will prevent me from the otherwise
easy task of being an academic critic. I shall not be able to
branch off, like G. B. S., into discussions of ethical, theological or
political questions, for on such questions I am singularly ill-
informed. I have not that well-considered attitude towards life
which gave a kind of unity to G. B. S.'s worst inconsistencies
about art. In a word, I don't quite know what to do with the
torch that G. B. S. has handed to me.

Of the literary quality in any play, I shall perhaps be able to say
something, but I shall be hopelessly out of my depth in criticising
the play itself. The mere notion of criticising the players simply
terrifies me, not because I know (as, indeed, I do) nothing about
the art of acting, but because I have the pleasure of personal
acquaintance with so many players. One well-known player and
manager is my near relative. Who will not smile if I praise him?
How could I possibly disparage him? Will it not be hard for me
to praise his rivals? If I do anything but praise them, what will
become of the purity of the Press? Most of the elder actors have
patted me on the head and given me sixpence when I was "only *so*
high." Even if, with an air of incorruptibility, I now return them
their sixpences, they will yet expect me to pat *them* on the head in
the "Saturday Review." Many of the younger actors were at
school with me. They will expect me to criticise them as an old
playmate should. With most of the others I have, at least, a nodding acquaintance. To one of them I had nodded so often that,
only the other day, we wrote a play together—a play which, by the
way, no manager will now be able to accept, lest he be thought
venal. How can I criticise the acting of a collaborator? If I do
not care for one of his impersonations, how can I do aught but
write an eulogy in these columns and put my true opinion into a
sealed envelope to be opened after my decease and immediately
destroyed? My whole position is unfortunate. I have the satiric
temperament: when I am laughing at any one I am generally
rather amusing, but when I am praising any one, I am always
deadly dull. Now, such is the weakness of my character that I
cannot say in print anything against a personal acquaintance. I
think I have met all the habitual playwrights in my time. Therefore, in criticising an average production, I shall be obliged to

confine myself to slating such members of the cast as I have never met. If they have acted well, this will undoubtedly be hard on them. Even if they have not acted well—and I for one shall not know whether they have or not—their punishment will be out of all due proportion. The only advice I can offer them, meanwhile, is that they should make haste and meet me.

It has struck me, in reading this article, that I have not given my readers much hope of edification. Let them console themselves with the reflection that they are less to be pitied than I am. I shall miss G. B. S. quite as much as they will, and they will not be compelled to read the articles which I *shall* be compelled to write. This absurd post which I have accepted will interfere with my freedom in life, and is quite likely to spoil and exhaust such talent as I might otherwise be exercising in literary art. However, I will not complain. The Editor of this paper has come to me as Romeo came to the apothecary, and what he wants I give him for the apothecary's reason. I daresay that there are many callings more uncomfortable and dispiriting than that of dramatic critic. To be a porter on the Underground Railway must, I have often thought, be very terrible. Whenever I feel myself sinking under the stress of my labours, I shall say to myself, "I am not a porter on the Underground Railway."

"CYRANO DE BERGERAC"

July 9, 1898

The tricolour floats over the Lyceum, and the critics are debating, with such animation as they can muster (at the fag-end of an arduous season) for a play written in a language to which they secretly prefer their own, whether "Cyrano" be a classic. Paris has declared it to be a classic, and, international courtesy apart, July is not the month for iconoclasm. And so the general tendency is to accept "Cyrano" in the spirit in which it has been offered to us. I myself go with that tendency. Even if I could, I would not whisk from the brow of M. Rostand, the talented boy-

4

playwright, the laurels which Paris has so reverently imposed on it. For, even if "Cyrano" be not a classic, it is at least a wonderfully ingenious counterfeit of one, likely to deceive experts far more knowing than I am. M. Rostand is not a great original genius like (for example) M. Maeterlinck. He comes to us with no marvellous revelation, but he is a gifted, adroit artist, who does with freshness and great force things that have been done before; and he is, at least, a monstrous fine fellow. His literary instinct is almost as remarkable as his instinct for the *technique*—the *pyrotechnique*—of the theatre, insomuch that I can read "Cyrano" almost as often, with almost as much pleasure, as I could see it played. Personally, I like the Byzantine manner in literature better than any other, and M. Rostand is nothing if not Byzantine: his lines are loaded and encrusted with elaborate phrases and curious conceits, which are most fascinating to any one who, like me, cares for such things. Yet, strange as it seems, none of these lines is amiss in the theatre. All the speeches blow in gusts of rhetoric straight over the footlights into the very lungs of the audience. Indeed, there is this unusual feature in M. Rostand's talent, that he combines with all the verbal preciosity of extreme youth the romantic ardour and technical accomplishment of middle-age. Hence the comparative coldness with which he is regarded in Paris by *les jeunes*, who naturally do not like to scratch Mallarmé and find Sardou. Not the debased Sardou himself has the dramaturgic touch more absolutely than has M. Rostand. But M. Rostand is not, like M. Sardou, a mere set of fingers with the theatre at the tips of them. .On the contrary, he is a brain and a heart and all sorts of good things which atone for—or, rather, justify—the fact that "Cyrano" is of the stage stagey. It is rather silly to chide M. Rostand for creating a character and situations which are unreal if one examine them from a non-romantic standpoint. It is silly to insist, as one or two critics have insisted, that Cyrano was a fool and a blackguard, in that he entrapped the lady of his heart into marriage with a vapid impostor. The important and obvious point is that Cyrano, as created by M. Rostand, is a splendid hero of romance. If you have any sensibility to romance, you admire him so immensely as to be sure that whatever he may have done was for the best. All the characters and all the incidents in the play have been devised for the glorification of Cyrano, and are but, as who should say, so many rays of lime-light converging upon him alone. And that is as it should be. The romantic play which survives the pressure of time is always that which contains some one central figure, to which everything is subordinate—a one-part play, in other words. The part of Cyrano is one which, unless I am much mistaken, the great French actor in every future generation will desire to play. Cyrano will soon crop up in opera and in ballet. Cyrano is, in fact, as inevitably a fixture in romance as Don Quixote or Don Juan, Punch or Pierrot. Like them, he will never be out of date. But prophecy is dangerous? Of course it is. That is the whole secret of its fascination. Besides, I have a certain amount of reason in prophesying on this point. Realistic figures perish necessarily with the generation in which they were created, and their place is taken by figures typical of the generation which supervenes. But romantic figures belong to no period, and time does not dissolve them. Already Ibsen is rather out of date—even Mr. Archer has washed his hands of Ibsen—while the elder Dumas is still thoroughly in touch with the times. Cyrano will survive because he is practically a new type in drama. I know that the motives of self-sacrifice-in-love and of beauty-adored-by-a-grotesque are as old, and as effective, as the hills, and have been used in literature again and again. I know that self-sacrifice is the motive of most successful plays. But, so far as I know, beauty-adored-by-a-grotesque has never been used with the grotesque as stage-hero. At any rate it has never been used so finely and so tenderly as by M. Rostand, whose hideous swashbuckler with the heart of gold and the talent for improvising witty or beautiful verses—Caliban + Tartarin + Sir Galahad + Theodore Hook was the amazing recipe for his concoction—is far too novel, I think, and too convincing, and too attractive, not to be permanent. Whether, in the meantime, Cyrano's soul has, as M. Rostand gracefully declares, passed into "vous, Coquelin," I am not quite sure. I should say that some of it—the comic, which is, perhaps, the greater part of it—has done so. But I am afraid that the tragic part is still floating somewhere, unembodied. Perhaps the two parts will never be embodied together in the same actor. Certainly, the comic part will never have a better billet than its first.

I have said that the play is unlikely to suffer under the lapse of

6

time. But though it has no special place in time, in space it has its own special place. It is a work charged with its author's nationality, and only the compatriots of its author can to the full appreciate it. Much of its subtlety and beauty must necessarily be lost upon us others. To translate it into English were a terrible imposition to set any one, and not even the worst offender in literature deserves such a punishment. To adapt it were harder than all the seven labours of Hercules rolled into one, and would tax the guile and strength of even Mr. Louis Parker. The characters in the "Chemineau" had no particular racial characteristics, and their transportation to Dorsetshire did them no harm. But there is no part of England which corresponds at all to the Midi. An adapter of "Cyrano" might lay the scene in Cornwall, call the play "Then shall Cyrano die?" and write in a sixth act with a chorus of fifty thousand Cornishmen bent on knowing the reason why, or he might lay it in any of the other characteristic counties of England, but I should not like to answer for the consequences. However, the play will of course be translated as it stands. And, meanwhile, no one should neglect this opportunity of seeing the original production. There is so much action in the piece, and the plot itself is so simple, that even those who know no French at all can enjoy it. And the whole setting of the piece is most delightful. I was surprised on the first night to see how excellent was the stage management. Except a pair of restive and absurd horses, there was no hitch, despite the difference of the Lyceum and the Porte Saint Martin. Why, by the way, are real horses allowed on the stage, where their hoofs fall with a series of dull thuds which entirely destroy illusion? Cardboard horses would be far less of a nuisance and far more convincing. However, that is a detail. I wish all my readers to see "Cyrano." It may not be the masterpiece I think it, but at any rate it is one's money's-worth. The stalls are fifteen shillings a-piece, but there are five acts, and all the five are fairly long, and each of them is well worth three shillings. Even if one does not like the play, it will be something, hereafter, to be able to bore one's grandchildren by telling them about Coquelin as Cyrano.

"MACBETH"

October 1, 1898

Shakespeare had his short-comings. Love of him does not blind me to his limitations and his faults of excess. But, after all, the man is dead, and I do not wish to emulate that captious and rancorous spirit—inflamed, as it often seemed to me, by an almost personal animosity—in which my predecessor persecuted him beyond the grave. *Nil de mortuis nisi bonum*, say I : else, what is to become of the classics? In that they were directed against one who could not defend himself, I regarded Mr. Shaw's attacks as cowardly; in that Mr. Shaw was a dramatist himself, I regarded them as suspect. Yet would I have heartily approved of them, had I imagined that they would induce managers not to revive certain of Shakespeare's plays quite so frequently. But I have just said that defamation of the dead will tend to destroy the classics. And so it may, if it be used discreetly. And if it do, so much the better for Shakespeare. When a play has become a classic in drama, it ceases to be a play. It may become a classic in literature without any detriment to itself, but, when it becomes also, like "Hamlet" or "Romeo and Juliet" or "Macbeth," a classic in drama, all, if I may be allowed to say so, is up with it. One of the reasons for the recent success of "Julius Cæsar" was that so few persons had ever seen "Julius Cæsar" acted. The characters and the situations were moving and impressive, were, in a word, dramatic, because, not having seen them more times than one would care to count, one did not know them all by heart; one saw the play as a play and so derived æsthetic pleasure from it. Now that the dramatic qualities of "Julius Cæsar" have been demonstrated, it will be revived often in various theatres. Seeing how good are the parts of Antony, Brutus and Cassius, eminent actors will always be seizing an opportunity to play them. The thing will become a classic in drama, and one will be able to regard it only as a vehicle for acting. One will be as deadly familiar with the forum-scene as with the screen-scene in "The School for Scandal," or the balcony-scene in "Romeo and Juliet." All its dramatic savour will have been lost. Its interest will be merely

8

histrionic:—"Is Mr. * so powerful as **?—you never saw **? Ah, what a performance! Not so subtle as ***'s perhaps—but oh! the way he said 'Was this ambition?' He just put his hand in his toga and—why, * holds his hand straight in front of him— misses the whole point of it! For my own part, I always thought that, in some respects, ****'s idea—" . . . Nothing could be drearier than this kind of comparative criticism; yet a classic play makes it quite inevitable. The play is dead. The stage is crowded with ghosts. Every head in the auditorium is a heavy casket of reminiscence. Play they never so wisely, the players cannot lay those circumambient ghosts nor charm those well-packed caskets to emptiness. "Hamlet" and "Romeo" and "Macbeth" can be revived, but not in the literal sense of the word: live again they do not, nor will they ever do so, unless all managers —metropolitan, suburban and provincial—enter into a solemn compact not to revive them for a period of (say) thirty years. Give us but time to forget them and their interpreters, and then they will once more be plays. At present they are but so many parts and so many scenes, so many tests and traps for eminent mimes. For the sake of those mimes no less than for the sake of Shakespeare, let all managers forthwith enter into the compact which I have suggested.

Of all Shakespeare's plays, "Macbeth" is, perhaps, the most often enacted. It is the only one that contains two great parts, each of which, susceptible of many interpretations, can be equally well fitted to the temperaments and methods of various mimes. According to Aubrey the play was first acted in 1606, at Hampton Court, in the presence of King James. It is stated that Hal Berridge, the youth who was to have acted the part of Lady Macbeth, "fell sudden sicke of a pleurisie, wherefor Master Shakespeare himself did enacte in his stead." One wishes that Aubrey had given some account of the poet's impersonation. It would be amusing to know Shakespeare's own view of the part— more amusing, however, than valuable, for the actor is the interpreter of the dramatist, and the creative artist is always the least competent interpreter of his own work; besides, as I have said, there can be no final or binding interpretation of so complex a part as Lady Macbeth. Different actresses will always act the part in their different ways, and every way will have its champions among the critics, and every champion will have right on his side. Meanwhile, I find the Macbeth controversy rather tedious. Most critics of the latest production have been talking non-sense about the *Zeitgeist* and about neurotic subtlety and Pre-Raphaelitism and all the rest of it, as though the play had hitherto been acted only in the blood-and-thunder convention of Mrs. Siddons. Mere fallacy! We may be sure that "the gentle poet-philosopher" himself acted in much the same way as Mrs. Patrick Campbell or, for that matter, Miss Ellen Terry. In Pepys' diary, too, there is certain evidence that Mrs. Knipp's famous impersonation was of much the same kind as that which our critics suppose to be a strange phenomenon of 1898. "Thence to the Cockpitt Theatre," writes Pepys in the autumn of 1667, "to witness my dearest Mrs Knipp in the Tragedie of Macbeth, than which as I did this day say to Mr Killigrew I do know no play more diverting nor more worthie to the eye. Did secure a prime place in the pitt, whereof I was glad, being neare under my Ladie Dorset and her good husband. The latter did twice salute me with effusion, and I was pleased to note that those around me perceived this. Methought Mrs Knipp did never play so fine, specially in the matter of the two daggers, yet without brawl or overmuch tragick gesture, the which is most wearisome, as though an actress do care more to affright us than to be approved. She was most comickal and natural when she walks forth sleeping (the which I can testify, for Mrs Pepys also walks sleeping at some times), and did most ingeniously mimick the manner of women who walk thus." Obviously, then, the critics are wrong in regarding Mrs. Camp-bell's performance as something peculiar to the spirit of this generation. In the sleep-walking scene, Mrs. Campbell was not "comickal," but she was very "natural," and throughout the play she made her appeal to the sense of beauty and to the intellect rather than to the sense of terror. Mr. Forbes Robertson acted in a similar way. Both took the line laid down for them by their natural method. I thought that both performances were very beautiful. It does not matter in what method Macbeth and Lady Macbeth be played, so long as they be both played well in the same method. A violent Lady Macbeth and a gentle Macbeth, or *vice versâ*, would be a nuisance. Mrs. Campbell and Mr. Forbes Robertson act in perfect harmony. Mr. Taber is most admirable as Macduff. Indeed, the whole production is a great success. I trust that it will be the latest production of "Macbeth" for many years to come.

AT THE TIVOLI

December 3, 1898

A lady of heroic proportions, accoutred as a life-guardsman, strode upon the stage just as I was edging my way to my seat. There was patriotism in her every curve, and I presume that her song, to which I did not listen, was about the Twenty-First Lancers. My thoughts were far away, coursing sentimentally through the Past and lingering among the many evenings I had frittered at the Tivoli in the period of earlier youth. Here, in these very stalls, I would often sit with some coæval *in statu pupillari*. Lordly aloof, both of us, from the joyous vulgarity of our environment, we would talk in under-tones about Hesiod and Fra Angelico, about the lyric element in Marcus Aurelius and the ethics of apostasy as illustrated by the Oxford Movement. Now and again, in the pauses of our conversation, we would rest our eyes upon the stage and listen to a verse or two of some song about a mother-in-law or an upstairs-lodger, and then one of us would turn to the other, saying, "Yes! I see your point about poor Newman, but . . ." or "I cannot admit that there is any real distinction between primitive art and . . ." Though our intellects may not have been so monstrous fine as we pretended, we were quite honest in so far as neither of us could have snatched any surreptitious pleasure in the entertainment as such. We came simply that we might bask in the glow of our own superiority—superiority not only to the guffawing clowns and jades around us, but also to the cloistral pedascules who, no more exquisite than we in erudition, were not in touch with modern life and would have been scared, like so many owls, in that garish temple of modernity, a Music Hall, wherein we, on the other hand, were able to sit without blinking. Were we, after all, so very absurd? It was one of our aims to be absurd. Besides, does not every man see something absurd in the things he did four or five years ago? Assuredly, that is a law of nature. A man may not have progressed in intellect—he may even have deteriorated—but he cannot regard himself, as he was, without some measure of contempt. I fancy that even an octogenarian must (if his memory be unimpaired) think that he was rather an ass at the age of seventy. Men who paint pictures or write books or produce anything that abides tangibly with them, may look at their old work and find much that is good in it; but, the greater their admiration, the greater their wonder that they, being what they were, contrived to do it. I myself was reading lately a little essay on Music Halls, written by me in the period to which I have alluded. I find it excellent. Yet I can but blush for the fatuous creature I was in the days when I wrote it—just as I shall be blushing, five years hence, at my present personality, in which I cannot now detect any flaw.

The foregoing words are a more or less amplified version of the reverie I indulged in while the lady of heroic proportions held the rest of her audience in spell. The loud applause in which, at length, she marched off the stage, also put a term to my reverie. I remembered that I had come, not for the old purpose of being superior, but to lay the foundations for an article. And so I listened attentively to Mr. Tom Costello. I do not remember what either of his songs was about. I remember only that he wore two false noses, one for each song. It is one of the old traditions of an English Music Hall that the male comedians must make themselves as unsightly as they can. Indeed, ugliness, physical or moral, always seems to be the chief feature of the characters represented by the male artists. The aim of the Music Hall is, in fact, to cheer the lower classes up by showing them a life uglier and more sordid than their own. The mass of people, when it seeks pleasure, does not want to be elevated: it wants to laugh at something beneath its own level. Just as I used to go to Music Halls that I might feel my superiority to the audience, so does the audience go that it may compare itself favourably with the debased rapscallions of the songs. Perhaps this theory would apply even better to the case of the outlying Music Halls, where there is no prosperous element in the audience. At the Tivoli most of the audience is prosperous. Music Halls have become, in recent years, a feature of the "West End," a rival to the theatres. Gradually, they are becoming less and less Music Halls in the old sense—places, I mean, where songs are sung in succession throughout the evening. The "turns" are now interspersed with such items as juggling, bell-ringing, limb-contorting. The Tivoli is in a state of transition. But the old convention—the convention of unalloyed ugliness—still lingers and will, I fancy, die hard. It is significant that most of the younger men on the Music Hall stage adhere strictly to the old convention. The most gifted and popular of these younger men, Mr. George Robey (who was educated at Cambridge and is, in my opinion, one of the few distinguished men produced by Cambridge within recent years), nightly presents himself in the most hideous guise and makes the most hideous noises. Shortly after Mr. Robey's "turn," the other night, appeared Mr. T. E. Dunville, whom I saw for the first time. He is, in all respects, a replica of Mr. Robey. He has the same kind of make-up, the same kind of manner—the Cambridge manner, I suppose—and the same kind of songs. Evidently the old convention has life in it. Personally, I do not like it. I can bear it from Mr. Dan Leno—genius reconciles one to anything. From Mr. Robey, clever as he is, and from Mr. Dunville, it jars on me. At the same time, it is interesting; also, it seems to give great pleasure; and so no student of life can afford to ignore it. And I feel that, in saying that I dislike it, I may be betraying my own limitations. I hasten, therefore, to say that I yield to none in my enjoyment of that fatuousness which, in the old convention, is as necessary to the songs sung by women as is ugliness to the songs sung by men. Who (I have often wondered) writes the words? Of the rate at which they are written I had an interesting glimpse not long ago, in the report of a case in the County Court at Brighton. The defendant, asked by the Judge to state his occupation, said that he wrote the words of songs for Music Halls, receiving the sum of one pound for every song. Asked how much he made in the course of a year, he replied simply, "Three hundred and sixty-five pounds." I blame the Judge for not having pushed his inquiries further. I should have liked to know something of the spirit in which the defendant wooed his Muse. Was it a rough wooing, for the most part, or a timid? Was she never coy? Would he say that on some days she yielded to him with greater ardour than on others? Did he discriminate between the fruits of their union, regarding this one as fine, that one as puny? Would he hotly maintain that some of his songs were underrated by the public, and others esteemed beyond their deserts? Would he give a fig for what the public thought of his work, or did he, in the silence of his Study, strive only to please himself and to satisfy his own conscience? If he did sometimes write merely to tickle the ears of the groundlings, did he find the groundlings knowing by some subtle instinct of their own that he had trifled with them, and refusing to react to his humour or his pathos? I think it probable that all the really successful songs are written in straight sincerity, to the utmost of the writers' powers. And yet—I don't know.

> In the lane where the violets nestle,
>   In the lane where the lilies grow,
> When Jack comes home from his vessel
>   He will meet me again, I know.
> Hand in hand we will wander together,
>   For his heart beats true, it is plain;
> On the deep blue sea he is waiting for me
>   And the day when we'll meet in the lane.

That was the song sung by Elementary Jane, in Mr. Richard Pryce's delightful novel; and in real life, I am sure, it would go as straight to the heart of the public as it did in the book. Yet Mr. Pryce is far from being an unsophisticated writer. "Since I came to London" was sung by one of Jane's elder rivals, and I wish Mr. Pryce had not kept it to himself. Its sprightliness must have been so traditional, so restful—something in the manner of what Miss Alice Lloyd was singing at the Tivoli the other night:

> You don't know you're alive!
>   That's so—oh, no!
> A girl like you of twenty-one,
>   Nothing done, and had no fun!
> You say you've never heard
>   How many beans make five?
> It's time you knew a thing or two—
>   You don't know you're alive!

That is exquisitely in the tradition. But for my own part I adore the sprightly style less than the pathetic.

MORE IN SORROW——

January 14, 1899

I wish this were an illustrated paper. There are situations which can be described so much better with a pencil than with a pen, and one of these, pre-eminently, is the situation I found last Saturday at the Globe Theatre. I wish my Editor would accept, instead of the following article, the cartoon I drew on Sunday morning. "Going back to 'School'" is its title, and it represents the British Public, as Mr. Bultitude *in toga puerili*, being received by Mr. John Hare, as Dr. Grimstone. Prettily suggested in it are the speechless indignation and reluctance of the former figure, the dreadful geniality of the latter. It lies before me as I write, mocking and paralysing "the hand that wields the pen."

I have seen few things more melancholy, more spectral, than the first night of "School." What an atmosphere of stale perfume pervaded it! The freshness and sweetness of 1869 all withered, desiccated, yet given to us with a light pretence that it was the same as ever! "Time—The Present," said the unblushing programme. "Scene—A Glade in the Forest." One looked at the Glade and saw that it had been painted to represent the verdure of midsummer. Yet I vow there was a rustle of dead leaves whenever any of the players crossed the stage. "1869. Very curious." "1869. An unique specimen."—Such were the labels affixed to those modern costumes in which the players strutted with so false an air of jauntiness and uptodation. "Time—The Present," indeed! Every scene, every speech, had its obvious date on it, and in vain did the players try to palm the play off as a thing with life in it. Their effort was as irritating to the audience as it must have been fatiguing to themselves. Everything (I thought) fell flat until the end of the last act, when the audience uprose and protested with loud cheers its ineradicable affection and admiration for Mr. Hare, that artist, and showed by its persistent cries of "Speech! Speech!" how anxious it was for any modern thing—even a managerial speech—which might purge from its mouth the adulterated old-world flavour of the play.

And "School" might have been so enchanting, had Mr. Hare

but produced it in the right way, with the costumes appropriate to its period. Surely, it was obvious folly to produce it as a modern play which would appeal dramatically to a modern audience. One does not expect a stuffed bird to sing. If the skeleton of the dodo soared into the air, one would be surprised. And yet this play has been produced as though it had just been written. Surely, with the precedent of "Trelawny" at the Court, such folly is inexplicable. There need, I think, have been no great stretch of imagination or of daring to foresee that the public which had flocked to sentimentalise over a faked portrait of the early 'sixties would be quite as eager to see a genuine portrait of the late 'sixties. The language of the 'sixties had been caught deftly enough by Mr. Pinero. But here, in "School," we have the very quintessence. "What a singular girl!" soliloquises Lord Beaufoy, in the third act. "As fresh as nature and as artless as moss! So different from the young persons one sees in Paris, and from the splendid tame tiger-lilies one meets in town!" That is quite perfect. Imagine how it would have entranced one, had it been spoken by an actor made up as a young "swell," with glengarry, cheroot, and "Crimean beard"! Spoken, as it was, by an actor who was laboriously dressed up to the 'nineties and was in terror of creating a laugh, it only made one curse the management's ingenuity in ruining a production. To preserve that impossible formula, "Time—The Present," there was a resort to two or three touching little subterfuges. Thus "Tel-el-Kebir" had been substituted for "Balaclava." Of course Balaclava and the appearance of Mr. Fred Kerr are not congruous; but equally incongruous are Tel-el-Kebir and the character of Jack Poyntz. This kind of tinkering is, indeed, worse than useless. If the management was blindly determined to produce the play in a modern way, Mr. Carton, or some one else who is in sympathy with the Robertsonian spirit, should have been commissioned to revise every line of the original version and bring it up to date. But that would not have been enough. Merely verbal revision would not have brought "School" up to date: reconstruction—fundamental reconstruction—would have been necessary. There is, as you may have heard, such a thing as social evolution. Customs, institutions, the relation of classes, the whole fabric of life—these things do not stagnate during three decades; certainly, they have not stagnated here since 1869. Human nature may be pretty much as it was; but it is ever being expressed through new conventions, before new backgrounds. As a sentimental Tory, I dislike new conventions and new backgrounds. There they are, nevertheless; one cannot ignore them, and it is silly to mix a little of one period with a little of another. To transfer "School" into the late 'nineties, would entail the complete transformation of its background and the excision of its main motive. As touching the background, I need hardly say that Dr. Sutcliffe's Academy for Young Ladies is quite obsolete. The moment the curtain rises on the first act, we are confronted with anachronism—school-girls in modern costume sitting in a wood, whilst a pupil-teacher reads to them the story of Cinderella. Either the girls should be dressed as in '68, or the pupil-teacher should be replaced by a young woman with a Cambridge Local Certificate, and "Cinderella" by the current issue of "Answers" or "Home Chat." The curtain of Act II rises on anachronism even more glaring. The pupil-teacher, discovered, is shelling peas. Now, if there is one occupation peculiarly redolent of the 'sixties, it is the shelling of peas. Even in the 'seventies it had almost entirely died out, and I suppose it is now done by machinery. The modern Bella— her name, by the way, is very '68—would have to be discovered with a typewriting machine or a copy of "The Perfect Wagnerite." The pupils singing "seconds," the pupils curtseying to Mrs. Sutcliffe—these little touches of temporal colour would have to be obliterated. Bella and Naomi would not be sent to look for Mrs. Sutcliffe's goloshes, for goloshes are no longer worn; nor would the pair be chased by a mad bull, for the modern bull is invariably sane. Dr. Sutcliffe and Krux, the usher, would be cut out entirely, and Mrs. Sutcliffe, whose every sentiment shows her to be a lady with *paniers* and *pouffes* to her dress, and to be the proud possessor of a "Grecian bend," constant envy of her pupils —would not the whole of her character have to be very thoroughly overhauled? Indeed, the whole atmosphere of the play would have to be changed before it could be enacted in modern vesture with any result but absolute, irritating disaster. Its main motive would, as I have hinted, have to be changed also. It is, most essentially, a snobbish play. All the drama in it has snobbishness for its foundation. Perpend! A young peer meets a young lady of humble position and unknown parentage. He falls in love with her. She is duly overwhelmed by his condescension, and she accepts him. He gives her a ring, but forbids her to say what it portends. Her employers ask who gave it her, and, hearing that the young peer gave it her, they dismiss her, as a matter of course. Six weeks elapse. Every one believes the worst. Enter the young peer. He announces that the young lady is living with him, and, though he is dressed as a bridegroom, no one ventures for one moment to suppose that he has not merely seduced her. After an interminable scene of mystification, enter the young lady dressed as a bride. The young peer declares that he has married her. But that, according to the canons of the 'sixties, would be an unhappy, a painful, ending to the play. Unhappy endings had not yet become popular, and so Tom Robertson took steps to assure the audience that the young lady was the long-lost grandchild of Beau Farintosh, a gentleman of highest fashion. And thus, when the curtain was rung down, the audience went away perfectly satisfied, admiring the romantic self-sacrifice of the young peer, and rejoicing that his action had not, after all, involved him in a union which would have been too hideous to contemplate. Well! to a modern audience the frank snobbishness of "School" is a trifle offensive. A modern audience would not mind if the play were presented as a picture of the dark, undemocratic 'sixties— as such, it would be most delightful; but it is quite intolerable as a picture of contemporary life—it is a gross libel. Snobbishness still exists, no doubt, but we try to veil it. A Lord is still a Lord, but we do not call his attention to the fact quite so persistently as we did in the days of Tom Robertson. In our hearts, we adulate him as much as ever, but, thank Heaven! we have the decency to pretend to treat him as one of ourselves. And, just as we do no longer fawn on our betters, so do we not now bully our inferiors. Just as we try to conceal our respect for our betters under cover of an almost brusque manner, so do we, by parade of a too elaborate courtesy, try to make our inferiors feel how utterly we despise them. If there existed now any girls' school with a disagreeable usher and a pupil-teacher of lowly origin, it is quite certain that the former would not send the latter for a clothes-brush and tell her to brush his coat. The situation is impossible and, therefore, not dramatic. The refusal of Bella to brush Krux's coat may have been a highly effective "curtain" in the 'sixties. It is a very weak one in the late 'nineties. If, on the other hand, the play . . . but why should I lay any further stress on the inanity of the Globe production? I trust I have written enough to persuade Mr. Hare to atone ere long by producing "Caste," or some other play of the Robertson repertory, with due respect for archæology, sentiment and common-sense. If he will do this, I can promise him that he will have not only a good notice in the "Saturday Review," but also a great artistic and commercial success.

"GRIERSON'S WAY"

February 11, 1899

"Why was not this experiment made on the whole of that vile body, the public, rather than on that small fraction of the public which is so amenable to the mesmeric beck of Mr. Archer, Mr. Massingham and Miss Robins that it will sacrifice an afternoon or two in the cause of serious drama?" That is a decolloquialised version of the problem I was propounding to myself and others during the entr'actes of "Grierson's Way." I propound it here. Why did not Mr. Harrison and Mr. Maude buy "Grierson's Way," instead of merely lending their theatre for a furtive and limited production of it? That their loan is regarded as a sign in them of the utmost daring is shown by the perfervid and Heaven-bless-you-kind-gentleman-may-you-never-want-for-anything effusion of gratitude with which Mr. Archer covered them, preliminarily, in the "World." When Mr. Esmond's "Cupboard Love" was produced at the Court Theatre, nobody seemed to be impressed by Mr. Chudleigh's daring. Yet "Cupboard Love" had absolutely no merit of any kind, and "Grierson's Way" is the best English play of its kind that has been produced in London. How hideous a condemnation of the public, that the one was taken (by a manager) and the other left (to the New Century Theatre). Hideous—and hasty? The one ran for only six nights, being, apparently, below even the public's level. Might not the other have run for (say) sixty? Might not the dereliction of the one have been taken as augury of some hope for the other? Had the other been but a curious effort in dramaturgy—a bad play written exquisitely by a poet, or thoughtfully by a philosopher, or strenuously by a propagandist—then, of course, I could not have hoped for it more than a success of esteem. But this play of Mr. Esmond's, remarkable in many ways, is primarily remarkable for its stage-craft. Personally, I think that the modern glorification of stage-craft is a thing to be deplored. Stage-craft is not the same thing as dramatic power: one can have either without the other. But the amount of stage-craftiness required in the making of a play which shall be good according to modern canons is quite enormous, and among other lamentable results of this tyranny is the fact that playwriting is now confined to so small a ring of writers, most of whom are personally men of second-rate to tenth-rate ability. We have first-rate writers in whom the sense of drama is paramount—Mr. Hardy and Mr. Gissing among them. Why do not they enrich our stage-literature? Simply because the novel is a wide medium for drama, the theatre a narrow one; and because they do not deign to spend their time in studying and assimilating the thousand-and-one meticulosities of restriction and imposition which have gradually adhered to the art of writing plays. At present I do not hear on Primrose Hill, or on any other of our mountains, the feet of him who shall redeem our drama by showing the people that these meticulosities are no more essential to true drama, no less injurious to it, than was the Pharisaism of nineteen centuries ago to the Jews' religion. Here I sit, straining my ears patiently, but . . . but, alas! I have digressed. What I meant to say was merely that Mr. Esmond is, in the truest and widest sense, a dramatist, and also that he has expressed himself in "Grierson's Way" without violating any of the modern conventions. He has not slipped off the tight-rope. Not one of the egg-shells has he broken. His play is in four acts, all most neatly constructed; the curtain falls every time on a climax; all the action takes place in one room; there is no character which does not definitely and directly contribute to the plot's progress; and so on, and so on, insomuch that no one could deny that the play is perfectly "well-made." What, then, prevented any manager

from producing it? Its gloom, I suppose. The public, as its
members are always asserting, does not "go to the theatre to be
harrowed." To me such a play as this is far less painfully harrowing than any of those rattling farces or bustling romances which
the public loves. I do not like being *actually* harrowed. To be
æsthetically harrowed, however, gives me great pleasure. The
trouble with the public is that it has not enough art-sense to be
æsthetically harrowed by a modern tragedy—it cannot take the
thing impersonally, and is depressed by it actually. A tragedy
that is remote from modern conditions, a tragedy cast in another
age and in another country, may give it some kind of æsthetic
pleasure. From "Hamlet," as being a glimpse of Denmark in the
dark ages, it does not shrink. But, conceive what a frost that
play would be if it were brought up to date: if Claudius were just
a prosperous merchant who had become sole partner in his business and master of a commodious residence at Blackheath through
poisoning his brother and marrying his sister-in-law; if Hamlet,
his step-son, were a young man who had just taken a first in Greats
at Oxford; if Ophelia were the daughter of a dear old vicar in the
neighbourhood. Would even Mr. Harrison and Mr. Maude
connive at the production of such a play? Should not even I
protest against it? And, if I, how much more strongly the
public! Yet, when it is merely a matter of "*Scene*, Elsinore.
Time,—" the public derives no more pity and awe than is quite
pleasant from the spectacle of Death bowling over Polonius,
Ophelia, Gertrude, Claudius, and Hamlet, with unerring aim, as
though they were so many ninepins. If Mr. Esmond had only
written, in his stage-directions, "Elsinore" for "London," and
"——" for "The Present," commercial success might have been
his. In "The Jest" Messrs. Parker and Carson showed us a main
situation very similar to the main situation in "Grierson's Way"
—a husband advised by a lunatic to commit suicide because he
had married a woman who loved another man. "Cesare," like
"Grierson," was "the shadow between her and the sunlight,"
but then, luckily for him, his name was Cesare, and he was
Mediævo-Florentine, and Mr. Wyndham knew that the public
would not be frightened by him. Except their fatal dilemma,
Grierson and Cesare have nothing in common. Poor Grierson
could never have cut a dashing figure in chain-armour. He is a

sweet, weak creature, whose very unselfishness seems due to the lack of any power to assert himself. After he has done one thing on his own initiative—married the girl he loves, in order to save her from the disgrace of her seduction by another man—all volition ebbs out of him. He simply sits down and lets things take their course, until it is time for him to commit suicide. In fact, he is rather a muff. As presented by Mr. Esmond, he is by no means an impossible or unlikely character; on the contrary, he seems terribly real. But, much as one pities Grierson, I cannot help thinking that Mr. Esmond would have done well to endow him with a little more "kick." If, having married Pamela, Grierson tried to make her love him, if he did not give her the opportunity of reading letters from her seducer, if he forbade the seducer to call at the house—if, in a word, he once struggled against destiny—his final extinction would have been even more dramatic than it is. It is all very well to talk about "inevitableness": no doubt there is much drama to be got out of the "relentless march of fate," and out of a man's helplessness against fate. But I maintain that such drama is far more poignant when the man struggles and rebels than when he mildly acquiesces. However, I do not wish to find fault with Mr. Esmond—my general gratitude is too great for that. Grierson is, at least, a *real* character, and so is every other character in this play. I am grateful for this play because it shows me real and human characters, behaving in a real and human way, under stress of circumstances that are conceivable. I am grateful, in fact, for a privilege seldom vouchsafed me by any dramatist. When I read the play, and again, when I saw it acted, it gave me a real emotion. The end of Grierson really moved me, and on the future of Pamela I am still speculating. Will she marry Captain Murray, her old lover, or will the revulsion from him, caused by her husband's suicide, be permanent in her? Mr. Esmond—rightly, as I think—does not settle that question. As a dramatist, he is concerned with Grierson's Way, not with the success or failure of that Way, and, as soon as Grierson is dead, the play is, strictly, at an end. Murray comes, however, and rings at the door of Grierson's flat. We hear him ringing and ringing. Finally, we hear him going away. His partial introduction is no more, really, than the introduction of Fortinbras at the end of "Hamlet"—no more than a symbol that, though the play is over, there is a future. It is merely one of those vague symbols which are the fit conclusion to a work of art.

Mr. Titheradge played the part of Grierson exactly as it ought to have been played, suggesting at once the feebleness and the fineness of the man's nature. It would be difficult for any actress to make the part of Pamela seem unreal, but no actress could have intensified its reality better than Miss Lena Ashwell. She did not move gracefully on the stage or use her voice beautifully, but she played with intense sincerity and power. And in a realistic play of this kind grace of movement and diction are of less importance than sincerity and power. Actresses may be divided into four classes: those who comport themselves beautifully on the stage and give the impression of real life; those who only comport themselves beautifully; those who only give the impression of real life; and those who do neither of these things. The last of these classes is the largest, and the first, in which only the greatest actresses can be placed, is, of course, the smallest. Mr. Fred Terry, as Captain Murray, had the least good of the parts, but made the most of one fine scene. Mr. Esmond, as the half-mad cripple, realised the author's intention with commendable fidelity. There was also a baby in the play. As soon as it appeared on the stage, the audience distinguished itself by continuous peals of inane laughter. It did not matter that the baby (begotten by Captain Murray) was brought on simply to point the tragedy of Grierson's position. Babies on the stage are supposed to be objects of mirth, and so the audience roared. Remember that this audience was, so to say, a picked audience—one that had come deliberately to see a serious play. If the baby had been shown to an ordinary first-night audience, I tremble to think what would have happened—I suppose the play would have had to proceed entirely in dumb show. Perhaps it is well that the play was not given to the whole public. Oh, the public, the public! It will never be described better than in Mr. Bumble's famous epigram.

COMPARISONS

March 18, 1899

Except Miss Geneviève Ward, none of the mimes did well in the new piece at the Adelphi. Miss Ward herself had very little to do, and even that little was of slight importance to the play. So far as I can remember—plays like "The Man in the Iron Mask" make slight claim on one's memory—there was no particular reason for the Queen Mother to appear on the stage at all. Appear she did, however, in the person of Miss Ward, and then, for the first and last time in the evening, one saw a performance that did not utterly violate all those canons to which, in romantic melodrama, mimes must conform. Miss Ward conformed magnificently to all those canons. She strode across the stage, bearing herself reginally. She struck the ground with her stick sharply. She threw back her head, and her eyes were blazing. She rolled forth her words with bitter passion. Her every syllable was resonant, and with her every gesture she swept the house. And she won a full, immediate victory for the old tradition, for the grand manner. The moment she appeared on the stage, her presence—and she has indeed a presence!—thrilled us to attention. After our prolonged oppression in a sultry atmosphere of amateurishness, it was as welcome as a thunderstorm. Though it did not exactly clear the air—as soon as it was over, sultriness set in again—it was, while it lasted, intensely stimulating. It was fine to hear, and its flashes were a wondrous spectacle.

Altogether, a sorry evening for the new school of acting! Do not take me to mean that the new school is inferior to the old. In many ways it is far superior, though it cut so very poor a figure on Saturday night. Weigh the two methods in the scales of modern comedy or modern tragedy, and the new method comes down with a triumphant clash. Weigh them, however, in the scales of romantic melodrama, and that method flies lightly, ingloriously, up. The new method of acting is corollary to the new method of drama, just as was the old method of acting to the old method of drama. It is always (if I may say so without wounding the Actors' Association) the dramatist who makes the mime, and

24

not (as some mimes fancy) *vice versâ*. And as the new drama will
wax inevitably, and the old will wane, the importance of the new
acting and of the old will wax and wane in relative proportion.
As one who likes to be on the winning side, I should be, therefore,
the last to pooh-pooh the new acting. It is only when I am
forced to see an imitation of the old drama that I champion the old
acting. "But," some one may object, "how dare you imply that
romantic melodrama is an old-fashioned form? Haven't we been
deluged with it for months?" We have. The public will always
want to be deluged with it. When I call romantic melodrama an
old-fashioned form, I mean that it is no longer a form to which
any vital English dramatist devotes himself. The best plays that
are written now are realistic tragedies, like "Grierson's Way,"
or realistic comedies, like "The Liars." All the romantic melodramas that are written now are very poor stuff—"The Man in the
Iron Mask" is, by the way, very poor stuff indeed—and the best
of them is as inferior to "The Lady of Lyons" as are the tame,
niggling, gripless little efforts of Mr. Anthony Hope or Mr.
Stanley Weyman to the novels of the elder Dumas. When "The
Lady of Lyons" was written, romantic melodrama was a form
which the good dramatist still loved, which he still took quite
seriously. Now it is left to accomplished hacks, who fake it up
to the best of their ability. In dramaturgy, as in literature and
painting, real highfalutinism is just now a lost art. Bombastes
has been suppressed. Ercles' vein is off. Regret this, if you like
—I myself often do regret it—but don't deny the patent fact.
Art is never stagnant. It is always moving, heavily, irresistibly,
now in one direction, now in another. During recent years, it
has been moving in the direction of realism—when I say "realism,"
I use the word in its general and proper sense, not as signifying
any crude presentation of suicide, disease, or incest. Fifty years
ago, literary and pictorial genius was all for rainbows, waterfalls,
palaces, princesses, zephyrs, lakes, ruined towers by moonlight.
These things were shaken and taken by the best artists and by
them glorified with the utmost rhetoric. The writer orated over
them in words, the painter in pigments. They were called the
Good, the Beautiful, and the True, and were the stock-in-trade
of every self-respecting artist. In those days, the artist's aim was
to shut his eyes to the actual world as tightly as he could, to see

nothing as it was, and to create for himself a remote and roseate phantasmagoria. Sometimes this aim had very beautiful results. The pictures painted by Turner, even the romances of Bulwer, had passages of very real, even tremendous, power. Certainly, the neo-romantic movement in England was by no means barren. But it could not last for ever. Reaction came gradually. One after another, the younger artists refused to throw in their lot with the Good, the Beautiful, and the True. They opened their eyes to the world around them. They began, like babies, to "take notice." And what they saw interested them. They vowed that life itself and the little facts of various lives, their own characters and the characters of other men and women, had far more fascination than was to be found in the phantasmagorias of the masters. Whether they were right or wrong, I am not going to discuss. The important thing is that they held this opinion, and that they acted on it. Timidly at first, they drew near to life, and began to describe what they saw. In painting, literature, dramaturgy, new schools were founded, schools which are still flourishing, and realism was the motto of them all. Realism was the chief motive of the pre-Raphaelites as essentially as it was, later, the chief motive of the Impressionists. From George Eliot to Meredith and Hardy, all the novelists have been imbued with this one primary aim: to get nearer to actual life, deeper into it. Mr. Hardy professes to have found in it the Bad, the Ugly, and the False; Mr. Meredith, to have found the other things. But though the discoveries of the two men have been so different, their method has been the same. Both are realists, both constantly inquisitive of life. They have had their ears at the same key-hole, though they have not overheard the same things. And the best of the younger writers, they too are realists. The realistic novel is the only kind of novel that has any life in it now. And, as in painting and in literature, so also in dramaturgy the trend has been, and is, all towards realism. Maeterlinck himself, though, like the pre-Raphaelites, he wears a romantic halo, is as much a realist as Ibsen: it is the various emotions of men and women, as they are, that he is always seeking to describe. There is significant irony in the fact that Tom Robertson, the first man to introduce realism on the modern English stage, has long since been swept away by the revolution he created. It was he who first tried to make his puppets life-like, and in doing so, he created, also, that new school of acting which is one theme of my article. He created the Bancrofts. Since that time, the whole method of acting has changed. The old method was useless in the portrayal of modern human beings. For such portrayal, sympathy, intelligence, the power to observe character accurately and to render with delicacy fine shades of emotion, are of far greater importance than are a voice of thunder and an imperial manner of walking about the stage. The new method, quiet and subtle, is the only method by which modern drama can be interpreted. And it has killed the old method. On the metropolitan stage, Miss Ward is now one of the very few exponents of the old method. Nearly all the others have been driven forth into the provinces. There, indeed, the old method is still flourishing. There one finds infinitely better acting in romantic melodrama than one ever finds in London. There, too, Shakespeare's plays are performed much better than in London, for in Shakespeare's plays the poetry and the rhetoric are of far greater importance than the psychology. The metropolitan mimes squeeze out of them the last drop of psychology, and add many more on their own account; but of the splendour of the verse they can give us little or nothing: the plays languish under a load of delicate, irrelevant subtlety. And if the old method is the best means of interpreting Shakespeare, in whose plays there is always more or less psychology, how much more is it the best interpreter of romantic melodrama, in which there is no psychology at all! I think it a great pity that the author of "The Man in the Iron Mask" did not insist, in his contract with Mr. Norman Forbes, that all the parts should be assigned to old-fashioned mimes. If there were not enough of them—the cast is large—in London, then others should have been brought up from the provinces. For "The Man in the Iron Mask" is just an essay in the thunder-and-lightning *genre*, and in that *genre* one demands from the mimes something more deafening than the homely chirp of the cricket, and more dazzling than the modest radiance of the night-light.

AN ASIDE

April 8, 1899

I saw a play last week. It was extremely dull. There was not one moment of drama in it. It was in five long acts. It was written in verse, most of which was spoken in long speeches by the two principal characters. Whenever the curtain fell, it fell not on a dramatic climax, but simply on some especially elaborate peroration. And yet the audience seemed to enjoy itself immensely. The applause was frequent, and full in volume.

I need hardly say that I saw this play in Paris, not in London. In London such a play would not be possible. If it had been produced by some mad and wealthy manager, it would have been inevitably withdrawn after the first night. And yet it is the kind of play which runs, in Paris, for many weeks; the kind of play, even, that Parisians love better than any other. For, like the Athenian and the Elizabethan audiences, a Parisian audience loves listening to the declamation of verse; will sit and listen to it, unyawning, rapt, for three and a half consecutive hours, and will then pronounce the play "bien beau" with absolute sincerity. It does not need any bribe of "sumptuous production." A few shabby scenes, a few shabby supers, are all that the manager need provide, if he has secured a play written in sonorous Alexandrines, and has engaged actors and actresses who can roll out their speeches, beautifully, in the grand manner. Our public cares not at all for the sound of words, and will not tolerate poetry on the stage unless it gets also gorgeous and solid scenery, gorgeous and innumerable supers. It generally happens that the scenery and the costume for these occasions are hideous and, æsthetically, worse than worthless. But that does not matter. So long as the things look as expensive as the preliminary paragraphists have declared them to be, the public is well satisfied, and will, for their sake, condescend to tolerate a certain measure of poetry. Not a great measure, certainly. The poetry must be short and split; must be subordinated to the action of the piece, and to the expensive scenery and the expensive costumes. In fine, the London public is lacking in that attribute which has been given to the Parisian

28

public: a sense of beauty. I wonder whether this is in any way the result of our environment? I have often thought that Paris, λιπαρὰ πόλις, with the dry and glittering air on its trees and statues, and on the grandeur of its wide, white-grey streets, must indeed always foster the sense of beauty in its citizens. In London, here and there, one can find buildings that are beautiful. But they are rare and devious. Ugliness, formlessness, is the keynote of the whole city. Certain poets and painters have, in recent years, declared London to be beautiful; insomuch that we have been bullied into a vague belief that, in some mysterious way, it is so. As a matter of fact—there is no use in blinking the fact— it is quite hideous. Painters may have painted it well, and poets written good sonnets about it; but the beauty lies in their work, not in their subject. So far from quickening the sense of beauty in its citizens, London must tend to deaden it. Or am I mixing cause and effect? Is it rather because we, as a nation, lack sense of beauty that London is so ugly, and because the Parisians have sense of beauty that Paris is so beautiful? Perhaps that is the sounder theory. In any case, it is undeniable that the most obvious characteristic of modern art in England—and especially of dramatic art—is its lack of beauty. A few weeks ago, in these columns, I was pointing out that during the past forty or fifty years the movement of all English art has been steadily towards realism, and that in none of our arts is this movement so evident as in our drama. The obvious beauty of poetry and romance is almost uncultivated now by our dramatists. In France, however, it is still cultivated, is still regarded as the best and most important thing. France, alike in drama and in literature, is faithful to its old tradition of beauty. True, it has produced realists, has coquetted with realism. But it has never for one moment taken realism seriously. Balzac, Zola, Maupassant—it is only in England that they are, as writers, taken seriously. The Frenchman regards realism merely as an amusing short-cut to impropriety, and he takes it accordingly. He will never salute as a great writer any man whose first aim is not literary beauty. In other words, it is the classic tradition which still governs French taste. Beauty of subject, beauty of treatment, are still held to be essential. In England, on the other hand, the critics and the public are quick to crown with laurels any one who, with acute perception and with vigour and sincerity, writes about anything at all. It does not matter how ugly the subject may be, or how unlovely the treatment of it: if the thing be "true" it is unreservedly acclaimed. Had Mr. Kipling been born a Frenchman his talent would have found no recognition at all. Indeed, it is probable that he would never have extricated himself from the necessity of journalism, and would at this moment be known to us only as a particularly virulent Anti-Semite, Chauvinist, and fulminator against "*perfide Albion.*" Luckily he was not born under the French standard of literary taste. He was born an Englishman, and thus his talent has expanded to the utmost and is in no immediate danger of being underrated. No national standard of taste is perfect. We, in England, are inclined nowadays to care too little for beauty in literature, and to think that the lack of it is no great fault; just as, conversely, the French are inclined to see no great merit in any work of art that does not conform to beauty. Which is the sounder standard—the French or the English? The standard by which a writer like Mr. Kipling would be ruthlessly excluded from the hierarchy of letters, or that by which he is placed promptly at the head of it?

AN OBJECT LESSON

May 6, 1899

Dinner done and cigarettes alight, I said to the foreigner who was my guest, "No doubt, you are right. London has no obvious air of gaiety. By daylight and candle-light, we enjoy ourselves without seeming to do so. We have not, in fact, what you have well defined as the 'spirit of the carnival.' But, believe me, open-air cafés, which you recommend as a panacea, would not be any good at all. Our climate, and our manners (which are the result of our climate), would make such cafés quite barren and impossible. You belong to a talkative nation. Your people go to the café to talk. Bock, absinthe, syrup, whatever it may be, is the mere little pretext. Englishmen, on the other hand, have no con-

versation—at least, not when they are sober. When they are
drunk, they do, indeed, talk, and do attain even a certain degree of
disinvoltura. Some become sentimental and retrospective; others,
quarrelsome; others, gay. The first kind tends to tears; the
second, to blows; the third, to horseplay. But do not imagine
that in a café such as you have prescribed for us there would ever
be any general air of animation. There could be no general
animation till the majority of the people were in their cups; and
even then the question would arise whether an atmosphere of
frowns and whispers be not, on the whole, preferable to one of
tears, blows and practical jokes. However, I do not suppose one
would ever get so far as to find that a burning question. For the
English are a sober and sensible race, and the small percentage
that is dissolute would not be tolerated in a café built for the
greatest pleasure of the greatest number. So, my friend, you
may take it from me that such a resort would be not appreciably
more cheerful than the National Gallery which you admired so
much this afternoon. Nevertheless, do not run away with the
impression that we English do not habitually enjoy ourselves.
We *do*, though we have no means of showing it. Even those of
us who have private worries or anxieties derive a real and constant
solace from the knowledge that they are Englishmen. If one of
your compatriots broke his leg or lost a large sum of money, he
would, for a time, suffer unalloyed misery. But an Englishman,
in similar case, would be upheld through his affliction, and kept
inwardly cheerful, by the thought of that great Empire which is
ours. Believe me, there is not an Englishman to whom that
Empire is not a source of continual and personal pleasure."

"The Empire! But yes," said my friend. "I have often
heard to speak of it."

"Heard of it?" I cried, laughing at the narrowness which is
characteristic of even the most intelligent Frenchmen. "Heard
of it? I should rather think you had!"

"By example, yes! And I have great envy of to see it. It
ought to be an affair well amusing, well gay."

"Scarcely amusing, perhaps. But very great, very solid, very
gratifying."

"Could we not accompany us there this evening?"

I smiled interrogation.

"Is it not that it finds itself in la Place Leicester? Is that then so far from here?"

... Presently, we descended at the portal of that great establishment which is the reputed hub of all the wild gaiety in London —that Nirvana where gilded youth and painted beauty meet, to the strains of music and the twinkling of Terpsichore, in a glare of electric light. I had not wanted to come to it for my own sake. But I had thought that a visit might perhaps explain to my friend the point which I had been trying to impress on him : that obvious gaiety is not possible in London. So I had consented to show him the place. We bought two seats. As we passed, on our way to them, into the far-famed Promenade, I asked my friend to walk slowly, and to observe carefully the throng's demeanour. Everything was the same as it had ever been. The same glare, and the same music ; the same congestion of silk hats and swallow-tails, pressed against the barrier of the circle, watching the ballet ; the same slow and serried procession of silk hats and swallow-tails, billicocks and racing-coats, moodily revolving along the space between the ballet-gazers and the long row of large-hatted ladies who, bolt upright on the crimson settees against the wall, conversed with one another in undertone ; the same old absence, in fact, of any gaiety, of any semblance of gaiety, of any wish or effort to contrive any little hollow semblance of gaiety. I saw that my friend was puzzled, disappointed. Around him were all the common ingredients for revelry—light, glitter, youth, money, beauty, dancing, alcohol ; all those things without which revelry is, indeed, quite possible, but with even a small measure of which revelry would seem, to the child of a Latin race, quite inevitable. I was amused by my friend's disillusionment. We loitered, contemplative. There was no need to clinch my previous argument by pointing for him with words the moral of the Promenade. As we descended the staircase to the stalls, "My brave," he said to me simply, "you had reason."

The ballet—"Alaska"—was winding to its conclusion. The battalions of slim and spangled limbs were whirling through their final evolutions, and the orchestra blared to the climax. Cavalazzi, the immense, the inscrutable—for any meaning she ever conveys to me, Cavalazzi is a sphinx indeed—came striding through the coryphées. She threw back her head and pointed to the ground. She frowned and folded her arms. She smiled, unfolded her arms and pointed with the forefinger of her right hand to the middle-finger of her left hand. She strode significantly away through the coryphées, leaving them and the orchestra to bring things to a satisfactory conclusion. When the curtain fell, two footmen appeared before it with brooms, and swept away stray flakes of the golden rain which had fallen in the ballet. A "celebrated operatic vocalist" being indisposed, the orchestra played a selection. (Surely "extra-turns" might be contrived on these occasions?) M. Delbosq appeared in due time —"comic tumbler and vaulter." Mr. Imro Fox followed him— "comic conjurer." This gentleman, though he spoke with an unique blend of the German and American accents, did not persuade me that conjuring, that gloomiest of the arts, can be brought into any kind of relation to comedy. A man may bring a rabbit out of a hat, and a pigeon out of a canister. A man may make puns, and may pretend, more than once, to trip up as he crosses the stage. But when these two different kinds of activity are combined they really are intolerable. Mr. Imro Fox combined them, and I could not bear him. Came the three Harveys, who walked very gracefully on wires. Their performance pleased me as an unusually finished example of that art which, as was once observed by a thoughtful critic of it, "seeming to defy the laws of gravity, owes its success to the completeness of its obedience to them." Their performance pleased me, too, as the one thing on the programme that was neither deadly dull in itself nor utterly unsuited to a vast stage and vast auditorium. Came Yvette Guilbert. She is one of the "turns" which are of no use in the Empire. Her art is an art of little niceties and nuances, of little half-tones and fine shades, and in singing at the Empire she is about as effective as the writer of the "Genius of Place" would be in addressing a mass meeting in Hyde Park. Of course, the audience applauds her—the educated part of it, lest it be thought not to understand her; the uneducated part of it, because she receives a fabulous sum for her every performance. So I suppose the management is wise to engage her. As soon as she had sung her last song, the orchestra played another long selection. Then came the most appallingly tedious thing I have ever seen in a place of entertainment. How long it lasted, I do not know: we left before it was over, before there was any symptom that it soon would be over. It may not have been for more than a quarter of an hour—it seemed an eternity—that we watched four young American men riding round the stage on bicycles and trying to project with their front-wheels a small ball into one or other of two small goals. "Bicycle Polo" was the name given to this cheerful pastime. When I go to a music-hall, I do not pay my money to see four young men doing what they might, on a winter's day, in the open air, possibly do with some enjoyment. Nor can I believe that any one is so inane as to enjoy seeing four young men do this thing in the Empire. I said as much, while I conducted my friend up the staircase. "Who knows?" he laughed. "It seems to be a droll of city, Londres."

As we threaded our way out, the Promenade was still glittering with its habitual gloom. I noticed in the distance two young men who seemed even more gloomy than the rest; my brain, I suppose, was a trifle dulled by the whole evening, for it was not until I came quite close to them that I recognised my friend and myself in a mirror. As we went out, mutes were still pouring in. Souls on the way to purgatory would have looked more cheerful. The only smile I saw was on the face of a drunken man whose entry was being barred by a tall commissionaire. I drew my friend's attention to the smile.

As we drove away, I conjectured that even if the man had been sober his smile would have disqualified him for admittance. But then, as my friend (apt pupil) reminded me, if he had been sober he would not have been smiling.

HAMLET, PRINCESS OF DENMARK

June 17, 1899

I cannot, on my heart, take Sarah's Hamlet seriously. I cannot even imagine any one capable of more than a hollow pretence at taking it seriously. However, the truly great are apt, in matters concerning themselves, to lose that sense of fitness which is usually called sense of humour, and I did not notice that Sarah was once hindered in her performance by any irresistible desire to burst out laughing. Her solemnity was politely fostered by the Adelphi audience. From first to last no one smiled. If any one had so far relaxed himself as to smile, he would have been bound to laugh. One laugh in that dangerous atmosphere, and the whole structure of polite solemnity would have toppled down, burying beneath its ruins the national reputation for good manners. I, therefore, like every one else, kept an iron control upon the corners of my lips. It was not until I was half-way home and well out of earshot of the Adelphi, that I unsealed the accumulations of my merriment.

I had controlled myself merely in deference to Sarah herself, not because I regarded the French prose-version of "Hamlet" as an important tribute to Shakespeare's genius. I take that version to have been intended as a tribute to an actress' genius, rather than a poet's. Frenchmen who know enough of our language to enable them to translate Shakespeare know very well that to translate him at all is a grave disservice. Neither into French poetry nor into French prose can his poetry be translated; and, since every element in his work was the direct, inalienable result of his poetry, it follows that any French translation is ruinous. I do not say that this particular translation is unskilful; on the contrary, it seemed to me very skilful indeed. The authors seemed to have got the nearest equivalents that could be got. But the nearest equivalents were always unsatisfactory and often excruciating. "Paix, paix, âme troublée!" for "Rest, rest, perturbed spirit!" is a fair sample of what I mean. Save that it reminds one—an accident which the authors could not foresee—of "Loo, Loo, I love you!" there is no fault to be found with this rendering. It is, I think, as good as possible. But it carries in it no faintest echo nor most shadowy reflection of the original magic. It is thin, dry, cold—in a word, excruciating. The fact is that the French language, limpid and exquisite though it is, affords no scope for phrases which, like this phrase of Shakespeare's, are charged with a dim significance beyond their meaning and with reverberations beyond their sound. The French language, like the French genius, can give no hint of things beyond those which it definitely expresses. For expression, it is a far finer instrument than our language; but it is not, in the sense that our language is, suggestive. It lacks mystery. It casts none of those purple shadows which do follow and move with the moving phrases of our great poets. In order to be really suggestive, a French poet must, like Mallarmé, deliberately refrain from expressing anything at all. An English poet, on the other hand, may be at once expressive and suggestive. That is a great advantage. It is an advantage which none of our poets has used so superbly as Shakespeare. None of our poets has ever given to his phrases shadows so wonderful as the shadows Shakespeare gave to his. In none of Shakespeare's plays, I think, are these shadows so many and marvellous as in "Hamlet"; and the quality of its theme is such that the shadows are more real to us, and reveal more to us, than the phrases casting them. Cut away those shadows, and you cut away that which makes the play immortal—nay! even that which makes it intelligible. One by one, they were cut away by the two talented Parisians who translated "Hamlet" for Sarah. Reluctantly, no doubt. But I am dealing with the translation as I find it, and (despite my colleagues) I must refuse to regard it as a tribute to Shakespeare. The only tribute a French translator can pay Shakespeare is not to translate him—even to please Sarah.

In England, as I suggested some time ago, "Hamlet" has long ceased to be treated as a play. It has become simply a hoop through which every very eminent actor must, sooner or later, jump. The eminent actor may not have any natural impulse to jump through it, but that does not matter. However unsuited to the part he be in temperament or physique, his position necessitates that he play it. I deplore this custom. I consider that it cheapens both Shakespeare's poetry and the art of acting. However, it is a firmly-established custom, and I must leave it to work itself out. But I do, while there is yet time, earnestly hope that Sarah's example in playing Hamlet will not create a precedent among women. True, Mrs. Bandmann Palmer has already set the example, and it has not been followed; but Mrs. Bandmann Palmer's influence is not so deep and wide as Sarah's, and I have horrible misgivings. No doubt, Hamlet, in the complexity of his nature, had traces of femininity. Gentleness and a lack of executive ability are feminine qualities, and they were both strong in Hamlet. This, I take it, would be Sarah's own excuse for having essayed the part. She would not, of course, attempt to play Othello—at least, I risk the assumption that she would not, dangerous though it is to assume what she might *not* do—any more than her distinguished fellow-countryman, Mounet Sully, would attempt to play Desdemona. But, in point of fact, she is just as well qualified to play Othello as she is to play Hamlet. Hamlet is none the less a man because he is not consistently manly, just as Lady Macbeth is none the less a woman for being a trifle unsexed. Mounet Sully could be no more acceptable as Lady Macbeth than as Desdemona. I hope he is too sensible a person ever to undertake the part. He would be absurd in it, though (this is my point) not one whit more absurd than Sarah is as Hamlet. Sarah ought not to have supposed that Hamlet's weakness set him in any possible relation to her own feminine mind and body. Her friends ought to have restrained her. The native critics ought not to have encouraged her. The custom-house officials at Charing Cross ought to have confiscated her sable doublet and hose. I, lover of her incomparable art, am even more distressed than amused when I think of her aberration at the Adelphi. Had she for one moment betrayed any faintest sense of Hamlet's character, the reminiscence were less painful. Alas! she betrayed nothing but herself, and revealed nothing but the unreasoning vanity which had impelled her to so preposterous an undertaking. For once, even her voice was not beautiful. For once . . . but why should I insist? The best that can be said for her performance is that she acted (as she always does) with that dignity of demeanour which is the result of perfect self-possession. Her perfect self-possession was one of the most delicious elements in the evening's comedy, but one could not help being genuinely impressed by her dignity. One felt that Hamlet, as portrayed by her, was, albeit neither melancholy nor a dreamer, at least a person of consequence and unmistakably "thoro'bred." Yes! the only compliment one can conscientiously pay her is that her Hamlet was, from first to last, *très grande dame.*

"G. B. S." AT KENNINGTON

October 7, 1899

For a dramatist who deliberately sits down to write something of a kind which he despises, one would predict failure. For a dramatist who, after two acts, sickens of his task and spends the last act in an endeavour to restore his self-respect by making the other two acts ridiculous, one would predict absolute disaster. Yet "The Devil's Disciple" is not merely a work of extremely fine quality, but a great popular success to boot. I know not which fact surprises me more—the fact that Mr. Bernard Shaw has done a romantic melodrama better than it is done by gentlemen with romantic hearts and melodramatic heads, or the fact that the public seemed quite delighted when the play suddenly tumbled into wild frivolity. For my own part, I had been simmering with laughter throughout the first two acts, but the good people of Kennington, not knowing the soul and the creed of Mr. Shaw, had been taking his play very seriously. I, in their place, should have done the same, for, I repeat, the play is most excellent. But its very excellence was for me the point of the jest. In a bad melodrama by Mr. Shaw there would have been no incongruity. But that he should write a really good one, in spite of himself—that was irresistible! And so I welcomed the farcical last act, not because it amused me more than the other acts, but as an opportunity for unburdening myself of all the laughter which I had been suppressing in deference to a rapt audience. Also, it was a relief to find that Mr. Shaw had not imposed too lengthy a strain upon himself, but had broken away just when it was becoming intolerable, none the worse for his penance.

"*Si ipsum audissetis!*" What scorn would Mr. Shaw have not poured down these columns on such a play? How he would have riddled the hero, the sympathetic scapegrace (called, of course, "Dick") who, for all his wickedness, cannot bear to see a woman cry, and keeps a warm corner in his heart for the old horse Jim, and the old servant Roger, and wishes to be hanged by the English in the place of another man, and tries to throttle the major for calling a lady a woman! What scathing analysis Mr. Shaw would

38

have made of this fellow's character, declaring that he, "G. B. S."
refused to see anything noble in a man who, having lived the life of
a wastrel and a blackguard, proposed to commit suicide by imposing on the credulity of a court-martial! Far be it from me to
attempt what Mr. Shaw would have done with conviction. Indeed, I confess that "Dick" seemed a very splendid fellow to me,
and I rejoice to think that, though he had been so cruelly misunderstood and had lived "with worthless men, aye! and with
worthless women," he had kept his powers of self-sacrifice intact.
Yes! "Dick" thrilled me. At least, he would have done so if
any one but Mr. Shaw had created him. As it was, I was intoler-
ably tickled by the irony with which Fate contrived that the first
really human and convincing character drawn by Mr. Shaw should
be a character which Mr. Shaw had drawn quite cynically and
with the express intention that it should be absolutely unlike anything in real life. When, as in his serious plays of modern life,
Mr. Shaw depicts life as he conceives it to be, and men and women
as he knows them, the result is not (for me, at least) satisfactory.
He imagines emotion to be an unfortunate and not inevitable
nuisance, and reason to be the pivot on which the world should go
round. His heroes and heroines are, therefore, absolutely rational
machines, unclogged by such accessories as flesh and blood. It
would be hard to imagine anything less like human beings than
they are. To Mr. Shaw himself they seem quite real, no doubt.
He would probably admit that they are a little in advance of the
age, belonging to the twentieth rather than to the nineteenth century. As a matter of fact, there is no reason to suppose that men
and women become more rational with the advance of civilisation;
still less, that they will ever approximate to Vivie Warren or
Leonard Charteris. And, incidentally, the fact that Mr. Shaw
quite honestly believes and hopes that they will, suggests that Mr.
Shaw himself is born after rather than before his time. His
touching faith in the efficacy of reason dates him right back into
the eighteenth century. There, had he lived in it, he would have
found many supporters—not leaders, of course, but many staunch
supporters. As it is, Mr. Shaw stands alone, apart from the tendencies of this bustling age, a trifle *rococo*. I would not he were
otherwise. I would not play pedagogue to him, as does Mr.
Archer, trying to persuade him to be this, and to leave off being

39

that, and to beware of becoming the other. On the contrary, I hope Mr. Shaw will always be just what he is—as delightful in the defects of his qualities as in the qualities themselves. Nor have I any doubt that my hope will be gratified. You may mould a child, but not, to any appreciable extent, a grown-up man. Mr. Archer forgets that. He imagines that there is yet time for what he takes to be Mr. Shaw's salvation. But let him cease to trouble. Mr. Shaw's salvation, like that of every one else, is in being himself. For the space of two acts, Mr. Shaw has pretended—for his own amusement and emolument, not to please Mr. Archer—to be not himself. The result is that those two acts are fine and moving drama. But no number of fine and moving dramas to come would compensate me for the permanent obliteration of "G. B. S." If Mr. Shaw had written his last act in key with the other two, his play would have been a better work of art, but how much less delightful! The success of "The Devil's Disciple" may tempt Mr. Shaw to write other melodramas, and I trust that he will never fail to intrude himself in the last act. That he will always be welcome is proved by the attitude of Kennington. I offer Mr. Shaw my congratulations on the amazing cleverness with which he has handled the melodramatic form, and on having the loud laugh over the thirty or forty London managers who have allowed his play to go a-begging. I trust that when, in the fulness of time, I leave off being a dramatic critic and become a dramatist, my successor in these columns may have reason to be half as jealous of me as am I of "G. B. S."

The play was admirably performed. Mr. Carson, as "Dick," kept the ball rolling at top speed. His humour and his full-blooded method are peculiarly well suited to the part. Interesting as he always is, I do not think I have ever seen him act better or with more obvious enjoyment. Even Mr. Shaw, had he been present at the performance, would have been convinced by "Dick." All the other parts seemed to me to be well filled, especially that of General Burgoyne, a part so exquisite in itself that the veriest duffer could not have seemed bad in it. Mr. Luigi Lablache played it deliciously. But I am impatient for the publication of the play, in order that I may see how Mr. Shaw himself, in accordance with his custom, analyses the General's character in his stage-directions. I hazard, as a conjecture: "It being his trade to kill off such of his fellow-creatures as do not see their way to being fleeced by his employers, he goes about the job with every desire to speedily bring it to a satisfactory conclusion, but has no enthusiasm, and, if he had, would be careful not to communicate it to his men, knowing well that enthusiasm has been the cause of ninety per cent. of his country's defeats. Finding himself outgeneralled, he accepts the situation with perfect good-humor, only regretting that the American climate and the dulness of the American generals prevent him from showing his contempt for his country by going over to the enemy. In fact, a realist, whose only illusion is that he is a very agreeable fellow. This (by any civilised standard) he is not; being, indeed, an aggravated type of English gentleman, whose previous professional success alone prevents him from being cordially disliked by the community which has prostituted him to its own ends, and which his failure as a butcher serves thoroughly well right. Withal" . . . but

"O most presumptuous! lay aside the pipe
Of that sweet elder shepherd."

WILLIAM ARCHER AND
A. B. WALKLEY

November 18, 1899

In "The Friends of the Rectory," that delicious example of medio-Victorian romance, you will find these words: "The two daughters of the Reverend James Thornton were both remarkable girls, differing widely in all things except the affection each had for the other. Miss Alice, the elder, was of a serious disposition, smiling seldom, thinking much, and a detester of gossip. Strangers thought her cold, not suspecting that beneath the surface beat a generous and kindly heart. Miss Emily, the younger, was noted for vivacity. In company she was never at a loss, but seemed to delight in laughing and poking fun at everything. . . . The neighbours thought her 'giddy.'" One is accustomed to couple Mr. William Archer and Mr. A. B. Walkley, inasmuch as

they were the pioneers of "live" dramatic criticism in our generation. Just now, these two books,* published at the same moment
and from the same source, seem to put them for me in still closer
juxtaposition. Driven to compare them, I find myself sharply
confronted with the shades of the Misses Thornton.

Miss Emily, as you may remember, had "many admirers," who
were more than a trifle "afraid" of Miss Alice; and I confess that
I am one of those who prefer Mr. Walkley's manner to Mr.
Archer's. Much as I admire W. A., I do not count myself an
"admirer" of him, as of A. B. W. I respect him, revere him, am
vastly impressed by him, always. In him I find my ideal of a
critic, but—is it not always a little disconcerting, even depressing,
to find one's ideal? Besides, I do not much care about good
criticism. I like better the opinions of strong, narrow, creative
personalities. There is more joy in my breast over one oath
roared by Mr. Henley than over the ninety-and-nine just opinions
which a man like Mr. Archer can produce at a moment's notice.
Mr. George Moore, prancing uncinctured through a forest of
mistakes, bruising himself and tumbling head over heels, groping
and groaning his way further into darkness, emerges sooner or
later, if only for an instant, into some brighter patch of sunlight
than is to be found in the cool Academe where sits Mr. Archer,
serene, amenable, scrupulously draped. Perhaps it is not quite
fair to suggest that Mr. Archer is academic. He is by no means
cold, or crabbed, or unapproachable. Indeed, he is a creature of
warm and complete sympathies. He radiates readily in any
direction. That is why he seems to me an ideally good critic.
But, if a man is always radiating at every point, it follows that no
ray can go very far. It is because men like Mr. Henley and Mr.
Moore are so narrow, and therefore, almost invariably, so wrong,
that they are, now and again, so brilliantly right—and, always, so
interesting. If Mr. Archer were less quick to "spot," and to be
grateful for, the soul of goodness in things artistically evil, he
would be a less good critic, but he would be more entertaining
and, here or there, more illuminative. I prefer him as he was in
the days of the Ibsen crusade, and I am delighted when he shows
some faint trace of his early prejudice. Perhaps with a view to

* "Study and Stage," by William Archer (Grant Richards). "Frames
of Mind," by A. B. Walkley (Grant Richards).

showing that he *can* go wrong if he likes, he calls "Mrs. Warren's Profession" a "masterpiece." But I prefer to think that this is a genuine opinion, the result of an old notion that unpleasant material makes a good play. And, I prefer to think him sincere in advising Mrs. Craigie and Mr. Anthony Hope to "tackle" serious themes. Such advice is obviously foolish. But ah, what a relief it is to find Mr. Archer astray! The feet of Gamaliel caught tripping! It seems to bring one into touch with him.

With Mr. Walkley I am always in touch. Not that he is one of those strong, narrow spirits which I love to watch in criticism! On the contrary, he is almost as broadminded as Mr. Archer. He is neither hater nor lover, but just a level-headed, tolerant student of things. In a way, he appeals to me less than Mr. Archer. For his is the scientific method, and I like art-criticism to be æsthetic. He is never quite able to forget that he once took a first "in Scientiis Mathematicis et Physicis," and he has cultivated his mind at the expense of those emotions which, in matters of art, are of infinitely greater importance. He does not, like Mr. Archer, love the theatre; indeed he is inclined to despise it. But fate has thrown him in the way of it, and he finds much in it to consider and to discuss. His attitude is not inspiring. Yet he makes it delightful for me. This, by simple means: he is always amusing. He seems "to delight in laughing and poking fun at everything." Humour always pervades the soundest of his theories, making fantasy of common-sense, and softening the dry light with rosy shades. And it is by reason of his humour that his judgments in dramatic criticism carry little weight for the public. Like Miss Emily, he is thought "giddy." In Paris, he would be taken very seriously indeed, for there, as we know, absence of humour is not considered essential to sound work. Mr. Archer's style is not dull, but, again, it is not bright. Consequently, he has attained to a solid "position," and his judgments carry tremendous weight —at least, among all those who do not go to the play.

Whatever the comparative merits of Mr. Archer and Mr. Walkley, there is no doubt at all that Mr. Walkley's is the nicer book. Both books consist of reprints from various papers—current criticisms of literature, drama and so forth. Mr. Archer's criticisms suffer, in a book, from the excellence of them as reviews for newspapers. His detailed considerations of books now forgotten and plays now withdrawn are very admirable, and will have, no doubt, great documentary interest in the future, but for the moment they seem almost superfluous. By Mr. Walkley subject-matter is less conscientiously treated, and thus his writings "wear" much better. It is not so much his aim to explain to his readers the merits and demerits of this or that work as to construct a theory or point a moral. He begins with a phrase, works round his subject, comes back to the phrase, and makes his bow. He is anxious to reveal himself—in other words to show how clever he is, and how amusing. In fact, he is more of an essayist than a critic, though his criticism is always sound and adequate, except when he is dealing with vast, elemental subjects, such as Balzac. These seem to annoy him. So much the more fun! Mr. Walkley's only irritating fault is his too great allusiveness. He lets Boswell, Aristotle, Sam Weller, Marcus Aurelius and other more recondite philosophers crop up just a little too often. I do not object to Mr. Walkley's erudition. A man cannot read too much. But he can remember too much of his reading. After all, every-thing has been said a great many times. No man can say a new thing, but he can always say it in a new (that is, in his own) way. And he cannot say it in his own way if he remembers exactly how a dozen other people have said it before him: he takes the mould handiest to him instead of making one of his own. Thus is literature impoverished. However, there are occasions when inverted commas have a peculiar value, giving point or weight to the context, and Mr. Walkley often strikes pretty effects from his bookishness. He quotes from Michelet a purple patch about women: "'It is with her as it is with the sky in relation to the earth: it is below and above and all round. In her we had our birth. Through her we live. We are enveloped by her; she is the atmosphere, our heart's blood.' 'Gents,' says the bagman in 'Pickwick,' 'I give you woman.' Michelet 'gives us woman' with a vengeance," &c., &c. It is for such things as these that I delight in Mr. Walkley.

Well! I am glad that two so gifted creatures as W. A. and A. B. W. are writing dramatic criticism. I wish very much that the general mass of dramatic criticism showed signs of being im-proved by their example. Mr. Walkley seems to contend that signed articles are a kind of panacea. But there is one insuperable

obstacle to the general use of signed articles in dramatic criticism :
most of the critics, I am convinced, cannot sign their names.
When I read their articles, I have a suspicion, amounting to a conviction, that reading and writing were not included in their upbringing, and that their articles are simply dictated to the com-
positor. It follows that, in most cases, the only authentic signa-
ture would be a simple " × ." But that would be little better
than anonymity. Besides, though well enough on a ballot-paper,
it might be bad for the dignity of the Press.

A VANISHED HAND

December 9, 1899

If I am not very careful, I shall soon have that deadliest of all
assets, a theatrical library. Week in, week out, they come drifting
to me from the office of this Review, these dreadful, innumerable
volumes about mimes dead and forgotten, plays and playwrights
dead and forgotten, theatres pulled down and forgotten. Why
are these volumes written? Why should any one presume to
remember things which are, and ought to be, forgotten by every
one else? Why these desperate raids on oblivion? Who wants
to know that "the mantle of Macready, which fell all too soon
from his sturdy shoulders, was modestly assumed by his brave and
faithful lieutenant, Samuel Phelps, one of the great actors of the
century whose noble work at Sadler's Wells can never be forgotten"? The fact is that the noble work of the nineteenth
century (or does Mr. Scott* mean Samuel Phelps' noble work?)
at Sadler's Wells *has* been forgotten, clean forgotten, except by
those persons who are old enough to have frequented Sadler's
Wells during its management by the nineteenth century (or
Samuel Phelps). For those who saw Samuel Phelps on the stage,
such reminiscence may be interesting enough. If Samuel Phelps
had possessed in his theatre a combination of phonograph and

* "The Drama of Yesterday and To-day." Clement Scott. 2 vols.
London: Macmillan. 1899. 36s. net.

biograph to enable us to appreciate his abilities as clearly as those of any actor who is disporting himself to-night, then, no doubt, he might mean something to us. Perhaps there will soon be some such invention, and then our grandchildren will not yawn when they listen to our reminiscences of early-twentieth-century mimes. Failing such an invention, we shall, I am afraid, have either to keep our reminiscences to ourselves or to be accounted tedious. So long as the mime's performances are inaudible and invisible after his retirement or decease, so long must he, as artist, forego the claim to anything like immortality. Reminiscences of Thackeray or Browning, Millais or Rossetti, are interesting to us; for great writers and painters are known to us through imperishable work. Criticism of them does not seem to us belated; for we can ourselves still criticise them. But Phelps, Macready, Webster, Buckstone—at them, gently but firmly, we draw the line. Gently but firmly, we protest against any effort to drive in the thin end of immortality's wedge. We understand and respect the motive of such efforts, we suspect that we ourselves shall hereafter be guilty of similar efforts; but that does not make us shrink from the painful duty of discouraging them.

In reading Mr. Scott's book, then, I have carefully skipped those parts of it which deal with "the drama of yesterday." About "the drama of to-day," however, Mr. Scott is very well worth reading. He is generally in the wrong (as must be any man who regards Tom Robertson as a terminus), but he is never dully in the wrong. If a man is dull, rightness in him does not conciliate me. If he is not dull, wrongness in him is for me no drawback. Mr. Scott has a personality, and therefore I delight in him. It is not, perhaps, a very fine personality, and it is, in many respects, a very absurd personality; but the fact remains that it *is* a definite, consistent personality; and, as such, it always claims some of my attention. Mr. Scott has had, moreover, a strangely chequered life. Hot water has been, and still is, his natural element. His life has been a dissolving view of scrimmages, and it is amusing to note how naïvely unconscious he is that the cause of his troubles lies merely in himself. Again and again, he suggests that dramatic criticism is the most exciting and dangerous career open to a young man. He speaks, ruefully, of "that fatal charger, dramatic criticism." He seems to think that an honest dramatic critic will always, of necessity, be embroiled with the objects of his criticism, and that disingenuousness is the only path to be trodden in peace. I need hardly point out that there is not, really, anything at all dangerous in the practice of honest dramatic criticism. Everything depends on the "tone" of your criticism, and on whether you make bosom-friends among the people whom you may be called on to criticise. Now, Mr. Scott has always been much more interested in the art of acting than in the art of dramaturgy; and his temperament, and the circumstances under which he has written, have always combined to make his "tone" one of violent ecstasy—ecstasy of blame, ecstasy of praise. Mimes, as I have often pointed out, are necessarily more sensitive to praise or blame than are other artists. It is probable, therefore, that they would have been very often very angry with Mr. Scott even if they had never seen him outside a theatre. But here, again, comes in the question of temperament. Mr. Scott's temperament is such that he cannot admire a mime without yearning to grip him or her by the hand. "I told Fred Charles, who had acted with Fechter, and was now at the St. James's Theatre with Irving, that there were few young actors I was more desirous of meeting." And so Fred Charles arrived at Mr. Scott's room in the War Office bringing young Irving in tow. The incident is typical. All through his life, Mr. Scott has lived in histrionic society. If he had cared nothing about acting, or if, caring, he had been able to express blame gently and temperately, there need have been no exciting consequences. But Mr. Scott has always cared more about acting than about anything else in the world, and, though a good performance has always filled him with a desire to grip the performer's hand, he has never felt restrained from lashing out at what seemed to him a bad performance by the fact of a previous handgrip. I do not pretend that so emotional a creature as Mr. Scott has never had his judgment warped by personal friendship (and personal enmity), but I incline to the belief that all the opinions he has expressed have been opinions in which at the moment of expression he did honestly believe. He has had his favourites, and his detestations. But he has always believed in the soundness of his superlatives in favour of his favourites, and of his superlatives in detraction of his detestations. And there have always come moments when he has turned and rent his favourites. What wonder that "bad blood" has been the result? What wonder that even those who were not favourites resented being wildly rent by one whom they knew personally, whom they often sat next to at supper? Ecstasy of praise is slightly discounted by personal acquaintance; but ecstasy of blame is very much aggravated by it. Mr. Scott wrote for a morning paper, and had never time for qualification. The critic of a morning paper must either confine himself to safe *clichés* or run riot in superlatives. Mr. Scott never confined himself to *clichés*, for he had theories about acting. Also, he had the lamentable distinction of being the most rapid writer on the press. He could write, in half an hour, more words than any other man—very long words, too, many of them. Thus, though he had not time enough for reflection, he had time enough to "rub it in." And if the embrocation happened to be a bitter one—well, then, no wonder he got himself disliked!

Personally (not being an actor), I regret Mr. Scott's voluntary exile in America. I console myself with the assurance that soon he will be again in our midst. The Americans do things on a far larger scale than we. If Mr. Scott could not stand our buckets of hot water, will he stand the scalding reservoirs in New York? No! I expect that he will soon be here, more deeply than ever convinced that honest dramatic criticism means martyrdom, and that his colleagues escape the stake only because they are not honest.

PUNITIVE PANTOMIME

December 30, 1899

"The Snow Man" is not a pantomime to which all children, indiscriminately, should be taken by their parents. But all naughty children should be taken to it at once. It is, I know, a stern measure that I am advocating; one from which many parents will shrink, partly in fear of the S. P. C. C., partly from an incapacity to see why the sins of the children should be visited on themselves. Nevertheless, I advocate it. The sentimental way of treating children has been tried, and it has failed. Our piteous appeal to their better natures has been intercepted by their worse. It is well known that naughtiness is alarmingly on the increase. Parents must make a stand. Let them make their stand now, in the Lyceum Theatre. Let all children who persistently tell fibs, tear their clothes, run away from home, stamp their feet, refuse to say their prayers, steal jam, fidget, make faces, blot their copybooks and slide down the banisters, be taken, summarily, to see "The Snow Man." Let them arrive for the rise of the curtain, and be kept there for its fall. Then let them be given fair warning that unless they reform they will be taken to see it again. So will naughtiness be stamped out.

But what irony! This sovereign remedy is itself a part of that system which has fostered the disease. Doubtless, in producing "The Snow Man," Mr. Comyns Carr imagined that he was offering to children something which they really would love—something to "spoil" them, and so make them the more beautiful and delightful. The modern system of child-culture, to which Mr. Carr thus conforms, is the system of treating children as decoration. It was inaugurated by Miss Kate Greenaway, developed by the late Mr. Stevenson, spun to a chaste perfection by Mrs. Meynell. Its basis is a feeling that childhood is not (as the world has hitherto supposed) a mere prelude to maturity, but the perfect flower of human existence. Our aim, therefore, should be, not to treat children in such a way as may tend to make them acquit themselves well in after-years, but to conserve in them, passionately, all their wild, little, pretty, untutored impulses. Children are here for our delight, and if we interfere with them we shall be robbing ourselves of our delight. How can we most surely keep them as they are? By making them happy. How make them happiest? By showing them, at all times and in all places, how much we admire them. Here we have the source of all the modern books for children. Instead of cautionary tales, illustrated by grim wood-cuts, we give children pretty little pictures of themselves walking down lanes in prettily-coloured and quaintly-fashioned clothes; and, very gently, we read aloud to them pretty little verses written by grown-up persons who try to remember and reproduce what was done in the green leaf; then we kiss them, and use every means to dissuade them from leaving

us on the plea that it is bed-time. We do not perceive that
children, though they are quick to take advantage of our devotion
and to use it for their own ends, are intensely bored by us, and
that our efforts to pose them as decoration evoke from them none
of the gratitude we have a right to expect. We do not perceive
that the kind of pantomime inaugurated by Mr. Oscar Barrett, so
delightful to us, bores them to extinction. Such pantomimes are
praised by the critics, as being "delightful for the little ones,"
"endless fun for the tots," and so forth. But if the editors, who
mostly engage for the criticism of plays men whose opinions
coincide as nearly as possible with those of the public, were consistent enough to engage children for the criticism of pantomimes,
the result would be that the kind of pantomimes supposed to
appeal especially to children would be so unanimously damned by
the Press as to necessitate their instant withdrawal. Children
have no more wish for "refinement" in pantomimes than in any
other things. They do not want graceful dancing or pretty songs.
Above all, they do not want idealised versions of themselves.
Stories about children, enacted by children, and illustrated by
ballets of children, drive grown-up persons into paroxysms of
delight, but they induce gloom into any one under the age of (say)
fifteen. What children want—no blame to them—is a show with
plenty of monsters, demons, noise and buffoonery. These things
are to be found at Drury Lane; but there, alas! unpleasantly
overlaid with didactic processions, allegorical ballets and all the rest
of it. The only pantomimes really suitable to children are to be
found in the suburbs and the provinces. The metropolitan
caterers (except Mr. Collins, who was caught very young by Sir
Augustus Harris) all seem to have fallen under the spell first cast
by Miss Greenaway. This is very delightful for us who are grown-
up. But it would not be so if "The Snow Man" were a fair
specimen of its kind. A more spectral entertainment one can
hardly imagine. It is all the more spectral by reason that many
of the big and little mimes engaged in it show glimpses of considerable talent: one is appalled by the utter waste made of them. It is
all the more spectral by reason of the very pretty scenery and
dresses: one wonders why should so much money and good taste
not have been kept to embellish something a little worthy of them.
Again, "Who," one asks, "is Mr. Arthur Sturgess? Why was

he asked to write the book of the play?" Mr. Carr's answers to these questions would be, I suppose, (1) "A Pantomime Librettist." (2) "Because he is a Pantomime Librettist." Well! I can understand that experience goes for something. One naturally expects that an experienced workman will be able to construct a story for the stage more or less clearly and dramatically. But that is just what Mr. Sturgess fails to do. I defy the most inexperienced duffer to produce a more opaque rigmarole than "The Snow Man," with its endless superfluities, and repetitions, and involutions, and blanks. But even if Mr. Sturgess had justified the confidence felt in his practical capabilities? Surely, in a writer of "refined" pantomime, one demands some measure of poetic feeling, metric talent, humour, fancy, and so on. Thus, in any case, a collaborator would have been necessary. And I fancy that the collaborator would have pointed out to Mr. Sturgess that the Snow Man was bound to be dreary on the stage, and would have offered to invent a superior substitute within half an hour. The idea of an animated Snow Man, who, with the best intentions, casts a chill upon all around him and freezes the heart of every one he touches, is not a bad symbolical idea for treatment in a book. But on the stage, where you see the actual process— and Mr. Sturgess lets you see it again and again—the Snow Man is quite intolerable. The auditorium seemed to be growing colder and colder. Our teeth chattered. We struggled into our greatcoats, and sat with upturned collars. Realism had been going too far. Mr. James Welch played the part of Snow Man. I suspect he was as much depressed by it as were the rest of us. I had, however, no means of being sure; for he was hidden from head to foot in an impenetrable costume of sheep-skin, and had as little chance of displaying any kind of emotion as a sultana bound for the Bosphorus.

Enough! If I have awakened parents to the chance they have in "The Snow Man" of undoing the evil which recent years of sentimentality have created, then do I forgive Mr. Sturgess the dreadful entertainment. Let every naughty child, forthwith, be taken to the Lyceum. One visit will be enough, surely. But there are matinées and evening performances. The very desperate offender might be taken twice in one day (thick bread-and-butter to be consumed, in the brief interval, at the nearest Aërated Bread Shop).

FIRST NIGHTS

January 6, 1900

One of the questions with which a fussy conscience loves to pose me is whether I ought not to abjure first nights. I am always driven to admit that I ought to. And yet—such is human frailty —I don't.

The fact is, I like first nights for their own sake. Partly, no doubt, this fondness for them is due to my being a seasoned frequenter of them. If accident order that you do a thing many times, your nature, imperceptibly, adapts itself to the function. Even if the thing be not, at first and in itself, congenial to you, it will become really congenial at last. The gods gave us Habit, lest the world, that mechanical toy which they had made for their laughter, should disappoint them by stopping and heeling over with a gr-r-r-r very soon after it had been wound up. I do not, however, mean to imply that I ever had a distaste for first nights. On the contrary, I always regarded them as rather a "treat." But now they are more than that to me. They are an integral part of my life, a recurring pleasure to which I look keenly forward. And that, I regret to say, is one of several reasons why I ought to keep away from them. The spirit in which I go is not the right spirit for a critic. I ought to go in a mood of serious æstheticism, merely to see a play acted by mimes on a stage. As it is, my mood is freaked with a kind of festivity. I have a kind of vague sense that I am "going it." Of course, we all have more or less of this feeling whenever we go to a theatre. When we open a book, or pass the turn-stile of a picture gallery, our hearts do not leap irrelevantly. But a theatre has magic of its own. The old Puritanism still survives just enough to make us feel that we are being rather bold. Besides, was not a pantomime the most mysterious, rare, delirious joy of us when we were small children, the most brilliant occasion for "sitting-up," the least exhaustible topic for weeks after? We cannot, even now, quite rid ourselves of the idea that there is in a theatre something which makes for exhilaration. And this idea is fostered by the hour at which plays are acted. Whatever is done after dinner has an air of recreation—

our senses override our thoughts, making fribbles of us. For this reason, I hope that when Mr. William Archer opens (as I trust he will, in the teeth of incivism and stupidity) his Ideal Theatre, the curtain will be rung up every morning not later than 9.30 A.M. That, I take it, is the hour when we are most receptive of serious art. Of course, the aim of drama, as of all arts, is to give pleasure; but before we can hope to raise drama to the level of other arts we must undermine, by every means in our power, the custom of regarding the theatre as a jolly place in which to digest food and sit in amity with our fellow-creatures. "Let us away with the glamour of the theatre!" is a hard saying, perhaps; but right and necessary, for all that. And never has the theatre so much glamour as on the first night of a play. Never is it so fascinating in itself. The familiar faces in the audience; the mutual bows, smiles, hand-shakes, hand-waves; the sprightliness of it all, and the frantic self-importance—these are gusts by which I, having a sociable temperament, am quickly carried off my feet. We are about to see something which has never been seen, and our anxiety to know what it will be like is eclipsed by pride in our strange privilege of being on the spot. That, in its turn, is eclipsed by the privilege of seeing and being seen by one another. In fact, it is almost as difficult to see a play at a first night as to see pictures at a private view. Apart from the social element at a first night, there is also the sentimental element, still more blinding to me. I cannot help remembering how much depends, for how many people, on the success or failure of the play. I think of the over-wrought manager, and of all it means to him. I see the mimes less as figures in a play than as men and women hoping for good "notices" in the newspapers, hoping they will not "fluff," wondering whether so-and-so is "in front." I see the box in which the author's family is sitting. I never fail to recognise that box, and I find myself glancing up to it throughout the play. How awfully calm are they who sit in it! Indifference how Olympian is theirs! Yet, if one watch them closely, one will see interchanges of encouraging smiles, pressure of hands, and other tokens that they are mortal. At the fall of the curtain, they keep up a vigorous applause under the ledge of the box; they shoot glances of scorn and hatred and defiance at the Gallery if there are any "dissentient voices" there. And in every entr'acte there will be mysterious retreats to the back of the box, where, maybe, pale in the impenetrable shadow, stands he whose work I have come to criticise. What drama could he write that would match, in human poignancy and significance, the spectacle of his box? Is it wonderful that my eyes wander to his box so often? "Perhaps not," he might answer. "But it would be more fair to me if you would come and see my play on the second or third night." And I should be bound to admit the pertinence of his reply. Or perhaps I should plead that I had been exaggerating. That is a plea which I might fairly make. It is true that the author's box always fascinates and touches me, and that the social aspect of a first night is distracting, also; but, on the whole, I am able to keep my attention fairly well fixed on the play. There are more really valid objections to a first night. One of them I have already noted: few mimes can, on a first night, do justice to themselves, and, accordingly, it is unfair to judge them. Another is that a good play seems, in its first performance, better than it would seem to one in any other performance, and that a bad play seems worse. All dramatic critics would, I think, bear me out on this point. Seeing a play for the second time, they must all have often wondered why they were so very emphatic, what reason they had for all those epithets. Nor is the explanation at all remote. Excitement, as we all know, is contagious, and the public at a first night is always in a state of peculiar excitement. The most detached creature in the world cannot help being to some degree affected by it. Insensibly, the balance of his judgment is disturbed. I do not mean that loud cheers and applause will make him think the play good, or that groans will incense him against it; the effect may be, as it tends to be in my case, the exact reverse. The point is that he is infected by the audience's excitement. His nerves are strung up to an unnatural pitch, even before the curtain has risen. All his impressions are tinged with hysteria. Therefore, if I really had the interests of the drama at heart, and if I really wished to do my full duty to my readers, I should take my imaginary playwright's advice, and go on the second or third night. Nay! I should go on the second night *and* on the third. No critic is able to criticise a play rightly after seeing it but once. If he write for a daily paper he has to exhaust himself with the effort to remember every turn of the plot, in order that he may write a clear *précis*. If he write for a weekly paper, he has to be on the alert for something which will make the basis for a theory—some salient feature on which he can fasten an idea. In neither case can he derive any of that untrammelled pleasure, emotional or intellectual, which a work of art should excite in him. Therefore, I suggest, let him go in a private capacity to the second night, and as a critic to the third. From the first night let him be absent. So will he have the chance of writing something really fine and just. Will the critics, I wonder, be swayed by this counsel of perfection? Not I, for one. Few plays deserve to be seen at all; on the other hand, I grow more and more fond of first nights.

HISTORIC CHARACTERS AND THE STAGE

January 27, 1900

There was a memorable experiment in a melodrama lately seen by me at the Princess' Theatre. The scene was Hyde Park—a review of troops ordered to the front, a stageful of supers in khaki. While the orchestra played the National Anthem, there appeared a landau, in which sat three female supers. One of them was meant to represent the Queen; the other two, Princesses. Yet I, who am an emotional loyalist, was quite unmoved by the sight of them. Of course, they were not really of the blood royal, not the real persons. But that does not explain my apathy. I have thrilled at the sight of Cleopatra on the stage, though I knew that she whom I saw was not really Queen of Egypt. In fact, I am as illudible in theatres as any one else. Why, then, did not the occupants of the landau stir my heart? This question suggests another: how far is it artistically possible to introduce into a play the figures of men or women who are known to exist or to have existed in real life?

Obviously, it is not well to show us a physically inexact representation of one whom we have all seen, whose appearance we know exactly. The representation must be exact; else, illusion is obviously impossible. At the Princess', the representation was not exact. Indeed, I have seldom seen any one less like the

Queen than the lady chosen by the management to represent her. Even had she herself carried any conviction to me, the two Princesses, picturesquely tousled and attired in the gaudiest and most unguelfish fashion, would immediately have robbed me of it. In point of fact, though the trick might have been done better than it was, it could not, in any circumstances, have come off. It is (practically) impossible to make on the stage a satisfactory representation of any one who is well known to us by sight; and even if the (practically) impossible feat were achieved we should be not illuded, but merely startled and amused. Thus it seems that notable living persons ought not to be introduced into plays. Does the same rule apply to the illustrious dead? Let me take the case of the Duke of Wellington. I never saw him. My knowledge of his appearance is derived from various prints, engravings, paintings, which, none of them exactly tallying with another, give me a general impression of him. An actor might be able to satisfy this impression of mine, without satisfying the people who actually saw him. The appearance of Mr. Fulton, in a dreadful play called "The Days of the Duke," was quite good enough for me. But did I derive the necessary illusion that the Duke was before me? Did the carefully-built bridge on Mr. Fulton's nose span the yawning gulf between illusion and me? Never for one moment. I knew quite well, could not for one moment rid myself of the knowledge, that here was a sound young actor, who had never saved his country and would never have his windows broken by his idolaters. On the other hand, I remember a play in which I had a real illusion of the Duke. In the third act of "Rosemary," the characters, as you may remember, were assembled in an upper room, waiting to see the pageant of the Queen's Coronation. One of them, who was looking out of the window, suddenly cried "Here's the Duke!" All rushed to the window, cheered, waved their handkerchiefs, crying "The Duke! The Duke!" I had a real illusion that the slim, bent figure was riding by on the big horse, stiffly saluting them. But had they said "See! He dismounts! He's coming up the stairs!" and had he come in, however well made-up, on however good a pretext, I know that my illusion would have left me precipitately. It is, indeed, much safer to keep great historical figures "off." In "Julius Cæsar," one believes in Cæsar so long as he does not

appear. Such, at least, was my experience at Her Majesty's.
When he was on the stage, presto! the illusion was gone. Again I
saw the solid bridge on Mr. Fulton's nose, and again (so to speak)
I would not trust myself on it. Yet Mr. Fulton was dignified and
sonorous. Had he played Antony, or Brutus, or Cassius, I should
have been illuded by him. And yet again, were not Antony,
Brutus, and Cassius great historical figures, in their degrees?
And Cleopatra, by whom I have been illuded on the stage, was not
she, in her sex, as great as Cæsar even? Why does Cæsar leave
me cold? It is because Shakespeare has not risen to the conception of him, and has made him a mere shadow. If he presents a
great historical figure, the dramatist must also be careful to make a
great part. It is not enough to bring the figure on and let him take
his chance of impressing the audience by his name. Small
historical figures can be brought on in subordinate parts and be
accepted quite readily by the audience. But one does not accept
Cæsar, unless the dramatist has charged the creation with something of the vast significance which the real Cæsar has for us.
One is merely amused or offended, and sorry for the actor who is
cast for the part. When I said just now that it was "safer" to
keep such figures "off," I was remembering how very few dramatists ever were themselves great enough to bring them on successfully. Shakespeare was great enough for the trick, though he
bungled in the case of Cæsar. And if he was great enough, Mr.
Stephen Phillips must, presumably, be great enough, also. But I
doubt whether there is any other living dramatist whom I would
quite readily trust. And so I would lay it down as a general rule
for dramatists, that the very illustrious dead had better be let lie,
for the present.

They who are living are to be barred for a reason which I have
already suggested, and for another reason. Shakespeare was able
to re-create Cleopatra, because she, like Hecuba, was nothing to
his audience. He could not have re-created Elizabeth, because
she was much to it—part and parcel of its times, indissociable
from its realities. She had not arrived at the time when it were
possible to be useful in fiction. Living characters cannot even
be used "off"; even so they would destroy verisimilitude. Moreover, figures of men not actually living, but belonging to the
immediate past, must not be used for theatrical purposes,

Mr. Gladstone, Mr. Parnell, Lord Randolph Churchill—the time is not yet come for them to be susceptible of any fictional treatment. It seems almost unnecessary to point this out; but I once saw a play called "General Gordon" (in which the chief part was acted by a favourite provincial actor with raven curls and a lisp), and so, perhaps, the warning is not really quite superfluous. When actual figures *do* become a fit subject for the dramatist it is almost impossible to determine. There is not, as in questions of copyright, any exact limit. One cannot say exactly how long an interval must elapse after a great man's death before we may, without breach of taste, discuss publicly his private failings—one cannot fix the date of his falling out of actual life into history. Likewise, one cannot say how soon he may be treated in drama.

"AU REVOIR"

February 3, 1900

It is almost a year since Mount Moore was in eruption. It is almost a year since from that flammivomous summit the torrents of baleful lava rolled down over London, entombing (for ever, as we thought) Mr. William Archer, Mr. George Alexander, Mr. Pinero and other men of sin. The flames have subsided, the torrents dried, the smoke has drifted from between us and the sky, and the victims have surprised us by emerging, scathed but not shrivelled, and going about their business. But I have ever kept my telescope towards the yawning summit, supposing that some more awful vengeance surely would issue. And now, indeed, the eruption has begun again. In this month's number of the "Fortnightly Review," Mr. Moore has a "Preface to 'The Bending of the Bough.'" But how different from last year's preface to "The Heather Field"! How very mild! If Primrose Hill were to pose as a volcano, it would not affright us less. Indeed, dealing with Mr. Moore's latest manner, I must altogether drop the simile of the volcano. Let me say rather, a little chaste star, infinitely remote, wistful, innocuous, unassuming.

"Much have I striven, and some things have I compassed, and
known sorrow and fear and the lovelessness of men. But now go
I back to my own land, even to that dear land overseas whence
I came. For there my heart is." So, in the legend, spoke a
hero of whom Mr. Moore has never reminded me much. So
speaks Mr. Moore in the "Fortnightly." True, he and Mr.
Martyn and Mr. Yeats "have turned our backs on London as men
turn their backs on a place which has ceased to interest them," but
Mr. Moore, at least, shakes the dust off his feet with a very gentle
kick, and looks back not without a smile and a sigh to the abandoned city. "We did not," he murmurs, "decide on our home-
ward journey without having considered the reformation of
London. After some doubts, some hesitation, it suddenly came
upon us that it was impossible." This, I confess, thrills me,
intrigues me vastly. I long to know the exact moment of the
fateful apocalypse. Was the world unconsciously revolving, and
we, its parasites, were we behaving quite in our usual manner,
making "the same old crush at the corner of Fenchurch Street,"
and exciting ourselves over the trivialities of our noisy humdrum,
when, suddenly in some sequestered room where they were sitting
silent, Mr. Moore, Mr. Martyn and Mr. Yeats started from their
chairs and said "We must pack up our things"? At that moment,
did no shudder run through the metropolis, as through one over
whose grave some one is walking? Did no stars fall, nor statues
perspire? *Can* such a seed be dropped without the whole earth
quivering under its impact?

But perhaps I overrate the significance of Mr. Moore's article.
Certainly, if Mr. Moore were to spend the rest of his life away
from us, our loss would be very great; we should lose an unique
and most stimulating person. But I suspect that he will not
really withdraw himself for long. A play of his will be produced
next month, at the Irish Literary Theatre in Dublin, and this
simple fact is quite enough to account for his elaborate valediction.
It is one of Mr. Moore's peculiarities that whatever is uppermost
in his mind seems to him to be the one thing in the world, and he
cannot conceive that there will ever be room for anything else.
He surveys the history of the world, in order to show that Art
cannot exist longer in England, and that it is probably about to
exist in Ireland. He argues that great movements in Art have

sprung only in nations after some great national struggle; that, so soon as a nation becomes great and wealthy and replete, Art cannot continue to exist in it, and never returns to it; that England, accordingly, is no place for him, and that Ireland is. "It is impossible," he says, "to write plays in England except for money." But is it? Have not we at least one thriving society for the production of plays written for love? Such plays, according to Mr. Moore, "are offered to the Irish rather than to the English public." But they are not offered to the Irish public. They are offered quietly, in a little hall, to a few Irish people. The Irish public does not want them at all. That, however, does not prevent them from being written. Nor does the indifference of the English public prevent Englishmen from writing similar plays and getting them produced. It may be that the Irish Literary Theatre marks the beginning of a great dramatic literature in Ireland, and that in England there will be no more great plays. Personally, I have great hopes of the Irish Literary Theatre; but I do not, on the other hand, despair of drama in England. I do not agree with Mr. Moore that Art cannot return to a nation. The genius of Elizabethans has not prevented the Victorian era from producing a great literature of its own. Why should it prevent us from an outburst of great plays? For my own part I think it improbable that the great wave of Victorian literature will recoil without washing up some fragments, at least, of great drama; and I am keeping a hopeful eye on the shore. However, my aim is not to refute Mr. Moore's interesting theories, but to assure myself and my readers that Mr. Moore is not lost to us for ever. His, as I have said, is a mind violently exclusive, and present disgust of London is amply explained by the impending production in Dublin. But even if the Keltic Renascence prove to be the most important movement ever made in Art it will not long enchain him. His blazing passions burn themselves out rapidly, and the white-hot core gapes for other fuel. At heart he is a dilettante, though he differs from most of his kind in that his taste does not diverge simultaneously to one thing and another. All his taste is concentrated always on one thing, but nothing can hold him long. That he was born in Ireland does not imply any probability that he will stay there. For the moment, he is fulfilled of patriotism, but only because the kind of Art in which he is immersed happens to have sprung from his native soil. A few weeks hence, if I hear that he has appeared in Edinburgh and declared that to be the only place to live in, I shall not be surprised. And I know that the prodigal will come back, at last, to London, the city which has harboured him through most years of his maturity. I hope I shall go to see his play in Dublin, for I suspect that it will be his only contribution to Irish Art. Already, even in his article, I find signs that his allegiance is straying. When he says "It were better to delight a moment in the little candour of the robin, and to admire the coral hedge of the irreparable year," I feel sure that he will soon be trumpeting the immortality of Mrs. Meynell.

TWO PERFORMANCES OF SHAKESPEARE

February 24, 1900

Mr. F. R. Benson is an Oxford man, and he is in the habit of recruiting his company from his university. Insomuch that, according to the "Daily Chronicle," "the influence of university cricket has been seen in the cricket fields of many provincial towns visited by Mr. Benson's company, as well as that of university culture on the boards of the local theatres. In the summer months cricket by day and dramatic art in the evening is a rule which he follows as far as possible." A delightful existence! The stumps are drawn, the curtain is rung up. All day long the sun shines while Mr. Benson and his merrymen wring from the neighbourhood respectful admiration of university cricket. But, when the shadows of the wickets lengthen across the pitch, the call-boy appears, and the tired but victorious mimes go to doff their flannels and to don the motley. I repeat, a delightful existence! But one cannot help wondering what Mr. Vincent Crummles would have thought of it. "Trace the influence of university cricket and university culture on histrionic art at the close of the nineteenth century" is likely to be a favourite question when the Drama, at length, gets its chartered Academy, with power to set examination-papers. University culture imbues the mime with some sense of blank verse, and saves him from solecisms in pronunciation. University cricket keeps his body in good training, enables him to move on the stage with the more agility and to posture with the more grace. In the old days, before the cult of athletics, and before acting was regarded as a genteel art, the strolling mimes were mostly illiterate and mostly fat. They knew little of anything but their art, and they spent their days in drinking, and smoking, and talking about their performances. They were not gentlemen, and as men they were very poor creatures indeed, vastly inferior to their successors. But as artists? That is another matter. The better man is not necessarily the better mime, nor does even gentility carry one very far in art. Art is a mysterious thing, in which cads and weaklings may often excel, and gentlemanly athletes may often fail. The old strollers lived a life of degradation; but it does not follow that their excess in alcohol and nicotine hurt them as mimes. The new strollers play cricket and other games, and are healthy and reputable fellows; but they do not necessarily act the better for that. Indeed, I should say (though it is a hard saying) that the old method was better than the new. The art of acting, more even than any other art, demands that the artist live on his nerves: the more highly-strung his nerves, the better he will act. The old stroller, living a sedentary life and indulging overmuch in stimulants, was a bundle of nerves. The new stroller is a bundle of muscles. Of course, as I have suggested, muscles are a very good thing for a mime to have. The ideal mime would be a bundle of nerves *and* muscles. But alas! the two things do not go together, and nerves are infinitely the more important of the two. The old stroller would cut a sorry figure on the cricket pitch: he would muff all his catches and be bowled out first ball. But on the wooden boards, behind the footlights, he seems to us more admirable than the members of Mr. Benson's eleven—company, I mean.

Alertness, agility, grace, physical strength—all these good attributes are obvious in the mimes who were, last week, playing "Henry the Fifth" at the Lyceum. Every member of the cast seemed in tip-top condition—thoroughly "fit." Subordinates and principals all worked well together. The fielding was excellent, and so was the batting. Speech after speech was sent spinning across the boundary, and one was constantly inclined to shout

TWO PERFORMANCES

"Well *played*, sir! Well played *indeed*!" As a branch of university cricket, the whole performance was, indeed, beyond praise.
But, as a form of acting, it was not impressive. Not one of the
parts was played with any distinction. There was not one that
stood out at the time or was remembered later. Every one rattled
along and bustled about and gave one the impression that he was a
jolly, modest, high-spirited, presentable young fellow in private
life; and there one's impression of him ended. The whole thing
was very pleasant, but it was not Shakespearian acting. It had
neither the sonorous dignity of the old school, nor the subtle
intelligence of the modern metropolitan school. It was simply
what the dramatic critics call "adequate," meaning "inadequate."
Now, there are some Shakespearian plays of which "adequate"
performances are tolerable. But "Henry the Fifth" is not one of
them. It should be done brilliantly, splendidly, or not at all.
Only the best kind of acting, and the best kind of production,
could make it anything but tedious. Except a few purple patches
of poetry, it contains nothing whatsoever of merit. It is just a
dull, incoherent series of speeches, interspersed with alarums and
excursions. As a spectacle, it might be made much of. Mimes
might, by exercise of much imagination, make the speeches
interesting and impressive. With a very keen sense of character,
they might give life and individuality to the puppets. But, since
Mr. Benson's system precludes spectacle, and since cricket tends
to exhaust in its devotees the energy which might otherwise be
spent in cultivating imagination and sense of character, those
members of the public who forgot to visit the Lyceum last week
lost very little and (I am tempted to say) escaped much. Before
these words appear, Mr. Benson will have produced "A Midsummer Night's Dream." That will be quite another matter.
It is, in itself, a play of surpassing beauty. So are "The Tempest," and "Antony and Cleopatra," and other Shakespearian
plays which Mr. Benson is to produce in due course. Even if the
performances of them be not better than the performance of
"Henry the Fifth," they will be well worth seeing. I trust that
Mr. Benson will have a successful season. His enthusiasm for
Shakespeare is very laudable and attractive. No one could help
wishing him well. But—but he must, really, break himself and
his company of this fatal cricketing-habit.

Last Wednesday, in Carpenters' Hall, the Elizabethan Stage Society played the "First Quarto Hamlet," "as it hath been diverse times acted by his Highnesse servants in the Citte of London." The aim of the Society is, expressly, "educational"; and, indeed, Mr. Poel does succeed in teaching us to pity the poor Elizabethans and to be thankful for the realism of the modern theatre. Now and again, however, he combines amusement with instruction. Now and again, he gives a production from which I can derive æsthetic pleasure. The "First Quarto Hamlet" gave me this kind of pleasure. I can imagine that any one who had not seen the authorised "Hamlet" so many times as I have, so many times that he could not regard it as anything but a series of perfect recitations which he had long known by heart, would have found the production more than a little tiresome. He would have wondered why a garbled and bedraggled version of this most beautiful play should have been produced instead of the original. Reminded that he was there to be educated and not to enjoy himself, he would have protested that he wished to learn about Shakespeare, and not about the havoc which some person or persons unknown had made of Shakespeare's work. He would have inquired, sarcastically, whether Mr. Poel had on his syllabus "The Midsummer Night's Dream" as produced by the late Mr. Augustin Daly, and whether that item would also be called "educational." And I should have been bound to admit that there was some reason in his protest. But I should have pointed out that, according to the best modern authorities, the good of education lies, not in what is actually learned, so much as in the function of learning. And I should have protested that I, for my part, had enjoyed the "First Quarto Hamlet" immensely. To me it came almost as a new play. It was not, of course, a good version of "Hamlet," but still it was "Hamlet." The young prince, "with his noble sorrows and weak rage," was again before my eyes. I could listen to him, be filled with pity for him, see all that encompassed him and all that was in his soul. And it is long since I was able to do that. It is long since Hamlet was real to me, a living and moving figure, something more than a part in which an ambitious actor was making a hit or not making a hit. And the reason why he now existed again for me is that he was differently presented. The verbal and structural

differences between the First and Second Quartos were just
enough to create for me a new Hamlet. And so I was grateful to
Mr. Poel.

"TESS"

March 3, 1900

I do not like to read a novel in an illustrated edition. The process is uncomplimentary either to the author or to myself. It
implies that he, on the one hand, is incompetent in one of the
essentials of his art: unable to project, through words, the images
of his characters; or that I, on the other hand, have not enough
imagination to see them for myself. It does not matter to me
that some illustrators draw decently, and do their work in personal consultation with the man whose book is entrusted to them,
and preserve an intelligent sympathy with his aims. For me, all
illustrators are equally objectionable. If I cannot see the characters in a novel, then they are not worth seeing. If I can see
them, then any other man's definite presentment of them seems
to be an act of impertinence to myself and of impiety to the author.
If my first reading of a novel is done from an illustrated edition,
I cannot see the characters for myself: my imagination is paralysed,
and I can see them only as they are shown in the pictures. Possibly these pictures coincide roughly with what my mind's eye
would have achieved for itself. The hero and heroine may be
exactly like the hero and heroine I should have drawn if, having
never seen them illustrated and being suddenly endowed with a
gift for perfect draughtsmanship, I had been compelled to project
upon paper, with pen and ink, the images of them conceived by
me. But that (very remote) possibility does not incline me to
forgive the illustrator. No embodiment, howsoever nearly
accurate, of a mental image can ever satisfy me, can do anything
but offend me. The mind's eye and the body's see too differently.
The mind's eye sees many things which cannot appear in a picture.
It sees things moving and in three dimensions. Also, it is blind
to many trivialities of detail which cannot be omitted in an actual

picture. It does not say "There is no high-light on the toe of the hero's boots"; for the hero's boots do not occur to it. But in a picture the hero must wear boots, and there must, accordingly, be a high-light on the toe; else the eye of the body would be offended. And this high-light, these boots, do offend the mind's eye. To it they are a superfluity, an encumbrance. So is the cut of the heroine's gown; so are the legs of the chair she sits on, the shape of the lamp, the pattern on the carpet. These things are a nuisance. But in illustrations they are a necessary nuisance. And that is one of the reasons why I shun illustrated editions. Especially do I shun such editions of books which I have read and enjoyed in an unillustrated form. It is bad enough to have your imagination cramped from the outset, so that you cannot see the characters otherwise than as they are presented in the wood-cuts or process-blocks. But it is infinitely worse when your imagination, having had free play, and having created for itself a dear gallery, is suddenly confronted and interrupted by the definite projections of some one else's hand. It is only too likely that these new projections, being so definite, will rout the delicate, intangible images which have abided with you. You will mourn over their flight, try in vain to call them back to you and to rally them round you. But they will have been frightened all away. They will not come back to one who has gazed on unspeakable things. You will be left alone with your illustrated edition, and, though you burn it in flames or bury it in a barren field, yet will it always haunt you. "Their eyes met"—"She came slowly along the avenue"—"'Then it is good-bye!'"—"The eminent physician shook his head very gravely"—"'Only tell me that I shall meet her somewhere again!'" All these horrors will abide with you ruthlessly—these nightmares of noble profiles, dramatic attitudes, sun-bonnets, drooping moustaches, elm-trees, French windows, cuffs and collars, rag-tag and bobtail. Certainly, to gaze on the Gorgon's head is less petrifying than to open an illustrated edition of a book which you love.

A dramatised version of a book which you love is like an illustrated edition (and it is—for dramatic critics—a sight less easily avoided). In the one, as in the other, you have a materialisation of your dreams—if you are very lucky. But I have suggested that even materialisation of one's dreams is painful. Even an actor and actress who corresponded in appearance and voice and manner with your previous notion of hero and heroine would give you a certain measure of pain. But to get such an actor and actress were more difficult even than to get an illustrator who would start from the basis of your own fancy. The chances that you will be affronted at every turn are infinitely greater than in the case of an illustrated book. The voice might be right, or the manner, or the appearance. But you are not likely to get all three. I cannot at this moment think of any actress who could, for example, embody Mr. Hardy's Tess without violating in at least two of these respects my conception of what Tess should be. Nor can I at this moment think of any actress less like my own idea of Tess, in all three respects, than Mrs. Lewis Waller, who was playing the part last week at the Coronet Theatre. Mrs. Waller is an accomplished actress. She is always intelligent, often powerful. In the third act (the scene of the murder), she acted very powerfully indeed; and throughout the play she gave proof of her natural intelligence. But her face has not, I think, one feature in common with the face of Tess; and, as for her voice and manner —well! Tess was a simple, romantic girl, sprung from the soil of Wessex. Mrs. Waller's voice and manner on the stage are always exceedingly sophisticated and metropolitan. She might go on trying to act Tess till doomsday, yet would never for one moment succeed in demonstrating anything but the impossibility of her task. Mr. William Kittredge was no more successful in the part of Angel Clare. He seemed to be a hearty, robust, commonplace youth, with no nonsense about him. Angel Clare was a dreamer, and the whole story hinged on the fact that there was a great deal of nonsense about him. All Mr. Hardy's skill in the delineation of character had to be employed in order to convince us that Angel Clare really would have left Tess on the wedding-day. It was only by very elaborate means, by a vast number of subtle touches in psychology, that we could be made to believe that he would have acted as he did. In drama, there is little time for this kind of delicate preparation. Such characters as Angel Clare demand of a dramatist an extraordinary amount of skill. What the novelist may explain at his leisure, the dramatist must make clear in a few lines. I do not think that Mr. H. A. Kennedy, the author of this version of "Tess," has contrived to prepare his

audience for Angel Clare's conduct in the second act. It seems
to me that he relied rather on the chance that the part would be
interpreted by some actor who, by his manner and appearance,
would lead the audience to believe him capable of his abnormal
behaviour. But dramatists have no business to be so sanguine.
They should make it a rule always to expect the worst of their
mimes, not the best. They should, so far as they can, contrive
every part so that it will carry conviction despite the worst performance imaginable. I do not say that Mr. Kittredge's performance of Angel Clare was the worst imaginable, but it was
certainly bad enough to make one regret that Mr. Kennedy had
not taken very much more care in writing the part. For the rest,
I am quite ready to admit that Mr. Kennedy has written his version of the book with considerable ingenuity. Indeed, I congratulate him on the manner in which he has done his task. There
was only one way in which it could have been done much better.
That way, of course, was not to do it at all. "Tess," more than
most books, should have been saved from the stage. Some novels,
as being merely melodramatic, deserve no better fate than being
foisted upon the stage. Others, as containing no melodrama at
all, and being, therefore, unlikely to attract the public, are allowed
to rest within their covers; but, if they were dramatised, at any
rate they would not be degraded so unspeakably as is "Tess."
For "Tess," as a book, is full of melodrama. The melodrama in
it is made beautiful by the charm of Mr. Hardy's temperament.
One sees it softened and ennobled through a haze of poetry.
One would vow, in reading it, that it was sublime tragedy. But
come the adapter, however reverent, and how fearfully one's eyes
are opened! A seduction, a deception, an intercepted letter, a
confession, a parting, a broker in the house, a relapse into impropriety, a taunt, a murder, a reunion, a death scene—that is all that
"Tess" is when it is translated to the stage. A wronged heroine,
a villain, a prig, some comic rustics—these, and nothing more!

"DON JUAN'S LAST WAGER"

March 10, 1900

"Mr. Martin Harvey's Latest Impersonation" would have been an apter title. And to all the characters pleasant English names should have been given, and a pleasant English background Not that these changes would have made the play a good one; but they would, at least, have mitigated its absurdity. Don Juan! "Some one else of the same name!" were surely the guess made by poor Juan, could he be lured one evening from the infernal flames to which Gonzalo beckoned him, and be consigned to the auditorium of the Prince of Wales' Theatre. No scorn would flash from under his tired eyelids. No sardonic grin would twist his still noble features. Neither to mirth nor to resentment would he be moved. He simply would not know himself in the *beau rôle* of Mr. Martin Harvey. As to the play, I am afraid he would be terribly bored by it, and that his one emotion would be a hope that perhaps it was not eternal. The true Don Juan, as portrayed by Tirso or by Molière, is not a *beau rôle*, not a "sympathetic" part. He is altogether brutal—a superb brute, but still (to a modern English audience, at any rate) a brute. It is not in such a part that a modern English actor, who has made a hit in romance, cares to show himself on the stage.

If he wished to play Juan at all, he would, of course, insist on a sympatheticised Juan—a Juan whose faults were the result of a careless upbringing rather than of original sin—a Juan with his heart in exactly the right place. Mr. Martin Harvey, for some mysterious reason, seems to have wished to play Juan. "Don Juan's Wager," as produced at the Prince of Wales', is the result. It is a curious play. It reminded me irresistibly of a tract which, some years ago, was thrust into my hand by a fellow-passenger on the Great Northern Railway—"When the Wicked Man, or, How Albert Simpson, after having lived in sin for upwards of fifteen years, found the light." Only, I was far less impressed by the play than I had been by the tract. Perhaps because it was on a night journey (when one's nerves are always somewhat over-strung) that I received and read this tract, I was, at the time, quite deeply impressed by the history of Albert Simpson. I do not remember the exact means by which he found the light, and probably they were not less miraculous than those by which Mr. Harvey's Juan finds it. But miraculous conversions, though they may sometimes be impressive in tracts, never are impressive in plays. In plays one is sceptical enough to demand a certain evolution of character, or, at least, some great stress of likely circumstances, as a prelude to the conversion. There is no such evolution, no such stress, in the conversion which overtakes Mr. Harvey's Juan on the Banks of the Guadalquivir. Soledad, whom he has duly abducted, weeps while he is making love to her. "Why do you weep?" he asks her. "Because," she falters, "because God has made you so good." She puts her hand in his. That is enough for Juan. The peripety is over in a moment. Behold him quite good! Enter Don Luis, whose betrothed he has stolen. Juan says "I have done you an irreparable injury!" and wildly abases himself. Luis is surprised at the change in his rival's temper. Juan proceeds to explain that Soledad has made him good: "Man, she just put her little hand into mine!" &c., &c. Enter the Commendador, furious at the abduction of his daughter. More protestations: "See! I kneel to you!" "I had never met a good woman before!" &c., &c. Juan has become a thoroughly "sympathetic" part. But the Commendador will have none of him, and insists on a duel. Juan is forced to defend himself. Of course, he does not kill the Commendador, the father of her whom he loves; that would not be at all "sympathetic." The Commendador kills himself. "You threw yourself on my sword!" cries Juan over the prostrate body, eager to put himself right with the audience. "Poor fellow!" sighs the audience. "How dreadful for him to feel that he has been a means of suicide to the father of her whom he loves! He is not in the least to blame, of course. We quite see that. But it is very dreadful, all the same. Poor, dear fellow!" So the death of the Commendador is but another leaf in the sudden laurel-wreath of Mr. Harvey's Juan. The old legend is altogether transformed. Since Juan did not kill the Commendador, and since he was only too anxious to lead Soledad to the altar, the subsequent behaviour of the statue strikes the audience as perfectly brutal—a malignant persecution which makes the victim more poordearfellowesque than ever.

That the statue finally forgives him does not excuse what it has done. What is there to forgive? Juan may have been "wild," like many other young men. But he has made ample atonement. He has suffered terribly. Heavens! how that man has suffered! The curtain falls slowly while Soledad, who has also become a statue (except as to her face, which retains its previous colouring), and stands on a pedestal between two little white German angels designed by Mr. George Frampton, A.R.A., bends gracefully sideways and clasps her marble arms around the hero of the play. But the audience feels that no amount of tenderness will compensate poor Juan for all that he has gone through. Thus the ending is not altogether happy. Never mind! "The Only Way" did not end happily.

I have been implying that the heart of the audience bleeds for Mr. Harvey's Juan. I may or may not be right. What is quite certain is that Mr. Harvey himself must have expected that heart to bleed freely; else he would never have outraged a very fine legend by producing so fatuous a version of it. That he did not wish to play the true Juan I can well understand. The true Juan, as I have said, was a brute; and Mr. Harvey's method in acting is the very reverse of brutal: he excels in ethereal romance. But an ethereally romantic Juan is an obvious contradiction in terms. Juan is, literally, a "term." He has passed into all languages. He stands out, for all peoples, as a definite type. And if his "Last Wager," despite the elaborate manner in which it has been produced, fails to please the British public, it will be because even the British public has too clear a conception of the true Juan to be coaxed into admiration of any one who, however prettily disguised with whitewash, bears the same name. I do not say that this will be so. Nor do I much care. The taste of the British public is not a subject in which I take a keen interest. But about British acting I do care enough to be still wondering why on earth Mr. Harvey wished to appear as Don Juan. And about British drama I care enough to deplore the result of his wish. Some of the dramatic critics have suggested that Mrs. Cunninghame Graham, whose name is printed with Zorilla's under the title of the play, may be responsible for the emasculation of the legend. It is only fair to that lady to say that the larger part of the blame lies on the shoulders of Zorilla, whose play she translated, and to record a persistent rumour that she had nothing whatever to do with such deviations as have been made from Zorilla's scheme and text.

At the Lyceum, Mr. Benson has been alternating "Hamlet" and "The Rivals." The latter play needs "go" in its interpreters rather than imagination; and, since cricket promotes "go" in its devotees no less than it saps imagination, Mr. Benson's company did far better in Sheridan's play than in Shakespeare's. But Mr. Benson himself, keen cricketer though he is, has little "go" in acting, and his Captain Absolute was suspiciously like his Hamlet. If his Hamlet had been at all distinguished, this likeness might have been condoned. Unfortunately, his Hamlet was dry, wooden, insipid—"adequate," in fact. His production, however, was interesting, inasmuch as the play was performed straight through, without "cuts," and thus achieved a freshness which is not usually to be found in it. One was enabled to see the King and Polonius in all their glory—and glorious parts they are! It is a pity that no "star," in producing the play, takes one of these parts himself and proportionately cuts down the other part and the part of Hamlet. The play is so vast, so full, that a versatile "star" could triumph on three consecutive nights, in a perfectly stelline manner, without repeating his performance. Might not the experiment be made? There is one other train of thought which Mr. Benson's production opens to me, and it is one which might well be pursued further than I can pursue it here. Mrs. Benson, who was Ophelia, played the mad-scene more shockingly than I (who am not unimaginative) could ever have imagined it being played. I should not be so ungracious as to call attention to her performance, were it not that Ophelias *in petto* might possibly profit by my remarks. About Shakespeare it should be remembered that he was both a dramatist and a poet. The less his lines are acted the more clearly is their poetry apparent. Dramatic emphasis, pauses, facial play, are all inimical to the music of words, which is best served by quiet recitation. But quiet recitation saves for the words their music at the expense of their dramatic force. And thus, as a rule, the best Shakespearian acting is a kind of compromise between poetry and drama. But there were some moments when Shakespeare was merely dramatist, others when he was merely poet. Ophelia's mad-scene is mere poetry. Ophelia is a nonentity throughout the play : sane or mad,

72

she is nothing to us. If in her sanity she had been made interesting, then her final lunacy would have some dramatic effect. There would be reason for playing the mad-scene more or less realistically, for sacrificing more or less of its beauty. As it is, such a proceeding is a mere impertinence. In recent years, most Ophelias have gone in the direction of realistic lunacy, and we have suffered accordingly. But no actress has gone so far, and made us fare so ill, as Mrs. Benson, who groans and gasps, glares, shrieks and gesticulates, so indefatigably as to make havoc of every beautiful line the poet has put into her mouth. The medical staff of Colney Hatch might find much to interest them in her antics and her kakophonies. But intelligent lovers of Shakespeare can only shudder, can only wonder. I wish that all promising young actresses could see this performance. Their sight of it would save us some suffering in the future. Here is a clear case for a "professional matinée."

"CYRANO" IN ENGLISH

April 28, 1900

One evening, some years ago, I had been dining with a friend who was supposed to have certain spiritualistic powers. As we were very much bored with each other, I proposed that we should have a *séance*. Though doubtful whether I should be "sympathetic," he was quite willing to try. The question arose, with what spirit should we commune? He suggested Madame Blavatsky. I was all for Napoleon Buonaparte. Finally—by what process I forget—we agreed on Charlotte Corday. The lights having been turned out, we sat down at a small table. Placing the tips of our fingers on it, we thought of Charlotte Corday with all our might. Many minutes went slowly by, and the table showed no signs of animation. My friend said it was very strange. After a fruitless hour or so, he seemed to be so much annoyed that I thought it would be only kind to press my fingers in such a way as to make the table tilt duly towards me for a moment and then tilt back. I did this. "Are you there?" asked my friend, in a low voice. I pressed again, producing the requisite number of taps for "Yes." "Who are you?" my friend rejoined. "Charlotte" I rapped out. I continued to rap appropriate answers to my friend until I thought he had had enough enjoyment for one evening. The spirit having evidently withdrawn to its own sphere, he turned up the lights, pronounced the *séance* a great success, and told me that I seemed to have some power as a medium. But I have never taken the advice he gave me to develop this power, and I recall our evening merely because I was irresistibly reminded of it, the other night, when I saw the English version of "Cyrano" at Wyndham's Theatre. I saw, with my mind's eye, the manner in which the whole play was written. There were Mr. Stuart Ogilvie and Mr. Louis N. Parker, seated solemnly on either side of a small table, trying to raise the spirit of Cyrano. "It is very strange," said Mr. Ogilvie, frowning; "the table does not seem to move." Genial Mr. Parker, hating that his friend should be disappointed, brought illicit pressure to bear on the table. "Are you there?" asked the author of "Hypatia," in a broken whisper. "Yes," rapped Mr. Parker, smiling inwardly. And so the mockery was inaugurated. So the collaboration went forward, hollow rap by rap, laboriously, portentously, with no more real evocation than was got in the *séance* I have described.

Alas, that any pretence of raising this ghost need have been made among us! When first M. Coquelin brought M. Rostand's play to England I expressed a pious hope that it would not be translated. Of course, I knew well that it would be. Cyrano, the man, got safely home from the Hôtel de Bourgogne, routing with his own sword the hundred rascals who lay in wait for him; but Cyrano, the play, would not escape its English obsessors so easily. It might slip through the fingers of one and another of the hundred desperate actors who were thirsting to produce it. It might keep the whole gang at bay for a while. But in the end it would, inevitably, be taken. And, of course, it could only be taken dead: the nature of things prevented it from being taken alive. I dare say that I explained that fact at the time. But of what use was it to argue against a foregone conclusion? Cyrano, in the original version, is the showiest part of modern times—of any times, maybe.

Innumerable limelights, all marvellously brilliant, converge on him. And as he moves he flashes their obsequious radiance into the uttermost corners of the theatre. The very footlights, as he passes them, burn with a pale, embarrassed flame, useless to him as stars to the sun. The English critic, not less than the English actor, is dazzled by him. But, though he shut his eyes, his brain still works, and he knows well that an English version of Cyrano would be absurd. Cyrano, as a man, belongs to a particular province of France, and none but a Frenchman can really appreciate him. An Englishman can accept the Gascon, take him for granted, in a French version, but not otherwise. Cyrano is a local type; not, like Quixote or Juan, a type of abstract humanity which can pass unscathed through the world. Nor is he, like Quixote or Juan, a possible individual, such as one might meet. Even in Gascony he were impossible. He is the fantastically idealised creation of a poet. In M. Rostand's poetry, under the conditions which that poetry evokes, he is a real and solid figure, certainly. But put him into French prose, and what would remain of him but a sorry, disjointed puppet? Put him into English prose (or into the nearest English equivalent that could be found for M. Rostand's verse) and—but the result, though it can be seen at Wyndham's Theatre, cannot be described. All this I foresaw, being a critic. But the actors, not they. Creatures of impulse, they saw nothing but the chance of playing Cyrano. Mr. Wyndham happens to be the man who ultimately got it. But as the part does not, from a critic's standpoint, exist, how am I to praise his performance of it? how, as one who revels in his acting, do aught but look devoutly forward to his next production?

"QUO VADIS" AND "NIL PRÆDICENDUM"

May 12, 1900

The moon is a chill substitute for the sun, and they who basked and revelled in Mr. Wilson Barrett's "Sign of the Cross" will not, I fear, take kindly to that pale shadow of it which rose, last

Saturday evening, from the horizon of the Adelphi. Mr. Stanislaus Stange, though he has copied most of Mr. Barrett's figures with all the passionate minuteness of a pre-Raphaelite, has not written a good melodrama. The steps in that progress whereby Marcus Vinicius becomes what is called a crease-chyarn are not, as in the case of Marcus Superbus, exciting steps. The progress is very slow. It might almost be described as uneventful, since all the chief marvels of the play happen "off," and are known by us only at second-hand. True, Mr. Stange's stage-directions provide for the burning of Rome before our very eyes. But the London County Council, more zealous for our safety than for our delight, does not permit real holocausts on any stage. Consequently, Nero's fiddling is accompanied by nothing more awesome than some pink magnesian light behind transparent back-cloths. Nor is Mr. Stange fortunate in his principal mimes. Mr. Taber has not Mr. Barrett's gift (which is, indeed, inalienable) of saying ridiculous things in a ridiculous way and so making them carry conviction. When little Aulus (Miss Valli-Valli) trips off the stage, trilling a roulade of the most sophisticated merriment ever emitted, Mr. Taber looks after her and says "Such innocent laughter is seldom heard in Rome!" so tenderly, so thoughtfully, with an air of such conviction, that the absurdity of the thing becomes almost indecent. Delivered in the quick, staccato voice and with the tremendous gesture of Mr. Barrett, the words would have come as a matter of course. And Miss Lena Ashwell! Why is her uncompromising intelligence, her almost uncouth sincerity, always chartered for melodrama, which it can but ruin, and so kept out of the serious plays which it would glorify? There are a hundred-and-one columbine-actresses who would have played Lygia (that is the queer name of Mr. Stange's heroine!) far better than Miss Ashwell. Utter lack of intelligence and of sincerity is as indispensable for such a part as are technical skill and a beautiful face. Miss Ashwell has the two last requisites, but they are not enough. Not having the first, she would ruin a much better melodrama than "Quo Vadis."

Though the play is bad, if you judge it by any standard of melo-dramatic art, I cannot join in the critics' outcry that it is objection-able on grounds of religion. The critics are angry because there are frequent invocations of the Deity, references to the Sermon on the Mount, verbal quotations from Holy Writ. They declare that the Censor ought to have interfered, and speak darkly about "exploiting religion." Why? If in them the old Puritan prejudice were so strong that they held playhouses in abhorrence, I could sympathise with their objection. But the fact that they frequent playhouses is proof presumptive that they take a more liberal and modern view. Not one of them, I believe, will pretend that dramatic art, more than literature, or painting, or any other art, makes for damnation. Nor will they pretend that books and pictures are not decent vehicles for religious sentiment. Do they, yet, pretend that religion must be barred from the stage? I could sympathise with their indignation against "Quo Vadis" if Mr. Stange had treated Christianity in any spirit of levity or scepticism. But he has done nothing of the kind. The whole purpose of the play is to glorify the Christian faith, and the martyrs who died for it, and the pagans who came under its spell. True, the unconverted pagans are dealt with in a somewhat lenient spirit. Nero becomes a kind of buffoon who is not really at all responsible for his actions. Petronius Arbiter becomes as harmless and wholesome as Mr. Pickwick. Allowances are made even for Poppæa. But this tendency to forgive is, surely, all in accord with the doctrine which the play is meant to extol. Artistically, of course, it is not defensible. From any pedantic standpoint, the play is shocking enough. "Lygia," of course, is an impossible name. "Vitelius" wants another l. "No one thought of that but thee, no one but thee!" is not a plausible translation of anything which Nero—*qualis artifex!*—might have said to Petronius. The whole play is full of such lapses. It will stand no test of history, or of grammar, or of tact. It is very vulgar throughout. That, I suppose, is why the critics object to the religious element in it. If it were a piece of refined work, they would not brand it for irreverence. I admit that there is no real reason why religious plays should always be vulgar. It is quite possible to combine religion with refined art. But to be shocked by a religious play because there is no refined art in it is not less absurd than to dismiss a good play because it has no religious purpose. The critics should remember that what seems vulgar to them does not seem vulgar to the public, and that what seems vulgar to them is really a very potent means of bringing religion home to the public. The method of such plays as "Quo Vadis" is the same kind of method as that which is used by the Salvation Army. As for the hints about "exploiting religion," we have no right whatever to assume that Mr. Stange has not written his play in good faith. If he is an infidel, his insincerity is no worse in him than were any other kind of insincerity. And if (as we must, in courtesy, assume) he is a religious enthusiast, he has as indisputable a right to his "royalties" as has every vicar to his tithes.

I attended one of the six *matinées* of "You Never Can Tell" at the Strand Theatre. "Such innocent laughter is seldom heard in London," murmured I, echoing Marcus Vinicius; for the house was quite full, and every one in it was roaring with laughter throughout the four acts of the play. Six *matinées*! Why are the commercial speculators who control theatres so obtuse as not to run Mr. Bernard Shaw for all he is worth? I assure them that he would be worth a very great deal to them. In the course of the next decade or two, they will begin to have some glimmerings of this fact. Meanwhile, they shake their heads and purse their lips at the sound of his name. "Very clever, no doubt," they pronounce him; "much too clever; over the heads of the public." Of course his head is over the heads of the public; but I protest that he is no mere cherub, that his feet are set solidly on the ground, and that his body is in touch with the crowd. Even had I not already witnessed Kennington's enthusiasm for "The Devil's Disciple," my visit to the Strand Theatre would have convinced me that Mr. Shaw, as he stands, is a man who might save many managers the trouble of going bankrupt over the kind of plays in which they see "money." I have never fallen into the error of overrating the public, but I take this opportunity of insinuating to purveyors of farce and melodrama that the public's stupidity has its limits. Several farces and melodramas have been withdrawn lately after the shortest runs, for the simple reason that they were not good enough for the public. To provide something beneath the public is quite as disastrous as to provide something above it. In the latter case, moreover, disaster is no ignominy. Might it not, sometimes, be courted? Even had it not already been proved that some of Mr. Shaw's plays have qualities which delight the public, it would still be surprising that no manager hastens to give them a fair chance.

"NIL PRÆDICENDUM"

It is rather difficult to determine how "You Never Can Tell" ought to be acted. Realism and sheer fantasy are inextricably entangled in the scheme of the play. Serious characters behave ridiculously, ridiculous characters suddenly become serious. Mr. Shaw sends all the persons of his play dashing round sharp corners, colliding with one another, picking themselves up, exchanging hats, and dashing off again. It is all very confusing. Of course, when serious elements and ridiculous elements are combined, the former disappear under the latter, even when they actually preponderate. It is but one step from the serious (or sublime) to the ridiculous, but once you take that step you cannot get back without climbing a sheer precipice. And thus I cannot regard seriously the serious characters and scenes in Mr. Shaw's play. Consequently, it worries me to see any of these characters and scenes seriously played. All would seem quite right and proper, I should have an impression of artistic unity, if Gloria and the dentist were played as extravagantly as Mr. Bohun and the twins. Of course, Mr. Shaw meant Gloria and the dentist to be played seriously, and believed them to be quite serious characters. And so they are, from time to time, as I can see when I read the play. But when I see the play acted, and have no time for detached thought, they are consistently ridiculous, and as I have suggested, serious acting distracts me with a sense of utter incongruity. For artistic reasons, then, the whole play ought to be acted extravagantly, and not, as by the company at the Strand, according to Mr. Shaw's stage-directions. I should enjoy it so, much more. And yet . . . I am not quite sure that I would rather it were played in that way. The very worry and distraction caused by the serious acting were, in a sense, an addition to my delight in the play; for they kept me in mind of the author's peculiar temperament and attitude, of which the manifold contradictions are so infinitely more delightful, even when they make us very angry, than the smooth, intelligible consistency of you or me.

DUSE AT THE LYCEUM

May 26, 1900

I have often wondered why Sydney Smith said he "would as soon speak disrespectfully of the Equator." After all, the Equator is a mere geographical expression. It casts no weird spell of awe over mankind. On the contrary, seafarers, when they come to it, put on false noses and play practical jokes. For "Equator" read "Duse," and then the remark has point. There never was an influence so awe-inspiring as Duse. At her coming, all the voices of the critics are hushed. Or rather, they are uplifted in unisonant dithyrambus. The heaven is rent with superlatives. And these are not the bright little superlatives we flick at Sarah—imagine any one calling Duse "Eleonora"!—but superlatives of a solemn, almost religious, order. The heaven is rent, and the entrances to the theatre are forthwith besieged by great concourses of people who don't know a word of Italian. Night by night, the English public sits solemnly at the Lyceum (having paid higher prices than it pays for a play in its own language), tremendously bored, tremendously edified. Whatever Duse may be in her own country, here she is a national institution, nay! a supernatural phenomenon, making for righteousness. If a fiery chariot were seen waiting outside the stage-door, no one would be much surprised.

Last week I said that I would write about Duse as soon as I had "seen her whole répertoire." That sounded a little pompous, perhaps; as though I were loth to deliver judgment until the whole bulk of the evidence had been adduced. As a matter of fact, it was mere cowardly procrastination. I wished to put off the evil hour of confessing that I could not bow down before the demigoddess. There are three ways of raving about an actress. One way is to rave about her technique; another, to rave about her conception of the part she is playing; another, to rave about her personality. Well! I am debarred from the first way by the simple fact that I know no more Italian than did poor Mrs. Plornish. This disability is the more humiliating for me, in that I am, evidently, the only critic who labours under it. All the other critics understand the language perfectly; else they would not be able to tell us unanimously that Duse's technique is beyond reproach. The technique of acting lies in the nice relation of the mime's voice, gesture and facial expression to the words by him or her spoken. Obviously, if those words are for you so much gibberish, you cannot pass any judgment on the mime's technique. You look on, and you see certain movements of the mime's face and hands, and you hear certain inflections of the mime's voice, but I defy you to know whether they are the right movements, the right inflections. You have to take them on trust. I am willing to take Duse's technique on trust, but I cannot rave about it: I can but consume myself with envy of my colleagues, and wish I had made a better use of my opportunities for learning Italian. It is of no use to have seen the play previously in a language which one understands. I have seen "Magda" and "The Second Mrs. Tanqueray," as played by Mrs. Campbell, and have seen them several times. I have seen "Fédora" in English and in French. I have read that tedious effusion, the "Princesse Georges." But I do not (nor do you) remember more than a few disjointed fragments of the dialogue in any scene, and I do not (nor do you) often manage to "spot" one of these fragments when the scene is played in an unknown language. If, by some wild chance, I do "spot" one of them, I am so surprised and excited that I forget to notice the manner of its delivery. Still less, if possible, am I likely to form any personal opinion of Duse's technique in "La Gioconda," of which there is nothing for me but a synopsis. Let her play in English or in French, and then, no doubt, I shall have the felicity of raving with the best of them.

I come now to the second way of raving: raving about the mime's conception of the part played. Here, of course, the unknown language is no barrier; it is merely a stumbling-block. If you have seen or read the play in a language which you do understand, you will, by dint of ordinary vigilance, be able to form a sound synthetic idea of what the mimes mean the characters to be. I know Magda, Paula, Fédora and the Princesse Georges well enough to praise or disparage an actress' conception of any one of them. I know them well enough to be convinced that Duse has no conception of any one of them. She treats them as so many large vehicles for expression of absolute self. From first to last, she is the same in Fédora as in Magda, in Magda as in Paula, in Paula as in the Princesse Georges, and in the Princesse Georges as in La Gioconda. "Io son' Io," in fact, throughout. Her unpainted face, the unhidden grey of the hair over her brows, are symbolic of her attitude. That Paula is a local English type, and the Princesse Georges a local French type, and that accordingly neither of them can be understood and impersonated by an Italian, matters nothing at all to her. She does not make it part of her business to understand and impersonate. It matters nothing to her that even an Italian equivalent for Paula or the Princesse Georges would be outside her range. "Io son' Io," and she cares not under what alias she comport herself. La Gioconda (known to me, as I have said, only through a synopsis) happens to be an Italian part, and it happens to suit Duse. It might be well realised otherwise than by her, but it could not, I imagine, be realised so fully. If I had never seen her in any other part, I should have raved about her conception. "She *is* La Gioconda," I should have exclaimed. As it is, I can only remark that La Gioconda is she.

This personal pronoun brings me to the third way of raving. Am I overwhelmed by the personality of Duse? Of course, I ought to be—there can be no question of that. But the wretched fact remains that I am not. True, I see power and nobility in her face ; and the little shrill soft voice, which is in such strange contrast with it, has a certain charm for me. I admire, too, her movements, full of grace and strength. But my prevailing emotion is hostile to her. I cannot surrender myself, and see in her the "incarnate womanhood" and "the very spirit of the world's tears" and all those other things which other critics see in her. My prevailing impression is of a great egoistic force ; of a woman overriding, with an air of sombre unconcern, plays, mimes, critics and public. In a man I should admire this tremendous egoism very much indeed. In a woman it only makes me uncomfortable. I dislike it. I resent it. In the name of art, I protest against it. . . . Thus do I, devil's advocate, resume my seat, trusting to the judge to suppress any disturbance in court.

DAY-BEFORE-YESTERDAY DRAMA

June 16, 1900

Had Mr. Gilbert been born into the world twenty-five years later than he was, his Pygmalion would be a very different person from the Pygmalion whom he did actually create in the 'seventies. For in recent years we have much concerned ourselves with the psychology of artists, and have drawn certain conclusions, formulated certain laws, in the light of which Mr. Gilbert's Pygmalion stands forth absurd and unreal, an embarrassed anachronism. Were he a mere dabbler and duffer in sculpture, his temperament, as expressed in the speeches given to him by Mr. Gilbert, might perhaps pass muster. But he is, on the contrary, a great master in his art, brimful of genius. This fact is essential to the scheme of the play. Let us see by what means Mr. Gilbert impressed it on the 'seventies. That great artists are arrogant fellows was known already, and the keynote of arrogance is struck with Pygmalion's first entry. An art-patron has sent his slave to bid the artist wait on him. Pygmalion is furious. So far, so good. But listen to the manner of his fury!

> "Tell him from me that, though I'm poor enough,
>   I am an artist and a gentleman."

Now, if there is one fact we have learnt about great artists, it is that their arrogance is founded solely on their mastery in art. Whether they be gentlemen or not is a question which never troubles them for an instant. If a great artist were to say "I am a gentleman," he would say so merely as one stating a fact; it would never occur to him that the fact could at all enhance his self-esteem or the esteem in which others held him. Also, he would be telling a lie; inasmuch as great art and gentility (I use the word in its proper sense) are things which are not, and cannot be, combined. (This, indeed, is another fact which has been discovered since the 'seventies: that except in the narrow sense of birth, great artists never are gentlemen, and that they are more often not so even by birth, since the strenuous vitality which is needed for great art can hardly be drawn but from peasant-stock.)

Pygmalion, having already made himself incredible, proceeds to make himself more so. He declares to his wife Cynisca that wealth is the only thing he can work for. Even the 'seventies must have shied at that. At any rate, Cynisca does. She cannot understand such words

> "from one whose noble work it is
> To call the senseless marble into life!"

This is Pygmalion's cue. He utters a long-pent rigmarole to the effect that he can only copy life, not create it, and curses

> "those proud gods,
> Who say, 'Thou shall [*sic*] be greatest among men,
> And yet infinitesimally small."

Of course, this is utterly absurd. A great sculptor may torment himself with his failures to attain absolute perfection in his form; but he would never find fault with the form itself, never wish to outstep its glorious limitations. . . . You think me pedantic, a breaker of butterflies on wheels. "Mr. Gilbert's play," you point out, "is a sheer fantasy. His aim in the first act is to provide some motive for the animation of the statue. You do not, we imagine, object to the idea of an animated statue?" "Not in the least," I answer. "But," you rejoin triumphantly, "statues never really come to life. Why worry because Mr. Gilbert makes Pygmalion cry out against the cold stone of Galatea? It is a quite legitimate step in what is, we repeat, a sheer fantasy." Having allowed you to work out your theory to the end, I hasten to contradict it. No fantasy is good unless it be founded in solid reality. None revels more than I in the impossible, but it must spring from the possible, else it is without meaning and gives no illusion. That is an æsthetic truth which any worthy weaver of fantasies would admit. Mr. Gilbert would admit it. Working in the 'seventies before men had begun to take an interest in the souls of artists, he, doubtless, imagined that he had made his Pygmalion such as a great sculptor might be, and that the ensuing fantasy was well founded. Were he a young man, writing the play to-day, he would have profited by the accumulated data of recent years, and would have cast the legend into quite another scheme. The only profit one can derive from seeing or reading the play as written then is to speculate what it would be like were it written now.

Not that I would advise Mr. Gilbert to revise his play on the lines laid down by me. Had I been at his side in the 'seventies, I should have tried hard to dissuade him from tackling the idea of an animated statue, even though I might then have accepted his notion of a great artist's character and proclivities. For that particular idea is poetical, and Mr. Gilbert, for all his metrical skill, is as unpoetical as any man who ever lived. He has a sense of humour; and there is, of course, no end of fun to be got out of an animated statue. But it could only be got by a humorist who was also a poet, for it lies in the contrast between the prosaic, complicated circumstances of actual life and the poetic, elementary simplicity of the creature woken to them. If the creature be a minx, like Mr. Gilbert's Galatea, with the kind of poor-girl-didn't-know-you-know innocence which is familiar to us in the Music Halls, the fun of the situation is lost utterly. However, the fun is a secondary matter: it is the poetry of the idea which one wants to have developed, and, as I have just suggested, Mr. Gilbert is the last man who ought to have undertaken the job. When he did so, he saw, no doubt, that the play ought to be mainly poetical. The statue was to awaken and be a woman, and to love him who had fashioned her, and to be loved by him; and he was to suffer evil through love of her, and she, knowing there was no other way of saving him, was to set herself again upon her pedestal and be again a stone. What a chance for a really poetic play! Down sat Mr. Gilbert, in all his power of writing correct blank-verse. But alas! not one spark of poetry would fly from a single iamb. Nor, try as he would, could he see the idea except through a tangle of those complications which were so popular in 'seventy farce. Galatea is told that a soldier is a man who is hired to kill human beings. On comes Leucippus (a soldier, and the prospective brother-in-law of Pygmalion) holding a fawn which he has just shot. Galatea thinks the fawn is a human being, and upbraids the murderer. Exit Leucippus, with fawn. Enter his betrothed. Galatea makes her believe that Leucippus has murdered a woman. Re-enter Leucippus. More cross-purposes, till he, exasperated, exit declaring he will have no more of her. Later, much time is expended in order to lead up to this situation: the elderly art-patron discovered by his wife with his arm round Galatea's waist. Thus, in one way and another, most of the wearisome rag-tag and bobtail of farce is dragged in to pass the time which Mr. Gilbert had meant to spend in developing the poetry of the idea. Not less tedious are the scenes which the author, pulling himself together, devotes to the relations between Galatea and Pygmalion. "Relations" is the very word. Galatea, that "serio," makes advances towards Pygmalion. He is, at first, inclined to flirt. Then he remembers that his wife (who has gone on a journey) would make herself unpleasant if she found him out. He hustles Galatea away, makes arrangements—observe the invincible delicacy of the dramatist!—that she shall sleep in his sister's house. Next day, his wife comes back. She finds him out, and . . . but the last part of the play is of a piece with the first. If you have never seen or read the play, see it or read it now, and you will join me in thanking the Fates, who, soon after it was written, sent Sir Arthur Sullivan along and saved its author from writing others like it.

On the whole, I would advise you to read the play rather than to see it. One can skip a book without troubling any one, whereas it is selfish to dodge in and out of a theatre where the mimes are doing their best and most of the audience is anxious to take out its money's-worth in attention. If you do go to the Comedy, you will not see a particularly brilliant performance, though you will see a performance better than the play deserves. I do not think it is merely because I had been prejudiced in Miss Steer's favour by Mr. Gilbert's rather mean letter about her to the papers that I thought her performance really quite tolerable. Her voice and manner are not those of a simple creature just woken into life, but they are guilelessness itself in comparison with the part as it is written. Moreover, she acts with no little grace. Miss Repton, as Cynisca, reproduced to a nicety the mannerisms with which Miss Julia Neilson made her début, and which she has gradually got rid of. The rest of the mimes do not stand out in my memory, except (by reason of his cloddishness in the part of Pygmalion) Mr. Fuller Mellish.

HELLAS VIA BRADFIELD

June 23, 1900

The gods are dead—they, who were deathless. More than one writer has tried to explain this contradiction by evidence that, though Olympus is a desert now, the gods still live on. Heine, Pater and many others have been convinced that the gods do actually live in our midst, humble and unrecognised, earning daily bread by the performance of such odd jobs as their former state may have made them fit for. Vulcan, it is said, works to-day in some village-smithy, Mercury is a Queen's Messenger, Pan is attached to a Punch and Judy show. A fascinating belief! I myself am among the converts to it. Also, being of a habit both sentimental and sanguine, I hope and believe that I may yet live to see the day when these ex-Olympians will be able to throw off their disguises, and to rule over mankind, and be honoured by it, as in the past. But I cannot deny that my cult is a tiny one. Most people, obviously, believe the gods to be (if they ever existed) dead as door-nails. I have never seen so crude a sign of this general scepticism as in the overt theatre of Bradfield College, whither I went, last Tuesday, to see a performance of the "Agamemnon." This theatre, you must know, is within a stone's throw of the College Chapel. It is an exact replica of a real Attic theatre, and in the midst of its round orchestra stands a little white altar, green-garlanded, inscribed with the legend $\Delta IONY\Sigma O\Sigma$. Thereon burns a flame—a little flame, pale under the sunlight of an English June. From time to time (even as in Hellas, centuries ago), the Coryphæus tends it, shifting the fuel so that it burn brightlier. In Hellas, however enthralling a play might be, the actors never forgot that their first duty was one of reverence to him from whose worship drama was evolved; and here, at Bradfield, the old reverence is scrupulously reproduced, under the supervision of the Headmaster. He sits there, the Headmaster, watching the play, clad in the scarlet robe worn by him in a Christian university; and among the audience, seated on the stone benches which rise in circular tiers around the arena, are many other clergymen, most of them accompanied by wives, sisters, offspring, pupils. The white altar stands there in the midst, with its garland and its legend and its constant flame; yet not a word of protest is uttered, not a brow contracted. Imagine what would happen if this were a community of early Christians, of men still going in fear and hatred of the idols which they had shattered! But here, in 1900, it does not occur to any one that there is anything at all dangerous or apostatic in rites performed round the altar of the son of Semele. The clergymen beam through their archæologistic glasses—"very curious and interesting! Very well done indeed!" I hope poor Dionysus (now clerk to a wine-merchant in Oxford Street) had not got a day off, last Tuesday, to see this play. The sight of it would have been the last blow to his pride. Even in his helplessness, he might have been tempted to do something rash—he, whose nature was so resentful of any disrespect that he sent a hideous madness on Lycurgus of Nemea and caused Pentheus of Thebes to be torn in pieces by the fauns. In none of the gods was pride so jealous as in that twice-born god. I have often thought how bitterly he must have chafed at the development of the drama —the transformation of those agrestic revels, held for him, into an artistic celebration of other gods and of mortal heroines and heroes. If ever he go to the play nowadays, he must surely find a grim satisfaction in the sterility to which the dramatic form has come, and the contempt in which it is held.

For me there is no such satisfaction. Indeed, it was primarily as an escape from the stuffy atmosphere of modern drama that I enjoyed my visit to the Greek theatre at Bradfield. Here, at least, I was to see a beautiful play, and to see it, as I soon found, under beautiful conditions. The way to the theatre lay down a long, steep dingle, through whose leaves the sunlight could not penetrate. When I came to the end of it, I seemed to emerge into the sunlight of ancient history. That altar, that flagged orchestra, those rough-hewn tiers of benches rising from the hollow; and above them, all around, the green trees, and wild flowers in full bloom! A trumpet was blown. A herald came upon the stage, and thrice hailed us—citizens! The minstrels, attired in many colours, trooped across to their appointed places, holding their strange lyres and flutes. With the first notes of their music, slowly and solemnly, through a green avenue that flanks the columns of the stage, came the chorus, κατὰ ζυγά—the chorus of Argive

Elders, leaning on their staves. Into the round orchestra they trooped, there to sing of Troy, of the gods implacable. To them, through the royal door, came the murderous Queen. After she had hung a chaplet of roses around the gold statue of Aphrodite, she told them of the beacons which proclaimed the war's end. Came the conqueror Agamemnon, in a chariot drawn by Trojan slaves and preceded by his own soldiers. Behind him crouched one in whose face was terror. She who foresaw all doom, Cassandra, shrank away from the palace in which Agamemnon and she were fated to die. With joyous words, the Queen welcomed her lord. Fair carpets were spread for his entry. We, like Cassandra, knew the inexorableness of the gods, and how heavy lay the curse on the house of Atreus; we knew, as Agamemnon passed through the royal door, that soon we should hear his death-cries. We waited, appalled nearly as much as though we had been Greeks ourselves. We waited, while in the air swallows darted hither and thither, careless and impudent. One of them perched for an instant on the very stage where Cassandra gave her terror to the Elders. A stock-dove began to coo from one of the bushes—what did *it* care for the house of Atreus? And so the afternoon wore on, while we listened to the words of Æschylus, in such sunlight and to such an accompaniment of birds as they had in Hellas, in such a theatre as that for which the poet wrote them.

In the whole production there was little that struck me as being wrong. That the long-suffering watchman should first appear on the stage, and then run up the steps to look for the beacon, is rather unfortunate. But that is the fault of no one except the architect who built the Bradfield theatre without a διστεγία. On the other hand, there were one or two corrigible errors in the stage management. Agamemnon's sandals ought to be made in such a way that they can be taken off quickly, or else he ought to continue his speech while the slaves are taking them off. Last Tuesday, his entry into the palace lost much of its poignancy during the enormous interval spent by him in silence while his sandals were being removed, and by us in silent wonder whether they ever would come off. Another mistake occurred in the scene where Clytæmnestra is wheeled forth on the eccyclema, standing over the bodies of her lord and his prophetess. The Queen steps down from the machine, and it is wheeled off, at the end of her first address to the

Chorus. Thus the dialogue that follows loses all its dramatic force. It is all very well for Clytæmnestra to say

"οὗτός ἐστιν Ἀγαμέμνων, ἐμὸς
πόσις, νεκρὸς δέ, τῆσδε δεξιᾶς χερὸς
ἔργον, δικαίας τέκτονος,"

but if Agamemnon is not there—not οὗτος, in fact—she cannot expect to make our flesh creep. Another objection which I have to offer is of a larger and more important kind. It is against the decision not to let the actors appear in masks. Why this decision was arrived at I really do not know. On the programme it is said that "all the essential features of a Greek Tragedy will be reproduced, except the masks and the high *cothurni*, which are considered unsuitable to the conditions of modern art." But the Greek language is, surely, no less unsuitable. "Modern art" has nothing to do with the case. The aim of the undertaking was, I imagine, to treat with thorough archæology an ancient work of art. Why stop short of any detail? Buskins may be too difficult for boys to walk gracefully in without years of practice, and I am quite ready to waive them. But to masks there is no practical objection. They were constructed by the Greeks in such a way that they rather helped than impeded the wearer's utterance. Why, then, should not they have been reproduced at Bradfield? Even if they had not acted as sounding-boards (as which indeed, by reason of the boys' admirable elocution, they were not needed), they would have saved their wearers a great deal of self-consciousness. And they would have saved us our sense of the incongruity between wholesome, pleasant, public-schoolboy faces and the characters of Clytæmnestra, Agamemnon and Cassandra. Even Mr. (or Master) L. Harvey, who acted the part of Cassandra with so much real imagination and power, using his voice so skilfully and gesticulating always so appropriately, was quite unable to import into his features a trace of anything more fateful than a love of cricket and football. Given a κατάκομος, he would have been quite perfect. Even supposing the production had not been primarily archæological, and that, moreover, it had been acted by professional mimes with a command of facial expression, masks would have been better than no masks. For Æschylus' characters are not human beings, like those of his two successors. They are grandiose abstractions,

terribly and wonderfully made—superb puppets destined to sin
and suffer elementally. They are all "larger than life," and
simpler. They are statuesque, static, invariable. In a play of
Sophocles or Euripides, there might be something to say against
masks; but, even then, not if the play were acted at Bradfield, by
boys. However, it is ungracious of me to be cavilling at anything
in so good a performance, given under conditions so beautiful. It
is long since I enjoyed a day so much as my day at Bradfield. I
fancy, after all, that Dionysus himself would have enjoyed it. The
sound of his old language (despite the strong English accent) would
have been music to him, surely. And as for the altar—well! there
might have been for him more sweetness than bitterness in its reminder that he was once a god.

PLAYS REPEATED

June 30, 1900

The war has kept a great fraction of the public away from the
theatres. Plays, therefore, have had shorter runs than usual, and
two or three productions have been necessary in playhouses for
which, in time of peace, one production would have been quite
enough. Well! the greater the number of new plays, the greater
is likely to be our rate of progress in drama. If the war had multiplied that number, there would be a real addition to the blessings
which we are supposed to have derived from it. But such is not
the case. New productions are not necessarily of new plays, and,
in point of fact, though there have never been more first nights
than during the present season, there have never been so few new
plays. Most of the managers, knowing that no play would have
the chance of a long run, have discreetly and economically fallen
back on "old favourites." If the gates of Thespis had closed
automatically when those of Janus were opened, vital drama would
have forfeited little or nothing, and dramatic critics would have
been consoled for being thrown out of work by not having to live
in agitated wonder as to what on earth they should say next.

I presume that Mr. William Archer has not, like the rest of us, been living in this state. He, as you know, holds it to be "an almost universal experience that our keenest theatrical enjoyments have come to us in seeing plays with which we were perfectly familiar, on the stage and off." As a playgoer, then (if not as a critic), he must have been having lately a high old time, and imagining that everyone else was likewise blest. At the risk of saddening him, I suggest that the experience which he calls "almost universal" is a very rare experience, if it be not, indeed, actually confined to himself. Our "keenest theatrical enjoyments" (or, as I should prefer to say, the moments when we most greatly enjoy ourselves in theatres) are derived, surely, from plays whose power or beauty takes us by surprise. Mr. Archer contemns the element of surprise. "Curiosity and suspense," he says, "are not indispensable factors; if they were, no one would ever go to see a play a second time." Quite so; but it does not follow that when we see a play for the second time our enjoyment of it is not diminished by our knowledge of what is going to happen. Nor does Mr. Archer appreciate the element of "surprise" at its true value. The advantage of seeing a powerful or beautiful play for the first time is not merely that we do not know what is going to happen (or know only through reading the play in dim book-form). Plot and situation are not the only things which are glorified by surprise. Character, idea, diction, affect us far more really when they are new to us than when they are familiar. True figures on the stage, revolving round a fine idea, expressing themselves beautifully—when we see them for the first time, are we not enraptured? We do not criticise. There is no self-consciousness in our pleasure, nor any express opinion that this or that point is fine. We do not admire the playwright's skill, nor the mimes'. We merely sit there, forgetting ourselves, full of nothing but illusion. We are spell-bound. We are "bowled over." And that, I insist, is the keenest, truest kind of æsthetic emotion to which we can attain—simply to be "bowled over." When next we go to see the play which has thus affected us, we have time to appreciate, to discriminate the details, to admire the whole work in conscious reference to our temperaments or our standards of taste. These active functions, they too are pleasant; but they are not comparable, surely, with that first passive pleasure which is forfeit. And the pleasure we take in the

active functions is always marred somewhat by actual consciousness that we are not enjoying ourselves as we did the first time.
Our anticipation having been so keen, there is always a measure of
disappointment in the reality. We ask ourselves whether, after all,
the thing is so wonderfully well done as we had thought it. We
cast side-long glances at the friends whom we have brought with
us, wondering whether they are wondering at our recent rhapsodies.
We pull ourselves together, fix our attention on the stage, and try
to convince ourselves that we did not say a word too much. As
often as not, we succeed in convincing ourselves. We may even
recapture, here and there, some moments of unconscious delight;
but usually, and at best, our second sight of a fine play brings but
a detailed confirmation that it is a fine play. At our third sight
of it, and ever after, we take its fineness rather as a matter of
course, and our chief interest is centred in the performance:
"are the mimes as good as they were on the first night?" or,
in some cases, "is the play as well cast as it was when we first
saw it?"

It is almost inevitable that, when we see an old play with a new
cast, we should be disappointed in the performance. If a part has
been finely created for us by one man or woman, we cannot bear
that another man or woman should play it. We can hardly rid
ourselves of our first sharp impression. Were "Pelléas and
Mélisande" wholly recast, we should struggle desperately before
we could be induced to admit that the new Mélisande was nearly
so good as Mrs. Patrick Campbell's, the new Pelléas as Mr. Martin
Harvey's. Luckily, in the present matinées at the Royalty, Mrs.
Campbell and Mr. Harvey are still playing their old parts. I
watched them narrowly, and cannot report any deflection from
that path of dim and delicate beauty which they first trod two years
ago. But alas! Mr. Forbes Robertson no longer is Golaud. Mr.
Frank Mills is. Doubtless, if he had been Golaud two years ago,
I should have had nothing but good to say of him. Even as it is,
I can see that his performance is, strictly, more "in the picture"
than was Mr. Robertson's. He is quieter, more monotonous—
more Maeterlinckian, in fact. Yet I deplore and resent him. I
cannot banish from my memory that other Golaud. Those wistful and poignant heart-cries cannot, for me, be rightly uttered
but by Mr. Robertson himself. Even the uncouth violence of

Mr. Robertson's performance was right, in a sense—for was not Golaud, too, "out of the picture"?

I hope that, when the war is quite finished, Mrs. Campbell will renew my emotion of two years ago by producing some other play of Maeterlinck. Can she resist the temptation to be Selysette, or Ygraine, or Alladine? London contains quite enough Maeterlinckians to make such ventures profitable to her as a manageress. The only fear is that she may be discouraged by the idiotic behaviour of people who, without sense of poetry, insist on going to see poetic plays. When I went this time to "Pelléas and Mélisande" there were, as usual, enough of these people to make a widespread titter at various points in the play. The scene of the turret in the garden was, as usual, punctuated with laughter. I spent some time in wondering why. A girl leaning from a turret window, combing her long hair, and, beneath, looking up to her, her lover—what *is* there funny in that? People don't do such things in real modern life, of course. And that is apparently the reason why to some people such things seem funny. It is not in the power of every one to adapt his mind to other conditions than those under which he lives. These asinine titterers are really no worse than the critics who solemnly brand as "unpleasant" the scene in which Golaud holds up his child to spy through Mélisande's window. Indeed, they are better, inasmuch as they do not pretend to pass judgment on works of art. "Unpleasant"! Fancy a man treating a work of remote, symbolic art in the same spirit as that in which he would write a leaderette about yesterday's sensational divorce-case!

MELPOMENE AND MR. W. L. COURTNEY

July 7, 1900

A good criticism of a good criticism must wear always a rather ungracious air. It must be hostile; else it is useless, and were better dumb. In criticising the work of a creative artist whom he admires, a man may devote himself to reverent interpretation.

Indeed, that is always the highest kind of criticism—to translate, through one's own temperament and intellect, the fine work of another man, to cast new lights on its beauties, to reveal things hidden in it, to illustrate and to extend its meanings. But this method would be absurd if it were applied by one man to the use already made of it by another If the other man has interpreted well, obviously he needs no interpreter. His work is there, finally, for all men's profit; all one could do were to repeat it; which would be useless (æsthetically), and (morally) an infringement of copyright. If he has said all things well, his critic can but congratulate him and ever more hold his peace. But the chances are that he has said some things ill, for even the best critic is fallible. The only means of writing about him profitably is to search for these things, and—when found, strike a spark out of. But to insist thus on the things which are said ill—that is, the things which, seeming to be mistaken, give the secondary critic a chance of expressing himself—is to risk an impression of not giving the primary critic due credit for the general goodness of his work. The secondary critic must, therefore, be very careful to preface his remarks with a generous, expansive congratulation to the provider of his subject. Let me not forget to do this to Mr. W. L. Courtney, whose "Idea of Tragedy"* I am taking for my theme. Let me, before I come to my one or two points of disagreement, hasten to say that this little book is full of erudition, sanity, acumen. True, its author is not one of the critics whom I most delight in, not one of those who startle me with new ideas, sometimes aweing me to silence with strange rightness, sometimes raising me to loud revolt. But he wields the old ideas in a way of his own. He has a temperament, a charming manner. His erudition is never dry. He does not, "pointer" in hand, mumble a pedantic discourse between us and an articulated skeleton of Melpomene. Rather, he drives round the town with that Muse, in an open carriage, as one has seen some courtly official drive round with some royal stranger from overseas. Though he bears himself with deference—with his back to the horses, as it were—he is quite at his ease with that living Muse, in whose kingdom he has himself travelled widely. And—the metaphor breaks here—he explains her to us as fluently and gracefully

* "The Idea of Tragedy," three lectures delivered at the Royal Institution by W. L. Courtney. London: Constable. 1900.

as Sir Rennell Rodd (for instance) would doubtless explain us to the Khedive. In fact, there is "a bloom on his scholarship." Admirable as are his analysis of the elements in all tragedy, and his comparison of the conditions which evoked tragedy in Greece and those which govern it in the modern world, he is never happier than when he is attacking the pedantic critics of an art in which, as in all arts, emotion is more than logic, or when he is flouting their futile efforts to measure this or that transcendent artist by rule of thumb. But, no matter what heads he break, he breaks them always urbanely, even playfully. He behaves always to the Oxford manner born. . . . Have I not paid as many of my handsome compliments as were needed? Let me proceed to business.

My first objection shall be made, not on a matter of opinion, but on one of manners. It seems to me that, in one instance, Mr. Courtney has carried his playfulness too far—indeed, quite beyond the bounds of good taste. I have no objection to his inclusion of Mr. Pinero's name in his syllabus. To begin with Æschylus, then to work through Sophocles and Euripides to Shakespeare, and from him to Maeterlinck and Ibsen, and to finish up with *Pinero, Mr., profound significance of*—!—that, I admit, was a quite happy thought. To trumpet Mr. Pinero among the Immortals, in the rarefied air of the Royal Institution, without a smile—that was a well-deserved hit at the kind of illiterate folk who, having no standards of taste, shriek "masterpiece!" over anything that comes along. "Hereafter," said Mr. Courtney with a delicious air of gravity, "we shall know better, I think, than we do now how great an achievement Mr. Pinero's 'The Second Mrs. Tanqueray' is, how true a tragedy in form, management and style. *We stand too close to it at present to see its true proportions.*" The italics are mine—a necessary suggestion of the ironic emphasis with which Mr. Courtney, I am sure, made deadlier his shaft. Of course, no discerning person who heard the lecture or has read the book suspected Mr. Courtney of speaking here otherwise than through his hat. Perhaps, since undiscerning people have been known to slip even into the lecture-theatre of the Royal Institution, it would have been better to say outright that Mr. Pinero's masterpiece was (not is) no more than a brilliant *pastiche* of Ibsen, grafted on an ordinary commercial melodrama of coincidence, and that its author (for all his cleverness) has yet to betray one symptom of intellectual originality or sincerity. But, for the rest, irony is a keener weapon than denunciation, and I am glad that Mr. Courtney (in bidding us stand a few leagues further off, that we might the better appreciate the majesty of the molehill's "true proportions") made so very swift and terrible a use of it. My objection is that he carried his cruelty too far, in allowing his publishers to invite Mr. Pinero to preface the printed lecture with an introduction. Perhaps it never struck him that Mr. Pinero would come solemnly up to the scratch. Yet that is, actually, what has happened. Actually, Mr. Pinero, as critic, has come forth to beat his drum round the gibbet whereon Mr. Pinero, as writer, hangs. "My dear Courtney" . . . "Your obliged friend, Arthur W. Pinero," and, between those two lines, a modest, heartfelt assurance that "when the scholar and thinker speaks of immortal poets, and of their development of an idea which has proved a source of noble inspiration to man through innumerable ages, the playwright of to-day, seeking illumination, must surely be among the humblest of his listeners"! Thus, and much more besides, with not a glimmer of perception that modesty, in such a case, is an impertinence, and that no gnat is expected to apologise for finding itself in a group of elephants, or to compliment the elephants on their size. Altogether the inclusion of this preface is a false note. It is too painful. Mr. Courtney should not have let his love of tragedy carry him so far.

Mr. Pinero relieves any possible monotony in his compliments to Æschylus and Shakespeare by adopting an attitude of reserve towards Ibsen. "Scandinavia's greatest poet," he admits, "and one of the most potent dramatic influences of our day. [I would pay sixpence for a glimpse at Mr. Pinero's list of the others.] Yet . . . I felt grateful that the tragic idea had developed in a larger atmosphere than the smoking-room of a Norwegian hotel." I quote this regret, not for its intrinsic importance, but because it echoes from Mr. Courtney's lecture a passage to which I have a strong objection. Mr. Courtney, on the whole, is as acute as usual in his view of Ibsen, both as man and as artist in dramaturgy. In parenthesis, I may suggest, however, that he is wrong in thinking that "a self-satisfied idiot like Helmer" goes to prove that "mankind must seem very despicable to" Ibsen. Helmer is not an idiot at all. He is a very decent, very capable person. Ibsen shows no sign of hating or despising him. What he hates and despises is the social tradition and convention which has made the man an unsatisfactory husband of his wife. But this is by the way. The view against which I wish to protest especially is the view echoed by Mr. Pinero: that Ibsen's genius is parochial. Mr. Courtney hedges by saying that "perhaps the time has come when literature ought no longer to belong to the centre but to the circumference," but he leaves no doubt that his own private opinion is (like Aristotle's, which he quotes) that tragedy ought to deal with gods, kings, heroes. But to quote Aristotle is no great support here. Aristotle lived long ago, and, meanwhile, evolution has been at work on tragedy as on everything else. When drama was still connected with religious worship, grandiose figures and noble backgrounds were obviously indispensable. But now that drama has, as Mr. Courtney elsewhere remarks, substituted a purely æsthetic for a religious aim, the tragic dramatist is at liberty to take whatever figures and backgrounds please him best. Mr. Courtney suggests that the tragic dramatist ought to be more pleased with "Glamis Castle, Melrose Abbey, Carisbrooke, or even with Carlton House Terrace" than with "a back parlour in South Hampstead." Why? Because they are more of "the centre," says Mr. Courtney. But are they? Surely, the test of a tragic dramatist's centrality is whether he has penetrated into the permanent elemental passions of humanity, rather than whether he has penetrated into the places where the "*vie quotidienne*" is most "*auguste*." The modern development of drama has been all towards realism. Dramatists have been trying to discover whether they can get from the common materials around them motives for lasting, universal art. This is what Ibsen has been trying to discover, and of his success one need ask no better proof than Mr. Courtney's identification of Dr. Stockmann with Prometheus. Out of the petty politics of a parish, Ibsen obtained a motive identical with that which Æschylus obtained from Attic mythology. Had he made Stockmann a King of Norway and Sweden, instead of a provincial doctor, what should we have gained? If Aubrey Tanqueray had been made a Duke, would the play in which he figured have been any nearer than it was to "the centre" —less parochial, in the true sense of the word? If the stories in the "Family Herald" had a back-parlour in Hampstead for their background, instead of Glamis Castle and Carlton House

Terrace, would Mr. Courtney read them, every week, with less avidity?

Another mistake which Mr. Courtney makes is in attaching too much importance to the fact that tragedy originated from the people. He constantly speaks of tragedy "belonging" to the people. As a matter of fact, even at Athens, where it was a religious ceremony, it appealed so little to the people that (as Mr. Courtney elsewhere remarks) the people had to be lured to it by the performance of "a satyric drama, which was a piece of buffoonery like the farce which so often forms the afterpiece of a theatrical performance in the provinces." Tragedy belonged rather to the dramatists who invented and developed it as an art-form. It died away when those dramatists ceased to exist. There had never been any real, æsthetic demand for it. Nor can I dare to hope, with Mr. Courtney, that the present war in South Africa, and the national excitement caused by it, is likely to produce such a demand in the English people during the twentieth century. There is no doubt that the great movements in art have always arisen after some crisis in national life—in other words, that great artists are apt to be born when great deeds are being done. But it is not every big war that has this desirable effect. There is no true analogy between our present war and the Greek struggle against the Persians, or our own struggle against the Spaniards or Napoleon. Says Mr. Courtney, "are we not living at present under a wave of indignant emotion, which is sweeping away class distinctions, destroying the false notion that wealth is a form of nobility, bringing down the rough estimate of things to the bare human level, the qualities which make a virile and efficient man?" No; frankly, we are not. We are engaged in no struggle for national existence. So incomparably stronger are we than our enemy that our emotion in subduing him can (in comparison with the emotion we should have felt over the Armada) be little stronger than that of a magistrate who sends a juvenile offender to a reformatory. The war was a necessary incident in our imperial policy. At one time, it seemed as though it might be a very complicated incident. But the end of it was never for one moment in any real doubt. We knew that England and the Empire would come out all right in the end—that we should, at worst, "muddle through." And that is not the spirit which produces in the next generation great works of art. Moreover, the conditions of modern life are such that this spirit could hardly arise even in a real national crisis. In former times, wars were much longer than they can be now, and the two nations at war lived in a state of vague, exalted suspense. News came to each slowly, little by little. Now, however, there are cables, and special correspondents, and halfpenny newspapers. These things intensify the emotions of the nation no doubt, but they intensify them by means of congestion. The excitement is tremendous, but it is soon over. Nature works slowly, and is not likely to produce children of exceptional genius in circumstances so pressing. Already, the nation is but languidly interested in the South African war. Its eyes are turned towards China. When the Chinese difficulty is settled, there will be some other difficulty to settle. And this reminds me that there is no instance of a great empire producing great movements in art. "With the Assyrian, Chinese, Persian, Roman, and British Empires," says Mr. George Moore in an admirable essay, "contrast Egypt, Greece, the Italian States, Venice, Holland, and the English island." The energy of a nation which runs an Empire is concentrated on imperial affairs. It has no time for great art. Mr. Courtney must make up his mind to accept this fact. After all, though we cannot expect a regeneration of great drama, there is no reason why our drama, such as it is, should not continue to improve. Mr. Courtney will find solace in that likelihood, I am sure, even though our drama travel, as it will, further and further from Carlton House Terrace into the backwoods of Hampstead.

"LAST ACTS"

July 14, 1900

It is remarkable how many modern plays are ruined by their conclusions. It so often happens that all goes well to the end of the penultimate act. The development has been natural, and the culmination is really moving, or exciting, or interesting. Then comes the last act, and very soon after the rise of the curtain our fingers flutter to our watches, even to our hats. Why is this? The dramatic critics, next morning, will declare in chorus that "after the thrilling *dénouement* which brings down the curtain on the third act, the remainder of the play was necessarily something of an anti-climax." Their ideal in construction is a play where the excitement is kept up to the final fall of the curtain. They want the curtain to fall with a "bang!" and the audience to leave the theatre as excitedly as though it were being shot from the mouth of a cannon. If that does not happen, they cry "anti-climax," and believe that they have explained what was the matter with the last act. Foolish fellows! Every play should end in an anti-climax; and there are few cases in which that anti-climax ought not to have a whole last act devoted to it.

I dare say that the best modern dramatists would, if they were appealed to, endorse the critics' disparagement of anti-climax. The truly creative artist never knows how things ought to be done in his art. He has no theories, and is always quite ready to accept such theories as may be dinned into his ears. Fortunately, he does not act on those theories. He acts by instinct, and instinct guides him in the right path. It is for the sake of the dramatists who, not having the divine flame, are apt to trim their work to the fallacious standards of the moment and so to make it even less good than it might otherwise be, that I am going to drop a few hints on the subject of anti-climax—a few hints, some of which Professor Lewis Campbell, in his turn, has (accidentally) dropped to me, from the current number of the "Fortnightly." Certain modern critics have sought to reconcile their reverence for the Greek and Elizabethan dramatists with their knowledge that final anti-climax occurred invariably in Greek and Elizabethan drama by a theory that anti-climax was used simply because there was no curtain to the stage. Obviously (they argue) these plays could not end on a poignant climax unless a quick veil were drawn between the stage and the audience; for instance, the last words in a play could not be the last of the dying hero, when the hero immediately after his last gasp, would have to get up and make his exit in full view of the audience; and, therefore, some kind of internal anti-climax—in a Greek play, a chorus; in an Elizabethan play, a subordinate character—had to be foisted in. Professor Campbell, quite rightly, believes that the "exodus" of the Greek chorus and the entry of (say) Fortinbras were not mere makeshifts, as these modern critics imagine, but were inherent in the right æsthetic effect. He quotes Cicero's "De Oratore," in support of his theory. Why, by the way, will no professor ever rely on himself? Cicero was a man whose word no one would take, even in his lifetime. How much less weight can it carry now! Professor Campbell, on the other hand, is one whose opinion would carry considerable weight. How much better had he given it to us untainted!—had he said, simply, the things which now I must say for him.

No drama is rightly wrought unless it decline from its culminating point gradually to its close, even as gradually it rose to that point from its outset. A drama should be like the well-rounded life of a human creature; it should end in as low a key as that in which it began. To end it in an outburst would be as great an error as to begin it in an outburst. A drama must descend as surely as it ascended, and we who follow it must be left on the same level as that from which we started—on the same level, though (of course) on the other side of the hill. Despite the dubious formula "*in medias res*," no one has ever argued that a work of art ought to begin on a high key. That formula is interpreted, rightly, as meaning "waste no time over irrelevant preliminaries; don't palter; come straight to your material." No one takes it to mean "come straight to the extreme use you are going to make of that material." There are two reasons for this. One is that the reader of a book or the seer of a play requires time before he can be lifted out of the common atmosphere of his own life; the process must be a kind of gradual wooing. The other is that he cannot be made to feel acutely about things which have not been explained to him, and that a crisis of any kind would be wasted on him until he were prepared for it. Thus, though a novelist may begin with "You brute!" he is obliged to add immediately "The speaker— a girl with flashing eyes, was standing," &c., &c., and then enter into an account of what led up to the scene before he can proceed further. Then he will repeat the words "You brute!" The scene will begin as though they had not been written before. As in literature and drama, so in other arts. In music the analogy is obvious. In painting it is not so obvious, because the effect made by a picture is not so definitely progressive an effect. But the analogy is there, too. The painter works up from low tones to high, and, though at first sight it is the high tones that catch our eyes, we do, thereafter, in examining the picture for our pleasure, start unconsciously from the low tones. It occurs to me that perhaps we don't, and that I am out of my depth. No matter; the analogy of painting is not essential to my case. I have shown clearly enough why no play ought to begin in a high key. As no one ever supposed that a play ought to do so, my reasons may have seemed superfluous. I gave them merely because they will explain equally why a play ought not to end on a high note, and will thus confute the anti-anti-climax party. Even as the dramatist has to raise us gradually from ordinary life, so is it his duty to conduct us safely back into ordinary life, to take leave of us with a bow. He must no more dash us down than he must wrench us up; else we shall have no æsthetic pleasure—shall merely be stunned. At both ends his work must put forth tendrils on the common earth. The entry of Fortinbras spans the gulf between Hamlet and reality. It sends us away with our illusion unhurt. It brings the play, moreover, into relation with the mimic world which is its background: Hamlet is dead, but he was only one of many men in that world; his destiny was one of many destinies to be yet fulfilled. It soothes us, and makes more impressive what has gone before, even as does the Old Testament's invariable formula after some kingly tragedy—"and ——, his son, reigned in his stead;" even as do Æneas' words, "Cessi, et sublato montem genitore petivi," after the burning of his city. That is what the entry of Fortinbras does for us. That irrelevance is really an inherent part of the play's art. Accursed be that manager who removes it from his acting-edition!

Thus the first reason I gave for ascent in plays holds good for descent. So does the second reason. Even as you cannot be really excited about matters not yet explained to you, you cannot to the full appreciate the pinnacle in a play unless you are given time to think about it—to look back at it. The pinnacle in "Hamlet" is the Prince's death, and it is Fortinbras who gives you time to mourn over him. But where the highest point in a play is not a death, but some great situation, portending great consequences, anti-climax is not merely desirable, but necessary. You must know what the consequences are, what the solution, how the knot is to be unravelled. In fact, you must have anti-climax. In most of the serious modern plays the highest point is a situation of this kind—a catastrophe to be made the best of. And this scene comes usually at the end of the third act. Thus the fourth act must be one long anti-climax. So much the better, as I have suggested. The reason why the fourth act so often spoils a play is, not that it contains an anti-climax, but that the anti-climax contained in it is clumsily or improbably worked out by the author. Sometimes the trouble is that the author, though he can invent an exciting situation, does not know enough of human nature to know what effect it would have on the human beings involved in it. Sometimes the trouble is that the situation itself (though it seemed, at the time, dramatically possible) was actually impossible, and that its consequences are seen by us, in cold blood, to be impossible accordingly. Most often the trouble is that the author, having made a situation that logically demands an unhappy ending, employs a cowardly and futile energy in the up-faking of a happy one. (A skip over twenty years into Christmas Eve used to be the favourite method. Less naïf methods are in vogue nowadays, but they are no more really effective.)

In future, let the critics not shake their heads over the thought of an anti-climax. Let them remember that if an anti-climax is tedious the fault is not its own, but the dramatist's.

MR. JONES BELOW STAIRS

October 6, 1900

Some time ago I suggested that the dramatist's horizon might be extended beyond the drawing-rooms of the upper and upper-middle classes. I hinted that the lower class really did exist, and might be translated into serious dramatic art. And I hinted (fearing that such a transition might be too sudden, too staggering, for a gentleman who had envisaged nothing but what is visible on the first-floors of Mayfair or Bayswater) that the dramatist might break his fall by dallying with that peculiar race which hangs half-way between the lower and the higher class—the race of servants. Hitherto, the dramatist had been content to use servants merely

as a means of unfolding the past of their betters at the beginning
of the first act, after which they were allowed to subside into fitful
and bald announcements that dinner was served or the carriage
waiting. Once or twice, indeed, a kitchen had been made the main
scene of a play; but then it had been treated only in a spirit of
broad, coarse farce, in the spirit of the "Yellow-plush Papers."
Thackeray had atoned for that dreary *jeu d'esprit* by his creation of
Major Pendennis' valet; other novelists, since Thackeray's time,
had concerned themselves seriously and objectively with servants.
But the dramatists, as their wont is, had been blind to the possibility of keeping pace with novelists. "Jeames" and "Sary Hann,"
"lawks" and "leastways," were for them the insuperable bound-
aries to what might be done with servants. They perceived not
that the anomalous life led by servants cried aloud for serious comedic treatment. So I threw my hint out to them. I never supposed
that they would take it. I should like to suppose that in "The
Lackey's Carnival," at the Duke of York's Theatre, Mr. Henry
Arthur Jones has fulfilled for me my touching ambition to shape
the history of the modern stage by taking the hint which I threw
out. Alas! I have gone into the matter, and have discovered that
his play was in Mr. Frohman's hands a few weeks before the hint
was thrown out. I may, however, solace myself with the knowledge that my mind converged unconsciously with the mind of
him who is always, in alertness and intelligence and sense for life,
a league or so in advance of the ordinary dramatists. There is,
also, this glad thought for me : that the ordinary dramatists, impervious to a critic's precept, will probably be fired by the example
of Mr. Jones. We shall have, at length, serious comedies about
servants. And that, after all, was the finer part of my ambition.

"The Lackey's Carnival" is a play with many technical faults.
All these faults have been unctuously exposed by the critics; for
the critics are ever eager to avenge themselves on a dramatist who
gives them anything to think about; and Mr. Jones, therefore, even
at his technically best, seldom gets a good word from the fraternity.
The good word deserved by "The Lackey's Carnival" is, as I have
suggested, that here is the first effort made by a dramatist to
penetrate the character of servants. Having said this good word
as loudly as I can, I feel that I may, decently, proceed to pick holes.
I may, in the first place, express my regret that Mr. Jones has not

devoted his whole play to his main effort. Instead of dealing solely with servants, and using masters and mistresses only in so far as servants are by masters and mistresses inevitably affected, Mr. Jones has made the affairs of his drawing-room as prominent as those of his kitchen. More prominent, indeed; for the servants are (dramatically) important only in so far as they affect the destinies of their masters and mistresses. This is a pity. These servants, seen for the first time on the stage, are infinitely more interesting than their employers, seen from time immemorial, and overshadow them, and prevent us from caring what befall them. Conversely, the uninteresting employers prevent us from seeing so much as we should like to see of the servants: they waste much of the time which ought to be spent by us in studying the servants alone. Even if Mr. Jones had taken as much trouble with his employers and made them as real as his servants, I should still object to the portmanteau form, on the ground that our inexperience of servants on the stage demands for them exclusive attention. But Mr. Jones has not done this. He has breathed no life into the employers; he has been content that they should be the familiar, old-fashioned figures of insanely jealous husband, innocent (but on one occasion indiscreet) wife, eminent Q.C., who is an old friend of the husband and tries to set everything right, &c., &c. They have no value, these figures, save for the stale purposes of dramatic intrigue. The servants, on the other hand, have a very real value. They are human beings—human beings of a new kind. They have characters. In fact, the two sides of the portmanteau do not meet. Mr. Jones' delight in depicting the servile character interferes with his conduct of the intrigue, and the intrigue mars the accuracy of his portrayal of the character itself. The whole of the third act is devoted to a ball given by a valet to his fellow-servants in his employers' absence. But this ball, interesting in point of character, merely retards the intrigue. Nothing comes of it. The valet (blackmailer of the wife) is reduced to harmlessness by two circumstances which have nothing whatever to do with the giving of the ball. When, finally, he is led off to prison and silence, one feels that for the purpose of the intrigue it would have been much better and simpler to make him an ordinary villain of the drawing-room. Mr Jones, in order to get a link between the drawing-room and the kitchen, has made him a kind of dual creature who, in the interval between his past and present "situation," has been palming himself off on society as a gentleman at large. And thus Mr. Jones has come within an ace of ruining the best of all the characters in the play. It is, of course, possible that a valet might, as in this play, be so clever and so well graced as to have got into a good club and made a well-bred woman flirt with him. But such a man, surely, would never have gone back to his old life. Found out by his new associates, he would hardly have sunk below the level of a flash adventurer. Even if he had, it would not have amused him to give a dance to his fellow-servants. He would, as does Thomas Tarboy, dine quietly at the Savoy when he got the chance; but he would not, like Thomas Tarboy, arrange an orgy for the simple folk whom he despised all the more bitterly because he was one of them by accident of birth. If Mr. Jones' dramatic scheme made it necessary that the valet should be a blackmailer, the valet's blackmail ought to have been levied on account of indiscretions committed by a lady not for his sake but for the sake of some man in her own class. Thomas Tarboy's out-of-class exploits may be possible in real life. But they are, at least, so rare as to be not typical. They smack of romantic fantasy. They mar what would otherwise have been a consistently realistic character, and they make improbable that servants' ball which might otherwise have seemed inevitable.

Stripped of the circumstantial unreality in which Mr. Jones has clad him, Thomas Tarboy is a fine and memorable creation—a study of the moral derangement and the pathetic aspirations which are produced by the conditions of domestic service in modern times. In all times, of course, domestic service has been a demoralising state of existence. To belong to one class and to live in close contact with another, to "live hardly" in contemplation of more or less luxury and idleness, to dissimulate all your natural feelings because you are forbidden to have them, and to simulate other feelings because they are expected of you—this has always been an unnatural life, breeding always the same bad qualities. The instinct to spy, to flatter, to peculate were common among the slaves in Plautus' time, as among the servants in our own time. But the Plautian slaves—the slaves, indeed, and the servants in all times but ours—were fairly content with their wretched lot; though they were eager to improve it by snatching little surreptitious comforts, it never occurred to them that they deserved a better lot. They envied their employers, but they never realised that they might themselves (but for an accident) be leading a delightful life. They felt themselves to be of a caste lower than that of their employers. They felt themselves brutish, ignorant, good for nothing but to serve. Plato somewhere suggests that, if a rich man were by some god rapt away into a wilderness with his retinue of slaves, his orders would be ignored, and he would be reduced to fawning on those over whom the social system had enabled him to tyrannise, and to making all kinds of concessions, sorely against his will. But Plato reckoned without the servile tradition. The Greek slaves would have been as docile in the wilderness as in Athens. They never had been educated. We, during the last thirty years, have been smiling over the blessings of universal education, and we are just beginning to realise, with horror, that we ought to have postponed that system until all menial duties could be performed by machinery. We are beginning to find that the only servants who are willing to perform those duties well are they who will soon be past their work. The younger generation of servants is almost as learned and as graceful as are we ourselves. It asks itself, "Why should we be treated as though we were dogs?" It begins to claim privileges—privileges that cannot be granted without upsetting the household. What are we to do? There is nothing to do but to rescind the Compulsory Education Acts, and to look forward to being served well in twenty years or so. Meanwhile, we suffer. The servants themselves suffer. They are seething for rebellion; yet they know well that, though they are too good to be servants, they are not quite good enough to be anything else. They must perforce continue to serve, and content themselves with serving as badly as they can without actually losing their means of livelihood. They hate us for the advantage we still have over them, and they try to be even with us in secret. Their aspirations are pathetic, as I have said. We, who are to blame in the matter, may at least acknowledge the pathos. But we cannot help seeing that these aspirations are bad for the character, and that they involve an amount of hypocrisy far greater than that which vitiated servants in other ages of the world. In projecting Thomas Tarboy Mr. Jones has brought upon the stage something that is (despite excrescences) as true essentially as it is new. What is painful in life is, if it be realised, delightful in art. Therefore I thank Mr. Jones. But I hope that he will soon write a play in which *all* the chief characters shall be servants.

"ALICE" AGAIN AWAKENED

December 22, 1900

I conceive the illustrator of books as an active fiend, who clips with long sharp shears the tender wings of illusion. I hate him. Especially do I hate him when he illustrates a work of fantasy. It is bad enough to be robbed of my own vision of a realistic scene, even when the illustrator's vision happens, by some rare chance, to strike me as better than my own. It is far worse to see materialised a scene of sheer fantasy, even if, by another rare chance, the illustrator's vision of it has coincided with my own. But, though I deplore all illustrations, I do discriminate. Though I should prefer that "Alice in Wonderland" and "Through the Looking-Glass" had never been illustrated at all, by Sir John Tenniel or any other artist, I do admit readily that Sir John's illustrations are the best imaginable. I rejoice in the goodness of them, if only because they are so good, so sure, that they have permanently benumbed the hundred-and-one hands which would otherwise have been itching to illustrate "Alice." It is a good thing, also, that there never was an edition of "Alice" unillustrated. We have never read the book save under Sir John's auspices. He, mercifully, clipped our wings before they had fluttered ever so little, and so his ingenious flying-machine has never really chafed us. The true fiend of illustration suffers us to soar alone ere he swoops with his shears. We ought, also, to thank Sir John for this mercy: that he has so paved the way that the inevitable dramatic version of "Alice" need not be painful to us. Imagine what would have happened if "Alice" had never been illustrated at all, or had been illustrated badly by various ladies and gentlemen! However well-inspired the conceiver and the costumier of the play, how we should have shuddered! As it is, we have but one common vision of all the characters and monsters whom Alice met—Sir John's vision. And we are perfectly content if these characters and monsters realise that vision. In the present production at the Vaudeville Theatre, they do realise it, obediently and fully. One and all, they are as we know them in the book. Poor Alice herself is the sole disturber of our preconception. That Alice's appearance should be wrong is a very serious pity; but it is not the fault of the management, nor of Miss Ellaline Terriss, altogether. A child could not play so long and important a part. No actress (to adapt a well-known aphorism) can play Alice till she is twenty, and then she doesn't look the part. She may produce an illusion of childishness, but she cannot give us the prim, Medio-Victorian childishness of Alice. The short petticoats of Alice, and the straight-combed hair, are not quite possible. Their severity has to be sacrificed. Some measure of alien softness and picturesqueness has to be contrived; else were the result a monstrous caricature. But I cannot help thinking that Miss Terriss, in her necessary desire to translate 'twenties into 'teens, has gone further than she need have gone in the matter of softness and picturesqueness, further than she need have gone from very Alice. Her curls need not fall in quite so wilful a tumult; nor need her dress be silken, with accordion-pleats; nor need her pinafore seem quite so costly a symbolic film. Her whole appearance is a defiance, rather than a compromise. However, for the others, I have nothing but praise to offer. The Mad Hatter and the Knave of Hearts, the Mock Turtle and the Duchess, and all the other creatures, are precisely as Sir John gave them to us, only with the added graces of colour, mobility, voices, and three dimensions. These added graces would, of course, be mere aggravations, were not Sir John's forms copied faithfully, or had not these forms existed at all. Wherefore, once and away, I may be entirely grateful to an illustrator. I beg leave to withdraw my wish that "Alice" had never been illustrated at all.

Often as this dramatic version has been performed, I had never seen it before. Its ingenuity is delightful. Lewis Carroll was not less fortunate in having Mr. Savile Clark as his dramatist than in having Sir John as his illustrator. None of the most delightful incidents in either of the two books has been omitted, and none of them has lost its savour, and all of them grow out of and into one another in the right kind of reasonably-unreasonable sequence.

The result is a perfect little pantomime. Every adult must revel in it. I cannot so safely answer for children. Between us and children—even the least "reserved" children—there is always a certain veil of mystery. It is not safe to dogmatise about their tastes by reference to what *we* should have liked at their age; for children are probably as different as are adults in different generations. The punning of which Lewis Carroll was too prodigal, and which delighted us as children, may, for aught I know, bore children nowadays as greatly as it bores us. Their ringing peals may be a mere affectation. Again, do they, I wonder, really share our delight in Carroll's philosophic *aperçus*? We laugh long when someone, to whom Alice has declared that she likes the Carpenter better than the Walrus "because *he* was just a little bit sorry for the poor oysters," replies "Yes, but he ate more of them;" we find in that reply a more deliciously just indictment of sentimentalism than ever was made, even by Mr. Meredith. The children laugh, too; but their laughter may be hollow mimicry of ours. Through the veil of mystery, we can but make wild shots at their true tastes. My own personal shot is that they do really like "Alice," as a story, by reason of its perfect blend of fantasy with moral edification. I believe the love of these two separate things to be implanted in the child for all time, and I believe that Carroll's inimitable conjunction of them keeps, and will keep, "Alice" really popular in nurseries. Behind Lewis Carroll, the weaver of fantastic dreams, the delighter in little children, there was always Mr. Dodgson, the ascetic clergyman, the devoted scholar in mathematics. And the former had to pay constant toll to the latter—to report himself, as it were, at very brief intervals. It was as though the writer never could quite approve of his deviations into the sunny path that he loved best. When he was not infusing mathematics into his humour, he was stiffening out his fantasy with edification. In his later books, mathematics and morals triumphed. Humour lay crushed in "The Tangled Skein," fantasy in "Sylvie and Bruno." Readers of Walter Pater will remember the story of Prior Saint-Jean; will remember how the last volume of that treatise on mathematics which had occupied his life never was completed. "Whereas in the earlier volumes you found by way of illustration no more than the simplest indispensable diagrams, the scribe's hand had strayed here into mazy borders, long spaces of hieroglyph, and as it were veritable pictures of the theoretic elements of his subject. Soft wintry auroras seemed to play behind whole pages of crabbed textual writing, line and figure bending, breathing, flaming into lovely 'arrangements' that were like music made visible. . . ." Well! (as Pater himself would have said) Lewis Carroll's history was the history of Prior Saint-Jean reversed. In him the fair luxuriance of a Pagan fancy was gradually overcome by the sense of duty to his cloth, and by the tyranny of an exact science. In the two books about Alice, however, you have a perfect fusion of the two opposing elements in his nature. In them the morality is no more than implicit, and the mathematics are not thrust on you. Though modern adults are apt to resent even implicit morality in a book for children, children delight in it. They delight in feeling that, in some way or other, Alice is being "improved" by her adventures. Orally, she seems to be an awful prig, but various internal evidence makes them suspect her of having "a past"—of having been naughty; and they feel that, somehow or other, the Caterpillar and the Red Queen and all the rest of them are working out her redemption. This human, commonplace element in Alice, and the delight depending on it, are, I think, missed in the production at the Vaudeville. Not merely does Miss Terriss look more like a fairy than a child: she *behaves* as such. She gives no hint of "a past" behind a priggish manner. She seems as one born to patronise, from a pedestal of solid virtue, Red Queens and White Queens and other potentates. For her no monster, how grotesque soever, has any terrors; she is secure, with the security that comes of a conscience utterly untroubled. Nor can she from any sage beast acquire any knowledge that is not hers already. To every one alike, she is all smiles, and sweet superiority, and honeyed graciousness. She is not merely a fairy: she is the fairy-queen. This is a pity. It robs the play of what would be, as I conceive, its primary appeal to children. It does not, however, mar very grievously the enjoyment of adults. And is it not for us adults, after all, that these pantomimes are intended?

THE VESTURE OF MIMES

January 12, 1901

In its "palmy" days our drama suffered by the too shabby aspect of its mimes. Now it suffers by the overpowering "dressiness" of them. When it lay under the purple dominancy of Bulwer and Bulwer's apes, the costumiers ought to have had *carte blanche*. Those reams of rhetoric, emitted by Emperors, Cardinals and Troubadours, needed as much of satin and velvet, ermine and silver-gilt, as of lung-power and florid articulation and lack of humour. Buckram and dingily-painted cardboard, darned hose and cloaks of napless velveteen, must have been very palpable drawbacks; but they were, for pecuniary reasons, inevitable. Those pecuniary reasons are no more. The nation has been prospering, and the price for playgoing has been raised. Managers of theatres have so much money passing through their fingers that they can afford displays of expensive costumes. The public, moreover, has learnt to expect these displays, to resent any lack of them. Well! if our drama were still wallowing in rhetorical romance, this state of things would be most beneficial. But our drama left Bulwer and Bulwer's apes long ago in the lurch. Except Mr. Stephen Phillips, all the current dramatists who matter a jot are devoting themselves to realistic comedy of modern life. To produce "Herod" properly, no expenditure of money for costumes (with proportionate expenditure of taste) would have been too great. The theme and tone of the play demand gorgeous display. Nor, from the artistic standpoint, can too much money be spent on any of Shakespeare's plays. But Shakespeare, though he is produced often, has nothing to do with the drama that we are trying to create—the drama that really matters to us. He has, doubtless, influenced Mr. Stephen Phillips; but there is no likelihood that Mr. Phillips, in his turn, will influence any one. He is walking alone through a remote wood from whose branches no apes dangle. Modern realism is the one thing that has vitality, present and future vitality. The dramatist's aim being to produce an illusion of contemporary life, it is important that the mimes be clothed like the real men and women whom one sees otherwise than across footlights. But, as a rule, they are not so clothed. They look too brand-new, too glossy, too expensive. They, and the managers who rule them, have not yet grasped that ideal which I have just suggested—the ideal of verisimilitude. They are still aiming at the ideal of gorgeous effect, though it is now quite incongruous with the scheme of the dramatist. What the producers of Bulwer ought to have done, but could not do, these others succeed in doing, without having any business to do it.

"But," you might murmur, "*is* gorgeous effect quite incongruous with the scheme of the dramatist? Doesn't he, almost invariably, disdain to deal with any class but the upper or the upmost upper middle, neither of which looks anything if not gorgeous?" I admit that the dramatist is, at present, very haughty. He is very shy of the suspicion that he knows anything about any one unworthy of a "social par." The kind of people used by him as subjects for his art are (with few lapses) people who spend a great deal of money at their dressmakers' or tailors'. Accordingly, it is well that the finances of the modern theatre enable the mimes to be dressed at great expense. In the afternoon, when they are driving, and in the evening, when they are dining, the upper and upmost upper-middle classes do look very gorgeous, no doubt. But it is not true that they always look gorgeous. If you are early a-foot in any modish thoroughfare of London, you will see ladies whose lives are spent in a whirl of "social pars" walking about in garb which (though, doubtless, worth a king's ransom) is quite simple, quite sober, quite unobtrusive. Do you, on the other hand, remember the confections of those ladies in the third act (time: very early morning) of "The Liars"? And they, those rainbows of silk, twinkling firmaments of jewellery, fleecy clouds of lace, were no rare phenomena on the stage. They were familiar and typical instances. It matters not what time of day be fixed by the dramatist, nor whether the scene be laid in London or in the country, all the actresses impersonating smart women on the English stage are dressed up to the nines, and as far as possible above that level. In "The Liars" I remember there was a typical instance of their disregard for place as well as for time. The second act of the play passed in a riverside hotel, where two or three ladies appeared, having just stepped out of canoes or punts. They, again, were dressed as for some elaborate urban

function—were rainbows, firmaments, clouds, and all the rest of it.
A frequenter of the river has told me that, last summer, most of the
women actually did navigate in this kind of attire. But they certainly had not done so before the production of "The Liars." It
is the business of mimes in a realistic play to mirror, not to set,
fashions. In romantic plays, the fashion-setting business would be
well enough. But in realistic plays it is as great a solecism as would
be the pronunciation of leisure as *leesure*, or homage as *'omage*.
Romance being "off," mimes no longer pose as authorities on the
pronunciation of words: they try to speak like us. Why do not
they dress, also, like the real people whom they are there to represent?

It is some salve to our national pride to reflect that the convention of inappropriate gorgeousness is not confined to the English
stage. Even Duse, reputed to be the most realistic of living
actresses, is a slave to it. In "La Gioconda," last year, at the
Lyceum, she impersonated the wife of a sculptor—a woman living
in the country, rapt in the love of her husband and her child, caring
nothing at all for the world, looking down on the world from a
pinnacle of noble dowdiness. How was she dressed? Exactly
after the fashion of her Mrs. Tanqueray, or her Magda, or her
Princesse Georges. I confess that I was surprised. I should have
wondered less if she had come upon the stage wearing the coat and
hat which she had worn on the way from her hotel to the theatre:
such a proceeding would have been but a corollary to her refusal
to annul the effect of footlights by putting paint or powder on her
face; it would have been but another piece of false realism. Indeed, seeing that she never made up her face even for the part of
a radiant woman of fashion, I was always surprised that she should
go out of her way to change her clothes for it. That she should
go out of her way to dress up gorgeously in "La Gioconda" was a
fact which could be explained on no hypothesis but that she loved
fine clothes for their own sake and was anxious to show them off.
If Duse, the austerely transcendental, has this little weakness, we
cannot very well blame our own (comparatively trivial) actresses
for having it too. But why do not the dramatists whom they interpret prevent them from yielding to the little weakness on inappropriate occasions? Or why do not the male critics cancel the
gushing encouragement given to the over-dressed actress by those

female critics who are sent to first-nights to describe the millinery?
Why do not the male critics make a point of always telling the
over-dressed actress how absurd she looks?

"Artistically," you murmur, "that is all very well. But the
theatre is a commercial undertaking. Much of the success of such
plays as 'The Liars' is due to the public's desire to go and see
pretty women gorgeously dressed. In London no young actress
can be brought to the footlights unless she is pretty. The public
does not want to see plain actresses, however great may be their
talent. And it wants to see them tricked out in such a way as
makes them most strikingly attractive." Again I meet you half
way. I am quite prepared to look at the matter from a commercial
standpoint. I admit the lamentable fact that our public likes its
mimes (male and female) to be selected for the shape of their
figures and faces rather than for the quality of their brains, and
that the managers must reckon with this preference. Handsome
actors do much to attract into the theatre the female section of the
public. Handsome actresses do much to attract the male section.
I have no doubt that the female section likes the actresses to be
overdressed, even as the male section, possibly, likes the actors to
be overdressed. But that consideration is not important. It is,
primarily, the male section which goes to see the actresses, and
whose tastes have to be catered for in that connexion. And it is an
utter fallacy to suppose that men's admiration of a woman is
spurred by gorgeous frocks and jewels. On the contrary, these
accessories are obstacles to admiration. "'A cloud of millinery,'"
said Lord Palmet, in "Beauchamp's Career," "'shoots me off a
mile from a woman. In my opinion witches are the only ones for
wearing jewels without chilling the feminine air about them.
Fellows think differently.' He waved a hand expressive of amiable
toleration, for this question upon the most important topic of
human affairs was deep, and no judgment should be hasty in
settling it. 'I'm peculiar,' he resumed. 'A rose and a string of
pearls: a woman who goes beyond that's in danger of petrifying
herself and her fellow man.'" But Lord Palmet was not really
"peculiar." Expressing (quite palpably) the views of his creator,
he was expressing also the views of mankind in general. Women
dress elaborately to please themselves, to please or displease other
women. If they imagine that they please men by their elaboration

they make a very great mistake. But probably they imagine no such thing. It is significant that in this age, as in all other ages of the world, she whose especial mission is to attract some man, the young unmarried girl, is by her mother shown with the least possible amount of ornamentation—no jewels, no furbelows. Furbelows are but an obscuring cloud, even as jewels, in Mr. Meredith's witty phrase, petrify. It is only the simplest kind of frocks that really give beauty its fair scope. And thus, accepting the idea of the playgoing public as Pasha, I find one reason the more against the prevailing "dressiness" of female mimes.

I do not know enough about the psychology of women to assert that they, in their turn, are chilled and disconcerted by the "dressiness" of male mimes. So I will base on merely artistic grounds my plea that actors should not wear patent-leather boots (or boots of brightest yellow) with tweed suits, and that they should never snatch an opportunity of displaying the latest vulgarity and monstrosity in the fashion of waistcoats. On the whole, however, the actor is less culpable than the actress in the matter of gorgeousness. The cut and colour of his clothes are generally similar to those of the clothes that would be worn by the real person whom he impersonates. The main fault of his costume is that it looks always much too new. The crease down the front of his trousers is so hard that one fancies it would cut his hands if he touched it. His coat sets so stiffly that one doubts if there be really a human body within it. He looks more like one of the figures in a tailor's fashion-plates than a man. His waistcoat is "a vest," his trousers are "trouserings," his coat is "a cheviot lounge" or "a frock braided." And so he is really little better than the actress, who looks like a Paris model touched up by the Queen of Sheba.

Rational dress for mimes is a necessary adjunct to rational drama. It will come in time, I hope. But it will never come unless my fellow-critics join me in my spirited effort to hurt the mimes' feelings.

MR. SHAW CRESCENT

January 26, 1901

Having regard to the commonweal, Mr. Shaw bemoans the existence of "reputations" in art, and vents a hope that the attractive specimen acquired by himself will decay quickly. If he is sincere in this protestation, he must change his tactics. He is not going the right way about the business. His new book * will increase the bulk of his reputation, and will make it more durable. In these "Three Plays for Puritans" he has made a perceptible advance from the point he occupied in those "Plays, Pleasant and Unpleasant."

When a well-known writer is, like Mr. Shaw, in his forty-fifth year, people are apt to assume that he cannot further advance. He may, it is thought, increase his reputation by repeating himself, but cannot increase it by doing anything better than, or in kind different from, what he has done before. And usually this popular assumption is quite correct. Nine lustres exhaust from a writer any vital stuff that may be in him. The question is not of the amount he has to express, but simply of the time during which he has tried to express it. The small writer aged 30 will have relatively as much left in him as the great writer aged 30; and neither will have anything to express fifteen years later. Be there never so great an amount of vital stuff in a man—in other words, if he be a genius—he will, nevertheless, be on the shelf (however devoutly he may believe himself to be *sur le tapis*) so soon as his ninth lustre is fulfilled. But to this rule there are, here and there, a few glaring exceptions, and Mr. Shaw happens to be one of them. I care not that he is in his forty-fifth year: he is, I assure you, a young writer; he is still in an early state of development. I will not try to determine whether he be a great writer or otherwise. But I do insist that you should regard him as a young one. Perhaps it will help you if I venture for a moment into that first-personal manner which Mr. Shaw himself has used to such effect. I am, I believe, regarded as a young writer. On the other hand, you think you know all about Mr. Shaw. You think his ideas and his methods are

* "Three Plays for Puritans." By Bernard Shaw. (Grant Richards.)

fixed, and that he, as a writer, must continue to be exactly what he already is. Now let me give you a striking proof of your error. Mr. Shaw and I, as writers, are exactly connate. Thirteen years ago, when the writing-instinct first stirred in me, one of my relatives was writing a weekly "London Letter" for a well-known journal in Scarborough. I implored that I might be allowed to write it for him, claiming no reward. He assented. I well remember that the first paragraph I wrote was in reference to the first number of "The Star," which had just been published. Mr. T. P. O'Connor, in his editorial pronunciamento, had been hotly philanthropic. "If," he had written, "we enable the charwoman to put two lumps of sugar in her tea instead of one, then we shall not have worked in vain." My comment on this was that if Mr. O'Connor were to find that charwomen did not take sugar in their tea, his paper would, presumably, cease to be issued. I believe the paragraph had a great success, in Scarborough. Recalling it, I do not think much of it. I quote it merely to show that I, who am still regarded as a young writer, am exactly as old as Mr. Shaw. For it was in this very number of "The Star" that Mr. Shaw, as "Corno di Bassetto," made his first bow to the public. Thitherto he had confined himself to speaking on platforms, talking to his friends, reading books. He had never, before the year 1888, been induced to express himself in writing. And thus he is as young a writer as I am. He is still perched on the lap of the gods. Almost every man who has a vocation to writing takes to his pen, as I did, when he is fifteen years old. Mr. Shaw did not take to his before he was twenty-eight. As I have already suggested, the amount that a writer has still to express, and the possibility of novelty in its expression, depends entirely on the time during which he has been writing. Thus, since the writer who begins at the normal age becomes barren at the age of forty-five, Mr Shaw, glaring exception that he is, will have celebrated his fifty-eighth birthday before we can pass any definite judgment on his powers. If his future progress in dramaturgy be in ratio to his progress during the past three years, he will leave behind him an immortal name. So I advise him to "slow down" at once.

When he published his "Plays, Pleasant and Unpleasant," I, knowing him to be quite young and malleable, thought it well to urge him not to go in for serious drama. "Arms and the Man" and "You Never Can Tell" seemed to me much better, much more sincere and genuine, as comedic farces than were "Mrs. Warren's Profession" and the rest as serious plays. Nor has my opinion changed in the meantime. In his serious plays Mr. Shaw was not himself. He was still the youth groping his way to self-expression, and groping, as so many youths do, in the wrong direction, under the wrong master. Hanging on to the coat-tails of even the wrong master is healthy exercise for a youth; it strengthens his muscles, and so forth. But such exercise must not be overdone. Mr. Shaw has loosened his hold on Ibsen's coat-tails not too soon. I admit that his serious plays were exceedingly good *pastiches* of Ibsen, and that in time he could have written serious plays to which one could have given higher praise than that. Nevertheless, he was not born to write serious plays. He has too irresponsible a sense of humour. This sense he never could have suppressed so utterly as to prevent it from marring his plays; and, as it is his greatest gift, one does not wish him to suppress it at all. Again, he is (though he may deny that he is) incapable of portraying satisfactorily those human passions which must form the basis of serious drama. In all his serious plays, he tried (and tried very cleverly) to reproduce Ibsen's women. These creatures are tolerable and admirable because they are warmly human, warmly alive. But Mr. Shaw never could get further than their surface-characteristics. And the result was that his heroines were quite appalling. They were just dowdy and ill-conditioned shrews—wasps without waists. I am glad to think that I have seen the last of them. Now that Mr. Shaw has got clean away from the Ibsen formula, and makes no attempt at dealing seriously with the great issues of human life, his heroines are quite delightful and (as far as they go) quite real.

The first of the plays in this book is a melodrama, the second an extravagant historical comedy, the third a romantic "adventure." In fact, the *form* of them is quite frivolous. Seriousness enters into them now and again, but inheres in them never. In "Mrs. Warren" and the rest it was the form that was serious, and the frivolity that could not be kept out. The change in Mr. Shaw's method is welcome because he himself is a jester with serious interludes, not an occasionally jocular seer. The new method is for him the artistic method. All three plays are presented on a large, loose scale which is about as far as anything could be from the strait, strict form of his early plays—as far from it as Mr. Shaw's true self is from Ibsen's. And Mr. Shaw uses this large, loose scale in a thoroughly masterly way, having found it for himself by the light of nature, and not having imposed it on himself as a duty. I admit that the last play, "Captain Brassbound's Conversion," is not masterly. The admission is, indeed, wrung from me by the fact that I elaborately disparaged the play in these columns a few short weeks ago. Nevertheless, it marks a distinct advance from the serious plays : it is much more capable than were they of being treated with respect. Of the first play, "The Devil's Disciple," I have also written here, and, reading it, I have nothing to subtract from the praises I heaped on it after seeing it acted. The second play, "Cæsar and Cleopatra," is quite new to me. It is, I think, far the best thing Mr. Shaw has yet done. Every scene in it is delicious. Most of the scenes are mere whimsical embroidery, a riotous sequence of broadly humorous incidents. But some of them, very cleverly woven in, are true psychological comedy. Both Cæsar and Cleopatra are perfectly credible studies. Of course, if Mr. Shaw had tried to portray Cæsar in some really serious love affair, or to give us Cleopatra in the Antonine phase, he would have failed utterly. But here, merely, is Cæsar as an important public man who knows that a little chit of a girl-queen has taken a fancy to him, and is tickled by the knowledge, and behaves very kindly to her, and rather wishes he were young enough to love her. This kind of emotion Mr. Shaw can delineate sharply and truly. Nor could the kittenish admiration of Cleopatra for her hero have been more sympathetically shown to us. I wish very much that this play could be produced. But it would cost many thousands of pounds, and managers are coy of a vast production which is not the setting of some vast dramatic motive. Indeed, there is, as I have more than once demonstrated, an artistic, besides a financial, objection to such a production. Nevertheless, if I were a very rich manager, I should produce the play, if only to watch how a modern British audience would be affected by the early Briton whom Mr. Shaw has foisted into his play. Mr. Alfred Bishop would be engaged by me for this part. He would be immense in it.

I am not sure that Mr. Shaw's prefaces, notes, and stage-directions are not even more delightful than the plays themselves. In them, too, I find that Mr. Shaw has made real progress. He has always had a "style," in the sense that he has always been able to express accurately, in a live manner, the thoughts that are in him. But now he is evidently beginning to realise that a style may be beautiful, and ought to be beautiful, in itself. In one of the prefaces, especially, in which he describes the career and character of Mr. Cunninghame Graham, he introduces some really graceful and charming prose. The Puritan, paying homage to the Cavalier, decks himself with some of the Cavalier's own plumes, and looks, I am bound to say, very well in them. But I hope Mr. Shaw will not, like so many of our young writers, pay attention to manner at the expense of matter. I notice, with misgiving, his use of the word "stupent." He must beware the fascination of archaisms. On the other hand, I am glad to find in his prefaces evidence that he has just been reading Plato. To quote Plato freely, as he does, is a very proper habit in a young writer.

"THE DRAMA OF THE DUSTBIN"

February 23, 1901

This phrase was not coined by me; I never alliterate. It came lately from the humming mint of one whose last words (long may they remain unuttered!) will probably, through lifelong habit, be alliterated. Mr. Clement Scott issued it into our currency as a description of "Mr. and Mrs. Daventry." As such, it seems to me hardly apt. For, whatever faults that play may have had, it was, at least, fresh and vital; thrown by Mr. Frank Harris upon the stage, it was an explosive bomb rather than a heap of stale and negligible refuse, and many of the critics were seriously injured by it—none more seriously than Mr. Scott himself; and for some months it has been exploding nightly, with great noise and shock. To connect it with the dustbin is, therefore, quite manifestly absurd. However, Mr. Scott's phrase must be dear to him, and I should not like to make him drop it. Merely would I urge him to apply it more carefully. There is a kind of drama to which it really is quite applicable. Of this kind an obvious sample is the play now claiming my attention. For this play I regret to say Mr. Scott himself is partly responsible. But let not that consideration prevent him from following my lead and applying his phrase as I do. For here is stale and negligible refuse indeed. Here are the picked bones and the broken eggshells and the potato-parings of drama, embedded, with many other nameless scraps and shreds, in the dust of ages. Time, one had thought, had carted them away long ago. But Nature is an idle vestry, and the opened lid in the area of the Garrick Theatre wafts to our nostrils the faint unwholesome savour of "Peril." Here, I protest, is "The Drama of the Dustbin" indeed.

Why was the lid opened? Why were the mimes sent down to rummage? What lost jewel did any one hope to recover? Had Mr. Bourchier really found, throughout the length and breadth of the MSS. submitted to him as a manager, so lamentable a dearth of anything like talent for dramaturgy that "Peril" seemed to him the best and only policy? I will not believe it. I prefer to think that in reviving this play he was actuated solely by a tender desire to cheer Sardou's declining years, to prove to that outmoded manipulator that the beer now thought of him is not so small in London as in Paris. Such a motive is very creditable to Mr. Bourchier as a man. But I would urge him to take a hint from Count von Bülow and wear his manly heart in his managerial head. "Peril" was a very good entertainment in its generation. But its generation is past, and therewith is past the vogue of those little tricks and dodges and wheezes which were Sardou's sole stock-in-trade. We may not have progressed very far; but we are far enough on to have left Sardou out of sight; and, when Mr. Bourchier doubles back and returns breathless with Sardou in his arms, none of us, I fear, can contrive to force a smile or welcome for the rescued derelict. We have reached that stage at which we demand from the writer of a comedy that he shall make his characters live, and that he shall develop his theme more or less as life might develop it. We cannot pretend to be interested in characters which have utterly failed to evoke a spark of interest in their creator, or in a theme out of which he has not attempted to make anything but one stage-situation. In "Peril" Sardou's primary characters are (1) the elderly married man, (2) the juvenile wife, (3) the young man intervening. But he does not attempt to show us the character of one of them. He merely dumps them down on the boards—A, B, and C—and proceeds to show us what might happen if a door were locked and a window were open, and if a chair were overturned and a bell-rope snapped in two, and if the shutters closed easily from within and the balcony were twenty feet above the ground, and if a lady's-maid had gone to bed and a family doctor was still sitting up. It was in order to lead up to this door - *cum* - window - *cum* - shutters - *cum* - chair - *cum* - bell-rope - *cum* - lady's maid - *cum* - family-doctor accident, and not with any particle of interest in anything else, that Sardou (as was his wont) wrote "Nos Intimes." When Mr. Clement Scott and Mr. B. C. Stephenson adapted the affair, the result was quite popular, no doubt. . . . At that time, if I am not mistaken, Mr. Bourchier was in Eton collars. He is no longer in them. And he might put away, also, those other childish things of which "Peril" is a type.

"Peril" is not merely childish: it is (to me, who am no prude) positively offensive. By the second act of "Mr. and Mrs. Daventry" I was not at all offended. The play was a serious reflection of life, and its showy "situation" was purged of offence by the fact that it was a necessary episode for the development of certain realistic characters. It meant something. It led from one interesting point to another. Yet Mr. Scott was horrified by it. Sardou's showy situation in "Nos Intimes" is, in itself, identical with Mr. Harris' in "Mr. and Mrs. Daventry"; a man violently "tempting" an unwilling married lady in a locked drawing-room. But, whereas for Mr. Harris this situation is merely a means to an intellectual end, for Sardou it is the end itself, and also the beginning and the middle. For him nothing else exists. From him we get nothing but the unmeaning representation of illicit sensuality. And this, I am prude enough to admit, is "shocking." The sight of Mr. Graham Browne (as C) slowly stalking Miss Violet Vanbrugh (as B) round a sofa, emitting sundry grunts and gasps, and finally catching her and fastening his pent-up kisses on her, does seem to me a really unwholesome sight; inasmuch as we are asked to see it merely for its own sake, and for sake of nothing before or beyond. Now that I have shown cause why I dislike Sardou's situation, and not Mr. Harris', Mr. Scott might occupy a spare quarter of an hour worse than in justifying the obvious opposition of his attitude to mine.

The parts of A, B, and C are so conventional that they give to their interpreters no chance of anything but a display of histrionic technique. Mr. Brandon Thomas is technically good as A, and so is Mr. Graham Browne as C; but Miss Vanbrugh is not so as B, inasmuch as her part is (except for a few moments) a comedic part, and she has not a drop of comedic blood in her veins. In highly coloured tragedy she is a valuable actress, but in comedy she is forced. Her eyes, which dilate naturally, sparkle only under protest; her groans or shrieks have quite the true ring, but her smiles are merely muscular expansions. However, it matters very little to me whether a Sardou heroine be played well or ill. In the whole of "Peril" the only part which deserves to be well played is the part of Sir Woodbine Grafton—one of the figures with whose irrelevant antics the dramatist has drawn the play out to the required length. This part, in itself an amusing piece of burlesque, is a good opportunity for "eccentric character." Of this opportunity Mr. Frederick Kerr makes the most. But the Grafton jewel is not so precious as to compensate us for the opening and ransacking of the aforesaid dustbin.

You will be able to view the contents of another dustbin if you go to the Prince of Wales' Theatre. There the rubbish is called "Peg Woffington," though why it is not called "Masks and Faces," as Tom Taylor, its shooter, called it, I really cannot conjecture. It will not seem to you quite such sorry rubbish as "Peril." Not being literally, it is not metaphorically "offensive." Moreover, the fact that it is a costume play will save you the full shock of its old-fashioned technique. Hoops and coifs and scarlet heels will enable you to connive at its puerile construction—to treat it with some measure of that consideration which you extend to (say) Oliver Goldsmith, but which you could not possibly extend to Tom Taylor if one of his other plays were revived in the costume of to-day. (I trust Mr. Bourchier is not meditating such a revival, and hasten to nip the possibility in the bud.) You will have the further consolation of not having to search frantically for the reason why *this* dustbin has been opened and overturned. The reason is obvious. *This* dustbin was known to contain two jewels among the refuse. The parts of Peg Woffington and Triplet are admirable parts; and whenever a new mistress of sentimental comedy appears, or a new master of it, "Masks and Faces" is pretty sure to be revived for his or her benefit. Rubbish it is, and I doubt whether any impersonations, how brilliant soever, of the two valuable characters in it, could make a modern audience quite tolerant of it as an evening's entertainment. But, as I have often pointed out, it is the mimes and not the members of the public who ordain that certain old plays shall be revived. You must reconcile yourselves to the probability that "Masks and Faces" is dust that will always be shovelled from its bin whenever there is a histrionic talent to blossom in it. Whether to see the play, or to stay at home, is a question which you must settle according to the proportion between your dislike of dramatic refuse and your delight in histrionic blossoms. To me, personally, Miss Marie Tempest as Peg Woffington is a sufficient consolation for seeing the play. I have seen one or two other Pegs in my time, but not since I came to years of discrimination. Consequently, my pleasure in Miss Tempest's bonny and spirited performance is not interrupted by favourable or unfavourable comparisons with her predecessors. Miss Tempest has the comedian's temperament: laughter and tears come readily from her, commingling, helping each other. Laughter, indeed, in the literal sense, comes rather too readily from her. She laughs too persistently at the end of her sentences. But this is merely a fault in technique, the result of her training in a form of drama in which the chief aim is, not to produce an illusion of naturalness, but to keep up the spirits of the audience. Miss Tempest will soon rid herself of this fault. Meanwhile, she is to be congratulated as a very fragrant blossom in the dust. A solitary blossom, too; for she wins her success despite what must be the great difficulty of acting well in connexion with so stodgily unimaginative a Triplet as Mr. Frank Cooper, whom one can congratulate only on his success in refuting the tradition that Triplet is "actor-proof."

BY-GONES UP TO DATE

March 2, 1901

"Andromache," the play written by Mr. Gilbert Murray and produced by the Stage Society, is an interesting experiment. This sounds as though I had been very much bored but were anxious to be as polite as possible. Certainly, other things being equal, these uncommercial plays deserve from the critic more politeness than he would bestow on plays written in hope of lucre: be they bad, they deserve more forbearance; good, more enthusiasm. But please do not assume that "Andromache" bored me. I have given it the epithet "interesting" in all sincerity. Indeed (thus do I convict myself of an otiose phrase), every experiment is bound to be interesting. Its interest is not greater or less accordingly as it succeeds or fails, but according to the materials used, and the manner of their usage, and the kind of discovery that is hoped for. If the flying-machine be consummated, or the North Pole danced on *pede libero* by a live explorer, or the philosopher's stone at length alchemised into actuality, so much the better, of course. But the fascination of these emprises, and the amount one may learn from them, is independent of their success. Mr. Murray's attempt to make a good modern play out of Hellenic materials does not, in my opinion, "come off." But it is not the less interesting on that account. And the Stage Society did well to give Mr. Murray a chance of repeating behind the footlights the experiment lately made by him between covers.

In one sense the experiment is actually successful. It proves to me beyond doubt the impossibility that any one hereafter will achieve what Mr. Murray fails to do. I do not mean that Mr. Murray has done his work as well as it could be done. (On the contrary, and with due deference, I shall chide him for several faults in workmanship.) But he has tried to do a thing which no one else has tried to do—a thing of which, till it was attempted, I could not have predicated utter impracticability. Suppose that ere I had read or seen the play some one had come to me and said "Look at Hellas! Think of those tremendous legends from which the Hellenic dramatists inspired themselves into immortality! Why should not these immortal legends be looted for display on the quite modern stage? That which Æschylus and the rest told in their way why should not a modern dramatist tell in his? Archaism of form is not necessary to matter which is eternal. Such matter ought to receive the form of every successive age. Therefore let us enliven ourselves with revised versions of Greek drama. Let these characters speak simple English prose. Let the unities be violated. Let there be entr'actes. Away with the chorus! Why not even a little comic relief here and there? Given the proper dramatists, there is no reason why the Greek drama should not be effectively Anglo-modernised." Had such suggestions been made to me I might have swallowed them. I know not whether they were made to, or evolved by, Mr. Murray; anyhow, he has acted on them. He has fixed Neoptolemus and Andromache, Orestes and Hermione, into modern form, giving them three acts and two scenes, substituting comic for choric relief, and classic English for classic Greek. And the result is that we ourselves see the play with modern eyes. We form modern opinions of the characters, and of their deeds and destinies. When these things are shown to us in the manner of Æschylus or Euripides we are taken out of ourselves, are spirited into the skins of ancient Greeks: we see and feel the things as the ancient Greeks saw and felt them. But at a modern demonstration of them we are just ourselves. That is a state foreseen by Mr. Murray and by my hypothetical agitator. If, as the latter said, the Greek legends are for all time, then we can be moved by a contemporary version of them as deeply as were the original Greeks. But the fact appears that we cannot be moved by a contemporary version. Mr. Murray's "Andromache" proves that we cannot. Instead of being purged, according to the ancient prescription, by pity and awe, we are utterly unaffected. We are even disaffected. The superstitions that were impressive to us in the old version become definitely absurd in the new. The deeds that were inevitable and pitiable become merely incredible phenomena of brutality. We feel as though we had stumbled into a conclave of moonstruck butchers. And thus we realise that the Greek legends are not for all time. What is immortal is the form in which they were presented. And that is the only form in which they should ever be presented.

Every age has its own beliefs or tendencies, formulable in contemporary art. Presented to posterity in their original art-form, these beliefs or tendencies are (through the imagination which that art-form stirs) as potent, or nearly as potent, as ever they were. Æschylus is a force hardly less accessible (to those who can understand Greek) than Ibsen. Shakespeare is as near to us as Mr. Henry Arthur Jones. But to present Æschylean things well in modern English form is as a task not more hopeless than would be the writing of a good modern English play in Elizabethan blank verse or in Greek rhythms for three actors and a chorus. In the latter case we should be attuned to the ancient Greek or Elizabethan spirit, and so should be unable to make head or tail of the characters. In the former case we are attuned to our own spirit, and our receptivity is limited to the things cognate with that spirit. It matters not how conscientiously and cleverly the dramatist may have done his job. The job should not be done at all. That Mr. Murray has done it I am glad, inasmuch as, no one having done it before him, its futility had not been proven. Mr. Murray has added a little new fact to our store of knowledge. Let us be duly grateful.

Now that I have declared the whole scheme of "Andromache" to be impossible, it may seem rather unnecessary that I should point out to Mr. Murray how he might have made the play better than it is. However, if a dramatic critic were to refrain from writing anything uncalled-for, his occupation would be all but gone. So let me proceed to chide Mr. Murray for turning Andromache into a modern Christian. By doing so, he has made his play even more impossible than it need have been. The contrast of this Andromache, with her philosophic disbelief in the necessity for eternal bloodshed, makes the other characters even more grotesque for us than they need have been. Cast in their midst, she acts as a kind of deputy for us. She sees them with our eyes, and criticises them with our lips. She is not one of them. She is, in fact, thoroughly inartistic on the part of Mr. Murray. Another fault which Mr. Murray should have avoided lies in the technical construction of his play. The division of a play into several acts makes it necessary that every act shall be an organism in itself. An ancient Greek play, being undivided (except by choruses, which are actual links between one part and another), is judged only as a whole. But a modern play, interspersed with entr'actes, has to submit to interim judgments—has to be judged not only as a whole, but also in its separate parts. And neither the first nor the second act of "Andromache" would be in itself strong enough to pass muster even if the story unfolded in it were of a kind that appealed to us. Taken together and joined to the third act, without one interval for the stretching of our legs and the summing-up of our impressions, they might form a solid whole. Indeed, having read the play as a book, I can testify that they would. But, the unity of space being violated, a continuous production would not be possible, even if Mr. Murray had so far lapsed from his modernity as to desire it.

Mention of the book reminds me that the writing leaves much to be desired. Of course, Mr. Murray writes in a scholarly manner. But we look to him for something more than refinement of language: we look for a certain imaginative glow; and we do not get it. Throughout, the language is merely that of the Common Room, not always quite scrupulously filtered. Praying to Thetis, one of the characters says "Accept these offerings from the bondmaidens Aithra, and Pholoe, and Deianassa; and grant all good things to them and theirs." Them and theirs! Why not "their circle" at once? There are more than a few lapses of this kind, quite distressing. Another fault is that much of the dialogue is like a literal translation (than which nothing is less dramatic) of Euripidean stichomuthi. I select at random the following passage in which a priest questions Orestes about a gold chain that he wears:—

Orestes. A banished man must have his wealth in little compass.
Priest. A chain like that should buy an exile's return.
Orestes. I care not to return.
Priest. Are the friends of the dead so bitter against you?
Orestes. The friends of the dead are dead, and my friends are dead.

This is not the way to set about making the Greek spirit live in modern English drama. Perhaps it is not exactly the way in which a fourth-form boy construes his Euripides on a cold grey morning; but it is exactly the way in which his form-master, complacently, shows him how the thing ought to be done. . . .

However, dramatic critic though I am, I will buffet no more air. I cast the play from me, gently, and with all acknowledgments to the author; whilst of the mimes who interpreted it (and who, had they interpreted it never so brilliantly, could not have made it possible as drama) I will say merely that they were like a hutchful of white rabbits trying to behave like a cageful of lions, and failing.

"MRS. EBBSMITH" AND THE BENSONIANS

March 9, 1901

"The Notorious Mrs. Ebbsmith," now revived at the Royalty Theatre, belongs to that period when Mr. Pinero was respectfully begging to call your attention to his latest assortment of Spring Problemings (Scandinavian Gents' own materials made up. West End style and fit guaranteed). And the average critic, as he tries the suit on again, before the mirror of Time, and tugs at it and pats it and wags his legs in it, is protesting loudly that it looks as high-class as ever. Quite sincere though his protestation may be, I cannot echo it. The garment seems to show its age pretty clearly. It is of the fashion set six years ago. It is not threadbare, certainly. There is plenty of "wear" in it. It need not be given away yet. But it would need a good many alterations before one could look smart in it. In other words, the play is still an exciting, almost an absorbing, story; but on no one save the average critic could it possibly impose as being what it pretends to be: a solemn and wide-eyed consideration of life. Its two essential characters are not normal types; they are remarkably abnormal. They are not mere puppets, however. On the contrary, they are realised in a very intense manner; and their behaviour, in circumstances which are (except when the author fakes them for theatrical effect) quite credible, is (except when the author fakes it for theatrical effect) quite credible. But they are both abnormal, decentralised; whereas it is only from the study and projection of normal, central types that any philosophic expression of life can be made. That the irregular union of Mrs. Ebbsmith with Lucas Cleeve was a failure is no evidence at all that such unions must fail. The two characters happen to be utterly antagonistic to each other, and there's an end of it. That Lucas Cleeve was impatient of Mrs. Ebbsmith's theories is no evidence at all that a woman cannot be at once the darling and the intellectual companion of a man; for Mr. Pinero has deprived Lucas of any inkling that there might be a possible compromise between the two separate states. That Mrs. Ebbsmith pulls a Bible out of a stove does not prove that a woman cannot without the consolation of religion stand upright in the conflict of her emotions. If she had been, like many women, brought up in some kind of religious creed which circumstances had led her to reject and despise, then her action might have had some significance. As she was educated in unbelief, the suggestion that she would have (1) treated the Bible as the cause of her misery, (2) rescued it as her salvation, is a mere theatrical excrescence. So far from having any general significance, it is palpably untrue to her own particular self. It is an exciting incident, I admit readily. And, of course, it makes an effective appeal to the religious consciences of such playgoers as don't think. But any meaning that it has is nonsense, and I suggest to Mr. Pinero that he might have been as exciting and as "edifying" without so utterly disorganising his presentment of character if he had made Mrs. Ebbsmith throw the Bible (as she has previously thrown a bouquet) into the canal, from which it might have been retrieved by a pet spaniel. The dog, wagging its tail and shaking the water off its back, would have brought down the curtain quite as effectively, and not painfully, as does the lady, quivering over her scorched hand. The last act of the play, again, is a crude appeal to the "unco" but unreflective "guid." Mrs. Ebbsmith, had her maker dared to let her act for herself, would never have accepted the offer of that "retreat" to the Ketherick parsonage. The offer might have touched her; but the idea of accompaniment by the clergyman and his sister would have sent her off at a very sharp tangent. Again, being a woman of fine nature, she never would have consented, as Mr. Pinero makes her consent, to undertake the impossibly degrading position offered to her by the Cleeve family. Indeed, that such an offer would have been made seems to me hardly credible. During the third act, I suspected that Mr. Pinero had had it made in order that he might bring about the very effectively ironic scene when Cleeve imagines that Mrs. Ebbsmith has been won over to that which really, of course, she regards as a repellent impossibility. That she should, in the last act, agree to the proposal, merely because the legitimate Mrs. Cleeve shows signs of genuine emotion, is a development which must startle even the most gullible playgoer in London. However, I am ungracious in finding so many faults. I repeat that the play remains, as it always was, an exciting story. And, by reason of the admirably capable way in which it is constructed, and of the general vividness of the two chief characters, one is quite willing to tolerate (though not to overlook) its sacrifices of truth to effect, and to forgive (though not to approve) its pretentious air of being somehow philosophic and Ibsenish. That Mr. Pinero is a born dramatist I never deny. It is because of what he is not (and fain would have appeared to be when he wrote "Mrs. Ebbsmith") that I cannot give myself the pleasure of joining that chorus in which those others, a little uneasily, are always acclaiming him "our premier dramatist." I cannot find a more signal proof of his technical genius than that this play, despite its continuous and tedious implication that he is what he isn't, still retains in itself, after the lapse of six long years, a power of stimulation. Despite its inconsistencies, the part of Mrs. Ebbsmith is a fine one, and Mrs. Campbell invests it with all that quiet and haunting realism of which the secret is hers. Her glamour is as it has always been. Her art has become subtler, more potent. As Lucas Cleeve, Mr. Courtenay Thorpe, that most elastic actor, makes his usual success.

Æsthetically, there are many vulnerable points in the system upheld by the Benson company; nor is my rapier immaculate of its gore. As critic, I have partially condemned it. Yet do I, as man, revel in it without reservation. It is as cosy a thing as ever was invented. It is an unrivalled pander to what Daudet called "*l'habitude de l'habitude*"—that instinct shared by us all. To see over and over again, with brief intervals, the same mimes, on the same stage, is a true and cumulative pleasure. First sight of the Benson company is not, I admit, a ravishing experience. But I defy you to be not fascinated after the sixth or seventh time, and to be not more fascinated after the eighth than after the seventh.

Settled in your seat, you glance at your programme, and are soothed by the familiar bead-roll, wondering how the mimes named in it will "be" to-night. For every one of them, as he or she comes on, hall-marked with his or her own face and port and voice, you have a smile of welcome. They have become as brothers and sisters to you, even as to one another. They touch not merely the instinct of familiarity, but even the family instinct. And the fact that you never see them twice in similar guise saves you from that sense of sameness which in an actual family often alloys affection with boredom. The peculiar cosiness inherent in a stock-company cannot be diffused through a large theatre. Last year, when the Bensonians were figuring in the Lyceum Theatre, that subtle essence of theirs evaporated and was lost to us. Only a troupe of giants could in that dim immensity have wafted the family effect. But the little house in Panton Street is quite another matter. It is so little as to be almost homelike. Mimes in it are no midgets: they are life-sized. We are all very near to them, and feel as though we could almost shake hands with them across the footlights or converse with them *sotto voce* from our seats. Thus cosiness reigns supreme. From an artistic, as well as from this merely personal, standpoint, the removal of the Bensonian venue from the Lyceum to the Comedy is a welcome change. The cavernous stage of the Lyceum cannot be made a tolerable background except at great cost of time and money. Such cost the Bensonians cannot, by reason of their system, afford. Nor can they afford that cost which alone could make the stage of the Comedy a really good background. But such scenery as they have is enough to make the background passable: there is no distractive inadequacy. Also, the mimes' performances can be appreciated. To fill a great theatre, great acting is needed. In an ordinary stock-company there can be no great acting: good-all-roundness—or, say, excellent-all-roundness—is the pinnacle. At the Lyceum, therefore, the Bensonian acting was ineffective. But at the Comedy such good actors as Mr. Oscar Asche, Mr. Lyall Swete and Mr. George Weir produce the impression they deserve. If only Mr. Benson would not persist in grafting the star-system on the stock-system—two things utterly incompatible—his latest production, "As You Like It," would be really admirable. Shakespeare wrote some leading parts which

Mr. Benson can play very well. But Orlando is not one of them. Nor, emphatically, is Rosalind a part for Mrs. Benson. I wish Mr. Benson would, in his very genuine devotion to Shakespeare's memory, ask himself, whenever he is meditating a new production, "If the poet were alive to-day, and I were asking him to dictate the cast, would he make me and my wife play the two leading parts? If not, which are the two parts he would assign to us?" If Mr. Benson would think out the answers to these questions, and act according to them, he would be doing no more than justice to the modesty and the high intelligence for which we all like him. In "As You Like It" he might well have appeared as Jaques. Yet am I glad he did not do so, inasmuch as I should not then have heard Mr. Swete's extraordinarily skilful and touching treatment of the speech about the "seven ages." From playing the Duke he would have been debarred by Mr. Asche's obvious qualifications for the part. He might have fallen back on Touchstone, as who Mr. Weir is not good at all. Touchstone is a fantastic creature, needing imaginative interpretation. And Mr. Weir, whose solid and straightforward humour is very useful and delightful in such parts as Dromio, or Sir Toby Belch, or the First Gravedigger, is not an imaginative actor. Mr. Benson *is*. He would have been a very good Touchstone. The qualities which he lacks—ardour, "go," force, spontaneous self-expression, naturalness—are quite unnecessary for Touchstone. And without them poor Orlando is quite null.

MR. BOURCHIER ANALYSED

March 16, 1901

Devout study of human character leads to the conclusion that one man is identically the same as another. Every tendency produces in its owner a proportionate tendency in the opposite direction. Analyse his soul, and you will find nothing that is not cancelled by something else. One man has no tendencies at all, is null in the first analysis. Another—and he is more common—

has some very strong and obvious tendency, thus duping the superficial observer into the belief that this is the keynote and pivot of him, and that he is a definite, peculiar person in virtue of it ; whereas, really, there is an inevitable reaction that makes it (and with it him) naught. In some cases you will find the two tendencies alternating in lengthy "bouts"—supplementing, but (like Box and Cox) never stumbling across, each other. Usually, however, the two tendencies synchronise, one of them showing itself in one part of its owner's life, the other in another. Take the case of Mr. Arthur Bourchier. How would he by the superficial observer be summed up? As "breezy," of course. And very breezy he is, as an actor. Now what is the reverse of breeziness? Morbidness. Then be sure that Mr. Bourchier is as morbid as he is breezy. As he is always acting and so, demonstrably, is being breezy every night of his life (except Sunday) for two or three hours, it follows that his morbidness must occupy two or three of the remaining hours in every week-day. Fatigue, supper, sleep, probably prevent him from being morbid before he rises in the morning. Now, a few years ago it would have been impossible to prove, except by such circumstantial evidence as I have given, that Mr. Bourchier is ever morbid; still more impossible to determine what part of his days is especially overcast. Of Mr. Bourchier, except as an actor, one knew (or, at least, would have had to pretend to know) nothing at all. Only on the stage was he a public character. But now he is an actor-manager. He is a purveyor, as well as an interpreter, of plays. This is an arduous business, which means busy mornings. Thus by the policy of Mr. Bourchier as manager, by the quality of the plays favoured by him, we can see what his morning mood is. Does he produce bright, strong, fresh, astringent work? To "Peril" at the Garrick were such epithets applicable? Was that a play which could have been accepted for production by any man whose vitality was not at zero? Mr. Bourchier's undertaking of it was a clear sign of despondency, of despair. "There are no plays written now," he must have groaned. "The art of dramaturgy is a lost art. All is darkness. Muffle me in my cloak, give me my spade and lantern. 'Tis a starless night, and I would fain prowl among the tombstones. The owls and the bats and the quivering cypresses will suit well my grim humour. And maybe, with luck,

I shall disinter some poor bones that the public would like to see articulated. A ghoul's emprise! yet I am strangely eager for it. Listen to the wind, and expect me when you see me." So he stole forth, and "Peril" was subsequently jigged before our eyes. But that was not enough for him. It might have satisfied the reaction of an ordinarily breezy man. But Mr. Bourchier is so extraordinarily breezy that he must needs creep back to the graveyard, and shovel up another set of bones, to be exhibited at the Criterion. "Peril" at the Garrick, at the Criterion "Mamma": such is the horrid consequence of our carelessness in leaving two theatres under the control of an extraordinarily breezy actor.

With "Peril" I dealt so lately that I may spare you a detailed consideration of "Mamma." The two things are on all fours with each other. Both were adapted some years ago from the French— a number of years sufficient to have robbed them of any vitality that may not have been dried out of them in the actual process of transplantation. "Peril" is a dull and offensive comedy. "Mamma" is a dull and inoffensive farce. That is the only detectable difference between the two things. As I am not so utterly unblest with sense of humour that I can be amused by the situations and jests of farce which is even of the contemporary English kind, I will not base my declaration that this aged French farce is as dead as a door-nail on my own failure to be amused by it. Having no standard of my own, I cannot distinguish between farces that are good and bad of their kind. I can but evaluate the opinion of the public. So my condemnation of "Mamma" must be derived from the behaviour of the audience on the first night— from the hollow laughs evoked by the mimes, and the hollow silence that fell almost immediately after the curtain. Of the performance, too, I have little to say. Mrs. Calvert, in the principal part, which demanded rowdy accentuation, went quietly and solemnly through her mannerisms, and did not enliven me. Mr. Giddens wagged along in what I take to be the duly imbecile manner, and Miss Ethel Matthews did nothing in particular rather better than it could have been done by a mechanical doll. There was a *débutante*, Miss Beatrice Forbes-Robertson, who seemed very lively and intelligent. I hope to see her again, in happier circumstances. Mr. Arthur Bourchier was as breezy as ever. It is delightful to see such breeziness on the stage, but when I think of the price he has to pay for it—the price *we* have to pay for it—I wish Nature had withheld it from him, or that Fate had not cast him into management. However, Nature is inexorable, and so is Fate. We cannot alter their decrees. At the same time, we can mitigate the effects of them. Though a breezy actor-manager is a grave danger, and difficult to deal with, the resources of civilisation are not exhausted. We have a Censor. And why should not we bless this official with a *raison d'être* by empowering him to arrest the breezy actor-manager in his propensity to exhume old bones? To open a tomb that contains human remains is the most difficult thing in the world. You may win over the next of kin, and the Home Office itself; but the Cemetery Authorities, or the Consistory Court, or something of the sort, will surely crop up to foil you. That spirited lady who lately sought access to a ducal vault was backed up by the sympathy of a whole public athirst for sensation. Almost every one wished the matter to be sifted thoroughly and at once. Yet the lady availed nothing. The more she tried, the further was she bandied away from the goal. Does the public sympathise with the breezy actor-manager on his lugubrious excursions? Does any one wish him to exhume these skeletons of decently-buried plays? No one. And yet there is no power to divert him from his purpose. The only party he need consult is the owner of the grave, who—be he Mr. Grundy, or Mr. Scott, or any other—always seems to assent with alacrity. In the interest of dramatic art, a strong prohibitive power should be created. Things should be made as difficult for Mr. Bourchier as for Mrs. Druce.

LATIN AND ANGLO-SAXON MIMES

April 13, 1901

Periodically the cry goes up "How long is London to lack a Conservatoire, such as Paris boasts, for the making of mimes?" Pleaded are the indubitable facts that France produces a greater number than we of first-rate mimes, and that the companies supporting these mimes do their work admirably, whereas in London the subordinate parts are but so many vehicles for display of dufferdom. And these facts are attributed to the French care for, and the English neglect of, specific tutelage. Well! this seems to me a shallow theory, mistaken and misleading. The root of the mischief lies, I think, much deeper than our agitators pretend. I believe the mischief to be rooted rather in nationality than in national neglect—rather in the fact that, whereas the French are French, we happen to be English. As I am at this moment in France, and so have instant opportunity for comparison between the two sides of the Channel (without any opportunity for describing to you the new plays with which London, doubtless, bristles), and as the offer made (or *not* made) by Mr. Carnegie to endow us with a national theatre has duly revived that periodical cry to which I have alluded, I may as well set myself the holiday-task of explaining to you exactly why, in my view of the nature of things, our mimes are less good—incurably less good—than French mimes.

My "desk" is a little sunlit disc of marble outside the Café de la Paix. Excuse the kakophonous collision of those two nouns! There is no equivalent for either. Sound, even on a holiday, must defer to sense. I might say "I write on a little sunlit disc," &c.? But that, strictly, would imply a MS. that would never reach you—a pencilled scribble that not even the waiter would read ere he deleted it with his napkin. And truly, why should I not write this article even so—not on paper that endureth, but on faithless marble? The cosmic movement would not be impeded by the lapse. Nay! you might wear as an ornament my golden silence of one week. But I must not let the holiday-mood instil into me a sense of proportion. Though here, far from the foggy four-mile radius, I am peculiarly susceptible to that para-lysing poison, I can at least inoculate myself with an injection of commercialism—*aur: sac: fam:* as it is called in the prescriptions. Though I cannot persuade myself that there is any true justifica-tion for my hebdomadal excursus, I can at least write it, write it in time for the post. This process is the less irksome because study of the fresh folk around me is really relevant and necessary to my theme. At most of the marble discs two or three men are seated. In all of them I notice one common peculiarity. Though the

hour is not yet noon—not yet that hour before which Englishmen
never move their lips except for some very good reason, all these
Frenchmen are conversing with the utmost animation. They are
all excited about something or other. Were I deaf, or were their
language mere gibberish to me, I should conclude that some great
national crisis obsessed them, or that every one of them was in the
thick of some private crisis on his own account. But I can both
hear and understand the conversation of them who are nearest to
me. The three men to my right are differing as to the age of a
well-known Spanish dancer; the two men to my left are agreeing
as to the merits of a new kind of automobile which they saw
yesterday; in front of me two other men are deciding where they
shall breakfast to-day. It is fair to take these three conversations
which I can hear as typical of the others which I cannot—to
strike from them an average for the whole set of tables. I add
them together, divide them by three, and deduce that every one
around me is making a prodigious fuss about nothing. Going
a step further, I deduce that all the other natives of France are
making a prodigious fuss about nothing. Nor, I think, will any
one who knows them dispute my conclusion. The French people
are born with a natural gift and lust for expression. They do not
but talk, as do we, lingually. They talk with their hands, with
all the muscles of their faces, with all the resources of their lungs,
with their whole souls and bodies. They accentuate everything,
magnify everything, drive everything home. Such is their
natural manner, giving them (for me, at least) a constant fascination. From the national standpoint, possibly, it were better for
them to be more self-contained. We in England are wont to
regard this kind of *disinvoltura* as a sign of national decadence.
I am not sure, however, that we are right. Probably Frenchmen,
in the heyday of France, were as excitable and voluble in their
manner as now; and probably we ourselves shall (note the tact of
that future tense!) go down the hill as stolidly and silently as we
have come up it. But my point is one of artistic rather than of
political ethnology. It is simply this: that France is a nation of
born mimes, and that England is a nation of males and females who
cannot act. For who is the born mime? He or she, obviously,
who can transmit whatever the author has given to him or her
for transmission to the audience. This job of transmission can

only, *ob naturam theatri*, be done through quick concentration. For the mime, as for the dramatist, time flies very quickly. Like the dramatist, the mime must put a very great deal into a very little space, and must, moreover, shoot that very great deal far across the footlights. How is he to do this? Emotion and intelligence alone will not enable him to do it at all. He must have a variable face, a variable voice, variable gestures. His whole body must be always alert, always responsive to what is in him or to what has been put into him. Only so can he transmit the right effects to the audience. Such, then, is the root of the technique of acting. In any ordinary Frenchman it is innate. He does not have to acquire it. If he become an actor, his only technical difficulty will be in not overdoing the exaggeration. His difficulty will be one of degree merely. For the Englishman who becomes an actor the difficulty will be one of kind. The Englishman is unaccustomed to, and averse from, any expressiveness. He is by nature taciturn. When he breaks silence he breaks it merely in a mumble or a monotone. His face is a mask. His body is a log. His hands are useless except for manual labour. Inflect or gesticulate he cannot. Consequently, when he becomes an actor he has to begin his whole self over again. He has to take it in hand and force it into an unnatural dance. What wonder that it dances, like a bear, clumsily, sulkily? What wonder that the average of French acting is so much higher than ours, when the French actor starts with practically all the needed technique at his expressive finger-tips, and so can straightway devote himself to the cultivation of his intelligence and his emotions, whereas the English actor's intelligence and emotions are lying fallow throughout the long years spent by him in a forlorn endeavour to learn the indiscible? Of course there are exceptions among Englishmen. We have a few good English actors. Very few indeed. Most of the good actors on the English stage have some strong taint of foreign blood in their veins. (In "foreign" I include, of course, Jewish blood.) As a general rule, Englishmen cannot act, and they never will act. And as the English stage is, and will always be, mainly filled by Englishmen, it is, and always will be, vastly inferior to the French stage.

You will see now that I have no keen sympathy with the renewed wail for a British Conservatoire. Mr. Carnegie or another may found such an institution, and you may lead the young Englishman down to it, and you may make him drink from it; but what he drinks will certainly be no elixir of histrionic art. Acting cannot be taught. The most that a Conservatoire could do were to give a few tips—how to walk across the stage, how to fence, how not to speak through the nose, how to pronounce out-of-the-way words in Shakespeare's plays, and so forth. But really, I do not think that these benefits would be so important as to justify any one in spending a vast sum to confer them on us. There seem to me so many objects in the world more important and worthier of spare cash than the tuition of superficial deportment to our young mimes. Anyhow, at this distance from my native city, I cannot coax up any enthusiasm for such tuition. Here I might find myself indifferent to the phantom Conservatoire even if I thought its materialisation would do some real good to English acting. As it is, I dismiss the fad with a sneer. If our English mimes want to improve themselves, let them be born again, of French parents.

"THE WILDERNESS"

April 20, 1901

The Garden of Eden being closed to us *sine die*, there must needs be in every human lot some proportion of unhappiness. Also, ours being a fallen nature, some proportion of humbug must needs infect the behaviour of every social class. These proportions of unhappiness and of humbug vary, of course, according to the lot and the class. I am inclined to think that riches are rather a blessing than otherwise—that the rich man (other things being equal) is happier than the pauper. Also, I have a suspicion that the upper class, inasmuch as it frankly makes pleasure its chief aim, and has, moreover, no model but itself, harbours less of hypocrisy than do the classes below it. But then, I am of a philosophic temper, and can detach myself. Most other persons who happen to be not rich, and to be of the middle class, have com-

fortably convinced themselves that wealth is a burden indeed—
an excoriant pack for poor Pilgrim to stagger under; and that
"high life," moreover, is a kind of Juggernaut—a horrible, overriding deity, insatiable of sacrifices of virgin souls. The rich
man (these good people are happy to believe) is cut off from all
worthy communion with his fellow-beings. No one loves him.
Every one is agog to get at him. He can trust nor man nor woman.
Not for him, poor wretch! the hand-clasp of comradeship, not for
him the rays of unblemished love from a girl's blue eyes. Against
such demonstrations he must steel his heart, for, in his direction,
they are all false, false, false. Though he see passing him through
the needle's eye a whole procession of camels, himself cannot set
foot in even a fool's paradise. Lord Rosebery, with his sure
instinct for saying what will give the greatest happiness to the
greatest number, recently set his seal on this popular view of the
rich man's lot. The whole population exchanged glances.
"Hear that?" and "Told you so!" was murmured throughout the
gratified Isles. Lord Rosebery, and other capitalists, and a few
detached seers of life, were the only people who saw where the real
cleverness of the speech came in. I suggest that Lord Rosebery
should not let slip the chance of fostering now that other pleasant
illusion which I have mentioned—the illusion of general hollowness and unreality in "high life." Let him come down to us and
assure us that the atmosphere in which he lives has prevented him
from ever being honest and frank (except, of course, on the occasion when he proclaimed the vanity of riches). Let him asseverate
that in Society no true self ever comes to the surface; that every
one there wears a mask behind whose pink and white surface is a
very sallow skin; and that through those eyelets peep eyes void of
lustre, and under those tinselled robes are stomachs unnourished
by any fare but Dead Sea fruit. So will he be yet more highly
commended of the people. Meanwhile, he has allowed Mr. H. V.
Esmond to steal a march on him.

Mr. Esmond, crying in "The Wilderness," has the advantage
not only of priority but also (I suspect) of sincerity. He was born
into the same social class as I, and, being a sentimental creator
rather than a thinker, he has probably accepted as truth that
class's view of the class above it. One may assume that he is
honestly compassionate of "the upper ten thousand." Also, the

fact that he has till lately shown an industry in acting not less than mine in criticism may be taken as proof presumptive that he was not born heir to vast private means. Nor has he yet (though, doubtless, he soon will have) written a great enough number of popular plays like "The Wilderness" to make a capitalist of him. Being, then, a man who does not yet know by experience what it feels like to be really rich (and being, as aforesaid, a sentimental creator rather than a thinker), he has probably accepted as truth the poor man's theory of wealth. And thus his indictment of wealth and his indictment of fashion have for me the true ring of conviction. If he were making these indictments directly, in his own person, I should not attempt the unpleasant task of disillusioning him. But he makes them indirectly, through the mouth of a *dramatis persona* who is a young and healthy Baronet with £30,000 a year; and so, as a critic, I find inevitable the duty of exposing to him his fallacy. This young Baronet, as drawn by him, offends my sense of artistic truth. Such a man would not, in real life, be convinced that riches were a curse; nor would he (unless, like Lord Rosebery, he had a motive for ingratiating himself with the public) proclaim them to be a curse. Nor would he find, or profess to find, fashionable life a hollow and tedious mockery. On the contrary, he would take things as he found them, enjoying them all thoroughly. Mr. Clement Scott, the other day, said rather quaintly of some one that "he took his good fortune smiling, like a gentleman." That is what this young Baronet would do. He would know well that if such a man as he had no true friends the fault was his own, not his wealth's fault, and that if he thought the people of his class were but so many sinister automata the fault was in his own stupidity. But the creature of Mr. Esmond's fancy, Sir Harry Milanor, moves through life in a mood of gloomy protest. "There are no wildflowers," sighs he, "in Bond Street." He has no "friends"— he "might have had friends" but for his horrid, horrid wealth. And every one is oh! so false. Even his own mother is an imposture through which he sees in the twinkling of an eye. In a rather jarring scene with her he asks her to compare herself as she appears before him and "the world" with herself as she appears when her maid wakes her in the morning. Certainly this "world" is no world for him. It is a void so appalling to him in its desolation that he mixes the metaphor of his very catchword, conjuring his sweetheart to "come out of the wilderness into the light." The topic which the Fat Knight arrives at only on his death-bed is the one topic on which the yearning Baronet can ever discourse without bitterness. On this topic he spreads himself out indeed, insomuch that his "Uncle Jo" rouses in my breast quickly responsive echo when he ejaculates "Look here, young man! If I went out for many of these walks with you, I should do you a mischief." Doubtless, Sir Harry Milanor's incessant prattle about fairy rings and what not is very pretty. But it is not the kind of prettiness of which any grown-up man on the earth would be guilty. From a grown-up man on the stage a very little of it goes (not for the public, I know; but for me) a very long way. For me, it soon degenerates into mere sickly fatuousness. For prettiness—even pretty-prettiness—in the right place I have as great a taste as any one else. But I submit that it is not in its right place when it is uttered by an adult male in a realistic comedy. If Sir Harry Milanor had been otherwise a character which convinced me I should have been much more exasperated by his pretty outbursts than I was. But from the first, for reasons which I have explained, he never convinced me at all. He seemed to me as flimsy and unreal a phantom as was ever projected for the public's pleasure. Consequently, he spoilt for me the whole play, and disabled me from enjoying much that I perceived to be good in it. But for Sir Harry, I should have taken keen pleasure in the skill with which Mr. Esmond has drawn the character of the heroine. A real character, this—a real creation, sharp and true in all the lights and shades of it; but, in juxtaposition to the unreal hero, a character wasted.

But for Sir Harry, I should have taken keen pleasure in the skill with which Mr. Esmond has developed his story throughout the first two acts, and should have been seriously vexed by the collapse of his skill in the third and last act. But for Sir Harry, I should, in writing this criticism, have perhaps confined myself to praise of the first two acts. As it is, let me skip them, and merely demonstrate why the third is bad. (Indeed, since the rest of the critics seem to have been unanimously praising all three acts, and especially the third, I shall thus make myself more useful to Mr. Esmond than I should otherwise have been.) During the first two acts the story has been evolved naturally from the characters. There have been no dramatic tricks, and all the characters (except, of course, Sir Harry) have been behaving like human beings. But in the third act, apparently, Mr. Esmond discovered that he had not left over enough story to give the play its regulation length. The situation to which he had brought his characters was easily soluble. But the obvious solution would not fill up the whole of the last act. And so Mr. Esmond faked the probabilities. This he did in two ways. He wrote in a very long scene for the wife and the former lover, making the wife keep the former lover for a long while in the dark, and even lead him on to suppose that she cared for him as much as ever. All that she would have done, but for the exigencies of the stage, is to have told the young man that she now loved her husband, and to have suggested that, unless he gave up the acquaintance altogether, he must purge his mind of any notion of mutual romance. Even worse, because more mechanical, is the other intercalation made by Mr. Esmond. Before the wife confesses the motive she had for marrying, the husband learns, quite unnecessarily, from a miscarried letter the motive to be confessed. Thereupon he pours out his grief to an impossible confidant, imagining that his wife is still indifferent to him, and blaming himself for having ruined her life. Considering that he has been seeing her hourly for some months, his misapprehension is obviously as impossible as his confidant. How Mr. Esmond could have spun out the last act without interfering with the probabilities, it is not my business to suggest. I merely point out that the method chosen by him was a bad one.

A PUZZLE IN LITERARY DRAMA

May 11, 1901

What, precisely, was Mr. Henley's share in the plays done jointly by Robert Louis Stevenson and himself? This is a baffling problem, meet to be mooted rather in the long Winter evenings than when Spring hovers airily over us to unknit our brows. Nevertheless. . . .

To evaluate, from a work produced by A and B, the share of B, your best way is to proceed by elimination. Analyse the work into its component parts—its matter, method, style, and so forth. Then set aside all that in it might be due to A, as A is known to you through the work done by him single-handed. The residue, presumably, must have been done by B. This presumption becomes a certainty if, referring to any work done by B single-handed, you find that any of it coincides with that part of the joint work which does not seem to have been done by A. You may now, of course, find in the joint work things that could have been done either by A or by B. Some of the things that were A-like may, in the light of B's other work, seem to be equally B-like. For them you must give half-credit to both men. You may, on the other hand, find things that you can attribute neither to A nor to B. For these, also, you will divide the credit. They are the result of fusion.

Apply this method to the two plays which were performed last week at Her Majesty's, "Macaire" and "Beau Austin." Take "Macaire" first. "A Melodramatic Farce" it is called, though it is rather a farce suddenly transformed, at last, into a melodrama. Stevenson, single-handed, was prolific of both these forms in his books. As examples of his farce we have the immortal "New Arabian Nights"; of his melodrama, "The Pavilion on the Links," "Dr. Jekyll and Mr. Hyde" and the greater part of every romance that he wrote. Therefore there is no reason why he should not have alone conceived the plot of "Macaire." There is (I forestall, unscientifically, the proper working of the process) very good reason to suppose that Mr. Henley did not conceive the plots of the plays written with Stevenson, inasmuch as he has never by himself shown any tendency to story-telling. As critic, as lyric and descriptive poet, he has been active. In fiction he has done nothing. Even if he had, the plot of "Macaire" (as also the plots of "Deacon Brodie" and "Admiral Guinea") would obviously be Stevenson's. No one that has read "A Penny Plain and 2d. Coloured"—and who with any love for the art of writing has not read that perfect essay many times?—could for one moment doubt the source of these plots. Out of Stevenson, by Skelt:

that is their one possible pedigree. The horrific scenes and figures that the small boy Stevenson used to cut out from Skelt's pages, and to paste upright, and to manipulate on the stage of his own toy theatre, they are the self-same figures that he projected in his prime. Fondly he remembered "those pages of gesticulating villains, epileptic combats, bosky forests, palaces and war-ships, frowning fortresses and prison vaults," and these horrific plays were not less the obvious outcome of that piety than was "A Penny Plain and 2d. Coloured." In plot, then, "Macaire" was his. The choice of Macaire as protagonist is, surely, his also. Not only was Macaire among the figures enumerated by him as being in Skelt's repertory, but the whole conception of Macaire— its difference from the traditional conception—is essentially Stevensonian. This eloquently philosophic scoundrel, this tatter-demalion with transcendental schemes for subjugating his fellows, is too like Stevenson's Villon and Stevenson's Dynamiter not to have sprung fully-equipped from Stevenson's own brain. His companion, too, Bertrand—how could one attribute him to any one but that writer who always so persistently revelled and excelled in delineating a timid nature thrown into perilous affairs? The passion of fear was the one passion that Stevenson never could keep out of anything he wrote. A score of instances will occur to every reader of him. The rest of the characters are mere supernumeraries. They could have been conceived by Stevenson or any one else. How about the actual writing of the play? Here, again, one is confronted with the certainty that it is all Stevenson's. "Blessings on that frontier line—the criminal hops across, and lo! the reputable man." The little verb "to hop," and, in opposition to it, the pompous Latinity of "reputable," when "honest" was the so obvious thing to say! That is a trick which only Stevenson's subtly humorous sense for words could have played for us. Again, "your soul is incorporate with your stomach," "I find you all—permit the expression—gravelled," "Where is my long-lost child? produce my young policeman, show me my gallant boy"—who but Stevenson could have made these phrases, which are fair examples of the play's manner throughout? It remains to be wondered whether Stevenson did the technique, the construction, of "Macaire." He might well have done it. It is just what one would expect from an amateur dramatist who did not take the stage at all seriously. The sudden change of key from sheer farce to sheer melodrama, and the monotony and superfluity of much in the opening scenes, smack sharply of the trifling tiro. At the same time, one could not assert surely that they were Stevenson's. Now that we have analysed the play, let us sum up the residue from what Stevenson might have done in it. Lo! there is no residue at all. Stevenson might have done the whole thing out of his own head. Appearances lead one to believe that he conceived the plot, drew the two important characters, wrote the dialogue. There is, on the other hand, nothing to stamp him surely as drawer of the subsidiary characters or as technical constructor. Thus the present inference from the evidence is that Mr. Henley may have constructed the play and drawn all the characters but Macaire and Bertrand. To test this inference, turn to Mr. Henley's record. He, as I have said, is a critic and a lyric and descriptive poet. Those qualities through which, in the arts of criticism and poetry, he has won his high reputation do not, certainly, obtrude themselves from "Macaire." Much in the play is characteristic of Stevenson, of Mr. Henley nothing. That Mr. Henley may have drawn the subordinate characters is, nevertheless, possible. As I said, any one could have drawn them. Also, being, like Stevenson, an amateur in dramaturgy, he may have been responsible for the construction. Such is the conclusion one draws as to Mr. Henley's share in the play. It is a conclusion not satisfactory to our general admiration of Mr. Henley. However, it is but an interim-conclusion. Mr. Henley, as I shall show, must have done more than what we can give him credit for at first sight.

With "Beau Austin" the case is much the same as with "Macaire." True, this play is a comedy, and comedy was not a form in which Stevenson dealt. At the same time, he, as being a creator in fiction, seems likelier than Mr. Henley to have conceived the plot of it. Moreover, the character of the Beau himself, round which everything revolves, is as thoroughly Stevensonian as the character of Macaire. It is, indeed, the character of Prince Florizel of Bohemia, realised on a comedic plane. Florizel as foreign potentate in modern London was farcical, but Florizel as dandy on the Pantiles becomes perfectly possible and comedic. That magnificence, that "stately and agreeable demeanour," that

infinite span of condescension, become matter for smiles, for tears
even, though before they could evoke only one's roars of ecstatic
joy. Yes! surely, the Beau is Stevenson's. The paternity of
Dorothy Musgrave is dubious. She is a shadow, and Stevenson,
as we know, never could draw a woman. But then, the chances
are that Mr. Henley, likewise, never could draw a woman. So
let the credit for Dorothy Musgrave be divided between the two.
Also the credit for the Aunt, the valet, and the other characters,
who, though there is no reason to attribute them to Mr. Henley,
do not remind one of any characters in Stevenson's books. The
construction of the play—not inconsistent like the construction of
"Macaire" but timid and frail—may be due to either of the
authors. But the writing—again the writing seems authentically,
exclusively, Stevenson's. "I am the rejected suitor of this young
gentleman's sister, of Miss Musgrave. . . . See in how laughable a
manner fate repaid me! The waiting-maid derided: the mistress
denied, and now comes this very ardent champion who insults
me." The voice is the voice of Florizel, in all its clear and melli-
fluous cadences, and there are none of those bristles that might
betray to us the prose of Mr. Henley. Mr. Henley's prose-style
is admirable, but it is essentially a bristling style. It sprouts, it
pricks. It sprouts in uniformly brief sentences, pricks with uniformly sharp "points." It never waves and caresses, as did
Stevenson's. The dialogue in "Beau Austin" waves and caresses
in the truly Stevensonian mode. I am convinced that Mr. Henley
did not write it. So far, then, the inference we have come to is
that in "Beau Austin" Mr. Henley may have drawn Dorothy and
the other minor characters, may have done the construction, and
may, improbably, have conceived the main idea of the story, and
that Stevenson did the rest. Again the conclusion leaves something to be desired by us admirers of Mr. Henley. Let me try to
supply that something.

There must be some fallacy in the evidence from which we
deduce that Mr. Henley played so small a part in the collaboration.
If he had not played a part greater than it appears, the collaboration would have been a farcical affair, and Mr. Henley never would
have allowed his name to be tacked on to plays with which he had
had practically nothing to do. Can we reconcile the difference
between what seems and what must have been? "Dexterously,

good madonna." Mr. Henley, brought into contact with Stevenson, was so affected by the fascinating personality of his companion that he lost his own identity, and became Stevenson, thought like Stevenson, felt like Stevenson, imagined like Stevenson, wrote—no, I cannot believe that any of the script was his. Stevenson wrote the plays, and Mr. Henley, to balance the collaboration, invented them. In the other collaborated works of Stevenson we do not wonder at our difficulty in determining what he did not do. Reading "The Dynamiter," we remember that the cleverness of all wives is soon assimilated to the cleverness of their husbands. Reading "The Wreckers," we easily extend this rule to clever step-sons. But that a material so definite, so tough, so trenchant as the mind of Mr. Henley should ever have been transformed by any one, is certainly, as the journalists say, "matter for no small surprise." It implies an elasticity of which we never should have suspected Mr. Henley, and for which we admire him all the more. And it is unique testimony to the glamour of "R. L. S."

THE TAME EAGLET

June 15, 1901

There are they who would encore eternity. Some of these folk, I make no doubt, were at the first night of "L'Aiglon," and felt, when the thing ceased, that they had been spending a very happy four—five—five hundred-and-five—how many hours, by-the-by, *was* it? Would that I could classify myself among these happy inexhaustibles! But I cannot; nor (it comforts me to believe) could the vast majority of my fellow-first-nighters and of them who have seen the play since its production. You call us insular? We hang our heads, pleading in extenuation that we live on an island. Were we Frenchmen, probably we should enjoy "L'Aiglon" very much. For this probability there are two reasons. Firstly, Frenchmen can listen with pleasure to reams of rhetoric in theatres. If the rhetoric be good in itself, they care not at all whether it be or be not dramatically to the point. Secondly,

Frenchmen have an enthusiastic cult for Napoleon. Now, "L'Aiglon" is composed chiefly of reams of excellent but irrelevant rhetoric about Napoleon, and reams of details about him. Little wonder, then, that Paris took kindly to it. But how should London follow suit? Unless it be dramatic, rhetoric, however good, bores us: such is our fallen nature. Moreover, Napoleon is our fallen foe. Time was when we were frightened of him. Naughty children expected him momently to appear down the chimney. Good grown-up people expected him momently to appear off Dover. But these fears never were fulfilled. We laugh at them now. We feel nothing but a mild pity for the inspirer of them, who, having duly succumbed to the superior genius of "the Dook," was not (it seems) made so comfortable as we could have afforded to make him, in the flush of our conquest, at St. Helena. A live dog being more formidable than a dead lion, we (though, as Englishmen, we will not admit that there was anything leonine about Napoleon) are inclined to be less afraid of Napoleon than of General Mercier. But General Mercier does not (to use one of our favourite phrases) loom large enough to interest us in any five-act play that might be written in his honour. How much less so *le petit caporal*!

On us, then, M. Rostand's main appeal is wasted. Take away from us the capacity for Napoleon-worship, and what remains of "L'Aiglon"? Everything, according to the author, who exclaims, prefatorily, "Grand Dieu! ce n'est pas une cause Que j'attaque ou que je défends. . . . Et ceci n'est pas autre chose Que l'histoire d'un pauvre enfant." But that is only pretty Fanny's way of stopping Marianne's mouth. "L'Aiglon" is obviously a pæan composed to the greater glory of Napoleon. The "poor child" is but the excuse for it. In France he is taken as such, the audience concentrating its sentiment, duly, on his father. But in England he becomes, actually and indeed, the central figure—the one point of interest. And he is not a large enough figure, not interesting enough, to make the play "go." If M. Rostand had simply come to London, and, rising after the public banquet which we should have organised for the author of "Cyrano," had exclaimed "Gentlemen, three tears for the Duc de Reichstadt!" we should have shed three times three there and then, and sung "For he's a poor little fellow" with the utmost heartiness. This eaglet does cut a very pathetic little figure in history. We know that it was not his fault that he was the son of his wicked father: it was his misfortune, and we blame him not at all for it. We pity him even as we pity any one else who, being the son of an eminent person, has the wish but not the power to distinguish himself in the same line. We have had, and still have, many such eaglets in our own country. On the bushes of St. Stephen's, of the Law Courts, and of other public resorts, they perch by the score. They are tame. They feed from our hands. Our hearts go out to them as they flutter round us. But our hearts do not go out to the extent that is covered by five interminably long acts in Alexandrines. We must draw the line somewhere. We must draw it at M. Rostand's latest achievement. "Tame eaglet: tame play" is our inevitable verdict.

Big plays must have themes proportionately big; and, since for us the little Duc is not merely the ostensible theme but also the actual theme, "L'Aiglon" wearies us beyond measure. Had M. Rostand curtailed his play by (say) one half, we could delight in it. In a play written to last from (say) nine to eleven o'clock, the little Duc, so tenderly delineated by M. Rostand (yes! the excuse has been concocted very elaborately), would throughout hold our sympathies. But from eight o'clock to midnight! In a play of such vast structure, with a cast of more than fifty persons! The little Duc fades, evaporates, under such tremendous pressure. He becomes simply a little bore, whose oxymoronically belated-premature death we hail (if we have not already hailed a hansom and been driven home to well-earned rest) as a merciful release for all concerned in his brief-inordinate life. "Mountains in labour" is no adequate description of this play. The phrase suggests, at any rate, suspense. *Nascetur ridiculus mus*, but how are we to know that? Though, when this creature is born, we may feel that we have been fooled, we have had, at any rate, the pleasure of being on tenter-hooks for something colossal in scale. But when, from the very outset, we see the ridiculous mouse running healthily about, with a background of maternal mountain-peaks grazing proudly down on it, we, with the best will in the world, can neither bless its pretty little heart nor admire the scenery. To the pretty little heart of M. Rostand's Duc we are quite indifferent by reason of the enormous circumstances in which it is

shown to us.   To M. Rostand's technical skill in handling enormous circumstances we are quite indifferent because there is no
reason why they should be handled here at all.   No reason, that is,
so far as we English are concerned.   If only we were Frenchmen!
As we are not, our best plan were simply to read the play and not
see it acted.   In the study we are more patient than in the theatre:
we measure time less jealously; besides, we can "skip."   Remember, too, that crowds and "sets" and "properties" when they are
merely imagined are much less overwhelming than when they are
seen.   Let us read the two hundred-and-fifty pages of "L'Aiglon"
by all means.   From five acts of him Heaven defend us!

It were no disaster not to have seen Mme Bernhardt as the Duc.
Of course, her performance is very brilliant: that is a mere postulate.   It is also wonderful as a feat of endurance.   I admit, too,
that she, of all living mimes, seems born to interpret Rostand.
Her luxuriance and flamboyance in acting are precisely analogous
to his in dramaturgy.   As Mr. Arthur Symons has wittily and
unkindly said, M. Rostand appeals to the public as a millionaire
appeals to Society; and the remark might have been made with
equal truth of Mme Bernhardt.   Nevertheless, this impersonation of the Duc is a mistake, a thing to be forgotten quickly and
forgiven at leisure.   The trouble is not that Mme Bernhardt
looks too old: on the contrary, her youthfulness is astounding.
Nor is the trouble merely that to students of history she does not
look like any known miniature of the Duc de Reichstadt, and does
look like every known photograph of Miss Nellie Farren as "Little
Jack Shepherd."   The trouble is that to every one she looks like a
woman, walks like one, talks like one, *is* one.   That primary fact
upsets the whole effort, mars all illusion.   As the part would be
tedious even if it were played by a man, I may seem captious in
grumbling that it is played by a woman.   My displeasure, however, is not that the eaglet is played by Mme Bernhardt, but that
she plays the eaglet.

ALMOND BLOSSOM IN PICCADILLY CIRCUS

June 22, 1901

Our own almond-trees have duly shed their blossoms, to be blown out of sight by the blasts of our own spring. But, just where we should least hope to find it, an exotic specimen has been planted, and blooms there fairer and more fragrant, assuredly, than any native growth. There, in Piccadilly Circus, where the chaotic shoddiness of modern civilisation expresses itself most perfectly; there, in that giddy congestion of omnibuses, advertisements, glossy restaurants and glossier drinking-bars, glossy men and glossier women; there, in that immediate inferno of ours, this gracious almond-tree is in flower. Let us tend it lovingly. Let us make the most of its brief season—the brief "season" for which the players from the Imperial Court Theatre of Tokio have leased the Criterion.

There seems to be something appropriate in the coming of these players to the very centre of our vulgarity. For have not we, in our greedy occidental way, made a very great point of vulgarising down to our own level the notion of Japan? The importation of a few fans and umbrellas and idols set us all agog. Forthwith Brummagem could not turn out a big enough supply of cheap and nasty imitations to keep us happy. The trade began about twenty years ago, waxing ever faster and more furious. "Japanese Stores" sprang up on every side. Japanese musical comedies were produced. "Jolly Japs" peddled around and about. Now at length we have had our surfeit. We are eager to vulgarise some other national art. And lo! suddenly in the midst of us, appear these players from Tokio, to remind us how much nicer the real thing is, and to warn us against making any more such spurious imitations as those which we have made of them. Their warning is likely to be the more effective through the shock which their presence gives us. In the fulness of our national pride, we had believed that the old Japan was no more. We had flattered ourselves that the Japanese were now as vulgar and occidental as we. And yet here, classic and unperturbed, untouched

by time or by us, these players stand before us, as though incarnate
from the conventions of Utamaro and Hokusai.

Straight from the prints and drawings of Utamaro and Hokusai
these creatures have come to us. Those terrific men, bristling
with hair, and undulating all over with muscle and showing their
teeth in fixed grins; those pretty little ladies, with their little sick
smiles, drooping this way or that as though the weight of their
great sleek head-dresses were too much for them—here they all
are, not outlined on flimsy paper, but alive and mobile in the
glory of three dimensions. Here they all are, magically restored
to the very flesh in which the limners saw them. See! Two of
the men have drawn their broadswords and are planting their feet
far apart in the classical attitude that one knows so well. They
are grunting, snorting, gnashing their teeth. They are athirst for
each other's blood, both loving Katsuragi, the Geisha (whom, by
the way, they do *not* call the jewel of Asia). The swords clash
noisily, and sparks fly from them. The grins and the grunts
become more and more terrible, as the combatants stamp round
and round. And she, the cause of the combat, sways this way and
that, distracted, yet with a kind of weary composure on her face
and in every fold of her red kimono, watching for the moment
when she can throw herself between, to separate and soothe and
save them. Whether she succeed or fail we care not. Merely
are we entranced by the sight of her, by the realisation of the
dreams that the colour-prints wove for us. Again, when her
lover has deserted her and to escape her vengeance has hidden
himself within a Buddhist monastery, we care not whether by her
dancing she shall persuade the monks to admit her within their
gates. She dances, and that is enough for us. She divests herself of her kimono. Swathed and rigid, she averts herself from us.
Faint, monotonous music is heard, and a crooning voice. Gradually she turns towards us. Her left hand is across her mouth, in
her right hand she holds aloft her shut fan. The music is insistent. Still she stands motionless. Suddenly, with a sharp
downward fling of the arm she shoots open her fan. The left
hand flutters upon the air. She sways, droops forward, and
sidles into her dance—a dance of long soft strides, indescribable.
Presently she sinks on her knees under an almond-tree, and claps
the palms of her hands delicately. Down from the branch falls a

light shower of petals. These she sweeps together, imprisons them between her hands, runs away with them, scatters them from her, and, always in some mysterious accord to that mysterious music, chases them round and round.

Some symbolism there is, doubtless, in these evolutions. For us the grace of the kitten suffices. Anon, she does another dance, wearing on her head a hat that is like a pink plate and is tied with a pink riband across her lips. Anon, she is beating a tiny drum as she dances. See with what strange movements of her arms she waves the tiny drum-sticks! She is never still, and yet her every gesture imprints itself on our gaze as though it were the one arrested gesture of a figure in a picture. Nothing is blurred by mobility. Nothing escapes us. It is as though one were not seeing actual life in unrest, but inspecting at leisure a whole series of those instantaneous plates which are contained in a cinematograph, and wondering at the strange secrets revealed in them—those movements which are impalpable and unsuspected because only within the fraction of a second can they be caught. And yet, though we see everything thus separate, we see it also in its general relation to the rest. Though we see those quaintly exquisite postures and gestures which the limners recorded for us, we see also how they were made, and what——no! what they expressed remains for us a mystery. We, who do not even know the Japanese language, how should we penetrate the mysteries of the Japanese spirit? We, to whom all these men and women look respectively (and delightfully) just like one another, how, in the name of goodness, are we to know what their souls are driving at?

True, "arguments" of the two plays performed at the Criterion are duly included in the programme. Thus one knows roughly what is going on. One knows that one person is jealous, another frightened, another pleased, and so forth. And, as I have suggested, one doesn't care. So differently are the emotions expressed in Japan that illusion is completely merged for us in curiosity. When an Englishman is indignant because the mother of his betrothed has given her in marriage to another man, he expresses himself ebulliently. Yet when Yendo Morito meets Koromogawa, the mother of Kesa, and learns from her how badly he has been treated, he merely grunts and snarls. That (in the light of the argument) is his way of expressing anguish and rage.

Naturally, we are more interested in the situation than touched by it. When he draws his sword and bids Koromogawa prepare for instant death, she does not, as would an Englishwoman, scream or kneel or try to run away; on the contrary, she remains perfectly still, rolls her eyes and grunts.

Such is the form that fear takes in Japan. Again, our sympathy is unaroused, tightly though our attention is held. Such is our experience of every climax in the play. We understand it, from the argument; but we cannot feel it. And between every climax is a long interval, which the argument does but very faintly illuminate. In these intervals we see the figures moving, gesticulating; we hear quaint sounds made by them. The hands wave and the lips curve and the arched eyebrows move up and down and the bodies sway to and fro and everything of course means something, but nothing reveals a hint to us. And we, if we are wise, do not try to penetrate the veil. We do not try to think: we merely look on. For sheer visual delight, nothing can match this curious performance. All who have eyes to see should see it. The one fault to be found with it is that the figures are seen against very elaborate and gaudily-painted backgrounds. Plain, pale backgrounds were needed to make them "tell" worthily of their own quaint perfection.

INCOMPARABLES COMPARED

June 29, 1901

In the art of acting, obviously, the personality of the artist is more important than in any other art. To excel in any art postulates an excellent personality; but in literature, or painting, or sculpture, or musical composition, the personality of the artist lurks in the background, to be divined by us merely through the work, whereas in acting the personality (itself being the artistic medium) is equally and simultaneously visible with the work achieved through it. When we are told of a great writer whom we have never read, our impulse is to ask for a description of his work: what is its subject-matter, style, method? But, when we are told of a great actor whom we have not seen, our first question is "What kind of a man is he?" Having heard whether he be tall or short, Jew or Gentile, robust or ethereal, and what kind of a voice he has, we ask for details about his artistic skill. To know what kind of a man he seems is necessary before we can imagine the effect his acting would produce on us. For, be he never so objective, an actor cannot elude himself; at least, no great actor can. The great actor must have a great personality, and that personality is the starting-point for everything. Impersonate he never so wisely, he cannot much discount it. He may try to sink it utterly into his part, but only to a slight extent can he succeed in doing so. Often the great actor makes no such attempt: he tries merely to absorb the part into himself—to reveal himself through it. Thus on the stage there is frequently a contradiction between good art and great art, and the two things have a difference in kind, and not merely, as elsewhere, in degree. The great actors are never the good actors. They cannot, even when they do try to, merge themselves. Neither great nor small actresses ever try to. Any attempt to disguise her face or voice would precipitate an actress into the grotesque. She may play tragedy one night, and comedy the next, and be equally fine in both; but in both she will be frankly the same woman, seen from different angles of herself. (The most we can hope is that she will not, like Duse, be visible from only one angle, having only one angle to be visible from.) And thus, in the case of a great actress even more surely than in the case of a great actor, the first question must be "What manner of woman is she?" If the great actress be a foreigner, you may even forget to ask subsequently for details of her art. In a foreign language which you do not understand you cannot appreciate the *nuances* of the acting. In a foreign language which you do understand you cannot (unless you know the language as perfectly as you know your own) appreciate so well the art of acting as in your own language. But, though so much of this art loses its savour in crossing frontiers or seas, a woman's personality is equally impressive everywhere—more impressive perhaps (as I shall suggest) away from her own land than in it. Thus especially in the case of those exotic actresses who come annually hither, in more or less force, to gladden summer, we are occupied with what they are rather than with what they do or how they do it. What is the secret of Sarah's appeal to us? Why do our hearts go out to Sada Yacco? Why is Réjane enchanting?

If I, Paris-like, were called on to decide which of these three goddesses was most admirable, the apple would (I think) be adjudicated to Sada Yacco. But there would be a long, embarrassed pause before the award, and after it I should beg the empty-handed couple not to treat it too seriously, it being merely impressionistic, and in no sense judicial. "This lady from Tokio," I should insinuate, "may not be nearly so gifted as either of you who come from the city named after me. She may be reckoned by her compatriots as positively plain, positively clumsy and quite unintelligent. In point of her art she may be accounted 'a stick.' But for me, an occidental, a simple shepherd on Mount Ida, somehow she surpasses both of you. It is, doubtless, because she is so remote from my understanding—because her face is a mere inscrutable oval, and her gestures have for me no meaning, and to her gait I know no parallel—that I (deeming fair her face, and fair her gait and gestures) have set her thus above you. She is new to me, and you (daughters of the Latin race) know the tag 'quidquid novi.' She is mysterious to me, and 'omne ignotum' you remember. And now, excuse me, I must herd my sheep, which have strayed sadly during this arbitrage." So, bowing inclusively as I shouldered my crook, I should away to my work. But perhaps, ere I had taken many steps down the mountain-side, I should hesitate, halt, look round, and, as a rider to my judgment, bid Sada Yacco let Réjane and Sarah take each a bite of the apple—Réjane, a big bite; Sarah, a small one.

For both those Parisians I have a strongly sentimental admiration. Both are delightful. Sarah, however, delights me now much less than of yore, much less than Réjane delights me. I said just now that no actress ever tried to disguise herself. I was forgetting Sarah. She does try, and the result is (as I said it must inevitably be) ludicrous. As L'Aiglon and other young men, she loses herself, but becomes no one else: she becomes merely a coruscating *thing*. The feat is amazing, but it is not serious art: it is showmanship, or (one needs a monstrous word for it) showwomanmanship. Soon, it seems, we are to inspect her as Romeo. Why not (while she is about it) as Romeo *and* Juliet? Some years ago I found in a music hall an "artiste" made up as Faust on one side and Marguerite on the other singing "Notte d'Amor" in alternate voice and profile. If Sarah had seen him, I am sure she would have taken the hint. Perhaps she will take it now. The more absurd her absurdities become, the better shall I be pleased, for the sooner will she, sick of them, revert to her art and to herself. Her own fascinating self—that is what I miss most keenly. And it is because soon I shall be seeing it again in "Phèdre," and in other parts within its range, that I should so far relent as to allow Sarah that small bite of the awarded apple. It is because Réjane is, duly and consistently, herself, that she would have the privilege of that far bigger bite. Do not mistake my tone for one of patronage. I do not expect her, who is a goddess, to descend upon Mount Ida for my approval. It is I who have been climbing Notting Hill to behold her and kneel to her in the little theatre that caps that windy peak.

But "goddess" is not an appropriate word for her. She excels in virtue of seeming so essentially a mortal woman. Her rareness is not in any peculiarity, but in displaying on the stage, to a supreme degree, every peculiarity of her sex. She sums up in herself her whole sex, with all its typical qualities, good and bad. Sarah—I mean, of course, Sarah proper—might be, aptly enough, called "goddess," inasmuch as she is quite unlike any other woman. Her voice and her face, her repose and her unrest, her expressions of love or hatred, of despair or gaiety or what you will —none of them ever recalls to you anything else of the kind. Generically feminine and specifically Parisian though she is, she has always a kind of lurid supernaturalness. And, for me, this quality gives her something of that mystery which involves Sada Yacco. Thus, in the tripos of fascination, I should class Sarah proper above Réjane, who has not a smile nor a spread of the hand nor a toss of the head that is not instantly typical of her sex at large. Of course, there is no woman resembling Réjane. It is she who resembles the whole lot of them put together. She is a unique synthesis. That is the secret of *her* charm.

Considering them strictly as actresses, not merely as women on the stage, one finds not a pin to choose between Sarah and Réjane. Each is equally perfect mistress of her art. Each can use it with equal sureness as medium of self-expression. Creatures so different need, of course, different kinds of drama, and, just as Sarah needs a romance or a classic tragedy, so must Réjane have a play of modern realism. "Sapho," "Ma Cousine," "La Course du Flambeau," "La Parisienne"—it matters little in which you see her. In all of them she is at her very best. In all of them she is Réjane, incarnate woman, seen from one angle or another. She being so, it matters little whether the play you happen to see be good or bad—whether it be an amusing satire, like "La Parisienne," or a "Zaza" down from date, like "Sapho." Réjane, not the play, is "the thing." See her in all her plays. Climb Notting Hill nightly, to see her from all angles and to study all her art. You will not grudge the hardness of the ascent. The air is exhilarating up there, and enthusiasm comes all the more easily by reason of a slight dizziness.

MR. PINERO PROGRESSES

September 28, 1901

During the off-season, it seems, Mr. William Archer has not been idle. He has been practising the delicious functions of a private detective, and, with the luck of the novice, has made a most sensational discovery. Scotland Yard looks silly, and the myrmidons of Slater hide their diminished heads, while the novice, flushed with triumph, tells us of a dastardly plot against the art of Mr. Pinero. There exists in our midst "a little knot of critics whose chief glory and accomplishment is to despise Mr. Pinero . . . anti-Pineroites," who are going to make "assaults" on "Iris." I applaud Mr. Archer's enterprise. I am touched by his anxiety to save, with these preliminary cracks of the whip, his darling from the dogs. But where are the dogs? Those quivering nostrils, those gleaming fangs, those taut tails—where are they all? In a mare's nest, surely. Mr. George Moore, it is true, did not like Mr. Pinero's work. Nor did Mr. Shaw. But neither of those two delightful Irishmen is engaged now in dramatic criticism. To the best of my belief, Mr. Walkley, Mr. Symons and I are the only current dramatic critics who have shown any reluctance to acclaim Mr. Pinero as a builder of masterpieces. And none of us, I am sure, rejoices in this churlishness. None of us lies in wait to make "assaults" on Mr. Pinero's latest plays. Rather do we hope to share the raptures of our brethren. In the case of "Iris" this hope has been, for me, partially fulfilled. I admire the play very much indeed.

According to Mr. Archer, any one who denies to Mr. Pinero "the quality of genius" must be "the victim of a paralysing prejudice." If that is true, mine is a clear case of paralysis. But possibly my reluctance to hail Mr. Pinero as a genius may be due to a laudably nice sense of words—a sense which is not to be deflected by the electric atmosphere of a successful first-night. If Mr. Pinero is a genius, what are we to call Ibsen, for example? "Genius" seems to me a term which must be reserved for men who are distinguished by some great force of originality, men who bring into the world, out of their own souls, something that the world has not known before. Such a definition of genius may be faulty. Genius is a thing that can hardly be summed up in words. But, even as Mr. John Morley knows a Jingo when he sees one, so do I know a man of genius. I never read or saw any one of Ibsen's plays without feeling that Ibsen was a genius (however limited and unlovely his genius may have appeared to me). I never read or saw a play of Mr. Pinero's without admiring his skill; but genius I never scented there. Ibsen I scented there, and Tom Robertson and Thackeray and many other influences; but Mr. Pinero himself never leapt forth to impress me. He ever seemed to me a catholic adapter of other men's discoveries; one who sympathetically observed life through other men's eyes, and told us very cleverly as much as he dared tell us of what he had seen. That he is a born playwright I have never denied. But artistry, though it is essential, is not all-sufficient in art. It is but the means of expression. One is concerned also with the quality of what is expressed. What did Mr. Pinero express in "Mrs. Tanqueray," "Mrs Ebbsmith" and his other serious plays? Nothing that other men had not expressed before him. He went nearer to seriousness than any other Englishman had gone in writing for the stage. That was all. And when you penetrated beneath the superficial boldness you found a timid conventionality; beneath the superficial sincerity, cunning substitutions of stage-tricks for human character. Those plays were little more, really, than good entertainments. Like them, "Iris" is a thoroughly good entertainment. You may always rely on Mr. Pinero to hold your attention, to keep you excited in his story. You may rely, in fact, on good craftsmanship. What you cannot rely on is intellectual honesty, intellectual originality. It is because "Iris" seems to me more honest and more truly observed than any other of Mr. Pinero's plays, because in it life is less faked to yield theatrical effect, or to soothe the average burgess, that I have headed this article with a compliment to the author.

Drama of the best type is that in which the situations are evolved from, not imposed on, the conflicting characters. "Iris" answers to this test much more nearly than any previous play of Mr. Pinero. The characters have been well realised from the outset, and are, except at certain points, allowed to act consistently with themselves. Their inconsistencies are of that consistent kind which . . . no! I will spare the overdone reference. I hope that by laying stress on the few points at which Mr. Pinero, in my opinion, has strayed into theatricalism, I shall not incur the charge of "paralysing prejudice." My motive is merely to spur Mr. Pinero to still deeper self-respect in his future work. The first point at which he yields to temptation is when Iris refuses to go with Laurence Trenwith to the colonies. The antecedent circumstances are these. Iris is a rich widow who must sacrifice her fortune if she marry again. She loathes the idea of poverty as deeply as she loves Trenwith. Therefore Trenwith must go and make money before she will join him. On the eve of his departure she learns that all her money has been embezzled and that she is as poor as her lover. Trenwith urges her to come and be poor with him. "No," she says, "I must stay behind. I must go through a period of probation." She has a long and ingenious series of arguments to prove that she must not accompany him. But we know that in real life she would not have used them, would have merely told her maid to pack her boxes. We know that she is only repeating, like a parrot, what Mr. Pinero has taught her to say. If she did not stay behind, poor Mr. Pinero would have to sacrifice practically the whole of his play. So here she remains, fallen far in our estimation of her as a human being. Again, (limited space or laziness, compels me to write on the assumption that my readers know the outlines of the play) she would not have accepted the millionaire's cheque-book with such alacrity after her lover's departure. In course of time, no doubt, she would have drifted into that acceptance. Mr. Pinero should have given her a respite. His introduction of a young girl whom Iris is eager to help out of financial difficulties is ingenious, but it is not convincing. Even if Iris, in real life, would have used the cheque-book for that girl's sake, we know that in real life that girl would not have entered thus in the nick of time. Her entry is a stage-trick, unworthy of the play. Again, consider the conduct of Trenwith when, returning love-sick from the colonies and finding Iris under the protection of the millionaire, he refuses to take her away with him. In real life, Trenwith would either have forgotten Iris after his three years' absence, and would not have returned to claim her, or, coming back and finding her, he would have forgiven her everything. That he loved her, and that she loved him, and that she was unhappy, would have been (unless he was a hopeless prig, as Mr. Pinero does not suggest) the only considerations to sway him. Here Mr. Pinero has made a concession of truth to conventional morality. He did not dare to let an "erring" woman end happily. The stalls, even the pit, might have forgiven him, but the dress-circle never. There is another point at which I suspect Mr. Pinero of inartistic timidity. I mean the scene of the first parting between Iris and Trenwith. As written, it is quite otiose. It takes place in Iris' room, where the lovers have been sitting up throughout the night to see the last of each other. The dawn breaks, the moment comes for Trenwith's departure. Certainly the scene is a beautiful one; very true and pathetic is the way in which, at the last moment, the two lovers stand making little feeble jokes, awkwardly, unable to find words for grief. But the scene is not necessary to the play, develops nothing, reveals nothing essential. Mr. Pinero is too sound a craftsman, surely, to have conceived it thus. If the lovers had been behaving more in the manner of Romeo and Juliet, it would have point. It would materially increase the poignancy of the subsequent drama. And I suggest that Mr. Pinero must have conceived it thus, but then had not the courage to execute it. However, this is merely speculation from internal evidence, and it is the last of the objections I have to make to Mr. Pinero's drama as drama.

The rest of my strictures are but against the actual writing of the play. It seems to me the worst-written of all Mr. Pinero's plays. In an unlucky moment, years ago, some rash creature hazarded the opinion that Mr. Pinero wrote well. Since that time, the dramatic critics (who, as a class, have as little sense for literature as is possible in human bipeds) have with one accord been prating of Mr. Pinero's "polished diction" and his "literary flavour" and so forth. The consequence is that Mr. Pinero, elated, has been going from bad to worse, using longer and longer words, and more and more stilted constructions, under the impression that he was becoming more and more literary. In "Iris" he has horribly surpassed himself. Not one of his characters but talks as a leader-writer for a small provincial newspaper writes. When the millionaire in the play makes a speech in honour of Trenwith's departure, one or two of the other characters object to the pomposity of his language. Why? They themselves use exactly the same vocabulary even in ordinary converse—nay! sometimes even in moments of utmost agitation. Trenwith himself, bidding farewell to a friend of his *fiancée*, exclaims "I shall always think of you—it will be a consolation for me to do so—as being at Iris' side." Iris dilates gaily on the advantage of having "a fashionable solicitor—*one whose practice is rooted in the gay parterres of Society*"! The *ingénue*, glad to have been asked to a dinner-party, murmurs "It was so sweet of you to *include* me!" Looking at the view from a window, she exclaims, "Oh, I could gaze at this *prospect* for ever, Aunt!" "Shall I *assist* you?" says a smart woman to a man who is taking off his overcoat. "You *resemble* the pictures of angels," cries Trenwith gazing into the eyes of his beloved. "*I fear*" and "*I surmise*" are frequently placed (between commas, too) in the mouths of Mr. Pinero's unhappy interpreters. I do solemnly assure Mr. Pinero that these tricks are not "literary." Even if they were, they would be inappropriate to a modern realistic play. By all means let us have literary graces (if we can get any playwright to supply them) in artificial comedy or in romance. But in modern realism the only proper "style" is that which catches the manner of modern human beings in conversation. If that style is beyond Mr. Pinero's range, he ought to have his future MSS. completely rewritten by some one within whose range it happens to be.

After all, though, how the characters in a play talk is much less important than how they feel and act. In "Iris," I repeat, Mr. Pinero has made his characters feel and act more convincingly than in any other of his plays. When all has been said, "Iris" remains a fine play, a work worthy of its author's great talent for play-writing. Mr. Pinero has progressed. And (though Mr. Archer may not believe me) I am glad accordingly.

A MEANS OF GRACE FOR THE DRAMA

October 5, 1901

Cursorily, some time ago, I suggested that theatres ought to be opened, and plays enacted, in the morning, not in the evening. Were I a public speaker, this suggestion would doubtless have been punctuated by the reporter with "(a laugh)." Being merely a writer, I have not even the solace of knowing that it amused any one. It certainly did nothing more. Yet it deserved very serious discussion. For, were it carried out, we should soon have something very like a respectable national drama.

No unbiased person will contend that we have anything like that at present. Serious plays draw the public only when they are supposed to be "risky." Prosperity bends her beaming face down on the music halls and on the theatres devoted to musical comedy, and the overflow from these places of delight finds its way either to such farces as "Why Jones Left Home," or to such sentimental comedies as "When We Were Twenty-One"—farces that are to art as practical jokes are to wit, sentimental comedies that are to art as the mingled sobs and chuckles of a man ejected from a public-house are to true tears and laughter. Why does the public thus neglect dramatic art? Not, as the dilettanti tell us, because there is no dramatic art for it to neglect. We have several dramatists who show themselves capable of doing fine work, and who occasionally do it. But the public does not encourage them, unless it suspects them of trying to undermine its morals. In France, in Germany, such artists would have their reward, immediately and constantly. Why not in England? The obvious answer is that England is not an artistic nation; and the answer is true, so far as it goes. We are a nation of practical men, whose genius is commercial. It is said by many experts (whether truly or not I cannot judge) that as "shopkeepers" we are falling off, growing rusty and letting other nations get ahead of us. But nobody ever attributes to us any attempt to compensate ourselves for diminishing prosperity by becoming artistic. Art and great commercial success seldom thrive together in one nation, and it is probable that in Germany dramatic art will be less encouraged proportionately as her citizens grow richer and richer. In time her drama will sink to the level of ours. But, instead of waiting placidly for that time, might we not make, meanwhile, a spirited effort to put our drama on a level with hers? We need not fear that this would be a forlorn hope. "Not an artistic nation" means, not a nation incapable of artistic emotion, but a nation whose capacity for such emotion is not spontaneous. There are ways of choking such capacity, and ways of fostering it. The surest way to choke it in regard to drama is to fix the time for playgoing after sunset—that is, after dinner or after high-tea, as the case may be. The surest way of fostering it would be to fix that time in the early morning—to make breakfast the preliminary tonic to drama, and lunch, as supper is now, the anodyne.

At present, we have to playgo either in the evening or in the afternoon. Neither time is propitious. In either of them the most artistic creature is not truly fit to cope with art; how much less so, the average Englishman! The morning always has been recognised as the time when the functions of the brain and the heart are best performed. In the morning all our faculties are agog. We are fresh from sleep. We come into the sordid world purged by our repose from it, with all that in us is divine and elemental restored to us, ascendant in us, for a little while. Our hearts, so slack when we went to sleep, slack from the thrumming fingers of day, are tight-strung again now. A touch makes them vibrant. Solemn or enchanting chords quiver from them. In fact, we can feel finely. And, just as our emotions are in proper trim, so are our brains. We cerebrate clearly, cleanly, assimilating facts, detecting fallacies, at a glance. We are as receptive as tiny children, yet, unlike them, able to reason from our learning. Like the shining day itself, we are young. In the afternoon, like the day, we are middle-aged already. The dust and dirt of actual life cling about us. We are tired, disillusioned, sedentary, looking back wistfully at the mistakes we have made, wishing, with I know not what of bitterness in our hearts, that we could live our lost morning over again. For after lunch we cannot originate. We are still in possession of all our faculties, but we cannot make them do for us anything new. In a word, we are middle-aged. As the sun westers we become old men, and as it sinks we die. At dinner-time we are born again. But the new life that dinner gives us is a horribly inferior article in comparison with that new life which is the gift of generous sleep. A jolly life, if you will, yet hectic, treacherous, and, in its essence, gross. The glow of meats and wines and artificial lights recreate you after the lassitude produced by your day's work. They make a man of you. But what kind of a man? Emotionally, a sensualist, and a sentimentalist, too. Intellectually, a windbag. You have the capacity for feeling, but only the grosser, with the sillier, human emotions find entry, coming in their grossest and silliest forms. You have (I address, of course, the average reader) the capacity for thinking, but you think only in rough outlines and gaudy tones. You exaggerate, loquaciously. Your tongue runs away with you, and you enjoy the sensation. You enjoy the sound of your own voice. You are impatient of other voices, for you wish to give forth what is in you, and have no room to take in what comes from any one else, dinner having robbed your brain of all its receptivity. It is in this aggressive, irreceptive mood of the brain, and in that gross mood of the heart, that you do habitually go to the play. What is the kind of play likeliest to satisfy such a spirit? The kind of play that makes no demands whatever on your intellect, while it appeals through false pathos to your sentimentalism, or through horse-play to your high spirits, or to your sensuality through a pretty chorus dancing to the sound of cheery little tunes. No wonder, then, since the managers of our theatres are mostly wise in their generation, that drama, as an art-form, does not thrive among us. In France, in Germany, it thrives, despite evening performances, because the French and the Germans are naturally artistic, and can, even after dinner, more or less apprehend and appreciate fine art. But it would thrive there far more fully if plays were acted in the morning, for the morning is the time when all human beings think and feel to the utmost of their capacity. Even as for transaction of important business, or for solemn rites of religion, the morning is everywhere recognised as the proper time, because the requisite qualities of brain or heart are then untainted, so should the morning be recognised as also the ideal time for playgoing. Perhaps you have never seen a play performed in the morning. I happen to have seen many plays rehearsed so. And I assure you that I have always appreciated them—their goodness or their badness—far more keenly than when I have seen them, later, in the usual way. Draw on your own experience in other arts. You may once have heard, early in the morning, some fine familiar piece of music, and been thrilled by it with a thrill that it had never given you before, and have wondered, when next you heard it at some concert in afternoon or evening, that you could not recapture that ecstasy. Or, with tourist-like determination to "do" thoroughly some foreign town in which you have found yourself, you may have gone early in the morning to a picture gallery, and been enthralled there by some picture, which, in the afternoon, when you came back to see it, somehow disappointed you, not seeming quite so wonderful. The fault, believe me, was not in the picture, but in yourself—in the self that the day had been busily blunting and marring. Art does not reveal her secrets unless you go to her as a child might go. And it is only in the morning that you are child-like. It is only then that your soul is fresh and free, worthy of the sacrament.

In the morning, then, in the quite early morning, the London theatres should be open, and in the evening never. Imagine a musical comedy on which the curtain rose at 9 A.M.! How rightly we should be revolted by it, seeing it in its true colours, in all its grossness and inanity! Or imagine what in these conditions would become of such plays as Mr. Esmond and Captain Hood now confect for our maudlin pleasure! We should shift away all such trash very quickly, should we not? On the other hand, we should make a good deal of our masterpieces. We should cry out for more masterpieces, and our cry would be answered. In every theatre . . . Utopian, am I? In the morning the community is hard at work? Then let all the houses of business be closed in the morning and remain open in the evening. But we are still by way of being a business-like nation? And the morning, as I said, is the only proper time for business? Well, I admit that you have posed me. But an idea is not the less serious because it cannot be realised. A dream is not the less true for unfulfilment.

A CURSORY CONSPECTUS OF
G. B. S.

November 2, 1901

Assuming that Mr. Shaw will live to the age of ninety (and such is the world's delight in him that even then his death will seem premature), I find that he has already fulfilled one half of his life span. Yet is it only in the past seven years or so that he has gained his vogue. One would suppose that so distinct a creature, so sharply complete in himself, must have been from the outset famous. But the fact remains that every morning for some thirty-seven years Mr. Shaw woke up and found himself obscure. Though, of course, his friends and fellow-workers recognised in him a being apart, for the Anglo-Saxon race he did not exist. I have often wondered what was the reason : was it the world's usual obtuseness, or was it that Mr. Shaw was unusually late in development? I had no means of deciding. I did not possess any of Mr. Shaw's early work. Thus very welcome to me is the reprint of a novel * written by Mr. Shaw in the flush of youth. Of the novel itself Mr. Shaw himself evidently thinks no great shakes. For on this excursion he takes with him even more than his usual armful of light baggage—prefaces, notes, appendices, quotations; he has also a new portable dramatic version of his book. And, as he bustles along the platform with these spick-and-span impedimenta in his grasp, he seems hardly to care whether or not that battered old resuscitated trunk of his be thrown into the van. Yet for me that is the real object of interest. I rush to examine it,

* "Cashel Byron's Profession." By Bernard Shaw. London: Grant Richards. 1901. 6s.

and tears of joy well up at the sight of "G. B. S." printed on it, as on the new hand-baggage, in letters of flame.

Yes! "Cashel Byron's Profession" is quite mature. Mr. Shaw is fully himself in it, and throughout it. It tallies with all his recent work. Such differences as may be found in it are differences of mere surface, due to the fashions of the decade in which it was written, not essential differences in the writer. Apart from them, it might be his latest book. It has all his well-known merits and faults, and who shall say whether his faults or his merits are the more delicious? His own quick strong brain is behind it all, darting through solid walls of popular fallacy to the truths that lie beyond them, and darting with the impetus of its own velocity far beyond those truths to ram itself against other walls of fallacy not less solid. All through the book we hear the loud, rhythmic machinery of this brain at work. The book vibrates to it as does a steamer to the screw; and we, the passengers, rejoice in the sound of it, for we know that tremendous speed is being made. As a passage by steam is to a voyage by sail, so is Mr. Shaw's fiction to true fiction. A steamboat is nice because it takes us quickly to some destination; a sailing-yacht is nice in itself, nice for its own sake. Mr. Shaw's main wish is to take us somewhere. In other words, he wants to impress certain theories on us, to convert us to this or that view. The true creator wishes mainly to illude us with a sense of actual or imaginative reality. To achieve that aim, he must suppress himself and his theories: they kill illusion. He must accept life as it presents itself to his experience or imagination, not use his brain to twist it into the patterns of a purpose. Such self-sacrifice is beyond Mr. Shaw. He often says (and believes) that he is, despite his propagandism, a true delineator of life. But that is one of his delightful hallucinations, due to the fact that his sight for things as they are is weak in comparison with his insight into himself. In fact, Mr. Shaw is not a creator. He cannot see beyond his own nose. Even the fingers he outstretches from it to the world are (as I shall suggest) often invisible to him. Looking into his own heart, he sees clearly the world as it ought to be, and sees (as I have already suggested) further still. Of the world as it is he sees a clean-cut phantasmagoria, in which every phantom is his own unrecognised self. When he describes what he has seen, himself is the one person illuded. Some novelists fail through being unable to throw themselves into the characters they have projected. They remain critically outside, instead of becoming the characters themselves. This is not the explanation of Mr. Shaw's failure. He does not stand outside his characters: a man cannot slip his own skin. Mr. Shaw fails because the characters are all himself, and all he can do is to differentiate them by "quick-changes." But these disguises he makes in a very perfunctory way—a few twists of diaphanous gauze, a new attitude, nothing more. Thus it is in "Cashel Byron," as in his plays. Take Cashel himself. Mr. Shaw means to present him as a very stupid young man with a genius for pugilism. But soon he turns out to be a very clever young man, with a genius for introspection and ratiocinatory exposition. These powers are not incompatible with a genius for prize-fighting. But quite incompatible with it are physical cowardice and lack of any sentiment for the art practised. Mr. Shaw makes Cashel a coward, and lets him abandon prize-fighting without a pang at the first opportunity, in order to prove his thesis that prize-fighting is a mere mechanical business in which neither sentiment nor courage is involved. As usual he goes further than the truth. It is untrue that prize-fighters are heroes and artists and nothing else, as the public regards them. But it is equally untrue that you can use your fists (gloved or ungloved) without courage, or that any man with supreme natural ability can care nothing for the channel in which it exclusively runs. Thus Cashel does not credibly exist for us: he is the victim of a thesis. Besides, he is Mr. Shaw. So, of course, is Lydia, the heroine, the imperturbable, strong-minded, blue-stockinged heroine, who, like the rest of Mr. Shaw's heroines, has nothing to do but set every one right—a sinecure, so easily does she do it. The only characters that really illude us are the subordinate characters, of whom we see merely the surfaces and not the souls. Mr. Shaw has a keen eye for superficial idiosyncrasies, and such figures as Mellish and Mrs. Skene are as possible as they are delicious, though even they are always ready to dart out on us and ratiocinate in Mr. Shaw's manner.

After all, it is Mr. Shaw *qu'il nous faut*. My analogy of the steamship was misleading. Though Mr. Shaw's chief aim, indeed, is to proselytise, we enjoy his preaching for its own sake, without reference to conviction. We enjoy for its own sake the process by which he arrives at his conclusions. At least, we do so if we take him in the right way. We must not take him too seriously. An eminent scholar once said to me that what he disliked in Mr. Shaw was his lack of moral courage. I pricked up my ears, delighted : here was a new idea ! Urged by me to explain himself, the eminent scholar said "Well, whenever he propounds a serious thesis of his own, he does so in a jocular vein, not being sure that he is right, and knowing that if he is wrong he will have saved his face by laughing in his reader's"—or words to that effect. I was disappointed. My interlocutor had betrayed simply his incapacity to understand the rudiments of Shawism. The fact that he is a Scotchman, and that Mr. Shaw is an Irishman, ought to have forewarned me. To take Mr. Shaw thus seriously is as inept as to believe (and many folk do believe) that he is a single-minded buffoon. In him, as in so many Irishmen, seriousness and frivolity are inextricably woven in and out of each other. He is not a serious man trying to be frivolous. He is a serious man who cannot help being frivolous, and in him height of spirits is combined with depth of conviction more illustriously than in any of his compatriots. That is why he amuses me as does no one else. The merely "comic man" is as intolerable in literature as in social intercourse. Humour undiluted is the most depressing of all phenomena. Humour must have its background of seriousness. Without this contrast there comes none of that incongruity which is the mainspring of laughter. The more sombre the background the brightlier skips the jest. In most of the serious writers who are also humorous there is perfect secretion between the two faculties. Thus in Matthew Arnold's controversial writings the humorous passages are always distinct interludes or "asides" consciously made, and distinct from the scheme of the essay. They are irresistible by reason of the preceding seriousness. But in Mr. Shaw the contrast is still sharper and more striking. For there the two moods are, as it were, arm in arm—inseparable comrades. Mr. Shaw cannot realise his own pertness, nor can he preserve his own gravity, for more than a few moments at a time. Even when he sets out to be funny for fun's sake, he must needs always pretend that there is a serious reason for the emprise ; and he pretends so strenuously that he ends by convincing us almost as fully as he convinces himself. Thus the absurdity, whatever it be, comes off doubly well. Conversely, even when he is really engrossed in some process of serious argument, or moved to real eloquence by one of his social ideals, he emits involuntarily some wild jape which makes the whole thing ridiculous—as ridiculous to himself as to us; and straightway he proceeds to caricature his own thesis till everything is topsy-turvy; and we, rolling with laughter, look up and find him no longer on his head, but on his heels, talking away quite gravely; and this sets us off again. For, of course, when seriousness and frivolity thus co-exist inseparably in a man, the seriousness is nullified by the frivolity. The latter is fed by the former, but, graceless and vampire-like, kills it. As a teacher, as a propagandist, Mr. Shaw is no good at all, even in his own generation. But as a personality he is immortal.

BJÖRNSON AT THE ROYALTY
THEATRE

November 16, 1901

Lately I wrote about commercial success and failure in the management of theatres. I took the Haymarket as the type of a successful theatre, and ascribed its triumph mainly to the fact that its present managers had an innate *flair* for what the public wanted, and had supplemented this *flair* with so much scientific study that they could gauge exactly the chances of any play sent to them. But, let me say, theirs is not the only way to prosperity though it is perhaps the only way to untold wealth. The Royalty Theatre, for example, has prospered in Mrs. Campbell's hands. It was, before she came to it, one of the "unlucky" theatres, whereas the Haymarket always had been "lucky"; and thus what Mrs. Campbell has in a small way achieved for it is commercially not less striking than what Messrs. Harrison and Maude have achieved in a large way for the Haymarket. Yet Mrs. Campbell makes no effort to give the public what it wants. Her policy is simply to give the public what she herself likes. As she has no passion for sentimental comedy, or melodrama, or farce, or musical comedy, a thoughtless person might wonder how it is that such a policy has not spelt ruin. For most managers it undoubtedly would spell that so easily spelt word. For her it has spelt the more difficult word success, not so much because she is a great actress, but because the gods have endowed her with the added grace of a personality—magnetism, call it what you will—which the public is quite unable to resist.

Her latest offering is a series of matinées of "Beyond Human Power," an English version of a play in two acts by Björnson. It is a gift which none but she would have dared to offer, even in the afternoon, and which, if any one but she had offered it, would have been rejected with every expression of scorn and ribaldry. Last Saturday, however, I found the public respectfully entranced by it. The first act ended in a storm of applause. Simple Norwegians, of whom I saw several in the vestibule, were evidently elated by Björnson's triumph. "Skohl!" they murmured, gazing at the large photograph of the master which hung beneath a laurel-crown upon the wall. A fine head is Björnson's. A square head, with an electric shock of hair upsprouting from it; and beneath it a pair of beetling brows and gleaming spectacles, and a stubborn, invincible nose, and a mouth ground between the millstones of upper lip and nether chin. The face of a tremendously dynamic and forthright person, strenuously imposing himself on the enfeebled nations of the South, and wringing from them the homage he knows to be his due. And yet, impressive though the photograph was, or rather because it was so awfully impressive, I could not help smiling. For I knew well how ill this brawny Viking would have fared here, had not that frail-looking Southern lady, with the dreaming eyes, stood sponsor for him—had she not bent down and lifted him in her arms, affectionately, and carried him, and cooed over him.

If these words should meet the eye of any simple Norwegians, they must not suppose me to be sneering at Björnson's play. I sneer rather at the conventionality of people who cannot appreciate for its intrinsic goodness a play which does not conform with the current fashions of dramatic art in their own country. In the second act, as I shall suggest, Björnson defies not only our own current and negligible conventions in dramatic art, but also those eternal, universal conventions which inhere in the art—conventions which every dramatist should respect. And the result of this violence is that most of the second act seems to me (and must seem to any other impartial creature) hopelessly undramatic, dull and trivial. But with this rather large reservation, "Beyond Human Power" seems to me a fine and inspiring work. The irony of its story (I need not warn you of the sense in which I use the word "irony") is quite magnificent. Pastor Adolf Sang is a buoyant saint, practising the precepts of Christianity according to their most literal significance, a giant rejoicing in the strength of his faith and in the strength that his faith gives him. There is no danger he will not encounter, so sure is he of Divine protection. There is no miracle he cannot work among the peasants who are in his charge. Over their weak and simple natures his simple strength has such sway that he can cure them of all sicknesses. He is a prophet not without honour in his own country, but (here is the first irony) he is a prophet without honour in his own home. His wife has never believed in him as an agent of Heaven, and has always taken a rationalistic view of his miracles. His two children, now that they have grown up, are also unbelieving. There is this further irony, that the children, loving him devotedly, are yearning to take him at his own valuation, and failing signally to do so. His effect on his wife is a matter of still deeper irony: in the knowledge that he, through his literal Christianity, is ruining the worldly prospects of the children, and in the constant struggle between her love for him and her desire for their welfare, she has suffered such torments that her health has broken down utterly. She is partially paralysed. She cannot sleep. She is always in pain. The omnibeneficent Pastor has ruined the life that he loves best of all. His wife's is the one affliction he cannot cure. Even *his* self-confidence is undermined by this salient failure. But he shakes off doubt, determining to put forth a vast effort. And it is on the success or failure of this vast effort that the interest of the play is centred. Pastor Sang goes away to pray in his church. Presently, a bell is heard tolling. It is the signal that his prayer has begun. His wife falls into a quiet sleep. Scarcely have the children realised this wonder when they hear an ominous crash in the distance. They start up, knowing it to be a landslip from the mountains, knowing that nothing can save the church where their father is praying. Nearer and nearer comes the noise of crashing and crumbling. It passes, subsides, and through the silence comes the steady sound of the bell, tolling still. . . . That is the end of the first act, and if you, reader, do not think it a finely dramatic end, then my writing must be lamentably inferior to Mrs. Campbell's stage-managing. Let us skip now to the end of the second act. In the room outside that in which the sick woman is still sleeping sits a company of Pastors. Pastor Sang is still in his church, praying. Will his prayer be granted? Will the woman rise from her bed and come among them before the sun sets? The light of the setting sun reddens the cross above the door, and a strange silence falls on the room. The door slowly opens, and through it, slowly and vaguely, with extended arms, comes the arisen woman. The peasants troop in, singing a hymn of praise. The Pastors join in the hymn, gazing awestruck at the miracle. And, at last, he who has wrought the miracle rushes in and clasps his wife in his arms. In his arms she dies. "Oh," he gasps, "this—this is not what I meant." He has killed his wife by a miracle, and by that same token his own faith. This is not what he meant. The final irony of his fate is accomplished. He dies.

My suggestion that we should skip thus to the end was made in order that I might not spoil the description of what is fine in the play by describing with it what is ineffably tedious. Those Pastors! six or seven of them, every one of them with his own view as to how modern faith-healing ought to be regarded by the Norwegian Church. What they say is in itself, doubtless, quite sensible and interesting. But they have no business to say it in this play. It has no possible bearing on this play. The dramatic point is whether a particular miracle will or will not be accomplished. What is the attitude of Norwegian clergymen towards miracles in general is a question quite beside the point. If the opinions of these clergymen were likely to affect in any way the life of Pastor Sang, they might be dramatically excusable. But such is not the case. The clergymen are strangers from a distance, here by chance, and going away directly; and their discussion is purely academic. Dramatically they are quite impertinent, and in a work of art whatever is not pertinent is bad. Even in Norway, where, possibly, "Faith-healing and the Church" is a topic of acute controversy, these clergymen must have been a sorry dead-weight. That in England the audience did not throw things at them is a great tribute to the goodness of the play as a whole—or, at least, to the glamorous power exercised by Mrs. Campbell, even when she is not visible on the stage.

If difficulty be the measure of achievement, Mrs. Campbell has never done anything so good as her impersonation of the bed-ridden woman. No problem in histrionics could be harder than this: how to hold the attention of an audience, throughout a long act, without raising your voice or moving your body. Glamour, how great soever, will not alone enable a mime to solve this problem. Mrs. Campbell solved it, somehow, through the working-out of certain abstruse equations in facial expression and vocal inflection. She wrought the triumph of technical skill over difficulties. Mr. Titheradge was duly spiritual as the faith-healer. But I do not think his personality is well suited to the part. He has too intellectual an air. It is the strength, and the weakness, of such a man as Pastor Sang that he cannot think, that he can only feel. Mr. Titheradge seemed obviously capable of both functions, and so failed to satisfy me. Mr. Du Maurier, as the Pastor's son, had the kind of part in which a self-conscious young Englishman would be bound to feel that he was making a fool of himself. Youth and self-consciousness go hand in hand, and to feel that one is making a fool of oneself is a sure means of doing so actually. But Mr. Du Maurier did nothing of the kind. Advancing years have made an artist of him.

"A MOST HARD-WORKING PROFESSION"

November 30, 1901

The eminent lawyer so amusingly drawn in Mr. Reginald Turner's novel, "Cynthia's Damages," describes his histrionic client as "a young lady who, by indomitable courage and application, has become a leading light in a most hard-working profession." This notion of stage life is not confined to lawyers.

There is a quite general impression that to be a mime is to follow a frightfully arduous calling. As most mimes (say nine in ten of them) are almost always out of work, this impression seems to be rather false. Setting aside the submerged nine-tenths, let me inquire whether the buoyant tenth leads quite so laborious a life as we suppose.

Let me take, first of all, a cursory glance at other professions. I see the "man of business" leaving his home after an early breakfast and returning to it only for a late dinner. Half of one of the intervening hours he devotes to his lunch. Throughout the rest he is at work in his office. I see the civil servant at his desk from ten or eleven A.M. till five or six P.M. (Against his brief interval for lunch must usually be set a whole evening devoted to literary work.) I see the clergyman going his perpetual round between Matins and Evensong. All day long I hear the naval officer shouting his orders from the quarter-deck, in the intervals of "cramming" for some imminent examination, and the barrister pleading for clients whose affairs he has mastered through prodigal expenditure of midnight-oil. The doctor's bell may be set clanging at any hour of the night, and out of bed must the doctor stumble forth into the night, to pit his skill against Death's. Never, while light lasts in the heavens, will the jealous painter spare one moment from his canvas. From the sculptor's hand the chisel drops not till . . . But enough of my cursory glance. I need not labour my point that most professions are worked at from morning to night without much cessation. In point of hard work, how do they compare with the peculiar profession of acting? The average play lasts from eight to eleven. A mime who appears both in the first and in the last act must reach the theatre at (say) half-past seven, in order to change his clothes and paint his face. Having removed the paint and resumed mufti, he leaves the theatre at (say) half-past eleven. Suppose that the distance between his home and the theatre is a distance of half an hour. We then credit him with a working-day of four hours. Suppose that there is a matinée both on Wednesday and on Saturday. We then credit him with working for eight hours on two days in the week. But really we are too generous. The two hours spent by him in going backwards and forwards come rather under the head of healthy exercise than of actual labour. And in the three hours of the play's duration he is not working all the time. Deducting time for entr'actes, we find that a play lasts rather less than two and a half hours. We assume, too, that an actor who is not playing "lead" is not actually on the stage for more than half an hour altogether. During the greater part of the performance he is lounging at the "wings," or in the green-room, or in his dressing-room. So that the averagely successful mime is not actually practising his art for more than four hours in the course of the week. "But," you interject, "how about 'study'? And rehearsals?" True, I had forgotten them. But there is not nearly so much of them as there used to be. One must allow for the long-run system. In the old stock-companies there were, perhaps, daily rehearsals. But in the modern touring-company, which sets out on a wide nomady with but one play to bless itself with, there is after the outset no rehearsing at all. And I suppose that the London theatres have between them a yearly average of four productions apiece. Assuming that the average play is rehearsed for three weeks, and the average length of every rehearsal is three hours, we find that the averagely successful mime puts in yearly some two hundred and sixteen hours of preliminary work. But we bring it down with a rush from that not very stupendous total, when we remember that only during one small part of every rehearsal is he himself rehearsing. Say that he himself is on the stage for three-quarters of an hour. That leaves fifty-four hours as his yearly average. I do not (judging by results) imagine that to actual "study" he devotes much more time than is required for learning his words by heart. Let us suppose, charitably, that he *thinks about* a new part for two hours altogether. That brings up his yearly average for extra work to sixty-two hours. I have not the patience to work out from my previous calculations his yearly average of hours of actual work before the public, and to collate this total (plus sixty-two) with the yearly average of hours spent in work by the doctors, sailors, lawyers, financiers, painters and other unfortunates. But I have said enough, surely, to gladden the hearts and stiffen the backs of all those stage-struck girls and stage-struck boys who are being checked in their aspirations by their parents' solemn warning that the stage means very hard work.

Let me carry encouragement a step further for them. In considering the exigency of any profession, one must take account not

merely of the number of hours that must be devoted to work in
the course of the year, but also of the degree of vital energy—force
of body, force of intellect, force of emotion—which in every hour
it absorbs from you. Now, to be a great actor, you must have
these three forces in a high degree. Unless you are physically
strong you cannot get through the performance of such a part as
Hamlet, for example, without showing obvious signs of fatigue.
You cannot, moreover, give a worthy rendering of that part unless
you have brought to bear on it a large brain and a large heart.
But to give a worthy rendering of the average part is not so difficult
an affair. To walk and talk for half an hour in the course of the
evening makes no great strain on your physique, even though you
have to walk gracefully and to talk in a loud tone. Moreover, the
amount of brain-power you require for "studying" the average
creation of the average dramatist is—well, not above the average.
Nor is the emotional power that you require for "feeling" nightly
all that is in it. However, doubtless the aspirants whom I am
addressing do not wish to be average mimes, and feel that they
are cut out for great things. Even so, they need not fear that their
art will "take it out of" them, to any alarming extent. In acting
a great part they will have to spend a good deal of physical force.
But their intellectual force will be spent merely beforehand:
once their conception of a part's meaning is clear, their minds may
be set at rest. They will not have to elucidate the part every
evening. Nor will they even have to "feel" it after (say) fifty
consecutive evenings. Even if they then be still able to feel it
(which is doubtful), they need not bother to do so. They will be
able to produce on the audience, without any trouble, exactly the
same effect as they produced at first through throwing their whole
souls into every line. Their facial expression, their vocal inflections, their gestures—all these will come of their own accord,
through force of habit. The long-run system is often deplored
on the ground that the mimes "walk through" their parts. This
is not quite just. Really, it is very seldom, even after two hundred
nights, that one sees a mime acting with less evident strenuousness
than at the beginning of the run. Nevertheless, any one who
knows anything about the inner side of histrionics knows that this
strenuousness, however convincing, may be but an illusion, that
the mime may be merely producing his or her effects automatically.

A curious instance of this detachment in mimes after a long run was given me, some years ago, by a candid actress. She was playing the principal part in a play which had had a very long run. Her part was that of a Russian countess, and her great scene came in the third act, when she determined to take poison. Sitting down at a table, she wrote a letter to her lover, speaking it aloud, sentence by sentence, according to the time-honoured convention, while her quill scoured the paper. "Ere you read these words, Ivan, I shall be far away, tasting a tranquillity which, since you came into my life, has been denied me. You have wronged me foully, Ivan, and broken my heart. But now, in the shadow of death, I forgive you—forgive you for the sake of those few brief days of rapture when I knew myself loved by you. Already the shadow of Death is" &c., &c. It was a longish letter, and I quote from memory, but that was the effect of it. And the effect of it on the audience was very poignant. The sobs of the Countess, her chokings, the real tears that fell from her eyes, all had their counterparts in the audience. And yet it is a fact that, on most nights after the first flush of the play's run, Mrs. —— was taking the opportunity of writing some little note which she had forgotten to write before coming down to the theatre. "Dear Mr. ——. If you have nothing better to do, won't you come and dine with us quite quietly on Sunday? It seems such an age since I saw you. And I want to tell you all about" &c., &c., or "Mrs. —— is much surprised that Madame Chose has not sent the dress which she promised faithfully would arrive last night. Unless it is delivered before noon to-morrow" &c., &c.

How arose the general notion that mimes are a hard-worked race? The true answer to this question is, I think, suggested in " Cynthia's Damages." Commenting on the eminent lawyer's description of Miss Walpole, Mr. Turner says "it was always remarkable how hard-working all the actresses for whom he appeared seemed to be." The British public holds a brief for all actors and actresses. The fascination of their atmosphere has conquered the public. And, ever moral, the public is determined to convince itself that it has been won not by fascination but by moral worth.

SOLILOQUIES IN DRAMA

December 7, 1901

Talking to oneself has this obvious advantage over any other form of oratory or gossip : one is assured of a sympathetic audience. But it has also this peculiar drawback : it is supposed to be one of the early symptoms of insanity. Wrongly so, perhaps. A mad-doctor might rule the habit out of his diagnosis. Nevertheless, the popular belief is firmly rooted. And it is for fear of this belief, doubtless, that we talk to ourselves, even as we dress our hair with straws, so rarely. It may be said that we never do address our-selves at any length except in the delirium of a fever. In moments of ordinary excitement, of course, we utter to the wind some sort of appropriate ejaculation. Delight wrings from us a cry of "Hurrah!" or "Thank Heaven!" even though there be none by to echo us. Similarly, in any disgust we emit one of those sounds whose rather poor equivalents in print are "Ugh" and "Faugh" "D——n" and "Tut." Much further than this we do not go. "Why, what an ass am I !" cries Hamlet in one of his soliloquies. Omitting the first word, and transposing the last two, the ordinary modern man does often soliloquise to that extent. But he could no more soliloquise to Hamlet's extent than he could speak in decasyllabics. Nor is there any reason to suppose that that class of the community with which, contemptuous of his own fluency, Hamlet compared himself, is or ever was more prone to soliloquise than any other. In the matter of soliloquies we cannot accept Hamlet as an unbiased authority. We merely find in him the possible origin of the belief that talking to oneself is a bad sign.

Now, the aim of modern dramatists is to come as near as possible to reality—to present life without accepting any convention which is not a convention necessary to theatric art. The classic instance of an unnecessary convention is the "happy ending"; of a neces-sary convention, the three-sided rooms inhabited by the dramatis personæ. Then there are other conventions, whose necessity or negligibility is not quite so clear. For instance, the preservation of the two unities, time and space, does undoubtedly increase verisimilitude. It has often been argued that a dramatist ought to handle only such themes as can be handled without breaking those unities. But the effect of that argument were such a restriction for drama as none but the most hardened academic mind would welcome. The best rule for the dramatist is to defer to time and space until they become insufferable tyrants, when he may kick them out remorselessly. Another convention round which doubts have raged is the convention of the soliloquy. This is, of course, opposite in kind to the time-and-space convention, for that it is a convention not of restriction but of licence. In real life, as I have demonstrated, people don't soliloquise. "Therefore," said Ibsen, "my puppets shan't soliloquise." After a decent interval, when Ibsen's general ideal of realism had forced itself into the European mind, our own dramatists began to echo this particular determination. Mr. Jones, Mr. Pinero and others, not to be outdone, brought their fists down on their writing-tables, firmly exclaiming "*Our* puppets shan't soliloquise." For some years now their puppets haven't soliloquised. Insomuch that whenever we have heard the puppets of less accomplished playwrights unbosoming themselves to the audience, we (none loudlier than I) have protested against the miserable, outmoded, illusion-destroying little trick. Ten or fifteen years ago that trick would have passed without rebuke. We regarded the soliloquy as not less essential to drama than the three-walled room. So we accepted it calmly, without hurt to illusion. But now, persuaded that it is unnecessary, and that it can always be avoided by due technical skill, we are disilluded and enraged by it. Not, of course, in poetic drama. For there the aim is to show us not life as it is, but life through certain conventions of formal beauty. Such additional conventions as the soliloquy make there no difference to us. No one who had not a train to catch would prefer "Hamlet" without the soliloquies of the Prince of Denmark. Mr. Stephen Phillips, then, and all those others who tend the faint flame of poetic drama, may skip this article with light heels: the embargo on soliloquies does not affect *them*. It does, however, very really affect the prose-dramatist. It makes his task considerably harder. And it does much to ward away from dramaturgy those literary persons who might do much to improve our drama. Let not these persons skip this article. I hope to throw into it some rays of hope for them.

Though in real life we do not talk to ourselves, we do think to ourselves, and many of these thoughts we could not or would not divulge to any other creature, however dear a friend he might be. Perhaps these incommunicable thoughts are the most important we ever have—the thoughts which, if they were divulged, would best elucidate our characters and our actions. To elucidate the characters and actions of his puppets is the novelist's first duty. His best means of doing this is to throw himself into the brains of those puppets and admit us through the breach. This, in fact, is what he is always doing. "The door closed, and John Smith was left alone. At first his mind was a mere tumult of doubts. 'Why,' he wondered bitterly, 'had . . . Of course, it must be that she . . . Yet no, surely, it was he himself who had always . . .' He was filled with self-loathing. He looked into the depths of his soul, fascinated by what he found there. He realised now for the first time that the motive of all that he had done throughout his life had been . . . A torrent of indignation at the world—the world that had made him what . . . A strange calm fell on him. 'After all,' he thought . . . Yet again there rose up and confronted him . . . And then a strange idea crept, like a thief, into his mind. . . . 'No, no, anything but that' . . . 'Yet' . . . His mind was made up. He looked at the clock. He had been communing with himself all through the night. Already there came a faint sound of twittering from the garden . . ." We all know the kind of thing. And a very necessary kind of thing it is. What would the serious novelist be without it? Something very like the modern dramatist. For the modern dramatist there are many occasions when it is essential that the audience be admitted into a puppet's brain. But he himself cannot, like the novelist, come forward, bow, and admit them. Of course, it might be argued that such occasions are to be avoided—that the inner workings of the mind are not *du théâtre*. But no one were quite such a fool as to use that argument. What then is the novelist to do? Even the most accomplished mime cannot be trusted to convey in dumb-show to even the most intelligent audience a really complicated train of thought. Soliloquies, I admit, are to be avoided, if avoided they can be, as being an unrealistic convention. Is there any other way-out? What is the ordinary modern way-out? It is our old friend the Confidant. True, our old friend comes before us elaborately disguised. He is

not the simpleton we knew of yore—the gaping simpleton with
no excuse for his presence except his pricked-up ears. He is now
endowed with a *locus standi* in the form of a character and a real
connexion with the plot. But, for all that, the Confidant he
remains. I do not like him. I do not like him, because to him
are so often confided things which in real life would be confided to
no one. The confiding of such things to him is an offence against
fundamental reality, whereas the confiding of them through
soliloquy to the audience is but an offence against reality of surface. It should be easier, in such cases, to accept soliloquy as a
conventional substitute for silent thought than to accept confidence
as an actual substitute. In such cases, then, our best dramatists
are on a false tack in using the Confidant. Perhaps they are now
too hardened in their method to use the soliloquy. But let the
soliloquy be used without qualms by the trembling neophyte—
without qualms, and with the happy knowledge that it is technically much easier to use than the Confidant. They need not fear
that I shall blame them. Like other critics, I have in my day
sweepingly condemned the soliloquy. But I had no right to do so,
and I apologise. I shall not do so again.

Only (the trembling neophytes must not wholly cease to
tremble), I shall persist in condemnation of soliloquies that do not
seem to me inevitable. Soliloquies must be used for no other
purpose than to let the audience into secrets which a puppet
would not as a human being, even if he could, reveal to any one else,
and which the dramatist cannot reveal except through that puppet's lips. Soliloquies must not be used as a convenient way of
letting the audience know (for example) how many minutes it
takes some puppet to walk from his house to the railway station, or
whom he met at dinner on the preceding night, or how old he is.
Such things as these must, of course, be overheard by us in his
conversation with another puppet. In 1901 it is hardly necessary
to warn the neophytes against that crude form of soliloquy, the
"aside," which consists of a few words spoken by a puppet in the
presence of others to keep the audience mindful of something
already explained to them. In the palmy 'sixties it was all very
well for the villain to look over the heroine's shoulder and shout
"I do but dissemble." For the audience was composed of simple
folk whose minds, untrained by any Board School, were mostly

incapable of grasping clearly any fact or of retaining it for more than a minute. Also, the average actor of that period, untrained by any psychologic drama, probably knew no way of expressing deceit except a contraction of the brow and a side-long smile at the audience. Nowadays, a dramatist must not proceed on the assumption that his mimes will be mere vocal dolts or that his audiences will be incapable of taking a single point that is not hammered into them. Neither of his mimes nor of his audience must he, however, expect too much. He must strike the mean. As to where exactly that mean is to be struck, he must use his own discretion.

"THE IMPORTANCE OF BEING EARNEST"

January 18, 1902

Of a play representing actual life there can be, I think, no test more severe than its revival after seven or eight years of abeyance. For that period is enough to make it untrue to the surface of the present, yet not enough to enable us to unswitch it from the present. How seldom is the test passed! There is a better chance, naturally, for plays that weave life into fantastic forms; but even for them not a very good chance; for the fashion in fantasy itself changes. Fashions form a cycle, and we, steadily moving in that cycle, are farther from whatever fashion we have just passed than from any other. The things which once pleased our grandfathers are tolerable in comparison with the things which once pleased us. If in the lumber of the latter we find something that still pleases us, pleases us as much as ever it did, then, surely, we may preen ourselves on the possession of a classic, and congratulate posterity. Last week, at the St. James', was revived "The Importance of Being Earnest," after an abeyance of exactly seven years—those seven years which, according to scientists, change every molecule in the human body, leaving nothing of what was there before. And yet to me the play came out fresh and exquisite as ever, and over the whole house almost every line was sending ripples of laughter—cumulative ripples that became waves, and receded only for fear of drowning the next line. In kind the play always was unlike any other, and in its kind it still seems perfect. I do not wonder that now the critics boldly call it a classic, and predict immortality. And (timorous though I am apt to be in prophecy) I join gladly in their chorus.

A classic must be guarded jealously. Nothing should be added to, or detracted from, a classic. In the revival at the St. James', I noted several faults of textual omission. When Lady Bracknell is told by Mr. Worthing that he was originally found in a hand-bag in the cloak-room of Victoria Station, she echoes "The cloak-room at Victoria Station?" "Yes," he replies; "the Brighton Line." "The line is immaterial," she rejoins; "Mr. Worthing, I confess I am somewhat bewildered," &c., &c. Now, in the present revival "the line is immaterial" is omitted. Perhaps Mr. Alexander regarded it as an immaterial line. So it is, as far as the plot is concerned. But it is not the less deliciously funny. To skip it is inexcusable. Again, Mr. Wilde was a master in selection of words, and his words must not be amended. "Cecily," says Miss Prism, "you will read your Political Economy in my absence. The chapter on the Fall of the Rupee you may omit. It is somewhat too sensational." For "sensational" Miss Laverton substitutes "exciting"—a very poor substitute for that mot juste. Thus may the edge of magnificent absurdity be blunted. In the last act, again, Miss Laverton killed a vital point by inaccuracy. In the whole play there is no more delicious speech than Miss Prism's rhapsody over the restored hand-bag. This is a speech quintessential of the whole play's spirit. "It seems to be mine," says Miss Prism calmly. "Yes, here is the injury it received through the upsetting of a Gower Street omnibus in younger and happier days. There is the stain on the lining caused by the explosion of a temperance beverage—an incident that occurred at Leamington. And here, on the lock, are my initials. I had forgotten that in an extravagant moment I had had them placed there. The bag is undoubtedly mine. I am delighted to have it so unexpectedly restored to me. It has been a great inconvenience being without it all these years." The overturning of a Gower Street omnibus in younger and happier days! Miss Laverton omitted "and happier." What a point to miss! Moreover, she gabbled the whole speech, paying no heed to those well-balanced cadences whose dignity contributes so much to the fun—without whose dignity, indeed, the fun evaporates. In such a play as this good acting is peculiarly important. It is, also, peculiarly difficult to obtain. The play is unique in kind, and thus most of the mimes, having trained themselves for ordinary purposes, are bewildered in approaching it.

Before we try to define how it should be acted, let us try to define its character. In scheme, of course, it is a hackneyed farce —the story of a young man coming up to London "on the spree," and of another young man going down conversely to the country, and of the complications that ensue. In treatment, also, it is farcical, in so far as some of the fun depends on absurd "situations," "stage-business," and so forth. Thus one might assume that the best way to act it would be to rattle through it. That were a gross error. For, despite the scheme of the play, the fun depends mainly on what the characters say, rather than on what they do. They speak a kind of beautiful nonsense—the language of high comedy, twisted into fantasy. Throughout the dialogue is the horse-play of a distinguished intellect and a distinguished imagination—a horse-play among words and ideas, conducted with poetic dignity. What differentiates this farce from any other, and makes it funnier than any other, is the humorous contrast between its style and matter. To preserve its style fully, the dialogue must be spoken with grave unction. The sound and the sense of the words must be taken seriously, treated beautifully. If mimes rattle through the play and anyhow, they manage to obscure much of its style, and much, therefore, of its fun. They lower it towards the plane of ordinary farce. This was what the mimes at the St. James' were doing on the first night. The play triumphed not by their help but in their despite. I must except Miss Lilian Braithwaite, who acted in precisely the right key of grace and dignity. She alone, in seeming to take her part quite seriously, showed that she had realised the full extent of its fun. Miss Margaret Halstan acted prettily, but in the direction of burlesque. By displaying a sense of humour she betrayed its limitations. Mr. Lyall Swete played the part of Doctor Chasuble as though it were a minutely realistic character study of a typical country clergyman. Instead of taking the part seriously for what it is, he tried to make it a serious part. He slurred over all the majestic utterances of the Canon, as though he feared that if he spoke them with proper unction he would be accused of forgetting that he was no longer in the Benson Company. I sighed for Mr. Henry Kemble, who "created" the part. I sighed, also, for the late Miss Rose Leclerq, who "created" the part of Lady Bracknell. Miss M. Talbot plays it in the conventional stage-dowager fashion. Miss Leclerq—but no! I will not sink without a struggle into that period when a man begins to bore young people by raving to them about the mimes whom they never saw. Both Mr. George Alexander and Mr. Graham Browne rattled through their parts. Even in the second act, when not only the situation, but also the necessity for letting the audience realise the situation, demands that John Worthing should make the slowest of entries, Mr. Alexander came bustling on at break-neck speed. I wish he would reconsider his theory of the play, call some rehearsals, and have his curtain rung up not at 8.45 but at 8.15. He may argue that this would not be worth his while, as "Paolo and Francesca" is to be produced so soon. I hope he is not going to have "Paolo and Francesca" rattled through. The effect on it would be quite as bad as on "The Importance of Being Earnest"—though not, I assure him, worse.

MR. SHAW'S TRAGEDY

February 1, 1902

The promptest notice of "Mrs. Warren's Profession" would have been too late to guide any one as to whether he should or should not go to see the play. And the belatedness of my notice matters the less because the play, though performed only twice, lives lustily in book-form, and will assuredly live so for many years. Not that it seems to me "a masterpiece—yes! with all reservations, a masterpiece," as Mr. Archer hastily acclaimed it. Indeed, having seen it acted, I am confirmed in my heresy that it is, as a work of art, a failure. But the failure of such a man as "G. B. S." is of more value than a score of ordinary men's neat and cheap successes, even as the "failure" of a Brummell is worthier than a

score of made-up bows in the gleaming window of the hosier
"Mrs. Warren" is a powerful and stimulating, even an ennobling
piece of work—a great failure, if you like, but also a failure with
elements of greatness in it. It is decried as unpleasant by those
who cannot bear to be told publicly about things which in private
they can discuss, and even tolerate, without a qualm. Such
people are the majority. For me, I confess, a play with an unpleasant subject, written sincerely and fearlessly by a man who has
a keenly active brain and a keenly active interest in the life around
him, is much less unpleasant than that milk-and-water romance
(brewed of skimmed milk and stale water) which is the fare commonly provided for me in the theatre. It seems to me not only
less unpleasant, but also less unwholesome. I am thankful for it.

Gratitude, however, does not benumb my other faculties.
With all due deference to Mr. Archer, "Not a masterpiece, no!
with all reservations, not a masterpiece" is my cry. The play is
in Mr. Shaw's earlier manner—his 'prentice manner. It was
written in the period when he had not yet found the proper form
for expressing himself in drama. He has found that form now.
He has come through experiment to the loose form of "Cæsar and
Cleopatra," of "The Devil's Disciple"—that large and variegated
form wherein there is elbow-room for all his irresponsible com-
plexities. In "Mrs. Warren" he was still making tentative steps
along the strait and narrow way of Ibsen. To exhaust a theme in
four single acts requires tremendous artistic concentration. When
the acts are split up loosely in scenes the author may divagate with
impunity. But in four single acts there is no room for anything
that is not strictly to the point. Any irrelevancy offends us. And
irrelevancy is of the essence of Mr. Shaw's genius. Try as he
would, in admiration of his master, he could not keep himself
relevant to Mrs. Warren. We find him bobbing up at intervals
throughout the play, and then bobbing down again, quickly, ashamed
of himself. In the loose form which he has now found for himself
he can bob up as often as he likes, and always we are overjoyed to
see him. But in the old constricted form we frown at him. We
frown not merely at the waste of time, but also as at a breach of
good taste. Mr. Shaw is a comedic person, Mrs. Warren a tragic.
The Restoration is over, and no dramatist could treat her from any
but a tragic standpoint. It is from this standpoint, of course,

that Mr. Shaw has treated her. And thus we are jarred by the involuntary intrusions of Mr. Shaw's self. They give a painful effect of levity, though we know well that nothing can be further from levity than the spirit in which Mr. Shaw regards his theme. Theme, spirit: that brings us to the root of the matter. The main secret of the play's failure is that we have a comedian trying to be tragic. To create a tragedy, you must have a sense of that pity and terror which——"Agreed," Mr. Shaw will interrupt "and I have nothing if not that sense. If you don't find it in this play of mine, you must be blind." "Agreed," I rejoin. But I proceed to suggest that a man may be more than a comedian in himself, yet fail to be tragic in dramaturgy, and that Mr. Shaw does not feel the pity and terror of life in the way that a tragic dramatist must feel it. His sense of it is a sincere and fine one. But it is the satirist's sense. He is sorry for things as they are, and afraid of things as they are, and angry that they are not otherwise, and laudably anxious to reform them. His is a fine civic ardour, which I should be the last to disparage. But it does not constitute him a tragic dramatist. The tragic dramatist must feel pity and terror in a certain specific way. It is through the hearts of men and women that he must feel them. He must be able to see into their hearts, and show us what he has seen there. He must be able to create human beings. Comedy's main appeal is to the head, tragedy's to the heart. We can be intellectually interested in figures that do not illude us as real, but we cannot feel for such figures. Thus in comedy a subjectively created figure will do well enough, but in tragedy it is useless. Mr. Shaw cannot create a figure objectively, and thus he cannot communicate to us through drama a tragic emotion. Tragedy, of course, can appeal not only to the heart, but also, incidentally, to the head. From the intellectual point of view, "Mrs. Warren" is, as I have said, a most stimulating affair. We admire the writer's grip of his subject. We cordially agree with his views. We praise the trenchancy of his expression. A remarkable little pamphlet! We really must have it bound! . . . With a start, we realise that this is not a pamphlet whose leaves we are turning, but a play which is being acted. . . . Our mistake was rather a stupid one. For if this play had been a pamphlet, it would have been appealing to our hearts and our heads simultaneously. The fact that it appealed (despite its theme) only to our heads ought to have reminded us that it was an ill-created tragedy. So tragic a theme could not otherwise have failed to touch us.

In order to rouse public opinion against those economic conditions by which a Mrs. Warren is produced, Mr. Shaw, as dramatist, could not have chosen a better means than that of juxtaposing Mrs. Warren with a grown-up daughter who is ignorant of her mother's history and occupation. There you have the makings of a fine tragic conflict. Only it is necessary that the daughter should be of flesh and blood. And there you are bumped up against one of the limitations in Mr. Shaw's genius. Doubtless, Mr. Shaw will say that Vivie is of authentic flesh and blood. I am ready to believe that there may be, here and there, a well-brought-up girl who would behave as (admirably, if Mr. Shaw likes) Vivie behaves. Only, such girls are very rare, very abnormal; and, in any case, Mr. Shaw has not succeeded in making this one seem like anything but a figment created by him to show how, in his opinion, a girl in such circumstances ought to behave. But even if he had made her real, that would not be enough. The tragic dramatist must not only be able to make a character real: he must also be able to select the kind of character that is right for his purpose. In "Mrs. Warren," obviously, the character of the daughter ought to be normal. Were she a normal girl, the situation would stir us to pity and awe. As she is but an unsympathetic figment dangled before our eyes, we are merely interested. The whole play becomes a mere academic debate. Mr. Shaw has called attention to certain things, and has moved a resolution, and we have all voted for the resolution, and there is an end of the matter. Perhaps I go too far. The moving of a resolution does give a kind of artistic finish to a debate. But there is no kind of art in the conclusion of Mr. Shaw's play. We leave Vivie Warren precisely the same as we found her. She has passed through her ordeal without turning a hair. At any rate, any hair that may have turned has been pressed back severely into its place. The girl is not at all to be pitied, and since we cannot pity her, we lose all the emotion that the play might have given us. As an acute critic, Mr. Shaw must have known that it was essentia to his play that Vivie should be made human. The fact that he did not make her so proves that he could not. The fact that he could not puts him out of court as a tragic dramatist. As an acute critic, he has realised this third fact, and is acting accordingly —doing the kind of work that he ought to do, in the way in which only he can do it. I felicitate him. I felicitate everybody.

A TRAGIC COMEDIAN

February 22, 1902

The monotony of the outcry for a National Theatre is broken, now and again, by an outcry for a National School of Acting. I think that such a School would be a rather cumbrous and expensive means of teaching our mimes those little technical tricks which they contrive to master for themselves at cost of a brief experience. It would not, of course, be a means of creating great mimes, or even good mimes. It would not evoke genius or talent where genius or talent was not. Let the outcriers for it remember (and such of them as happen to be playgoers cannot fail to remember) that we have in England a quite sufficient number of mimes who "know their business." In London, in the suburbs, in the provinces, you do not often see any obvious amateur on the professional stage. When you do see one, you may be quite sure that there is some definitely financial or romantic reason for the engagement, and that the management could have found, at a moment's notice, a score of efficiently professional substitutes—a score of mimes who could have walked and talked without suggesting to us what must have been the port and elocution of Charles I half an hour after his head was cut off. Without any School, the supply of mimes who "know their business" is already far in excess of the demand for them. Nor would a School do anything to save us from the obtrusion of an amateur here and there. If, on the other hand, any of our outcriers harbour the delusion that a School would inculcate something more than technical tricks, let them reflect that we have already more than a sufficient number of decent actors to go round. We very seldom see a play that is not really beneath notice, but we constantly see in one play two or three quite admirable actors. It is not so much actors as dramatists that we lack. Had we merely a greater number of good actors, we should have merely an even greater amount of talent being thrown away on unworthy materials. I admit that we have very few good actresses. I do not profess to explain the rarity. Acting is supposed to be the only art (except singing) in which women may excel equally with men. But the fact remains that in this country, and in this age, the superiority of the male to the female sex is almost as obvious in the art of acting as it is in the other, more directly creative, arts. However, there remains this fact, also: that the small number of good actresses at our disposal is quite large enough to cope with the worthy chances given by our dramatists. Thus, even if a School could drill histrionic talent into girls, it were not the less a superfluous institution. A School that could drill dramaturgic talent into boys— that is what we need now. If cry out we must, let it be rather for an impossibility that we need than for one that we don't.

Of the good actors whose gifts, spent unworthily, are always shaming us for our lack of playwrights, perhaps the sharpest and strongest example is to be found in that irresistible creature, Mr. James Welch. That example is being adduced for us nightly at Terry's Theatre, in a farce called "The New Clown." The second act contains a scene which seems to have been written in order that the full force of the example be driven home into our hearts. Mr. Welch plays the part of a weak aristocrat who, through farcical complications, wishes to become a clown in a circus. The ring-master tells him the kind of thing which the public will expect of him: he must grin, and jump, and crow, and be frequently knocked down. The novice demurs. "Isn't it all rather mediæval?" he pleads. "Couldn't I introduce a few subtle effects of my own, such as——" "Certainly not," roars the ring-master. "What the public likes is to see a man being knocked down. And that's what you've got to give it." Throughout this scene, there was in Mr. Welch's acting a note of tragedy deeper than was needed for art's sake. There was a vibrating note which must have been sounded from the depths of his own private soul. Was not the scene a precise epitome of Mr. Welch's career on the stage? Is it not always his inexorable fate to grin, and jump, and crow, and be monotonously buffeted? And, to him, being what he is, must not this seem a cruelly, stupidly unjust fate? Year in year out, we see him in a sequence of inane farces, with never a chance of doing real justice to his qualities. It is true that he has established himself the prince of knock-about artists—of being-knocked-about artists, at any rate. The public loves him devotedly, and is well content that he should continue to be what he is till crack of doom. But for us others, who revere an artist when we see him, and who hold that no true artist should be a being-knocked-about artist, Mr. Welch's career is a matter of irritation and distress hardly less poignant than it must be to Mr. Welch himself. The more lurid glimpses we catch of what he might do, the more are we distressed by what he actually is doing. In his every impersonation Mr. Welch gives us more or less frequent glimpses. We can always descry in him a true comedian, and occasionally a master of pathos. His strongest point, perhaps, is pathos. In "The New Clown," the other night, there was one moment at which, if I had been an irresponsible playgoer, not a critic on the look-out for points, the tears would have come into my eyes. The would-be clown, ordered by the ring-master to give a taste of his quality, has retired to the side of the tent, taken the tips of his coat-tails between finger and thumb of either hand, bounded into the air, uttering a hideous yell, and waddled to the ring-master's side. He has looked up eagerly into the ring-master's face, but has seen there no shadow of a smile. Abashed, he repeats his performance, this time for the benefit of the "strong man" of the show. He peers up into the averted face of the giant, who is staring blankly into distance. The giant slowly turns his head, and the would-be clown, thinking that he is going to meet a glance of approval, catches up his coat-tails again, and begins to smile. The coat-tails are dropped, the smile flickers away, under the scorn of the giant's gaze. . . . The episode lasts but a moment, with no word spoken. It is but the momentary twitch of Mr. Welch's eyelids, lips and fingers. And whatever passes thus in a moment, inarticulately, cannot be well described through the medium of writing. You must take it on trust that what I have tried to describe is a very rare and exquisite moment—one of those moments when the genius of an actor is revealed. Nor is comedic pathos the only kind of pathos in which Mr. Welch excels. If ever I heard the note of tragic pathos struck,

I heard it struck authentically by Mr. Welch in "Macaire," in the lament of the little scoundrel over the dead body of the great scoundrel, his master. In the cry "I didn't blab on you, Macaire!" Mr. Welch had that in his voice and face which could have been heard in the voice, seen in the face, of none but a born tragedian. Strange, that into one small body should have been packed thus together the souls of a comedian and a tragedian!

It is this very smallness of body which has prevented Mr. Welch from using in "high" classical tragedy the power which he undoubtedly has for it. That he would be a spiritually magnificent Othello I have no doubt at all. But even if, following a famous tradition, he blacked himself all over, he could not make a hit in the part. The process of his make-up would not have occupied sufficient time. Yet, though he is debarred by Nature from impersonating the normal heroes of tragedy, there is no reason why his tragic power should be revealed to us only in accidental glimpses—no reason, except the lamentable sterility of our modern dramatists. Who will write the tragi-comedy in which Mr. Welch will be able to use the full measure of his endowment? Generally, I disapprove the system of writing plays "round" this or that mime. But Mr. Welch is one of those exceptional beings in whose favour a critic willingly waives a principle. He is a tragic comedian, of the highest grade, measuring in height fewer inches than I should care to count. It were quite possible to create a play in which his tiny stature would be consistent with his towering talents. It would not, of course, be so easy as it is to write a play with a view to nothing but his tiny stature. But whoever did it would earn all my gratitude, and all the gratitude of every discerning playgoer.

MR. CRAIG'S EXPERIMENT

April 5, 1902

In October, 1899, we went to war with the Transvaal and the Orange Free State. That war is still going on. In March, 1902, at the Great Queen Street Theatre, there was a production of a little opera and a masque, remarkable for that in it Mr. Gordon Craig had made, for our wonder and delight, certain strange and lovely experiments in the management and decoration of the stage. That production is not still going on. No such time-limit was set to it, originally, as was set to the war. It was to go on as long as the public would encourage it. Yet it did not outlast one week. Well! Though the direct concern of my life is with art, not with politics, my sense of proportion enables me to see that the brevity of Mr. Craig's campaign is a less serious matter than the length of Lord Kitchener's. I admit that I have collated a small matter with a great. Yet do I make no apology for the collation. For I take it that both matters spring from the same cause, and illustrate the same peculiarity in the nation.

It is often said and believed that the English are a political people, the French an artistic people—that the average Englishman has a flair for politics, the average Frenchman for art. This idea is quite false. It is based on faulty observation, and on a radical blunder in psychology. The average Englishman is no more political than he is artistic. The average Frenchman is no less political than he is artistic. A feeling for art and a feeling for politics have the same roots. Both feelings come from a temperament which can be quickened in its owner by things abstract from his own person, his own private and immediate circumstances— a temperament which can imagine and generalise. You cannot have either feeling without the other. Having either, you must have the other. The temperament of the average Englishman is not imaginative. His interests are all narrow, domestic, personal. What lies beyond his own hearth has no meaning for him. He knows his own hob, fender, and fire-irons, and loves them with a surpassing love; but of all that is in him of love and knowledge these articles have a strict monopoly. This stolid apathy was a very good thing for the commonweal so long as England produced great statesmen. A great statesman, having at his back a solid mass of compatriots too inert to question his policy, or to do aught but what he bids it do, can work wonders for his country. But when the stock of greatness fails! When there is but a crew of little-minded and frivolous and improvident politicians! Then the commonweal requires a strong, energetic force of public opinion, to keep these politicians up to the mark and out of mischief. Making a virtue of apathy, we pride ourselves on the calmness displayed by the nation during this long-drawn war "What," we cry unctuously, "would have happened in France?" There would soon have been frettings, fumings, upheavals. Yes, but by those very eruptions might have been thrown up a wonder-working statesman. By them, at any rate, the small men in public life would have had their heads knocked together, and would have been forced to take things seriously—to stop the war altogether or to strain every nerve towards its quick conclusion in victory. The average Englishman, however, is well content to let things be. He sits in smugly rapt contemplation of his hob, fender, and fire-irons. He is a triumph of domesticity. And the same tempera-ment in him which lets the Government do as little as it likes for as long as it likes has prevented Mr. Gordon Craig from displaying his achievements for more than a week at the Great Queen Street Theatre. And, as these achievements were so fresh and fascina-ting that I should have liked to see them many times, I take leave to deplore the effect of the national temperament on art as well as on politics.

Had Mr. Craig offered to Paris what he kept for London, he would have been the maker of a venture generally discussed and admired. But who in London wants "to tell or to hear some new thing" in any art? Twice a year the public will leave its hob, fender, and fire-irons, to visit Burlington House. It will go to Her Majesty's or elsewhere, now and then, to sit under Shake-speare, and Dickens descends often from its book-shelf. If a modern dramatist be substituted for Shakespeare, that author must be conventional or be mistrusted. So must another novelist than Dickens. Artistic curiosity is a gift confined to a tiny and embarrassed number of the dwellers in London. Go to any little picture-gallery where some new kind of work is being exhibited, or to any theatre lent for the production of a play written by an unknown or foreign dramatist, and you will find always the same little public—the same wan and dishevelled men and women. Which sex preponderates in this little public it would be impossible to determine, for each looks so very like the other. But one thing is certain: always there are the same men and the same women. Occasionally you see among them some being from the outer world; but that is a rare and startling sight. The artistic public in London is a hole-and-corner public, an *eccentric* public, quite distinct from the rest of creation, and numbering not more than 200—perhaps 250—members. Perhaps, then, 250 people patronised Mr. Craig's experiment. Any one else must have strayed into the theatre by chance and been horribly bored. Commercially, the experiment was doomed from the first. Needless to say, that, with a few exceptions, the critics, not having seen anything like it, decried it as absurd. And yet it was a very serious and delightful experiment, for which Mr. Craig deserves many thanks and puffs.

Even if I knew anything about music, I should not be so rash as to trespass on J. F. R.'s* ground. But I know nothing about music. I know not at all whether Mr. Craig's mode of production was appropriate or inappropriate to the spirit of Handel's "Acis and Galatea" and Purcell's "Masque of Love." All I know is that the production was in itself delicious, and that Mr. Craig's spirit and method would be invaluable in the mounting of certain kinds of plays. It would not be suitable to such plays as "Pilkerton's Peerage." But for plays of fantasy or of mystery it would work wonders. I hope Mr. Craig will be called in, somewhere, and soon, to devise and superintend the production of a children's pantomime or of a Maeterlinck play. How enchantingly pretty the one, and how hauntingly mystical the other would grow under his hands! I am sorry that my fatal habit of generalisation has left me no space in which to describe and analyse Mr. Craig's ideas of background and costume, "lighting" and "grouping"— the simplicity of that pale, one-coloured background, rising sheer beyond our range of vision, uninterrupted by "flies" or ceiling; the fluttering grace of those many-ribanded costumes, so simple, yet so various —every one of them a true invention; the cunning distribution and commingling of the figures and colours; the cunning adjustment of shadows over light, making of Polyphemus in "Acis and Galatea"a real giant—the one and only real and impressive giant ever seen on any stage, or ever likely to be seen till Mr. Craig is given the chance of giving us another. This cowled and terrible giant singing in his huge arbour, and those white-frocked children dancing beneath a flight of pink and white air-balls, and those solemn and slow-moving harlequins, with

* J. F. Runciman, musical critic of "The Saturday Review."

surcoats of dark gauze over their gay lozenges, setting the huge
candles in the candelabra of the Prison of Love—they and the
rest are ineffaceable pictures in my memory. Mr. Craig must give
us many more such pretty pictures.

THE ADVANTAGE OF WRITING PLAYS

April 12, 1902

Among the many curious phenomena which differentiate this
era from past eras, and (dare one hope?) from future eras, are
those innumerable little penny magazines, published under the
auspices of this or that prosperous news-company, for the tickling
of a certain taste in fiction. "Girls' Chat," "Sunny Hours,"
"Rosy Thoughts," and the rest! The news-companies batten
on them, the bookstalls groan under them. Examine them, and
you will find not much to choose between them. All of them
consist mainly of serial and short stories, anonymously written, and
interspersed with smudgy little process blocks. The illustrations
do not vary: always we see the same young hero in flannels, with
the same creases down his trousers, the same elderly clergyman
with fleecy white hair, the same girl directing a punt or dreaming
under the leafy porch of her father's (the clergyman's) house.
And the stories themselves are not less invariable, are written
always with the same lack of anything in the way of humour or
imagination or observation, and with the same weak and clumsy
pretence to prettiness of sentiment. Who reads them? Half-
educated girls, presumably, read them. Who writes them?
From internal evidence it is obvious that they are written by half-
educated girls. Lately, from a friend who is in a position to know,
I learnt what is the scale of payment for these stories. Considering the enormous profits made out of them, this scale is appallingly
low—a starvation wage, indeed. Yet it seems that many of the
writers have no other means of subsistence. I conceived pity for
these unfortunate, unknown writers, who are doing what is,
after all, a form of skilled labour for so tiny a pittance, and with no

prospect of fame or even credit. I wish to help them. I think I can help them, if they will listen to me. For sake of convenience, let me so far disregard their anonymity as to call them all, generically, Miss Evie Simpson.

Miss Evie Simpson, never having had public attention paid to her, is probably modest in right proportion to her lack of talent, and would recoil if I sprang my suggestion on her suddenly. She would think I was laughing at her, suggesting that she should do something quite beyond her powers. Therefore, let me preface my suggestion, and clear the ground for it, with a few remarks at large. Let Miss Simpson consider this general proposition. A and B are doing two different kinds of work. But the difference between these two kinds of work is superficial, not essential. Both kinds require the same qualities in the workers. Now if, by examination of A's little efforts, it could be proved that A, doing B's work, would produce something exactly like B's little efforts, and that he could not produce anything better than B's little efforts, what deduction would you draw? Miss Simpson is ready with her answer. Her deduction is that if, conversely, B did A's work he would be able to produce something not less good than A's little efforts. Quite right. Now, fiction and drama are two different kinds of work. But their differences are merely formal. Both of them depend on the same creative qualities—the power to observe and to imagine things, to project human or inhuman characters, to invent possible or impossible circumstances, and so on, and so on. Therefore, if the work of A, the dramatist, be such that we know that any stories he might write would have exactly the qualities so remarkable in the stories of B, and would have no other qualities beyond, then we may be quite sure that if B wrote plays they would be as good as A's. Now, we have already defined Miss Simpson as a writer of stories. Captain Basil Hood will allow us to define him as a writer of plays. But what sort of plays does he write? Some of his activity goes to the writing of libretti. But them we need not take into account. We need consider him merely as contriver of plays written in prose and in relation to modern life. Nor need we plod back through all his achievements in this kind. For "My Pretty Maid," which was produced last Saturday at Terry's Theatre, is a perfect specimen. We find in it all the usual attributes of Captain Hood, with no additions or subtractions. What do we find in it? Not very much, certainly. There is a beauteous girl, whose father is a dear old school-master. She loves, and is loved by, a "double-blue." Both the lovers are very poor—she because her father is much too "sympathetic" to make his business pay. There is an ugly usher, horrid and mean, who loves her, and can make or mar her father's school, and uses his power to win her hand. But there is a Lord. He is very rich, and is the friend of the "double-blue," whom he makes agent of his estate; and so all ends happily, not far from where it began. Reading my précis of the plot—and so little plot is there that I have hardly needed to compress anything—Miss Simpson will recognise a plot which she herself, in her time, has used again and again. If she will go and see the play, she will recognise also that the characters are exactly as she herself has always drawn them, or left them undrawn, and that the dialogue is instinct with just that mild futility which she, poor girl, knows to be the hall-mark of her own dialogue. What inference will she draw? This, of course: that if Captain Hood were with her on the staff of "Rosy Thoughts" his "copy" would be so exactly like hers that one or the other of them would have to go. And then, remembering that general law which she and I have just worked out together, her eyes will open very wide, and, bewildered, she will hold her breath.

At first, she will shrink from the inevitable corollary. She will be miserably sure that there must be some flaw in our reasoning— "it is too good to be true." Nay, let her be re-assured. The formal difference between fiction and drama need not affright her. She, doubtless, has no formal talent for dramaturgy. She would not know how to knit together and how to unravel, how to prepare and how to progress, and to do all those other things which are the peculiar secrets of the craft. But does Captain Hood know? Not he. Or, if he does know, how blithely he ignores his knowledge! The second act of "My Pretty Maid" does not require the first; the third would get on quite well without the second. Such as it is, the play consists of two acts, which are called the third and fourth. And even in them how wonderfully little there is! And I defy you, Miss Simpson, to find in them anything that you could not have done yourself. Self-confidence is the one thing you need. Cultivate that. And then, go in and win. For exactly that amount and quality of talent which have been winning you a handful of silver, you will receive a large cheque "on signing contract," another large cheque "on production," and yet another large cheque every Friday night of many ensuing weeks, to say nothing of other yet larger cheques for provincial, American, and Colonial rights. Yes, there is a good time coming for you— coming not only for your exchequer, but also for your self-respect. O hitherto inglorious girl, your features shall be made familiar to us through all the illustrated weeklies, your name shall be written in scarlet—EVIE SIMPSON—along all the omnibuses, and to you, even as to the Captain, will a daily paper presently devote a whole column of its valuable space, wherein will be solemnly set forth your "methods of work." And the dramatic critics, sitting in judgment on the results, shall pronounce them "singularly dainty," "undeniably fresh," "eminently wholesome," and "altogether delightful." Have the literary critics ever turned to praise you? Never. So different are the standards which are applied to fiction and dramaturgy. If I myself, after the production of your first play, do not praise you, you need not be downcast. I am so foolish as to imagine that what is negligible in a newspaper is negligible also on the stage. I am so dense as to see no difference between the Miss Simpson that is and the Miss Simpson that shall be—between the Miss Simpson and the Captain Hood that are. But this very folly and denseness I have displayed to you, Miss Simpson, for your salvation. And, as a rich and popular dramatist, you will be able to laugh at me—me, splashed with mud by the wheels of your highly-swung barouche, or, at best, riding on an omnibus emblazoned with your name.

AN ACTRESS, AND A PLAY

May 24, 1902

"Sapho," at the Adelphi, is not a play to be admired very warmly by any one who knows Daudet's book, or by any one who does not. Quite evidently, Mr. Clyde Fitch's aim was not to do full justice to Daudet or to himself, but to give a set of glorious chances to Miss Olga Nethersole. And here the chances are, and here is Miss Nethersole, taking them. In part-payment of this debt to America, she has left there nearly all her mannerisms; and thus there is little of the old impediment to our admiration of her great qualities—her originality, her intelligence, her wonderful technique. "What an actress!" is our thought, from first to last, while she glides in and out of innumerable moods, and ranges all the emotions to which humanity is liable. From first to last she has authoritative hold on our attention, and "brava!" is ever on our lips. On the first night (some time ago, now), the critics of the morning-papers were vexed that the curtain did not fall before midnight: how, they asked, were they to get their notices done before their papers went to press? But were not their notices already written out, verbatim, in their heads? Did they have to sit down and enubilate from a general impression of rapture the reasons why they had been pleased? Surely they knew, at every single point in the performance, by what means pleasure was being produced in them. Their pleasure was in the conscious appreciation of those means. They were not surrendering themselves, humbly, to a dramatic illusion. They were taking note of a fine display of histrionic art, a demonstration impressive by reason of its exquisite lucidity. There was nothing to make their hearts beat, but there was a large consignment of furniture delivered in an orderly and businesslike way, for the cells of their brains.

There you have the limitation of Miss Nethersole as an actress. She never touches you through the character impersonated. It is of her art that you are always conscious. Why should this be? The reason is apparent: Miss Nethersole is always conscious of her own art. She stands aloof from her conception of a character and calmly, though lavishly, supplies it with the resources of her art. According to Diderot, of course, this is the one and only right method. But the famous Paradox, though it is quite sound as an academic theory, flatly falls to the ground of experience. We learn by experience that, if a mime lose not himself or herself in his or her part, he or she leaves us inilluded. Now, the state of inillusion is all very well in the case of broad comedy. For, as Elia suggested, in such comedy illusion is not needed—not, as least, to its full extent: there the mime may, and should, exercise a critical as well as a creative faculty. And thus we can account for the posthumous encouragement given to Diderot by M. Coquelin and other comedians who can compass none but the comedic method. Tragedy is quite another matter. In tragedy we must be illuded, touched, thrilled. And this effect can be wrought on us only by a mime whose whole heart and soul are fused indissolubly into the part assumed. Acting is a form of hypnotic suggestion. If a mime believe that he or she is what he (confound the English lack of a common personal pronoun in the singular!) or she is pretending to be, then are we, too, credulous. If there be pity and awe (see how I am trying to dodge that confounded lack!) in the mime's own bosom, then are we, too, sorry and afraid. At least, we are so if the mime's technique, consciously acquired and unconsciously used, be so good as to fit, and to express, exactly and inobtrusively, the mime's own emotions. Then it is for the critic to acclaim a truly great performance in tragedy. This pious office is not imposed on him, and never will be, by Miss Nethersole. But she does afford him the æsthetic pleasure of studying a technique which is, in itself—in its strength and suppleness and sureness—as perfect as a technique can be. And, if he do not recognise, and acclaim loudly, that perfection, he writes himself down a brute impervious to the art of acting.

I apologise to the Stage Society for being so belated in my tribute to its production of "The Lady from the Sea." My only excuse is that the production itself seemed to be belated. Try though I would to blink myself into a belief that my eyes were deceiving me, I had to acknowledge the gaunt solidity of the confronting fact that Ibsen was already old-fashioned. Try as I would to hear the play ringing true, my ears insisted that it was ringing, aye! pealing, false. "Byron is dead!"—can that message have fallen with a more awful suddenness on our grandfathers than "Ibsen is old-fashioned!" falls on us? The news from Missolonghi was at first discredited, and so, in a sense, was broken gently. Similarly, only those who attended the private production of "The Lady from the Sea" will read my news without a hopeful doubt. For us, who were on the spot, the best course is to dash away our tears, see if we can find out the cause of the tragedy, and draw some moral from it. As we listened to the play, was it the technique that seemed out of date? No, that seemed out of date only in the sense that Ibsen is still several years ahead of all his competitors. Was it . . . but there is no need for a process of elimination. It was Ellida, the Lady herself, who was the trouble, diffusing over the footlights the scent of things long kept in lavender. Ellida, as you may remember, is the usual Ibsenist heroine, propounder of the regular Ibsenist ideas. Ah! those ideas, how quaint and tedious they have become! How often we seem to have heard them! How little we care to hear them again! That is the dangerous thing about new ideas : they are old so soon. They are delightfully exciting for a time. But presently one of two sad fates befalls them. Either we accept them, and they become truisms; or, as is the case with Ibsen's femininistic propaganda, we reject them, and they become irritating little old paradoxes, and woe betide the dramatis persona who mouths them for us. If this creature be an authentic human creature, behaving as such, then perhaps we are appeased. But—and here is another danger for the dramatist with ideas—the chances are that the creature has been built primarily as a mouth-piece. Our friend Ellida has been built that way, and so we think of her not as our friend at all, but as a very old acquaintance whom we are anxious to drop. A few years ago we should have been much impressed when she suddenly abandons her aspirations of her soul because her husband gives her leave to elope if she wishes to, or to do anything else that takes her fancy. But then Ibsen's insistence on the equal rights of the sexes—or rather, on the lesser rights of the male sex—was a new idea in drama. We should have overlooked the crude falseness of the psychology, in our excitement over the idea for whose illustration the character had been twisted. But when an idea is old and tattered it is no longer a garment in which a lay-figure can compete with a thing of flesh and blood. Certainly, Ellida must be dropped. And Nora, and all those others? I suppose so. But Time is a cyclist. The things of the day before yesterday are nearer to us than the things of yesterday, and nearer still are the things of the day before the day before. Ellida and the rest, creatures of yesterday, will grow gradually younger, and will doubtless be much admired at the close of the century. Meanwhile, our discovery that they do belong to yesterday is a cruelly sharp reminder of our own advancing years

HONOUR AMONG DRAMATIC CRITICS

June 7, 1902

I have been reading a pamphlet which evoked some fuss in the seventies. In contrast with its title, which sounds curiously modern, its contents are quite ghastly in their obsoleteness. Of the scores of persons satirised in it hardly one is alive now, hardly one has not been forgotten by us since his death. So fleet are the wings of Time that the names bestowed on the various butts of this elaborate pasquinade—names which at the time were flimsiest disguises—are now disguises penetrable only by strong erudition and ingenuity. To understand a tithe of the allusions, which at the time doubtless raised instant laughter throughout the town, we should need now an immense mass of notes composed by elderly and indefatigable commentators. Not in the comedies of Aristophanes himself do we find a denser plexus of petty points to be elucidated than in this pamphlet over which has passed only one quarter of a century. Ah! let the enemies of the satirist, in every age, soften their hearts. Time wreaks on that poor gentleman so summary a vengeance. So soon do the bells of his cap jingle rustily against his skull.

In all this pamphlet nothing has seemed to me more quaintly remote than the section in which are scourged the critics of the contemporary drama. The scene is a tavern near Fleet Street, where various disreputable persons of both sexes foregather in a state of more or less inebriation. This, apparently, is the favourite haunt of the dramatic critics. What is thought of them there is suggested in the speech made by an actor for the instruction of the stranger who has just strayed in. The speech runs thus (but let me save space by writing the verses continuously): "Don't be hard on the critics, sir. Poor things! They've got their little weaknesses, no doubt. They 'cut up' hardly, foolishly they praise; they're apt to sit out first performances at the refreshment-bar or nearest 'pub,' where they'll ask 'How's it going?' and record a triumph or failure from the answers. . . . They've all three acts somewhere about them, acts that must be played, acts that must find a manager, a stage, a company. What would you have them

15   209

do? Why damn the wittols who won't hear of it, and puff the houses where they have a chance." How infinite a gulf yawns between now and then! Of course, one narrows it with a margin for satirical exaggeration. The dramatic critics were never, doubtless, even in the seventies, quite so desperate a gang as is here depicted for us. There are some white sheep in every fold. Nevertheless, if you consult any trustworthy cockney who is old enough to have been behind the scenes of that period, he will give you an account tallying roughly with the account given in this satire. Also, if you consult the average provincial whose knowledge of things is based on vague hearsay, he or she will tell you that in London to-day the dramatic critics are beset with all kinds of temptations to dishonesty, and that they more often than not succumb. Thus does the secret truth of one generation become the common fallacy of the next. I am afraid it would be useless for me to try to enlighten the provinces: they would construe my protest as merely an ebullition of *esprit de corps* and guilty conscience. But for my own pleasure, and for the pleasure of any one else who knows the true facts, it is worth while to inquire how and why it is that dramatic criticism has, in so short a time, undergone so great a change, becoming so very respectable indeed.

To a certain extent, an art is affected in its welfare by the quality of its critics. Good critics are good for it, bad critics are bad for it. But only an art that is by way of doing well can hope to have good critics. An art that is sunk in a slough of incompetency will cry in vain to good critics to rescue it. If it struggles out of the slough and begins to cleanse itself, then the good critics will draw near and show a friendly interest. Well! you must remember that in the seventies and early eighties English drama was almost wholly in the hands of miserable hacks whose highest accomplishment was the making of adaptations from French plays. As an art, it did not exist: it was simply one of the less lucrative trades. Accordingly, the task of criticising it was tossed to the fools. In the newspaper offices any reporter was considered good enough to "do" a new play. The only doubt was whether he were not *too* good, whether he had not better be kept in on the chance of a fire or a murder or some other event of real import. But towards the close of the eighties a strange thing happened. English drama began to struggle in the slough. Crying aloud for help, it struggled, slowly and painfully, towards hard dry ground. It has now, for some time, been out of the slough. It has been making honourable efforts to purge itself of the mire that cakes it—efforts great enough to conciliate quite intelligent and artistic persons who would not, previously, have touched it with a barge-pole. At first there were but one or two of these tardy good Samaritans; but their number has multiplied apace. Now even the editors of the daily papers—some of them, at any rate—have so far moved with the times (and with the "Times") that they prefer to have their dramatic criticism done well. Like the editors of weekly papers, they seek a man of real ability, a man who can observe, and think, and feel, and perhaps write. But, of course, this kind of man is not going to devote himself wholly to dramatic criticism. He has other stakes in life or in art, and it would not pay him to withdraw them. Thus, if one analysed a list of the intelligent dramatic critics (and this would be a fairly exhaustive list, since almost all the duffers have died out), one would find two civil servants, a barrister in good practice, two poets, an essayist, a political secretary, a caricaturist, the editor of a monthly review, several men whose main business is in reviewing books, and other men in various other callings. Indeed, I do not think there is one who is merely a dramatic critic. There are only two whom one would describe as being primarily dramatic critics. With these two exceptions, the men who write about plays regard the work as a mere parergon. They are in the theatre, but not of it. They treat it seriously enough, but it is for them only a small thing in their lives. Now, for the average dramatic critic of the seventies the theatre was by no means a small thing. For him it was the predominant factor in his life. A man of no account, with merely the knack of reeling out ungrammatical copy, he was delighted to find that the task of writing about the theatre gave him an actual importance in one sphere—the theatrical sphere. He found that mimes made up to him, and he blushingly culti-vated the society of these, the only people who did not ignore him. He found them willing even to pay him, in one way or another, for favours received—him who had never, in his most sanguine hour, dreamed of being able to confer the smallest favour on any human being. He found that he could make money through plays which could never be acted, if he offered them to the right managers.

The poor fellow's head was turned. And he became a scamp—he whom Nature had intended to be only a fool.

The modern dramatic critics are immune from moral danger because they have, as I said, greater interests outside the theatre than inside it. They do not cultivate the society of mimes and managers: their ways are far aloof. Of course they do, now and again, in the chances of social intercourse, meet mimes and managers. And, being human, they cannot but be affected in favour of persons who behave agreeably to them. But their heads are not turned, their integrity is not undermined, for they are already accustomed to being treated agreeably. They may alter the manner, but they do not alter the matter, of their future criticisms of a mime or manager whom they have met. They have too much respect for their work, and too much care for their reputations, to let themselves be really "got at" through sentiment. Of course, if one of them happens to write a play, and that play is accepted by a manager, he does feel unwilling to attack other plays produced by that manager. But then, if his play is a success, he instantly retires from dramatic criticism and devotes himself to dramaturgy. If his play is a failure, his aforesaid self-respect and caution save him from doing wrong. He is so afraid of being deceived by his gratitude, and of being thought venal, that he errs invariably on the side of harshness whenever he criticises his champion's other productions. . . . But all this is well known in London. I find myself, after all, addressing the provinces. They mayn't believe me, but I do assure them that we dramatic critics are, like the Metropolitan Police Force, a very fine body of men.

"LA VEINE"

July 19, 1902

Luck—a hateful thing, is it not? As moralists, you hate it. As rationalists, you hate it. However deplorable your own conduct, you wish, as you watch the struggle of life, bad people to go under, and good people to come up smiling to the top. Yet are

you often forced to own that the old comparison between the unrighteous and the green bay tree still holds good. And alas! not
only the clever unrighteous, but also the stupid unrighteous, often
flourisheth before your eyes. "Why," you ask, "has So-and-So
got on so well? He is not brilliant. In fact, his brain is rather
below the average. Yet . . . ." Your rational sense insisting on
some sort of explanation of So-and-So's success, you murmur
something about "force of character." But, as often as not, So-
and-So happens to have a receding chin and a wandering eye.
You find yourselves brought up—bump!—against the dead wall of
Luck. M. Maeterlinck has lately scaled this wall, and peered
over it, and assured you, for your comfort, that there is something
on the other side of it—something really rational. A lucky man,
according to M. Maeterlinck, is one who, in a previous incarnation, was a sage. In him, hidden deep down in his soul, the old
wisdom and foresight linger unsuspected, prompting him to do
or not to do this thing or that; and he, unconsciously, obeys these
promptings, and so, mysteriously, prospers. This is a pretty
explanation, and one is eager to accept it. I fancy that M. Capus,
however, would laugh it to scorn. It is quite impossible that
Julien Bréard, the hero of "La Veine," was ever a sage, even in the
remotest incarnation, so grossly sensual and earthy a creature is
he now. And yet, through no quality except luck, he rises triumphantly from point to point, and is still rising when the final curtain hides him from us. M. Capus evidently regards the incidence
of Luck as a pure fluke. "Je crois," says Bréard (and the speech
is one of those in which the author, rather than the character,
seems to be speaking), "je crois que tout homme pas trop sot, pas
trop timide, a dans la vie son heure de veine, un moment où les
autres hommes semblent travailler pour lui, où les fruits viennent
se mettre à portée de sa main . . . Cette heure-là, c'est triste à
dire, mais ce n'est ni le travail, ni le courage, ni la patience qui
nous la donne. Elle sonne à une horloge qu'on ne voit pas, et
tant qu'elle n'a pas sonné pour nous, nous avons beau déployer
tous les talents et toutes les vertus, il n'y a rien à faire, nous sommes
des fétus de paille." There you have the whole philosophy of the
play. "Comme c'est faux, ce que vous dites là, et surtout
décourageant!" cries the woman to whom Bréard has expounded
it. Nevertheless, it turns out to be not at all false in Bréard's

case. The hour of luck strikes presently for him, and he, though he is weak and lazy and of no more than average intelligence, becomes a rich and famous man, apparently self-made, with a brilliant future in the Chamber of Deputies. Naturally, this demonstration by M. Capus has made most of the dramatic critics very angry. Like Charlotte Lanier, they declare it to be false and discouraging. Discouraging it may be. But that it is not wholly false is testified for any one of us by a score of instances in life. It is, at any rate, much less false and frivolous than that notion which the average critic accepts so respectfully from the average dramatist—the notion of virtue triumphant in the end.

M. Capus has been chidden also for the low moral tone revealed by every character in his play. "They have," writes one shocked critic, "no more morals than have monkeys." Precisely. And that is the very reason why it is absurd for any one to be shocked. You are not shocked by the thought of what goes on in the branches of a primeval forest, for there, as you know, there is no consciousness of moral law. Monkeys are not wicked, because they are not consciously wicked. If we sent into their midst missionaries who could learn their language and teach them clearly the differences (as determined by us) between right and wrong, and if, thereafter, the monkeys still persisted in their traditional licence, we should have the right to regard them as wicked, and to be shocked by them. Turn, now, to the characters in this play. The first scene is the interior of a Parisian flower-shop. Three girls, wiring flowers, discuss the comparative advantages of being and not being "honnête." Two of them think that a girl who is so has the better chance of being happy and successful in the long run. A third inclines strongly to the opposite view. She does her duty in her present state of life, but her ideal is to be the mistress of a millionaire. Enter the "patronne" of the shop, an amiable, respectable, hard-working woman. The question is referred to her. She replies, "Si c'est un conseil que vous me demandez, je vous dirai de rester honnêtes le plus longtemps que vous pourrez; d'abord vous ne risquez rien. Mais le jour où le hasard vous fera rencontrer un homme qui vous aimera et que vous aimerez aussi, tâchez de ne plus le quitter" etc., etc. Later, enters a gentleman to buy a button-hole. A millionaire, he offers leisure and luxury to the girl who has been dreaming of him.

When he has gone, the girl reports to the patronne the offer and its acceptance. "Vous ne me gardez rancune?" she asks. "Moi?" laughs the patronne. "Je te souhaite qu'une chose, c'est d'être parfaitement heureuse. Tu vas mener la vie que tu désirais. Tâche de ne pas perdre la tête." Try not to lose your head: that is the one golden rule of sexual conduct known to the characters throughout the play. Conventional morality in sex is not flouted by them: it does not exist for them. They are, for the most part, honest, industrious, kindly, unselfish folk; but the notion of chastity or continence as a good thing, and of unchastity or incontinence as a bad thing, in itself, is a notion of which no glimmer is revealed to them. Consequently, they are blameless, one and all, for their wrong-doing. To be shocked by them argues a hopeless confusion of mind. Let our dramatic critics reserve their indignation for those other plays, in which the characters are self-conscious winkers and gigglers over their own misconduct, taking us into their confidence, and inviting us to wink and giggle with them. Such plays are not at all uncommon on our virtuous native stage, and no man need be ashamed of being shocked by them.

Perhaps the play's wholly non-moral atmosphere detracts somewhat from the value of it as a picture of life. In life such an atmosphere is found only in places where there is wealth and leisure. The characters in "La Veine" belong mostly to the poor and hard-working class. In France—as will be granted by any one whose knowledge of France is not based wholly on hearsay—this class is even more strongly under the influence of morality than it is in England. And thus, M. Capus . . . But here I have been solemnly weighing the play as a philosophy of life, and as a representation of life, when all the while I ought to have been writing of it as what it so pre-eminently is: a little comedy shimmering all through with a humour that is not quite like any other. I shall return to it next week.

COMEDY IN FRENCH AND ENGLISH

July 26, 1902

Certainly, in my province, the prime event of this season has been the introduction of M. Capus. "La Veine," and now "Les Deux Écoles"—how fresh, tart, bubblesome a beverage, briskly refreshing our palates and dispelling the taste of so much foregoing stodge! Last week, foolishly, I did not just quaff "La Veine," but gravely sipped it, rolled it over my tongue, held it up to the light, discussing it as though it had been some full-bodied and blood-making wine that must have a full and solemn justice done to it. True, there was more body in "La Veine" than there is in a dozen of our usual headache-giving native comedies. Throughout it was a philosophic idea, cunningly treated, and a central figure who was a general type delineated with acutest fidelity; and all the other figures in it were credible human beings behaving in accord to their several natures. But, for all that, the play's point, its pre-eminent merit, was in the exquisite fun and lightness of its dialogue. In a criticism of "Les Deux Écoles" ponderousness were even more amiss. This play, even more than the other, depends for its triumph on its dialogue. It is not, like the other, a philosophic comedy, but a philosophic farce. It is permeated by quite a good comedic idea; to wit, that a woman must choose between two kinds of husband—the solid, upright man who will be faithful to her, boring her all the while, and the high-spirited man against whose delightful presence must be set by her his frequent absence. But the idea is treated in the convention of farce. There is the young wife divorcing her light husband, and subsequently betrothed to "der solide Mensch." (Why does this German phrase seem more expressive than "l'homme sérieux"? The type indicated is really quite as common in France as in Germany. The only difference is that, whereas in Germany it is extolled, in France it is laughed at.) And there is the husband lightly turning to a cocotte. And then there is a quadrille. The "solide Mensch" wearies his betrothed, who forgives and remarries her divorced husband, while the cocotte is fascinated by the 'solide Mensch," and he in his turn is fascinated by her. The whole action of the play is wrought thus in a prescribed pattern. The characters are not left, as in "La Veine," to do what they like. Realistic enough on the surface, they are but conventional puppets, manipulated for no purpose but that of laughter. The play, in fact, is a farce. As such, rightly, it is performed by the company. One member of the cast is somewhat too farcically farcical. M. Guy, as Le Hautois, has not the right kind of solidity. He does not preserve the proper surface of realism. A Sir Willoughby Patterne was evidently the intention of M. Capus; but M. Guy appears as a Chadband. No woman in the world could respect such a creature, could deem him not altogether ludicrous and impossible from the outset. And thus is queered the necessary balance between him and the divorced husband. Moreover the fun of his ultimate downfall thus loses all its edge. The part of Le Hautois is a good instance of the much-broken law that in farce the characters must not necessarily be made ridiculous by their interpreters. In farce, very often, the fun of a character is proportionate to the seriousness with which its interpreter takes it, or to the charm with which he invests it, or to . . . But again I wax ponderous—ponderous though M. Capus' dialogue is still ringing so lightly and brightly in my ears. How shall I describe to you that delicious sound? What is the peculiar quality of it? I might quote for you instances of M. Capus' wit, as when one of his characters remarks "La foule est aussi une solitude. Qui a dit cela?" and another replies "C'est un homme qui n'est jamais allé à un rendez-vous." Or I might quote for you instances of the humour—that soft, irresponsible humour, so much more Irish than French—pervading and illumining every scene in either play. But of what avail is it to snap-shot summer-lightning? The virtue of M. Capus' humour, as of all good dramatic humour, is in its context. You cannot separate it, cut it out, transfer it. Besides, it is a humour made to be spoken, not written. A delicate Irish humour, expressed in the French language, spoken by French voices—that is the nearest expression I can find for the secret of the delight offered to us at the Garrick Theatre.

What a perennial delight there is in hearing the French language spoken! A year or two ago I evoked in these columns, unwittingly, a long and ardent discussion by saying that the French language seemed to me an unsatisfactory vehicle for the higher kinds of poetry, for that it was too clear, too neat, too keen—incapable of leaving anything to the imagination. And that opinion is still fixed in my insular mind. But, though I thus depreciate the French language in its appeal to the soul, I yield to none in my admiration of it as a supreme means to slighter ends. For languages, as for animals, there are, it seems to me, two sexes. There are masculine languages and feminine languages. Of those of which I can speak with any familiarity, ancient Greek is the only one that seems to me hermaphroditic, combining fully in itself masculine strength and feminine grace. Latin, of course, is wholly masculine; but French, its descendant, is wholly feminine. And, even as among human beings the great things are conceived always in the brains of men, and executed by men's hands, while many little things can be conceived and executed incomparably better by women than by men, so are the feminine languages incomparably better adapted than the masculine to such lighter tasks as ordinary conversation, though they cannot compete with the masculine in those graver tasks, of which poetry is an example. In French how quickly, how neatly, how gracefully, you can say just what you want to say to your interlocutor! How blunt and heavy and ugly an old instrument, in comparison, English seems! And, since one of the aims of realistic modern comedy is to reproduce succinctly the language of ordinary life, it follows that the French comic dramatist starts thus far happily ahead of any English rival. His words are winged. They fly straight across the footlights of their own accord. They do not have to be packed up in bundles and hurled at us. They come flying to us of their own accord, swiftly, unerringly, ever so prettily. Certainly, were I a dramatist, I should never forgive Fate for not making me a Frenchman too. As a critic, whenever I see a French comedy, I am always glad that I am English, for that so I have a standard of comparison enabling me to realise and enjoy those blessings which the Frenchman (contemptuously ignorant of any language but his own) takes simply as a matter of course.

Nor is the language which is his medium the sole handicap for the English comic dramatist. The French dramatist is always likelier to be well interpreted by his mimes. In French acting we are conscious always of something that is lacking even in the best of English acting. We may assure one another, patriotically that if French mimes were acting English characters they would fare as ill as English mimes acting French characters, and that the sole difference is the difference of nationality. But we know, in our heart of hearts, that there is an intrinsic superiority in French acting, not to be explained away. The fact is, of course, that the French are a naturally expressive race. It is natural for them to express themselves through facial play and gesture, as mimes must, and through modulations of the voice. It is not natural for us to do so. And thus, whereas the English mime has to use art to cover up the fact that he is doing what Nature did not mean him to do, the French mime need use art merely to do as well as possible what Nature did intend him to do. This is a great saving of time. And, accordingly, the French mime is like to acquire a far greater proficiency than the English mime in the various tricks of his art. His personality may be no more—may be much less—impressive or amusing than the personality of this or that English rival; but he has the pull of superior art. To say that there are not bad French mimes were as absurd as to say that there are not good English ones. My contention is merely that the average French mimes are better than the average English, and that the best English are inferior to the best French. I should like to know in what English theatre we could hope to see a comedy played so perfectly as "La Veine" and "Les Deux Écoles." And yet none of the performers is an imposing genius. Madame Granier lacks magnetism, and has no peculiar charm. Yet, so perfect is she in her art, that one would willingly give in exchange for her a round dozen of our leading-ladies, and would even throw in one or two of our actresses. M. Guitry, again, brings nothing save his art; yet the gift is ample. As for Madame Lavallière and M. Brasseur, each of those drolls is quite unlike any other creature in the world; and I feel that life in England without a stereoscopi-cinematophonograph of them both will hardly be worth living.

A PRETTY PLAY SPOILT

September 20, 1902

The theme of "Quality Street" (produced last Wednesday a the Vaudeville Theatre) is that of "The Finding of Nancy." Mr. Barrie sets out to show us, as did Miss Syrett, the tragedy of a girl in whom joy of life is being sapped by years of drudgery—a girl growing old without benefit of girlhood. But nothing could be more different than the spirit in which the two authors have touched their theme. Here we have the essential difference between masculine and feminine. Miss Syrett it is who sounded the masculine note, Mr. Barrie now chiming in with the feminine Miss Syrett went straight to the root of the matter, strong and unflinching. Mr. Barrie hovers around it, smiling and sobbing in a very pretty and becoming manner, and quite sure that we shall all liken him to an April day. Commercially, it is well for Mr. Barrie that he behaves thus, since the average playgoer loves this kind of behaviour as deeply as he is disturbed and annoyed by Miss Syrett's kind. Artistically, too, it is well for Mr. Barrie Neither his humour nor his pathos blends well with any attempt to create seriously from the materials of real life. In his description of Thrums he was always delightful, for the very reason that his Scotch peasants were as remote from reality as are the Irish fairies of Mr. Yeats. They were just the creatures of his humour and pathos, to be irresponsibly enjoyed by us. But when Mr Barrie begins, as he began in his book "Tommy and Grizel" and in his play "The Wedding Guest," to try to tackle seriously the serious real things around him, then his pathos runs to mawkishness, and his fun is apt to jar; then, moreover, his fundamental ignorance of any kind of life outside the local colour invented by him degenerates into something of a nuisance. So I am glad that of his latest theme he has made merely a little fairy story, with characters not pretending to be more than shadows cast by characters of Miss Jane Austen, and performing a shadow-dance of a strictly theatrical kind. Into such characters and incidents as we have here may be infused quite agreeably any amount of Mr Barrie's famous mixture—I refer not to the most famous one of all known to us through the advertisements of tobacconists, but to that tears-and-laughter mixture, which, I am glad to think, must have been found almost equally saleable. "Quality Street," in fact, is a thing done in Mr. Barrie's right manner. I cannot describe it better than by saying that it is "sweetly pretty." It is perhaps the sweetliest prettiest thing yet done by Mr. Barrie. And if it do not become in England one of his most lucrative things, the fault will be not his, but rather the fault of its English interpreters.

Ironically enough, the play suffers in interpretation through the very fact which is its main motive: that women are ashamed of being no longer young or of not looking young. When first is shown to us the parlour in Quality Street, Miss Phœbe Throssell is twenty years old, Miss Susan thirty or so. Miss Phœbe is held to be marriageable, but Miss Susan is regarded as being far past the period of her attractions—a creature irremeably on the shelf. Yet I vow that Miss Marion Terry, as Miss Susan, might have passed, physically, for an ingénue. And in exactly similar case were three ladies who impersonated three spinsters coæval with Miss Susan. After the first act (according to the programme) nine years elapse. Not with so much as a wing of gossamer do they touch Miss Susan. The lady has not aged by one fraction of a second. Nor have her three coævals. Nor has her little sister. And yet, according to Mr. Barrie, the little sister is now a confirmed sufferer from headache and "tired eyes" and other grievous symptoms of eld, hastened by the drudgery of keeping a school. Insomuch that Valentine Brown, remembering her as she was, and now, after long years of absence, seeing her as she is, is stung to the quick by the horrid pathos of it all. So is the elder sister. So is every one—every one, I mean, who does not happen to be on the other side of the footlights. To every one who does happen to be in that position, and who sees on the stage not a single female arrived at years of discretion, all this talk about the tragedy of growing old and forfeiting all that in life is lovely does not ring truly enough to draw the number of tears which intrinsically it deserves of us. Without the illusion of coming eld Mr. Barrie's play is pointless. I urge Mr. Barrie to go angrily down to the theatre and call a dress-rehearsal and insist on his rights. Of course, Miss Marion Terry and Miss Ellaline Terriss and the rest

might argue that the notion of a woman being necessarily les
attractive at the age of thirty than at the age of twenty was a
absurd notion, refutable by thousands of cases to be found in rea
life. But let not Mr. Barrie be drawn into any consideration o
modern actuality. He has a perfectly sound case to go on. It i
true that in England, at this time, women remain young in aspec
and in spirit for an unconscionably long time. But the fashion i
quite recent. You need not go so far back as to the daguerreo
types in quest of a time when women put all grace or coquetr
aside, resigning themselves to middle age, as soon as their thirtiet
birthday was upon them. Even a lustre ago, the woman of thirty
dressed and behaved like an old maid, even as the youngest mar
ried woman dressed and behaved like a matron. Even to-da
you need go no further than Germany to find an exact parallel t
that curious state of things. The standards by which youth and
age are judged (and, therefore, youth and age themselves) vary i
various times and places. I suppose that the more artificial th
society, and the more self-conscious its pursuit of life, the greate
is the tendency to prolong that period of life which is regarded a
most pleasant. In any case, the fact remains that in the early par
of last century, which is the period of Mr. Barrie's play, wome
looked, and felt themselves to be, well-stricken in years at an ag
that seems to us vernal. And the wilful disregard of that fact b
the ladies engaged at the Vaudeville is a fault crying for rectifica
tion. It is strange that even the best actresses are inclined to b
women first and artists afterwards. And it is a pity that author
and stage-managers do not strive more manfully to reverse tha
order.

I wish it were half so easy to explain what good acting is as t
explain what isn't good acting. Such is the disparity between th
two tasks that one is always laying oneself open to the charge o
ungraciousness. How much more pleasant it would be now t
spend my time in praise of Miss Marion Terry, with ever so brie
a disparagement of Miss Ellaline Terriss, than to spend it in th
following manner! But what can I say of Miss Terry, excep
such words as "sensibility" and "grace" and "sincerity" and s
forth? I might add how glad I was to see a woman really feelin
the part she was acting, really identifying herself with it (in spirit
though not in aspect). But how tame all that would be, ho

unilluminating! I might try to analyse Miss Terry's technique; but with what chance of success? Is not the whole virtue of technique to be invisible, to defy analysis? On the other hand, Miss Ellaline Terriss offers a handle for something better than vague platitude, by reason of the very fact that she does not even begin to act—not, at least, in any strict sense of the word. She walks and talks very prettily, and is very pretty altogether. But never for one moment does she forget herself, still less merge herself for us, in the part she is playing. And in "Quality Street," alas! she is playing a very important part—a part on which rests quite a half of the play's burden, a part requiring infinite skill. All she does with it, in the lighter scenes, is to coo and nestle appealingly towards the audience, as though she were speaking the tag of an old English comedy; whilst in the emotional scenes she is like nothing but a school-girl repeating a lesson at the top of her voice. The voice, I repeat, is very pretty, and—but no! why qualify? Miss Terriss, flushed by the applause of her un-critical audience, and by the pæans of critics who think it safer not to discriminate between chalk and cheese, can face with equani-mity my little plain truth. Of Mr. Seymour Hicks, as Valentine Brown, all that can be said is that from the moment of his first entry into the Miss Throssells' parlour he behaves only as though he were playing football; and all that can be hopefully suggested to him is that he might try, by degrees, to make it parlour-football. The rules of the latter game are, I believe, quite simple—simpler far, anyhow, than the rules of acting.

ILL-CHOSEN BACKGROUNDS AT DRURY LANE

October 4, 1902

Whether Oxford have reason to curse the memory of Mr. Rhodes is a point which Time alone can settle. Whether those forthcoming bevies of young Colonials *sans peur et sans reproche*, and of similar young Americans, will be easily absorbed, with all their perfections on their heads, and adapted to their environment, or whether they will produce atmospheric disturbances, unsettling the traditions of a place whose whole charm and use is in the placid maintenance of its traditions—whether, in fact, the newcomers will or won't be a great nuisance, we cannot tell until we have seen something of them. Meanwhile, the Benign Mother has acquired a fame wider than ever came to her in the past. She has been enormously puffed by the popular press. Her history has been recounted in long special articles, and the eccentricities of her character have been touched off, not unkindly, in innumerable paragraphs. Her name has been bandied freely and knowingly among those classes which had hitherto regarded her merely as an annual excuse for a bet. And now comes for her the proud corollary of being introduced by Mr. Cecil Raleigh, with a flourish, into the latest melodrama at Drury Lane.

Her début, I regret to say, was not an unqualified success. She was there to display her well-known accomplishment of "whispering to us the last enchantments of the middle age"; and she did her best; but somehow the whispers did not get across the footlights. One sighed for the Lawn at Ascot, or for the Promenade of the Empire Theatre, or for the Central Lobby of the House of Commons—for any of those more lurid scenes which Mr. Raleigh had lavished on us in other years. Oxford in Oxfordshire is as irresistible a city as was ever built by Time; but by very reason of one of her own dearest charms Oxford is unable to quit herself creditably in Drury Lane. She is not hustling enough. Some grey walls and towers, some old men in long black gowns, some young men in short black gowns—these, with nothing more (and what more is there?), do not compass much of an effect in the kind of melodrama which is made to be spectacular before all things. Mr. Raleigh felt this instinctively. So, to enliven the milieu, on he brought a circus procession, with Mrs. John Wood as Britannia, and other sops for the eager jaws of his patrons. And Oxford had to take a back seat.

Poor Oxford! Will she, I wonder, ever be made successfully the background for a play, or for a novel? It is curious that of all the stories devoted to a portrayal of Oxford "Verdant Green" is the only one in which Oxford's spirit has been caught. And "Verdant Green" is avowedly farcical. What is it that prevents the serious novelist from catching the spirit of the place? I suppose it is his fear of eliminating sex. Without sex, he is sure, there can be no human interest; and so the mainspring of every Oxford story is the love of an undergraduate for Miss So-and-So; and so every Oxford story falls right out of focus. It is true that since the Fellows have been permitted to marry, and to take unto themselves little red-brick villas in the environs, and since the foundation of Somerville and Lady Margaret Hall, Oxford has in itself quite a large feminine element. But the spirit of the place, so far as the undergraduates are concerned, is still the ancient spirit of celibacy. Roughly, it is true that in a young girl the desire for erudition is never allied to physical comeliness, and that to be a Don's wife in the Parks is not a choice ever made by a woman who has the chance of any other kind of married life. But the spirit of celibacy among undergraduates is not explicable through these incidental rules. There are exceptions to these rules. Now and again feminine comeliness occurs in Oxford, and you will hear undergraduates professing admiration of it; but only a very light, remote kind of admiration is theirs, by no means distracting them from the usual tenour of their life. Sport, athletics, books, and, above all, good-fellowship—these are the things that make up the lives of the undergraduates, these are their true interests. The instinct of sex is dormant, and, even if it happen to be stirred in vacation, it quickly relapses in term. And thus, to any one who knows Oxford well, the kind of novel which has hitherto been written about Oxford rings persistently false. There is a great chance for the novelist who shall accept the limitations of Oxford as a milieu, and write sincerely in the plenty of room left to him. But though fiction is ripe for a treatment of these academic materials—friendship, intellectual development and so forth—the stage is not yet, never perhaps will be, ripe for them. Certainly, nothing could be more unripe for them than the stage of Drury Lane. And, since Oxford does not afford the kind of scenic excitement which Drury Lane demands, I think Mr. Raleigh should have shunned it altogether. True, having got the circus into it, he bundles us out of it, so far as South Africa, with all possible speed. Nor are we again reminded of its existence, except at one delicious moment when a Boer who has got through the British lines is saved from instant execution by the plea that he, having been educated at St. Simon's

16   225

College, Oxford, has just remembered that it is Boat Race day and has slipped in to drink success to the crew with an English officer who had been his contemporary at the dear old place. Nevertheless, the atmosphere of Oxford, that damp and insidious atmosphere, seems to overhang the rest of the play, and South Africa seems positively relaxing.

I doubt whether South Africa could, in any case, have been exhilarating. Had Mr. Raleigh treated the war from a sternly patriotic point of view, showing the Boers to be cunning and cowardly savages, the audience would not, I think, have been roused to enthusiasm. Two years ago that kind of thing would have gone down very well; but now that the war is over, the shrill voice of Jingoism would, I fancy, somewhat jar the public's ear. The very fact that Mr. Raleigh, avowedly a man who tries to write exactly the kind of thing which the public wants, did not assume that shrill voice is proof presumptive of the change in the public's feeling. I welcome the change, and I am glad to think that the voice which Mr. Raleigh has assumed this year is a voice better attuned to the public's ear. But I protest that he goes rather too far in his dulcet chivalry. He hardly gives the English a look in: almost everything is sacrificed to a sympathetic statement of the Boer case, to an exposition of Boer simplicity and bravery; and in the whole play the one really well-drawn character, the one part of which an actor can make anything, is the part of an aged commandant. The British officers are so many insignificant nine-pins, dotted around, while the aged commandant, as large as life, stands firmly in the middle of the stage, in a blaze of lime-light, being most awfully pathetic, all the time. Mr. Raleigh might argue that at Drury Lane a golden mean turns to lead—that you must run to one extreme or the other. Doubtless, that argument would be quite sound. But it would merely clinch my point, that Mr. Raleigh ought to have left South Africa severely alone. The war is now remote enough for the public not to hate the Boers. But it is not so remote that the public can regard the Boer cause as something infinitely finer and more sympathetic than its own. The sporting instinct to favour the weaker side cannot be expected of the stronger combatant until the combat has passed into remote history. And therefore, at present, South Africa can make no wide dramatic appeal. I offer to Mr. Raleigh, too late, another, a simpler, reason for leaving the war alone. We are all so heartily sick of the very mention of the war. It continued for a long time, and there was a horde of professional and amateur writers incessantly describing it for us; insomuch that now we sicken at the sight of such words as "kopjes" and "khaki," and sicken accordingly when we see kopjes and khaki on the stage.

Altogether, it seems to me that in the selection of backgrounds which will please the public—and that is the art (if Mr. Raleigh will excuse the word) of writing dramas for Drury Lane—Mr. Raleigh has not shown his usual tact. I have no doubt that the public will go in its myriads to Drury Lane. But it will go rather by force of annual habit than by force of desire to see what is to be seen there.

THE VALUE OF "SYMPATHY" IN DRAMA

October 25, 1902

What we call "sympathy" is essential to a tragic play. To a farce it is fatal. If a man pursued by the Furies evoke from us nothing but a sporting interest as to which will win the race, Melpomene will disown him. Conversely, if he, sitting down on a basket of eggs or collapsing through a cucumber frame, wring from our hearts the tribute of pity and awe, the Muse of Farce—'Arriet, or whatever her classic name may be—will none of him. There are not Furies in every tragic play, nor cucumber frames and baskets of eggs in every farce. The persons and properties may be precisely the same in a farce as in a tragedy. The two forms differ essentially not in their materials but in the emotions at which they aim. Equally promising material for either form is, for example, a man unhappily married to one woman and in love with another. It is quite easy to make us weep with him or laugh at him, to make him tragic or farcical, without making the slightest addition to or subtraction from his actual circumstances. All that the dramatist need do is to make him either a sympathetic or a ridiculous person.

Midway between the forms of farce and tragedy lies the form of comedy. And here there is no necessary inclusion or exclusion of sympathy. Comedy may make her appeal either to the emotional or to the intellectual side of us, she may make us either care what happens to her puppets or merely be interested in seeing what happens to them. Comedy, in fact, may have it both ways. But not, I gather, in England to-day. There seems to be a decree that to-day in England comedy shall be ever thumping the lachrymal chords in us: "hands off" is the shriek if she stretch a tentative finger towards our intellects. The dearth of intellectual comedy is, indeed, one of the most lamentable features of our stage. In France such comedy is not at all rare: there is a veritable school of it, flourishing blithely. Why this difference? I suppose because we are such a solemn race, a race believing that laughter must necessarily be a frivolous function, quite incompatible with any working of the brain, and believing that the only good excuse for laughter is a plenteous admixture of those tears which we, being also a very sentimental race, have always on tap. And I hazard the further reason that we, being what we nationally are rather in virtue of stubborn strength of character than in virtue of brain-power, and having indeed remarkably little brain-power, but having a certain shrewdness of our own, are anxious to husband such brain-power as we have, jealously storing it for business-hours, and sternly refusing to waste it over an art which, so far from putting anything into our pockets, takes something out of them. Yet another possible reason is to be found in the mimes themselves. The acceptance or refusal of plays at almost every theatre depends, directly or indirectly, on the will of some eminent mime. And almost always the dear desire of an eminent mime is to appear in a sympathetic part. A long part, a strong part, a part demanding keen intelligence, a part giving scope for display of technical skill—these, in their way, are all very well for him, but ever his loadstar is a sympathetic part. I believe this preference to be a thing of recent growth. In every age, of course, the mime has confused himself with the parts assumed by him, and has been confused so by the public. That is in the stupid nature of things. But in the old days, when the mime, outside the theatre, was regarded as an uninteresting outcast with no private life to speak of, it mattered little to him whether or not the public liked him personally. But now that he is as illustrious off as on the boards, it does matter to him very much indeed. Confronted with an unsympathetic part, he sees social ruin staring him in the face—sees his most important friends in the audience gazing with strange cold eyes at him, whispering to one another behind their programmes, determining to drop him. By a definitely anti-pathetic part he is not affrighted. Called on to forge and foreclose, to seduce and murder, he struts bravely forth; for nobody would suspect him, the well-regulated, of doing in his off hours such far-fetched things. But it is not impossible that he might be suspected of not being a really nice man—not a really kind and generous and truthful and sweet-tempered paragon on his inner hearth. And so the untried young dramatist, even the acclaimed and mature dramatist, who submits to him a play without a part to make the hearts of the audience throb in sympathy with him, is sure of a very cold welcome. Of course, there are exceptions—eminent mimes in whom enthusiasm for their art outstrips self-respect. But the rule is as I have adumbrated. And doubtless it is one of the causes of the dearth deplored by me.

An audience's sympathy for one set of characters usually involves antipathy for another set of characters. And it is one of the tests of tact in a dramatist whether the sympathy and anti-pathy fall plump in the directions intended by him. Sometimes the audience shies from his lead, refuses to love his darlings or be appalled by his bogies; and the result is a disagreeable friction between its own instinct and its consciousness of what is expected of it. This is what happens at the Avenue Theatre while "Mrs. Willoughby's Kiss" is being enacted. Mr. Frank Stayton, the author, is said to be very young; and I have high hopes of his future, for his youth betrays itself not in ineptitude for putting a play together, but in ignorance of the public's feelings. That is a fault which time will remedy. It is not a fault at all, so far as the art of dramaturgy is concerned. But it is a deadly fault in point of commercial success. So perhaps Mr. Stayton will bear with me for a few moments of instruction. I find no fault with the outline of his idea. Two married women simultaneously receiving home their husbands who have been in another part of the world for a period of eleven years or so; one of the married women mistaking in the twilight the other's husband for her own and being similarly mistaken by him; a passionate embrace, electric light turned on, mutual embarrassment; later, the woman's discovery that her actual husband is utterly unsuited to her, and the man's discovery that his actual wife is utterly unsuited to him; and their common discovery that they are both perfectly suited to each other; and the doubt whether or not they had better elope. Quite a promising scheme, I think. But it is spoiled (remember that I speak commercially to Mr. Stayton) by the manner in which it has been filled in. Obviously, the sympathy of the audience is claimed by the two lovers. The audience is expected to feel with them the unkindness of the fate which mated them apart, and of the conventions which keep them asunder. But, in order that the audience may come up to scratch, there must be cast at least a rudimentary halo of nobility around the pair, while the other husband and the other wife must appear comparatively bestial. Mr. Stayton has not taken these precautions. He, in the face of a moral public, has drawn no moral difference between the would-be sympathetic characters and the would-be antipathetic. Nay! he has left the latter far better off morally than the former. His plea for the former he bases entirely on æsthetic grounds: Mrs. Willoughby dresses smartly, and has kept her figure, whereas Mrs. Brandram is rather untidy and rather stout. True, they both inhabit the same set of flats in West Kensington, but that is merely for dramatic convenience: in mode of life they are leagues asunder. Mr. Brandram, again, wears a large beard and a shapeless ulster, and orders a glass of milk and a bun. How very different from clean-shaven, well-coated Mr. Willoughby, with his cry for a tankard of ale! But, Mrs. Brandram is a sweet-natured and affectionate wife and mother, and we have no reason to suppose that Mr. Willoughby is not a very good fellow. Mr. Brandram and Mrs. Willoughby have thus a merely snobbish grievance, and a merely snobbish affinity. They fall in love because they think each other "good form." Far be it from me to suggest that such a motive is unnatural or even rare. And far be it from me to suggest that snobbishness is a thing likely to be unintelligible in this island. But I do suggest, and insist, that in the theatre the English public cares much more for morality than for social distinctions, and that it excuses a breach of morality only if the breach be made by strong sentimental passion. With such passion Mr. Brandram and Mrs. Willoughby have not been endowed by their creator. And therefore they win no sympathy at all. Such sympathy as there is goes all to that decent, homely pair, Mr. Willoughby and Mrs. Brandram, who, if they said to each other "What a pity it is that we two comfortable, genial, honest souls should be tied to those two maundering snobs!" and if they forthwith eloped together, would not, I do believe, be blamed by any one. But this kind of sympathy does not save a play. It is no use to have the audience pulling one way and the author another. There must be a sweet consensus.

A WELCOME PLAY

November 15, 1902

I think "The Admirable Crichton" is quite the best thing that has happened, in my time, to the British stage. New ground has been broken before. But the breakage has ever been made too furtively to attract other miners, or too clumsily not to scare them back to the old congested camp; nor, indeed, has the new ground been invariably of the kind that is worth breaking. Keen, then, is my gladness that Mr. Barrie has broken triumphantly, in the eyes of all men, the very ground whose infinite possibilities I have in these columns boomed so long and wistfully. Had the play been written by a tiro, Mr. Frohman would have deserved all our thanks for his courage in producing it. But it needed no courage to produce a play by Mr. Barrie. Is not he established as the prime purveyor of "a good cry"? And was not it quite certain that the whole tear-loving public would come flocking from "Quality Street" to "The Admirable Crichton" for long enough to insure the management against actual loss on the production? The only doubt was whether they would catch the intention of the latter play. It was on the cards that they might treat the butler-hero of it as an excruciatingly pathetic figure, and weep floods of tears over his ultimate fate. In that case, so much the better for the box-office. As it happened, the public seemed on the first night really to understand what Mr. Barrie was driving at, and seemed to delight in his meaning and his method. Not even the interminable entr'actes, due to a strike of stage carpenters, affected the consensus. Always, when a terrified gentleman in evening dress comes before the curtain, and apologises for delays, and appeals to "the British love of fair play," he may absolutely rely on a rapturous salvo from the cosmopolosemitics who make up two-thirds of a first-night audience. But the other third, composed of unflattered Britons, is apt to be rather brutal. Not a sound of brutality assailed the apologist at the Duke of York's. Innumerable last trains were lost without a murmur. Thence my glad deduction that the public is ripe for the drama of modern fantasy.

You might, of course, remind me that the public is unripe for any other kind of drama. It is undeniable that the most successful modern plays are those which are most fantastically untrue to real life. But Mr. Barrie's play differs from them in that it is frankly, and of a purpose, untrue to life. Here we have impossible people, dressed in the fashion of to-day, doing impossible things, and yet (what a relief!) we are not asked to take them seriously (though, as I shall show, there is a quite serious side to them). In the first act, we are not quite in key. Force of habit is too strong for us, and we object that if a nobleman invited his servants to tea once a month, the good breeding of his sons and daughters would enable them to carry the thing off gracefully: they would not, at least, behave as do the sons and daughters of Lord Loam. Also, we object that all Lord Loam's servants (except Crichton, the philosophic butler) belong to a bygone generation—the generation before board-schools. We are not yet attuned to the fantasy, do not yet see the point of the fable. For the play is fable as well as fantasy. It is not, like the "New Arabian Nights," which in many ways it resembles, a mere farcical distortion of modern actuality. It is formed and conditioned by a philosophic idea which bears on a problem of modern life—the problem of domestic service. Slavery was justified by Aristotle on the ground that a certain proportion of men are born with servile natures. "Quite so," says Mr. Barrie, "but *which* men?" He proceeds to show that servility is merely a matter of environment, and that the most servile of slaves may become, in a place where there is free competition, the most masterly of masters, and *vice versâ*. This may not strike you as in itself a startlingly new idea. But it is startlingly new for the theatre. It has been circulating in the outer world only during the past five years or so. It never occurred to us before we began to realise the results of compulsory education. Our slaves are still servile enough, superficially, but we know that many of them are in all respects our superiors. And we feel very guilty and uncomfortable in their presence. We have given to them, and cannot now take away from them, the power to meet us and beat us on our own ground; and who knows how soon they will have the courage to exercise that power? Crichton, the butler, is the type—the fantastically faked type—of these potential monsters blindly created by us. So soon as the Loam family is stranded with him on a desert island, he becomes absolute master of them all. He has not changed in any inherent sense, nor have they. The difference is merely the difference of locality. There is no longer that veneer of custom and tradition which alone prevented Crichton from asserting himself at first. Mr. Barrie might have made us more uncomfortable if, when the Loam family was rescued by a warship and taken home, Crichton had retained something of his influence. As it is, Crichton retires gracefully to a public-house at "the fashionable end" of the Harrow Road, much as Prince Florizel of Bohemia (whom I hope now to see some day upon the stage) retired to a cigar divan in Rupert Street. Nor does the ironic invention mar the logic of Mr. Barrie's lesson. It merely enables even the most thoughtful and nervous of us to smile. Mr. Barrie has always been able to amuse us. But this is the first occasion on which he has succeeded in making us also think. And so he will excuse me for having insisted on the meaning of a play whose chief charm, from first to last, is in the uproarious fun of it.

Bestowing not on Mr. Barrie's name (nor, indeed, on his own) the giddy benefit of capital letters or separate line, "Charles Frohman presents

Miss Irene Vanbrugh

and

Mr. H. B. Irving

in" Mr. Barrie's modest little effort. The form of the announcement is roughly significant of the relative commercial value of mimes and dramatists on the other side (perhaps, too, on this side) of the Atlantic Ocean. But it is rather hard on the two "stars," of whose general lustre and magnitude Mr. Barrie here takes but slight advantage. Neither of them is allowed to shine with more than a modest radiance among the rest, and the authentic "star" of the evening is a no greater person than small-typed, smuggled-in "J. M. Barrie" himself. Admirable is Mr. H. B. Irving, as Crichton, for his air of dignity and authority, and admirable for the appropriate solemnity with which he takes the ironic humour of the part. He is clearly cut out to play the aforesaid Florizel. The only fault in his present performance is a fault of omission: Crichton ought surely to betray an occasional trace of a cockney accent. That he shall be, in our eyes, socially as inferior to his servants on the island as to his employers in England is not less important a point than that throughout he shall seem to us morally and intellectually superior to them. Mr. Irving seems to be socially the equal of the Loam family throughout. And thus something of the irony implicit in the family's subjection is lost for us. His love-scene with Lady Mary, his chivalrous determination to raise her to his own (insular) social position, would be much funnier, and more significant, if there were between the two characters the difference of tone that marks the plebeian from the aristocrat. That Mr. Irving made himself too distinguished was the more a pity for that Miss Irene Vanbrugh, as Lady Mary, made herself too little so. When an actress succeeds signally in one part, she is told evermore by the critics that she has not yet ridded herself of that part's influence. Often this charge is quite unjust—a mere parrot-cry. But it does seem to me that Miss Irene Vanbrugh has indeed not yet shed the slough of Miss Sophie Fullgarney. She lacks the repose that once was hers. She is always making little skittish efforts, nodding and becking and wreathing smiles out of season. All these tricks were right and proper in the portrayal of such a young person as Miss Fullgarney. But the part of Lady Mary needs the quietism of good breeding, to bring out its irony and the irony of the whole theme. Miss Vanbrugh should live among poppies for a while.

MR. BARRETT AS KING ALFRED

December 27, 1902

"Elusive" is not, perhaps, the obvious epithet for Mr. Wilson Barrett. Yet, despite the strength and substance of his being, he is the most elusive creature that ever came to baffle the poor intelligence of mankind. When we see him in a modern play, purporting to be a merchant or a barrister or some other familiar modern type, we protest that it is impossible to accept him as such. He is not of our time, we say, but rather a throw-back to some erst glorious and now fallen, forgotten empire of the past. For us that lucent top-hat perches as an accident on his brow, hiding a yet more lucent diadem of barbaric gems. His frock-coat is buttoned across harness of gold and silver. Superficially like a walking stick, that which he bears in his right hand is a curiously-wrought sceptre. From no hansom or four-wheeler has he just alighted, but from some high-pooped galley. His talk is not as our talk, and his walk is in time to some strange music made from shawms and sackbuts by a thousand virgin slaves. Of the truck of our sordid world he is all ignorant, all unconscious. An old-time tyrant, he.

Now, Mr. Barrett does not always appear in plays of modern life. Often he favours some quite remotely antique period. Herein, we are sure, our awe of him will not be tempered by sense of anachronism. But we ought never to be sure of anything in regard to Mr. Barrett. Antique in modernity, he appears not less modern in antiquity. The resources of the costumier's wardrobe avail him nothing. Lightly or heavily clad, according to the fashion of the period required, he is yet altogether of our own time. His voice, his port, his manner, all have a contemporary ring. A tyrant he is still, but a familiar tyrant. True, the form of tyranny suggested by him varies from scene to scene. Sometimes we think of an eloquent Nonconformist divine swaying his congregation; at other times of a headmaster "taking" the fourth form; at other times of a magistrate reading the Riot Act. But whatever form of tyranny he suggest to us at the moment, the form is always a modern one. And thus, whether he appear in ancient or modern

garb, Mr. Barrett is always an august anachronism—a whale out
of water. The truth is, of course, that himself is neither ancient
nor modern : he seems one or the other only by force of the contrast
with whichever thing he try to seem. He belongs, really, to no
time at all. There is not, and never was, any one to resemble
him. That is the secret of his hold on us.

He is now on view at the Adelphi Theatre, enacting the title-
part of a play written by himself—"The Christian King, or Alfred
of Engle-land." The play is conceived in a large spirit, and is, I
hope, the first of a series in which Mr. Barrett will deal with all
those English Kings whom Shakespeare left unexploited. The
play has, at least, one very real merit. It is inspired by a serious
effort to show us the greatness of a great man. Mr. Barrett tries
to show us the great man, not (as is the usual case) involved in
some love affair merely, or making merely a picturesque background to some one else's love affair, but actually doing the things
on which depends his reputation for greatness—planning cam-
paigns, transacting affairs of State, and so forth. True, the effort
does not quite come off. The task of making us fully realise in
the theatre the genius of any great man can come off only if the
dramatist himself be, in his own line, an equally great man. Mr.
Barrett's greatness is a greatness rather of personality than of
dramatic invention. Unimpressive, for instance, is the scene
in which Alfred cross-examines a lady whom he suspects of
attempting to poison another lady. "Why did you put poison in
that cup?" asks Alfred. "I didn't," says the lady. "You did,"
says Alfred. " I didn't," repeats the lady. "You did," repeats
Alfred. We feel that Alfred is not doing himself justice—not
revealing that intellectual potency with which Mr. Frederic
Harrison and other admirers have credited him. Spiritually, too,
he leaves something to be desired. "Tell King Guthrum," he
cries, "that Alfred of Engle-land will meet him in the field—
meet and defeat him." The Scandinavian to whom he entrusts
this message is a man of spirit, who declares that, on the contrary,
Alfred's own doom is at hand. Alfred is inexpressibly shocked
"Sir," says he, "that shall be as God wills." But why thus
rebuke the messenger for overlooking a point which had just
been overlooked by himself? Years ago, in statu pupillari, I
knew a youth who was ploughed three or four times in the Divinity

chool. As he was destined for holy orders, this was a serious
matter for him. And, every time he failed, after reading very
hard for that very simple affair, he impressed me by his pious
acquiescence in what he declared to have been decreed from above.
The impression thus produced on me was nullified by him when,
at length, he succeeded in passing his examination. His talk was
full of having "romped through"—"floored the examiners"—
"no mistake about it this time." Even as to that undergraduate,
so to Alfred seems it that he need hold Providence accountable
only for his misfortunes. Not an edifying theory!

The Alfred whom Mr. Barrett has created is not nearly so grand
a person as the Alfred whom Mr. Barrett impersonates. And yet I
fancy that the former has more than the latter in common with
the Alfred of actual history. The latter, as I have suggested,
seems to belong to our own age. When he seals up a letter and
says to the bearer of it "If he be not at home, search till you find
him, and bring a written answer to this my message," we feel
(despite the exquisite archaicism of the words) that he has rung
up a messenger-boy after failing to "get through" on the tele-
phone. Again, the actual Alfred was essentially English—or so
we imagine him to have been. Mr. Barrett speaks the English
language with perfect fluency, and may, so far as I know, be of
purely English extraction. But to me he gives the impression of
being unbounded by any nationality. He transcends place, even
as he transcends time. Infinity and eternity are his.

He takes infinite pains to put us at our ease. Even as in a
previous play he entered bearing a lamb (or was it a sheep?) in his
arms, so now, when he first appears, he lays a caressing hand on
two handsome deer-hounds. One of his retainers has already
been made to say, reassuringly, "He has the tenderest and most
considerate heart I wot of." And, in case these precautions be
inadequate, Mr. Barrett proceeds to hold a long and tenderly
facetious conversation with a little ragged child. But, somehow,
the more he tries not to overawe us, the more are we overawed.
When he says of his kingship "I dare not hope that I shall fill the
rôle," his modesty seems more terrific than any amount of bluster.
And in his relation to the two ladies who appear in the play he
overwhelms us utterly. One of them is a good lady, the other
a bad lady. The good one is a blonde, the bad one a brunette.

The bad one appears with a hawk—a stuffed hawk—on her wrist
the good one with a dove—a real live dove—in the hollow of her
hand. They both love Alfred simultaneously. And Alfred loves
them both in succession. But what an Olympian lover he is
Jove himself, condescending to this or that nymph or mortal
cannot have had more of the grand manner. It is true that Alfred
leaves off loving the bad lady in time to save himself from misconduct, and marries the good lady in due form. But the romance
is pervaded by a subtle odour of mythology.

Sometimes I suspect Mr. Barrett himself of being a myth.

THE INVARIABLE BADNESS OF
AMATEUR ACTING

January 24 and 31, 1903

There is much to be said for the amateur in other arts. There
is nothing to prevent us from taking him quite seriously. His
work, at its best, or even at its second best, yields us a quality of
pleasure which we could not win elsewhere.

As "amateur" is a rather dubious word, let me explain that I
mean by it one who practises an art by the way, as a recreation
from some other kind of work, or as a recreation from leisure, and
not with any need of emolument from it, nor devoting to it his
whole life. Work done with this motive, done under these conditions, may often be trivial, but it never can be vulgar. Professionalism is a very dangerous thing. It tempts a man to accept
a popular standard, and to ignore his own standard of what is
right and wrong in his art—to aim at what passes muster, not at
what himself thinks worthy. Necessitating, moreover, not merely
constant labour but also constant output, professionalism tends
to foster a fatal fluency, enabling a man to say anything anyhow
robbing him, at length, of the power to express anything from
himself. From such dangers the amateur is safe. Working
solely for his own pleasure, he is not seduced into doing less than
his best for sake of a public which does not exact, or positively
will have none of, his best. Under no contract to stand any

deliver at stated hours, he can linger over his work as long as ever he care to. He need take no short cuts to sufficiency. He may treat, with deliberate footsteps, the high-road to perfection. He never acquires a cheap ready-made knowledge of "how to do things." Thus he must always be finding out for himself how a thing—how on earth even the easiest, most obvious thing—can be done. And thus the way, when he finds it, is his own way; so that even the easiest, most obvious thing achieved by him has some distinction, some personal flavour and significance. Some beauty, belike, too; for his is "the hand of little employment" that "hath the daintier sense"—the lingering hand, delicately refining. The most exquisite work, in other arts than the art of acting, is always the work of an amateur.

Take an example. No one, I suppose, will dispute that in the art of writing prose the most exquisite work done in our time was the work of an amateur. Essentially an amateur was Walter Pater. There was no worldly need for him to write. Writing was his recreation, his way of enjoying himself. To the last, he was an amateur. And the peculiar value and beauty of his work came from the very fact that he was so amateurish. He never mastered, because there was no need for him to master, the rudiments of writing as a business. He never could express anything off-hand. He had always to fumble and grope in the recesses of his consciousness before he could set down on paper the simplest thought. He had infinite leisure for fumbling and groping there before he need express thoughts more complicated. And thus it is that we have in his writing so exact and vivid a presentment of himself, and a beauty so distinct from any other kind of beauty that is known to us (except, of course, in the work of his disciples). Suppose that Pater had failed to win a Fellowship, and had come "down" to London, there to make worldly use of the specific instinct that was in him. Suppose that he had become a professional writer. And then try to imagine yourself reading with any pleasure such books as he might have left behind him. Pater not exquisite! A poor sort of Pater that would be.

I have taken in Pater, of course, a pre-eminent example—the kind of man bound to do pre-eminent work as an amateur. The average amateur has but little true impulse for the art which he pursues—nothing that is worth expressing, nor much of the gift for achieving a beautiful expression of it. His work does not matter much; but it has, at least, a kind of fragile charm and distinction. The faint reflection of a faint thing is better than the harsh reflection of nothing in particular. And the difference between those two reflections is the difference between the work of the average amateur and the average professional.

Not that I would altogether decry professionalism. Its power for evil is not unlimited; and it is to some extent a power for good. It kills only the exquisite talent. To that rarer phenomenon, genius, it is of real service. Pater was a great man in a small way, and professionalism would have been fatal to him; but, had he been great in a great way, he would have been all the better for having to earn his bread by writing. Take the case of any absolutely great writer who has been beset by that necessity. Take, for example, Balzac. Had he had enough money to keep him in ease and comfort, had he not laden himself with that appalling load of debts, he would not have written more carefully than he did write. Merely, he would have written less. Professionalism is a kind of pump. It soon pumps out of a small artist what might have been valuable had it been expressed by the small artist, slowly, of his own accord. It does not, on the other hand, exhaust the great artist. It does but keep him in a constant state of effusion. How much leisure the great artist has for his work is a question which does not at all affect the quality of his work. He is so strongly himself that his hastiest work bears always his own authentic stamp. The great artist is always at his best. If ever he tried (and he never does try) to be exquisite, he would not succeed in being so. Exquisiteness is within the reach only of certain smaller artists. And it is within their reach only when they are working as amateurs.

As in literature, so is it in painting and in music. For example —but oh, bother examples! Or rather, I beg you to take them on trust. I am a simple dramatic critic: I refuse to do more than make general assertions about music and painting. A priori, of course, one would expect that a rule deducible from the arts generally would hold good in the art of acting also. It is among amateur mimes that one would look to find the most delicate and various interpretation of finer shades of character. One would not look to find great tragic acting, or even great comedic acting. But one would expect, at least, a certain exquisite subtlety in the portrayal of "character parts." The average professional mime offends us with his roughness and readiness. His experience is such that he never has to think anything out freshly for himself. He repeats mechanically the tricks which he has played before, and which, maybe, he had picked up, in the first instance, from other mimes. If he is one who confines himself to a single "line of business," he does the same thing, over and over again, in the same way. If he is "versatile," he does different things, over and over again, in the same way. Never is he the character as drawn by the author. Never is he even himself. He is but a tissue of tedious conventions. Now, the average amateur has little or no experience. Therefore he must think for himself. A part is put into his hands, and he must excogitate what will be the best means of conveying his idea of it to the audience. And it is likely (on the analogy of the other arts) that he, if he have a true bent towards acting, will give a very original and delicate performance. Well, let us test these likelihoods by our experience of amateur acting. We have all, in our time, seen a good deal of amateur acting. For it is acting which has been in our time the most popular of the art-forms, and therefore the most ardently practised by the greatest number of amateurs. In the early part of this century, poetry bore away the palm. So pervasive was the force of Byron that thousands of ladies and gentlemen, who else would never have thought of rhyming love to dove, began to scribble innumerable verses in innumerable albums. Then came Queen Victoria, who was no poet, but was fond of sketching in water-colour. Forthwith, the albums were laid aside, and easels were set up in their stead, and the faltering fingers that had been stained with violet ink were now stained with moist paints. Later came Jenny Lind, and the genteel world sketched no more in water-colour, but warbled. Last of all came Mr. Henry Irving; and the genteel world ceased to warble, and began to act, and has been acting ever since. Acting, indeed, has had, and still has, a greater vogue than came to any of the other art-forms. For, in a sense, it is the easiest of them all. Not every one can write a metrical line, or draw a straight line, or sing a note in tune. But any one who is not dumb and paralysed can come and speak a few lines across a row of footlights, and can imagine that he is speaking

17

them rather nicely. The greater the number of amateurs, of course, the greater the number of duffers. But there is no reason to suppose that among even the greatest number there will not be some persons of real skill and talent. And yet, and yet, did any one of us ever behold an amateur mime whom he could praise without insincerity, or whose performance seemed comparable with even the worst professional performance? None of us ever beheld that amateur mime. Why?

That the vast majority of amateur mimes should merely flounder does not, of course, surprise me. What else should they do? They go in for private theatricals, not with any inward impulse for the art of acting, but just for the fun of the thing, as a variation from the common round of amusements in country-houses. As on the professional stage, so on the amateur stage, the conditions foster a certain freedom between the sexes, and many amateur mimes regard their art less as an end in itself than as a means to flirtation. In such diversions as sport or gambling there can be no sexual element. A woman who rides to hounds, or goes out with the guns, is doing a mannish thing, and ceasing, for the time, to be a woman. She does not distract attention from the fox or the birds, and presumably does not seek to distract it: she, too, is exclusively a minister of death. Similarly, when men and women play cards, their aim is to win one another's money; and this stern enterprise precludes any kind of dalliance. But in rehearsing a play there is nothing to prevent, and much to encourage, a tender familiarity. There is nothing to make either the man forget his manhood or the woman her womanhood. And the fact that the man is impersonating by the way another man, and the woman another woman, creates for them a vague sense of greater freedom and less responsibility. Innumerable other motives there are by which amateur mimes are made. A middle-aged man told me, the other day, that he had taken to amateur acting because of an accident which had slightly injured his eyesight. He had no longer been able to shoot straight, and consequently there had been a heavy fall in the quantity and quality of his invitations. As he was a bachelor, and not very rich, and fond of the country, and gregarious, this had been for him a serious matter. And so he had taken counsel with himself, had thrown himself enthusiastically into the art of acting, and had now won his way back to the favour he had forfeited. "I know I can't act for nuts," he said. "But then, *they* can't act for nuts, either. So what does it matter?" Perhaps a real efficiency in acting would be as disastrous for him as had been his crooked shooting.

Not many amateur mimes are, like this gentleman, conscious of their own defects. And this brings me to one of the solutions for their mysterious badness. They are never told—never told personally—how bad they are, or even that they are not very good indeed. I know that the professional mimes get very little in the way of frank criticism. The average critic finds far greater difficulty in understanding the rudiments of acting than in understanding even the intricacies of dramaturgy. So he takes the safe course of peppering every cast with such epithets as "manly," "sincere," "polished," "sympathetic." In his opinion, what the leading man does is always "perhaps the best thing he has yet done"; and "nothing could" ever "be better than the performance of" the leading lady; and even the small fry always give "valuable assistance" and (as though one might expect them to be treacherous) "loyal help." Nevertheless, there are a few critics who really can (and dare) discriminate bad from good acting. And for these critics the performers have a wholesome respect, and from them learn many wholesome lessons in their art. The amateurs, on the other hand, move in an atmosphere of untainted adulation. Their friends, and their servants, and their villagers, vie with one another in loudness of applause. And even the expert dramatic critic never dreams of being anything but dulcet. Of course, he is not often there at all. Books by amateurs are published, and paintings by amateurs are exhibited, and so are criticised by the experts. But (thank Heaven!) private theatricals are nearly always given in private or remote places, and the expert escapes them. Now and again, however, Fate drops him into one of these private or remote places. And he, basely, does not attempt to improve the occasion by telling the truth. Last year, a well-known expert went to stay at a house in ——shire. His hostess was a lady of much lustre and importance in the county. The expert, when he arrived, found her rehearsing a play. It appeared that the rector of the village church had set his heart on an east-window, and that his appeal for subscriptions had not had a very hearty response. So the expert's hostess had organised a theatrical entertainment, to be given in aid of the fund. Two playlets, of an old-fashioned and unpretentious kind, were to be enacted in the village schoolroom. In each of them the expert's hostess had assigned to herself the leading part. This she had done, not because she had ever acted before, nor because she had any great wish to act now, but rather because she owed it to her position not to appear in a subordinate capacity even on the stage. Her husband disapproved strongly of the whole scheme. It was only under strong protest that he attended the performance. The expert happened to be sitting next to him; and the notion that the husband was with difficulty repressing his contempt and mortification made it the more difficult for the expert to repress his own hysterical mirth at what was passing on the stage. The helpless awkwardness of the untried amateur is not in itself amusing; but when it is brought into an even conflict with the dignity and easy grace of a great lady moving in her own sphere of influence, the result (according to the expert) is something quite irresistibly droll and delightful. Throughout the evening, the husband sat silent. When the curtain fell, he turned to the expert and said, in perfect seriousness and good faith, "Well, I never could have believed it. Of course, she can't do anything really great in such parts as those. Nobody could. But I should like to see her as—well, say as 'La Dame aux Camélias.'" Later, the expert found himself saying to his hostess, for want of anything better to say, "I should like very much to see you as 'La Dame aux Camélias.' It is a part that would suit you." The other day, he heard that the rector was agitating for a new font, and that "La Dame aux Camélias" was in rehearsal.

Certainly, the absence of criticism is one of the blights on amateur acting. But the real mischief lies deeper. It is inherent in the art of acting. Acting is essentially a public art. A man might paint or write, with some pleasure, on a desert island. But he could not act there. Not less than the orator, the actor must have an audience to work on. Now, it were no great gratification to an orator to address none but small and select audiences, even if these audiences were composed of finely critical persons. The fact that his work does not endure beyond the moment of its performance makes it essential for him to be heard at large. Similarly, the man who has any real impulse for acting will not be satisfied with private or semi-private triumphs—would not be satisfied by them even if the private or semi-private audiences were composed of finely critical persons, and not of persons who applaud with equal enthusiasm whatever he may happen to do. Such triumphs may be gratifying enough to the vanity of the duffer but the man who feels that he has it in him to act will crave for a wider field. To that wider field he cannot attain if he continue to be an amateur actor. Consequently, he becomes a professional actor as soon as ever he can. And thus the amateur stage is always automatically deprived of such persons as might, if they tarried on it, become its ornaments. Only the duffers tarry on it.

KIPLING'S ENTIRE

February 14, 1903

"George Fleming" is, as we know, a lady. Should the name Rudyard Kipling, too, be put between inverted commas? Is it, too, the veil of a feminine identity? If of Mr. Kipling we knew nothing except his work, we should assuredly make that conjecture. A lady who writes fiction reveals her sex clearlier through her portrayal of men than through any other of her lapses. And in Mr. Kipling's short stories, especially in "The Light that Failed" (that elongated short story which "George Fleming" has now adapted to the stage), men are portrayed in an essentially feminine manner, and from an essentially feminine point of view. They are men seen from the outside, or rather, not seen at all, but feverishly imagined. If to a lady who writes fiction you declare that men are not as she draws them, she will say (or, at least, think) that if they are not they ought to be. Mr. Kipling would say or think likewise about his own men. "*My* men—*my* men!" cries Dick Helder when a regiment of soldiers passes his window. He is not their commanding officer. He was at one time a war-correspondent. He is now blind, and his cry is wrung from him by his anguish in not being able to see what was to him the fairest sight on earth. He had always doted on the military. And so has Mr. Kipling. To him, as to his hero, they typify, in its brightest colours, the notion of manhood, manliness, man. And by this notion Mr. Kipling is permanently and joyously obsessed. That is why I say that his standpoint is feminine. The ordinary male fictionist has a knowledge of men as they are, but is preoccupied by a sentiment for women as he supposes them to be. The ordinary female fictionist has a knowledge of women as they are, but is preoccupied by a sentiment for men as she supposes them to be. (Between these two propositions lies the reason why so little of our fiction can be taken seriously.) Mr. Kipling is so far masculine that he has never displayed a knowledge of women as they are; but the unreality of his male creatures, with his worship of them, makes his name ring quaintly like a pseudonym.

In men's novels you will find, for the most part, that virility is taken for granted. The male characters are men, and, so far as their creator can see, there's an end of the matter. But, for a creatrix, there's only just the beginning of the matter. She *insists* that her male characters are men. That is a lurid fact which she herself constantly remembers, "and don't you," she seems to say to her reader, "forget it." The point is laboured by her both in the first person and through the lips of the male characters themselves. Into whatever circumstances of joy or sorrow she cast them, always they are acutely conscious of their manhood and acutely nervous of being mistaken for women. However urgent the other calls made by Fate on their attention, always they keep the corners of their eyes on the mirror, to assure themselves that their moustaches are bristling, and their chests expanding, and their pipes "drawing," satisfactorily. They are never quite sure of themselves. They tremble at the sound of their own footsteps, fearing that the soles of their boots are not heavy enough. In ever-present dread of a sudden soprano note in the bass, they tremble at the sound of their own voices. They would beware of talking much, even were they sure of their lungs. They must, at all costs, be laconic, taciturn, as becomes men. Their language must be strong but sparse. No babbling fountains must they be, but volcanoes of whose inner fires we are to catch through infrequent cracks terrific glimpses. In real life, men are not like that. At least, only the effeminate men are like that. The others have no preoccupation with manliness. They don't bother about it.

That is the difference between them and the male creatures of female writers. It is, also, precisely, the difference between them and the male creatures of Mr. Kipling. Manliness on the one hand, manlydom on the other. Manlydom: find for me, if you can, a word more apt to Mr. Kipling's heroes.

Strange that these heroes, with their self-conscious blurtings of oaths and slang, their cheap cynicism about the female sex, their mutual admiration for one another's display of all those qualities which women admire in men, were not, as they so obviously seem to have been, fondly created out of the inner consciousness of a lady-novelist. There are, however, some respects wherein they differ from the heroes whom the average lady-novelist has made so painfully familiar to us. Women are rather squeamish, for the most part, and, though they idolise in men the strength which has been denied to themselves, they shrink from the notion of its excess. Brutality of word or deed is a notion which affrights them. Their heroes are never brutal. The oaths and the slang and the cynicism are kept beyond the confines of coarseness. There is always a certain atmosphere of gentility. And thus the ingenious commentator of the future will perhaps be saved from the fallacy (to which otherwise he would fall surely victim) that "Rudyard Kipling" was a lady's pseudonym. For Mr. Kipling is nothing —never was anything—if not unsqueamish. The ugly word, the ugly action, the ugly atmosphere—for all these he has an inevitable scent; and the uglier they be, the keener seems his relish of them. Strength, mere strength, is not enough to make a hero for him: his hero must be also a brute and a bounder. Writing of George Sand, Mr. Henry James once suggested that she, though she may have been to all intents and purposes a man, was not a gentleman. Conversely, it might be said that Mr. Kipling, as revealed to us in his fiction, is no lady. But he is not the less essentially feminine for that.

No one but himself, I should have thought, could so adapt his peculiar fiction to the stage that nothing of its flavour were lost. As he was averse from dramaturgy, the point was for him to select the second best person for the job. No man need have applied: only a woman could preserve the point of view. And it seemed likely that the point of view could be preserved in its entirety by no woman who had not spent her life in the fish-market of Billingsgate.

Such women are averse from dramaturgy. And so, in course of time, the job fell to "George Fleming," in whom are the two qualifications that she is a woman and a clever dramatist, and the one disqualification that she has a charming and fastidious talent. Of her two qualifications she has made very good use, and she has contrived, somehow, to triumph temporarily over her one disqualification. Examining her script with a fresh eye, she must have been surprised (and pained) by its fidelity to the original. All the atmosphere is there—an atmosphere charged pungently with the triple odour of beer, baccy and blood. And in this atmosphere the characters speak that abrupt jargon of alternate meiosis and hyperbole which is Mr. Kipling's literary style. It is wonderful, too, how exactly Miss Fletcher has caught the "way of a man with a maid" as conceived by Mr. Kipling. "I want you, Maisie—I want you badly" sounds rather like the echo of a coon-song, but it is also good Kiplingese. And "You're a woman, Maisie, from the top of your dear little head to the toes of your blessed little boots" is Kiplingese of the purest kind, inconfusible with any other kind of vulgarity. In some passages Miss Fletcher has "lifted" the dialogue verbatim. It is a pity that she has omitted Dick's immortal description of his inamorata as "a bilious little thing." You remember that he was walking in Kensington Gardens, meditating on Maisie's lonely life, wondering whether she took proper care of herself. It occurred to him that perhaps she did not eat regular meals. For some girls, he reflected, this would not matter, "but," he cried in an agony of tenderness, "Maisie's a bilious little thing." In the dramatic version, much of this soliloquy reappears as an address to Maisie; but, somehow the immortal phrase has dropped out of it. "You're a bilious little thing, Maisie" is a line that we listen for eagerly and in vain. We miss, too, that scene in which Dick gloats eloquently over the traces of physical disease on the face of a middle-aged editor (or was it a picture-dealer?) who has called on him with a view to cheating him out of some money due for work done. And we miss, above all, that night-scene in the armoured train, when Dick, after blindness has overtaken him, ecstatically yells to the soldiers who have been ordered to fire the machine-gun on some skirmishing Arabs, "Give 'em Hell, men—oh, give 'em Hell." Sad not to have heard that noble heart-cry uttered on the stage—a heart-cry so inalienably characteristic of the Kipling hero. Still, despite these and other omissions, Miss Fletcher has given us a marvellously close adaptation of the book. The play she offers us is a frothing draught of the authentic brew. It is Kipling's Entire. I raise my glass, and, in Kiplingesque parlance, "I looks towards" Miss Fletcher, but with a look that is meant to convey reproach.

Men are less pliant than women. Mr. Forbes Robertson cannot, try as he will, throw off that air of distinction and nobility so inconsistent with the Kipling ideal of manlydom. As Dick Helder, he may be likened to a stag in a baboon's skin. Some of the other actors in the cast, by dint of much growling and grunting and scowling and lumbering, come within measurable distance of the ideal.

A "DREARY" PLAY

May 2, 1903

Ten years ago it was the fashion to call "unwholesome" any play which presented sincerely a not altogether jolly side of life. Well, the critics who encouraged such plays, and who were supposed to discourage any other kind of plays, have not dropped and died, one after another, to prove the aptness of the epithet. They are still among us, not apparently ailing. So another epithet has been hit on—"dreary," to wit. "Dreary" was much bandied last Monday afternoon, at the Imperial Theatre, in the entr'actes of "The Good Hope." Ten years ago, the emergents into the foyer would have been angrily grimacing, gasping for what they would have called "a whiff of fresh air," and complaining of (a favourite phrase, then) "a nasty taste in the mouth." Last Monday, they merely looked glum. One of them, regarding me with a faint twinkle in an otherwise lack-lustre eye, asked "Is this dreary enough for you?" I assured him that I was enjoying myself immensely. And so I was. Indeed, I had hardly ever felt so happy, so braced-up and buoyant, in a theatre. True, the play was a tragedy, and a very horrible one at that. But I do not see how it could produce a feeling of dreariness, and could fail to produce a definitely tonic effect, on any person capable of intelligent æsthetic pleasure. One salient defect of the average Englishman is that he is incapable of such pleasure. If a work of art remind him of cheerful things in real life, he is exhilarated; if of cheerless things, he is downcast. The reminder of cheerful things may be dully given. That does not matter to him. The reminder of cheerless things may be given beautifully, strongly, and therefore joyously. That does not matter to him. For he was born inartistic.

There, I take it, is the reason why our drama is so weak in modern tragedies—the reason why, if the artistic few wish to see a modern tragedy, they have to import it from France or Germany or elsewhere. I do not suppose that we have in England no man capable of writing as fine a tragedy as that which Hermann Heijermans has written. But I do know that such a play as "The Good Hope," produced publicly, would be in England as signal a failure as it has been a success in Holland. And therefore (since, by the nature of his work, the dramatist, more than any other artist, needs encouragement) such a play is not written. Not from every kind of tragedy does our public flinch. It will tolerate Shakespearian tragedy, because it is not thereby reminded of realities. It will sometimes tolerate even a modern tragedy, for there is a way of writing modern tragedy without trenching on anything within our actual experience. A playwright can take a tragic theme from real life, and found a play on it, and yet make his characters and his atmosphere so unreal that no offence is given. No offence, did I say? Nay, very great pleasure. Our public loves to cry, to cry copiously, so long as its tears are not shed over something that is not a quite palpable figment. I can imagine a really popular British play made from the very same materials that Heijermans used for "The Good Hope." The title itself is promising. Nor is the theme unfamiliar or unwelcome. Fisher-folk, living their lives in a constant tussle with the elements, are part and parcel of our national romance. "Men must work and women must weep"—"They who go down to the sea in ships"—"For those in peril on the sea"—does not every one of our households contain, somewhere, at least one engraving or oleograph to illustrate these phrases? Well we know them, those impossibly young and buxom wives, standing on rocks, shading their eyes with their hands, seawards, while their tresses stream becomingly in the gale from beneath their sou'westers, and their impossibly old and decrepit grandfathers in the foreground crouch prayerfully so as not to obstruct our tear-dimmed vision of neat ankles. Long and well have we known them pictorially; long and well on the stage, also. It is strange with how slight ingenuity might the exact situation chosen by Heijermans be turned into the kind of play that has often enriched our own dramatists. Take the principal characters: pathetic "lead," a very woman whose husband and two of whose sons were drowned years ago; hero, one of her surviving sons, a handsome, daring fellow, recently dismissed from the Navy, and sentenced to a term of imprisonment, for knocking down a superior officer who had foully slandered the heroine; heroine, a bonny, high-spirited girl, cousin of hero, loving him dearly, dearly loved by him; villain, wealthy shipowner, who heavily insures and sends to sea vessels which he knows to be unseaworthy; comic relief, younger brother of hero, a coward, afraid of the sea, anxious to get employment on land. All these characters are ranged before us in the course of the first act. The villain compliments the heroine on her good looks, and hints at his own sensuality. In the second act the hero, after making many verbal scores off the villain, whom he regards as a lazy tyrant, puts out to sea in a vessel which we know to be doomed. Here are all the makings of a successful British drama. It seems almost superfluous to indicate how the successful British dramatist would deal with them. Of course, the villain would in the third act renew his odious advances to the heroine, and be repulsed indignantly. Later would come the news that the vessel had gone down with all hands aboard. The heroine, in deep mourning, would again repulse the villain, who, stung to fury, would boast that he had killed the hero on purpose, and would gloat over her bereavement. She, in her turn, stung to fury, would stab him with a stray clasp-knife to which our attention had been previously drawn. And then—then there would be two courses open. If the successful British dramatist wished to increase his reputation for profound thought, the villain would be mortally wounded, and the curtain would fall on the heroine giving herself up to the police. The public would go weeping out of the theatre, but (for a reason which I have already explained) not really at all depressed or resentful. The other, and perhaps the safer way, would be for the villain to wrest the knife from the heroine's weak hand after receiving a very slight scratch, and to turn the weapon vindictively against her. The door would burst open. "Are you his ghost?" the villain would cry. "No," the hero would shout, "I am flesh and blood. Unhand her! I have swum ashore. Come to my arms, dearest. As for you, you scoundrel, you shall pay the penalty of your misdeeds. Constable! [*Enter constable*] You have here a warrant for this man's arrest, on the charge of murdering my shipmates. [*Exeunt constable and villain*.] And now, my darling, now that the clouds which overshadowed us have rolled away, and the glorious sunshine," &c. That were the way to make "The Good Hope" acceptable in England. It is, however, not at all the way Heijermans has gone about *his* business.

In the play, as it stands, there is practically no love-interest. Very little stress is laid on the fact that Greet and his cousin Jo are lovers, and the tragedy of his death at sea is marked for us quite as much through the bereavement of his mother as through that of his betrothed. Nor, indeed, are we called on to weep for him especially. The fate of his brother, and of the rest of the crew, seems not less lamentable than his. No one character predominates much over another. There is practically no story. The play simply represents a typical episode in a little fishing village. Most of the characters are fisherfolk, possessing much the same peculiarities of temperament as we may find in the fisherfolk in Cornwall or elsewhere, and possessing none of the peculiarities of fisherfolk as seen by us on the stage. There is nothing consciously heroic about them. They are ordinary creatures, with certain modifications and exaggerations produced by their peculiar life. And herein lies one of the sharpest differences between the work of Heijermans and the work of any English dramatist. Heijermans has deigned to take a respectful interest in humble life, and shows to us humble people as they are, not as every fool knows them not to be. An English dramatist, having to show a group of peasants, would be content to multiply the conventional stage-peasant. In the group of peasants shown to us by Heijermans every one is distinct from another, and all are human beings, and all, moreover, are normal human beings. Equally real and normal are the characters who do not happen to be peasants. I notice that some of my colleagues decry the ship-owner, Clemens Bos, as a conventional villain. Are they themselves so saturated with convention that they failed to notice that his hinted desire for Jo in the first act was not succeeded by persecution of her in the later acts? As a matter of fact, the man takes no further notice of the girl. To pretend that he is a conventional villain merely because he speculates in unseaworthy ships is to deny the possible existence in Holland of what the late Mr. Plimsoll proved to exist in England. Perhaps it was some vague memory of Mr. Plimsoll's crusade that led these critics into the deeper absurdity of decrying the play as "a pamphlet." Certainly it is a criticism of certain things in life which the author holds to be horrible and unjust. In that sense it is a pamphlet. But it is also a very fine and scrupulous work of art. There is nothing incongruous in this duality. True, there is always the danger that an artist who is inspired by a moral purpose may distort life so as to make his moral the more striking. But he does not necessarily do so. Certainly, Heijermans has not done so. I wish that some of our so purely artistic dramatists could, through their coldly observant eyes, see life half as clearly and steadily as it is seen through the somewhat flashing eyes of Heijermans.

MR. MARTIN HARVEY AT ST. HELENA

May 16, 1903

Captivity is dramatic or undramatic according to the nature of the captive. The fowler who ensnares from the empyrean an eagle, and coops him in a cage, is a purveyor of drama. Not only is our imagination stirred by the contrast between that boundless azure and these mean bars, and by the thought that one who was the tyrant and terror of his fellow-birds is turned now into a mere object for their pity, but also our sense of drama is stirred by the obviously active conflict between the eagle's soul and his lot.

The eagle remembers, pines, rebels. He never surrenders his right to that wild throne from which man has by subtlety deposed him. He is as strong as ever he was on the divine right of eagles. Us he regards as vile conspirators against heaven, and there is a world of scorn for us in the dim glare of his steadfast yellow eyes. His spirit never breaks, though himself wastes away, with moulting feathers and wings atrophied. Regard yonder canary. He, too, is a pathetic figure, when we come to think of it. Had he his rights, he would be even now fluttering from sunlit branch to branch of whatever tropical trees best pleased his fancy. Only, he has surrendered his rights. He has adapted himself, quite agreeably, to durance vile. He enjoys his little cold bath every morning. From perch to perch he flutters, all day long, piping servile notes to his gaolers, and pecking with servile relish at the groundsel that they thrust contemptuously between the bars. Perhaps he is a philosopher. Perhaps he is only a fool. In either case, he is not at all dramatic. His behaviour precludes that sense of conflict without which drama cannot begin to be for us. We incline to the theory that he is a fool. We do not, however (to use a famous distinction) think him a damned fool. And how, except as a damned fool, could we regard an eagle that were behaving in his manner? Imagine a caged eagle pirouetting, and cocking his head coquettishly to one side, and feeding from our hand, and entertaining us with whatever vocal noises are made by eagles at large, and generally exhibiting the Christian qualities of resignation and cheerfulness, as a lesson to us all. We should not be edified. We should but say "This bird is undramatic; and, worse, he is undramatically ridiculous."

Let us take now the case of a human captive. Perhaps because Jupiter's bird was the minister of his sufferings, Prometheus springs into my memory. Why is it that Prometheus Bound is so finely dramatic a theme? It is because his spirit, though his limbs were bound to the rock, was still unfettered. It is because he was for ever indignant, unrepentant, undaunted. His spirit never was broken. He was always writhing and wrenching for freedom, and, had he freed himself indeed, would again have scaled Olympus and therefrom filched some other element desirable for mankind. And thus he is the eternally dramatic symbol of the conflict between soaring personal genius and the dull general force that hates it and overpowers it. Now, suppose that Prometheus, on his rock, shrugging his shoulders as far as his chains would permit him, had acquiesced in the gods' verdict. Suppose his sentiments had been merely a distaste for the cramped monotony of his life, and a regret that he was not still lightly at large. Suppose him, if you can, saying "tweet" to the eagle. Then in all history no figure will seem to you a less dramatic figure than he. Nay! having regard to his past, you will deem him of all figures the most undramatically ridiculous.

Not incomparable with Prometheus Bound is Napoleon at St. Helena. Of course, the destructive egoist in captivity does not cut so noble a figure as the beneficent altruist; but Napoleon, not less than Prometheus, is an eternally dramatic symbol of the aforesaid conflict. A handful of dull English dragoons and duller English civilians lording it and martinetting it, in an out-of-the-way islet, over him who from the fire in his own breast had set Europe blazing, and in whose own breast that fire was still smouldering and, in its suppression, choking and stifling him—what finer psychologic theme could any dramatist find in the world's history? But suppose history to be here inaccurate. Suppose that, when he disembarked at St. Helena, Napoleon so "ranged himself" as to become a gentle, agreeable, sentimental, unambitious old gentleman, such as you might meet at any moment in the smoking-room of any club in London. Met there, the type is not ridiculous. The old gentleman in the armchair next to yours has not, in his day, set Europe blazing—has never even, you conjecture, cherished sinister designs on the Thames. So you "mock him not." But he is not dramatic. Nor would Napoleon, behaving at St. Helena as this old gentleman behaves here, have been dramatic. And ridiculous, most ridiculous, such a Napoleon would, assuredly, have been. And just such a Napoleon it is that Messrs. Lloyd Osbourne and Austin Strong have from their joint fancies evolved for Mr. Martin Harvey.

Conscious that a sudden, unprepared sight of Napoleon—even of Pelléas in Napoleonic costume—would suggest to us the wrong old notion which they have discarded, these authors wisely keep Napoleon off the stage till the curtain is falling on the first act. Meanwhile, we have been told what manner of man we are to expect. We hear, among many other things to his advantage, that what most preys on his mind is not the loss of his empire, but the enforced separation from his dear wife and child. The children of other people are, however, a very great solace to him; and in the second act, on his birthday, he holds a review of them, all armed by him with toy muskets and taught to march just like real soldiers. Bless his heart—his gentle, uncomplaining, tenderly-humorous heart—but do not imagine there is no warm corner in it for deserving adults. Notice that young English lieutenant, a most deserving case. He is in love with yonder English maid, but too poor to buy his promotion and wed her. Napoleon, like the good fairy god-father that he is, will find, though he can ill afford, the money to buy him his promotion. There must be a peal of wedding-bells to gladden Napoleon's old heart. His thoughts are all for others. Others' are for him. Others plot that he may escape, but they do not take him into their confidence. They say that his health would not stand the excitement, but we suspect that what they really fear is that he would refuse to participate in anything underhand. When all their plans are laid, and they try to rush him into the enterprise, he does, for a moment, waver, seeming as though he would allow himself to be rushed. He is only human. But in a moment his better nature asserts itself. "No," he says firmly, "I will not spill the blood of France *in a purely personal cause*." The young lieutenant has a little surprise for him—a portrait of the little Duc de Reichstadt. "Leave me alone with my son," falters Napoleon. They leave him alone with his son. And there we, too, are asked by Messrs. Lloyd Osbourne and Austin Strong to leave him.

To the people whose one desire in playgoing is "a good laugh" such a Napoleon will be a safe attraction. Those who are fond of drama, will be bored by it. Those who are fond both of drama and of history will be much annoyed by it. Indeed, I never saw a worse specimen of historical drama. Usually, as in the case of "Dante," the mischief is that the playwright takes from history some undramatic material which he twists painfully into dramatic form, thus creating an uncomfortable friction between our knowledge of the real thing and our sense of the imaginary thing. That is bad enough. But how much worse is it when, as now, in "The Exile," finely dramatic material is taken from history and twisted painfully into quite undramatic form! Napoleon at St. Helena

vas inwardly the same Napoleon that had terrorised the world.
There is the dramatist's chance, and he goes out of his way to miss
t if he makes Napoleon a sympathetic old dodderer. Napoleon
oved his son, doubtless; but only in a Napoleonic sense, only as
he possible heir of his own greatness. Napoleon may (I believe
here is evidence that he did) drill a squad of small children. But,
f so, his motive was the wish to realise in his own dramatic way
he full irony and bitterness of downfall; it was not a delight in
attering feet and chubby cheeks and piping voices. Napoleon
did not escape from St. Helena. But the reason was not, you may
be sure, that he, who, in the old days, would ever have so gladly
sacrificed to his purpose those "six cent mille soldats qui marchent
avec moi, pour moi, et comme moi," had become squeamish at
he sight of blood "spilled in a purely personal cause." I cannot
see why the authors of "The Exile" have gone so far and wilfully
out of their way. I can but conjecture that their play was the
result of a wager made by them that they would induce Mr.
Martin Harvey, of all actors the least likely, to appear as Napoleon.
Mr. Harvey is all for dreamy and ethereal and contemplative
romanticism, and would flinch from the notion of playing Napoleon
as he was. So they sat down to project Napoleon as he pre-
eminently wasn't. They have won their (hypothetical) wager.
And Mr. Harvey plays their (hypothetical) Napoleon in exactly
the right key.

AT THE COURT THEATRE

June 20, 1903

You are allowed to shed a tear or two when you see the owls
building their nests in some palace that was erst a setting of gaiety
and pride and riches. During this week the Elizabethan Stage
Society is performing "Twelfth Night" at the Court Theatre.
In days gone by, this pretty theatre had a very great vogue.
Popular little comedies were enacted in it by constellative little
companies, and throughout the stalls and boxes diamonds of the

18   257

first water flashed on bosoms heaving with mirth. Sloane
Square is no further now than then it was from the centre of
things. If anything, it is a trifle nearer. Yet, somewhy, the
popular little comedies and the constellative little companies are
things of the past there, and the diamonds of the first water are
a-flash elsewhere. The Court is still a pretty little theatre, but
forlorn. Indeed, were it less spruce, had it something of a ruin's
aspect, its estate would seem less piteous. When the roof of a
palace has fallen in, and the walls are clad in moss and lichen, one
does not grudge the owl his building operations. But it is bitter
to see him where all is yet fit for human habitation. I do not
dissemble a pang at seeing the Elizabethan Stage Society in possession of the Court. Deeply though I respect that Society for the
enthusiastic scholarship which is the cause of it, its operations
are somewhat too owlish to be pleasant here. I use the word
"owlish" as implying a certain rather morbid and inhuman
solemnity and a detachment from the light of day. The aim of
the Society is to show us the plays of Shakespeare and his contemporaries as they were enacted in their own period. To see them
thus is instructive, but it is not, except for a few exceptional
persons, delightful. Shakespeare wrote at a time when the
science of scenic production was in its infancy, and he himself, as
he has told us, was conscious and resentful of the limitations.
We have developed that science, and it is only when Shakespeare's
plays are produced with due regard to this development that they
seem to us works of living art. Doubtless, the Elizabethan
audience was not, like the quicker-witted poet, conscious of the
defects in the Elizabethan productions. But we, in the twentieth
century, cannot project—or rather retroject—ourselves into their
state of receptivity. We cannot forget what we have learned.
Living in the light, we cannot accustom our eyes to the darkness
of the dark ages. The epithet "owlish" is inevitable of a Society
which finds in the darkness of the dark ages its natural element.
To go back into those ages for instruction is one thing; to do so for
pleasure is another; and there is no doubt that members of
the Elizabethan Stage Society really do enjoy themselves. Long
may they blink and flutter and hoot. Only let them not be held
up to us as examples, as illustrators of how the thing should be
done. They love darkness, and have a perfect right to disport

hemselves in it. But don't let us be awed into admitting that hey, not we, are the children of light.

It seems absurd that we should have to make a stand in the natter. Yet it is a fact that the mode of the Elizabethan Stage Society is by some authoritative persons pretended to be the one and only dignified mode of presenting Shakespeare's plays—to be a mode in comparison with which ours is tawdry and Philistine and wicked. This pretence is not, I think, made by Mr. William Poel or by his coadjutors. They are modest and sensible men, claiming no more than that they pander to our passion for archæology. Enough for them, to be our instructors : for amusement, for æsthetic satisfaction, we may go elsewhere, without hurting their sensibilities. Yet are they used by the authorities aforesaid, as a stick to beat us with. Some people are born with a sense for poetry, but with no dramatic sense. Such people detest the theatre. That is in them a quite reasonable sentiment. For the theatre aims at presenting poetic drama as something more than mere poetry ; and that something more, if you don't care for it, mars the pleasure that the mere poetry gives you. Some people, again, care for drama, and are dead to poetry. Accordingly, they detest "the study." They don't sit down there to read Shakespeare's plays. That, again, is quite reasonable in them. But they would be behaving unreasonably if they said to the students "Come! Get out of this. You are not legitimately enjoying yourselves." And that speech is the converse of what some of the more arrogant students are saying to the playgoers. These students, seeing a poetic play performed by the Elizabethan Stage Society, are blissfully conscious that the dramatic element is eliminated. True, there are footlights, instead of a reading-lamp ; and there are dressed-up ladies and gentlemen instead of a printed page. But at any rate "there is no damned nonsense about" drama. Poetry reigns supreme, alone, unquestioned. The student can almost imagine that his feet are on his own fender. And so "This," says he, "is the way in which Shakespeare should be acted." Thus "an eminent Man of Letters writes" to the Elizabethan Stage Society that its performance of "Twelfth Night" is "one of the most inspiring and most poetical at which I have ever been present." In other words, he had not been made conscious of the dramatic significance of the verse which he loved. He had heard a

series of recitations—the next best thing to reading them to him
self. "You have trained your actors," he says, "to treat the play
with the maximum of respect." Not much interlineal ingenuity
is needed to grasp the meaning of that little pæan. Men of
letters, for the most part, cannot abide mimes who know their
business. For such mimes give (though under the system of the
Elizabethan Stage Society not even they can give) dramatic signi
ficance to the verse spoken by them, making it illustrate the feeling
of the characters by them impersonated, making it point the situa
tions into which those characters are thrown. From my own
standpoint, from the standpoint of any one in whom some
dramatic sense is combined with some sense for poetry, the ideal
interpreter of a Shakespearean part is one who effects an exactly
fair compromise between the poetry and the drama, giving to the
words as much of the beauty of their rhythm as is compatible
with their reflection of mood and character. These ideal interpreters are, as is the way of ideal things, rare. But, when found
they would not satisfy the kind of man who is most easily described
as "of Letters." What he wants is mere reciters—mimes who
know only the one side of their business, or who have been
"trained" not to show through the mists of an undramatic Society
that they do know the other. Hence this eminent one's joy in
the present stars of the Elizabethan Stage Society. Perhaps
because he is so accustomed to solitary reading, he is not a good
judge even of the art of recitation. Or it may be that the company
had put forward for him a best foot that was not protruded last
Tuesday evening. Though Malvolio appeared as a brisk, pleasant
meaningless squire, and Olivia as a subdued tragedy-queen, and
though none of the other characters, except Sir Toby Belch, was
graced with characteristic qualities, my eager ears did not catch
any triumphs in declamation. Indeed, I had seldom heard—or
rather, tried to hear—such poor efforts in elocution. But I sup
pose it is more important, to the art of an eminent Man of Letters
that mimes be undramatic than that they be audible and
euphonious.

"COUSIN KATE"

July 4, 1903

In "Cousin Kate," the latest play by the latest playwright, the character which for me stands out most distinctly, and gives me the most amusement, is the character of the Rev. James Bartlett, a curate. I have seen many curates on the stage. Indeed, without a comic curate a comedy is held to be hardly complete. Curates, from time immemorial, have been one of the national butts. It has always been felt that there is something absurd about them. And I fear that the instinct is a sound one. Only, the absurdity of the average curate is not of the kind that is commonly attributed to him. He is not a fool, a prig, a molly-coddle, or any of those other things as which he is presented to us. He is quite an ordinary young man. But he occupies an extraordinary position. And it is in the contrast between what nature made him and what circumstances have made him, in the contrast between what he is and what he tries to be, that we find the true reason for the smiles which he provokes in us. Of course, there are other ordinary young men in extraordinary positions. There is the young doctor, there is the young solicitor. Each of these has to assume a measure of oracular wisdom, telling us sharply, gravely, what we must do and what we must not do, and knowing well that his advice may turn out to be quite wrong. The matters on which we consult a doctor or a solicitor are generally matters of which we, with our especial knowledge of ourselves, are quite competent judges; nor is the average doctor or solicitor endowed with such a gift of penetration as will raise him to our level; nor has he more common sense than we have. Yet we insist on sitting at his feet, and gaping for such words of unwisdom as he, lordly, shall vouch-safe us. We refuse to see that he is ridiculous. In the average curate we refuse to see anything else. There is a reason for this unjust difference. The doctor or solicitor practises his craft during certain hours of the day, in appropriate places, for fixed fees. For the rest of the day he is an ordinary, unspecialised human being. He does not have to cheapen himself and bring himself into ridicule by striking always a doctorial or solicitorial

attitude for every emergency, or for no emergency at all. Th
curate is less lucky. Wherever he is, at whatever hour, he mus
exemplify those qualities which in church he prays may be im
planted in us all. Of no finer clay than we are, he must appear t
be always gentle, cheerful, high-minded, simple-hearted, fulfille
with universal sympathy and love. He must behave, in fact, as
saint. Now, saints are rare, and not all of them are put into hol
orders. Consequently, the number of really impressive curate
is quite infinitesimal, and the number of really ridiculous curate
is quite enormous. Elderly clergymen are often impressiv
This is partly because their natures have by years of effort—ca
it pretence, if you will—been actually elevated some way toward
saintliness, so that between what they really are and what the
ideally ought to be there is no staggering distance; and partl
because they have, at least, gained ease of manner, and can con
port themselves with apparent naturalness. The young curate
necessarily ill at ease. He does not feel saintly, and he does n
know how to seem so. There are times, doubtless, when he is in
really gentle and cheerful frame of mind. But there are othe
when he is in a bad temper and depressed. His mind is n
always high, nor his heart always simple; and as for univers
sympathy and love, he has his likes and dislikes, even as the re
of us. In course of years he may develop a personal manner t
conceal these failings. But at present he has to adopt a conver
tional manner—to squeeze his voice and vocabulary and th
expression of his face into a conventional mould of saintlines
He has to cut himself hastily on a pattern. And the result mu
needs be ludicrous. He does not seem like a human being.
we happen to have known him before he was ordained, and kno
him to be quite a good fellow really, the ludicrous shock is double
for us. I remember reading in some novel (though I do n
remember in what novel) an amusing treatment of this situatio
The hero meets in London an old college friend who has just bee
ordained. He invites him to dinner, eager to renew the friendshi
But, try as he will, the friendship presently dissolves in his ow
irrepressible laughter. "If," he reflects, "I had never met hi
before, I could at least have kept my countenance." That is th
tragedy, or the comedy, of the average curate in real life: the co
trast between the saint that he isn't and the good fellow that he i

On the stage, hitherto, this contrast has been missed. There the curate has always figured as a merely absurd person, whose mannerisms are just what one expects of him. But in "Cousin Kate" Mr. Hubert Henry Davies lets us see a curate who is quite human despite his mannerisms. The Rev. James Bartlett, as he calls him, is a man of like passions with ourselves, to be hailed and taken seriously by us. And for that very reason he is irresistibly comic. The girl with whom he is silently in love is about to be married to another man. Almost on the eve of the wedding, the bridegroom disappears, and there is a general impression that he means to jilt the bride. The curate pays a call on the distressed household. As a man, he is, of course, overjoyed. But as a curate he has to offer that consolation of which he is universal provider. "May I," he says to the girl's mother, "sympathise with you very deeply in this visitation?" He sighs gently. "It is all lamentable—lamentable," he exclaims. "May I," he asks again, "hope that, though your path now seems dark, all may ultimately prove to be for the best?" The girl herself is presently handed over to him for ministration. "Be patient," he tells her, "and be assured that all shall be made plain." Later, when he has declared his own private feelings, the bridegroom reappears. "As," says he to the mother, "your daughter is about to take what is perhaps the most important step in her life, would it not be well to pause whilst there is yet time?" In all these passages we have exactly the diction of the average curate. The fatuousness is not exaggerated. Having to express broadcast, in and out of season, sentiments which he does not feel, the average curate must, as I suggested, reel off an artificial lingo. But Mr. Davies' cleverness is not so much in that he has caught this lingo and given it without the usual exaggeration of the comic playwright as in that he provides for the first time the foil by which the full absurdity of that lingo and of its utterer is made manifest. I think that the vicar of every parish in the land should send his curate or curates to the Haymarket before this play is withdrawn. . . . On second thoughts, I withdraw that suggestion. Our curates are conscious of their own defects, already; and, as these defects are an inevitable part of an inevitable system, to quicken that consciousness were an act of sheer brutality.

A PASTORAL PLAY

July 11, 1903

The most commonplace things must ever be the most signi
ficant. (This saying is itself a commonplace, and significan
accordingly.) Our trite form of greeting springs from the ver
root of things. That we say invariably "How are you?" is
analysed, an admission that the most important element i
human happiness is physical health. In every country the greet
ing is equivalent to ours, except in America. There the struggl
for wealth is so fierce, the pace to it so swift, that they take it a
a matter of course that no one is well. Every one there—ever
man, at least—is suffering from overstrained nerves. And
believe that when two male acquaintances hurry past each othe
on the street their greeting is a perfunctory "What have you?"
But in our hemisphere health is still the topic of prime importance
and nowhere is it so constantly debated as in that fleck on ou
hemisphere which is called England. For health depends ver
much on climate, and nowhere else is the climate so capricious
We never know what the weather will be, and how we shall be
to-morrow. Our interest in the weather is based on our will t
live. I do not see why among us any one should be sneered a
for opening a conversation with a reference to the weather. Th
wonder is that this fascinating and absorbing topic is ever—a
sometimes it is—subsequently dropped by two English inter
locutors. Of course, if meteorology were to become an exac
science, we should know where we were, and the weather, as
topic, would not so tyrannously dominate us. But, as meteoro
logy seems to be not yet a science at all, but simply a name given t
certain kinds of practical jokes lightly played on us at our ow
expense, we must needs continue to dabble in weather-wisdom o
our own account. Perhaps, in time, Science will atone for som
of the many burdens it has piled upon the frail shoulders o
humanity by discovering some means of not merely detecting, bu
also directing, the intentions of the elements. Utopian, I loo
forward to a time when there shall be erected, at Greenwich o
some other convenient place, an elaborate contrivance whereb

the clouds shall be "compelled," as erst by Zeus, and the winds be held in thrall, as erst by Æolus, and Phœbus himself be forced to smile pleasantly on us throughout all his daily tour. Rain shall fall in the country, as much of it as the farmers need; but in the cities never, save for a light shower, between three and four A.M., to lay the dust for the traffic of the coming day. Breezes shall come from the west to flatter us, and from the south to caress us. None shall be admitted from the other two points of the compass. We shall have entered on a Golden Age, wherein, among many other things, Pastoral Plays shall have become really delightful.

"Really possible" I was about to say. But had not Mr. Philip Carr, conning the bright lexicon of youth, found that they were not impossible even here and now? And had not he stepped lightly forth, an Ajax defying the rain, the snow, the wind, to say nothing of the lightning, to which we are, at all seasons, coweringly liable? "Quel geste!" I am glad to say that last week, when the Society which has been founded on his gesture produced "Comus" and "The Hue and Cry after Cupid," the elements, staggered by the sheer audacity of the thing, could not gather themselves together in time to punish it. And I am equally sorry to say that I was not able to witness their discomfiture. This week I attended a performance of "The Faithful Shepherdess," and alas! the elements were thoroughly themselves again. True, the rain, perhaps with a sneaking kindness for young insolence, held itself aloof from the concert of powers. But I felt that at any moment it might fall into line. Anyhow, as I entered the Botanical Gardens, I was shivering slightly.

Slightly shivering, but determined to spend a happy evening. I had often read and rejoiced in reading this delicate Pastoral. It had always conjured round me in my study an Italianised England. No Englishman, of course, could have made the play from his own unaided fancy. It needed first Guarini to set those sanguine shepherds and shepherdesses roving over the sunburnt grass. Such folk are not imaginable by a quite original English poet. Yet can they be stolen for us, and seen by us in the light of our own firesides. There, but hardly elsewhere. Remember that though Fletcher's poem was very much admired by contemporary critics, it was a failure on the stage, even though it was acted indoors, and even though there is good reason to believe that this island was warmer in the sixteenth century than now. However, I had always cherished the hope that my imaginings of the Wood before Clorin's Bower, and of the Wood with the Holy Well, might some day be actually realised for me. And, despite that slight shiver as I entered the Gardens, I was very receptive. The spirit was more than willing in me. I sighed, I slackened my pace, as though the evening were intensely hot. I *would* be attuned. I looked neither to the right nor to the left of the path, ignoring "This Way to the Gipsy Fortune-Teller" and "This Way to the Lucky Tub" and other similar lures whereby the cunning authorities tempt the ordinary visitor to believe that the open air isn't so bad after all. I would think only of Clorin and Amarillis, and Amoret, and those others. "Where," I asked of a man with a peaked and gold-braided cap, "is Clorin's Bower?" He was unlettered: I had to be more prosaic. But the taint of prose disappeared when I came within sight of what I sought. Entranced, I sat down and gazed at it. Others were seated beside me, but I was unconscious of them. My eye travelled over the undulating sward to that little forest of old trees. Trees were there of many kinds—cypresses, alders, willows, beeches, poplars. I do not, in point of fact, know one tree from another by name. But for the sake of style and colour, whether in thinking or in writing of them, I always hazard a guess at their names. Poplars, beeches, willows, elders, elms (I wanted a monosyllable, but could not think of one just then), cypresses—there they all were in their wistful and immemorial beauty, and over them all was the dim bloom of a summer twilight, and all of them, without exception, were shuddering in the wind. I shuddered in sympathy. I went, involuntarily, further than they: I sneezed. What if Clorin had heard me? Even now perhaps she was gazing reproachfully at me through the leaves. I dared not meet her steadfast eyes. I looked away from her bower. Yonder was a little lake, fringed with bulrushes. Them I can swear to. On the surface of this little lake were swimming two swans. One of them suddenly dived his head under the water. I looked quickly away—too late: I sneezed not once but twice. I had already noticed in the water the reflection of the moon, and I thought that perhaps the moon might help to keep me in the right key till the shepherds and shepherdesses should appear. I looked steadfastly up at the moon. It was at the full. I repeated to myself that it was at the full. It reminded me of a harvest-moon. Encouraged, I began to rehearse the epithets customarily applied to it. Honey-coloured . . . melancholy, inconstant, chaste . . . cold—I sneezed not twice but thrice. And at that moment, as by a miracle, three moons suddenly shone out from a bush—an oleander-bush—on the right-hand of the overt auditorium. Simultaneously, from the other side, came the music of flutes and viols. The performance was going to begin. Yes, there was Clorin herself, coming from the shadow of the leaves, to mourn that matchless shepherd who was dead untimely. "Hail, holy earth," she cried, "whose cold arms do embrace"—and the second line was lost to me through my own iambic sneezes. "Thus I free myself from all ensuing heats and fires," and again I succumbed, envying her power of imagination. There she stood, in the cold radiance of the quadruple moonlight, on the damp grass, in the almost whistling wind, vowing eternal maidenhood to the memory of a swain who, if he was worthy the sacrifice, must have been mutely imploring her from heaven not to stay out there catching her death of cold. The three additional moons, by the way, were merely the limelight. On the evening of my visit, the one ordinary moon would have been enough illumination; but Mr. Philip Carr was, of course, right not to have relied on it. Only, though limelight had to be there, it ought not to have been quite so obvious. It marred the naturalness of the scenery, and was the one blot on an otherwise impeccable essay in the art of producing a pastoral play. Had there been a little less artificial light, and a great deal of artificial warmth, everything would have been quite perfect. Even as it was, I enjoyed the performance immensely. I write "immensely" without exaggeration. But, if I were to attempt a conscientiously phonetic spelling, "ib-bedsely" would be, I regret to say, the correct version. "Et ego in Arcadia," but without a greatcoat.

MR. SHAW'S NEW DIALOGUES

September 12, 1903

Aristotle, often as he sneered at Plato, never called Plato a dramatist, and did not drag the Platonic dialogues into his dramatic criticism. Nor did Plato himself profess to be a dramatist; and it would need a wide stretch of fancy to think of him dedicating one of his works to Aristotle as notable expert in dramatic criticism. On the other hand, here is Mr. Bernard Shaw dedicating his new book to "my dear Walkley," that pious custodian of the Aristotelian flame, and arguing, with Platonic subtlety, that this new book contains a play. Odd! For to drama Mr. Shaw and Plato stand in almost exactly the same relation. Plato, through anxiety that his work should be read, and his message accepted, so far mortified his strongly Puritan instincts as to give a setting of bright human colour to his abstract thought. He invented men of flesh and blood, to talk for him, and put them against realistic backgrounds. And thus he gained, and still retains, "a public." Only, his method was fraught with nemesis, and he is generally regarded as a poet—he, who couldn't abide poets. Essentially, he was no more a poet than he was a dramatist, or than Mr. Shaw is a dramatist. Like him, and unlike Aristotle, for whom the exercise of thought was an end in itself, and who, therefore, did not attempt to bedeck as a decoy the form of his expression, Mr. Shaw is an ardent humanitarian. He wants to save us. So he gilds the pill richly. He does not, indeed, invent men of flesh and blood, to talk for him. There, where Plato succeeded, he fails, I must confess. But he assumes various disguises, and he ventriloquises, and moves against realistic backgrounds. In one direction he goes further than Plato. He weaves more of a story round the interlocutors. Suppose that in the "Republic," for example, there were "Socrates (in love with Aspasia)," "Glaucon (in love with Xanthippe)," etcetera, and then you have in your mind a very fair equivalent for what Mr. Shaw writes and calls a play. This peculiar article is, of course, not a play at all. It is "as good as a play"—infinitely better, to my peculiar taste, than any play I have ever read or seen enacted.

But a play it is not. What is a dramatist? Principally, a man who delights in watching, and can portray, the world as it is, and the various conflicts of men and women as they are. Such a man has, besides the joy of sheer contemplation, joy in the technique of his art—how to express everything most precisely and perfectly, most worthily of the splendid theme. He may have a message to deliver. Or he may have none. *C'est selon.* But the message is never a tyrannous preoccupation. When the creative and the critical faculty exist in one man, the lesser is perforce over-shadowed by the greater. Mr. Shaw knows well—how could so keen a critic fail to detect?—that he is a critic, and not a creator at all. But, for the purpose which I have explained, he must needs pretend through Mr. Walkley, who won't believe, to an innocent public which may believe, that his pen runs away with him. "Woman projecting herself dramatically by my hands (a process over which I have no control)." A touching fib! The only things which Mr. Shaw cannot consciously control in himself are his sense of humour and his sense of reason. "The man who listens to Reason is lost: Reason enslaves all whose minds are not strong enough to master her." That is one of many fine and pro-found aphorisms printed at the end of the book, and written (one suspects) joyously, as a private antidote to the dramatic tomfoolery to which Mr. Shaw had perforce condescended. Well! Mr. Shaw will never be manumitted by Reason. She is as inexorable an owner of him as is Humour, and a less kind owner, in that she does prevent him from seeing the world as it is, while Humour, not preventing him from being quite serious, merely prevents stupid people seeing how serious he is. Mr. Shaw is always trying to prove this or that thesis, and the result is that his charac-ters (so soon as he differentiates them, ever so little, from himself) are the merest diagrams. Having no sense for life, he has, neces-sarily, no sense for art. It would be strange, indeed, if he could succeed in that on which he is always pouring a very sincere con-tempt. "For art's sake alone," he declares, "I would not face the toil of writing a single sentence." That is no fib. Take away his moral purpose and his lust for dialectic, and Mr. Shaw would put neither pen to paper nor mouth to meeting, and we should be by so much the duller. But had you taken away from Bunyan or Ibsen or any other of those great artists whom Mr. Shaw, because they had "something to say," is always throwing so violently at our heads, they would have yet created, from sheer joy in life as it was and in art as it could become through their handling of it. Mr. Shaw, using art merely as a means of making people listen to him, naturally lays hands on the kind that appeals most quickly to the greatest number of people. There is something splendid in the contempt with which he uses as the vehicle for his thesis a conventional love-chase, with motors and comic brigands thrown in. He is as eager to be a popular dramatist and as willing to demean himself in any way that may help him to the goal, as was (say) the late Mr. Pettitt. I hope he will reach the goal. It is only the theatrical managers who stand between him and the off-chance of a real popular success. But if these managers cannot be shaken from their obstinate timidity, I hope that Mr. Shaw, realising that the general public is as loth to read plays as to read books of undiluted philosophy, will cease to dabble in an art which he abhors. Let him always, by all means, use the form of dialogue—that form through which, more conveniently than through any other, every side of a subject can be laid bare to our intelligence. It is, moreover, a form of which Mr. Shaw is a master. In swiftness, tenseness and lucidity of dialogue no living writer can touch the hem of Mr. Shaw's garment. In "Man and Superman" every phrase rings and flashes. Here, though Mr. Shaw will be angry with me, is perfect art. In Mr. Shaw as an essayist I cannot take so whole-hearted a delight. Both in construction and in style his essays seem to me more akin to the art of oral debating than of literary exposition. That is because he trained himself to speak before he trained himself to write. And it is, doubtless, by reason of that same priority that he excels in writing words to be spoken by the human voice or to be read as though they were so spoken.

The name of this play's hero is John Tanner, corrupted from Don Juan Tenorio, of whom its bearer is supposed to be the lineal descendant and modern equivalent. But here we have merely one of the devices whereby Mr. Shaw seeks to catch the ear that he desires to box. Did not the end justify the means, Mr. Shaw's natural honesty would have compelled him to christen his hero Joseph or Anthony. For he utterly flouts the possibility of a Don Juan. Gazing out on the world, he beholds a tremendous battle of sex raging. But it is the Sabine ladies who, more muscular than even Rubens made them, are snatching and shouldering away from out the newly-arisen walls the shrieking gentlemen of Rome. It is the fauns who scud coyly, on tremulous hoofs, through the woodland, not daring a backward-glance at rude and dogged nymphs who are gaining on them every moment. Of course, this sight is an hallucination. There are, it is true, women who take the initiative, and men who shrink from following them. There are, and always have been. Such beings are no new discovery, though their existence is stupidly ignored by the average modern dramatist. But they are notable exceptions to the rule of Nature. True, again, that in civilised society marriage is more important and desirable to a woman than to a man. "All women," said one of Disraeli's characters, "ought to be married, and no men." The epigram sums up John Tanner's attitude towards life even more wittily than anything that has been put into his mouth by Mr. Shaw. John Tanner, pursued and finally bound in matrimony by Miss Ann Whitefield, supplies an excellent motive for a comedy of manners. But to that kind of comedy Mr. Shaw will not stoop—not wittingly, at least. From John Tanner he deduces a general law. For him, John Tanner is Man, and Ann Whitefield is Woman—nothing less. He has fallen into the error —a strange error for a man with his views—of confusing the natural sex-instinct with the desire for marriage. Because women desire marriage more strongly than men, therefore, in his opinion, the sex-instinct is communicated from woman to man. I need not labour the point that this conclusion is opposite to the obvious truth of all ages and all countries. Man is the dominant animal. It was unjust of Nature not to make the two sexes equal. Mr. Shaw hates injustice, and so, partly to redress the balance by robbing Man of conscious superiority, and partly to lull himself into peace of mind, he projects as real that visionary world of flitting fauns and brutal Sabines. Idealist, he insists that things are as they would be if he had his way. His characters come from out his own yearning heart. Only, we can find no corner for them in ours. We can no more be charmed by them than we can believe in them. Ann Whitefield is a minx. John Tanner is a prig. Prig versus Minx, with the gloves off, and Prig floored in every round—there you have Mr. Shaw's customary formula for drama; and he works it out duly in "Man and Superman." The main difference between this play and the others is that the minx and the prig are conscious not merely of their intellects, but of "the Life Force." Of this they regard themselves, with comparative modesty, as the automatic instruments. They are wrong. The Life Force could find no use for them. They are not human enough, not alive enough. That is the main drawback for a dramatist who does not love raw life: he cannot create living human characters.

And yet it is on such characters as John and Ann that Mr. Shaw founds his hopes for the future of humanity. If we are very good, we *may* be given the Superman. If we are very scientific, and keep a sharp look out on our instincts, and use them just as our intellects shall prescribe, we *may* produce a race worthy to walk this fair earth. That is the hope with which we are to buoy ourselves up. It is a forlorn one. Man may, in the course of æons, evolve into something better than now he is. But the process will be not less unconscious than long. Reason and instinct have an inveterate habit of cancelling each other. If the world were governed by reason, it would not long be inhabited. Life is a muddle. It seems a brilliant muddle, if you are an optimist; a dull one, if you aren't; but in neither case can you deny that it is the muddlers who keep it going. The thinkers cannot help it at all. They are detached from "the Life Force." If they could turn their fellow-creatures into thinkers like themselves, all would be up. Fortunately, or unfortunately, they have not that power. The course of history has often been turned by sentiment, but by thought never. The thinkers are but valuable ornaments. A safe place is assigned to them on the world's mantelpiece, while humanity basks and blinks stupidly on the hearth, warming itself in the glow of the Life Force.

On that mantelpiece Mr. Shaw deserves a place of honour. He is a very brilliant ornament. And never have his ornamental qualities shone more brightly than in this latest book. Never has he thought more clearly or more wrongly, and never has he displayed better his genius for dialectic, and never has his humour gushed forth in such sudden natural torrents. This is his masterpiece, so far. Treasure it as the most complete expression of the most distinct personality in current literature. Treasure it, too, as a work of specific art, in line with your Plato and Lucian and Landor.

AN ÆSTHETIC BOOK

September 19, 1903

I revere the expert in an art; but I prefer the occasional critic. The mischief of being an expert is this: long before you have fairly earned the title, you have exhausted what you had to say; and, moreover, your knowledge of life and of the other arts has been rusting. Mr. Arthur Symons, whose new book* is my theme, must certainly be deemed an occasional critic of drama. He has gone, in his time, to many theatres, and written about what he saw in them; but he has not lingered in them exclusively; still less has he regarded them as his goal. By him they had merely been marked down among the many sights to be "done" by him as generally curious tourist. The notes he made of them are inevitably refreshing. True, we do not (for a reason which I will adumbrate anon) feel that here is a man who is in close touch with life. In that respect the book might be the work of a theatrical expert. Where it differs from such work is in the sense it gives us of a writer who has nourished his æsthetic sense by the study of diverse art-forms, and so can judge this particular art-form by a more general standard and with a larger vision. The expert is always tempted to pettifog. The occasional critic would hardly know how, even had he the desire, to pettifog. Yet in one branch of theatrical criticism, Mr. Symons is more knowing, more meticulous, than almost any of the regular critics. Theatrical criticism concerns itself with two arts, dramaturgy and acting. The ordinary critic devotes all his intelligence to the first, partly because it is the more important, and partly because, being itself a form of literature, it can more easily be written about. Many of our dramatists can get useful hints from many of our critics. But our mimes can derive no benefit save such pride as there is for them in knowing that they are "admirable," or have "never done anything better," or have "seldom been seen to greater advantage," and such shame as there may be in the consciousness that they are "somewhat disappointing" or "evidently suffering from the proverbial nervousness incidental to a first-night performance." On

* "Plays, Acting and Music." By Arthur Symons. Duckworth.

the other hand, I can imagine that the eminent mimes who in this book are so very sensitively and acutely appreciated might hail Mr. Symons as a wizard, in that he knows better than they how they make their every effect, and which of their effects is right, which wrong, and the why and the wherefore of all their fluid and elusive art. I can imagine that any young mime, reading attentively what Mr. Symons has to say of Coquelin and Bernhardt and Hading and many others, would derive real profit for his or her own work. I do not agree with all Mr. Symons' estimates. But the point is that they are estimates—keen and patient observations, made from a sound basis of first principles, and not merely the usual peppering of fortuitous epithets.

One reason why this book is so fresh and welcome is that we see for the first time the Pateresque manner and method of criticism applied to current dramatic art. "Pateresque" is no slight on Mr. Symons. I use it merely because "Symonsesque" would not, at present, be so quickly indicative. Mr. Symons is no mere servile imitator, though Pater had the good fortune to be born before him, and the bad fortune to die too soon to see how well his work would be carried forward. To say that the mantle of A has descended on B is usually but a polite way of saying that B, in his master's clothes, looks as like his master as a valet looks like his master. But there is no hidden sting to my image of Mr. Symons in Pater's mantle. Superficially, no doubt, Mr. Symons has indulged in some conscious imitation. His frequent "Well!" for the resumption of an argument is a conscious echo. But for Pater, again, he would not be so shy of showing us his sense of humour—would not swathe his jests in such solemn wrapper before venturing to slip them into his scheme. Nor would he so multiply his commas. But his conscious imitation does not go far. Essentially, he is himself, and that self merely happens to have been Pater's—a sensitive, fastidious, ever-ruminating self. The quietism of his style is, not less than Pater's, a genuine growth from within. The most salient point of likeness between the two men, that which is at once their cardinal strength and their cardinal weakness, is that for each of them (as, indeed, for every quietist) art matters more than life, and form in art more than meaning. Life was too harsh, chaotic an affair for the timid and exacting soul of Pater. He could not relish or digest it till art had minced

for him. He seldom mentioned it directly. When he cast his
riticism in the form of fiction, it was always some antique or very
loistral phase of life that he handled, some secretive and remote
oul that he dared finger. Once, indeed, he did venture out into
he open. But "Emerald Uthwart" is itself the greatest monu-
ient to his horror and ignorance of the hurly-burly. His aim
herein, his explicit aim, was to describe an averagely stolid
.nglish boy going to a public school, and subsequently going into
he army and dying heroically for his country. "See him as
e stands! counting now the hours that remain, on the eve of that
rst emigration"—that is, on the evening before he goes to school
or the first time. "That first emigration" is a whiff of smelling-
alts, to save the author from swooning on the threshold of awful
ctuality. "As Uthwart passes through the old ecclesiastical city,
pon which any modern touch, modern door or window, seems a
iing out of place through negligence, the diluted sunlight itself
ems driven along with a sparing trace of gilded vane or red tile
i it, under the wholesome active wind from the East coast. . . .
Uthwart duly passes his examination; and, in their own chapel in
ie transept of the choir, lighted up late for evening prayer after
ie long day of trial, is received to the full privileges of a scholar
·ith the accustomed Latin words:—*Introitum tuum et exitum
uum custodiat Dominus!*" Uthwart's whole school-life is treated
i this vein, as though it were a kind of passionate monasticism.
'he grim realities of warfare, when we find him later in the thick
f them, are described as one would describe a stately minuet,
anced by shadows. The story ends with an extract from the
iary of a surgeon. But, though this device savours of Miss
raddon, the surgeon himself, describing the post-mortem, is
idowed with all the lingering and exquisite melancholy of Pater's
pecial style. Only so, at that ceremonious distance, through
.ose veils, could Pater look life in the face. Not vivid, therefore,
ot very bracing and filling, is the impression he transmits. When
Ir. Symons deals directly with life, we suffer from a similar inani-
on. Life has no formal curves and harmonies. It is not an art.
Ir. Symons thinks that it is, if you can but see it rightly, and that
: is therefore in duty bound not to omit it from his syllabus.
As life too is a form of art," he says in his preface, "and the
sible world the chief store-house of beauty, I try to indulge my

curiosity by the study of places and of people." But the result
of this very discreet and tentative attitude is that Mr. Symons
hardly conveys through his writing that his subject is alive and
kicking. When he writes, as he often has written, of the cities
that he has visited, and tells us, with very delicate art, of the many
impressions they made on him, I always feel that they are, somehow, cities of the dead. I do not feel that pervasive animation
which is the keynote of a city's life. "Dear God! the very houses
seem asleep," and Mr. Symons, a still and solitary figure, muffled
seems to be crooning over them a delicious lullaby. In this book
he naïvely convicts himself of incapacity to write about actual
things. He confesses, like a certain statesman, but probably
with greater truth than he, that he never reads a newspaper.
The man who does not skim through at least one newspaper every
day is not a man who is interested in life, and not, therefore, a man
who can write well about it. Even when, as in this book, Mr
Symons is dealing with life only as filtered through art, his innate
quietism is sometimes a stumbling-block. Thus he argues that
Sir Henry Irving was an ideal Coriolanus because "he never
ranted." The truth, of course, is that Sir Henry failed as
Coriolanus because he was incapable of that harsh robustness
which is the very essence of the part. However, I do not deplore
such errors. They are the necessary defects of a quality. If Mr
Symons were not such a quietist, he would not be, on the whole
so patient and penetrating an art-critic. He would not, moreover
be himself. A definite self—that is what one most needs in a
critic. "It takes all kinds to make a world." And the habit of
demanding all kinds in one man is a stupid habit, due, no doubt
to that modern spirit of hurry-skurry which makes us so impatient
of all learning that cannot be absorbed quickly and easily from
one compendious source. Every quality has its defect, and it is
only by eclectic reading that we can behold that monster, the
perfect critic.

AN HYPOCRISY IN PLAYGOING

October 10, 1903

Eecosstoetchiayoomahnioeevahrachellopestibahntamahntafahnta
. . shall I go on? No? You do not catch my meaning, when I
write thus? I am to express myself, please, in plain English?
If I wrote the whole of my article as I have written the beginning
of it, you would, actually, refuse to read it? I am astonished.
The chances are that you do not speak Italian, do not understand
Italian when it is spoken. The chances are that Italian spoken
from the stage of a theatre produces for you no more than the
empty, though rather pretty, effect which it produces for me, and
which I have tried to suggest phonetically in print. And yet the
chances are also that you were in the large British audience which
I saw, last Wednesday afternoon, in the Adelphi Theatre—that
large, patient, respectful audience, which sat out the performance
of "Hedda Gabler." Surely, you are a trifle inconsistent? You
will not tolerate two columns or so of gibberish from me, and yet
you will profess to have passed very enjoyably a whole afternoon
in listening to similar gibberish from Signora Duse. Suppose
that not only my article, but the whole of this week's Review were
written in the fashion which you reject, and suppose that the price
of the Review were raised from sixpence to ninepence (proportionately to the increased price for seats at the Adelphi when Signora
Duse comes there). To be really consistent, you would have to
pay, without a murmur, that ninepence, and to read, from cover
to cover, that Review, and to enjoy, immensely, that perusal. An
impossible feat? Well, just so would it be an impossible feat not
to be bored by the Italian version of "Hedda Gabler." Why not
confess your boredom? Better still, why go to be bored?

All this sounds rather brutal. But it is a brutal thing to object
to humbug, and only by brutal means can humbug be combated,
and there seems to me no form of humbug sillier and more annoying than the habit of attending plays that are acted in a language
whereof one cannot make head or tail. Of course, I do not resent
the mere fact that Signora Duse comes to London. Let that
distinguished lady be made most welcome. Only, let the welcome

be offered by appropriate people. There are many of them
There is the personnel of the embassy in Grosvenor Square
There are the organ-grinders, too, and the ice-cream men. And
there are some other, some English, residents in London who have
honourably mastered the charming Italian tongue. Let all this
blest minority flock to the Adelphi every time, and fill as much of
it as they can. But, for the most part, the people who, instead of
staying comfortably at home, insist on flocking and filling are
they to whom, as to me, Italian is gibberish, and who have not, as
have I, even the excuse of a mistaken sense of duty. Perhaps they
have some such excuse. Perhaps they really do feel that they are
taking a means of edification. "We needs must praise the highest
when we see it"; Duse is (we are assured) the highest; therefore
we needs must see her, for our own edification, and go into rhap
sodies. Such, perhaps, is the unsound syllogism which these good
folk mutter. I suggest, of what spiritual use is it to see the highest
if you cannot understand it? Go round to the booksellers and buy
Italian grammars, Italian conversation-books, the "Inferno," and
every other possible means to a nodding acquaintance with
Italian. Stick to your task; and then, doubtless, when next
Signora Duse comes among us, you will derive not merely that
edification which is now your secret objective, but also that gratification which you are so loudly professing. I know your rejoinder
to that. "Oh, Duse's personality is so wonderful. Her temperament is so marvellous. And then her art! It doesn't matter
whether we know Italian or not. We only have to watch the
movements of her hands" (rhapsodies omitted) "and the changes
of her face" (r. o.) "and the inflections of her voice" (r. o.) "to
understand everything, positively *everything*." Are you so sure
I take it that you understand more from the performance of an
Italian play which you have read in an English translation than
from the performance of an Italian play which never has been
translated. There are, so to say, degrees in your omniscience
You understand more if you have read the translation lately than
if a long period has elapsed since your reading of it. Are you
sure that you would not understand still more if the play were
acted in English? Of course you are. Nay, and equally of course
you are miserably conscious of all the innumerable things that
escape you, that flit faintly past you. You read your English

version, feverishly, like a timid candidate for an examination, up
to the very last moment before your trial. Perhaps you even
smuggle it in with you, for furtive cribbing. But this is a viva
voce examination: you have no time for cribbing: you must rely
on Signora Duse's voice, hands, face and your own crammed
memory. And up to what point has your memory been crammed?
You remember the motive of the play, the characters, the sequence
of the scenes. Them you recognise on the stage. But do you
recognise the masquerading words? Not you. They all flash
past you, whirl round you, mocking, not to be caught, not to be
challenged and unmasked. You stand sheepishly in their midst,
like a solitary stranger strayed into a masked ball. Or, to reverse
the simile, you lurch this way and that, clutching futile air, like
the central figure in blindman's buff. Occasionally you do catch a
word or two. These are only the proper names, but they are
very welcome. It puts you in pathetic conceit with yourself, for
the moment, when from the welter of unmeaning vowels and con-
sonants "Eilert Lövborg" or "Hedda Gabler" suddenly detaches
itself, like a silver trout "rising" from a muddy stream. These
are your only moments of comfort. For the rest, your irritation
at not grasping the details prevents you from taking pleasure in
your power to grasp the general effect.

I doubt even whether, in the circumstances, you can have that
synthetic power fully and truly. It may be that what I am going
to say about Signora Duse as Hedda Gabler is vitiated by incapacity
to understand exactly her rendering of the part as a whole. She
may be more plausibly like Hedda Gabler than she seems to me.
Mark, I do not say that she may have conceived the part more
intelligently, more rightly, with greater insight into Ibsen's meaning. And perhaps I should express myself more accurately if I
said that Hedda Gabler may be more like Signora Duse than she
seems to me. For this actress never stoops to impersonation. I
have seen her in many parts, but I have never (you must take my
evidence for what it is worth) detected any difference in her. To
have seen her once is to have seen her always. She is artistically
right or wrong according as whether the part enacted by her can
or cannot be merged and fused into her own personality. Can
Hedda Gabler be so merged and fused? She is self-centred.
Her eyes are turned inward to her own soul. She does not try to

fit herself into the general scheme of things. She broods disdain-
fully aloof. So far so good; for Signora Duse, as we know her, is
just such another. (This can be said without offence. The
personality of an artist, as shown through his or her art, is not
necessarily a reflection, and is often a flat contradiction—a comple-
ment—to his or her personality in life.) But Hedda is also a minx,
and a ridiculous minx, and not a nice minx. Her revolt from the
circumstances of her life is untinged with nobility. She imagines
herself to be striving for finer things, but her taste is in fact not
good enough for what she gets. One can see that Ibsen hates her,
and means us to laugh at her. For that reason she "wears"
much better than those sister-rebels whom Ibsen glorified. She
remains as a lively satire on a phase that for serious purposes is out
of date. She ought to be played with a sense of humour, with a
comedic understanding between the player and the audience.
Signora Duse is not the woman to create such an understanding.
She cannot, moreover, convey a hint of minxishness: that quality
is outside her rubric. Hedda is anything but listless. She is sick
of a life which does not tickle her with little ready-made excitements. But she is ever alert to contrive these little excitements
for herself. She is the very soul of restless mischief. Signora
Duse suggested the weary calm of one who has climbed to a summit high above the gross world. She was as one who sighs, but
can afford to smile, being at rest with herself. She was spiritual,
statuesque, somnambulistic, what you will, always in direct
opposition to eager, snappy, fascinating, nasty little Hedda Gabler.
Resignedly she shot the pistol from the window. Resignedly she
bent over the book of photographs with the lover who had
returned. Resignedly she lured him to drunkenness. Resignedly
she committed his MS. to the flames. Resignation, as always, was
the keynote of her performance. And here, as often elsewhere, it
rang false.

However, it was not the only performance of Hedda Gabler.
There was another, and, in some ways, a better. While Signora
Duse walked through her part, the prompter threw himself into
it with a will. A more raucous whisper I never heard than that
which preceded the Signora's every sentence. It was like the
continuous tearing of very thick silk. I think it worried every
one in the theatre, except the Signora herself, who listened

placidly to the prompter's every reading, and, as soon as he had finished, reproduced it in her own way. This process made the matinée a rather long one. By a very simple expedient the extra time might have been turned to good account. How much pleasure would have been gained, and how much hypocrisy saved, if there had been an interpreter on the O.P. side, to shout in English what the prompter was whispering in Italian!

A MAGNIFICENT DIS-PLAY

October 17, 1903

If only Mr. Pinero would be simple! They say that he took two years to write "Letty"—three thousand hours or so, maybe, of solid labour. And not one too many. The modern form of dramaturgy is the most difficult of all the art-forms. Ibsen himself, even in his prime, was strictly biennial. Let Mr. Pinero be quinquennial, if so disposed. It is right for a work of art to be elaborate, in the literal sense of that word. But the elaboration of "Letty" is especially in the other sense. And to this difference I attribute the failure of "Letty" to evoke from me something beyond admiration for the author's amazing skill. An artist should labour to whittle away all that is superfluous to his main theme or idea. Even as an athlete is "trained" for the annihilation of every ounce of flesh that would impede the strong free play of his muscles, so must the work of art be "trained" till nothing is left but what is sharply essential to its effect. In Strasburg there is another mode of "training." Certain of the geese there are enclosed in hutches, and are given as much food as they want, and, having eaten that, are given by force very much more than they want. This system, hideous though it is, produces, at last, pleasant results for the epicure in food. But a similar system applied to works of art will not gratify the artistic epicure. That similar system has been applied by Mr. Pinero to "Letty." The play is too "rich."

Using the word in another sense, I declare Mr. Pinero himself

281

too "rich." It may sound paradoxical, but it is not the less true that Mr. Pinero would write better plays if he were a less richly endowed playwright. We all know the danger that lies in actual riches. We all know how the mere possession of fabulous wealth seems to crush the imagination of the millionaire, and to prevent him from regarding his means as a means to an end—except the end of empty ostentation. Tritely, by acquisition of yachts, motors, palaces, picture-galleries, grouse-moors, the millionaire seeks to dazzle us. And dazzled the majority of us is. When we are faced by an exceptional millionaire, who uses his money in pursuit of some ideal, we exchange glances and tap our foreheads significantly. Nobody, so far as I remember, accused "le petit sucrier" of being a lunatic. He scattered his gold down the customary channels, content with the flash of it, as were also we. But this other M. Lebaudy, who actually eludes our gaze, and will presently sail to a remote part of the world and try to work out an ideal—well, well, well! poor fellow! what a shame that he has no one to look after him! Similarly, there would not be such a general bowing-down to "our premier dramatist," if Mr. Pinero were less eager to dazzle us with a generous display of his perfectly-appointed technique, and more eager to illustrate simply a philosophic idea, or to develop simply a human theme. Just as do very great actual riches, so do very great dramaturgic riches seem to crush originality in their owner, and to foster ostentatiousness. A Henrik Ibsen is as rare as a Jacques Lebaudy—or (since this young man may prove to have not much in him beyond the mere power to break away from tradition) let me say, rather, a Cecil Rhodes. If Mr. Pinero were less brilliant in his specific way, there would be more room in him for ideas. As it is, there is no room at all. Mr. Archer, rather touchingly, ventures to hope that this absence of ideas is but "a transient phase of Mr. Pinero's development." As Mr. Pinero never has harboured ideas, it is rather too much to expect that he will proceed to do so now. A horse-dealer, commending the points of a pony, does not suggest that the pony is passing through "a transient phase of development" and will presently be a horse. Even so, Mr. Archer should not try to raise hopes that cannot be entertained—much less fulfilled. But, though the smooth and luscious fruit of Mr. Pinero's genius can no more prick us with underlying ideas than can thistles be gathered from grapes, there is in Mr. Pinero no lack of power for treating a human theme sincerely and fully. Mr. Pinero has a keen insight into human nature, more especially into the nature of women. And he might create really great pictures of life if he could but forget to show off his technical skill by bedevilling, as in "Letty" he bedevils, his main theme with a glittering congeries of inessential things. Let Mr. Archer concentrate his desires, not on making Mr. Pinero think, but on making him make us feel. A good quality cannot be implanted, but you can sometimes eliminate a bad one.

The essential conflict in "Letty" is strong, and the two conflicting characters are strongly imagined and set forth. On the one hand, we see a rich and rather sentimental profligate; on the other a very sentimental type-writer, rebellious against the shabbiness and drudgery of her existence. He is in love with her, she with him. She has wild hopes that he will marry her. The hopes are dashed: he is already married. There is another rich man, anxious to marry her; but he is definitely "a bounder," and she is vaguely "genteel." Here comes a conflict between her gentility and her desire to do nothing but wear pretty frocks. Gentility wins the day. Then comes a conflict of her inherited sense of propriety with her love of pretty frocks and her love of her lover. Shall she be mistress of the profligate? She wavers, consents, withdraws her consent. Subsequently she marries a "genteel" person in her own class, bears a child, and is fairly happy. Both she and the profligate are quite real people, behaving quite really. Their story is in itself extremely interesting and moving. And yet, somehow, one is unmoved by it; nor has one a keen sense of the reality of the two persons. This may be partly due to the performance. Miss Irene Vanbrugh catches exactly the tone of the type-writer whom she impersonates—the tone of the partially refined Cockney, "not quite a lady," but very lady-like indeed. She suggests perfectly the girl's social aspirations; but she does not compass a suggestion that the girl is in love. All the surface is there, but not the romantic soul. Mr. H. B. Irving, as the profligate, is ardent enough, but his ardour seems to belong to another time and place. As a fashionable young man of to-day and of London, he must be taken with several grains of salt. He is too remarkable. Give him a strong and odd character part, and he can be reconciled with modern life. But as young "Mr. Nevill Letchmere," leading in a flat in Grafton Street a life of frivolity, he compels us to remember that he is really a grim visitant from Olympus. We are not quite sure which of the gods he is. (Vulcan perhaps, without the limp.) But, whichever he be of them, we are frightened. That high collar round his throat, that hat perched so jauntily upon his head, are, we feel, the work of some practical joker, and the Olympian is going to avenge himself on *us*. Outwardly, he still preserves that air of sleek humility which he learnt from the Admirable Crichton; but we can see through it that he is raging within, and we tremble. At least, we should be trembling were not our sense of reality so outraged. Certainly, we must take his performance, and Miss Vanbrugh's, as accounting to some extent for the play's failure to give us so much illusion and emotion as we should expect from a play with so dramatic and so true a motive. But the main reason is that this motive is obscured for us by Mr. Pinero's passion for the extraneous. His skill is such that he can handle a whole mass of extraneous things with masterly ease, making them seem, at first glance, quite necessary. And that is the reason why he handles them. He must needs exercise and display his skill, perform feats of which all other men are incapable. Behold how many characters he can manipulate! Behold in how many exciting scenes he can place them without loss of verisimilitude! He will give you almost as much of the cinematographic method as can Mr. Cecil Raleigh, yet without the least strain on likelihood. Here is a fashionable restaurant, with waiters, and a manager, and different brands of champagne, and electric lights that can be switched off because it is the midnight of Saturday. And here are the leads of a housetop, with all the chimneys and the soot, and a piano-organ grinding out the latest popular tune from the street below, and a view of various steeples in the West End. And here is the anteroom of a fashionable photographer in Baker Street, with all the details. And every thing seems to be quite relevant. There was one moment, in the crucial scene of the play, when Miss Vanbrugh, rising from a sofa, inclined her body backwards and dangled her hands. I thought there was to be a cake-walk. I had been waiting for it, and I cannot understand the omission. Everything else of up-to-date actuality and "snap" is introduced so plausibly. Some of the subordinate characters, though all are amusing, are not quite so cinematographic. The tout for an insurance-agency, and the commercial traveller, seem like unpublished fragments of Dickens. The "bounder," though he is an outside broker, and is admirably played by Mr. Fred Kerr, might have stepped out of the pages of Samuel Warren, so remote is he from current reality. He is not a "bounder" but a "snob." It is strange that Mr. Pinero should have these lapses into bygone literature; for no one has a keener eye than he in studying from the models of living vulgarity. There is in this play a dressmaker's assistant whose every sentence rings phonographically true. Some of the effect produced by this part is due to the clever acting of Miss Nancy Price; but the part itself is an exquisite one, and only a pedant would grudge the author's extreme elaboration of it. One need not, however, be a pedant to deplore the elaboration of so many other things that are irrelevant to the central scheme of the play. If only, I repeat, Mr. Pinero could be simple! Why was it that the first act of "The Finding of Nancy," wherein we had almost exactly the same situation and problem as we have in "Letty," gave us so keen an illusion of reality, and moved us to so keen a sense of pity, while "Letty" leaves us cold and critical? It is because Miss Syrett, knowing little about her specific art, went straight to life, and threw us a bit of life, for what it was worth, with no clever superfluities. After the first act, her play fell to pieces, because she had not enough technical skill to carry the tale steadily forward. But that first act, for which little technique was needed, remains with us as a clear memory. And "Letty" shrivels in the light of it. Had Miss Syrett possessed one tithe of Mr. Pinero's technical skill, "The Finding of Nancy" would have been a fine whole. And could Mr. Pinero have made over to her nine-tenths of his technical skill, "Letty" would have been a fine whole. I have likened Mr. Pinero to a plutocrat. And, as erst in Galilee, he who has "great possessions" will be loth to part with them even for his salvation. But I don't want to dash Mr. Archer's hopes.

About the literary style of "Letty" I have more to say than can be said at the fag-end of an article.

MR. PINERO'S LITERARY STYLE

October 24, 1903

The previous instalment of my hebdomadal adventures into the variegated realm of things theatrical involved me in a consideration of that recent contribution to national dramatic art which is known by the homely but euphonious diminutive of Lætitia, and which is at this moment on public view at the playhouse whose cognomen is derived from a whilom namesake of the august deceased personage who similarly supplies a certain well-known columnal structure situate not a hundred miles from that rendezvous of the eminent, the Athenæum Club. In other words, I wrote about "Letty." But the unavoidable exigencies of that tyrannous goddess, Space, prohibited me from inquiring into, and animadverting upon, that special and particular department in the comprehensive emporium of the author's endowment which may succinctly be described as "literary style." In other words, I had not space in which to write about Mr. Pinero's literary style. I venture to surmise, however, that inasmuch as the manner in which Mr. Arthur Wing Pinero habitually wields his pen has earned for him from not a few quarters, from time to time, enthusiastic applause which is, in my opinion, by no means entirely merited, I may be pardoned for devoting a separate article to the same. In other words, here goes.

"Here goes!" The phrase ought not to be used here. But I plead the law of reaction. One cannot parody Mr. Pinero's manner without flying across into curt colloquialism. Likewise, for any one who goes to see "Letty," there comes—comes not long after the rising of the curtain—a time when he longs to throw things at the dramatis personæ and provoke from them a curt colloquial phrase or two, however irrelevant to the play's action. Mr. Pinero, I fancy, would be shocked by this impulse, and would have a good many long words to say about it. He would refuse to accept as establishing a desirable standard for his own professional endeavour the demands of those who are notoriously congenitally incapacitated from extracting personal gratification from the presence of literary style. Doubtless he really does think that he has literary style. Doubtless, many other innocents think so too. To clear the ground, let me begin by making him and them realise what *is* literary style, generally, and in plays particularly. Then we shall soon be agreed that Mr. Pinero hasn't it.

Generally, it is the exact expression of a writer's self through means of written words. Some people—most people—die inarticulate. A few can exactly express themselves in talk, a few in public speaking. The specific gift for conversation or for oratory is always denied to the man who is born to express himself in writing; for one means precludes another. Shut him in a room, with pen and ink and paper, and then only will he reveal himself. Words will come to him at his bidding, even as to some people (we know not why) birds will come. They are not shy of him, and he knows them one from another, and can make them do what he wills. His little game, like the talker's or the orator's, is self-expression; and his material is the same as theirs, but must be very differently used. *They* can make words live, and live variously, by modulations of the voice, by movements of the hand, by facial play. These tricks are quite as apt to the purpose of self-expression as are the words themselves. But for the writer words are the all-important and the only means, and they have to be used so cunningly as to supply all that in the medium of literature is lacking. Special words, special constructions, which would be ridiculous and unmeaning from live lips, must be used for just this or that effect which from live lips could be produced. Good writing is a thing of infinite formality. Yet the formality must not reveal itself. So soon as that happens, the writing ceases to be good, becoming lifeless. Such, then, is the making of a literary style. And happy he who can compass it! But there are pleasant and unpleasant literary styles. A man may express himself exactly, yet not please us. He is the man who lacks inward harmony, and so cannot use his medium beautifully. The man who expresses himself both exactly and beautifully is the man for us. He, none other, is the true stylist.

So much for the matter at large. Now come and determine with me what is literary style in that particular kind of writer, the dramatist. Obviously, it must be something very different, so very different are the conditions. The dramatist writes words not to be read, but to be spoken, and to be spoken not by himself for self-expression, but by other human beings for expression of certain puppets. From the first of these two differences it follows that the words must be far easier, more colloquial and familiar, than the words of the ordinary writer. In poetic drama, of course, where one has already the convention of metre, licence is given for elaborate dignity in words. But even here is made a reservation. There must be a tincture of oral style throughout the speeches. The exact nature of this difference is not easy to explain. Perhaps you can grasp it best by a comparison of the style in Shakespeare's sonnets with the style in his dramatic soliloquies. However, I am dealing here more particularly with style in those modern realistic plays of which "Letty" is one. The first essential is that the persons must speak in the manner of human beings. Or rather, they must *seem* to be speaking in that manner. For human beings talk so irrelevantly, so raggedly, so much, that a verbatim reproduction would be quite dreadful : the play would never end, nor should we know what it was all about. Selections, compressions, sharpenings, are all needful. But they must be made inobtrusively. We must not be conscious that the characters are not wasting the breath that would certainly be wasted if they were real. And not only must every character talk like a real person : they must all talk like different persons. So that, whereas in ordinary writing style is the perfect expression of the writer's self, in plays it is the perfect expression of various selves. But not that only. Just as in ordinary writing true style is a beautiful thing in itself, so in drama the true stylist will make his characters talk beautifully. This is a hard saying, perhaps, in relation to the law which I have been laying down. But, hard though it be, you must receive it. Human beings, doubtless, are not more apt to talk beautifully than to talk expressively and to the point. But, just as the persons of a play can be kept expressively to the point, so can they be made to use musical cadences, with no loss of verisimilitude. The trick is difficult. But it can be performed. And the dramatists by whom it cannot be performed must not be hailed as stylists.

Now, when a writer of books takes it into his head to write a play, his characters, almost inevitably, talk like his books. If his books happen to be permeated with style, the result may be charming, but it is not the less wrong. He is not a stylist "ad hoc."

His style is "matter out of place," and should be swept away. It would be all very well if his characters talked like various books and were dramatic embodiments of various literary ladies and gentlemen. For you will find that literary persons always talk in a literary way. Accordingly, they are not good talkers, in the strict sense. Their manner clashes with their medium. Listening, you would much rather write down the spoken words and read them at your leisure. Their talk is, indeed, a form of dictation. So is the talk of journalists—of busy journalists, at least. Suppose that all the characters in "Letty" were very busy journalists, all on the staff of one very inferior provincial daily paper, Mr. Pinero might be credited with a certain measure of literary style. We could congratulate him on having got so far as to make his characters talk as they would in real life. You see I have already plunged from the abstract into the personal side of our inquiry. I am sorry to have let the horrid truth out so abruptly; but there it is: Mr. Pinero's "literary style" is nothing but the lowest and most piteous kind of journalese.

After all, my attempt at parody had prepared you for that truth. Let a few quotations from "Letty" now drive it home. A visitor to Mr. Letchmere's flat complains of the heat. "My man," says the host, "has been neglecting to lower the sun-blinds." What a ghastly equivalent for "my man hasn't pulled down the blinds"! He complains to the valet: "This room is as hot as Hell." "Not quite so hot as that, I think, Sir." "We will not discuss that now. You will have ample opportunity for testing the truth of that simile at some future date." Mr. Letchmere, sending the valet to bed: "I shall require nothing further." Invited to join a supper party: "let no one be incommoded." Reassuring a lady who overhears a quarrel: "These little differences are invariably settled amicably." Very angry: "The result, now that I view it closely, is none the more palatable." I dare not quote longer instances of Mr. Letchmere's manner (which is also the manner of all but the intentionally comic persons in the play): those which I remember seem so grotesque that I may not have remembered them accurately. I wish to be quite just to Mr. Pinero. But I think I have quoted enough to show that no tempering with mercy, however gently rain-like and thrice blest, could prevent justice from condemning him to perpetual banishment

among the penny-a-liners from whom his style is borrowed.
Nay, these penny-a-liners have an excuse that cannot be pleaded
by him. They are paid by the line. They live by the length and
number of their words, whose quality matters not at all. Mr.
Pinero just receives a "royalty" for every performance of his play.
His style is, therefore, penny-a-lining for penny-a-lining's sake.
Rather a monstrous anomaly, that, is it not?

THE CRITIC AS PARIAH

October 31, 1903

We are not liked, we critics. The creators of art do not like
us, nor do the men in the street. And why not? Let us probe.
To account for a misfortune is to purge away half its bitterness.

We may be divided roughly into two schools: the ancient or
academic, and the modern or temperamental. Of course, these
two classes overlap. No man, however steeped in academicism,
can quite rid himself of his own prejudices and predilections.
No man, however intent on making the most of his own egoism,
can keep himself unspotted from the world of ready-made judgments and classifications in which he has been reared. Still, the
distinction is real and useful. Let us separately consider the
two distinct schools from the two distinct standpoints of artist
and man in the street.

Whereas the temperamentals are newcomers, the academics
have been with us for centuries, and the prejudice against them is
accordingly easier to analyse. Our literature—every literature,
indeed—teems with denunciations of them by artists. Often
these denunciations have been merely outcomes of wounded
vanity. But there is underlying most of them a wider and deeper
sentiment. We find there the contempt felt by the man who can
do something, and does it, for the man who cannot do it, but does
talk a lot about it. We find, also, the wrath of the doer, who works
in passionate concentration on one kind of thing, against the
arrogant outsider who just comes along and glances at the result,

and gives it a good or bad mark in relation to a host of other things beyond this doer's ken. Both the wrath and the contempt are very natural feelings, surely. "You think it good? Confound your impudence. You think it bad? Go and do it yourself." That is for the artist an inevitable attitude. Of course, it is a wrong attitude. No one should ever say "yah." If the academic critic could do the thing half so well as the artist, he would be accordingly less capable of wide appreciation. It is his impotence that keeps his taste in proper working order. But the artist, who knows his taste in his own work to be much finer than the critic's, and cares not a rap about taste in other kinds of work, cannot be expected to make the just allowance. As for the men in the street, they may be anxious to learn from the critic. But a thirst for learning does not involve a love for the teacher. Ever since the schoolmaster stood revealed by the lifting of the dark ages, his name has been a by-word for unpopularity. Nor have the little pupils in his charge more cordially disliked him and his rough-and-ready, cut-and-dried authority than have the quite adult and independent observers of him. And he, after all, is not lording it over the makers of the facts which he teaches. He does not indicate the line of attack or defence which Cicero ought to have taken in his conduct of this or that lawsuit. He is not down on the technique of Sophocles. He asks you to tell him the capital of Russia : he does not tell you what city ought, in his own very final opinion, to be the Russian capital. If he went on in that way he would soon be hounded from his own form-room. The academic critic does habitually go on in that way; hence the impulse, as irresistible in the average man as in the artist, to bid him go and do something himself and then let us see what it looks like. I think that this contemptuous impulse is shared, in some degree, by the very critic himself. He is confronted with a work of art which he knows to be bad, and which he promptly shows to be bad. The exercise may exhilarate him; but all the while a still small voice is whispering in his ear, "You couldn't have done it so well yourself. You hadn't the pluck or talent even to attempt it." He tosses his head, and "Pshaw!" he says, "the other fellow would be equally incapable of writing this criticism. It is a piece of very admirable criticism. It is a very fine work of creative art. I am every bit as creative as the other fellow." This theory of the

creativeness of criticism is strongly upheld by Mr. Walkley in hi
delightful treatise, "Dramatic Criticism." It is a very speciou
and comfortable theory. Up to a certain point, it is a quite tru
theory. I agree that "criticism, like any other art, is a mode o
self-expression," and, like any other art, "a channel for the com
munication of ideas and emotions between man and man." Th
critic, like the mime or the player of a musical instrument, has
right to be called creative. Virtue comes out of him. But i
does not do so of its own accord. The critic has to be wound u
from the outside. And thus he is not so creatively a creator a
the artist whose work is his theme. He is on a lower plane
Therefrom he may tower higher than the man on the plane abov
him. Even so, a lay-brother in a monastery may be much fulle
of faith and good works than some of the regular monks; yet h
sits below the salt, and his place imposes on him a sense o
inferiority. The critic suffers from just that sense, and wit
better reason. To lull it, he gives himself airs. Less wonder
then, that the rest of the world can't abide him.

The greater part of what I have been saying is as applicable t
the case of temperamental critics as to the case of academic critics
Both schools are disliked because they consist of talkers rathe
than doers. But though the temperamentals do more than th
academics, and though they have not that fatal affinity to school
masters, they are not less disliked both by artists and by men in th
street. Why is this? Of course, an artist likes (in a condescend
ing way) the critic to whose temperament his work happens t
appeal truly. But there are many kinds of temperament, and on
artist's work cannot truly appeal to more than one of these
Therefore, every artist can tolerate only one kind of tempera
mental critic. The rest he dislikes. The reason why one and al
are disliked by the man in the street is that they are professedl
selfish. It is something in their favour that they do not wish t
instruct other people; but it is not less heavily against them tha
they wish merely to amuse themselves. Their pleasure is i
determining "the exact quality of pleasure" derived by them
from this or that work. Incidentally, they may help their fellow
creatures towards a similar pleasure. But that is not their aim
They have an abstract air—an air of self-sufficiency. From Walte
Pater and Anatole France downwards, they have a way of smilin

o themselves and talking under their breath. They might be nicknamed "the Hornerists" of literature. You need no more exact description of Pater or France than that he sits in a corner, eating a Christmas pie, and puts in his thumb, and pulls out a plum, and says "What a good boy am I!" As with the masters, so with the disciples. They seem quietly greedy, and not anxious to share. Thus the possible exquisiteness of their palate does not affect your disapproval of them. To a perfect cook you are grateful, but not to the solitary consumer of a perfect dish. Very similar is the difference between your attitudes to the creative artist and to the temperamental critic. Of course, if you would pause to think, you would have to admit that the creative artist is as self-centred as the temperamental critic. He likes your applause, but it is not to please you that he writes. And, even as from his work, so can you, and do you, derive pleasure from the work of the temperamental critic. But it is quite natural that you should harbour an unreasonable prejudice against himself. So many unreasonable things are natural. All natural things are tainted with unreason.

"THE TEMPEST"

November 7, 1903

Over certain of the plays of Shakespeare broods darkly the superstition that they don't "act well." Whenever a manager dashes in, undaunted by this shadow, and produces one of these plays, we are startled to find that the play does act very well indeed. "Julius Cæsar," "King John," "Richard II," "A Midsummer Night's Dream," were all of them, within recent years, regarded as forlorn hopes. "The Tempest" was in like case. More artistically compact, and therefore more modern, in form than any other Shakespearean play, it was yet scouted as apt only to "the study." True, Mr. Benson had it in his repertory (as, indeed, he had also two, at least, of those other plays which I have named). But somehow, admirable though they are in many ways, Mr.

Benson's productions do not make a sharp and durable impression.
They are enjoyed, but not cherished in recollection. Though Mr.
Benson proved to London, two or three years ago, that "The
Tempest" was apt to the stage, the lesson, conclusive at the
moment, has been forgotten. Here comes Mr. J. H. Leigh, to
teach it again. But do not run away with (or rather from) the
idea that Mr. Leigh is a mere educationist. The unfamiliarity of
his name, and the deviousness of his venue (the Court Theatre),
and the report that his cast is recruited from an histrionic academy,
might make you—probably *have* made you—a trifle shy and
suspicious. Courage! Hold not back! Press boldly on to
Sloane Square! For Mr. Leigh's production is quite vivid and
pretty, quite untainted by pedantry. Some of my colleagues have
called it a compromise between the spectacular method and the
method of the Elizabethan Stage Society. That fosters a false
impression. To the method of Mr. Poel (quem, I hasten to add,
honoris causa nomino) there is not in Mr. Leigh's method the
faintest affinity. The play is treated here, not as a dead thing, at
which in its shroud we may be permitted to peer, but as a live and
kicking organism, as a thing visible from a modern standpoint,
susceptible to a modern method—in fact, as a classic, in the true
and full sense. The method is not the less spectacular because
the spectacle has to be on a small scale. No vast sums of money
could be forthcoming for a venture of this kind; but there has
been no stint of taste and ingenuity. From so small a stage as
the Court's we cannot gain that illusion of airy distance which we
need for a full sense of the mysterious island. But the scene-
painter has done his best, and a very decent best it is. The fairies
and nymphs and other spirits cannot swarm here, as ideally they
would; but we behold very respectable samples of them. In one
sense, the smallness of the stage is a positive gain for us. Against
the advantages of a very big stage must be set always this defect :
the characters become less than life-size, and thus shed much of
their proper dignity and importance. To atone for their tininess,
the mimes proceed to make terrific efforts, talking at a far higher
pitch, forcing their feet to take far longer strides, and their hands
to make far more comprehensive arabesques, than can be reconciled with the true expression of nature. They cease to be men
and women impersonating men and women. They seem rather

like a multiplied incarnation of the frog in the fable. Of course, there are mimes in whom the effort is not painfully apparent; but the effort is always there, a drag on the art of acting; and from the purely physical standpoint, there is not a single mime who can make the right effect, for giants find it more lucrative to be exhibited singly in side-shows than to take their chance on the legitimate stage. On a very big stage the fairies at Prospero's command would be of exactly the right size. At the Court they are of the wrong, the human, size. But Prospero himself is of the human, the right, size. And that is the more important point, surely. Sprites are nearer to humanity than is the gravely predominant Prospero to spritedom.

It is mainly from Prospero that "The Tempest" draws for us its peculiar interest and fascination. Of course, its technical difference, to which I have alluded, is an interesting and fascinating point. Here, one might say, is the least Shakespearean of all Shakespeare's plays. For what is the salient thing about Shakespeare? Surely, the careless exuberance, the headlong impatience, of his art. Like the age in which he wrote, he was essentially young. In the heat of his creative power, he cared not at all—could not pause to bother—how he expressed himself. Everything came out anyhow, shot by blind and irresistible impulse. Consider that debauch of uncontrolled fancy, "A Midsummer Night's Dream." With it "The Tempest" is often bracketed, by reason of the supernatural element in either play. But the two are at opposite poles. The one is a debauch, the other a work of art. True lovers of Shakespeare must needs prefer the debauch. "The Tempest" seems, by comparison, cold and calculating. One misses the headiness, the mad magic, of the youthful work. The divinely-overdone poetry has been chastened and straightened into something akin with prose. We have been transported from Thebes to Athens. Or say, we have passed from the rose of dawn into the twilight of evening. Yes, "The Tempest" is essentially the work of an elder. And for that very reason it seems, as I suggested, so modern. Art triumphs only over impoverished vitality. The reason why modern artists are so artistic is that they are not overwhelmed with a surplusage of emotions and ideas. They can practise restraint only because they have little to restrain. So it was with Shakespeare, when, before letting fall the pen from his hand, he wrote "The Tempest." Yet of all his plays "The Tempest" is not only the most artistic, but also the most original. I say "yet," for a paradox must be broken gently, that its truth be accepted. "Therefore" were the right conjunction. Not in the heat of creativeness are artists ever original. Having so much to give forth, and being by that impulse so pressed for time, they snatch at the handiest means. Into ready-made moulds they can pour quicklier their genius. In fact, like other spendthrifts, they will beg, borrow, or steal. But their unscrupulousness comes of wealth, not of poverty. That is the paradox, and the tragedy, at the root of all great literature. In some other planet there may be, but never will be in ours, a great writer expressing the full vigour of his greatness in his own way, and with exquisite care. An artistic conscience, and the desire for originality—a desire bred of self-consciousness and pride—will find entrance only when the breast shall have been eased of its tumultuous and surging contents. I have called "The Tempest" the least Shakespearean of Shakespeare's plays. It is that because into it Shakespeare put more of himself than into any other. Generation after generation of German and other commentators has been groping dustily, fustily, mustily, for "the sources" of this play. Every other play has been tracked down to the place it was filched from. "The Tempest" alone is unproven a theft. Mustily, fustily, dustily, the commentators are groping, everywhere, still, at this moment. But their labour is in vain, I think. I think the reason why this one story has not been tracked down to Italy or elsewhere is that Shakespeare invented this one story. Enchanting though it is, perhaps it is not in itself a great story. But as an allegory it is perfect. Obviously, Shakespeare, at the close of his career, wished to write an epilogue to his work, an autobiography, in allegorical form. That was a very natural wish. And what more natural than that he could not lay hands on any ready-made story whereby to symbolise his meaning? And what more natural than that he should proceed to evolve from his own brain, now at leisure for the task, a story after his own less quickly-pulsing heart? The very difference in form, the neat unity, of "The Tempest" may be taken as internal evidence that here the poet was working untrammelled from without. Though age had checked his diffuseness in other plays, too, "The Tempest" is the only one that satisfies the modern standard of art. And age, alone, is not enough to account for the singularity.

To impersonate Prospero is a solemn and difficult task for any actor. He has to impress us, not merely as a rightful Duke, endowed with supernatural powers, and now quitting his enchanted place of exile for his native duchy, but also as Shakespeare, retiring from dramatic authorship into privacy and leisure. By the way, I ought to have qualified my assertion that the allegory is perfect. The island is a perfect symbol for the theatre. Ariel is a perfect symbol for the genius which had served Shakespeare to weave his spells and was now to be hard-worked no more. Caliban (beyond his merely topical symbolism for the Virginian as slave) is a perfect symbol for the "groundlings" whom Shakespeare, having tried in vain to elevate them, was glad to leave in untroubled possession of the theatre. But one does not see why Shakespeare, a bourgeois, relapsing to obscurity from the sphere in which his genius had shone so lustrously, should sneer so persistently at his own "rough magic," and at theatrical art in general, and should imply that he is returning to a nobler and worthier sphere. Had he been, besides a dramatist, a master of scientific philosophy, believing, like Bacon, that " it is not good to stay long in the theatre," and had he, as had Bacon . . . but I am treading on a volcano, and I will not risk that eruption of fury which immediately overwhelms any definite refusal to treat a still open question as settled for ever. Enough that he who impersonates Prospero impersonates also the creator of Prospero, and that so we need of him a double dignity and weight. Mr. Acton Bond acts in a scholarly and charming way, and has enough authority to carry him well through the part of Prospero proper. But he does not quite satisfy our hunger for a realisation of Prospero's creator. Mr. Leigh himself plays Caliban, and is duly "savage," but ought surely to be more "deformed." Miranda, that extremist among ingénues, loses nothing by Mrs. Leigh's interpretation of her, and Mr. Charles Lander speaks well the lines of Ferdinand. Ariel is less lucky. Better the suggestion of a mere human being, however helpless, than of a pantomime fairy, however capable.

THE OLDER AND BETTER
MUSIC HALL

November 14, 1903

"An octogenarian in the hunting-field" is the title of annual paragraphs in the daily press. Annually one reflects that "an octogenarian in bed" were better news. One may be wrong. There are men incapable even of growing old—men so insignificant that Time overlooks them. Let such men pursue foxes even to the brinks of their own graves. As with the body, so with the mind. There are they who never cease to be intellectually receptive. A new idea, or a new movement, appears in their senile course, and lightly they "take" it, undaunted by the five bars or so, and gallop on. One admires them as showy exceptions to the law of nature. But one knows that they could not be so receptive if in their youth and prime they had ever deeply understood, or felt strongly, anything. They are shallow, and they are cynics, these genial old souls. What shall be said of those others who, having long ago exhausted their curiosity and keenness, do yet, in sheer vanity, pretend themselves keen and curious? How graceless an eld is theirs! See them riding to the meet, laced and stayed to a semblance of jauntiness! See them furtively leading their horses through the gaps, and piping, at last, a husky "view holloa" over the fallen fox! (Any reader who is also a sportsman will amend my metaphor if it is wrong.) Such impostors deserve no mercy from us. To us the prejudices of eld are sacred, and should be yet more sacred to their holders. I, for one, in the fulness of time, shall make no secret of them. I am too closely in touch with things now, too glad and eager, to be elastic in the dim future, and as for pretending to be elastic . . . no! I look forward to a crabbed and crusty old age. I mean to be a scourge of striplings.

The history of a keen soul in relation to a live art falls usually into three parts: (1) The soul lives in the future, the art lagging behind. (2) The soul lives in the present, the art having caught it up. (3) The soul lives in the past, left behind by the art. My soul, in relation to dramatic art, is still in its first stage. (Or rather, dramatic art, in relation to my soul, is still in its first stage.

For the soul itself is always static.) So far as the theatre is concerned, I am still a beckoner, a "progressive." But in the matter of music halls, I am already a staunch, even a passionate, reactionary—not a beckoner, but a tugger-back. There never was a time when the music halls lagged behind my soul. To me, as stripling, they seemed perfectly delightful. I dislike the fashion that now dominates not merely the specific "palaces of varieties" but also such places as the Pavilion, the Tivoli, and even that titular home of lost causes and impossible loyalties, the Oxford. The stripling reader tries politely to repress a sneer. Let him sneer outright. I can justify my prejudice. I may be old-fashioned, but I am right. The music-hall entertainment ought to be stupid, as surely as the drama ought to be intelligent. In every human creature is a mixture of stupidity and cleverness, and for both qualities we need nutrition. How can we satisfy our cleverness in a music hall? What comes to us but a sense of confusion and fatigue from the fashionable gallimaufry of clever poodles, clever conjurers, clever acrobats, clever cinematographs, clever singers and clever elephants? No good can be done to the intellect where no mental effort can be sustained and concentrated. A music hall, by its inherent nature, precludes such good. On the other hand, it can appeal very pleasantly to the stupid, or sensuous, side of us. It did this in the good old days, when there was an unbroken succession of singers, alternate males and females, each singing a couple of songs written and composed in accord to certain traditional conventions. We did not come away wiser and better men; but an inward unity in the entertainment had formed for us a mood. All those so similar songs were merged into our senses, pleasing and amusing, subtly sedative, warm. That old lilt in the veins of us—how bitterly we miss it! Even such songs as are still sandwiched in at the modish halls have lost all their charm. Patter leaves but a corner to tune. Like many other men of original genius, Mr. Dan Leno broke the form provided for his expression. We gladly barter tune for a full sense of so delightful a personality and so accomplished an actor as Mr. Dan Leno. But the others, the imitators, do not make good our loss. Clever they are, more or less, but we—we who are not of a generation that knows no better—would gladly sacrifice their cleverness in return for straightforward tunes.

Can we anywhere recapture the olden pleasure? Indeed, yes.
I have found a place. Let me guide you to it. Half way up the
Edgware Road we come to a very signally illuminated building.
Nothing could seem more brand-new than the front of this
Metropolitan Music Hall; but enter, and you will be transported,
deliciously, into the past. The system of ventilation is quite
perfect, yet the atmosphere is the atmosphere of a decade since.
Look, listen!

> "If *you* don't trouble trouble
> Trouble doesn't trouble *you*,
> So don't—you—worry over me!"

Is it—no—yes—it must be—it *is* Mr. Harry Freeman. That
simple, jolly, straightforward singer, dancing as he sings—how
long is it since we saw him? We tremble lest he have truckled
to changing fashion. Not he! No patter: just a short, sharp
phrase uttered through the music between the chorus and the next
verse—no more. A thousand memories sweep back to us from
that beaming face under the grey bowler hat. That face radiates
the whole golden past, and yet, oddly enough, seems not a day
older than when last we looked on it. We—we have changed.
Our taste, however, is as of yore, and we always did delight in
Mr. Harry Freeman. We beat time to his familiar music. We
sit again at his ever-moving feet. He always was a philosopher,
in his way. He was always a Stoic. A Stoic he remains. As of
yore, he is overwhelmed with misfortune. Fate still smites him
hip and thigh. He has just been robbed by one man and knocked
down by another. His home has been broken up. He has been
recently in prison. But

> "If *you* don't trouble trouble
> Trouble doesn't trouble *you*,"

and no sympathy is craved by this joyous dancer. The attitude
has a more than personal significance. Not long ago, Mr. Arthur
Symons wrote an essay about the very thoroughfare whose inhabitants Mr. Freeman is now delighting. He suggested that the
dominant characteristic of these inhabitants was a dull acquiescence in the sordidness of their lives. Acquiescent they are, but
not dully so. Mr. Symons, very naturally, cannot imagine a man

leading with pleasure their kind of life. They who have to lead it, however, take it as a matter of course, and are quite cheerful about it. They are, in fact, Stoics. This is one of the advantages of the old music hall over the new: it does reflect, in however grotesque a way, the characters of the class to which it consciously appeals. And so, after all, accidentally, one gets from it a mental stimulus. . . . Who is this vast man in evening dress? A "Lion Comique"? Not quite that. But something contemporaneous: a "Basso Profondo." He urges us to tak' the high road; he himself is going to tak' the low road. Loch Lomon', in 1903! Delightful! . . . And here is a "Serio," with the true Serionian voice and method:

> "Do not complain,
> I'll single remain,
> Of sweethearts I want no other."

The gallery-boys take the chorus from her, and she sways silently from side to side in measure to the waltz, smiling the smile of triumph. Comes a "Burlesque Actress," dressed daringly. The diamonds flash, but the heart is in the right place, and the song is about some one whose

> "Sweet face so glad
> Brings smiles to the sad."

Comes a "Comedienne." She strikes a rather more modern note. There is, according to her, one, and only one, way of putting the War Office on a sound basis, and that is the instant instalment of Sir Redvers Buller. The audience unanimously endorses her scheme, and she is, no doubt, right; but we regret the introduction of any names that were not names to conjure with in our boyhood: they are anachronisms here. Mr. Harry Randall, with his patter, is another anachronism. Several other turns, admirable though they are, we could spare also, for that they interrupt in us the luxurious development of the true music-hall mood.

But, certainly, the Metropolitan is a great discovery. Let us go to it often, magically renewing there our youth. And in those dreary other halls let us nevermore set foot.

"THE LOWER DEPTHS"

December 5, 1903

Lately I was writing harshly about the English people's contempt for the things of the mind. But I think I prefer that stolid contempt to the gushing superficial curiosity evinced in certain little private circles. The attitude which may be called "the literary tea-party attitude" seems to me of all attitudes the most dreadful. I will examine it for you—a painful duty—as soon as the season of good will is past. I am sure that in recent months the properest topic of conversation at literary tea-parties, or rather the properest means of initiating those brief and frantic little conversations into which the guests at literary tea-parties plunge as though they had something worth saying, and as though there were something worth hearing, has been Maxim Gorki. Gorki! I hear the tinkling of those tea-spoons. I catch the echoes of those fatuously earnest questions, those fatuously playful answers. Gorki, Gorki! But never for long do these initiatory topics reign supreme. They come and go, yielding place to others, very quickly. Sharp's the word, in that flighty and fickle kingdom. Gorki, I wager, is gone already. The last, so far as literary tea-parties are concerned, was heard of him at the beginning of this week, when the Stage Society produced "The Lower Depths." The attendants at literary tea-parties are not, as a rule, readers of books. Reviews of books are more to their taste. But they do, one and all of them, attend the productions of the Stage Society. And the dose administered on Sunday evening and on Monday afternoon will have sufficed to purge their minds of Gorkism. I strain my ears to catch the succeeding topic. I am sure there is one.

To no habitual reader of these articles need I explain that I am all for relaxing the girths of modern drama. The modern technique is much too tight, in my opinion. The difficulty of writing a technically good play is such that the best men prefer other modes of self-expression, and the task of play-writing falls mostly to duffers who, having nothing to express, have time and patience to master the needful (but not essentially needful) little tricks. Any sign, therefore, of a movement towards looser form is always sped very heartily by me. But looseness of form is one thing, formlessness is another. Such devices as prologues, and epilogues, and scenes of mere conversation, are all quite defensible, quite commendable. But the line must be drawn somewhere, and drawn a long way before we come down to "The Lower Depths" of Gorki. There must be some kind of artistic unity—unity either of story or of idea. There must be a story, though it need not be stuck to like grim death; or there must be, with similar reservation, an idea. Gorki has neither asset. At any rate he does nothing with either asset. Enough that he gives us, honestly and fearlessly, "a slice of life"? Enough, certainly, if he did anything of the kind. But he doesn't. "The Lower Depths" is no "slice." It is chunks, hunks, shreds and gobbets, clawed off anyhow, chucked at us anyhow. "No thank you" is the only possible reception for such work. We are not at all squeamish. But we demand of the playwright who deals with ugly things, just as we demand of the playwright who deals with pretty things, something more than the sight of his subject-matter. Mere gall is no better than mere sugar. It is worse. Mere sugar is not disgusting. Nor is gall disgusting if it be rightly prepared. In other words, horrible subject-matter ceases to be horrible when it is treated by a fine artist. The subject-matter of a tragedy is, in itself, necessarily horrible. Some tragedies are horrible. These are the bad tragedies, ungraced by any beauty or nobility of treatment, or ungraced by an idea, and so meaning nothing, leading nowhither, merely affronting us with their own horrors. Æsthetic pain or pleasure depends not at all on the artist's material: it does depend, entirely, on the artist. A convenient proof of this law may be made through comparison of "The Lower Depths" with another foreign play, "The Good Hope," which the Stage Society produced in its past season. Heijermans, its author, had taken a not less ghastly theme than Gorki's. Fisher-folk doomed to starve or to sacrifice their lives for the enrichment of an unscrupulous shipowner are not less ghastly a theme than are drink-sodden wastrels in a "night refuge." But Heijermans had an idea, and this idea he expressed, very beautifully, through a coherent story. He evoked, through art, a sense of pity and awe; and so he sent us away happy, despite our very real indignation that in real life such things should be. I would willingly subscribe something to any "fund for the amelioration of the condition of Dutch fishermen." But, also, I cherish the memory of a delightful afternoon. On the other hand, no "fund for the amelioration of the condition of wastrels in Moscow" would extract from me a brass farthing. I am not interested in them. I may become so, in the future. I shall become so, if some Russian artist arise and handle well the theme which Gorki has botched. If ever I meet Gorki, who is said to be an impressive person in real life, or if ever I read one of his books, which are said to be impressive, I shall be awakened doubtless, to a quick sympathy with Russian wastrels. But Gorki on the stage is merely a bore, and a disgusting bore. I dare say the characters in "The Lower Depths" are closely observed from life. But so are the figures in the lower depths of Madame Tussaud's quaint establishment. I defy you to leave the Chamber of Horrors a wiser and a better man, or a man conscious of an æsthetic impression. Where there is no meaning, no unity, nothing but bald and unseemly horror, you must needs be merely disgusted and anxious to change the subject. It is just possible, as I have hinted, that Gorki may have meant to express some sort of an idea. Let us credit him with having meant to express a very noble idea. But that idea is not enubilable from the muzzy maunderings of the wastrels. They maunder muzzily on, these wastrels, just as they would in real life; but no ray is cast from without on their darkness. There is an old man, who appears suddenly, and in whom we dimly descry a "raisonneur." But he disappears, not less suddenly, leaving behind him no lesson except a vague sentimental optimism. This lack of any underlying idea would not matter if there were any narrative unity. An artist has the right to tell a story without any criticism of its meaning. The story itself produces that artistic unity which, if there is no story, can be produced only by an underlying idea. But Gorki as story-teller is not less far to seek than Gorki as thinker. Two or three clumsy little bits of a story are wedged in here and there. But they have nothing to do with the play.

I wonder why the committee of the Stage Society had anything to do with it? To change the subject for literary tea-parties is hardly a great enough need to justify so difficult a production. Yet on no merely æsthetic ground could the thing have been deemed worth while. Snap-shot photographs are all very well in their way. But one keeps them in an album. One does not put them together into a large gilt frame. Such a frame one uses only for a large single painting. Gorki's work is to dramaturgy as snap-shot photographs are to the art of painting ; and a proscenium (literally a gold frame) deserves something better than the misuse of being made to nullify such value as such work may have.

AN INQUIRY INTO A CONVENTION

December 19, 1903

In the world, as the world appears to us through the medium of our best-loved form of dramatic art, are many startling and mysterious creatures. But I think that of all the stock-figures in musical comedy none is so startling and mysterious as the young man of fashion. Our wonder at him is never blunted. Yet he is always the same. Always he wears the same vacuous face, into which a monocle is screwed. Always he utters, with the same drawl, the same jargon. Always he has no occupation, except the passive one of being attended by the same, or rather by a similar, bevy of girls. He addresses them collectively as "girls." He is "a bit chippy," but thinks it would be "awf'lly beastly jolly" if they would lunch with him at a restaurant which he names. (The name of the restaurant varies from year to year, and is the one thing that ever varies.) The "girls" seem to have a poor opinion of him, and make pert answers. "Oh, come now, I say, by Jove," he rejoins, "you're awf'lly beastly severe. Give a feller a chance." But I need not further describe his mannerisms and mode of life. We all know them by heart. Sometimes this young man of fashion cuts an amusing figure. Such actors as Mr. George Grossmith, the younger, and Mr. G. P. Huntley bring to the impersonation of him a quaint skill and humour. More often this young man of fashion is merely tedious. Tedious, except in his constant power to puzzle us. For whence came he? Where, in the actual world around us, are we to look for the like of him—to look for anything how faintly soever resembling him? Apparently, he is offered as a satire on an actual type. We send forth experience and imagination, hand in hand, to follow up the clue.

Like to like; so perhaps in the surrounding stalls and boxes we shall find a stray solution? There are many authentic young men of fashion in the stalls and boxes. But sight of them does but thicken the plot. For instance, not one of them wears a monocle; that ornament is in these days peculiar to middle-age. Nor does the face of one of them betoken vacuity or languor. They all look quite alert and intelligent. Masks, perhaps? But wait until the entr'acte, circulate among them in the foyer, take notes of their conversation. Their elocution does not support your mask theory. They talk briskly, clearly, without affectation—a trifle loudlier, perhaps, than need be, but one has no other complaint to make. And the matter of their conversation, as apart from its manner? Well, they are not discussing the fundamental truths of the spirit. You catch mostly the names of ladies, of horses, of the various kinds of motor-cars, of electoral constituencies, and of stocks and shares. Many of these youths are on the Stock Exchange, assiduous brokers or jobbers. Others are in the House of Commons. Others are private secretaries. Others are in the Guards. Very few indeed of them have no definite occupation. You are struck by the strenuousness of their minds. The things they talk about may not be of the highest or deepest kind; but the talkers have their wits about them; and there is a very decent flow of shrewdness and humour. Mental ability is not safely gauged by height or depth of topic. The value of the thing said depends not on the value of the thing it is said about. We are compelled to rank higher the mind of the average young man of fashion than the mind of the average "intellectual" at those literary tea-parties which I lately mentioned here. Good sense about trivialities is better than nonsense about things that matter. Musical comedy, by the way, has not yet attempted to portray these "intellectuals." A painter, wearing a velveteen jacket, and singing as he paints the heroine with a mahl-stick, is the furthest point from its accustomed area. And its occasional painter seems to us not less verisimilar than its constant young man of fashion.

How came the convention? Was it always quite fantastic, or was it once grounded on a fact that has slipped away? Let us try to trace it back. Musical comedy began only in the 'nineties, but this convention existed certainly before that decade. I can remember the burlesques of the later 'eighties, and in them was just the same young man of fashion that we know now. The only difference was that his interlocutors called him "chappie"—a name which, like its later equivalent, never had been heard except on the stage. He flourished, also, I am told, in the burlesques and farces of the 'seventies and 'sixties. His début appears to have been when Edward Sothern created the part of Lord Dun-dreary. In that dark age he wore "Piccadilly weepers"; but otherwise he was as now he is: he had the monocle, and the vacuity, and the whole bag of tricks. But, though Sothern first gave him to the stage, he had existed for some time in the pages of "Punch." It is likely that Sothern derived him not from life but from the drawings and legends of John Leech. Did Leech, in his turn, derive him from life? I think it likelier that Leech derived him from the pages of Thackeray. There the figure was, ready-made, in the person of the Marquis of Farintosh. We can-not trace him back any further than that; and we may assume that Thackeray was his creator. Did Thackeray draw this type from observation or from his own inner consciousness? There is nothing to show that in that period the average young man of fashion was a fool. The Georgian dandies had been no fools. They had been, on the contrary, wits. The graces of intellect had been cultivated by them hardly less than the physical graces. Their tradition was kept bright by their followers in the Early-Victorian epoch. Count d'Orsay was no fool. We may be sure that among the young dandies, to whom he gave laws, there was no cult for fatuousness. Thackeray was not personally acquainted with them. He did not move in "the highest circles." Now, nothing can be so surely deduced from Thackeray's writings as that he would have liked to move constantly in those circles. He had a very real love for them. But whosoever loves the unattain-able is bound to hate it also. The instinct of mankind against satire is really a very sound instinct. Satire is always dishonest. For it is always the expression of hatred for a thing hopelessly coveted. Who satirises humanity? None but he who, not having the common human advantages, is obsessed with admiration of them. Who satirises plutocracy? The pauper who is warmed

by the notion of wealth. Who satirises aristocracy? The man
who wishes he had been born an aristocrat. Thackeray wished
that; and the Marquis of Farintosh was one of the natural outcomes of his wish. It must have pleased him to see this figment
gradually accepted as a type. He may have had the further
gratification of knowing that the figment reproduced itself as a
fact. Art does often react on life, and it is quite possible that
Farintosh, through Leech and Sothern, may have cropped up as a
type in the actual world. But an extinct fact is as negligible as a
figment.

"RUY BLAS"

February 20, 1904

Transport yourself, in fancy, to Paris . . . It is a sunbright
morning in Spring. You are in the Bois. The young leaves
glitter so beneath the sun that everything seems to you unreal—
refreshingly, deliciously unreal. You expand, you sparkle, you
are greedy of impressions. You catch a faint distant sound that
puzzles you. It comes a little nearer. You recognise it as the
sound of a big drum; and anon is faintly audible its accompaniment of brass. Anon you can distinguish the notes of the "Mar-
seillaise," and through the green trees you have glimpses of a
steely cavalcade that is coming with the tune. Anon they are
passing you, a company of Dragoons, prancing and caracoling
past you, clattering and gleaming past you, aloft on their big
chargers, with their big red plumes all a-nodding to the little green
leaves, while the blood in your veins dances in time to the blaring
and booming of the national hymn. Yes, you let yourself go.
You are swept out of yourself. You forget that it is all quite
unreal—a mere effect of the theatre, signifying nothing. Here,
you would vow, are no supers against a backcloth, but real heroes
among real trees. And you shout in correct French, at the risk of
being arrested by yonder vigilant gendarme, the hope that the
army may live.

Now transport yourself back into London. It is a raw wet

afternoon. You are walking, under an umbrella, along Gower Street. Everything looks very real indeed. The area-railings, the brown bricks, the wire-blinds—there can be no doubt at all about them. You behold coming towards you, tramping slowly in the middle of the road, an unfamiliar procession. Who are these men? You stand to watch them. They look highly respectable in their broadcloth, but very uncomfortable, mistrustful, gloomy. There is an air of Passive Resistance about them. Yet somehow they do not seem to be English. Swart are their faces, and their hair bristles in a distinctly Latin manner. Are they from Soho? "Nay," says a little voice at your elbow, "do you not remember them?" Looking down, you behold the good fairy who came to your christening. You tell her, curtly, that you have never seen anything like them before, and that you hope never to see anything like them again. "These," she pouts, "are the lovely soldiers you saw that morning in the Bois. I thought you would like to see them again. I thought it would cheer you up. So I wafted them hither. I think you might say 'thank you.'" Mechanically you thank her. She is appeased. "Fancy," she cries, "your not recognising them! That is the fault of the bad fairy who was not invited to your christening. She vetoed the uniforms, and the horses, and the music, and the sunshine, and the green leaves. Wasn't it horrid of her? But it hasn't made any real difference, has it? These were the very men." She vanishes with a smile of satisfied benevolence. The good fairy, you reflect, always *was* a fool.

I suspect it is by the good fairy that "Ruy Blas" has been "wafted hither" for our delectation. All honour to her for her well-meaning; but even she might have had the sense to know that the bad fairy, inevitably intervening, would spoil all the fun. French dragoons, dismounted, and thrust into mufti, and unaccompanied by music, would be, at any rate, a not more depressing sight than the usual passengers through Gower Street. But a dramatic romance by Victor Hugo, with sober blank verse instead of its own intoxicated alexandrines, and with a cast of mimes who (for the most part) have neither the training nor the innate sense for the art of declamation, or for those beautiful extravagances of port and gesture which are of the essence of romantic acting— ah, show me where, in the whole range of our depressing native drama, I need go in fear of a more depressing phenomenon than this! Strip a romance of its proper romantic trappings, and you behold but a "damned silly story"—a community of idiotic frogs trying to puff themselves to the semblance of bulls. It matters not at all whether Mr. John Davidson, adapting and abbreviating "Ruy Blas" for home consumption, have or have not made it less credible by this or that compression. The point is that he has transferred a wild and inflated lie from a plane where we could accept and revel in it to a plane where we must needs reject it with a yawn. I do not say that he could have done his work better. I do say that he ought not to have done it at all. His blank verse has many fine qualities. But it is blank verse—a medium for stateliness, grace, tenderness, sincerity and so forth, but no medium at all for the jolly headlong unreality and monstrosity of Hugoesque romance. Mr. Davidson might, at least, have preserved rhyme? No; rhymed decasyllabics are merely pretty, dainty—perhaps not even that, to our ears, through their degrading association with the annual pantomimes. He might have tried English Alexandrines? That would have been a doomed endeavour. The genius of our language forbids it. He might have invented some new rhymed measure? A waste of ingenuity. There is no means of truly conveying into English the spirit of "Ruy Blas," just as there is no possible synonym in our vocabulary for the word "panache." And so, avaunt, good fairy! No more of your kind intentions, we beseech you. Only by knowing the French language, and by seeing "Ruy Blas" in the original version, can we, solidly sentimental Anglo-Saxons, project ourselves into receptivity of this inspired balderdash.

MR. ALEXANDER'S COUP

March 26, 1904

During the past week England has had one hero:—Mr. George Alexander. Like a water-spout from a smooth ocean, there has shot vertically up into the empyrean a sudden column of marble,

with Mr. Alexander (blushing, doubtless; but I have no telescope)
upon its capital, and with John Bull and Britannia labouring under
strongest emotion around its plinth. Up, and ever up, flies the
beaver of John Bull; down, and ever down, fall the tears of gentle
Britannia; both these worthies feeling that there can be nothing
much the matter with a world in which so brave and good a man as
Mr. Alexander came to birth. A stranger from some less blest
planet might ask what exactly Mr. Alexander had been doing—had
he saved the State? had he endowed a national theatre? had he . . .
No, stranger; you will never guess the undying deed of derring-do
that has sent us and our newspapers rightly mad with wonder and
adulation. Listen! Hold on to something, in case you should
fall down. Now! On Thursday, 17 March, Mr. Alexander
produced, at the S. James' Theatre, King Street, S. James', S.W.,
a play entitled "Love's Carnival," being an English version of
Otto Erich Hartleben's play entitled, "Rosenmontag." On
Saturday, 19 March (steady, lad, steady!), Mr. Alexander withdrew the production.

At first sight, this great renouncement seems all the more
grandly brave for that it is somewhat un-English. The Englishman never knows when he is beaten. Who first made this remark
I cannot trace. Evidently, he was some sneering foreigner. But
the Englishman never knows when he is being sneered at. It is an
idiosyncrasy in him to take every sneer as a more or less obvious
compliment. "A hypocrite? Well," he smiles, "I grant them
I have the appearance of virtue, and so must seem hypocritical to
them. But why should I dissemble my virtue? I am not ashamed
of it." "Perfidious? I am certainly far-seeing—devilish subtle
and diplomatic, as they know to their cost." "A shopkeeper? I
have a genius for finance." "A glutton? None of your kick-
shaws for *me*." "Intemperate? There is no beer like British
beer, and no whisky like Scotch." "A snob? I have, it is true,
a sense of proportion in social as in all other matters." "Gloomy?
I am, thank Heaven, no fribble." In like manner, incapacity to
realise defeat is attributed by the Englishman to strength of
character, not to anything in the way of stupidity, and seems to
him a very admirable thing indeed. Thus, one would expect him
rather to despise the acumen of Mr. Alexander. But here one
must take into reckoning another of his idiosyncrasies. He loves,

above all things, a failure. Mr. Cunninghame Graham, not long ago, wrote a beautiful essay in praise of failure; and people thought this a very eccentric thing to have done, for they regard Mr. Graham as a generally eccentric man, and they always do refer everything that a man says or writes to their general notion of him. As a matter of fact, Mr. Graham was only expressing a sentiment in which the whole of England is steeped through and through. In England nothing so endears a man to his fellows as a good, straightforward, downright, deadly failure. In the South African war, the General who was acclaimed with the truest enthusiasm was he who seemed to have fallen most signally short. How different from any other country in Europe, where the unsuccessful General is hounded down as a malefactor! This preference is, perhaps, a rather lovable trait in Englishmen. Or it may be merely an offshoot of egoism and envy—preference for men who do not rise above the common level of mediocrity. Anyhow, there the feeling is. And on it Mr. Alexander has gone Nap. He produced a play that was not very favourably received (few plays are) on the first night. And forthwith he snatched the opportunity of saddling himself with a fiasco. It was the stroke of a master-mind. And I offer to Mr. Alexander my heartiest congratulations on his cleverness, not in knowing when he is beaten, but in pretending to be beaten when he isn't. For, as he confessed (rather indiscreetly) to the representative of a daily paper, he might easily have run the play to good business for at least six weeks. But he knew a trick worth two of that, and off the play came ingloriously. Gloriously, before the eyes of a public whose delight at having been so quickly deferred to is outdone by their joy in a man who has failed so signally, and by their admiration for his marvellous courage and his sweet humility in confessing himself crushed. In the general uproar, I pause to shed a tear over poor Herr Otto Erich Hartleben, who might, but for Mr. Alexander's happy thought, have been going to draw pleasant fees "for at least six weeks." I hope he will have enough pride to return the miserable three-night cheque which Mr. Alexander will have posted to him.

From time to time, one hears dark hints of "organised opposition" on first nights. I wonder if Mr. Alexander himself, the other night, had—no, it would have been unnecessary. You can

always count on a fairly hostile demonstration against a play that
ends sadly. And "Love's Carnival" had not merely a sad ending:
it was tedious throughout. My belief in the skill of Mr. Alexander, as manager, does, however, drive me to the conclusion that
the withdrawal of the play was not a sudden happy thought, but
an end for which he had been secretly working. Such is his skill
in management that he could not possibly have expected a real
success for "Love's Carnival." "Six weeks," perhaps, it might
have had; but not more than that—not enough to have induced
him, in the ordinary course of business, to try it on. Had success
been his objective, he would not have followed "Old Heidelberg"
with a play of exactly the same local colour. German uniforms
and German beer would have had a well-earned rest. Nor was
"Love's Carnival" a play which could, like "Old Heidelberg,"
be transplanted without becoming unintelligible. The persons of
it were not persons behaving in a generally human way. So far
as they were real at all, they were but locally real. Except under
the code of the German army, persons do not behave as they did.
(What a pleasant sensation it is to be writing of a dull play, for
once, in the past tense!) And the British public knows nothing
about that code, and cannot make allowances for its effect. Thus
the play was bound to seem unreal to the British public. Even to
German residents in England it was bound to seem unreal, for
another reason. The plot of it was just that which even our worst
novelettists have outgrown. A youth loved, and was loved,
truly. Both he and she were poor. Well-meaning wicked people
determined to part them, and told each that the other was faithless, and each believed the horrid tale, and never dreamed of
asking the other whether there was anything in it. Long time
they were parted. At length they met again, and were very glad
to find that it had been all a mistake; and the joy-bells—no, there
the "Family Herald" collided with the German military code,
and was smashed up: Edwin and Angelina—I mean Hans and
Else—did not go to church, but to a joint suicide's grave. You
see, now, that Mr. Alexander can neither have expected a great
commercial success nor have been impelled to a forlorn hope by
enthusiasm for the play as a work of art. Was there, you venture
to suggest, an irresistible part for Mr. Alexander? No. Mr.
Alexander could have easily resisted Hans. Hans was simply a

dehumanised version of the part he had been playing for many months. He must have known that, as Hans, he would easily be resisted by the public. And as though to make assurance doubly sure, he even withheld from Hans the outward charm that Hans demanded. A tremor ran through the house, and afar one seemed to hear a thousand and one picture post-cards rustling in vehement protest, when Mr. Alexander made his bow to the audience, wearing a wig that was evidently a mat of oakum woven by a convict. I protest, on grounds of political economy. What is to become of Mr. William Clarkson, and those other artists who have worked so long and honourably, if our actors are going to patronise prison-made goods? However, I don't want to be an alarmist. I recognise that this wig is not likely to create a wide precedent. It was an "ad hoc" wig; a wig to ensure the play's failure; a wrecker's wig. And Mr. Alexander will not wear it again, till, in the distant future, he decides that the popularity of his theatre is waning by reason of invariable success, and that the time is ripe for him to taste again those intoxicating sweets of failure which he procured for himself in the memorable month of March 1904.

SOME IRISH PLAYS AND PLAYERS

April 9, 1904

The other day I came to one of the rare oases that are in the desert of our drama. For one whole afternoon my feet were on very verdure, and there was clear cold water for my parched throat. We plodders through this unending commercial desert could not plod so bravely if it were not for the oases, dear in proportion to their rarity, offered to us by uncommercial little societies. "The sands are running out" somewhere, perhaps; but here, in this desert, they run on for ever, from every point of the horizon, down our throats. For ever and for ever we plod through "Lady Thingummy's drawing-room overlooking the Green Park" (a mirage, that Green Park), and for ever and for ever Lady Thingummy (played by Miss So-and-So with her usual grace and sensibility) gives her husband (whose rôle is sustained by the manager with even more than his usual sincerity and conviction) reason to suppose that her flirtation with Sir Blank Dash (Mr. Dash Blank has never done anything better than his impersonation of Sir Blank Dash) is a really serious affair, whereas, of course, all the while .... Add a "decimal point recurring" over that last dot. Imagine those dots running on, like the desert's grains of sand, for ever and for ever, and then you will be able to enter into the feelings of a dramatic critic, and to realise with what joy he, condemned to an eternity and an infinity of barren drawing-room comedy or drawing-room comedy-drama, turns aside to such accidents as the Irish Theatre.

The afternoon's programme included three little plays: one by Mr. Yeats, "The King's Threshold," and two by Mr. J. M. Synge, "Riders to the Sea" and "In the Shadow of the Glen." Very widely though the three plays differed from one another, from all one derived the same quality of pleasure—the pleasure in something quite simple and quite strange. There was in none of the plays any structural complexity, and yet none of them was not truly dramatic. It is fashionably supposed that a playwright, in order to compass a truly dramatic effect, must steep himself in some kind of black art—must become a very wizard, master of all manner of mysterious processes whereat we outsiders dare scarcely guess. Well, of course, dramatic effect can be produced through many complex means. But it is a fallacy to suppose that only through such means can it be produced. Out of a dramatic idea you can produce a dramatic effect, even though you go about it quite simply and straightforwardly. You must, however, first catch your dramatic idea. That is where the amateur often fails, afterwards attributing his failure to his ignorance of technique. That parrot-cry "technique"! How many a good literary man has been scared off by it; and of how much, therefore, dramatic literature has been baulked by it! My advice to the terror-stricken is quite simple, and quite sound: first catch your dramatic idea, and then go artlessly ahead with your expression of it. When your play is acted, you will be delighted to find that the audience finds it quite dramatic: the idea will have carried it through for you. Belike, your very artlessness is an advantage. For though dramatic effect may be compassed through very complex and highly specialised means, the man who has mastered those means is often, in his turn, mastered by them, insomuch that one cannot see the wood for the trees. Mr. Pinero is an instance of a man who shows us only trees. Fine, upstanding, thriving trees they are, but—where is the wood? Mr. Yeats showed me a wood quite clearly, and Mr. Synge showed me two woods. And the sight was all the more welcome because there was no fuss about it. Simplicity! That was, also, the keynote of the stage-setting. I have no objection to rich scenery and dresses—so long as the richness be not inappropriate or excessive. But, just for a change, how delightful to have a management which, so far from trying to dazzle us into awed calculations of its outlay, rather prides itself on its poverty. There is a prologue to "The King's Threshold," and in the printed copy of the play, Mr. Yeats notifies that this prologue was "not used in Dublin, as, owing to the smallness of the company, nobody could be spared to speak it." Of course, the pride of poverty is not in itself less ridiculous than the pride of wealth. But it has, for the London playgoer, at least, the charm of newness. Apart from that, it was fitting that a play about legendary Ireland, and two plays about peasants in modern Ireland, should be produced as simply as possible. As for the acting, I am not sure that so much simplicity as the players exemplified was quite artistically right. Mr. Yeats' poetry, doubtless —or any other man's poetry—gains by simple recitation. Dramatic inflections of the voice, dramatic gestures and so forth, do, of course, detract from sheer melody; but, equally, their absence detracts from drama. For dramatic poetry, therefore, the right treatment is a compromise. And when these players, trained to heed Mr. Yeats' poetry, and untrained to express anything dramatically, came to interpret Mr. Synge's prose, they did seem decidedly amiss. They, with their blank faces and their stiff movements, taking up their cues so abruptly, and seeming not to hear anything said by their interlocutors, certainly did impede the right effect of the play. For all that, I would not they had been otherwise. One could not object to them as to the ordinary amateur. They were not floundering in the effort to do something beyond their powers. With perfect simplicity, perfect dignity and composure, they were just themselves, speaking a task that they had well by heart. Just themselves; and how could such Irish selves not be irresistible? Several of our metropolitan players are Irish, and even they, however thickly coated with Saxonism, have a charm for us beyond their Saxon-blooded fellows. The Irish people, unspoiled, in their own island—who can resist them? But footlights heighten every effect; and behind them unspoiled Irish people win us quicklier and more absolutely than ever. And behind London footlights! There they have not merely their own charm, but that charm also which belongs to all exotics. Many people went many times, lately, to "In Dahomey," fascinated by the sight of a strange and remote race expressing through our own language things most strange to us and remote from us. Well, we are as far removed from the Irish people as from the negroes, and our spiritual distance seems all the greater by reason of our nearness in actual mileage. I admit that it was, in a way, more pleasant to see those negroes than to see these Irish folk. When we contemplate negroes, one clear impression comes through our dim bewilderment: we are assuredly in the presence of an inferior race. Whereas he must be a particularly dull Saxon who does not discern, and confess (at any rate to himself), that the Keltic race is, spiritually and intellectually, a race much finer, and also much more attractive, than that to which he has the honour to belong.

I spoke of the Irish Theatre as "an accident" only in reference to myself. I did not mean to imply there was not a good reason for the Irish Theatre, or that there was not an expansive future for it. For a national drama, you require dramatists and players. Acting is not a natural art to the inexpressive Saxon; but the inexpressiveness of Mr. Yeats' own particular players does not shake my conviction that to the Kelt the art of acting will come almost as naturally as to the Latin. Likewise, true dramatists are much likelier to crop up in Ireland than in England. When an idea occurs to an Englishman, his first impulse is to get it put into practice. An Irishman broods over an idea, and translates it into some symbolic form. For instance, it has occurred to Mr. Yeats that he is not taken seriously enough. People buy his books and compliment him very highly; but the State does not recognise him as a factor in public life. No title is bestowed on him. The Royal family does not make him its pet. He sees eminent statesmen, soldiers, lawyers, and other men of action, being petted and

decorated all the time; but he, the man of Thought, is not invited to step out of his niche and join that giddy throng. Were
Mr. Yeats an English poet, he would forthwith have written an
article for one of the monthly reviews, forcibly demonstrating how
necessary a part of the national life is Thought, and how extremely
impolitic it is, therefore, for the State to encourage and honour
only men of action. In fact, he would have done exactly what was
done, a month or two ago, by Mr. William Watson. Were Mr.
William Watson an Irishman, he would have written "The
King's Threshold," telling us, with exquisite lyric fervour, the
tale of the poet Seanchan, who, because King Guaire refused him
his right to sit at meat among the great councillors and warriors,
and thus dishonoured through him the majesty of all bards, lay
down across the threshold of the palace, and there would have
starved himself to death, had not King Edw—— I mean King
Guaire, relenting at length, kneeled down to him and offered to
him the very crown. As it is, I admired Mr. Watson s article
very much, and I readily admit that King Edward, a practical
man, would be less quickly perturbed by the dream-laden beauty
of "The King's Threshold" than by the urgent and unanswerable
arguments in that article. Only, one can't have it both ways;
and Mr. Yeats' way naturally seems to me, as dramatic critic, the
better way; and, as it is also the typical Irish way, I have high
hopes of poetic drama in Ireland.

There is plenty of poetry in "Riders to the Sea," modern
peasants though the characters are. The theme is much the
same as in Heijermans' play "The Good Hope"—a mother whose
youngest son is drowned, as all her other sons have been drowned,
at sea. Mr. Synge, being an Irishman, is content to show us the
pathos of his theme: he does not, as did Heijermans, try to rouse
any indignation. "So it is, and so it must be" is his tone. It is
the tone of the mother herself, whose acquiescence is deeper than
the acquiescence of the mother in "The Good Hope." She
submits not merely because it were vain to rebel. To rebel is not
in her nature. She has the deep fatalism of her race; and for her,
the things that actually happen, for evil as for good, are blurred
through the dreams that are within her. "In the Shadow of the
Glen," as a farce, is not less typically Irish than the tragedy. In
particular, it illustrates a very odd thing about the Irish people:

their utter incapacity to be vulgar. What this farce would be like if it were translated by an Englishman, into English life, and were enacted by English players, I shudder to conceive. But I delight in the recollection of it as it was. And still cherished in my ears are the soft echoes of the brogues ... Certainly, the Irish Theatre was an oasis. I will not trouble you, this week, with any samples of the sand I have since collected.

HYMENEAL DRAMATURGY

April 30, 1904

In the beginning, Mr. Carton fingered many modes of play-writing. We never knew what he was going to do next. We sometimes chid him for not knowing his own mind. Such an objection to him could not possibly be raised now. He, of all our playwrights, is now the most self-possessed. More precisely than any of them he knows what he wants to do, and how to do it, and has mastered the secret of doing it always. He stands alone, an intense specialist in a form of his art unessayed by any other man. He is the one and never wavering exponent of what may be called Hymeneal Dramaturgy.

Every choice has its advantage, and there is a very sound com-mercial advantage in Mr. Carton's choice. The public has a kindness for domesticity in theatrical art, or, indeed, in any kind of public work. Political economy is not a showily engaging science, and the books written about it do not fatten their pub-lishers. But there is, I am told, an exception. The books written by Mr. and Mrs. Sidney Webb sell really well. For them there is a steady demand in the booksellers' shops, and in the public libraries they are well thumbed. The "and Mrs." opens all hearts, and through that breach dash the battalions of dry facts and deductions to the storming of all brains. Even more potent is domesticity in the theatre than in the study. Husband and wife working together behind the footlights, shoulder to shoulder, as leading man and leading lady, husband leading wife, or wife leading

husband—there's a sight to gladden and moisten all eyes that
behold it. Mr. Carton, it is true, does not himself appear behind
the footlights. But sufficient that he has conceived the part which
his wife enacts, and has written every word that falls from her lips.
All hearts are opened. Yet, though such conjunctions appeal
very surely to the better side of our nature, some base æsthetic
instinct in us warns us of a possible danger in them. When leading man and leading lady are persons united in wedlock, there is
always, as I have suggested, the danger that one will be leading the
other. There is always the danger that whichever has the lesser
talent, however considerable that talent may be, will be wasting
himself or herself in an inappropriate part in a play chosen for the
sake of a part signally appropriate to his or her mate. Similarly,
there is the danger that a playwright whose leading lady is always
his wife will cripple either his own talent or hers. I do not profess
to say whether Miss Compton in acting or Mr. Carton in play-
writing has the more considerable talent. Each of them is
delightful. But I can so far distinguish between them as to
say that Miss Compton's talent is not versatile, whereas Mr.
Carton, in the beginning, proved that he could be versatile to a
fault. Lately doing the same thing over and over again, he has
acquired in the doing of it an extreme virtuosity, nor does he ever
lose his freshness of touch. Nevertheless, it seems rather a pity
that he doesn't, now and again, try something else. Suppose, for
example, that Shakespeare's wife had not stayed by the Avon, but
had come to London and gone on the stage. And suppose that
Shakespeare had been a more uxorious man than he was, and had
written all his plays round Mistress Shakespeare. What the
result? Let us assume that tradition is right, and that Mistress
Shakespeare was a shrew. We should thus have had the early
scenes of Katherine and Petruchio just as they stand; but the
whole charm of the play is in Katherine's conversion; and this
would have been sacrificed, as lying outside Mistress Shakespeare's range. And consider how different a play "Hamlet"
would have been, and how far inferior to the play that Shakespeare actually wrote, if it had been conditioned by the need for
making Ophelia not only a shrew, but also the central figure of the
scheme. Imagine the world well lost by Antony for the naggings
of Cleopatra; and the forest of Arden re-echoing to the shrill

tantrums of Rosalind; and even Cordelia merciless to the stricken King, her father; and Juliet fuming on the balcony. Imagine all Shakespeare's women as vixens, and all Shakespeare's plays as hinging on vixenishness. Then you will be able to imagine, also, how much we lose through the iron law made by Mr. Carton that his every play shall centre round a genial, good-natured, very modern-mannered woman of the world, with all her wits about her. I do not pretend that this actual loss is so great as that hypothetic one. Nevertheless, it is no small loss. I feel it and regret it.

"The Rich Mrs. Repton," at the Duke of York's—what new thing can I say about a play which is, albeit delightful, so little new? Enter Mrs. Jack Repton, after long spin on motor with Lord Charles Dorchester; and we know that Lord Charles will suggest a whisky-and-soda, and that Mrs. Jack will say, with a slow beatific smile, "Well, what do *you* think?" We know that she will ask for a very little whisky and a great deal of soda, and that she will say, when the tumbler is brought to her, "Now, don't speak to me for a moment," and, setting the empty tumbler down, "That was a great moment." We know her, and her slangy good-breeding, and her lazy good-humour, and her sharp capacity for getting people out of scrapes. We know all the hoops she will go through. Miss Compton impersonates her as deliciously as ever. Yet I have an unholy craving to see Miss Compton, just once and away, in some other part—to see her not quite so perfectly at ease, with a not quite so perfect grasp of the whole thing. I have said that hers is not a versatile talent; but even to see her floundering hopelessly would not displease me. And who am I, anyway, to declare that she is not versatile—I who do not remember seeing her in any but this one part? No doubt, her personality is better suited to this one part than to any other. But personality can shine more or less brightly through various manifestations. At any rate, it should be given the chance of shining through various manifestations. I do not urge Miss Compton to try her luck as (say) Lady Macbeth, or even in any modern version of that part. But there are many different kinds and degrees of geniality. And why should Miss Compton confine herself to just this one degree and this one kind among so many? Nor is Miss Compton, as the only actress whose husband writes plays, the only actress who is forced permanently along the line of least resistance. It is one of the pities of the modern stage that nearly all actresses and nearly all actors are thus restricted. So soon as one of them makes a hit, she or he is engaged again and again to make just that same hit elsewhere. And when the time comes, at length, he or she dies or retires in the act of making still that same dear little old hit. For players and managers alike, this is a safe policy; but it is not a glorious policy; and for the honour of the art of acting, and for the confounding of fools emboldened to deny that acting is a fine art, I should like to see it abandoned. The Duke of York's Theatre is controlled by a syndicate; and syndicates, especially, play for safety. There, accordingly, in "The Rich Mrs. Repton," one finds the safe policy in its fullest swing. All the principal parts are played by players who have made repeated hits in precisely similar parts elsewhere. It is a melancholy spectacle—all this high accomplishment in the doing of one thing, with all this inevitable loss of power for doing anything else; all these artists marking time so exquisitely, every one of them at his or her appointed post, never outstepping by half an inch the little square that has been chalked for her or his footfalls; and all the younger ones losing, as all the elder ones have lost long ago, the power to move in any direction whatsoever. Better than such stagnancy the blind-man's-buff of the old stock companies. One sighs for a mean.

Thus for Miss Compton's sake, not less than for his own, Mr. Carton really ought to write some other sort of play. Heaven forbid that I should try to deflect him from Hymeneal Drama-turgy. I do but ask him to put a wider interpretation on the thing.

MR. GILBERT'S RENTRÉE
(AND MINE)

May 14, 1904

A year or so ago a fearful thing befell me. Mr. Arthur Bourchier ceased to send me seats for the first nights at his theatre. Yet, cast thus into outer darkness, I uttered no cry of anguish. In the language of our police force, I "went quiet." The presump-

tive reason for Mr. Bourchier's sternness was that I had rather
regularly chidden him for playing comedic parts in a farcical
manner, and had rather regularly hinted that Miss Violet Vanbrugh's true vocation was not for comedy, but for tragedy, melodrama, romance. Now, these may have been horrid truths; but,
at least, they were—or seemed to me—truths; and I had had no
malicious intent in speaking them. Therefore, I suppose I
ought to have been very angry at being cast out. I suppose I
ought to have rushed through that outer darkness into print . . .
a free country, vanity of actor-managers, intolerable attempts to
stifle honest criticism, shall such things be? et patati, et patata.
But questions of principle, except when there is menace to my
own personal convenience, do not (I am ashamed to say) stir my
blood like a bugle-note. And it has been for me no personal inconvenience not to go to the Garrick Theatre. Were this a daily
paper, and I therefore a purveyor of news besides criticism, then
I should have come out strong on the question of principle. As
things are, I am free to pick and choose among theatres and plays.
So long as I have enough material for a weekly essay, all is well.
And it has so happened that whenever Mr. Bourchier has produced
a play, some other subject was at my service; and it has not so
happened that any of Mr. Bourchier's productions (very admirable
though they all were, doubtless) was one which I felt I *must* see
for my own delectation. Besides, I am a philosophic, sympathetic person. I never can be angry with any one, never having
been able to cure myself of the power to see other people's points
of view. It is, as I have more than once demonstrated, very
natural that mimes should be sensitive—more sensitive than any
other artists, except singers—for that themselves are the medium
of their art. How, then, could I have grown angry with Mr.
Bourchier? The histrionic temperament is a thing apart. I was
sure Mr. Bourchier was sure I had been malignantly persecuting
his wife and himself. It seemed so natural that he should wish
me, scoundrel of the deepest dye, never to darken his doors again.
So, delicate-minded, I was glad not to be darkening them. An
excess of delicacy? A cat may look at a king! But suppose the
king to be one who can't bear to be looked at except with blinking
admiration. Then, surely, any right-feeling cat would direct elsewhere its steadfast yellow gaze. On the whole, I think it was too

bad of me that I did, at length, last Wednesday, insinuate myself
into the Garrick Theatre. But the temptation to see a new play
by Mr. Gilbert was too strong for my better nature. I plead also,
in extenuation, that I chose a place very remote from the stage.
Mr. Bourchier did not see me. He did not blench behind his
make-up. The words did not die on his lips. The curtain was
not rung down.

Anyhow, I could not have left unsampled anything done by Mr.
Gilbert. He has given me so many hours of pleasure, and is so
illustriously enshrined among my minor gods. I think the lilt of
his lyrics is always running somewhere in my sub-conscious mind.
And the "Bab Ballads"—how shall I ever express my love of
them? A decade ago Clement's Inn was not the huddle of gaudy
skyscrapers that it is now; and in the centre of it was a sombre
little quadrangle, one of whose windows was pointed out to me
as the window of the room in which Gilbert had written those
poems, and had cut the wood-blocks that immortally illustrate
them. And thereafter I never passed that window without the
desire to make some sort of obeisance, or to erect some sort of
tablet. Surely the Muse still hovers sometimes, affectionately,
there where "Bab's" room once was. Literature has many a
solemn masterpiece that one would without a qualm barter for
that absurd and riotous one. Nor is the polished absurdity of
the Savoy lyrics so dear as the riotous absurdity of those earlier
ballads, wherein you may find all the notions that informed the
plots of the operas, together with a thousand and one other
notions, and with a certain wild magic never quite recaptured. I
know nothing comparable, for extravagance, with the "Bab
Ballads." None but Mr. Gilbert could have written them. And
only in his hot youth could Mr. Gilbert have written them.
"The Fairy's Dilemma," his new play, is, in scheme, a very good
specimen of what is commonly called Gilbertian humour—that
later humour of carefully calculated extravagance, such as we find
in the Savoy pieces. But, good specimen though it is, I must
confess that I don't rejoice in it. Why, indeed, should I hesitate
to make the confession? One is naturally tender to the autumnal
work of a writer in whose genius one believes, but who has never,
even in his prime, triumphantly expressed his genius, and has
never made it clear to the multitude. But Mr. Gilbert is a

popular classic; and I may be frank without compunction. The only compunction were in pretending to confuse what bores me with that in which my soul revels. Frankly "The Fairy's Dilemma" bored me. Had it happened to be an opera, with music by Sullivan, I daresay I should not have been bored at all. But without the music, the machinery of the humour creaked for me, audibly. Perhaps, even without the music, I should have heard no creaking if Mr. Gilbert had written the play in verse. His humour and his versification are inextricably connected; for his sense of rhyme and rhythm are as humorous as his ideas. Take any favourite stanza from the "Bab Ballads," and translate it into prose, and see how poor a thing it will seem in comparison. It will still, indeed, be funny. Many writers of humorous verse are men whose humour lies wholly in their technique; and they, when they write in prose, surprise one by their deadly dulness. "Bab," on the other hand, is full of intrinsically humorous ideas. It is (for random example) an intrinsically humorous idea that the sexton and the beadle of the Rev. Hopley Porter were of exemplary character on Sundays, but were ready for any infamous deed during the week. One smiles at that. But one laughs aloud at

> "These men were men who could
>   Hold liberal opinions:
> On Sundays they were good—
>   On week-days they were minions."

It is needless to insist further on the difference between the effect of the original version and the effect of my own prose translation. And there is just that difference between the effect of "The Fairy's Dilemma" and the effect of (say) "Iolanthe." Nay, there is a greater difference. Mr. Gilbert's prose is, and has always been, peculiarly dull and heavy. It is possible to use the medium of prose wittily; though few people are aware of the possibility, and fewer still have the gift. Stevenson had the gift; and Whistler had it, too. They could play pranks with words—could set words playing pranks with one another. Mr. Gilbert's one notion of humorous prose is to use as many long words and as many formal constructions as possible—a most tedious trick, much practised by other mid-Victorian writers. In prose Stevenson or Whistler could have made that analysis of

the sexton and the beadle almost as funny as it was made in verse
by Mr. Gilbert. But Mr. Gilbert's own prose version would be
something to this effect: "These two individuals were, I may be
permitted parenthetically to inform you, of a somewhat abnormal
character, inasmuch as, whereas on the Sabbath their general
behaviour was such that not even the most censorious could discover in it any reasonable grounds for disapprobation, they were,
throughout the remainder of the week, notoriously predisposed to
the commission of the most nefarious actions imaginable."
Dickens often wrote rather like that. Mr. Pinero always writes
exactly like that. Mr. Gilbert handed on the torch. I hope it
will soon have burned itself out. In "The Fairy's Dilemma"
all the characters talk rather like that, except the Demon Alcohol
and the Fairy Rosebud, who talk mostly in verse. What a relief
those two are! When the Fairy Rosebud says to her attendants:

"Dance on the sward before these stucco portals,
Which, I may state, are Mr. Justice Whortle's,"

then, indeed, we get the true Gilbertian thrill. Yes, assuredly
the whole play should have been in verse.

Even so, however, it would not have quite "come off." Verse
is not the only thing that it ought to have been written in; it ought
also to have been written in the 'seventies. For in the 'seventies
pantomime was flourishing still. Demon King and Fairy Queen,
transformation scene and harlequinade, were familiar and popular
things. But to satirise them now, in the 'noughts, as Mr. Gilbert
does, is to shoot at a target long since removed from the range of
vision. Mr. Gilbert once wrote a delightful parody of Martin
Tupper. Surely he would not now sit down and write another
parody of Martin Tupper. Indeed, he evidently does recognise,
to some extent, the need to be contemporaneous in parody; for he
has a shot at the criticisms in the "Times." But this skit, like the
references to motor-cars and other recent things, seems queerly
out of key with the play as a whole. For the mortal characters
"date" not less obviously than the fairies. There *are* no mild
young curates, with side-whiskers, and with a horror of the stage,
nowadays. There *are* no young military baronets who compose
love-verses and sing them with a piano-accompaniment, nowadays.
There *are* no ladies who sit at their toilet-tables combing tresses of

false hair, nowadays. Such ladies ceased to exist when chignons ceased to exist. And the Rev. Aloysius Parfitt, M.A., and Col. Sir Trevor Mauleverer, Bart.—they too are as extinct as chignons. They are but the ghosts of the Rev. Hopley Porter and of Lorenzo de Lardy, arisen from between the pages of the "Bab Ballads." They are interesting enough to the connoisseur of changes in fashion. But there is little fun to be got out of them. Had "The Fairy's Dilemma" been written and produced in the 'seventies, and were this production of it a revival, then the satire in it would seem to us all (as the satire in 1880's "Patience" lately seemed) quite fresh and vital. But the novelty of the thing is fatal.

I hardly dare to say that Mr. Bourchier was very good as the clown in the harlequinade. He will think I am persecuting him. On the other hand, I hardly dare to say that as the Baronet he played with unusual naturalness and restraint. He will think I am cadging for invitations to first nights. What dare I say of Miss Vanbrugh? In a simple and glowing gown of dark blue, she looked marvellously like a Rossetti; and she gave to her part all the charm of her vivid intensity. Had Mr. Gilbert's genius been moulded by the P. R. B. . . . but enough! I will *not* say the wrong thing.

PATRIOTIC DRAMA AT THE HAYMARKET

May 28, 1904

England is, I think, the one country in which a play with an anti-national bias may have a popular success. I cannot imagine a Parisian manager daring to produce a comedy in which the hero, an Englishman, would score off the Frenchmen at every point. Yet "Monsieur Beaucaire," over here, was promptly folded to the public bosom. I can imagine New York's fury over a play in which not all the soldiers of King George would be scoundrels and poltroons, nor all the rebels heroes and saints. Yet our own melodramatists have, again and again, made up the converse prescription, very lucratively. There is no nation that we would not gladly see glorified in drama; and there is no nation that could tolerate any but a ridiculous presentment of us. How is it that we alone are graced with this sense of international chivalry? To answer this question, we must ask another. What is chivalry? It is the instinct of condescension felt by the stronger person towards the weaker, or, at least, by one person for another whom he imagines to be the weaker. If a lady steps into a full tramcar, the nearest man rises and proffers her his seat, on the principle that a man's power of endurance is greater than a woman's. He performs, with a pitying flourish, an act of condescension. International chivalry has exactly the same motive as personal chivalry. England, a nation in its prime, feels a contemptuous pity for France, a nation past its prime, and for America, a nation racked by growing pains. I give these three descriptions not as surely true, but as representing what seems surely true to the average Englishman. It may be that England is actually inferior both to America and to France. But in the average Englishman is ingrained the conviction of England's supremacy. If an Amazon, in complete steel, lightly bounded into a full tramcar, the nearest man, even if he happened to be partially paralysed, would rise and proffer her his seat. And she, doubtless, would take it. For in woman, as in man, is ingrained the principle of woman's physical inferiority. Even so, in France and America and other nations, as in England, the average man believes in England's almightiness. Therefore, when we would blame them for their intolerance, let us remember that it is but the defect of a good quality—modesty. And when next we preen ourselves on our chivalry, let us spare a passing blush for the defect that causes it.

Though we are conceited enough not to mind being belittled, and seeing our rivals magnified, we are also vain enough to enjoy being flattered, and seeing our rivals made game of, now and again. "Lady Flirt," the play produced last Wednesday at the Haymarket, has evidently been fashioned to catch this mood in us. It is a play *ad majorem gloriam Britanniæ*; and I doubt not that Britannia will bridle voluptuously at its pæans, with many a titter at its disparagements of Gaul. Ironically enough, the play is not a home product, but an importation from the very land which it, as doctored for the British market, compares so unfavourably with our own. I did not see "Mademoiselle Flirt" in Paris. But I assume that in that original version all the persons of the play were French. In France, as in England, there are some serious, solid, sterling folk, and some frivolous, light, worthless folk: "Les Deux Écoles" in fact. And I assume that, as in M. Capus' play, the contrast between them was a contrast between compatriots. But the sly British adapter knew a trick worth two of that. And his trick, though brilliant, is very simple. The good persons of the play become English; the bad ones remain French. No mere moral gulf yawns, the Channel itself heaves, between those opposite groups. On the one hand are two brothers; good men, and serious, solid, sterling; fine, square, upstanding; endowed with rough humour; lovable, admirable, in every relation of life. The younger of them is what the newspapers call "a mighty hunter before the Lord," and has just returned to Europe from shooting big game. The elder is a diplomat, working so strenuously for his country that his wife strays into a perilous flirtation with another man. That other man—what shall we say of him? What *need* we say of him except that he is a Frenchman? What *need* we have said of the two brothers except that they are Englishmen—Lord Melborough (*of the British Embassy*) and the Hon. Paul Harding? But though the national labels be in themselves sufficient, it is very pleasant, and does our hearts good, to see the national differences minutely worked out and illustrated on the stage. What a poor, poor figure is cut, between Lord Melborough and Mr. Harding, by M. le Comte de la Roche! Granted that the fellow has a sort of sparkle, such as might for a little while please some foolish woman. Granted that he has a sort of tact and insight, whereby he pleases that foolish woman, Lady Melborough. But very soon the most foolish woman in the world must see through him. We ourselves see through him from the moment we set eyes on him; and what we see through him is the whole French nation—frivolous, light, worthless. We see through him a falling birth-rate. We see Sedan and Panama. We see Fashoda and Dreyfus and countless other sights not less gratifying. How lamentably he bows and scrapes, shrugs and chants, in the presence of that grunting, commanding Briton! He knows he has done wrong. He shrinks from the explanation which is demanded of him in the billiard-room. He will have a drink first. He pours some whisky into a tumbler. It seems almost sacrilege that Britain's beverage should be savoured by such lips as his. For once, our adapter has erred in taste, erred in knowledge. Absinthe is the stuff which this Frenchman should, and would, have taken with a trembling hand. And the Englishman should, and would, have snatched it from his hand and poured it upon the carpet, sternly eyeing him the while. The Frenchman wants to fight a duel, does he? Why don't he use fists, as Mr. Harding very properly suggests? He won't, won't he? Ugh! Coward! He had thought, at one time, of going to fight on the side of the Boers, had he? Yah! He says something to imply that he does not take a cold tub every morning. Boo-o-ooh! Mr. Harding compares him and his kind—chatterers and grimacers—with the monkeys whom he has seen in the forests of Africa. Hear, hear, hear! A hit, a very palpable hit, rightly repeated at the fall of the curtain, when we see the Frenchman obediently answering to the call of "Monkey!" and skulking away to avoid the righteous wrath of a British husband.

On the French stage this British husband would be represented as a man with very long whiskers and very prominent teeth, dressed in a knickerbocker suit of enormous checks. Since the Frenchman in "Lady Flirt" accords altogether so exactly to the general notion we formed of Frenchmen in the days of John Leech, and as that notion is now but an empty and insincere survival, I should prefer that Mr. Cyril Maude, interpreting that French-man, should wear closely-cropped hair, waxed moustaches, a "Napoleon," a flat-brimmed hat, and peg-top trousers. But, superficially, the Haymarket is nothing if not modern; and Mr. Maude, with a small moustache curled upwards, and with his clothes made by an English tailor, is very like dozens of men whom you may actually see to-day in Paris, and not at all unlike dozens of men whom you may actually see to-day in London. Surely that is an error in judgment. It suggests the brotherhood of man—that queer and unpleasant fact from which the adapter had so tenderly shielded us. It hurts our pride. Away with it! and then will "Lady Flirt" achieve perfectly the purpose for which it was designed. For my own part, I confess, I wish the adapter had not so designed it. His dialogue is so unusually graceful and witty, without being in the least formal, and he has evidently so nice an appreciation of little points in character, and of little facts in life, that the play (artificial though it is in scheme) would have altogether charmed me, but for that grim determination to set Britannia voluptuously bridling.

SARAH

July 9, 1904

It is our instinct to revere old age. In this reverence, if we analyse it, we find two constituent emotions—the emotion of pity, and the emotion of envy. Opposite though they are, both are caused by one thing. It is sad that so brief a span remains, but it must be delightful to have accomplished so long a span. Any moment may be our last. A flash of lightning, a side-slip, a falling brick—always some imprevisible chance that may precipitate us into the unknown. And how foolish we should look then—we with so little to our account! Certainly, it is enviable to have accumulated so much as have those elders, and to know, as they know, that no power can steal it away. Romantic awe is stirred in us by the contemplation of anything that has been going on for a long time. Ruins are apt to leave us cold; but any upstanding and habitable old building must touch and warm our imagination. Undefeated by time, any old building, however humble and obscure, becomes for us majestic. But greater, of course, and more haunting, the majesty of an old castle or cathedral. To have towered illustriously through the ages, a centre of significance and pomp, and to be towering thus even now! As with buildings, so with human beings. The romantic quality of an old person is intensified in ratio to the prominence of his or her past and present. There has been in our own time one figure that incomparably illustrated this rule. I am glad to have lived in a time when it was possible to set eyes on the aged Queen Victoria. I can conceive no more romantic thrill than I had whenever, in the last years of her reign, I saw her drive past in that old-fashioned barouche, attended not only by that clattering cavalcade of material guardsmen, but also by the phantoms—not less clearly there—of

Melbourne and the Duke, Louis Philippe, Palmerston, Peel,
Disraeli the younger—of all those many successive sovereigns,
statesmen, soldiers, who were but great misty names to us, yet
had been sharp little realities to her, in the interminable pageant of
her existence. Strange, to see her with my own eyes—that little
old lady, in the queer barouche, on her way to Paddington Station.
In Queen Victoria I saw always something of that uncanny symbolism which Mr. Pater saw in the portrait of Mona Lisa. Hers,
too, surely, was the head upon which all the ends of the world were
come, and the eyelids were a little weary. . . . There is no one
now to give me that kind of emotion in like degree; but, certainly,
the person most nearly filling the void is Madame Sarah Bernhardt, who has played during the past fortnight at His Majesty's
Theatre. Year by year, when she comes among us, my wonder
and awe are intensified. Seeing her, a few nights ago, in "La
Sorcière," I was more than ever moved by the apparition. The
great Sarah—pre-eminently great throughout the past four
decades! My imagination roved back to lose itself in the golden
haze of the Second Empire. My imagination roved back to reel
at the number of plays that had been written, the number of
players whose stars had risen and set, the number of theatres that
had been built and theatres that had been demolished, since Sarah's
début. The theatrical history of more than forty years lay strewn
in the train of that bowing and bright-eyed lady. The applause
of innumerable thousands of men and women, now laid in their
graves, was still echoing around her. And still she was bowing,
bright-eyed, to fresh applause. The time would come when our
noisy hands would be folded and immobile for ever. But, though
we should be beneath the grass, Sarah would still be behind the
footlights—be bowing, as graciously as ever, to audiences recruited
from the ranks of those who are now babes unborn. A marvellous
woman! For all the gamut of her experience, she is still lightly
triumphant over time. All this has been to her, as to Mona Lisa,
but as the sound of lyres and flutes, and lives only in the delicacy
with which it has moulded the changing lineaments, and tinged
the hair. Hers is the head upon which all the ends of the world
are come, and the eyelids are not at all weary. . . .

Such was my first impression, when Sarah reappeared to me in
"La Sorcière." But presently I had to qualify it. Superficially,

it is quite true that Sarah triumphs over time. Her appearance, her voice, her movements are all as ever. But her spirit shows the inevitable signs of wear and tear. Time has succeeded in damping the sacred fire that burnt within her. Gone from her are the passion and sincerity that once held us in thrall. As Phèdre, as Fédora, as any of the characters created by her in her prime, she is as enthralling, doubtless, as in the past, forasmuch as her unimpaired energy and memory enable her to reproduce exactly the effects that she produced then. But when she plays a new part, as in "La Sorcière," you are definitely aware that she is not feeling anything—that she is merely urging herself to the performance of certain tricks. Very perfectly she performs these time-honoured tricks. The lovely voice is always in tune and time, whether it coo or hiss, and the lovely gestures are all in their proper places, and the lovely face is as expressive as ever. But the whole performance is hollow—art without life—a dead thing galvanised. Of course, the play—a play written by the venerable M. Sardou for no purpose but to show Sarah off in the ways in which she likes to be shown off—is itself an utterly dead thing. But there was a time when Sarah could have put life into it. And for her failure to put life into it now we may console ourselves with the implicit revelation that she, too, after all, is mortal, like the rest of us.

Though her genius has been touched thus by Time, all untouched is her love of adventure; and she has given a performance of "Pelléas et Mélisande," with herself as Pelléas, and Mrs. Campbell as Mélisande. I did not see this performance. I love the play too well, and am loth that my memory of it as performed by Mrs. Campbell in her own language, with Mr. Martin Harvey as Pelléas, should be complicated with any memory less pleasing. I am quite willing to assume that Mrs. Campbell speaks French as exquisitely as she speaks English, and that Sarah's Pelléas is not, like her Hamlet and her Duc de Reichstadt, merely ladylike. But the two facts remain that Sarah is a woman and that Mrs. Campbell is an Englishwoman. And by these two facts such a performance is ruled out of the sphere of art into the sphere of sensationalism. If Maeterlinck were a sensationalist, that would not matter.

A PANACEA

July 23, 1904

Spare me the task of reviewing the past season. I hate, especially in the dawn of a vacation, to be pessimistic; and what else could I be if I recalled the immediate past? So let me imagine some other kind of immediate past—a kind that would justify me in optimism. Let me compile for you the pleasant history of what might, and ought to, have happened, as though it really and truly had been happening. . . .

Extract from "The Court Circular" for 1 April, 1904

"This morning His Majesty received in audience the Earl of Clarendon (Lord Chamberlain), Mr. George Alexander Redford (Examiner of Plays), and the members of the London County Council committee for the licensing of theatres.

"In the evening His Majesty presided over the thirty-seventh annual dinner of the Actors' Benevolent Fund."

Extract from report in "Daily Telegraph" of Actors' Benevolent Fund Dinner.

. . . "His Majesty, who was looking (if we may say so without disrespect) the picture of health, had, with that unerring tact and kind-heartedness which have so endeared him to his subjects, elected to aptly signify his interest in things appertaining to the theatre by appearing simply attired in the costume affected by the wealthier section of playgoers. On rising to graciously propose the toast of the evening, the King was received with a ringing volley of loyal applause. His Majesty said 'My lords and gentlemen, it is with great pleasure that I am here to-night. I am myself a playgoer of many years' standing. I regard the theatre as a great possible factor in the intellectual life of my subjects. But I regret to say that the theatre does not fulfil its function in this respect. We have no serious drama, and there seems to be no prospect of our getting a serious drama. The few playhouses not yet given over to a certain vile and degrading form of entertain-

ment—I refer, my lords and gentlemen, to musical comedy—offer
us plays which have little or no perceptible relation to the realities
of life. How different it is in a neighbouring country with which
I may boast a close connexion—I refer, my lords and gentlemen,
to Germany. There we find Sudermann, Hauptmann, and many
other scarcely less serious playwrights; and we find that they
(whom I am proud to claim as, in a sense, my compatriots) are
intensely popular, and are rivalled in popularity only by Ibsen,
Björnson, and other alien masters. Why this distressing difference between Germans and Englishmen? Why should they, in
relation to the theatre, be joyfully serious, whilst we are dully
frivolous? These are not new questions. For years past, there
has been a great deal of talk on this subject. But none of the
talkers has done anything. I, my lords and gentlemen, propose
to do something. Since my accession, I have footed it, to the
national good, in statecraft and in diplomacy. I am now going to
exercise a not, I hope, less beneficent influence on art. I have
decided that all the theatres in my kingdom shall be closed forthwith, for a period of ten years. In that drastic interval the public
will, I earnestly hope, lose its taste for musical comedy, and be,
when once more the doors of the theatres are thrown open to it,
patient of what we call the legitimate drama. Hitherto that
term "legitimate" has hardly been deserved. But I think that
ten years hence there may be a crop of plays to deserve it. Our
dramatists will have had plenty of time in which to live—to
observe life. They will have returned to their work like giants
refreshed. They will have returned joyously realising that there
is an outer world to be mirrored by their art. Some of them, of
course, will never return. No matter. We can well spare those
who have not the true vocation. It may be objected that, in the
drastic interval, the mimes will forget their technique. Let them.
It is much more important that they should have time to observe
their fellow-creatures than that they should continue to be elaborately unlike their fellow-creatures. Better a knowing amateur
than an ignorant professional. Nor will there be anything to
prevent our mimes, ten years hence, from acquiring gradually a
new technique, founded on actuality. My lords and gentlemen, I
have done. It only remains for me to say that the new regula-
tions will be enforced with all possible despatch. I give the

managers three days' grace. On the fourth day the official seals
will be affixed to the various portals. I raise my glass and drink
continued prosperity to the Actors' Benevolent Fund, on whose
resources may my decision bring no undue strain.'"

Extract from leading article in same issue.

"His Majesty the King, with his unfailing grip of all that is
essential to the welfare of his lieges, foreshadowed last night a
scheme which must meet with the hearty approval of all thinking
men and women. It is a policy grounded on principles which we
ourselves have implicitly advocated for many years. Now that
his Majesty the King, with that peculiar courage and sagacity
which" . . .

*Extract from resolution passed unanimously by meeting of theatrical
managers, Sir Henry Irving in the chair, 3 April.*

. . . "and that we humbly beg to assure His Majesty of our loyal
appreciation of this the latest and not least of the many evidences
of His Majesty's gracious interest in our calling" . . .

Extract from "World," 4 April.

"Our readers will regret to learn that Mr. William Archer, so
long endeared to them by his wholehearted faith in the steady
progress of modern dramatic art, is seriously indisposed."

Extract from "Daily Telegraph," 5 April.

"The unfailing kindliness and thoughtfulness of His Majesty
the King were never more felicitously manifested than when he
consented, despite the pressure of those numerous other duties
which he indefatigably fulfils, to close some of the principal
theatres in person. Yesterday forenoon His Majesty, in the
presence of a large and brilliant assembly, performed this picturesque old ceremony successively at Wyndham's Theatre and
the New Theatre, affixing the seals with his own hand. Afterwards, he honoured Sir Charles Wyndham with his presence at
luncheon, which was served in a marquee erected in the Charing
Cross Road."

A PANACEA

Paragraph in "Daily Telegraph," 15 April.

"Some affecting scenes were witnessed yesterday at Liverpool Docks, where many actors, actresses, playwrights, costumiers, wigmakers, dramatic critics and refreshment contractors were waiting to embark on the emigrant ship. It was noticeable that, though there were many tear-stained faces in the crowd, and many 'longing lingering looks' were cast back at the old country, not a man or woman uttered a word of complaint. As the great ship sailed majestically out of port, the emigrants were heard to sing 'God Save the King.'" . . .

Paragraph in "World," 18 April.

"At the moment of going to press we learn that Mr. William Archer has passed a fairly good night. The fever has somewhat abated, and there is a marked improvement in his general condition. The patient is said to be determined, in the event of his recovery, to remain on British territory."

Paragraph in "Daily Telegraph," 19 April.

"It is pleasant to find that among the dramatists who are remaining among us are Captains Robert Marshall and Basil Hood, both of whom have just been re-gazetted into their former regiments. Mr. Hubert Henry Davies has entered his name as a candidate for matriculation at one of the colleges of Cambridge. Mr. H. V. Esmond has been sent to an excellent preparatory school."

Paragraph in "World," 25 April.

"Yesterday morning, Mr. William Archer, who is now happily convalescent, took up his position at the door of one of our leading theatres. He informs us from his camp-stool that since his recovery from his severe illness he is inclined to modify his previous convictions. 'It may be,' he says with characteristic honesty, 'that all was not so well with the British drama as I had surmised.' At the same time, he is confident of the future, and looks keenly forward, though without impatience, to the evening of 15 May, 1914, the date fixed for the next production."

A PLAY FOR THE POPULACE

September 24, 1904

There can be no shadow of a doubt that Mr. Zangwill has, in the language of the vulgar, done it this time. The time of "Children of the Ghetto" was some years ago, and my memory of it is dimmed; but I remember enough to know that it was a time when Mr. Zangwill, emphatically, did *not* do it. The play was a failure, for Mr. Zangwill had not enough theatrical instinct—or perhaps it was only experience that was lacking—to vivify on the stage a large and serious conception, such as he had vivified in books. Even had he vivified this conception, for you and me, the play might have failed commercially; for the public, as you know, has an obstinate predilection for futile things. Mr. Zangwill, older and wiser now, has gone, in the writing of "Merely Mary Ann," nap on that predilection. Not that he is yet so old or so wise as to hush up the cynicism of his procedure. Two of the persons in his play, musicians, are discussing the public's taste in music. "You know," says one, "what the public wants?" "Yes," says the other, "it wants treacle." "Ah," says the other "but it wants a special kind of treacle." "I know," says the other: "'Golden Syrup.'" I was afraid that this sardonic touch was going to ruin the play. Audiences, dog-like, cannot bear to be laughed at; and a playwright who puts his tongue in his cheek may as well put his play in his waste-paper basket. Besides, usually a man who does work beneath his dignity cannot do it really well His jokes may be bad, and his sentiment false; but somehow they lack just the particular requisite quality of badness and falseness "Merely Mary Ann" is a blest exception. The audience did not notice Mr. Zangwill's jibe at it and at himself, for, strange to relate the play rang quite true—the hollowness seemed really hollow.

The theme of the play is rather a good one. The central figure is akin to the poet in "Candida"—a young man of good family driven out of his home because he insists on following his natural bent and devoting himself to musical composition. He takes a room in a Bloomsbury lodging-house; and here he lives tormented in the liberty he has gained for his genius, by the sordidness and

338

solitude of his material existence. The servant who waits on him and the other lodgers is a pretty girl from Somersetshire; and for her, as supplying the one touch of poetry here, he conceives a romantic regard, which she more than reciprocates. An offer from a music-publisher enables him to pay the landlady her bill and to take a cottage somewhere in the country. The girl is heartbroken at his departure. Why, he reflects, should he not take her with him? Of course he has too much worldly wisdom to marry her; but, even on grounds of humanity, would it not be better for her to live with him than to be left in loneliness and drudgery here? A very good play of a serious kind might be based on the subsequent history of these two persons. Disparity of class, in its effect on genuine affection, is always an interesting subject. So, too, is the conflict between artistic genius and genuine affection. I can imagine that Mr. Zangwill would, in the epoch aforesaid, have treated his theme grimly. Of course, the musician would have belonged to that race to which musicians mostly do belong, and would have been an earnest believer in all the tenets of its faith. The barrier to matrimony would have been the barrier of faith, not of class. But, essentially, this would have made no difference; and the resultant play would have been, at least, an interesting failure. On his present tack, Mr. Zangwill knew full well that his musician must be an aristocratic gentile, and that his play must be a sort of fairy-story. A really good fairy-story, on this as on any other theme, I should welcome. Mr Barrie would have achieved it. He would have touched his theme with a whimsical magic, transporting it straight away from the plane of reality to the plane of fantasy. Mr. Zangwill has not this magic. He can only, as it were, doctor reality. His characters are everyday people behaving as no person would on any day behave—a compromise which is, I grant you, all that the public needs. They are not figments; they are merely askew. And the mischief is that they are not at all, for me, charmingly askew. Disparity of class between lovers is a very ticklish subject, especially in comedy. It requires the keenest tact and delicacy in handling. It is one of the subjects which can hardly be made to yield the same effect in art as in life. In life there is nothing repulsive in the fact of a gentleman falling in love with a servant-girl. But transfer this fact to the comic stage, and the effect of it

339

on a sensitive person will (barring that almost superhuman tact
and delicacy) be as unpleasant as were in real life the fact of a lady
being in love with her footman. Mr. Zangwill has failed, from
my standpoint, to do what almost everybody else would have
failed to do. But he has, also from that standpoint, failed deeplier
than a great many other people would have failed. His star rose
in or about the year 1890. At that period every new star gravi-
tated surely to one or other of two constellations. Every new
writer became straightway either one of Mr. Henley's young men
or one of Mr. Jerome K. Jerome's young men. Mr. Zangwill
became one of Mr. Jerome K. Jerome's young men. Mercifully,
the allegiance lasted not long, for Mr. Zangwill had in him fine
stuff which could only be developed outside the Jeromian sphere
of influence. But it seems that even in that short period was
absorbed an ineradicable virus. Mr. Zangwill in his prime,
deviating from serious literature to frivolous dramaturgy, recalls
to us, awfully, the manner of his early master. Jeromian through
and through is the atmosphere he infuses into the Bloomsbury
lodging-house. The lodgers are heterogeneous; yet at every
window we seem to see one face—Mr. Jerome's. On every stair
we hear one footfall—his. On every peg in the hall his hat is
hanging. The haughty aristocrat speaks sharply to the servant-
girl, and his friend tells him that there was moisture in her eyes as
she turned to go. "So much the better," says the haughty
aristocrat, "it will make her face cleaner perhaps." That is
perhaps a rather extreme instance; but it is only by extreme
instances that a general impression can be briefly conveyed; and I
had to justify the deep impression of Jeromism which the play
gradually wrought on me. Physical humour, too, in which Mr.
Jerome dealt always lavishly, is lavishly dealt in here One
character, in a fit of abstraction, squirts the carpet with a syphon.
Another, also in a fit of abstraction, holds the teapot in such a way
as to pour out all the tea on the carpet. (It does one's heart good,
or ill, to see the audience convulsed by these simple exercises.)
And, all the while, Mr. Zangwill is methodically spilling jar after
jar of the Golden Syrup aforesaid, and smiling bitterly while the
public sprawls and laps it up—sprawls and laps till at length (when
the servant-girl has inherited half a million pounds sterling, and
has, after an interval of separation, thrown herself into the arms of

the erst haughty aristocrat) the public is sated and sent home, smiling a sticky smile of gratitude. The play will run for a very long while—clashing, I hope, with other plays in which Mr. Zangwill will try to give to the stage something of his own remarkable and admirable self.

I have pictured him "smiling bitterly" for the present. I do hope the picture is a true one. But I have my hateful doubts. I am sure that he smiled bitterly when he wrote the play, and, later, when Mr. Frohman jumped at it for the Duke of York's. But human nature is a subtly involved affair. It is quite possible that, in the course of rehearsing the play for production, Mr. Zangwill gradually lost his sense of aloofness from his work. After all, the play was his. His name would be on the programme. He would be held responsible. And it is nice to have an artistic success. And it is not nice to have an artistic failure. Was there in the play anything really good? Mr. Zangwill (if I am right in my diagnosis of the mood of a dramatist on the eve of a production) eagerly asked himself this question. He tried hard to find a reason for answering himself in the affirmative. For, though a man is ready enough to scoff at his own work, as studied by him in private, with no necessity to show it to any one, he resents that people should scoff at it when he gives it to the world, and is anxious to convince himself that the scoffers—if scoffers there be—will be in the wrong. So he becomes tenderly indulgent to himself. If his work please the many, the many are right; if not, not. If his work displease the few, the few are wrong. "Merely Mary Ann" is giving intense pleasure to the many. I hope I err in my suspicion that Mr. Zangwill sides with them against me. I hope he is grasping me by the hand, stammering heartfelt gratitude and promises of amendment.

LITERARY MEN ON THE STAGE

October 8, 1904

One speaks of "mixed emotions" as though they were a rather rare and peculiar thing. In point of fact, emotional people—and they are the vast majority of mankind—very seldom have an emotion single and straightforward. One emotion merges automatically into another; and the chances are that these different emotions have no logical connexion. Take, for example, the emotion of pity. Some one has suffered a misfortune. People are very sorry for him. But they are not merely sorry for him: they find themselves also exalting him as a hero. If a man fail publicly and signally, he can always count on being for a moment deified at large. A few months ago I drew your attention to the great enthusiasm evoked by the fact that Mr. George Alexander had produced a play which ran for only four nights. The British press and the British people, smiling through their tears, were immensely proud of Mr. Alexander. They seemed to think that he had done a deed of rarest courage and nobility. And now again they are in just this mood over Mrs. Brown Potter. Only rather more so; for Mrs. Potter has produced a play which she withdrew after only three nights. Pluck? It seems that there never was such a plucky woman. Ascend, madam, to the hierarchy of heroines, and make yourself comfortable between Antigone and Grace Darling. . . . It must be very nice to be an emotional person. My regret for Mrs. Potter's misadventure is unaccompanied by any cheerful sense of her heroism, and so is unmitigated. So much of work and hope and anxiety is involved in every theatrical production that I must needs be saddened whenever a play fails. If so be that the manager, stonily staring failure in the face and insisting that it is success, proceed to run the play at all hazards, then I have the comfort of being impressed by a display of reckless courage. But if the manager climb quickly down I can merely recognise an act of wisdom. And wisdom is such a tame affair, after all.

One result of Mrs. Potter's alacrity is that I did not see the play. I had secured a ticket for Monday evening; but, when Monday evening came, there was nothing for me to do but sit in my study, from 8.30 to 11 o'clock, trying, with closed eyes, to imagine that the play was being performed before me. I had read some criticisms of it, and I knew that one of the principal characters in it was a literary man. Him, especially, I tried to visualise. Presentments of literary men on the stage are a special hobby of mine. They are always delightful. And I had gathered that this particular one was more than usually delightful. Had Fate been kind enough to let me see the play, I should probably have devoted the greater part of this article to the presentment of the literary man, with some general remarks about literary men on the stage. As it is, I can but make the general remarks.

Partly, no doubt, it is the actors themselves who are responsible. The histrionic and the literary temperaments are of all temperaments furthest asunder. Actors, having so little in common with writers, see as little as possible of them. When an actor cast for the part of a literary man, conscientiously penetrates into literary circles, to observe, he is very much disappointed. He wants a good make-up—something typical and sharply distinctive; and he looks for it in vain. Literary men look so very like other men. Their art, unlike the actor's, stamps no special seal upon their features and their gait. As for costume, and hair-dressing, the modern writer carefully shuns anything in the way of specialism. His dearest ambition is to be mistaken for a soldier. His ambition is unfulfilled; but he often succeeds in looking rather like a doctor. To make himself up rather like a doctor would be perhaps the most artistic course for an actor in the part of a literary man. But he feels that in the theatre there must be sharp certainty, even at the expense of truth. The audience must recognise him, at sight, as a literary man. How is he to achieve this end? I remember that some years ago, an actor, thus troubled, appealed to me privately and personally. I looked at myself in the glass, vainly. I searched the files of "The Bookman," vainly. All I could advise him to do, at last, was to stain the thumb and forefinger of his right hand with a little ink. I was touched to see, on the first night, that he had taken my advice. For the rest, he wore a jacket of brown velveteen, an Inverness cape, and a soft hat, irregular in shape. His face was painted very white—"sicklied o'er," as he would have said, "with the pale cast of thought." Further symbols of intellect were a pince-nez and a bald brow, behind which some brown hair streamed down upon his shoulders. He looked like nothing that is at present on the face of the earth. He looked rather like our idea of the Bohemians in the 'fifties. And that is just how other actors, in similar case, invariably do look.

Though writers have no hall-mark on their appearance, they do

343

acquire, through practice of their art, a rather distinctive manner. Accustomed to express themselves through a medium wherein there is no place for gesture, or play of features, or modulation of the voice, they become peculiarly passive in their mode of conversation. Obliged in their work to dispense with such adventitious aids, they lose the power to use them in their off moments. But the actor has never detected this obvious peculiarity. At any rate, he does not reproduce it. Impersonating a writer, he behaves with as strenuous an animation as if he were impersonating himself. When a real writer reads aloud to you something that he has written, his calmness, as you must have noticed, becomes intensified. He drones to you, with half-closed eyes, in an unctuously faint monotone. It is not often that the writer as shown on the stage has an opportunity of reading aloud his own works: usually, his genius is to be taken on trust. But, sometimes, a greatly daring playwright will venture so far as to let him give you a taste of his quality. And then the unreality of him becomes more than ever effulgent. For the actor feels that here is his chance; here is a recitation, to be done for all it is worth. He takes the bit between his teeth, and races forth, with terrific impetus. One of the dearest of my recollections is of a fairly recent play whose hero was a young poet. He was entertaining some friends at his room in the Temple, and they asked him to read them some verses that he had just composed. At first, he demurred. "They are nothing," he said, modestly. They were not, indeed, very much—three stanzas of mildly pretty sentiment; but oh, you should have heard the actor declaim them! He was seated at a table when he began to read, but for the second stanza he rose to his full height, with flashing eyes and dilated chest; and for the third stanza he came down to the footlights, and roared at us like a bull. I shall never forget it.

So much for the actors. We must not forget the playwrights. They, despite the sacred and indissoluble union of literature and the drama, seem to be almost as hazy as actors in their notion of what literary men are like. I search my memory in vain for one passable presentment of a literary man in modern drama. Even in the most obvious and rudimentary part of their task they fail. The sharpest point of superficial difference between a literary man and his fellow-creatures is not the lack of animation in his mode of saying things (for in England animation is always rare), but the fact that what he says differs in form from what his fellow-creatures say. The literary man would like, no doubt, to express himself in conversation with soldierly abruptness and crypticism; but he cannot help being literary—cannot shake off that lucid formality which is essential to the task of writing. It should be easy enough for a playwright to suggest this manner. And yet he never does suggest it, unless he happen to be a playwright who cannot make any of his characters talk except with literary constructions—in which case the suggestion is valueless. Nor can I remember a modern play in which there was any semblance of truth in the presentment of a literary man's life or mode of work. I can but recall a number of "howlers." In one play—a very clever comedy—a great writer gravely asked his amanuensis if she had yet had time to correct the proofs of his forthcoming book. In another, another great writer said to his wife "Stay! I have an idea for a novel. Wait a moment, while I jot it down." In another a poet of the highest genius was seen at his desk, in the dawn, having completed a poem, all but the rhyme in the last line. This rhyme eluded him. He injected some opium into his wrist, murmuring over and over again

> "The dark waves claim me for their own
> Making murmur with infinite . . ."

"Ah!" he shouted suddenly. "I've captured the little devil at last! I knew I should! 'Making murmur with infinite *moan*.'" And so the dignity of the Muse was upheld, and all was well.

Seeing our playwrights' babe-like ignorance of the plainest facts about literary men, one can hardly wonder that in no play has there been any attempt at a study of the literary man's inner soul. I doubt whether any playwright, however discerning, could succeed in presenting a great writer impressively. In the theatre we are so loth to take glorious things on trust. When some character is presented to us as a great explorer, or a victorious general, we don't succumb. We eye him suspiciously. We want some evidence. The great writer is similarly handicapped. Where are his books? On the other hand, though we are coy of believing in glorious things which cannot be verified, we are quick enough to take on trust absurd things, or even ordinary things. We are willing to believe that a character on the stage is a bad writer, or even a respectable writer. And the literary temperament is a thing not more common among good writers than among bad and indifferent ones. And it is an interesting thing. There ought to be a good play about it. I feel sure there will be one, some day, in Utopia.

AN HORTATION

October 15, 1904

I subscribe to the general opinion that the stage is a rather tragic profession. To fail in the art of acting, which is of all arts the most directly personal to the artist, is a specially bitter experience; and it is, owing to the glamour of the footlights, and to the consequent rush of persons who have no vocation for the art, an experience that falls to the great majority of mimes. I am sorry for the numberless derelicts who, down at heel, daily haunt the Strand in the vague hope of something turning up. Yet it is not in them that I find exemplars of the darkest tragedy of their profession. I think there are deeper depths. My heartiest ruth is reserved for certain highly talented and popular mimes. The deepest depths are, as it were, at the top of the tree.

The long-run system is, in itself, sufficient reason for pitying these ladies and gentlemen. It must be horribly tedious and galling for any person with an active mind to repeat nightly, for weeks and months, a certain series of words written by somebody else. How much worse must it be to enact nightly the same part for years and years! Yet that is the common fate of the successful mime. He will have made his success in one strongly-defined part, and thenceforth the managers will have preferred the certainty of his excellence in one "line" to the chance of his proficiency in another. Perhaps he becomes a manager on his own account. Then it is likely that he, unless his love of art greatly preponderate over his fear of bankruptcy, will take the safe path of monotony. The public likes him as it knows him; and the public is slow-witted, averse from change, and probably would not accept him, however good he might be, in a new kind of part; and so the poor man immolates himself, and will continue to immolate himself.

Take, for example, poor Mr. Lewis Waller, who produced a new play last week at the Imperial Theatre. Some time ago he began to be very successful as hero of cape and sword. He beat all competitors in that business. None was of mien so gallant and resolute and daring. None's eye and sword flashed so harmoniously. None could rescue with such neatness and despatch a maiden in distress, or render with such coolness, or such violence, unheard-of services to the King, his master, whom Heaven bless. And so the history of the Imperial Theatre under his management consists of "Monsieur Beaucaire," "Ruy Blas," "Miss Elizabeth's Prisoner," and "His Majesty's Servant," with a swashbucklement by the revered Mr. Crockett in the offing. "Always so dashing" was the fond criticism which the maiden lady in "Quality Street" passed on her nephew. Had he ceased to cause her anxiety, she might have forbidden him her door. "Always so dashing," dodders Britannia over Mr. Waller, and he takes the hint. But at what a cost! Imagine the tedium of being always, year in, year out, dashing, and nothing *but* dashing! Nor is it only at nightfall that Mr. Waller's lot seems piteous. Acting is, in a sense, one of the dangerous trades. Psychologists have explained that a man who industriously simulates something must, at length, absorb the simulated thing into his own being. An actor loses imperceptibly, but for ever, a little of his true self, and absorbs a little of an alien self, every time he performs a part. This process would have no ill effects in the case of an actor in a stock company: constant variety in impersonation would give no time for any one radical change in the actor's soul. But Mr. Waller's soul—how much, I wonder, remains of the original article? By this time, Mr. Waller must almost have lost the power to be anything except gallant and resolute and daring. And this disability must be a source of very great inconvenience for him. The conditions of modern life afford so very little scope for a hero of cape and sword. The time is not out of joint, and by a cursed spite there is no outlet for Mr. Waller's desire to set it right. I picture him sallying every morning from his front-door with flashing eye and swinging gait, all alert and mettlesome for some dread emprise in the service of the right. I picture him pausing suddenly in the neighbourhood of Buckingham Palace, and eyeing with eagle glance a mounted policeman who canters by. In another moment there follows a closed carriage, driven at great speed. Mr. Waller's hand flies to the back of the brim of his hat, and he uncovers with a circular sweep. But ah! by Mr. Waller's halidom, the King is in danger—is being spirited somewhither to his hurt by yon varlets. To seize the bridles of the horses, leap through the carriage window, send the treacherous equerry to his last account, shoulder the King and convey him to some place of safety, would be but the work of a moment for Mr. Waller; only . . . Mr. Waller has remembered reality. We leave him standing on the curb in a picturesque attitude, frowning a terrible frown, and wondering how he will get through the day in this drab world, and longing for nightfall and the footlights. Yes, I have no doubt that I was wrong in supposing that Mr. Waller was bored by his own performance on the stage. But I, certainly, am beginning to be bored by it. Heartfelt though it be, it has through infinite repetition the effect of being mechanical. And, since in art one is concerned only with effect, it *is* mechanical. I exhort Mr. Waller to try soon, before it is too late, to give us some other performance. Perhaps he never has done, and never could do, anything so well as what he has done in cape and sword drama. But he has done other things admirably, and might do them so again. I exhort him to a course of overcoat and umbrella drama. Better be a bankrupt artist than an ever so prosperous machine.

As for the present play, I have nothing to say about it. I do not understand melodrama. For me the excitement of a play consists in the conflict of characters who give me the illusion that they are alive. In melodrama there is no time for this illusion to be wrought. Everything must be sacrificed for a full series of incidents. And whether one lay-figure will be happily betrothed to another lay-figure, or whether a third lay-figure will succeed in intercepting a letter and running a fourth lay-figure through the body, is for me a matter of total indifference. "His Majesty's Servant" may be good—may be bad—of its kind. If you need a verdict, consult some other critic.

DAN LENO

November 5, 1904

So little and frail a lantern could not long harbour so big a flame. Dan Leno was more a spirit than a man. It was inevitable that he, cast into a life so urgent as is the life of a music-hall artist, should die untimely. Before his memory fades into legend, let us try to evaluate his genius. For mourners there is ever a solace in determining what, precisely, they have lost.

Usually, indisputable pre-eminence in any art comes of some great originative force. An artist stands unchallenged above his fellows by reason of some "new birth" that he has given to his art. Dan Leno, however, was no inaugurator. He did not, like Mr. Albert Chevalier, import into the music-hall a new subject-matter, with a new style. He ended, as he had started, well within the classic tradition. True, he shifted the centre of gravity from song to "patter." But, for the rest, he did but hand on the torch. His theme was ever the sordidness of the lower middle class, seen from within. He dealt, as his forerunners had dealt, and as his successors are dealing, with the "two pair-back," the "pub," the "general store," the "peeler," the "beak," and other such accessories to the life of the all-but-submerged. It was rather a murky torch that he took. Yet, in his hand, how gloriously it blazed, illuminating and warming! All that trite and unlovely material, how new and beautiful it became for us through Dan Leno's genius! Well, where lay the secret of that genius? How came we to be spell-bound?

Partly, without doubt, our delight was in the quality of the things actually said by Dan Leno. No other music-hall artist threw off so many droll sayings—droll in idea as in verbal expression. Partly, again, our delight was in the way that these things were uttered—in the gestures and grimaces and antics that accompanied them; in fact, in Dan Leno's technique. But, above all, our delight was in Dan Leno himself. In every art personality is the paramount thing, and without it artistry goes for little. Especially is this so in the art of acting, where the appeal of personality is so direct. And most especially is it so in the art of

349

acting in a music-hall, where the performer is all by himself upon the stage, with nothing to divert our attention. The moment Dan Leno skipped upon the stage, we were aware that here was a man utterly unlike any one else we had seen. Despite the rusty top hat and broken umbrella and red nose of tradition, here was a creature apart, radiating an ethereal essence all his own. He compelled us not to take our eyes off him, not to miss a word that he said. Not that we needed any compulsion. Dan Leno's was not one of those personalities which dominate us by awe, subjugating us against our will. He was of that other, finer kind: the lovable kind. He had, in a higher degree than any other actor that I have ever seen, the indefinable quality of being sympathetic. I defy any one not to have loved Dan Leno at first sight. The moment he capered on, with that air of wild determination, squirming in every limb with some deep grievance, that must be outpoured, all hearts were his. That face puckered with cares, whether they were the cares of the small shopkeeper, or of the landlady, or of the lodger; that face so tragic, with all the tragedy that is writ on the face of a baby-monkey, yet ever liable to relax its mouth into a sudden wide grin and to screw up its eyes to vanishing point over some little triumph wrested from Fate, the tyrant; that poor little battered personage, so "put upon," yet so plucky with his squeaking voice and his sweeping gestures; bent but not broken; faint but pursuing; incarnate of the will to live in a world not at all worth living in—surely all hearts went always out to Dan Leno, with warm corners in them reserved to him for ever and ever.

To the last, long after illness had sapped his powers of actual expression and invention, the power of his personality was unchanged, and irresistible. Even had he not been in his heyday a brilliant actor, and a brilliant wag, he would have thrown all his rivals into the shade. Often, even in his heyday, his acting and his waggishness did not carry him very far. Only mediocrity can be trusted to be always at its best. Genius must always have lapses proportionate to its triumphs. A new performance by Dan Leno was almost always a dull thing in itself. He was unable to do himself justice until he had, as it were, collaborated for many nights with the public. He selected and rejected according to how his jokes, and his expression of them "went"; and his best things came to him always in the course of an actual performance, to be incorporated in all the subsequent performances. When, at last, the whole thing had been built up, how perfect a whole it was! Not a gesture, not a grimace, not an inflection of the voice, not a wriggle of the body, but had its significance, and drove its significance sharply, grotesquely, home to us all. Never was a more perfect technique in acting. The technique for acting in a music-hall is of a harder, perhaps finer, kind than is needed for acting in a theatre; inasmuch as the artist must make his effects so much more quickly, and without the aid of any but the slightest "properties" and scenery, and without the aid of any one else on the stage. It seemed miraculous how Dan Leno contrived to make you see before you the imaginary persons with whom he conversed. He never stepped outside himself, never imitated the voices of his interlocutors. He merely repeated, before making his reply, a few words of what they were supposed to have said to him. Yet there they were, as large as life, before us. Having this perfect independence in his art—being thus all-sufficient to himself—Dan Leno was, of course, seen to much greater advantage in a music-hall than at Drury Lane. He was never "in the picture" at Drury Lane. He could not play into the hands of other persons on the stage, nor could they play into his. And his art of suggestion or evocation was nullified by them as actualities. Besides, Drury Lane was too big for him. It exactly fitted Mr. Herbert Campbell, with his vast size and his vast method. But little Dan Leno, with a technique exactly suited to the size of the average music-hall, had to be taken, as it were, on trust.

Apart from his personality and his technique, Dan Leno was, as I have said, a sayer of richly grotesque things. He had also a keen insight into human nature. He knew thoroughly, outside and inside, the types that he impersonated. He was always "in the character," whatever it might be. And yet if you repeat to any one even the best things that he said, how disappointing is the result! How much they depended on the sayer and the way of saying! I have always thought that the speech over Yorick's skull would have been much more poignant if Hamlet had given Horatio some specific example of the way in which the jester had been wont to set the table on a roar. We ought to have seen Hamlet convulsed with laughter over what he told, and Horatio politely trying to conjure up the ghost of a smile. This would have been good, not merely as pointing the tragedy of a jester's death, but also as illustrating the tragic temptation that besets the jester's contemporaries to keep his memory green. I suppose we shall, all of us, insist on trying to give our grand-children some idea of Dan Leno at his best. We all have our especially cherished recollection of the patter of this or that song. I think I myself shall ever remember Dan Leno more vividly and affectionately as the shoemaker than as anything else. The desperate hopefulness with which he adapted his manner to his different customers! One of his customers was a lady with her little boy. Dan Leno, skipping forward to meet her, with a peculiar skip invented specially for his performance, suddenly paused, stepped back several feet in one stride, eyeing the lady in wild amazement. He had never seen such a lovely child. *How* old, did the mother say? Three? He would have guessed seven at least—"except when I look at you, ma'am, and then I should say he was one at most." Here Dan Leno bent down, one hand on each knee, and began to talk some unimaginable kind of baby-language. . . . A little pair of red boots with white buttons? Dan Leno skipped towards an imaginary shelf; but, in the middle of his skip, he paused, looked back, as though drawn by some irresistible attraction, and again began to talk to the child. As it turned out, he had no boots of the kind required. He plied the mother with other samples, suggested this and that, faintlier and faintlier, as he bowed her out. For a few moments he stood gazing after her, with blank disappointment, still bowing automatically. Then suddenly he burst out into a volley of deadly criticisms on the child's personal appearance, ceasing as suddenly at the entrance of another customer. . . . I think I see some of my readers—such of them as never saw Dan Leno in this part—raising their eyebrows. Nor do I blame them. Nor do I blame myself for failing to recreate that which no howsoever ingenious literary artist could recreate for you. I can only echo the old heart-cry "Si ipsum audissetis!" Some day, no doubt, the phonograph and the bioscope will have been so adjusted to each other that we shall see and hear past actors and singers as well as though they were alive before us. I wish Dan Leno could have been thus immortalised. No actor of our time deserved immortality so well as he.

352

MR. SHAW AT HIS BEST

November 12, 1904

Had Mr. Shaw been born in France, or in Germany, he would be at this moment the most popular playwright in Paris, or in Berlin. There is not the shadow of a doubt of that. As it is, he is becoming popular in Berlin. In New York he is popular already. Another decade will, with luck, see him popular in London. Meanwhile, I suppose, we must be grateful that his plays do manage to get themselves performed, somehow, somewhere, on the sly. During the past two weeks there have been some matinées of his latest play, "John Bull's Other Island," at the Court Theatre. It seemed natural that the auditorium had not been warmed on the bitterly cold day when I found myself there. But the temperature made me feel rather anxious; for in England, a country whose natural breed is dullards, any intellectual activity—and it is only the actively intellectual persons who go out of their way to special matinées—generally carries with it some grave physical delicacy; and we cannot spare aught of such intellectual activity as is going on among us. A man might die worse than in seeing a play by Mr. Shaw. But it seems a pity that he should not live to tell the tale. Moreover, I am quite sure that if Mr. Shaw's plays were more seductively produced, they would appeal even to the dullards at large. In a warm theatre, within the regular radius for theatres, after nightfall—in fact, with just those cheerful commercial circumstances which are withheld from them—these plays would soon take the town. The dull middleman shakes his head, mutters some dull shibboleth, dives his hand into a pigeon-hole, and calls rehearsals of a new play which has nothing whatever to recommend it except its likeness to the present failure, and to the last failure, and to the failure before last.

The critics, for the most part, are scarcely less dull than the managers themselves. Over "John Bull's Other Island" they have raised their usual parrot-cry: "Not a play." This, being interpreted, means "Not a love-story, split neatly up into four brief acts, with no hint that the characters live in a world where other things besides this love-story are going on." In "John Bull's Other Island" there is a love-story. But it occurs only in the fabric of the main scheme. This main scheme is to present the character of a typical Englishman against a typically Irish background—to throw up the peculiarities of the Englishman by contrast with various types of Irishman and various phases of Irish life, and to throw up the peculiarities of Ireland by contrast with the invader. This scheme Mr. Shaw carries out in four long acts, two of which contain two scenes apiece. Not much actually happens in the play. The greater part of the play is talk: and this talk is often not relevant to the action, but merely to the characters, and to things in general. Pray, why is this not to be called a play? Why should the modern "tightness" of technique be regarded as a sacred and essential part of dramaturgy? And why should the passion of love be regarded as the one possible theme in dramaturgy? Between these two superstitions lies the main secret of the barrenness of modern British drama. The first of them wards away the majority of men of creative literary power, who cannot be bothered to pick up the manifold little tricks and dodges which go to the making of what the critics call "a play." The second prevents playwrights from taking themes which would both invigorate their work through novelty and bring the theatre into contact with life at large.

Of course, I do not pretend that every good novelist could write a good play. There are essential differences between dramaturgy and any other form of literary work. My contention is that the dramatic instinct is no more rare than the narrative instinct, and that any man who has the dramatic instinct will, with a little practice, be able to write a good play. It is lucky for us that Mr. Shaw has not, like the vast majority of creative writers, been frightened away from the theatre. He has—though not, I wager, in a greater degree than many other men who dare only write novels—an instinct for the theatre, and he can with perfect ease express his ideas effectively through the dramatic form. None of our most fashionable playwrights could give him points in such technique as is really necessary. None is less amateurish in essentials. Mr. Shaw evolves his "situations" with perfect naturalness, and brings his characters off and on, and handles a whole crowd of them simultaneously on the stage, without the least apparent effort. He has, also, this great natural advantage in the writing of dialogue: he can always express himself directly, in a clean-cut manner. He is a thinker, and often a very subtle thinker. But he is also a public speaker, accustomed to dispense with that form in which his thoughts can be pondered at leisure, and to make the best of that form in which they must be caught as they fly. From the stage, then, as from the platform, his thoughts never elude us. We never have to pause to consider what he meant in the last line. It is always well to read a play by him at leisure, when it is published as a book; for the thoughts in it fly too thickly for us to remember them all after a performance. But at the moment of its utterance his every thought flies straight to our brain. As his thoughts are, so (I apologise for the arbitrary distinction) are his jests. His humour always gets well across the footlights, even when the fun of the thing said derives nothing from the character of its sayer or from the moment in which it is said. Thus, when Broadbent, the English Liberal candidate in Ireland, talks to his Irish fiancée about the canvassing, and is met by her reluctance to talk to "common people," he cries "Oh, but we must be thoroughly democratic, and patronise everybody without distinction of class." That is not even a caricature of anything that Broadbent would say. It is just a critical conceit of Mr. Shaw's. It is, therefore, not stage-humour, in the strict sense. But it is stage-humour in so far as it is so delightfully simple and sudden—a joke which not a soul in the audience can miss. However, these detached jests are rare in Mr. Shaw's play. Most of the fun comes of a slight exaggeration on the things that the character actually would say. But Mr. Shaw has also the art of extracting a ridiculous effect from every scenic situation. Broadbent has been selected as candidate quite unexpectedly, and on the spur of the moment. His valet has not heard the news. "Now, Hodson," says Broadbent, "you mustn't be standoffish with the people here. I should like you to be popular, you know." "I'm sure you're very kind, Sir," says Hodson; "but it don't seem to matter much whether they like me or not. I'm not going to stand for Parliament here, Sir." "Well," replies Broadbent, dramatically, "I am." This passage is not excruciatingly funny to read. But it is, as any one with dramatic instinct can imagine, excruciatingly funny to hear. Again, I might describe for you the scene in which Broadbent suddenly, by moonlight, makes his proposal of marriage, and is supposed by the young Irish lady to be intoxicated, and is by her converted to that uncomfortable belief, and led gently home by her; or I might describe the scene in which Broadbent drives away with a peasant's pig in his motor; but these descriptions would seem to me tame in comparison with the actual thing. There you have one of the tests of true dramatic humour : the inadequacy of pen and ink for a proper reproduction of it. Of all our playwrights Mr. Shaw is by far the most richly gifted with this humour. And of all his plays "John Bull's Other Island" is fullest of this humour. Yet none of our managers, gloomily hovering around Portugal Street, will offer the play to a public against which the obvious (and self-made) indictment is that it goes to the theatre just to be amused.

"Just to be amused." There is much besides amusement to be got out of this play (a fact which would, I suppose, form the manager's silly excuse for not producing it). Indeed, I think that none of Mr. Shaw's plays has so much serious interest. From all his plays one derives the pleasure that there is in finding a playwright who knows, and gives us, something of the world at first hand—a playwright who, moreover, has a philosophic view of things, and can criticise what he sees. Such displeasure as we have in Mr. Shaw's plays comes from the sense that Mr. Shaw is a little too sure of himself and his philosophy—a little too loudly consistent about everything to be right about most things. In this latest play of his, he seems to have mellowed into something almost like dubiety, without losing anything of his genius for ratiocination. He himself figures largely, as usual; this time in the person of Laurence Doyle, a disillusioned Irishman. But he does not have it all so signally his own way. Indeed, he is altogether put in the shade by an unfrocked priest, a mystic, who touches a note of visionary wisdom that makes every other character seem cheap and absurd. However, the principal motive of the play is not to give us the philosophy of this mystic, or Mr Shaw's philosophy, but to give us Broadbent, the Englishman, just as he is. Certainly, Mr. Shaw never created so perfect a type as Broadbent. Some years ago, in "Cæsar and Cleopatra," he gave us a person named Britannus, illustrating the peculiarities of the modern Englishman against an antique Roman background. But

Britannus, albeit delightful, was only a sketch. Broadbent is a
full-length portrait, minutely finished; and, moreover, the figure
stands out more sharply against modern Ireland than Britannus'
figure stood out against Rome, inasmuch as the modern Englishman is more akin to the ancient Roman than to the modern Irishman. Broadbent in business, Broadbent in politics, Broadbent
in love, Broadbent in all the various relations of life, is certainly
Mr. Shaw's masterpiece of observation and of satire. The satire
is the more deadly by reason of (what Broadbent would call) the
"conspicuous fairness" with which it is accomplished. Mr. Shaw
sees all Broadbent's good points, and lays stress on everything that
is not absurd in him. The tone is always kindly, even affectionate.
We are quite sure that justice is being done. Fullest justice;
and so—poor Broadbent! All Englishmen ought to see Broadbent. No Englishman could deny the truth of Broadbent. Indeed, no thoroughbred Englishman would wish to deny the truth
of Broadbent. That is the cream of the joke.

THE CHILD BARRIE

January 7, 1905

"Peter Pan; or," adds Mr. Barrie, "The Boy Who Wouldn't
Grow Up." And he himself is that boy. That child, rather;
for he halted earlier than most of the men who never come to
maturity—halted before the age when soldiers and steam-engines
begin to dominate the soul. To remain, like Mr. Kipling, a boy,
is not at all uncommon. But I know not any one who remains,
like Mr. Barrie, a child. It is this unparalleled achievement that
informs so much of Mr. Barrie's later work, making it unique.
This, too, surely, it is that makes Mr. Barrie the most fashionable
playwright of his time.

Undoubtedly, "Peter Pan" is the best thing he has done—the
thing most directly from within himself. Here, at last, we see his
talent in its full maturity; for here he has stripped off from himself the last flimsy remnants of a pretence to maturity. Time was

when a tiny pair of trousers peeped from under his "short-coats," and his sunny curls were parted and plastered down, and he jauntily affected the absence of a lisp, and spelt out the novels of Mr. Meredith and said he liked them very much, and even used a pipe for another purpose than that of blowing soap-bubbles. But all this while, bless his little heart, he was suffering. It would have been pleasant enough to play at being grown-up among children of his own age. It was a fearful strain to play at being grown-up among grown-up persons. But he was forced to do this, because the managers of theatres, and the publishers of books, would have been utterly dumbfounded if he had asked them to take him as he was. The public, for all its child-worship, was not yet ripe for things not written ostensibly by adults. The managers, the publishers, the public, had to be educated gradually. A stray curl or two, now and again, an infrequent soap-bubble between the fumes—that was as much as could be adventured just at first. Time passed, and mankind was lured, little by little, to the point when it could fondly accept Mr. Barrie on his own terms. The tiny trousers were slipped off, and under the toy-heap were thrust the works of Mr. Meredith. And every one sat around, nodding and smiling to one another rather fatuously, and blessing the little heart of Mr. Barrie. All was not yet well, though—not perfectly well. By force of habit, the child occasionally gave itself the airs of an adult. There were such moments even in "Little Mary." Now, at last, we see at the Duke of York's Theatre Mr. Barrie in his quiddity undiluted—the child in a state of nature, unabashed—the child, as it were, in its bath, splashing, and crowing as it splashes.

The first of all the differences between a child's mind and an adult's is the vividness and abundance of a child's fancy. Silently in solitude, or orally among its peers, a child can weave an endless web of romance around itself and around all things. As a child grows into boyhood, this delicate faculty is dimmed. Manhood, in most cases, destroys it utterly. For, as we come to manhood, the logical side of our brain is developed; and the faculty for logic is ever foe to the faculty for romance. It is only in our sleep, when the logical side of the brain is at rest, that the romantic side is at liberty to assert itself. In our dreams we are still fluently romantic, fertile in curious invention. In our dreams romance rises up, laughing, to lord it over logic who lords it over her all day long. She laughs, and leads him a dance all through the night. Sometimes, if we wake suddenly in the night, so suddenly that we remember a dream clearly, logic in us is forced to admit that romance is no mere madcap—that there is, at least, a method in her madness, and that, as man to woman, he is no match for her at her best. Yes, sometimes, remembering a dream, we marvel at the verisimilitude of it, marvel at the soundness of invention in the dialogue that we were waging, or in the adventure that had befallen us. And, with a sigh, we confess that we could not compass consciously so admirable an effect. Even when, as usually happens, the remembered dream is but a tissue of foolishness, how amusing the foolishness is! Why cannot we be amusingly foolish in the manifold follies of our hours of vigil? On the whole, certainly, our minds work to better effect when we sleep than when we wake. Why cannot we sleep for ever? Or, since the mind of a man sleeping is equivalent to a child's mind, why cannot we be for ever children? It is only the man of genius who never experiences this vain regret—never hankers after childhood, with all its material and moral discomforts, for sake of the spiritual magic in it. For the man of genius is that rare creature in whom imagination, not ousted by logic in full growth, abides, uncramped, in unison with full-grown logic. Mr. Barrie is not that rare creature, a man of genius. He is something even more rare—a child who, by some divine grace, can express through an artistic medium the childishness that is in him.

Our dreams are nearer to us than our childhood, and it is natural that "Peter Pan" should remind us more instantly of our dreams than of our childish fancies. One English dramatist, a man of genius, realised a dream for us; but the logic in him prevented him from indulging in that wildness and incoherence which are typical of all but the finest dreams. Credible and orderly are the doings of Puck in comparison with the doings of Peter Pan. Was ever, out of dreamland, such a riot of inconsequence and of exquisite futility? Things happen in such wise that presently one can conceive nothing that might not conceivably happen, nor anything that one would not, as in a dream, accept unhesitatingly. Even as in a dream, there is no reason why the things should ever cease to happen. What possible conclusion can inhere in

them? The only possible conclusion is from without. The sun shines through the bedroom window, or there is a tapping at the bedroom door, or—some playgoers must catch trains, others must sup. Even as you, awakened, turn on your pillow, wishing to pursue the dream, so, as you leave the Duke of York's, will you rebel at the dream's rude and arbitrary ending, and will try vainly to imagine what other unimaginable things were in store for you. For me to describe to you now in black and white the happenings in "Peter Pan" would be a thankless task. One cannot communicate the magic of a dream. People who insist on telling their dreams are among the terrors of the breakfast table. You must go to the Duke of York's, there to dream the dream for yourselves.

The fact that Mr. Barrie is a child would be enough, in this generation which so adores children, to account for his unexampled vogue. But Mr. Barrie has a second passport. For he, too, even pre-eminently, adores children—never ceases to study them and their little ways, and to purr sentimental pæans over them, and finds it even a little hard to remember that the world really does contain a sprinkling of adults. In fact, his attitude towards children is the fashionable attitude, struck more saliently by him than by any one else, and with more obvious sincerity than by the average person. It is not to be wondered at that his preoccupation with children endears him to the community. The strange thing is the preoccupation itself. It forces me to suppose that Mr. Barrie has, after all, to some extent, grown up. For children are the last thing with which a child concerns itself. A child takes children as a matter of course, and passes on to more important things—remote things that have a glorious existence in the child's imagination. A little boy does not say "I am a child," but "I am a pirate," or "a greengrocer," or "an angel," as the case may be. A little girl does not say "I am a little girl, and these are my dolls, and this is my baby-brother," but "I am the mother of this family." She lavishes on her dolls and on her baby-brother a wealth of maternal affection, cooing over them, and . . . stay! that is just Mr. Barrie's way. I need not, after all, mar by qualification my theory that Mr. Barrie has never grown up. He is still a child, absolutely. But some fairy once waved a wand over him, and changed him from a dear little boy into a dear little girl. Some critics have wondered why among the characters in "Peter

Pan" appeared a dear little girl, named in the programme "Liza (the Author of the Play)." Now they know. Mr. Barrie was just "playing at symbolists."

MR. SUTRO'S NEW PLAY

February 18, 1905

The homilist, or setter-to-rights, is a very familiar figure in modern comedy. Who shall number Sir Charles Wyndham's impersonations of him? Who shall number the dramatic complications that he has unravelled, the rough places that he has made smooth, the foolish actions that he has, by his ripe knowledge of men and women, and by his irresistible personal magnetism, prevented in the nick of time, the true lovers that he has united, the all-but-erring wives that he has restored to their husbands? We all know him. We are all impressed by his easy yet judicial manner of listening to a man's account of a quandary. How apt are the questions he interpolates from moment to moment! How significant his "H'm. Go on!" How very sound the advice that he presently delivers, usually concluding with "My dear fellow, leave it all to *me*!" And then, his management of the lady in question—of any number of little ladies in question! He reads them like a book. Nothing in their fluttering hearts is dark to him. He puts them perfectly at their ease. He seems to agree, in theory, with every word they say. He merely insinuates the suggestion of other views to be taken, other courses to be pursued. But the insinuation, as made by him, is enough. He has sown the seed: the flower follows. His advice is followed to the letter, and all turns out exactly as he, and we under his guidance, had foreseen. And all, needless to say, is well.

Now, I take it that in real life no man has personal magnetism to such a degree that, if he went through life minding other people's business, and instructing every one exactly how his or her business ought to be transacted, he would not be politely asked to leave whatever house he set foot in. Further, I take it that in real life no man has so perfect a combination of acumen and luck that every human "case" undertaken by him would turn out exactly as he intended it to turn out. In fact, I regard our friend the stage-homilist as a fraud. And I have often wished that some satiric playwright would come and prick the bubble—show the homilist annihilated by the proved fact that his diagnoses had been incorrect, his advice absurd, his stratagems clumsy, and his general effect disastrous to all around him. "Mollentrave on Women," at the St. James' Theatre, is therefore very welcome to me. The bubble is pricked at last. It is true that Mr. Sutro does not show the homilist consciously annihilated. I, who have been so long exasperated by the homilist, would like to see him really suffering. But I am ready to admit that Mr. Sutro's subtler way of dealing with him is perhaps more really unkind. Mollentrave has not the sense to understand even his own senselessness. Having complacently complicated the quite simple affairs of his friends, having seen all his predictions falsified and all his plans miscarry, he is left at the end of the play preening himself on the fact that all has come out well—all having come out well quite accidentally, of course, and in despite of his well-meant efforts.

In Mollentrave Mr. Sutro has directed good satire not merely against a tiresome stage-figure. There are such homilists in real life, too. There really are persons who, studying humanity from a scientific standpoint, and classifying it into various genera and species, pretend to be able to say what such and such a person will do in such and such given circumstances, and are fatuously eager to be consulted in human crises. And these poor pedants pretend to wisdom especially in regard to women. The more incalculable their material the more blithely calculating are they. They are an admirable target for the comic spirit.

"A Comedy" Mr. Sutro calls his play. But it is not really that. "A Philosophic Farce" would be a much better description of it. In a comedy the characters presented are taken from real life without sharp exaggeration, and the incidents are just such as might quite likely be experienced in real life. Mollentrave is a very sharp exaggeration of a type. There's no fool like an old fool, but not even the eldest fool in real life would pretend to such formal and final omniscience in psychology as is pretended to by Mollentrave. Nor is the course of events in the play at all natural

or credible. A middle-aged man, Sir Joseph Balsted, has a female
ward, whose presence in the house is irksome to him. She is
secretly loved by a young man of her own age, but is herself
secretly in love with Balsted. Mollentrave, of course, supposes
her to be pining for her coæval, and determines to ease Balsted by
bringing the young couple together. Having made the young man
acknowledge his feelings, he proceeds to convey the offer of marriage to the girl. But he does his work so clumsily that she
imagines that the proposal comes from Balsted. Now, in real life,
the simplest thing in the world would be for Balsted to explain the
mistake. There, in real life, would be an end of the matter. But
in the play Balsted allows Mollentrave to insist on a ludicrous
scheme, by which the girl's affection shall be gradually alienated.
The total failure of this ludicrous scheme to alienate the girl, and
its success in deepening her passion, is the staple of the whole
subsequent story. The whole play is founded on an impossibility, and its details are worked out with a conscious disregard of
likelihood—with a conscious straining after sheer absurdity. In
fact, the play is a farce. I have no objection to that. The scientific expert in affairs of the heart might be well satirised through
comedy. But comedy is not the only good means of satirising
him. Farce is in itself an equally good medium. All that
matters is whether Mr. Sutro has the instinct for satirical farce.
Offhand, I should have supposed that he had not the requisite
high-spirits. Mr. Arthur Bourchier is still angry with me, insomuch that I have not seen Mr. Sutro's play at the Garrick Theatre.
But I gather from hearsay that it is a very strenuous piece of work.
Nor would Mr. Sutro's pious labour in the cause of Maeterlinck
predispose me to expect of him a genius for farce. Nor, especially,
would my memory of a powerful little tragic play which he published some years ago as a book. However, perhaps in none of
these fruits of his activity was to be found the true soul of Mr.
Sutro. Into "Mollentrave on Women," again, he may not have
infused his true soul. Farce may not be his true bent. But no
matter. Enough that he seems to have a very real spontaneous
instinct for farce. His high-spirits seem quite unforced, and he
has an unflagging inventiveness in absurdities. "Mollentrave on
Women" is great fun, from first to last. It would be well worth
seeing even if it had no serious satire in it. But the fact that it is a

serious satire, and that every part of it is carefully correlated to the satirical idea, does not make it the less a farce.

Every one who has read the translations of Maeterlinck's plays knows that Mr. Sutro has a nice sense for words and for cadences —a real gift for literary expression. In writing farce he has, therefore, an advantage that he would not have in writing comedy : he can give full rein to his talent for writing. In farce the characters need not talk a natural oral language. Additional fun may be compassed by making them talk like books. Usually farces are written (and, for that matter, so are the other kinds of play) by persons of no literary talent whatever. In avoiding colloquialism, and straining after some sort of classicism, the average writer of farce achieves only stodginess. "Mollentrave on Women" is distinguished by real grace and charm of dialogue. It is not merely the work of a man who knows our language thoroughly. (Scholars are often quite incompetent writers.) It is the work of a man who knows how to use our language, and who is revelling in an opportunity for using it.

On the first night, certainly, the performers spoke their lines too hurriedly. They did not give full scope to the dignity of the words, and so did not get the full fun out of them. Otherwise, they were mostly admirable. The part of Mollentrave is, as I have said, a twofold satire. To get the full effect of it in so far as it satirises a familiar stage-type, the part ought, of course, to be played by Sir Charles Wyndham. But, in so far as it satirises a type in real life—and this, after all, is its more important function —it could not be played more admirably than Mr. Eric Lewis plays it. This is the first time I have seen Mr. Lewis playing the principal part in a play. I should not have been surprised at being disappointed. For Mr. Lewis' method in acting is not unlike that of the pointilliste in painting. He makes his every effect, as it were, dot by dot. While he is acting you are always conscious of his method in art. It is only afterwards that the figure impersonated by him stands out in memory as a perfect whole, just as it is only when you retreat a few steps that a pointilliste canvas resolves itself into a picture. Pointillisme in painting is a method that can only be well applied to small canvases. By analogy, I should have feared that Mr. Lewis would not be at his best in a large part. Yet there can be no doubt of his triumph as

Mollentrave. With sure artistic sense, he has widened and loosened his method in proportion to the space he has to fill. Miss Marion Terry was charming in a small part. Mr. Faber, as the young man in love with Balsted's ward, acted with real sense of humour. And all the other parts had been well cast, except the part of Balsted. I cannot imagine why Mr. Alexander did not cast himself for it. Mr. Norman McKinnel is an actor whom I have often thought excellent in parts that need gravity and force. Balsted, I admit, is not a light weight. But in a farce even the heaviest character must be played with a light hand. The audience must not feel that the actor is grimly in earnest. They ought to feel that he is consciously contributing to the fun. Mr. McKinnel is very grimly in earnest. He handles the fun as though it were tragedy's own toughest stuff. A blacksmith in a pastrycook's shop could hardly be more amiss.

"THE THIEVES' COMEDY"

April 1, 1905

British drama is a thing rather of the future than of the present. It is a matter of seeds rather than of blossoms. I hope to see, within a generation, blossoms all over the town. Meanwhile, it is chiefly in Sloane Square that I find the seeds. Little and devious though the Court Theatre may seem to one who regards it in a purely materialistic light, it is to the eye of the imagination the least insignificant theatre in London, and is of all our theatres the nearest to the vital centre of things. The little seeds sown there, sometimes by the Stage Society, sometimes by Mr. Vedrenne and Mr. Barker, matter far more than all the gorgeous parterres of blossoms displayed elsewhere. For those blossoms are of wax—wax with nothing but fresh coats of paint to hide its antiquity, and with nothing at all to disguise its unreality. British blossoms, no doubt; and the seeds at the Court Theatre are mostly imported from abroad. But a natural exotic is better than a blossom of home-made wax. And it is a thing to be valued not merely for its own sake: it is valuable also by reason of the good effects that are likely—are sure—to come of it. It would be gratifying to feel that we needed no examples in dramatic art. But that we do need them is obvious. It is also obvious that we might, once we had taken a start, develop a drama quite as good as the modern drama of (let us say) Germany. Outside dramatic art, we have writers of greater distinction than any writers in Germany; nor is our crop likely to languish. As for audiences, there is no reason to suppose that German citizens are on a higher level of intelligence than our own citizens. The mischief is this; whilst in Germany the drama is taken seriously, and the citizens go to the theatre with their wits about them, in England the theatre is regarded simply as a place for fatuousness. If the British drama became a serious drama (and, need I say? seriousness does not connote dulness—does not, indeed, exclude the most rollicking fun), then, you may be sure, British citizens would patronise it in an appropriate frame of mind. The way to set about creating a serious drama is to attract to dramaturgy the talented writers who now hold aloof, supposing that dramaturgy is a kind of dark magic which only a very few peculiar persons can master (and they only by life-long devotion to it), and that in no case could it be made a medium for the expression of anything but crude artificiality. Such a play as "The Thieves' Comedy" (a translation from Hauptmann's "Biberpelz") is a salutary refutation of these fallacies. I trust that you have already gone to see it, and to profit by it. If not, there are matinées next Tuesday, Thursday, and Friday. You might do worse than go to all three.

The play is solely a play of character and (to use a wickedly over-worked word which I would gladly spare) "atmosphere." It has no story. It has but a few anecdotes, similar to each other, peeping out here and there from a presentment of uneventful every-day life. Frau Wolff, a peasant, steals a deer from the neighbouring forest. That is one anecdote. Here is another: Frau Wolff makes her husband steal some logs of wood that lie stacked outside the house where her daughter is employed as servant. A third anecdote is that a fur-coat is stolen, at Frau Wolff's instigation, from a certain Herr Kruger, and is sold by her to a pilot, who has acted as her "fence" in other thefts. Nothing much happens. Frau Wolff is not found out. The pilot is not found out. They easily bamboozle the local magistrate. They may be found out later. The play has no really conclusive end, just as it has no really initial beginning. It is but an arbitrary intrusion on a cottage interior, made with the sole intent that we shall have a good look at the inmates; and, so soon as we have had a sufficiently good look, out we go again, leaving them just as we found them. The play, which was a very great success in Germany, differs from the fashionable British play in that its technique is very loose and simple, whilst the technique necessary to a fashionable British play is very tight and artificial. An old-fashioned British critic (the fashionable one has forged far ahead of the fashion in drama) would probably say that Hauptmann had no technique at all. This, of course, would be a mistake. To make a set of characters reveal themselves naturally on the stage is a task that involves a considerable amount of technical skill. But certainly it is not so hard and frightening and esoteric a task as to invent and carry through a whole evening a single story, with a series of sharp climaxes occurring at regular intervals, and with a slick solution to finish up with. It is because the power to do that can only be acquired through years of study, supplementing a natural aptitude which is very rare indeed, that the vast majority of our best men give dramaturgy so wide a berth, leaving it almost entirely in the hands of men who, if they devoted to any other kind of writing such intellect and knowledge of life and sense of style as they possess, would fall somewhere between the twentieth and the twenty-fifth rank. In "The Thieves' Comedy" there is no technique that might not be acquired by any man of active and adaptable mind. What makes the play remarkable and delightful is Hauptmann's humour, and his knowledge of a certain phase in actual life, and his sense of human character. There are among us many writers not less well equipped in these respects than Hauptmann. Let them take courage of his success. Peculiarly local though his characters are, and much as they must lose through being interpreted in the English language by English ladies and gentlemen, "The Thieves' Comedy" is undoubtedly a success here, inasmuch as nobody seeing it—nobody, of however mean an intelligence—can fail to be amused and interested by it. How much greater the chance of success for a similar play about life in England!

Of the company engaged at the Court Theatre almost every one makes a "hit." The reason is simple. Every part is a good part. Every character has been drawn, with a sure hand, from life itself. Every character is real, life-sized, full-blooded. People often complain of the dearth of trustworthy mimes in England. The answer is that so few of our mimes are entrusted with anything. Bricks can be made without straw; but the task ought not to be set. A mime may, by dint of creative genius, infuse life into a dummy part. But let us not condemn our mimes generally as worthless because they cannot all so far transcend what may reasonably be expected of them as to make good the deficiencies in what may reasonably be expected of the dramatists. It is quite true that our mimes are inferior to the Latins in some respects. They do not, nowadays, declaim verse so well. That is because the tradition of declamation has been lost. Let the tradition be found again, and all will be well. Our mimes never will, on the other hand, equal the Latins in display of passionate emotion, or in lightness of comedic touch. The reasons are that we are not by nature passionately emotional (or, at any rate, are averse from expressing our feelings), and that lightness of touch is not one of our national characteristics. But the art of acting does not depend wholly on lightness or on violence. It depends also on many other qualities; and in these qualities our mimes, when they have the chance, show themselves to be as well endowed as any mimes elsewhere. It is difficult, always, to apportion praise or blame justly between the dramatist and his interpreter. I have often heard this or that mime complain, and justify his complaint, that he has been contemned for not achieving that which the dramatist had given him no chance of achieving. I do not think I ever heard a mime complain of not having been contemned for not having taken chances which the dramatist had offered him. But I have heard many a mime make this complaint in reference to many another mime. A good part: good notices from the critics, however bad the performance. A bad part, however well played: that absence of gush, or that modified gush, which is the critics' nearest approach to blame. Such is the view of "the profession"; and it is, I fear, a true one. I commend it to my colleagues, for general consideration. Meanwhile, I am wondering how much credit is really due to the mimes in this particular instance at the

Court Theatre. Miss Rosina Filippi, above them all, triumphs. How much of that triumph is due to Hauptmann, how much to herself? Could any actress have failed in a character so fully and so truly created as Frau Wolff has been by Hauptmann created? Could any actress have got more out of that character—realised it more fully? Could any other actress than Miss Filippi have taken so firm a grasp of it, and of us? To the last two questions I am bound to reply that I think not. So, when all deductions have been made over to Hauptmann, Miss Filippi has still a really very good notice indeed. Mr. James Hearn, as the husband of Frau Wolff, and Miss Sydney Fairbrother, as a little daughter of Frau Wolff, and Mr. Edmund Gwenn, as the pilot, and indeed all the members of the cast, have very good notices, too. All understand their several characters, and make (so far as I can judge) the most of them. Yet none tries to triumph singly at the expense of the others. All are in the picture. A signal virtue, this; and especially needful here, in a play which is so like an actual picture.

A ROMEO ON THE HUSTLE

April 29, 1905

I have no wish to see a perfect production of "Romeo and Juliet"; for I make it a rule to have no wishes that may not one day be fulfilled. There never can be even a satisfactory production of an English play whose theme is the fierce passion of love in extreme youth. For this theme is a thing which does not exist in England. In Italy, whence it was by Shakespeare borrowed, it does exist. But the climates of the two countries are very different. In England the fire of love takes a long time to burn up. The fuel is well laid, but damp. Vague, timid, sentimental, are the loves of the English adolescent. Physical desire, and its gratification, linger at a polite distance from spiritual exaltation. It is only in the prime of life that the spiritual and the physical elements come into partnership. It is only then that a man is capable of being fully in love, as were Romeo and Juliet with each other.

Consequently, an English girl and boy could not be adequate as Juliet and Romeo. They could only guess at the sort of thing demanded of them : nor, even if they guessed at it shrewdly, would they be able to express it naturally. It has often been said that no actress can play Juliet till she has ceased to look the part, inasmuch as the part is a heavy one, needing such technique as can be acquired only through very wide experience. The same remark applies equally to Romeo. But the impossibility of getting a good girl-Juliet and a good boy-Romeo lies deeper, as I suggest, than in the matter of mere technique : it lies in the very souls of the boy-actor and the girl-actress. A man and a woman will serve the purpose better. But only in the sense that they will fail less signally. It is not only a question of their appearance : their souls, too, will be found wanting. They can show us the mutual full love of man and woman. But just what Shakespeare shows to us, when we read his play—this, unhappily, and inevitably, they cannot show to us. For the first awakening of love in a mature bosom—a very beautiful phenomenon though it be—is not the same beautiful phenomenon as love's first awakening in adolescence. And it is only the former phenomenon that can be represented on the stage by an English man and woman. In Italy, where acting is a natural art, and technique is learned quickly and by instinct, we might see a very Romeo and a very Juliet, perhaps. But Shakespeare in a translation—I thank you : no. It is better to muddle along with the original.

I have not seen, and may never see, a better Juliet than Miss Evelyn Millard. In appearance she is an exception to prove the famous rule which I have quoted. And she has grace, and tenderness, and gaiety, and a very real pathos. To passion, however, she does not surrender herself. If she did so surrender her English self, we should instantly be conscious of her as a woman, and should lose our sense of Juliet as a girl. But a rather dispassionate Juliet is not, I need hardly say, the very Juliet. On the other hand, there is nothing dispassionate about Mr. Waller. He will barter nothing for boyishness, not he! He is frankly and sternly (as, indeed, he always is, and was, and will be) rooted in the prime of life. And he is frankly and sternly rooted in love with Juliet. The very Romeo loved Juliet frankly, but had not acquired that sternness which does to some people come with years of discretion. And so Mr. Waller is not the very Romeo. I am glad to see him in a part which depends more on love-making than on fighting and on orating about fighting. I am glad that he has diverged from his line of excellence. It breaks the monotony. Or, rather, it bends the monotony, which could be broken only if Mr. Waller could forget the line from which he has diverged. This he cannot do. From first to last he is the soldier in love, never the mere lover. When, emerging from the shadow of Capulet's garden, he cries "He jests at scars that never felt a wound," the words take an unusual significance for us: we are sure that the body of Romeo is scarred all over—an heroic document of all the principal Veronese fights in the past fifteen or twenty years. While he stands under the balcony we seem to hear, above Gounod's music (loudly played though that is), a clash of arms round the corner; and Romeo, we are sure, will be in the thick of it as soon as his interview is over. "Away to heaven, respective lenity, and fire-ey'd fury be my conduct now! Now, Tybalt, take the villain back that late thou gav'st me"—never did these words ring out so finely, and never was the villain repaid with so much compound interest. And Mr. Waller's behaviour in this scene differs only in degree, not in kind, from his behaviour throughout the play. His whole performance is "magnifique, mais—c'est la guerre," whilst Romeo, as we know him, was bellicose only in his off-moments. "Oh, sweet Juliet," cries Mr. Waller, "thy beauty hath made me effeminate, and in my temper soften'd valour's steel!" But it hathn't. A man in love does actually assimilate something of the woman's softness; and she, too, catches something of his strength. Juliet at the Imperial Theatre catches nothing of Romeo's strength, and Romeo assimilates nothing of Juliet's softness. Ecstasy, in the strict as well as in the usual sense of that word, befalls all lovers. But Miss Millard and Mr. Waller do not stand outside themselves for one moment. As I have explained, it is just as well that Miss Millard keeps herself in. But Mr. Waller would have nothing to lose by ecstasy, for he does not aim at the effect of boyishness: the prime of life for *him*; and a mature Romeo, lyrically amorous, were nearer to Shakespeare's conception than a mature Romeo whose love is of so very stern a stuff as is offered by Mr. Waller to Juliet.

371

I hope that some day our mimes will have learned to distinguish in Shakespeare's plays the passages which are purely poetic or philosophic from those which are also dramatic. At present they seem to think that every line written by Shakespeare was strictly relevant to action or character. Lately I wrote about the disastrous manner in which Miss Maud Milton at the Adelphi recited the exquisite little description of Ophelia's death-place. In "Romeo and Juliet" these dear irrelevancies abound. And the players, of course, instead of dallying with them delicately, go for them as blindly as courageous fox-hunters go for the five-barred gates that challenge them in their wild career. It is part of the dramatic fabric that Romeo should remember an apothecary—a neighbouring apothecary—an apothecary who was poor, and so would be likely to sell poison if he were well paid for it. But it is not part of the dramatic fabric that Romeo should give a long description of the shop, working it up as minutely as ever a Dutch painter worked up an interior. That was simply Shakespeare, going off at a tangent, and forgetting all about Romeo for the nonce. It would be an act of hideous vandalism to "cut" the lines. But better "cut" them altogether than race through them as though they really belonged to the agitated soul of Romeo. That is what Mr. Waller does. And the result is that we don't get the beauty of the passage, and that we do get the full absurdity of their being uttered at this juncture by Romeo. Uttered quietly, in a tone of gentle reminiscence, they would duly enchant us, and the anomaly would not be noticed. Again, when the apothecary brings forth the poison, "There is thy gold" are pertinent words; but when Romeo proceeds to say "worse poison to men's souls, doing more murders in this loathsome world, than these poor compounds that thou may'st not sell," he is merely gratifying Shakespeare's whim for moralising at large. Any stress laid on the passage is fatal. And oh the stress that is laid on it by Mr. Waller! Dr. Torrey himself never inveighed so wrathfully against the corrupting influence of wealth. I am sure that the more impressionable members of the audience go round to the stage-door and ask to be shown into the "Inquiry Room." I tremble to think what would become of Queen Mab if Mr. Waller were Mercutio. Mr. Esmond is an admirable Mercutio, as merry and debonair as can be; but even in the light hand of Mr. Esmond Queen Mab has a bad time of it. Mercutio should utter the speech with as much conscious pleasure as Shakespeare must have had in the writing of it. Shakespeare did not rattle it off. Mr. Esmond does, as though he were afraid of boring us, or as though Benvolio and those others must have been all the while chafing to foot it in the masque at Capulet's. Surely, Benvolio and those others would have been spell-bound by a worthy utterance of that divine speech. And, surely, so should we be.

AT THE ST. JAMES' THEATRE

May 6, 1905

"Holmes and I had just finished a somewhat late breakfast. I pushed the morning paper across to him, remarking 'That rising politician, John Chilcote, seems to have made a great speech in the Commons last evening.'

"Holmes puffed another cloud of tobacco smoke, and took no notice of my remark. I knew by the more than usual rigidness of his face that he was thinking deeply—probably about that somewhat gruesome problem of the driver-less van in Russell Square, which, I knew, was very much on his mind just now. A moment later the servant entered and handed a visiting-card to him. Before he had time to say that he was not at home, a fashionably-attired lady had followed the servant into the room. She was closely veiled, but I could see that her face, which was one of extreme beauty, was deadly pale. Her tightly-clasped hands betokened that she was labouring under some strong emotion.

"Holmes rose from his chair, and, fingering the pasteboard, directed a swift glance at me before he turned to his visitor and said suavely 'Mrs. John Chilcote?' I almost leapt from my chair, so strange did the coincidence appear to me.

"'To what,' asked Holmes, 'do I owe the honour of this visit?'

"The lady commenced a confused apology for intruding on us, but Holmes held up his long thin hand, and, with the words 'Pray compose yourself, Madam,' motioned her to a chair.

"'I see,' said Holmes, 'that you left your house in a great hurry this morning, and that you did not wish to be observed.'

"The lady started violently. 'How did you . . .'"

Evidently, I am growing old. Sherlock Holmes is dead, and to young readers it may be that he is not even a dear memory. But I was at an impressionable age when he burst upon the world; and so he became a part of my life, and will never, I suppose, be utterly dislodged. I cannot pass through Baker Street, even now, without thinking of him. Long ago I had decided exactly which were the two windows of the sitting-room where Watson spent his wondering hours; and, only the other day, I had a rather heated dispute with a coæval who had also long since "placed" that sitting-room—"placed" it, if you please, on the side of the street opposite to that where it really was (need I say that I mean the right-hand side as one goes towards Regent's Park?). My sentiment for Sherlock Holmes was never one of reverence unalloyed. Indeed, one of the secrets of his hold on me was that he so often amused me. I would have bartered a dozen of his subtlest deductions for that great moment when he said (presumably on the eve of his creator's departure for a lecturing tour in America) "It is always a joy to me to meet an American, for I am one of those who believe that the folly of a monarch and the blundering of a minister in far gone years will not prevent our children from being some day citizens of the same world-wide country under a flag which shall be a quartering of the Union Jack with the Stars and Stripes." I learned that speech by heart, years ago; and, to this day, I generally try it on any American to whom I am introduced—sometimes with most surprising results. Sir Arthur (then mere Mr.) Conan Doyle's own attitude towards life, and his own extraordinary versions of the familiar things around us—what would Sherlock have been without these assets? Last Monday evening, at the St. James' Theatre, it must have been the account of John Chilcote's speech in the House of Commons that first turned my thoughts Sherlockwards, and gave me a clue to what the play ought to have been. One of the characters rushed in to describe the triumph to Mrs. Chilcote—to tell how, when her husband resumed his seat, "there was one of those spontaneous outbursts of applause which no etiquette, no decorum, can quell." This picture of the House of Commons as a place in which the members sometimes so far forget themselves as to clap their hands, and are reminded by the Speaker that "a court of law is not a theatre," somehow instantly transported me into the sphere of Sir Arthur's innocent activities. I had been told in the first entr'acte that "John Chilcote M.P." was adapted from a book of the same name, and that this book was very popular. Yet I made no resolve to read this book. The theme of it was surely too ridiculous, too incredible, to be pursued seriously through many pages. Even for a magazine story . . . but ah! in that form Sherlock would have saved it. Why did not the novelist lay the theme at Sir Arthur's feet? . . . "'Tell me everything,' said Holmes—'you understand, *everything*. It is often in those points which seem at first glance inessential, that the key of a seemingly insoluble problem lies hidden.' Then he leant back in his chair, closed his eyes, as his custom was when listening intently, and pressed his finger-tips lightly against each other . . ." Mrs. Chilcote, after a pause, would have told her narrative clearly enough—how her husband was sometimes a brisk and brilliant man of affairs, ardently devoted to herself, but sometimes for days together was languid, irritable, a slave to chloral. Holmes, without opening his eyes, would now and again have interpolated a brief question of which Watson could not for the life of him imagine the relevance. Presently, Holmes would have bowed the lady out, refusing a blank cheque for his well-expressed hopes of giving the lady some good news within twenty-four hours.

"'Well, Watson,' said my friend, 'and what do you make of it?'

"I had to confess that I was entirely in the dark, and that I doubted whether even he, magician though he was, would be able to throw any light on this case.

"'Well,' said Holmes, reaching out for his Stradivarius, and regarding me with a humorous twinkle, 'let me see whether I can throw any light on that sonata in A minor by old Beethoven. We have plenty of time for that other little problem. Some time this afternoon, I propose we should drop in at the Houses of Parliament. I was able lately to render the Prime Minister a trifling service in that matter of the forged treaty with the Argentine Republic, and I dare say he will give us a pass for the Strangers' Gallery. And, by the way, Watson! Take your pistol with you. You may want it.'"

I cannot guess the exact procedure of the story from this point. I am no match for Sir Arthur in construction of the requisite little steps. But I, or any one, can conceive the final scene in which Sherlock, having revealed to Mrs. Chilcote her husband lying dead from an overdose of chloral, beckons from the adjoining room the brilliant and devoted double, and, joining his and Mrs. Chilcote's hands together, wishes them all possible happiness in the future, and once more refuses a cheque, but, in the interests of morality, conjures them to take the world into their confidence. At the St. James', Mrs. Chilcote and her husband's double, determining, as the curtain falls, to take the world into their confidence, inspire in us no conviction at all. Sherlock, thou should'st be with them at that hour! Indeed, they have need of thee throughout the play. But I doubt whether even thou could'st save them in dramatic form.

In fact, as I suggested, they should have started in the "Strand Magazine," and stayed there. There we would gladly have accepted the premiss that two men might be so exactly alike in face and figure and voice that the wife of one would mistake the other for her husband. Process-block illustrations make little strain on our credulity. But when Mr. Alexander and Mr. Thorold appear before us in flesh and blood, with the stage carefully darkened to hide their points of dissimilarity, we are straightway acutely conscious that this is a story of cock-and-bull. Even had it been treated as such by the dramatist, and presented by him as a wild romance or melodrama, we should soon have been wearied by the very absurdity of it. Mr. E. Temple Thurston takes the whole thing quite seriously—presents it as a sombre drama of psychology, relieved by scenes of high comedy. He is at fearful pains to make it realistically credible, making his characters talk about Mr. Adolf Beck, and about a book entitled "Other Men's Shoes" in which two men pass themselves off as each other with complete success. And, throughout, the appeal is not to any base appetite for excitement, but to our power of understanding the inner emotions of actual ladies and gentlemen. This is really a lamentable waste of Mr. Thurston's time, and of ours, and of the talent of Mr. Alexander, and Miss Marion Terry, and the other members of a very good cast. And all in the lifetime of Sir Arthur, who could so easily have been induced yet again to raise Sherlock from the tomb!

"SALOMÉ"

May 13, 1905

"Salomé" has a strange record. Written in the French language by an Irishman, it would, but for the Censor, have been produced in England by a French actress. Produced in Germany, after many years, and there acclaimed a masterpiece, it has now found a way back into England. The English translation of it was performed last Wednesday at the Bijou Theatre, Bayswater. This was not, however, a wholly auspicious vicissitude for it.

No blame must be laid on the translator, who seems, indeed, to have caught back very skilfully into English the characteristic cadences which Mr. Oscar Wilde had imported, not less skilfully, into French. The mischief, for me, lay in the quality of the acting and of the stage-management; and, deeper, it lay in my conviction that not even the best acting and the best stage-management could make this play so good to see as it is good to read. Of course, I do not mean that "Salomé" has less dramatic than literary fibre. Mr. Wilde was a born dramatist—a born theatrist, too. Not less than in his handling of the quick and complex form of modern comedy, there was mastery in his handling of this slow and simple form of tragedy—a form compounded, seemingly, of Sophocles and Maeterlinck in even proportions. The note of terror in "Salomé" is struck well in the opening lines, and then slowly the play's action advances, step by step, to the foreknown crisis; and it is mainly through this very slowness, this constant air of suspense, that the play yields us the tragic thrill. Kneeling for the fulfilment of Herod's promise to give her anything "even unto the half of his kingdom," the daughter of Herodias says slowly "I desire that they shall straightway bring me on a silver charger"— "On a silver charger?" echoes Herod, and rallies her for claiming a reward of such little compass, and turns to his courtiers and asks them if she is not a strange girl, and turns to her and tells her that she is beautiful, and so babbles on, all unconscious of what impends. By such tricks of "irony," throughout, the play is prolonged, and the tragedy of its theme is deepened. Certainly, it is a good "stage play" so far as the technique of its author is concerned. But, for all that, it is not a good play for the stage. It is too horrible for definite and corporeal presentment. It should be seen only through the haze of our imagination. The bitter triumph of Salomé's lust for John the Baptist, as she kneels kissing the lips of the severed head, is a thing that we can read of, and vaguely picture to ourselves, with no more than the thrill of horror which tragedy may rightly inflict on us. But when we see the thing—when we have it illustrated to us in sharp detail by a human being—then we suffer something beyond the rightful tragic thrill: we suffer qualms of physical disgust.

The right kind of acting, and the right kind of stage-management, could not save us from such qualms, but could certainly mitigate them. And it was just those kinds that were lacking in the production at the Bijou Theatre. It seems to me, for instance, very obvious that the severed head of John the Baptist ought not to be very obvious to the audience. Salomé, when she receives it from the executioner, ought to remain at the back of the stage, in as dark a shadow as can possibly be thrown on her. In the Bijou Theatre, Salomé brought the head briskly down to the footlights, and in that glare delivered to it all her words and kisses. This was wrong, not merely because it intensified our physical disgust, but also because it destroyed all our illusion. Even though we looked away, we were aware that this was not the head of the prophet, but simply a thing of painted cardboard—a "property," prepared with much labour and ingenuity. And the fact that we knew it to be no more than this did not make us one whit the less uncomfortable. Indeed, an unpleasant thing that proclaims itself a "fake" is worse than an unpleasant thing that illudes us. Cold cardboard lips kissed passionately by a young lady, on the pretence that they are the cold real lips of a man murdered at her behest, are really a more horrid spectacle for us than they would be if we believed for the moment that in truth Salomé was kissing the lips of John the Baptist . . . "A young lady." The phrase expresses just what was wrong in the acting at the Bijou Theatre. (The dread name Bijou, too, is almost equally expressive.) If Salomé were impersonated by an actress of mysterious charm and force, an actress vibrating with as much sense of beauty as power for horror, then might Salomé make us nearly forget, in very awe of her, our disgust. Were she, as once she was to be, Sarah

Bernhardt, all might be almost well. But the actress at the Bijou Theatre was just a young lady—a clever young lady, a conscientious and promising young lady, whose career I shall watch with interest, but who never for one moment last Wednesday began to become Salomé or began to cease to be a young lady. And so, while our æsthetic sense of awe was unstirred, our sense of decorum was very gravely offended. To think that a young English lady in the twentieth century could have been so badly brought up as to behave in so outrageous a manner! We looked severely at her mother. Was she not ashamed? But no; not a day older nor a degree less ladylike than her daughter, Herodias was behaving not a whit less outrageously on her own account. There was only one thing for us to do: to strike them both off our visiting-lists. And to think that in these days of enlightened democracy such a ruler as Herod . . . Steady, my pen! We did not really think of Herod in relation to our own time. Here was no apparent young English gentleman to bemuse us. Here, indeed, was Herod himself, incarnate from out the pages of the play—a terrible being, half-dotard, half-child, corrupt with all the corruptions of the world, and yet not without certain dark remnants of intellect, of dignity. I do not remember that I had ever before seen Mr. Robert Farquharson (for he it was); and this is strange, inasmuch as he is evidently an actor of great experience. Imagination, and sense of character, and sense of the beauty of words and cadences, may inhere in the breast of a tiro. But there they inhere: they won't come out. Only through experience can they be expressed. Mr Farquharson's performance was especially laudable in that he never let his minute expression of Herod's self in all its hideousness interfere with his musical delivery of the elaborate cadences. He performed two tasks in perfect fusion. Passages that might have been merely beautiful he made dramatically hideous, without loss of their beauty. Passages that might have been merely hideous he made beautiful, without loss of their appropriateness. Of course he played all the other people off the stage, figuratively. Literally, they remained there, I regret to say.

The Mermaid Society, this week, has been performing "The Silent Woman." As you may know, this comedy is mainly about an elaborate practical joke. I am not so pedantic as to disapprove of practical jokes, as such, in real life. Even a dull practical joke gives me pleasure, if I play it myself. And even as victim I can enjoy a practical joke, if it be amusing and harmless. And, with that reservation, I can even enjoy hearing about a practical joke in which I figured not at all, if it was played on somebody whom I know well. But I take no earthly pleasure in hearing about a practical joke played on a perfect stranger. Such a joke is amusing only if one can recognise its aptness to the victim, and can intimately imagine its effect on him. For this reason, I am always rather bored by a play of which such a joke is the mainspring. The joke itself may be quite ingenious, quite innocuous, but its victim would have to be a long-familiar reality to me before I could enter into the fun of it. When Ben Jonson props up a dummy— "Morose, a Gentleman that loves no Noise"—for the sole purpose that a practical joke shall be played on it, I (as owing a duty to my readers) sit the play out; but smile I really cannot; and indeed, as the joke happens to be a barbarous one, even according to the Elizabethan standard, I should be rather ashamed of smiling at it. It might be more tolerable to me if I could suppose that Ben Jonson himself smiled at it. I do feel that Shakespeare got true personal glee out of the pranks played on Malvolio; and that is *some* consolation, at any rate. But Ben Jonson's humour was ever purely intellectual. Ben Jonson had no high spirits. I shall make haste to forget "The Silent Woman." And so, I trust, will our very admirable Mermaid Society.

MME LE BARGY ET CIE

June 24, 1905

Accept an hypothesis. Suppose that an English actress, by no means in the front rank, and having had but slight experience in her art, but happening to be a fluent speaker of the French language, suddenly found herself in Paris, playing the principal part in an English comedy which had been translated into French, and in which the other parts were being played by a first-rate company of Parisian mimes. How would that lady fare? Would she be self-possessed? Would she hold her own among her alien colleagues? Would she perhaps make those alien colleagues look small in the eyes of their compatriots? Would she be commended by all the cognoscenti in Paris, and warmly pressed to the great heart of the French public? Would she . . . Enough! These questions are as brutal as they are foolish. We know full well that within two days that lady would be in England, nursing a broken heart, while the manager who had engaged her would be doing his best to forget her in the lunatic asylum to which his friends had promptly committed him. And yet the hypothesis that I offered is but the ethnological converse of what has happened at the St. James'. Mme Le Bargy is not a heaven-born genius. Also, she has acted only some half a dozen parts on her native stage. Also, the cast of "The Man of the Moment" is as good-all-round a cast as could be found in London. And, despite all this, Mme Le Bargy is still in our midst, and Mr. Alexander is at large—has, indeed, enhanced his reputation for acumen. Instead of being played off the stage in her attempt to vie with eminent and experienced mimes in their own language and on their own ground, Mme Le Bargy is the very hit of the season. Beside her, the majority of the ladies and gentlemen acting with her come out as clumsy fumblers—as people who don't know their business, and couldn't manage it if they did. The contrast is chastening. But it is certainly interesting. Every one has always admitted that French acting is superior to English acting. Now, for the first time, we have samples of these two things presented simultaneously, and so a valuable opportunity for verifying exactly the difference between them, and for catching the secret of the one's obvious superiority to the other.

The difference between naturalness and artificiality—that is the main difference between French and English acting generally, as exemplified particularly in "The Man of the Moment." Mme Le Bargy, is, above all things, natural. We should not especially notice this quality if she were acting with compatriots; but here it forces itself on us as a stark phenomenon. She walks as any real woman might walk across a drawing-room. She talks as any real woman might talk in a drawing-room. She does not seem to realise that the stage is an odd thing to be on, and that things can only be done in an odd way there. She does not, like our mimes,

grasp the fundamental difference between the stage and the home.
Purblind lady, she is at home on the stage. When happens something of a nature to arouse the character whom she impersonates
—when comes a crisis that in real life would make that character
stare, or gasp, or scream, or clench her hands—then Mme Le
Bargy is duly aroused, and ebullient, and unusual. But when it is
merely a question of talking trifles, Mme Le Bargy is a trifler.
And when there is nothing at all for her to do, Mme Le Bargy sits
still and does nothing. Not so her coadjutors. They must always
be doing something, and doing it strongly, doing it significantly,
blackly underlining it for us. If they leave a room, they must leave
it as though they were bidding it an eternal farewell. If they
remark that the day is fine, they must imply that there is a deep
philosophic meaning buried in this superficially trivial pronouncement. When they come to an emotional crisis, there is not
much left over for them to do. They can but keep well up to the
level of significance which they have already set for themselves.
The result is apt to be bathetic. All things are relative; and if we
can never be, like Mme Le Bargy, insignificant, our significance
will seem not quite adequate when there is good cause for it. Of
the English mimes in "The Man of the Moment"—of such of
them, at any rate, as have anything important to do—Mr. Alexander is the most restrained, the quietest and most natural, the
least fussy. But how much of unnecessary significance and strenuousness even he purveys! You remember the end of the third act,
for example? Mme Darlay has confessed her infidelity. Her
husband says that he is going to her lover. She implores him to
do nothing reckless—asks him what it is that he is going to do.
"I am going," replies Darlay, "to tell him that he had better not
stay to dinner;" and the curtain falls. Obviously, that is a
comedy line—grim comedy, no doubt, but comedy. There is in
the play another man whose wife had deceived him, and who had
promptly shot her lover. The words have an implied reference
to this crime of passion. They mean "Don't be afraid. There
will be no fuss. I live in a civilised community, and am going to
behave in a perfectly civilised manner. I would rather seem tame
to myself, and to you, than be marched off to prison for being a
hero." Darlay's words ought, of course, to be spoken in a calm,
deliberate, slightly bitter tone. Mr. Alexander thunders them

forth into the auditorium. The contrast between them and that peal of thunder provides a more exquisite example of bathos than I had ever dared hope to hear. Of course, it is also an extreme example of Mr. Alexander's tendency to over-emphasis. But there the tendency is. And, as I have said, Mr. Alexander gives way to it less than do the rest of his compatriots in the play. Most of them, by the way, have nothing to do with any dramatic crisis in the play's action : they are important only as figures of comedy. But they do not touch the vein of comedy : they are heavy clowns. If Mme Le Bargy were not in the cast, we should not especially notice their heavy clowning—should take it as we take the air that we breathe. But, having a foil in her light and airy little method, it becomes a grim obsession to us. I do not, of course, pretend that there are no light comedians in England, no heavy clowns in France, any more than I pretend that there are no seemingly natural actors in England, no obviously artificial actors in France. Nevertheless, lightness and naturalness are the exceptions on our stage, and the rule on the French stage ; and this general difference is brought sharply home to us by the particular object-lesson at the St. James'. The lightness of the average French comedian, and the heaviness of the average English comedian, are partly explained by the respective paces at which they speak. Mme Le Bargy has been accused of gabbling her part. The fault is really the fault of her interlocutors on the stage. Certainly, she talks there rather more quickly than talks the average Englishwoman in real life. But does ever an English person of either sex talk with half the deadly deliberation that is used by the mimes at the St. James'? One and all, with baleful eyes on the audience, they seem to be saying "Some of you—have—trains—to catch—after—the performance. . . . Others of you—are going—on—to supper. . . . We—are—determined—that those—suppers—shall be—forgone —and—those trains—missed." Usually, this pace in elocution does not madden me. But with Mme Le Bargy let loose on the scene as pace-maker, and enabling me to gauge how few in proportion to the time occupied are the words spoken by English mimes, I am moved to cry out against this idiotic tradition of snailishness. English people in real life do not talk so quickly as French people. But it is not less ridiculous than it is tedious that they should be represented on the stage always as though they were carefully picking their way through an unknown tongue, or dictating their memoirs under the shadow of death. English people are heavy in the hand, no doubt; but not so heavy as all that. Let no more than their natural weight be imposed on our creaking boards.

MR. CONRAD'S PLAY

July 8, 1905

I hope that "One Day More," which the Stage Society produced with "The New Felicity," is not the only alms that Mr. Conrad will bestow on our needy drama. Mr. Conrad is just the sort of person who ought to be coaxed into writing plays. It is awful to remember that every day throughout the length and breadth of the land, duffers innumerable are, with fervid industry, planning new scenarios, and turning out dialogue by the ream, and getting it type-written and bound in brown paper and despatched to the various managers, whilst, for the most part, the few people who might really help to improve our drama hold themselves aloof from it as surely as respectable Americans hold themselves aloof from politics. That American politics are a hot-bed of corruption is the excuse always pleaded by respectable Americans for their aloofness. That the English theatre is a hot-bed of stupidity and artificiality is the excuse always pleaded by English masters of fiction for *their* aloofness. It is a very poor excuse. Just as the obvious answer to the respectable Americans is that it is their duty to redeem American politics by dashing into them in the full armour of their respectability, so the obvious answer to our masters of fiction is that they cannot expect the English theatre to be other than bad so long as they refuse to help it. When one of these masters does actually condescend to write a play, we ought all to dance around him and pat him enthusiastically on the back, crying "Continue!" I hasten to dance thus around Mr. Conrad. But my gyrations recall painfully to me those of the famous bee who tried to "swarm alone." My colleagues in criticism have, for the most part, a primitive mistrust of strangers. They do not say

"Here is new blood. Let us help it to circulate," but "Here is new blood. Let us throw cold water on it." They do not say of Mr. Conrad "Here is the sort of man that is needed—a man with a wide knowledge of many kinds of life, and a man with acute vision, and with deep human sympathy, and with a passionate imagination—an essentially dramatic imagination, moreover," but "Mr. Conrad has much to learn," or something to that miserable effect. It is the old story of heaving half a brick; and the handiest half a brick is, of course, always to say of a new playwright that he has not mastered the tricks of the stage. Sometimes the criticism is true (though always it is trifling). But in the case of Mr. Conrad it is quite unjustified. Mr. Conrad has not worked on that scale which offers serious difficulties in technical construction. He has not written a full-sized play. He has but turned one of his short stories into a little one-act play. And the short story chosen by him for this purpose happens to be one which any child could dramatise effectively. Indeed, I am not sure that it was not originally conceived in dramatic form. I remember that when I read it in one of Mr. Conrad's books, I thought to myself "Here is a play which has been refused in the usual way by the usual managers; and the author, with a sigh, has now turned it into a short story;" for the action of the story was laid in one scene, and was continuous, from first to last, and was far more "external" than is Mr. Conrad's wont. I had no means of verifying my theory. It is possible that my theory was incorrect. But the fact remains that, as the story was written, practically all that Mr. Conrad had to do, in making a play of it, was to excise all the words that did not appear between inverted commas. The play, as it stands, is a quite straightforward and well-knit play. The characters come on and go off quite naturally. There is no technical blemish whatever. But, even if this play were evidently the work of an amateur, and scored all over with technical blemishes, how lamentable a lack of critical insight were revealed by a criticism insistent on these blemishes, and impercipient of the originality and the fine humanity and strength underlying them!

The play is a tragedy, set in modern times; and that fact alone is, of course, enough to damn it in the eyes of most critics. A man who detects and depicts anything like a tragedy in modern life is instantly by these critics suspected of "morbidness," and of not thinking that life, generally, is worth living. Of course, the "morbidness" inheres really in these critics themselves, whose taste for life is so slight that they shrink away in horror from any phase of life that is not delicious. The heroine of "One Day More" leads a not at all delicious existence, and consequently these critics scuttle away babbling about defective technique in order to drown their memory of this dreadful girl. Her father is a blind sailor, to the care of whom she has for years devoted her health and strength. He is not at all grateful to her—bullies her, will not give her an instant's rest. She is not so young as she was; and she has enough imagination to repine at the passing of her youth, and the utter vacancy of her life. Except her father, the only person whom she knows is an old and crazy man who lives in the next cottage. He, too, was once a sailor, but had always hated and feared the sea. His son, when he grew to boyhood, ran away to sea, and has never been heard of since. For years and years, the old man has lived only for the return of his son. It is always "to-morrow" that his son will come back to him, and from day to day he lives on in that certainty. His cottage is packed with an accumulation of things that he buys to make for his son a fine home. And, of course, there must be a wife for his son. This destined wife is the girl next door—"the only sensible girl hereabouts." And to her, during all these years, he has been talking about her future husband. She, of course, does not believe that the son will ever come back. She does not suppose that, if he did come back, he would want to marry her. Still, so utterly empty her life is that she finds some solace in a hope that she cannot really feel. In the story, as Mr. Conrad wrote it, she and the crazy old man were equally important and elaborately-drawn figures: our interest was divided equally between them. In the play, naturally, she is protagonist, and the crazy old man falls to the background, with the other characters. One day, the son does return. He wants money. The father bids him be off. He wants no beggarly impostors coming to get money out of him. His son is coming back to-morrow—to-morrow. He slams the door of the cottage. Knowing of old his father's obstinacy, the young man finally abandons the attempt to establish his identity. This girl here must help him. Women have always helped him out of difficulties, all the world over. She, in his presence, realises the pitiful absurdity of the hope that she had half held. He laughs aloud when she tells him that his father had wanted him to settle down at home, and laughs still louder at the notion of his ever marrying. He, the wanderer! He, the conqueror of hearts! It is five pounds that he wants. The girl has saved just five pounds. He prevails on her to give them to him. And, in return, he roughly catches her in his arms, and holds her there while he kisses her. At first she struggles, after a while surrenders. Having kissed her enough, he goes off, laughing. The girl stands there dazed. Her name is bawled out from within the cottage. Her father is calling to her. Again he calls, and she goes to him. There the play, like the story, ends. It is a terrible and haunting play, as you may imagine even from this bald description of it. In other words, it is a powerful tragedy. And, therefore, I delight in it. What I want from art is some kind of emotion. It matters not at all to me whether the emotion be in itself one of pleasure or one of pain. In whatever way I be quickened, I am grateful. I pity the critics who can find no æsthetic pleasure in "One Day More." They ought to give up criticism.

I was less moved by the play than I had been by the story. But this disparity is not due to Mr. Conrad's supposed lack of technical skill: the play, as a play, is not less good than was the story, as a story. Nor are the performers to blame. Miss Collier, as the central figure, played admirably in just that minor key which was needed for the particular pathos of the character; and Mr. Lestrange, as the wanderer, had just the right sort of panache. The reason why the play is inferior to the story is simply that the dramatic form is, generally and essentially, inferior to the literary form. In the one ... Hush! Am I not a dramatic critic? And is not my immediate aim to coax Mr. Conrad, for our drama's sake, to further dramaturgy?

A WORD TO MR. GILLETTE

September 23, 1905

Last week I laid down the law that "mimes ought never to write plays." I regret that "Clarice" at the Duke of York's Theatre does not move me to except Mr. William Gillette. Rather, it moves me to lay special stress on him; so sharply does it exemplify the vices inherent in all mimes' dramaturgy. There is in it one subsidiary character—an elderly negress, the hero's cook —who seems to me to have an air of reality. But this impression may be due to my ignorance of her kind; and I should not be surprised to hear that she is a stock-figure of the American theatre, with no counterpart on the American soil. My knowledge of that soil is very superficial; but even had I never scraped that soil's surface, I should be in a position to swear that none of the principal characters in "Clarice" bears any relation to reality. They are such stuff as mimes' plays are always made of, all the world over. They are puppets, adjusted to no purpose but that of catching "sympathy" or causing thrills. They are, in technical phrase, "fat" parts, all of them. But, behind the layers of adipose tissue in which they roll so comfortably about the stage, there is never a bone, never a nerve or a vein of blood. This way and that they roll, softly and smoothly, to the music of clapped hands, and under a gentle shower of tears. As a reporter, I acknowledge that the majority of the audience is touched. As a hedonist, I envy these simple souls. As a critic, I proceed to probe the causes of my own indifference.

The hero, Dr. Carrington, leads a quiet life in Southern Virginia. His ward, Clarice Marland, lives with him, acting as secretary, and as illustrator of some scientific book that he is writing. She is, of course, an attractive girl; and he, of course, is an attractive man. Gradually, they have fallen in love with each other. But neither suspects the sentiment of the other. In real life, of course, no two persons could in the circumstances be so obtuse. The mutual sentiment would be as plain as a pikestaff. But then what a chance lost—what "fat" forfeited! Where would be those wistful glances, those long-drawn sighs, that en-

gaging self-depreciation, whereby the hero and heroine are so
quickly endeared to you? Where would the first act itself be?
Where would be for you that wild, wild thrill of joy when at last,
by some happy accident, hero and heroine do at last make the great
discovery that their sentiment is reciprocal? The audience knows
of old, and imperiously demands, and never will be weary of, that
dramatic moment when the hero and heroine gasp, blush, gaze
into each other's eyes (unable yet to believe the evidence which
those eyes have been offering for months past), and then with cries
of joy, or maybe in perfect silence, are gathered to each other's
arms. Presently a shadow must fall unbidden—no, the audience
bids it fall—across the sunshine. Some awful misunderstanding or
other must intervene. Mr. Gillette, ever ready to oblige, supplies
a misunderstanding of a rather novel kind. The hero does not, in
the usual way, believe the heroine to be false. Instead, he tries to
persuade her that he himself is false. His lungs are rather weak,
and the doctor who has just been examining them tells him that he is
in an advanced state of consumption, and has only a year or so to
live. Shall he repeat this to the heroine? No, a thousand times no!
He will, and does, tell her that he finds he has made a mistake—
doesn't care for her. It would be painful to tell her the truth.
But oh, how much more poignantly painful to utter this noble fib,
with a cold but not pitiless eye for the girl, and a distraught eye for
the audience! Think, too, of the chance for the heroine, abased,
but not repelled—humbly eager to remain, resuming her previous
estate, and to go on with those illustrations for the book! Her
attitude creates a new situation. The hero must inflict yet more
anguish on himself and her. He must, and does, tell her that she
has been not a help but an incubus. Her drawings, he cries, are
all wrong. They would ruin the book. She must go. She goes.
Later, we see him standing at his window, handkerchief in hand.
He is going to cry? No, the hero is one of those strong silent men
who are Mr. Gillette's speciality. The handkerchief is merely to
be waved to the heroine in the railway train that will presently
pass at no great distance. The train is passing. The hero is
ready to wave. But he discerns no answering ensign. The train
has passed. The heroine has not waved to him. He supposes she
is angry with him. We refuse to believe any such thing of her.
Something over which she had no control must have prevented her

from waving. The extra sympathy for the hero involves not an instant's loss of sympathy for so indubitable a heroine. The whole thing will be satisfactorily explained later on. Meanwhile, there is another, graver misunderstanding to be cleared up—not for us, but for the hero. We, at the outset, were admitted to a conclave in which the villainous aunt of the heroine did, for her base purposes, urge and persuade the hero's medical adviser, who also loves the heroine, to become a villain and communicate to the sound-lunged hero that sentence of impending doom. A vague suspicion now creeps into the hero's mind. He has just been on the verge of drinking poison before our very eyes. He has raised the bottle almost to his lips. He has thus got nearly all the "fat" that there is to be got by killing himself. Huge slices may yet be carved by him off Life. What if that doctor had deceived him? He will probe the matter. But how? In the actual world, he would hasten to consult another doctor. But no such scrap of lean will satisfy Mr. Gillette. He might, again, as he is a doctor himself, sound his own lungs. But no; that contingency has already been foreseen by the female villain, and banished by the male villain's reply "Impossible! His instruments are hopelessly out of date." (A few years ago, it seems, medical science could only make dim guesses as to whether a lung were sound.) Our hero will, in the villain's presence, pretend to have taken poison, and thus (he doubts not) elicit the truth (if truth it be) that he is quite well. So he sharpens the carving-knife, and anon many hissing slices of "fat" have fallen to him. The villain confesses, and, cowed and abject, disappears. Enter the heroine (whose failure to wave her handkerchief has already been explained by the fact that she was not in the train). All the lights in the sitting-room go out, leaving the two occupants in a darkness dissipated only by a shaft of nocturnal sunshine which shoots in through the window and reveals their embrace.

It is easy to lay down a law. To make it respected is quite another matter. Mimes will, I fear, continue to write plays, since the practice is one which ministers hardly less to the main public's happiness than to their own. I must find such solace as I can in my prevision of the time when Mr. Gillette will have ceased to write anything but stage-directions. His method in dramaturgy tends ever more and more towards dumb-show. Many men—

Carlyle loudly, M. Maeterlinck softly, and so on—have praised
Silence. Mr. Gillette practises it. I feel that ere long he will
offer to us only that golden thing, sifted and cleansed away from
the rubble of dialogue that still clings around it. I feel that his
favourite portion of "Clarice" is that in which he, solitary on the
stage, takes from his pocket the flower that the heroine has given
him, and looks at it for a long time, eloquently, and then puts it
back in his pocket, and then walks slowly to the window, and
thinks, and takes the flower out of his pocket, and looks at it for a
very long time, very eloquently, and then restores it to his pocket,
and then walks very slowly to his writing-table, and seats himself,
and thinks very deeply, and then takes the flower out of his pocket,
and, after a while, begins to pick it to pieces, petal by petal, after
the manner of Marguerite. How long this scene lasted I do not
know. I did not time it by my watch. I was wrapt in contemplation of (that which my heart told me was) Mr. Gillette's own
innocent pleasure in being able to hold the attention of the audience
—his own innocent pride in his own magnetism. Yes, I am sure
that the "thinking part," despised by novices, is the ultimate goal
of Mr. Gillette's ambition. But why should he stop short at that?
With such magnetism as his, need he appear on the stage at all?
It would be still more glorious for him, and still less trouble, if he
diffused his hypnotic rays from his dressing-room, and never cor-
poreally appeared but to take his calls at the end of each act.
Personally I should miss him from the stage. My gladness that
he is so magnetic—to other people—is not so keen as my admiration of his great talent (whenever he uses it) for acting. So gifted
and so accomplished an actor can hardly be spared—could hardlier,
if at all, be spared by me if he appeared in somebody else's plays.

With him, at the Duke of York's, is an admirable company.
Nearly always, American companies give one the impression that
in America the acting is on a higher level than here—that it is
more natural and better disciplined. Much of its charm may be
the mere charm of foreignness. But, even so, there remains a
wide margin that cannot be ignored. One obvious advantage of
the American theatre is its full supply of competent ingénues. In
our theatre ingénues do not begin to approach competence till they
have long ceased to seem ingenuous. In America, apparently,
there is no such retardment. Miss Marie Doro, who plays the

part of Clarice, is an altogether exceptional person—so highly finished is her art, which can have only just begun. But, though I have not seen her match, I have seen many American ingénues who might be mentioned in the same breath with her. In England we never mention our ingénues. It would be brutal.

"THE RETURN OF THE PRODIGAL"

October 7, 1905

The story of the Prodigal Son is, of course, one of the best stories in the world, and one of the best themes for an artist to work on. It can be taken from so many points of view, and be interpreted in so many ways; and innumerable variations can be played on it. The most obvious way of treating it is to make it a story of penitence and forgiveness, of dead sea fruit and the inexhaustible kindness of a father's heart. Next to this, the most obvious way is to take as pivot the two brothers—the eternal contrast between good young man and bad young man. Mr. Hankin is, I imagine, temperamentally not a preacher, nor yet a man whose heart and pen throb readily to the music of what we call the great human motives. I can see him approving, and even envying, the perfect Jacobean cadence of "for this thy brother was dead, and is alive again; and was lost, and is found"; but I can see no tears in his eyes while he murmurs to himself the familiar passage. It is natural that he should have chosen to treat the story in the second of the ways I have mentioned. An emotional presentment might be made of the two brothers, with a fervid appeal to sympathy for one or both of them. But, unlike the father, they do not compel emotional presentment. They can be treated comedically, with a measure of sympathy claimed for one or both, or with no sympathy claimed for either. Mr. Hankin claims sympathy for neither. And he vanquishes the difficulty of the father by relegating him to be a mere tool in the hands of his first-born. Mr. Samuel Jackson is a wealthy manufacturer of cotton; but it is Henry, his first-born, who has made the business brilliantly solid;

and it is Henry, throughout, who directs what shall be done with the inconvenient prodigal, Eustace. Eustace has not, apparently, been wasting his substance in riotous living. He simply failed to succeed commercially in Australia, losing the thousand pounds with which he had been sent thither. Since that time, he has been through various vicissitudes of poverty, and, having worked his passage back to England, he goes to his father's house merely for the sake of a meal and a bed. Finding how very prosperous and important a person his father has become in the meantime, he determines to get something more than a fleeting hospitality. His father offers him a berth in the cotton business. But his brother vetoes that notion. And Eustace cordially acquiesces. He has no talent for business. Besides, he doesn't like work. He wants to be a man of leisure. But his father won't have him at home doing nothing, and orders him out of the house. Very well: he will go straight to the nearest workhouse. Father and brother see how fatal it would be to their rather precarious position in the county, and to the chance of Mr. Samuel Jackson's election for the local constituency, if Eustace were thrust on the parish. Thus Eustace is in a position to dictate terms. Mr. Jackson proposes to send him back to Australia with another thousand pounds. Eustace refuses that. He points out that it is just as easy to fail commercially in Australia as to do so in England: he has tried it, and knows. The brother sees the sense of this, and advises the father to accede to Eustace's demand for a yearly allowance of three hundred pounds. The father draws the line at two hundred and fifty, and a cheque, on these terms, for the first quarter. Presenting this to Eustace, he tells him that he may write from time to time to let the family know how he is getting on. "Make it three hundred," says Eustace, "and I won't write." But Mr. Jackson folds his hands behind him. Eustace with a shrug of the shoulders, and a friendly nod, goes forth into the world. And that is the end of the comedy.

A pure, undiluted comedy, as you may perceive from this slight sketch of it. As there is little in the way of action, and nearly all the fun depends on the adroitness with which one of the characters turns inside out the conventional arguments of the other characters, Mr. Hankin has been much likened by the critics to Mr. Bernard Shaw. It is quite true that Mr. Hankin has come—

what young playwright, nowadays, could fail to come?—somewhat under Mr. Shaw's influence. But the likeness of Mr. Hankin's play to what Mr. Shaw would have made of it is a merely technical and superficial likeness. Mr. Hankin does not set out to prove anything, or to probe anything. He merely observes what is going on in the world, and is moved to communicate to us his good-natured amusement. Mr. Shaw, observing a prodigal son, would have knitted his brows, outstretched his index finger, and harangued us to the effect that the prodigal was perfectly right, as a citizen, in his refusal to work under the present conditions of labo(u)r, and that these conditions are irrational, dangerous, and ought to be abolished. And this harangue would have been couched in the form of a delicious comedy. But let us not, merely because Mr. Shaw is ever a dramatist with a purpose, lend grudging ears to the dramatist without one. Mr. Archer is distressed by Mr. Hankin's failure to thrust under our eyes some "general idea, whether moral or social." He gropes industriously around for that idea, and is half-persuaded that Mr. Hankin intended "a scathing satire on our public schools." (What *would* life be without Mr. Archer?) Mr. Hankin "diagnoses" for him "a morbid condition, but gives no hint as to how it may be cured or might have been avoided." In fact, Mr. Hankin is not Mr. Shaw, and stands condemned therefore by Mr. Archer, who, oddly enough, is never tired of throwing cold water on the serious intentions that underlie Mr. Shaw's dramaturgy. Apparently, Mr. Shaw ought to be Mr. Hankin, and Mr. Hankin ought to be Mr. Shaw. Then Mr. Archer would be happy. But, as Mr. Archer is not a magician, had he not better take people as he finds them, and merely investigate whether this one and that are doing their own best? Mr. Hankin may be trusted to have found what is the line in drama best adapted to his own temperament and talent. And, as his latest comedy of observation is delightfully amusing, and true to life—qualities that Mr. Archer does not deny it to possess—why should we, like Mr. Archer, dismiss those qualities as "rather a meagre outcome for four solid acts"? Heaven forbid that I should discourage Mr. Hankin, or any other playwright, from putting into his plays as much as possible of what Rossetti, in a memorable phrase, called "fundamental brain-work," and of what Mr. Archer (not less hauntingly, I fear) calls "intellectual elbow-grease." But there is no lack of this commodity in "The Return of the Prodigal." And it is Mr. Hankin's own. That is a virtue, from my point of view. I should not rejoice with Mr. Archer at the sight of Mr. Hankin picking the brains of, or (let us say) rubbing elbows with, a person so entirely different from himself as is Mr. Shaw.

It seems to me absurd to blame Mr. Hankin for not telling us why Eustace is deficient in will-power—why, though he is far more clever than his highly successful brother, he continues to be an abject failure. Eustace himself does not know the reason. He supposes that he was born so. And he makes no effort to fight against the unlucky accident. He was born to loaf, if he should have the chance; and, so soon as he sees the chance, he uses all such energy as he has to grasp it firmly. He is the philosophic loafer—a type that exists in real life; and the type has been admirably drawn for us by Mr. Hankin. I have but one fault to find. Eustace declares that of course he, like every one else, "would *like* to be a highly respected, prosperous member of the community." I do not think that the true Eustace—the *widely typical* Prodigal Son—would have felt that. He would have had an innate aversion from respectability and prosperity. These things would have bored him, except perhaps for a while. I remember reading a sonnet, written by a not yet famous poet, describing the gloom that must have settled on the soul of the Prodigal Son after the first flood of sentiment was forgotten, and the novelty of comfort had lost its edge. How slowly and smugly the days passed in that admirable household, shut off from all the chances and changes that alone could make life worth living! Wistfully, the Prodigal looked back on his vagabondage, yearning as much for its miseries as for its pleasures—"Oh for the husks of freedom that were sweet!" I wish Mr. Hankin had adumbrated for us this side of the Prodigal's story. For a moment, indeed, there is a glimpse of it. "My life," says Eustace, "hasn't been successful. It hasn't even been honourable. But," he adds with a ruminating smile, "it was devilish interesting." That, however, is the only glimpse. For the rest, Eustace would evidently be well content to settle down permanently under his father's "roof," if his father would consent to the arrangement. So subtly right does the quoted sonnet seem to me that I wish Mr. Hankin would reconstruct his whole play in accord to it. But this would necessitate for Eustace a loving father, who would implore his son not to leave him; and the curtain would have to fall on a broken heart. It would, in fact, necessitate the sort of thing that is not at all in Mr. Hankin's line. And I must not let Mr. Archer catch me tripping just where I have caught him.

HENRY IRVING

October 21, 1905

One mourns not merely a great actor, who had been a great manager. Irving was so romantically remarkable a figure in modern life, having such a hold on one's imagination (partly because he left so much to it), that his death is like the loss of a legend. As an actor, and as a manager, he had his faults; and these faults were obvious. But as a personality he was flawless—armed at all points in an impenetrable and darkly-gleaming armour of his own design. "The Knight from Nowhere" was the title of a little book of pre-Raphaelite poems that I once read. I always thought of Irving as the Knight from Nowhere.

That he, throughout his memorable tenancy of the Lyceum Theatre, did nothing to encourage the better sort of modern playwright, is a fact for which not he himself should be blamed. It was the fault of the Lyceum Theatre. In that vast and yawning gulf the better sort of modern drama would (for that it consists in the realistic handling of a few characters in ordinary modern life) have been drowned and lost utterly. On a huge stage, facing a huge auditorium, there must be plenty of crowds, bustle, uproar. Drama that gives no scope for these things must be performed in reasonably small places. A more plausible grievance against Irving, as manager, is that in quest of bustling romances or melodramas he seemed generally to alight on hack-work. I think there can be no doubt that he was lacking in literary sense, and was content with any play that gave him scope for a great and central display of his genius in acting. He did not, of course, invent the "star" system. But he carried it as far as it could be carried. And the further he carried it, the greater his success. From an artistic standpoint, I admit that this system is indefensible. But theatres, alas! have box-offices; and the public cares far more, alack! for a favourite actor than for dramatic art. Justice, then, blames rather the public than the favourite actor.

It was as a producer of Shakespeare that Irving was great in management. He was the first man to give Shakespeare a setting contrived with archaic and æsthetic care—a setting that should match the pleasure of the eye with the pleasure of the ear. That was a noble conception. Many people object, quite honestly, that the pleasure of the ear is diminished by that of the eye—that spectacle is a foe to poetry. Of course, spectacle may be overdone. Irving may sometimes have overdone it; but he always overdid it beautifully. And there was this further excuse for him: he could not, even had the stage been as bare as a desert, have given us the true music and magic of Shakespeare's verse. He could not declaim. That was one of the defects in his art. His voice could not be attuned to the glories of rhythmic cadence. It was a strange, suggestive voice that admirably attuned itself to the subtleties of Irving's conception of whatever part he was playing. It was Irving's subtle conception, always, that we went to see. Here, again, Irving was an innovator. I gather that the actors of his day had been simple, rough-and-ready, orotund fellows who plunged into this or that play, very much as the water-horse plunges through the reeds. They were magnificent, but they had no pretensions to intellect. Irving had these pretensions, and he never failed to justify them. One missed the music of the verse, but was always arrested, stimulated, by the meanings that he made the verse yield to him. These subtle and sometimes profound meanings were not always Shakespeare's own. Now and again, the verse seemed to yield them to Irving only after an intense effort, and with a rather bad grace. All the parts that Irving played were exacting parts, but he had his revenge sometimes, exacting even more from them. This was another defect in his art: he could not impersonate. His voice, face, figure, port, were not transformable. But so fine was the personality to which they belonged that none cried shame when this or that part had to submit to be crushed by it. Intransformable, he was—multi-radiant, though. He had, in acting, a keen sense of humour—of sardonic, grotesque, fantastic humour. He had an incomparable power for eeriness—for stirring a dim sense of mystery; and not less masterly was he in evoking a sharp sense of horror. His dignity was magnificent in purely philosophic or priestly gentleness, or in the gaunt aloofness of philosopher or king. He could be benign with a tinge of malevolence, and arrogant with an undercurrent of sweetness. As philosopher or king, poet or prelate, he was matchless. One felt that if Charles the Martyr, Dante, Wolsey, were not precisely as he was, so much the worse for Wolsey, Dante, Charles the Martyr. On the other hand, less august types, such as men of action and men of passion, were outside his range, and suffered badly when he dragged them within it. Macbeth had a philosophic side, which enabled Macbeth to come fairly well out of the ordeal. But Romeo's suicide in the vault of Capulet could only be regarded as a merciful release. Unfortunately, though I saw and can remember Irving as Romeo, I never saw him as Hamlet. This is one of the regrets of my life. I can imagine the gentleness (with a faint strain of cruelty), the aloofness, the grace and force of intellect, in virtue of which that performance must have been a very masterpiece of interpretation. I can imagine, too, the mystery with which Irving must have involved, rightly, the figure of Hamlet, making it loom through the mist mightily, as a world-type, not as a mere individual—making it loom as it loomed in the soul of Shakespeare himself—not merely causing it to strut agreeably, littly, as in the average production. Above all, I can imagine how much of sheer beauty this interpretation must have had. Though, as I have said, Irving could not do justice to the sound of blank-verse, his prime appeal was always to the sense of beauty. It was not, I admit, to a sense of obvious beauty. It was to a sense of strange, delicate, almost mystical and unearthly beauty. To those who possessed not, nor could acquire, this sense, Irving appeared always in a rather ridiculous light. "Why does he walk like this? Why does he talk like that?" But, for any one equipped to appreciate him, his gait and his utterance were not less dear than his face—were part of a harmony that was as fine as it was strange. And, though the cruder members of the audience could not fall under the spell of this harmony, they were never irreverent until they reached their homes. Never once at the Lyceum did I hear a titter. Irving's presence dominated even those who could not be enchanted by it. His magnetism was intense, and unceasing. What exactly magnetism is, I do not know. It may be an exhalation of the soul, or it may be a purely physical thing—an effusion of certain rays which will one day be discovered, and named after their discoverer—Professor Jenkinson, perhaps: the Jenkinson Rays. I only know that Irving possessed this gift of magnetism in a supreme degree. And I conjecture that to it, rather than to the quality of his genius, which was a thing to be really appreciated only by the few, was due the unparalleled sway that he had over the many.

In private life he was not less magnetic than on the stage. The obituarists seem hardly to do justice to the intensely interesting personality of Irving in private life. He has been depicted by them merely as a benevolent gentleman who was always doing this or that obscure person a good turn. Certainly, Irving was benevolent, and all sorts of people profited by his generosity. But these two facts are poor substitutes for the impression that Irving made on those who were brought into contact with him. He was always courteous and gracious, and everybody was fascinated by him; but I think there were few who did not also fear him. Always in the company of his friends and acquaintances—doubtless, not in that of his most intimate friends—there was an air of sardonic reserve behind his cordiality. He seemed always to be watching, and watching from a slight altitude. As when, on the first or last night of a play, he made his speech before the curtain, and concluded by calling himself the public's "respectful—devoted—loving—servant," with special emphasis on the word "servant," he seemed always so like to some mighty cardinal stooping to wash the feet of pilgrims at the altar-steps, so, when in private life people had the honour of meeting Irving, his exquisite manner of welcome stirred fear as well as love in their hearts. Irving, I think, wished to be feared as well as loved. He was "a good fellow"; but he was also a man of genius, who had achieved pre-eminence in his art, and, thereby, eminence in the national life; and, naturally, he was not going to let the "good fellow" in him rob him of the respect that was his due. Also, I think, the process of making himself feared appealed to something elfish in his nature. Remember, he was a comedian, as well as a tragedian. Tragic acting on the stage is, necessarily, an assumption; but comedy comes out of the actor's own soul. Surely, to be ever "grand seigneur," to be ever pontifically gracious in what he said and in his manner of saying it, and to watch the effect that he made, was all wine to the comedic soul of Irving. He enjoyed the dignity of his position, but enjoyed even more, I conjecture, the fun of it. I formed the theory, once and for all, one morning in the year 1895—the morning of the day appointed for various gentlemen to be knighted at Windsor Castle. I was crossing the road, opposite the Marble Arch, when a brougham passed me. It contained Irving, evidently on his way to Paddington. Irving, in his most prelatical mood, had always a touch—a trace here and there—of the old Bohemian. But as I caught sight of him on this occasion—a great occasion, naturally, in his career; though to me it had seemed rather a bathos, this superimposition of a smug Hanoverian knighthood on the Knight from Nowhere—he was the old Bohemian, and nothing else. His hat was tilted at more than its usual angle, and his long cigar seemed longer than ever; and on his face was a look of such ruminant, sly fun as I have never seen equalled. I had but a moment's glimpse of him; but that was enough to show me the soul of a comedian revelling in the part he was about to play—of a comedic philosopher revelling in a foolish world. I was sure that when he alighted on the platform of Paddington his bearing would be more than ever grave and stately, with even the usual touch of Bohemianism obliterated now in honour of the honour that was to befall him.

Apart from his genuine kindness, and his grace and magnetism, it was this sense that he was always playing a part—that he preserved always, for almost every one, a certain barrier of mystery—that made Irving so fascinating a figure. That day, when I saw him on his way to Windsor, and tried to imagine just what impression he would make on Queen Victoria, I found myself thinking of the impression made there by Disraeli; and I fancied that the two impressions might be rather similar. Both men were courtiers, yet incongruous in a court. And both had a certain dandyism—the arrangement of their hair and the fashion of their clothes carefully thought out in reference to their appearance and their temperament. And both, it seemed to me, had something of dandyism in the wider, philosophic sense of the word—were men whose whole life was ordered with a certain ceremonial, as courtly functions are ordered. "Brodribb," certainly, was an English name; but surely Irving had some strong strain of foreign blood: neither his appearance nor the quality of his genius was that of an Englishman. Possibly, like Disraeli, he had Spanish blood. Anyhow, his was an exotic mind, like Disraeli's, dominating its drab environment partly by its strength and partly by its strangeness. Both men were romantic to the core, ever conceiving large and grandiose ideas, which they executed with a fond eye to pageantry. And, above all, both men preserved in the glare of fame that quality of mystery which is not essential to genius, but which is the safest insurance against oblivion. It has been truly said that Irving would have been eminent in any walk of life. Had Disraeli the Younger drifted from literature to the foot-lights, and had Henry Brodribb strayed from the schoolroom into politics, I daresay that neither our political nor our theatrical history would be very different from what it is—except in the matter of dates.

"THE VOYSEY INHERITANCE"

November 11, 1905

Messrs. Vedrenne and Barker have made no more signal discovery than Mr. Barker's new play; and I hasten to offer my congratulations. I have often inveighed against the plays written by mimes, and have even asserted that no mime could possibly write a good play. Mr. Barker is an exceptional person, in whose presence I bow, corrected. On him, somehow, the blight of the theatre has not fallen. He has continued to keep himself less interested in the theatre than in life. He is not, and may he never become, "one o' the boys." May he ever continue to be their antithesis, letting his mind range actively over the actual world, not wallow in that one little weed-covered pond, the theatre, which reflects nothing. May his very bright intellect never grow dim. I may have to suggest anon that he is too purely intellectual to be perfect. For the present, though, let there be nothing but praise.

It is always the most obvious and most promising themes that our playwrights most ostentatiously neglect. One of these themes is the fraudulent solicitor. Mr. Barker's mere choice of this theme is laudable; but far more so is his treatment of it. Having chosen his type, he has shown it to us from within, laying bare all its intricacies. Mr. Voysey, of Voysey and Son, is no mere arbitrary figure of a scoundrel. A scoundrel he is, but much besides; and we are supposed to understand the reason and the exact quality of his scoundrelism, and to gauge the whole of his character "all round." In a sense, scoundrelism has been thrust on him. When he inherited his father's business, he found that it had been based, all the time, on fraud. He threw himself into the task of setting the business on an honest basis, without doing violence to his filial instinct by letting the world know about his father. In time, he achieved his task; but, in doing so, he had acquired a taste for the ingenious manipulation of funds. He had found that he had a genius for finance. Consequently, he soon became bored by the humdrum of a well-regulated little business. Moreover, he had begotten a large family, to which he was devoted; and, except by manipulating his clients' funds, he could not "provide handsomely" for it. So he proceeded to manipulate, ministering thus both to his paternal feelings and to his financial genius. Scruples of conscience troubled him not at all in his strenuous life. "Let us realise," he says, "that religion is one thing, home-life another, and business another; and that each of these great things in life is to be practised separately. Then we shall be able to practise them with all our strength, and to get the full benefit that is in them." I quote from memory, and these are not, doubtless, the actual words. But I have preserved the spirit of the passage well enough to give you a grasp of Mr. Voysey's philosophy, and of the lines along which Mr. Voysey's character has developed. The one cloud on his horizon is that none of his available sons seems fitted to carry on the business when he dies. Edward, for example, is a prig, and has steeped himself in various ethical systems. Still, it is on Edward that he must depend. Edward is taken into partnership, and the first scene of the play (for it is only in the play's course, gradually, that one learns what I have told you about Mr. Voysey) is concerned with Edward's horror at the revelations that have been made to him, and with the inward conflict in him as to whether he shall desert his father, whom he still loves, or shall become an accessory to, and possibly a scapegoat for, his father's frauds. The conflict is admirably conducted by Mr. Barker, who leaves it, however, undecided till the end of the second act. This act is occupied mainly by showing us the family "interior." And Mr. Barker excels not less in incisive sketches of character than in elaborate portrayals. The Voyseys are a very large family, and a very ordinary family. Yet every one of them is made to stand out distinctly and amusingly. Their very colourlessness becomes lurid through the accuracy with which it is observed by Mr. Barker, and through the sharp and subtle irony with which he shows it to us. In the second act we see the Voyseys in their daily round—in all the decent pettiness and dulness of their ordinary selves. In the third act we see them tested by a tragic crisis. Their father has died a death for which the audience was "prepared" by a queerly felicitous little touch at the end of the third act. After the funeral, Edward, who did finally decide to take up the partnership in his father's business, has to break to the mourning family assembled the news of its founder's nefariousness. A hundred thousand pounds has been left by Mr. Voysey; but three hundred thousand would hardly cover the liabilities of the firm to its clients. Edward points out that it is clearly the duty of the various children, married and unmarried, to surrender their legacies. This notion, somehow, does not appeal to the Voyseys; and their attempts to reconcile their distaste for it with the rectitude on which they pride themselves, and their bewildered doubts as to how to reconcile their virtuous indignation against their father with a decorous attitude towards the deceased whom they have been so sincerely mourning, and all the other elements of doubt that are battling in their souls and making them dimly ridiculous even to themselves, suffice to furnish what I am tempted to regard as the finest scene of grim, ironic comedy in modern English drama. Both in conception and in execution, the scene is the work of a master. It is admirably played, too, by the many mimes who figure in it. People often ask, quite innocently, with a genuine desire for information, why the acting at the Court Theatre seems so infinitely better than in so many other theatres where the same mimes are to be seen. I should have thought that the two reasons were obvious. One is that the mimes at the Court are very carefully stage-managed, every one of them being kept in such relation to his fellows as is demanded by the relation in which the various parts stand to one another—no one mime getting more, or less, of a chance than the playwright has intended him to have. The other reason is that at the Court Theatre are produced only plays written by clever persons who have a sense of character, and who are thus enabled to create characters which are human, and which, therefore, repay the trouble that the mimes take in playing them.

After this conclave scene, which is, I repeat, masterly, comes a scene to remind us that the master is still, to some extent, a pupil— a member of Mr. Shaw's academy for young gentlemen. Edward Voysey is tempted to let his father's firm go bankrupt, and so extricate himself from the unpleasant life in which he has become involved. No retrospective blame could be laid on him. Technically, as a member of the firm, he would be responsible. But he could show that since his entry into the firm there had been no fresh irregularities, and that his influence had been all on the side of the clients. On the other hand, if he continued the business, a smash would certainly come sooner or later, and he would be sent to penal servitude. Why should he court imprisonment for doing a thing from which he revolted? There was one highly chivalrous reason. He might, if the smash did not come too soon, gradually rescue the money of the humbler investors. He determines that to this off-chance he will sacrifice himself. I have nothing to urge against this determination in itself. But it is made at the instance of a Miss Alice Maitland, with whom Edward is in love; and Miss Alice Maitland won't do at all. There may, conceivably, be young ladies like her in real life. But the point is that all the young ladies in Mr. Shaw's plays are exactly like her; and, however appropriate they may sometimes be to their own setting, a replica of them is just what is not needed, and what is injurious, here. Wanted, an ordinary human person, who happens to be in love with Edward Voysey. Miss Maitland has the customary Shavian allowance of coquetry; but she shows no sign that she is in love with Edward, or could possibly be in love with any one except herself. She wants to marry, of course; but whether or not she will marry Edward depends entirely on whether or not he shall startle her by contriving to live up to her own theories of general morality. That she might sympathise with him in his ordeal is the very last thing that would occur to her. She simply waits to see how he will acquit himself. Time passes, and Edward now has managed to rescue some of the money aforesaid, and is in daily risk of exposure and imprisonment. He really has become worthy of her perfect self, and she sets her seal of approval by offering to marry him. "But what," asks he, "if I am sent to prison?" "Then," she says, meditatively, "I shall have to be very careful." He asks her why. "Because," she replies, "my pride will be so great." I doubt if even a Shavian woman (granted her existence) in real life would, at such a juncture, merely utter this little, dry, academic, all-in-the-air paradox about her own prospective emotions. Certainly, any ordinary woman would shrink with horror from the prospect of her lover being sent to prison, and being parted from her. Master Barker, at his desk in the Shavian academy, has shrunk with not less horror from the notion of admitting an ordinary woman into his play. The British drama has been given over almost exclusively to the portrayal of sentimental emotions, and to false portrayal of them; so that the reaction of a gifted young dramatist against sentimental emotions in any form is quite natural. It is well that we should have a dramatic portrayal of moral enthusiasm. But moral enthusiasm can be distorted quite as easily as the sentimental emotions. And it has been distorted even so by Mr. Barker. A heroine with nothing in her soul but abstract ethics is just as foolish a contrivance as the heroine of the average conventional play. For Mr. Barker's special purpose, Miss Maitland ought to have been a woman in whom moral passion was combined with a very strong passion of love for Edward Voysey. Then she would have supplied in herself an interesting conflict that would have added much to the interest of Voysey's own. As it is, she is as undramatic as she is (despite the charm of Miss Mabel Hackney's acting) insufferable; and I cannot imagine a greater tribute to the play than the fact that she doesn't wreck it. If she had not been brought in at all, I should not have lamented the "lack of feminine interest." The play would have been quite all right without her. But, as she was brought in, I have to call Mr. Barker's attention to her as a warning not to be afraid of sentiment, and ashamed of it, merely because it isn't brain-power. Sentiment is a not uncommon thing in real life. It is a very common and potent thing, and worthy material for even the cleverest of dramatists.

ACTRESSES AND AGES

November 18, 1905

One sometimes sees, not often, an elderly actress playing the part of a girl. The sight is distressing, and mars any illusion that the play may have power to create. But, at any rate, one has the solace of knowing that the actress is doing her best, and is failing only because she is unevenly matched in the duel with Nature. One has not this solace when one sees, as one so often does see, a young actress playing the part of an old or middle-aged woman. It is as easy to simulate eld as it is difficult to simulate youth. Crow's-feet and hollows, though they cannot be painted out, can be painted in. Infirmity of movement, or mature deliberation of movement, can be easily assumed by youth, though youth's agility can only be mocked by the efforts of eld. And youth's inimitable voice can easily be toned to notes other than its own. Yet, simple though these tricks are, young actresses are never seen playing them. Cast for elderly parts, they will go so far as to powder their hair, à la Marquise. Thus far, and no further. Their faces must not forfeit the bloom and linelessness of youth. And the result is a pretty picture of eighteenth-century young womanhood, and needs but a "mouche" on chin and cheek to consummate the illusion. A very living picture, too—living with all the blithe intensity of youth, moving with kittenish grace and freedom, and sparkling, and mincing, and coquetting, ever so prettily, and melodious with notes of laughter yet more silvery than the aforesaid coiffure. It seems rather churlish to cavil at a thing so pleasant in itself. But one has to judge it in relation to what it was intended to be by the author of the play which it adorns, and in relation to the exact dramatic impression which it ought to make on us. And by such standards one is bound to deem it amiss.

I noted two strong instances of it lately, in a very successful play which, in deference to the two ladies who supplied the instances, I will not particularise. One of these two had to impersonate an old maid, whose heart of gold was obscured by a very sharp tongue. In the course of the play, she was more than once referred to as "that old harridan." Yet, facially, she was the most winning of most juvenile ladies from the court of Le Roi Soleil. In voice, too, and in movement, and in everything but the rude things she had to say, she was signally, and unremittingly, seductive. Thus these rude things were utterly queered in their "value." Said by an elderly woman, they would have seemed a pardonable form of eccentricity, as intended by the author. Said by a very young and pretty woman, they were quite unpardonable insults, for which this very young and pretty woman would anywhere have been excluded from decent society. Nor was this the sole mischief. The whole reason for the old maid's presence in the play was that she was to act as chaperon to a young man and woman who might otherwise have been compromised in the eyes of an audience ever jealous for the chastity of heroes and heroines. But, as she appeared to be practically a cœval of the heroine, her chaperonage lost its obvious force; and only by a hard effort of the imagination, made with shut eyes, could the audience take her at her proper value. The other instance was supplied by a lady who impersonated a married woman with a grown-up daughter. For some time after the curtain rose, I was under the impression that the mother and daughter were sisters; and when I did, at length, grasp the relationship, I had to exercise the greatest care not to let it slip from me. Of course, one has seen sometimes in real life a mother and daughter who, in the distance, and at a cursory glance, might pass for sisters. But such misunderstandings can be contrived only through great pains taken by the mother. And the mother in this play was a simple and admirable creature, with no jealousy at all of her daughter's youth. Thus even a momentary misunderstanding would have been a pity. How much more a pity, a misunderstanding that had to be guarded against throughout the whole course of the play!

Such instances could, if I ranged over other plays, be multiplied indefinitely. These two suffice to the plaint that I am making at large. I move a resolution that the refusal of young actresses to add, in any circumstances, one week to their ages, is deleterious to the interests of dramatic art, and ought to be abolished. Young actors do not err thus. They err, rather, in the opposite direction. Cast a young actor for the part of a man of sixty, and the chances are that he will insist on playing it with all the extremist symptoms of senile decay. His face will not be visible through a network of wrinkles; his hands will tremble like aspen-leaves; his voice will quaver in the topmost treble. All this he will regard as "a good bit of character," and will be wholly delighted. Why has our young friend no counterpart among mimes of the other sex? It might be urged that women have less power of impersonation than men have. That is true. They can hardly escape from themselves. But they wouldn't if they could, when it were a question of young actresses impersonating old women. All women have a far more intense abhorrence from the prospect of eld than any men have. To assume publicly the aspect and manner of eld would be for them a hideous reminder of their future in private life—a reminder which their comparatively shallow devotion to art would never suffice to make them incur. Of course, women who are married and have several children do not regard the prospect of eld with very great horror (though even they regard it with greater horror than does the average young bachelor). But these women are not on the stage. At any rate, none of them is among the actresses who are young. The young actresses, one and all, for reasons of nature, are passionately averse from the simulation of eld. But there are professional reasons, too, for the aversion—reasons of trade. Every young actress wants to be a great success, and to earn a great salary. Unless she happens to be also a great genius, her salary will cease to be great after her first youth. With great genius, she will be able to linger on, dictating her own wishes, and playing young parts after she has ceased to be young, at the rate of fifty or more guineas a week. Without that rare gift of genius, she will have no chance of playing parts that do not befit her years. She will have to be content with humdrum middle-aged parts, for which the remuneration is (however unjustly) small; and (according to the present policy of managers) she will not be engaged often even for these. Thus, the young actress beholds before her a brief career. She will have to make hay while the sun shines, and, incidentally, to keep the sun shining as long as possible, and to make it appear to shine even after it has set. So soon as she is definitely regarded as middle-aged, the game is, to all intents, up. Is it likely that she will, meanwhile, do anything which might serve to make the public forget her youthfulness, or might give a definite impression that she is no longer young? No, it is too much to expect of her that she shall play middle-aged parts artistically. It is too much to expect of even the most imperious stage-manager that he shall succeed in compelling her to play such parts in such a way. On the other hand, it is not too much to expect of the managers them-selves that they shall cease to offer her such parts. The middle-aged actress is not rare. It is to her that such parts should be offered. Her endeavour will be to play them youthfully. But, even so, she will not be able to mar the needed illusion so com-pletely as it is marred now.

MR. SHAW'S POSITION

December 9, 1905

It must amuse him, whenever he surveys it; and I hope he will some day write a comedy around it. It bristles with side-lights on so many things—on human character in general, and on the English character in particular, and on the particular difficulties that genius encounters in England, and on the right manner of surmounting them.

For years Mr. Shaw was writing plays, some of which, by hook or crook, in holes and corners, were produced. They were witnessed, and loudly applauded, by such ladies and gentlemen as were in or around the Fabian Society. Not that these people took their socialist seriously as a playwright. They applauded his work in just the spirit in which, had he started a racing-stable, they would have backed his horses. He was taken with some measure of seriousness by such of the professional critics as were his personal friends, and were not hide-bound by theatrical tradition. Here, they perceived, was something new in the theatre; and, liking to be in advance of the time, they blew their trumpets in their friend's honour. The rest of the professional critics merely sniffed or cursed, according to their manners. The public took no notice at all. Time passed. In Berlin, Munich, Vienna, and elsewhere, Mr. Shaw was now a popular success. Perhaps in the hope that England had caught an echo of this exotic enthusiasm, Messrs. Vedrenne and Barker ventured to produce "John Bull's Other Island." England had not caught that echo. There was only the usual little succès d'estime. But, not long after its production, the play was witnessed by a great lady, who advised an august person to witness it; and this august person persuaded a person yet more august to witness it. It had been withdrawn, meanwhile; so there was "a command performance." All the great ladies, and all the great gentlemen, were present; also, several paragraphists. That evening Mr. Shaw became a fashionable craze; and within a few days all London knew it. The Savoy restaurant is much frequented by fashion, and by paragraphy; and its revenues are drawn mainly from the many unfashionable people who go to feast their eyes on the people who are fashionable beyond dispute. No large restaurant can live by the aristocracy alone. Nor can even a small theatre. Mr. Shaw "pays" now because now the English middle class pays to see that which is seen and approved by the English upper class, and (more especially) to see the English upper class. Whether either of these classes really rejoices in Mr. Shaw, as yet, is a point on which I am doubtful. I went to see "Man and Superman" a few nights ago. The whole audience was frequently rocking with laughter, but mostly at the wrong moments. (I admit that Mr. Shaw's thoughts are often so profound, and his wit is always so swift, that to appreciate his plays rightly and fully at a first hearing is rather an achievement.) But it was obvious that the whole audience was very happy indeed. It was obvious that Mr. Shaw is an enormous success. And in the round-about way by which success has come to him is cast a delicious light on that quality for which England is specially notable among the nations.

His success is not gratifying to the critics. To those critics who are incapable of exercising their brains, and who have always resented Mr. Shaw vehemently, it is of course, galling to find themselves suddenly at odds with public opinion—the opinion which they are accustomed to "voice." Having slated "John Bull," and slated "Man and Superman," they must have been in a fearful dilemma about the play produced at the Court Theatre last week, "Major Barbara." Perhaps this, too, was going to "catch on." Would it not be safer to climb down, and write moderate eulogies? I suspect it was stupidity as much as pride that diverted them from this ignominious course. They really could not make head or tail of the play. They were sure that this time Shaw really had come a cropper—had really delivered himself into their hands. "A success, are you? Pet of the public, are you? We'll see about that. *We'll* pet-of-the-public you. *We'll*" etc., etc. The old cries—"no dramatist," "laughing at his audience," and the like—were not sufficient, this time. "Brute" and "blasphemer" were added. In the second act of the play, Mr. Shaw has tried to show some of the difficulties with which the Salvation Army has to cope. A ruffian comes to one of the shelters in quest of a woman who has been rescued from living with him. A Salvation "lass" bars his way, and refuses to yield. He strikes her in the face. The incident is not dragged in. It is necessary to the purpose of the whole scene. Nor has any one ventured to suggest that it is an exaggeration of real life. Nor is the incident enacted realistically on the stage of the Court Theatre. At the first performance, anyhow, the actor impersonating the ruffian aimed a noticeably gentle blow in the air, at a noticeably great distance from the face of the actress impersonating the lass. I happen to be particularly squeamish in the matter of physical violence on the stage. I have winced at the smothering of Desdemona, for example, when it has been done with anything like realism. The mere symbolism at the Court Theatre gave me not the faintest qualm—not, I mean, the faintest physical qualm: æsthetically, of course, I was touched, as Mr. Shaw had a right to touch me. And it seems to me that the critics who profess to have been disgusted and outraged must have been very hard up for a fair means of attack. Equally unfair, for that it may carry conviction to the minds of people who have not seen the play, is the imputation of blasphemy. Mr. Shaw is held up to execration because he has put into the mouth of Major Barbara certain poignant words of Our Lord. To many people, doubtless, it is a screamingly funny joke that a female should have a military prefix. Also, there is no doubt that Mr. Shaw's play abounds in verbal wit, and in humorous situations. But the purport of the play is serious; and the character of Major Barbara is one of the two great factors in it. With keenest insight and sense of spiritual beauty, Mr. Shaw reveals to us in her the typical religious fanatic of her kind. Sense of spiritual beauty is not one of the qualities hitherto suspected in Mr. Shaw; but here it certainly is; and I defy even the coarsest mind not to perceive it. (To respect it is another matter.) When Major Barbara comes to the great spiritual crisis of her life, and when she believes that all the things she had trusted in have fallen away from her, what were more natural than that she should utter the words of agony that are most familiar to her? That any sane creature in the audience could have been offended by that utterance, I refuse to believe. It was as inoffensive as it was dramatically right. And the critics who have turned up the whites of their eyes, and have doubtless prejudiced against the play many worthy people who have not, like them, had the opportunity of seeing it, must submit to one of two verdicts—insanity or hypocrisy. I have no doubt that of these two qualities they will prefer to confess the latter. It is the more typically British.

In that delicate comedy, "Mr. Shaw's Position," the parts played by these critics seem rather crude. There is a subtler fun in the parts played by some of the superior critics—the critics who were eager to lend helping hands to Mr. Shaw in the time of his obscurity. So long as he was "only *so* high," and could be comfortably patted on the head, they made a pet of him. Now that he strides gigantic, they are less friendly. They seem even anxious to trip him up. Perhaps they do not believe in the genuineness of his growth, and suspect some trick of stilts. That would be a quite natural scepticism. A great man cannot be appreciated fully by his intimate contemporaries. Nor can his great success be ever quite palatable to them, however actively they may have striven to win it for him. To fight for a prince who has to be hiding in an oak-tree is a gallant and pleasant adventure; but when one sees the poor creature enthroned, with a crown on his head and a sceptre in his hand, one's sentiments are apt to cool. And thus the whilom champions of Mr. Shaw's virtues are now preoccupied mainly with Mr. Shaw's defects. The old torches are still waved, but perfunctorily; and the main energy is devoted to throwing cold water. Whereas the virtues of Mr. Shaw used to be extolled with reservations for the defects, now the defects are condemned with reservations for the virtues. Mr. Shaw, it is insisted, cannot draw life: he can only distort it. He has no knowledge of human nature: he is but a theorist. All his characters are but so many incarnations of himself. Above all, he cannot write plays. He has no dramatic instinct, no theatrical technique. And these objections are emphatically reiterated (often with much brilliancy and ingenuity) by the superior critics, while all the time the fact is staring them in the face that Mr. Shaw has created in "Major Barbara" two characters—Barbara and her father—who live with an intense vitality; a crowd of minor characters that are accurately observed (though some are purposely exaggerated) from life; and one act—the second—which is as cunning and closely-knit a piece of craftsmanship as any conventional playwright could achieve, and a cumulative appeal to emotions which no other living playwright has touched. With all these facts staring them in the face, they still maintain that Mr. Shaw is not a playwright.

That theory might have held water in the days before Mr. Shaw's plays were acted. Indeed, I was in the habit of propounding it myself. I well remember that when the two volumes of "Plays, Pleasant and Unpleasant" were published, and the ordinary dramatic criticisms in this Review were still signed G.B.S., I wrote here a special article in which I pointed out that the plays, delightful to the reader, would be quite impossible on the stage. This simply proved that I had not enough theatrical imagination to see the potentialities of a play through reading it in print. When, later, I saw performances of "Mrs. Warren's Profession," "The Devil's Disciple," and "You Never Can Tell," I found, to my great surprise, that they gained much more than they lost by being seen and not read. Still, the old superstition lingered in my brain. I had not learnt my lesson. When "Man and Superman" was published, I called it "Mr. Shaw's Dialogues," and said that (even without the philosophic scene in hell) it would be quite unsuited to any stage. When I saw it performed, I determined that I would not be caught tripping again.

I found that as a piece of theatrical construction it was perfect. As in "John Bull's Other Island," so in "Major Barbara" (excepting the aforesaid second act), there is none of that tight construction which was in the previous plays. There is little story, little action. Everything depends on the interplay of various types of character and of thought. But to order this process in such a way that it shall not be tedious requires a very great amount of technical skill. During the third act of "Major Barbara," I admit, I found my attention wandering. But this aberration was not due to any loosening of Mr. Shaw's grip on his material. It was due simply to the fact that my emotions had been stirred so much in the previous act that my cerebral machine was not in proper working order. Mr. Shaw ought to have foreseen that effect. In not having done so, he is guilty of a technical error. But to deny that he is a dramatist merely because he chooses, for the most part, to get drama out of contrasted types of character and thought, without action, and without appeal to the emotions, seems to me both unjust and absurd. His technique is peculiar because his purpose is peculiar. But it is not the less technique.

There! I have climbed down. Gracefully enough to escape being ridiculous? I should like mine to be a "sympathetic" part in "Mr. Shaw's Position."

IDOLUM AULARUM

January 13, 1906

In the suburban music-halls one finds plenty of talent, rough but undeniable. The entertainments there are cheerier than in the "syndicate" halls. They have more élan, and less pretension. But their audience is what most interests me. In suburban music-halls the public lets itself go. You behold it naked and unashamed. In a metropolitan hall, to which it has come from various distances, it is not quite itself. But to a suburban hall nearly every one has come, as it were, from round the corner. All are neighbours, and all feel themselves at home, and behave with perfect naturalness. Listening to their volleys of laughter or of applause, marking their silences and their positive expressions of disapproval, and correlating all these with the entertainment, you have an unique chance of gauging their true character and tastes—for detecting just what they really think and feel and are. You may be disappointed in them. But you are bound to be very much interested.

In one of these palaces of truth, a few nights ago, I was especially interested in what I learned about the public as hero-worshipper. Two performers, a man and a woman, were giving what the programme called "A Pot-pourri Entertainment": they sang, performed conjuring tricks, and did various other things. As the final item, the man announced that he would impersonate some famous characters. Setting his back to the audience, he busied himself before a mirror, and presently turned round, wearing a tunic of khaki, a brown wig parted in the middle, and a moustache of the same colour. Thus disguised, he stared fixedly at us. Whether any one ever looked less like Lord Kitchener is a point which I will not dare to decide. The audience, having been told whom to expect, clapped its hands. A wild salvo of cheers, anon, greeted a somewhat weak-faced and untidy Mr. Chamberlain. There was some cheering for Lord Roberts, with a very considerable admixture of booing. "I am now," said our Proteus, "going to represent General Buller—the Man who Did his Best." I assure you I thought that the roof of the hall would come off. While Proteus was putting the final touches, and while the audience was still roaring itself hoarse, the female performer, who had vanished, reappeared unobtrusively, and, as General Buller wheeled round saluting to the audience, she struck a meditative attitude beside him. She was wearing a grey wig, a white veil topped with a small diamond crown, and a broad blue riband across her breast. The orchestra played the National Anthem. I have considerately prepared you, sensitive reader, for the grotesque and pitiful truth that took me unawares. The female performer represented the late Queen Victoria. The din continued. It was not louder than it had been when General Buller's name was first mentioned. No din, indeed, could have been louder than that. But I wished to detect in it some notes of disapproval. There was not one. The late Queen was superfluous

as an incentive to enthusiasm for General Buller; but it seemed to
the audience a quite natural thing, a thing quite right and seemly,
that she should take her stand beside him and share his triumph.
They loved and revered the memory of her. She was no intruder
in this heroic company. It was a graceful and pleasing thought
to have summoned her hither from her resting-place. It showed
a sense of the fitness of things. And thus, with Queen Victoria
resting her chin on her hand and gazing dreamily at the audience,
in juxtaposition to General Buller at the salute, the curtain fell,
amidst deafening and delirious enthusiasm.

I might dilate on the hopelessness of submitting any delicate or
beautiful work in drama to a public so coarse-fibred that it wel-
comes, instead of instantly hissing off the stage, the ghastly exhibition that I have described. But I will concern myself merely
with the public's taste in heroes, as here exemplified. Not that I
am going to be iconoclastic. I have no wish to dash an image
from its pedestal: I am merely wondering how it came there. Far
be it from me to rake up the details of a not very interesting war.
Further still be it from me to deny that General Buller is a brave
man, and a good-hearted man. No one, I suppose, will deny that
Lord Roberts also is a brave man, and a good-hearted man. Why,
then, should Lord Roberts stand so much less high in the esteem
of our emotional public? It is natural that General Buller should
be a pre-eminent hero in Devonshire; for Devonshire is his home;
and county-feeling is in Devonians almost as strong an instinct as
family-feeling or patriotism. But one may be sure that the
audiences of our suburban music-halls are not recruited mainly,
or even in great part, from Devonshire. Why, then, their passionate idolatry of General Buller? His name may have something to do with it, as being fraught with popular associations—
John Bull, bulldog tenacity, and so forth. But Lord Roberts, in
the reception of whose semblance, the other night, booing was
mingled with mild cheering, bears a name not less auspicious—a
name that conjures up "gags" that have passed into the language,
and "breaks" that never will be forgotten. The cause of the
difference evidently lies deeper than in nomenclature. We find it,
I think, in the fact that General Buller did not conquer the Boers,
and that Lord Roberts (to a certain extent) did. Just as Lord
Roberts made some mistakes, so did General Buller do some

things well. But, roughly, the one man was a success, the other a failure. And nothing appeals more surely to the average Englishman than failure on a large scale. He judges not by intentions, but by results. A successful man may have been animated by intentions quite as pure and noble as those of the man who has failed. But the fact remains that he has succeeded. He has achieved that which the average man would have bungled; and thus he can inspire no brotherly love. He may not be a genius—may not have just those qualities which the average Englishman most sharply abominates; but he must take the consequences of seeming to be a genius—must be judged by results. Failure is the surest conciliator of mediocrity. It makes, also, the surest appeal to sentimentality. The Englishman, because he is gruff and stolid in manner, is supposed by foreigners not to be sentimental; whereas, in reality, there is nothing he enjoys more than shedding tears. Give him the right to call you "Poor old fellow!" and there is nothing he will not do for you. Make yourself the cause of a lump in his throat, and he is your debtor for life. Of course, an unknown man cannot win popularity throughout England by the simple expedient of making a public failure. A man must previously have attained a certain eminence. He must fall from a height, so that the average men are flattered by finding themselves level with him, and so that they have a solid excuse for exercising the voluptuous emotion of pity. In other countries than England this business of falling from a height does not bring popularity; for, though mediocrity, all the world over, envies eminence, England is the one country which is sentimental to the core. Germans are, in their ponderous way, sentimental about youth and beauty, about wine, woman, and song. But they never let sentiment interfere with their keenness for the national welfare. A German who fails in some national task is regarded as a public enemy. Even more is this so among the Latin races, which have no sentiment about anything under the sun, and always hound down the maker of a national failure as swiftly and pitilessly as animals destroy an ailing member of their species. Of course, it must be very nice for eminent public servants in England to know that they can instantly become idols by making of this or that task such a muddle that their official career will be closed. And it seems very nice of the English people to be so complaisant. But I think it a pity that, with all our chivalry, we have no gratitude left over for the men who have succeeded. It seems to me not right that the semblance of Lord Roberts should be booed, while that of "the Man who Did his Best" is wildly acclaimed. Lord Roberts himself did his best. It ought not to be accounted a sin in him that his best was nearly good enough. In the midst of the war, when sentimentality was totally eclipsed by panic, we were very grateful to Lord Roberts. Now that the panic has passed, sentimentality ought not to concentrate all its beams on General Buller.

It is useless, though, to reason with sentimentality. One can but study it. And a suburban music-hall is certainly the best school in which to study the special forms of it that inhere in the English public.

"DOROTHY O' THE" BOWERY

April 21, 1906

It is very natural that the Americans, having no history worth mentioning, should be so much keener than we on the "antiquities" that abound in Europe. It is very natural that they, having no art worth mentioning, should eagerly covet for their own country the objects of art that we take as a matter of course and hardly notice. I have never been inclined to join in the outcry that is raised whenever some famous work of art (of whose existence so few of us had hitherto been conscious) is in danger of being spirited away across the Atlantic. Why, my dear "D. S. M.", should we play the dog in the manger? We are surfeited with beauty. Why grudge this or that morsel of beauty to our starving "cousins"? Especially, too, when these poor relations are prepared to pay so handsomely for the transfer! At this moment, many loyal subjects of the King are secretly aggrieved that the royal collection of Whistler's etchings has been thrown on the market and bought by an American. Yet the objects of art in Windsor Castle vastly outnumber the motor cars. Why, pray, should a few scratchings on copper be hoarded?

We, as a business-like nation, ought rather to rejoice that we are ruled over by one who knows the right moment at which to sell. If there were a sudden "boom" in the late Herr Winterhalter's portraits, or in the seascapes of the Chevalier de Martino, why should not even these august works be allowed to flutter back to the native lands of their respective makers? Italy, I admit, is rich already in art-treasures, and might be accounted greedy in retrieving the Chevalier. But Germany is still poor: why should she not grasp again the master-hand of her fugitive son? Poorer yet is America. It seems only right that she should have the chance of gathering to her wide and wistful bosom, at last, the works of him who basely deserted her in order that he might achieve them.

It is not for America's sake only that I am glad whenever some famous work of art, "this side up, with care," crosses the Atlantic. I am glad, also, for the sake of that work of art. Its beauty will be intensified, out there. I never visit any one of our national collections without wishing it could be all disbanded. I should like to give it all away, broadcast, in "lots" of two or three—a "lot" apiece to every respectable householder who applied. Set in separate shrines, the uglier the shrine the better—these treasures would radiate their full significance. Massed together, they do but mar one another. You cannot rightly see them. There are too many of them. They fatigue you. Now, in a somewhat modified sense, my objection to these public galleries may be applied to England itself. So many are the beautiful old houses throughout England that they, too, mar one another. They are not packed together, of course, like objects in a collection. Yet, however wide the parks that enclose them, these houses are too near together, too many, for perfect admiration. Take, for example, Haddon Hall—the place taken by Messrs. Paul Kester and Charles Major, American dramatists, as the scene of "Dorothy o' the Hall." It is a lovely place in itself; but there are in England so many other places not less lovely. We cannot concentrate our minds on it. If we suddenly saw it (say) on the outskirts of Chicago, how much lovelier would it have grown for us! I wish that not pictures and statues only, but whole mansions could be carried in triumph over the water. I should wave them a hearty send-off from the docks. On the other hand, I should be the first to protest if some American millionaire, entering into possession of Haddon Hall, began to tamper with it where it stands. If starred and striped sun-blinds were affixed to the crumbling casements, and spread eagles of brass were ranged along the coping, and brazen statues of honest senators along the terrace, I should be very angry indeed. Of course, no American millionaire would tamper thus. No, *Sir*! He would guard the character of the place more jealously than could any Englishman. His reverence for it would be in proportion to its remoteness from his experience. But though, in matters of actual architecture, Americans are the least vandalistic of all races, they—some of them, let us say—are a trifle barbarous in matters of literature. I dare say that Messrs. Paul Kester and Charles Major, like so many of their compatriots, have visited Haddon Hall. I dare say that they went there thinking pretty thoughts about Dorothy Vernon, and stood there imbued with an exactly right sense of Dorothy's romance. I see them lingering by the postern gate, silent, with a tender light in their eyes, with a true vision of Dorothy in their souls. The silence is broken : "*Say, Paul,* [or *Charley,*] *we must* USE *this!*" I conjecture that they mapped out the scenario, with native brisk-ness, on their way back to the railway station. And what a scenario! Perhaps they felt inwardly ashamed of it—did their fell work reluctantly. But the chances are that they saw no harm in it. A man may have the most exquisite sensibilities, the keenest vision ; and yet, when he has to express himself through an art-form, become coarse and stupid. No dramatist, moreover, ever yet achieved popularity by deliberately "playing down to" the public. The public instantly finds out that trick, and will none of it. Mr. Kester, I know, is a very popular dramatist in America. So, I dare say, is Mr. Major. The chances are that they both did their best for "Dorothy o' the Hall." And what a best! Messrs. Kester and Major may dispute the accuracy of the parallel that I draw by inference between their work and the desecration of Haddon Hall by an American millionaire. I offer them a less imaginative parallel. Suppose I went to America, and visited some "show-place" corresponding (*mutatis mutandis*) with Haddon Hall. Suppose, for example, I visited, with an intense interest in its associations, Tammany Hall. What would Messrs. Kester and Major think of me if I proceeded to write, for the American public, a play called "Croker o' the Hall," showing the famous Boss as an exquisite figure of romance, and involving him in some romantically exquisite adventure? They would say to me "This won't do, Sir, for the American public." I wish I could complete my otherwise exact parallel by assuring Messrs. Kester and Major that the British public won't stand "Dorothy o' the Hall." But alas! such sentiment as the British public may have for Miss Vernon, and such power as it may have to discriminate between her and a Bowery "tough," are as nothing against its love of tawdry melodrama. The audience at the New Theatre, last Wednesday, seemed to be almost delirious with enjoyment. I am sure that no Bowery "tough" could be quite so crude a creature as the Dorothy of Messrs. Kester and Major. No matter. The authors may be pardoned a slight exaggeration from the model. It was necessary to bring the figure into consonance with the peculiar quality of their historical invention.

Miss Julia Neilson and Mr. Fred Terry are very popular. I wish they were so popular that they could force the public to accept them even in good plays. Two or three years ago they did make a great effort for art's sake. But "Sword and Song" had to be withdrawn very soon after its production. One cannot reasonably blame them for persisting now in the one kind of thing that pays. Certainly they cannot be accused of selecting a play for no other reason than that the chief part happened to suit Miss Neilson's style of acting. The part of Dorothy is mainly comedic; and Miss Neilson has no comedy in her: comedy is somewhere far from her, a mysterious, hard god, that must be frantically invoked, and laboriously appeased. A comedian might soften the dreadful outlines drawn by Messrs. Kester and Major. Skimming lightly through (or rather over) her part, she might, in some degree, dulcify it. Miss Neilson, trying to wring the full value out of every line, and having no natural comedy of her own to cover that value up, impressed me with her strength of character, but did not artistically please me. I welcomed the romantic passages (though romance, as purveyed by Messrs. Kester and Major, is a hardly less fearsome article than humour); for then Miss Neilson quieted down, and was able to give us something of herself. Mr. Fred Terry, who plays Sir John Manners, is a born romantic actor. True, he does not, I think, ever sound any depth of emotion.

When Queen Elizabeth (who dances a duet with Miss Vernon) decrees that Sir John shall be parted from his inamorata for a year, Mr. Terry murmurs "A year!" several times, with a beatific gaze, and in a voice thrilled with lyric rapture, as though Sir John had at last attained his heart's desire. It is not the strictly right effect; but it is somehow a more romantic one than any other actor on our stage could compass. Romantic acting is a matter not of truth, but of atmosphere; and this atmosphere Mr. Terry diffuses unceasingly, without effort. Could any one but he, hiding behind a bower of roses, thrust his face through the flowers, in sight of the audience, without seeming ridiculous? Mr. Terry thrusts his face thus, and stays thus for several seconds; and yet manages to remain, as he would say, "mahnly." It is a remarkable achievement.

"THE FASCINATING MR. VANDERVELDT"

May 5, 1906

Mr. Sutro has two manners, for two moods, in dramaturgy. Sometimes life is real, life is earnest to him, and must be strenuously preached about. At other times life appears to him as a trifle in itself, to which he owes no duty except a graceful attitude. It is in this mood that I admire him the more. His sermons do not greatly stir me : they seem too much informed by the desire to say what the congregation expects. But Mr. Sutro's grace in writing, like his humour, is a thing that comes directly from his own inner self. He is, since Mr. Oscar Wilde, the most "literary" of our playwrights—has, more than any other, a fine sense of words, and a delicate ear for cadences. In calling him "literary," I do not mean that he makes his characters talk "like books." In realistic plays of modern life, it is, of course, essential that the characters shall talk with apparent naturalness. Suppose one of the characters in a play is a costermonger. Obviously, it would be wrong that he should talk with classical propriety. Here the playwright can show his sense of "style" only by selecting such locutions as are at once most characteristic of costermongers at large and most pertinent to the matter in hand. For good or ill, England has no academy of letters; and, indirectly, one result—certainly an ill result—of this refusal is that the people in every stratum of society talk hardly better than costermongers. They have not, of course, specifically the same slang; but their slang is not less ugly than that which prevails in the Mile End Road; nor is their vocabulary of decent English words less limited; nor is their knowledge of grammar more sound; nor is their sense of rhythm better developed. Like most of our playwrights, Mr. Sutro casts his lines among the leisured classes. To make them talk with real naturalness, he would have to jettison his literary classicism as surely as he would in reproducing the exact manner of a costermonger. But only apparent naturalness is needed. And because the "barbarians" have, as a rule, pretty manners, and pleasing appearances, it is no strain on us to invest them with other graces also. Much of Mr. Sutro's new play consists of a contest of wit between the hero and a Lady Clarice Howland. Neither he nor she uses any phrase or construction that would be pedantic in a talker in real life. But I have rarely heard in real life any one use the English language so tastefully. What matter? The words do not sound unnatural. We merely feel that we are listening to a lady and gentleman who happen to be accomplished talkers. And in listening to this dialogue we have as much pleasure as had Mr. Sutro in composing it.

The actual scheme of the play is according to the formula that Mr. Henry Arthur Jones has often used. Lady Clarice is the rather frivolous but quite virtuous woman; and Mr. Vanderveldt is the *homme à bonnes fortunes* by whom she is compromised; and "The Cow and Calf" is the name of the compromising wayside inn. Mr. Sutro conducts the story with much skill; and, if we are not much excited by it, the fault is not his, but its. We know it so well—know so exactly how it must end. Lady Clarice must be reinstated in the world's favour, and the exact means of her reinstatement can evoke but a technical interest. Mr. Sutro gives a new twist to the formula by making his couple arrive at the inn by motor, instead of by rail; and also by making the lady adopt, in the last act, a defiant attitude towards her doubters. The details of the motor-drive are quite plausible and, so far as I can judge, accurate. But the lady's defiant attitude seems to me not in

keeping with her character and with the circumstances of the case.
Having disappeared in the afternoon with a gentleman of lax
principles and not having returned before the following morning,
she would surely not resent the anxiety of her friends and relations
to hear some sort of explanation. A strong-minded, Ibsenesque
heroine, with a contempt for social conventions, might, perhaps,
draw herself up to her full height, and snub her interrogators, as
does Lady Clarice. But is it natural for Lady Clarice to do so?
She is a perfectly conventional woman, who has undoubtedly
compromised herself; and she would, in the natural course of
things, welcome the opportunities she has of explaining things
satisfactorily. "If women would only put more trust in one
another, they would be more likely to gain the respect of men" is
in itself an admirable apothegm. Sir Austin Feverel might have
composed it, and preserved it in the Pilgrim's scrip. But it
wouldn't have leapt, just then, to the lips of Lady Clarice.

It is a pity for Miss Violet Vanbrugh that Lady Cicely has no
other lines which need to be delivered with an air of serious and
intense conviction. For Miss Vanbrugh excels in effects of
serious intensity. I think she has improved in effects of comedy
during the past few years. But I doubt whether she will ever
improve so far that Fate will be forced to acknowledge itself
wrong in not having let her be born a comedian. Fate will, I
think, always prefer to see her in those romantic tragedies and
melodramas to which she was predestined. Fate must be pleased
to notice that Mr. Bourchier, born a comedian, is ceasing to over-
lay his birthright with crude buffooneries. It is two or three
years since I had seen him act; and I was delighted by a very real
improvement. Evidently Mr. Bourchier now forswears those
devices by which he used, so industriously, to raise a laugh at any
cost. I hope I have had something to do with his conversion.
So far as his talent, apart from his personality, is concerned, he
could not play the part of Mr. Vanderveldt better. I notice
among the critics a disposition to suggest that he does not make
Mr. Vanderveldt live up to the epithet bestowed by Mr. Sutro.
But what man shall lay down laws as to what exactly constitutes
fascination for women? The critics, probably, would say that
Mr. Vanderveldt ought to have a more caressing voice, curlier
hair, a lither figure, a more tender regard in the eyes. It is true

that, on the stage, Don Juan usually has these trappings. But it is equally true that Don Juan, off the stage, very often hasn't them, and that the man who has them is very often a complete failure. Nor is there, off the stage, any such thing as a Don Juan (in the accepted sense). No man, I mean, ever was irresistible to every woman. Different women are attracted by different kinds of men. Ardent temperaments fascinate one woman; cold temperaments another. Strength of character or weakness of character, bravery or brain-power, a loud voice or a gentle voice, coarseness or refinement, tallness or shortness—all these and other mutually exclusive opposites appeal to different types of woman. It is true enough that Mr. Vanderveldt, as impersonated by Mr. Bourchier, is not "fascinating" according to the conventions of the theatre. But to say that he would not have fascinated Lady Clarice, and various other women, is to adventure where we have no possible foothold.

IN THE PIT

May 12, 1906

It was with much diffidence that I wrote, last week, about Mr. Sutro's new play. Usually I am well up in my subject—have a vivid impression to analyse. But of "The Fascinating Mr. Vanderveldt" I had only a very faint and hazy notion. Had I not happened to read a description of the play before I visited it, I could hardly have gathered any notion at all. Only through previous knowledge of what the characters were, and what they were doing, was I enabled to form enough of an opinion to write an article. A very uninteresting article I thought it when I read it last Sunday morning. I did not blame myself, though. No man can write well about a thing which he has had no chance of mastering at first hand.

How, you ask, had this chance been withheld from me? Well, three or four years ago I began to get on Mr. Arthur Bourchier's nerves. He no longer wanted my hints on the art of acting, and so, as a hint on the art of criticism, he ceased to send me tickets for

his theatre. Since then, I have not intruded at the Garrick
Theatre, except once or twice when Mr. Bourchier has produced
something that I was really anxious to see. I wanted to see Mr.
Sutro's play; so to the Garrick again I went; but, on my arrival,
found myself suffering under the disability common to lads who
are going to carve out a future in this great metropolis: I had only
half a crown in my pocket. To find my way to the pit entrance,
thrust my coin through a pigeon-hole, clutch at a brass ticket, and
descend a narrow flight of stone stairs, was for me the work of a
moment. I had no misgivings. Though I had never happened
to see a play from the pit, and my heart was leaping with the sense
of adventure, I knew no fear. How often, passing this or that
theatre, hours before the performance, had I seen a serried row of
men and women doggedly waiting outside the door that led to the
pit! Was it likely that they would spend their valuable time thus
if there were not a great treat in store for them? The Pit! There
was a certain traditional magic in the sound. There was some
secret of joy that I had often wished to elucidate. "I enclose my
card, and am, Sir, your obedient servant, AN OLD PITTITE."
How often in the newspapers had I read letters with this conclusion! And such letters—so oracular, permeated with so notable a
pride! It had often been borne in on me that there must be in the
pit something—some mystic grace—that enables a man to judge
more surely, to take himself more seriously, and to spend a happier
evening, than elsewhere. . . . It was with a glad heart that I
bounded down the stone steps.

Gradually my eyes accustomed themselves to the darkness, and
I groped my way to a vacant space that I discerned on the back-
most bench. Not until I was seated did I realise that the play had
begun. Yes, there, at a distance of what seemed to be fifty dark
miles or so, was a patch of yellowish light; and therein certain tiny
figures were moving. They were twittering, too, these figures. I
listened intently. I strained my ears, I strained my eyes. And,
since both my sight and my hearing are excellent, and since, as I
have told you, I had read a detailed notice of the play, I was
enabled to get some sort of vague illusion—the sort of illusion that
one gets from a marionette show. I felt with my hand the back
of the bench in front of me, hoping to find there a steel cylinder
with a slot. Perhaps, however, it is just as well that a man in the

pit cannot obtain a telescope in the way he can obtain a pair of opera-glasses in the stalls. If the mimes were so clarified and magnified for him that he could realise the changing expressions of their faces, then the faintness of their voices would seem to him all the stranger—would be all the more detrimental to his illusion of reality. So intensely, at the Garrick, did I have to listen, in order not to miss what the mimes were saying, that I thought there was perhaps something peculiar in the acoustics of the Garrick pit. I have consulted several frequenters of pits, and they tell me that the Garrick pit is a rather good one. Certainly Mr. Bourchier, Miss Vanbrugh, Mr. Aubrey Smith and other persons engaged in "The Fascinating Mr. Vanderveldt" are not bad elocutionists. And yet, the other day, with all my attention, I was constantly failing to overhear them, and having to use my experience of plays in general as a means of guessing at the drift. I saw an infinitesimal miniature of Miss Vanbrugh cross the stage and lay its hands in the hands of another lady who was just visible to the naked eye. And I heard this sound: "Want—pew." From the context of the play, and from the deportment of the two actresses, I was able to guess that Miss Vanbrugh had just said, "I want to help you." Probably my guess was right. But still, it is a bore to be kept guessing; and I was kept guessing in this way, from time to time, throughout the performance. The only members of the cast who never failed to make their words easily audible to me were Miss Henrietta Watson and Mr. Charles Goodhart. To the latter I owed another debt of gratitude, inasmuch as I could see him smile. Mr. Bourchier's smile, also, I could see, quite distinctly. For the rest, no facial expression was anywhere discernible. Had I been sitting in the stalls, I should doubtless have accused Mr. Bourchier of "clowning"—of smiling more widely than he ought to in a not farcical part. You may remember that last week I complimented him on having acquired the restraint needed for comedy. But he must not preen himself overmuch on that compliment. What seems like restraint to the man in the pit may seem like violent over-acting to the man in the stalls. And what seems like restraint to the man in the stalls may be a mere blank, a vacuum, to the man in the pit. Everything depends on the point of view.

The relativity of things occupied my mind throughout the

entr'actes of the play. Here was I, who am accustomed to occupy a comfortable stall without paying anything for it, and to see the mimes life-sized, and to hear them quite distinctly. And yet I seldom enjoy a play—nearly always have to console myself with the reflection that I am going to be paid by this Review for my presence. Here, on the other hand, were people who are accustomed to pay for uncomfortable seats, and who are not going to receive any payment for sitting on them and straining their eyes and ears for sight and sound of distant marionettes. And these people, obviously, are not rebellious. They really are glad to be there. Strange! For the constant pittite, no doubt, the strain of eyes and ears is less than for me. His eyes and ears must have been somewhat habituated by time. Moreover, if he has never happened to sit in a stall, he will not be conscious how much of the play and of the performance he is missing. Like Plato's cavemen, who knew naught but the shadows cast against the inner wall, and who would have been sorely puzzled by the realities, the constant pittite, doubtless, accepts as real creatures the tiny puppets vouchsafed to him. He accepts them, I mean, as the nearest approach that can in a playhouse be made to reality. I imagine that as seen from the gallery, and even from the "upper circle," the puppets must be still less likelike than as seen from the pit. And, since these three parts of the theatre hold the majority of the audience, I begin to understand why there is so little demand for dramatic truth to life. To me, sitting in the stalls, the persons of a play look very like human beings, and I want them to be allowed to behave accordingly. I am in a position to take them seriously. But to the majority of the audience they are little more than performing fleas. If I went to criticise a troupe of performing fleas, I should not write and attack their trainer because the performance had not closely tallied with my experience of human beings. I should not go to be instructed. I should go to be amused. It is in this spirit, necessarily, that the majority of people go to the play. They know that they cannot see anything that will remind them of actual life. What matter, then, how great be the degree of remoteness from reality? The marvel to me, since my visit to the pit of the Garrick, is not that the public cares so little for dramatic truth, but that it can sometimes tolerate a play which is not either the wildest melodrama or the wildest farce. Where low tones and fine shades are practically invisible, one would expect an exclusive insistence on splodges of garish colour. . . . I shall in future be less hard on the public than has been my wont.

A NOTE ON THE BALLET

May 19, 1906

Ballet, as an art-form, inspires me with less of delight than of affectionate interest. It was at its perihelion in the time of our fathers. And for all men the time of their fathers is the most delicious time of all—just near enough to be intelligible, just far enough to seem impossible. I am glad I never saw Grisi, glad I never saw Taglioni. Their names would not make such music for me, had the vision been vouchsafed. Nor would those pale-tinted portraits of them, still to be seen in out-of-the-way places— Taglioni floating through a glade; Grisi perching on the boards with the tip of one foot—touch so agreeably in my bosom the chords of pathos. I am glad the tradition of the ballet has not been lost. I like to see the "haute école" not quite disestablished, after all these years, by skirt-dancers and cake-walkers. But the æsthete in me rejoices less than the sentimentalist. As a representation of life, ballet fails for me. I am a writer, and thus a lover of words, and where no words are is a void for me. At least, there is a void where words might have been but are not. In a painting I do not feel the need of words, for they are excluded by the nature of the art. But they are not excluded thus from ballet. Their exclusion, the substitution of mere gesture, is quite arbitrary. There is no essential reason why ballet should not, like opera, have words. It gains nothing by the sacrifice, and (for me) loses nearly all. There is (so far as I, in a theatre, am concerned) no reality in a wordless representation of life. And, however fantastic be a representation of life, it ought to awaken a sense of reality—a fantastic sense of reality. Ballet not merely gives me no illusion: it conveys no meaning to me. Here, I admit, its failure is due partly to a defect in myself. A man ought to be able to master the meanings of formalised gesture. When a ballerina lays the palms of her hands against her left cheek, and then, snatching them away, regards them with an air of mild astonishment, and then, swaying slightly backwards, touches her forehead with her finger-tips, and then suddenly extends both arms above her head, I ought of course to be privy to her innermost meaning. I ought to have a thorough grasp of her exact state of mind. Friends have often explained to me, with careful demonstrations, the significance of the various gestures that are used in ballet; and these gestures are not very many; and I have more than once committed them to memory, hoping that, though I could never be illuded, I might at least be not bemused. But, after all this trouble, the next ballet that I have seen has teased and puzzled me as unkindly as ever. Is it that gestures were given to the ballerina to conceal her thoughts? Or is it merely that the quickness of the hand deceives the eye? Unable to catch for one fleeting instant the drift of the lady's meaning, I concentrate myself on her merely visual aspect. And here, again, I am disappointed. Of course it is very wonderful that a woman should be fashioned—or rather, should have contrived to fashion herself—thus. How many hours (I have often asked myself), on how many cold grey mornings, and in what large, bare, locked room, at the back of what house, must have gone to the making of this strange shape? Nature is not, of course, a conscious artist. She aims at usefulness, not at beauty. The reason why arms are slighter than legs is not, I presume, that any first principle in beauty demands that they should be so. Arms are slighter than legs because they have not to sustain the burden of the body. And thus we, who know no first principle in beauty, and derive our ideas of beauty through what we know to be useful, would be really repelled at sight of a woman whose arms preponderated over her legs. Such a phenomenon might be achieved if a woman were trained from childhood to walk on the palms of her hands. Suppose, on the contrary, a woman who had been trained from childhood not to use her hands and arms for any purpose whatsoever. She, too, would be unsightly. The meagreness of her arms, in proportion to the rest of her, would seem to us unlovely. And yet her arms would be not more meagre in proportion to her legs than are the arms in proportion to the legs of a ballerina. I do not say that the structure of a ballerina is an offence against abstract beauty; for I have no means of knowing what abstract beauty is. But certainly this structure jars my æsthetic sense, as being an obvious deviation from what is natural. It is natural enough that a woman should dance sometimes, just as it is natural that she should walk, sit, lie down. But it is unnatural that dancing should be the business of her life. And Nature takes vengeance by destroying her symmetry, by making her ridiculous. Poor ballerina! Is it for this that she has been toiling, toiling, day by day, in that large, bare, back-room—toiling to become physically ridiculous? That is a question that has often asked itself in my brain during the performance of a ballet. All those trippings, and pirouettings, and posturings at incredible angles, are very wonderful of course, and are paid for at a very high rate. If the ballerina is not extravagant, she will be able to retire into private life, with a comfortable income, before old age shall have overtaken her. She will be able to cease to be ridiculous. Meanwhile my heart goes out to her. It comes in again quickly. There had been no need to pity her. Regret is all that was needed. Such power of thought as she may once have had was long since absorbed into her toes. She does not know that she is ridiculous. Her fixed smile is no assumption to hide an aching heart. She really fancies that she is admirable, admired. And so she is, in the way that a performing dog is admirable, admired. It is wonderful that a dog can learn to behave more or less like a human being. It is wonderful that a human being can learn to cut capers seemingly beyond human power. But dog and human being alike cause in us—in those of us, at least, who are a little thoughtful—more of sorrow than of pleasure. My sentimentalism rejoices in the survival of the ballet. But my humanitarianism is revolted by the survival of the ballerina . . . Mlle Genée? Ah no; I grant an exception there. No monstrous automaton is that young lady. Perfect though she is in the "haute école," she has by some miracle preserved her own self. She was born a comedian, and a comedian she remains, light and liberal as foam. A mermaid were not a more surprising creature than she—she of whom one half is as that of an authentic ballerina, whilst the other is that of a most intelligent, most delightfully human actress. A mermaid were, indeed, less marvellous in our eyes. She would not be able to defuse any semblance of humanity into her tail. Mlle Genée's intelligence seems to vibrate to her very toes. Her dancing, strictliest classical though it is, is a part of her acting. And her acting, moreover, is of so fine a quality that she makes the old ineloquent conventions of gesture tell their meanings to me, and tell them so exquisitely that I quite forget my craving for words. In "Coppélia," which is now being enacted at the Empire, Mlle Genée has a longer and better part than she has yet played. And the delight she gives us is accordingly greater than ever. . . . Taglioni in "Les Arabesques"? I suspect, in my heart of hearts, she was no better than a doll. Grisi in "Giselle"? She may, or may not, have been passable. Genée! It is a name that our grandchildren will cherish, even as we cherish now the names of those bygone dancers. And alas! our grandchildren will never believe, will never be able to imagine, what Genée was.

IBSEN

May 26, 1906

Sometimes, when a great man dies, it is difficult to believe that he is dead. In a sense, it is difficult to believe this of Ibsen. He was the only Norwegian who excited any interest outside Norway. He alone was "good copy" for the journalists who supply Europe with Norwegian news. And thus, during recent years, we had read again and again that he was dying. Finding that he always lived on, we had ceased, at length, to be credulous. We had begun to think Ibsen immortal. And now, something of the incredibility of those rumours that he was dying attaches itself to the very news of his death. Those ever-recurring rumours had seemed to be so essential a feature of the modern newspaper. It is difficult to believe that there will be no more of them.

Ibsen's, however, is not one of those deaths which are in themselves hard to realise. Had he died some years ago, when he was still one of the vital forces of the world, the sudden blank would indeed have taxed our imagination. But, as it is, the force had long ago been spent. Six years have passed since Ibsen gave us "When We Dead Awaken." And that play, interesting and valuable though it was in its significance, was the work of an evidently failing hand. It was evidently, moreover, meant to be an epilogue. The volcano was extinct. Had Ibsen died even after "John Gabriel Borkman," we should have suffered a tragic sense of loss, knowing not of what riches we had been robbed. But to the work that he began in 1850 he wrote "finis" in 1890. Nothing is not there that might have been. Our loss is a merely personal one.

Are we down-hearted? No. It was interesting to think of Ibsen as being still actually alive—as breathing the air that we breathed. But the thought sounded no echo in emotion. I can imagine that people must have been really touched and stirred by the thought of Walt Whitman's survival. I did not begin to read that poet till some time after he was dead. But I am old enough to have been thrilled by the fact that Robert Browning was still living, and to have felt the world emptier for me when he died. Great men may be divided into two classes: the lovable and the unlovable; and, as surely as Whitman and Browning are typical of the one class, Ibsen is typical of the other. "Friends," he wrote, in one of his letters to Georg Brandes, "are a costly luxury, and when one invests one's capital in a mission in life, one cannot afford to have friends. The expensiveness of friendship does not lie in what one does for one's friends, but in what one, out of regard for them, leaves undone. This means the crushing of many an intellectual germ." Ibsen had no lack of friends, so far as his genius attracted to him many men who were anxious to help him. And he used these men, unstintingly, when he had need of them. That volume of his correspondence, published not long ago, reveals him as an unabashed applicant for favours. Nor is this by any means to his discredit. The world was against him. He was poor, and a cast-away. He had to fight hard in order that he might fulfil the genius that was in him. It was well that he had no false delicacy in appealing to any one who could be of use to him. But, throughout that correspondence, one misses in him the sense of gratitude. One misses in him the capacity for friendship. Not one "intellectual germ" would he sacrifice on that altar. He was, indeed, a perfect type of the artist. There is

29

something impressive, something magnificent and noble, in the spectacle of his absorption in himself—the impregnability of that rock on which his art was founded. But, as we know, other men, not less great than Ibsen, have managed to be human. Some "intellectual germs" may thereby have perished. If so, they are to be mourned, duly. And yet, could we wish them preserved at the price that Ibsen paid for them? Innate in us is the desire to love those whom we venerate. To this desire, Ibsen, the very venerable, does not pander.

We need not, I think, condemn ourselves as sentimentalists, for being disappointed. I think we may fairly accuse Ibsen of a limitation. Out of strength cometh forth sweetness. The truth of this proverb is not always, I admit, obvious. The Dean of St. Patrick's, for example, was strong ; and sweetness did certainly not exude from him, except in portions of his private correspondence. (Some day, perhaps, it will be found that Ibsen had a soft side to his nature. But that will not affect our general view of him as a writer, any more than Swift's private use of baby language affects our general view of *him*.) Swift's strength lay in his intellect, and in his natural gift for literature ; and a gigantic strength it was. But his harshness was not symptomatic of strength. It was symptomatic of a certain radical defect in himself. He was a Titan, not an Olympian. So was Ibsen, who, without Swift's particular defect, was but a shade less harsh in his outlook on the world. He was an ardent and tender lover of ideas ; but mankind he simply could not abide. Indeed, I fancy he cared less for ideas as ideas than as a scourge for his fellow-creatures. Just now I spoke of him as having been an extinct volcano after "When We Dead Awaken" ; and the application of that simile was more apt than it usually is. Volcanic he had ever been, from "Catilina" onwards. His plays were a sequence of eruptions, darkening the sky, growling and sending out flashes of light more unpleasant than the darkness, and overwhelming and embedding the panic-stricken fugitives. Much has been written about his "purpose" in this and that play. "Purpose," in the sense of wishing to reform this or that evil, he never had. Primarily, he was an artist, pure and simple, actuated by the artist's joy in reproduction of human character as it appeared to his keen, unwandering eyes. But he had a joy within a joy : joy in the havoc he wrought.

Vesuvius has no "purpose": it does but obey some law within
itself. Ibsen obeyed some similar law, and differed from Vesuvius only in the conscious pleasure that he had in the law's fulfilment. Peace was repulsive to him because the world was
repulsive. The world's green pastures, smiling so smugly up at
him, must be scorched black with cinders: not otherwise could any
good thing ever grow out of them. And if the good thing actually
grew, of what use, pray, would it be? Down with it! Eruptions,
destruction: nothing else matters. Liberty! What is the use of
that, except as an incentive to unrest? "Rome," he writes to
Brandes, after the proclamation of the republic, "was the one
sanctuary in Europe, the one place that enjoyed true liberty—
freedom from the political tyranny of liberty ... The delicious
longing for liberty—that is now a thing of the past. I for one am
bound to confess that the only thing about liberty that I love is the
fight for it; I care nothing about the possession of it." At any
rate, he cared nothing about other people's possession of it.

Because the men in his plays are mostly scored off by the
women, he has often been credited with a keen sympathy for the
feminine sex. "Strong-minded" women used to regard him as
their affectionate ally. It was not them he cared for, poor dears;
it was only the scrimmage. Men were "up"; so "up" with
women. Had Nature placed women in the ascendant, Ibsen
would have been the first to tug them down. No dispassionate
reader of his plays can fail to see that his sympathy with women
is a mere reflex of his antipathy to their lords and masters. The
general impression that he had tried to help the cause of their
emancipation was enough to send him off at a tangent. You
remember how flatly he denied, at a banquet given some years ago
in his honour, that he had had any such purpose whatsoever. He
had merely, he declared, portrayed certain tendencies. For his
part, he considered that woman's sphere was the home. Quite
feminine tears were shed, thereupon, by strong-minded women
in every quarter of the globe. And to those "droppings of moist
tears" Ibsen, we may be sure, listened with grim pleasure.

It was a strange mind, this mind into which I have been peering.
Posterity, too, I think, will always, from time to time, peer into it,
with something of my own awe. Even when time shall have
robbed the plays of the sharp savour that for us they have, Ibsen

himself will be as dominant a figure as he is for us. Against his lack of love may be set the fact that he loved not even himself. Throughout his life an artist essentially, he wrote in "When We Dead Awaken" a savage attack on the artistic nature which he exemplified. And, feeble though this final play is in execution, it seems to me deadlier in intention than any of the others. Perhaps it is but another instance of Ibsen's egoism that he reserved his most vicious kick for himself.

YVETTE GUILBERT AND ALBERT CHEVALIER

June 23, 1906

I went one afternoon this week to the Duke of York's Theatre, and saw Mme Yvette Guilbert and Mr. Albert Chevalier in juxtaposition. It seemed appropriate that these two should be together. The name of each conjures up visions of the early 'nineties. Both were innovators in method and in subject-matter, Mr. Chevalier weaving a network of romance around costermongers, Mme Guilbert depicting in hard, sharp outline the tragedies and comedies of the least pleasant persons in Paris. Years have passed, revising somewhat the aspect of both artists. Both were ethereal. Both are normally plump. And their outlook, not less than their aspect, has expanded. Mme Guilbert's is no longer confined to "les trous dangereux," though she still keeps an eye on them. She ranges over the gay and harmless provinces of France, in the gay and harmless past. Poudrée, she sings of Brittany; and in a crinoline she warbles of Parthenay; and in a peculiar costume meant to suggest that of a bygone English peasant she essays the folk songs of our own counties. Mr. Chevalier, in like manner, is unfaithful to the Old Kent Road, and deems alien from himself nothing that is human. He does not, like Mme Guilbert, dally with the past; but his range over the present is unbounded. Altogether, there is a distinct kinship between these two artists. And thus the differences between them have a certain significance, as illustrating the differences between French and English art.

No one, I imagine, will dispute the platitude that French acting is better than English. The points of superiority are many; but the most noticeable of them all is the quickness and apparent ease with which (I speak, of course, generally) French mimes express as much as can by English mimes be expressed only with much deliberation and apparent effort. I cannot conceive a better illustration of this difference than is offered by Mr. Chevalier and Mme Guilbert in double harness. Mr. Chevalier is not, of course, thoroughly English. He has Italian as well as French blood in his veins. And this admixture accounts for the vivacity of face and figure that surprised us so much in the early 'nineties, setting him so far apart from the ordinary music-hall artists that we had known. But, despite his cosmopolitan breeding, it was only on the English stage that he graduated. And so, despite his vivacity, he has never picked up the knack of ease and quickness. Indeed, his vivacity itself seems to act as a stumbling-block. He makes a dozen gestures, a dozen grimaces, when one would be ample. He suits the action to the word so insistently that every word, almost, has an action all to itself. Often the action is a very elaborate one, insomuch that when the way is clear, at length, for the next word, you have quite lost sight of the last word but one. In one of his rustic songs—"Wot vur do 'ee lov oi?"—he speaks of a kiss and of holding hands. Before he comes to the word "kiss" he violently kisses the air for quite a long time; and when he illustrated the holding of hands I feared that he would never, never unclasp them. Mr. Chevalier might reply that in this song he is merely illustrating the slowness of an agrestic mind. To which I should retort that every one of his other very diverse impersonations is marred by just that same extremity of slowness. Every one of them is admirably conceived; and the words, written by Mr. Chevalier himself, admirably express the conception. If only Mr. Chevalier would allow them and the conception a certain amount of liberty to take care of themselves! If only he would not overwhelm them with illustration! We may be fools, but we are not such fools as he takes us for. His points do not need such an unconscionable amount of hammering, to drive them home for us. If he were the owner of an inexpressive face and voice and hands, then, perhaps, all this strenuousness of his would be indispensable. As a matter of fact, every part of him happens to be mercurial. Evidently he under-rates himself as much as us.

One reason why I deplore his passion for over-emphasis is that the songs, as songs, lose thereby their savour. The lilt of the music disappears. The accompanist sits at the piano, waiting patiently till Mr. Chevalier will sing another half bar or so; and we sit patiently wondering what sort of a tune it is. One of Mme Guilbert's virtues is that she never forgets that a singer's first duty to a song is to sing it. Always she obeys the rhythm of the music. All her acting is done within that right limitation. Yet is not lost one tittle of the acting necessary to express the full meaning of the words. I do not think that her face, voice, and hands are more naturally eloquent than Mr. Chevalier's. But she knows just how much use to make of them. Notice, in the famous "Ma Grandmère," how perfectly she differentiates the words of the girl from those of the old woman, yet with hardly a perceptible pause, with hardly a perceptible change of key. Something happens in her eyes, and we know that it is the girl speaking: we see the girl herself; and then again, in another instant, we see the old woman. One can imagine the pauses with which Mr. Chevalier would mark these transitions, and the violent contortions he would go through before he got under weigh. And yet he would not make us realise the old woman and the girl half so vividly as does Mme Guilbert. We should realise that he was performing an ingenious feat of character-acting. We should think him frightfully clever. But—well, it never strikes us that Mme Guilbert is clever. She does but fill us with a perfect illusion of whatsoever scene she sings, of whatever type she apes. How she does it is (at the moment of watching her) a mystery. And but for that mystery she couldn't do it.

Mme Guilbert's restraint is so exquisite, she so perfectly effaces herself in the subjects of her songs, that I cannot understand how she has let herself fall into the habit of flinging restraint to the winds and luridly revealing herself when she sings the last line. In some of her songs this habit is absolutely fatal to the effect. Obviously, for example, "La Grandmère" ought to end on the note of quiet melancholy that has been struck throughout. (You remember the refrain:

GUILBERT AND CHEVALIER

"Combien je regrette
Mon bras si dodu,
Ma jambe bien faite,
Et le temps perdu.")

When Mme Guilbert sings this refrain for the last time, she pauses after the third line, throws back her head, spreads out her arms to the audience and utters "et le temps perdu" in a tone of radiant ecstasy, as much as to say "*Haven't* I sung that well?" Again, at the end of "La Glu,"—"'le cœur disait, en pleurant, 'T'es tu fait mal, mon pauvre enfant?'"—it is obvious that the words ought to be spoken quite faintly. Mme Guilbert drives them home with an emphasis which not Mr. Chevalier himself could surpass. We lose all sense that it is the heart of the murdered mother that is speaking. We lose all the piteousness of the song. We are conscious only of Mme Guilbert demanding applause. I have often heard her sing both these songs. I am sure she used not to spoil them thus.

J. L. TOOLE

August 4, 1906

By a decorous tradition, the newspapers always "deeply regret to announce" the death of a well-known man. The formula rings false, because a less decorous tradition compels the newspapers to have accumulated in readiness for the saddening event a store of gladdening anecdotes, which shall be published the moment after the breath is out of the body. As applied to Mr. Toole's death, the formula struck another and especial discord. Every one who knew the circumstances of his life had for years been pitying him for his survival. Among those who knew him, this pity was still deeper, and was doubtless (like the affection they had for him) deep in proportion to their degree of intimacy.

The tragedy of his survival was brought into sharp relief, a few months ago, by the death of his greatest friend, Irving. It was quite possible for the newspapers to "regret to announce" that

death "deeply." As an actor, Irving was not far past the pleni-
tude of his powers. In him a flame was extinguished. But for
that very reason his death was, for him, a happy one. He was not
spared to feel the bitterness of decay. Thus had Toole been
spared, unmercifully, year after year. He had not "lagged superfluous on the stage." The nature of his illness had prevented
that, had given him a yet harder lot. He had lagged superfluous in
life, or rather in living death. He, the volatile low-comedian—
the little man with the elastic face and the eyeglass, the odd
gambols and catch-words, the ridiculous high spirits. A little old
man, sitting motionless, with features all rigid, speaking in a
hollow whisper. . . . Had Irving, the tragedian, suffered such a
fate as this, I think it would not have seemed so tragic. In his last
years, except when he was on the stage, Irving seemed to be a very
old man—very old for his years. It seemed almost inexplicable
that on the stage he could act still with such force and fire. But to
have pitied him would have been an act of impertinence, of which
no one was guilty. Eld, in him, was but an added grace, an added
power. It was a glittering thread in the spell he wove on you. It
may even have been, to some extent, an assumption. Even had he
suffered the fate of Toole, I think one would not have dared to pity
him. His dominancy would have been as great as ever. Always,
after his young Bohemian days, he had been a personage somewhat
aloof, somewhat enthroned. Toole, on the contrary, had never
ceased to be a thoroughgoing Bohemian, had never ceased to be
"a jolly good fellow," full of the rough-and-ready give-and-take of
friendship and acquaintance. Thus, when it was ordained that
this expansive creature should be contracted into himself, what
was there left? It were well had nothing at all been left.

Irving, by reason of his genius, had a perfect right to take himself seriously. As I only once saw Toole act, and was then a small
boy, to whom a play and a play's performance were matters of
slight interest in comparison with the great fact that I was actually
in a theatre, I cannot say certainly whether Toole had a right to
take himself seriously and was therefore the more to be admired
for not availing himself of it. I gather from hearsay that he was
not, indeed, much of an artist; rather, a droll, with a capacity for
pathos of a kind that would not nowadays, perhaps, seem very
pathetic. Fashions in drollery change more quickly than fashions

in pathos ; and I dare say that Toole's performances might not have made me laugh very much. But I should have liked to see him playing his practical jokes in private life. He seems to have been really an artist in practical jokes. They are out of fashion now. They are looked down on and discouraged. I, however, though I have not the gift for playing them, take a great delight in seeing them played, or even in hearing about them. Of course, I discriminate. Booby-traps and apple-pie beds are stupid. Such art as there may be in the making of them is a low form of art, and has been practised too much. It is perhaps because they and their kind have been overdone that people nowadays fail to do justice to the higher kinds, in which a genuine artistic gift may be used delightfully. The higher kinds of practical joke are not physical at all, but intellectual. To conceive a really good "mystification" is a test of imaginative faculty; and to execute one well is often a test of mimetic power, of moral courage and self-control, of personal magnetism and knowledge of men. Toole, like so many of the actors in his generation, seems to have spent a very great portion of his private life in playing practical jokes of this kind; and many of his achievements are classics. I dare say that they, and not his triumphs on the stage, were what he looked back on most wistfully in the last years of his life. I remember a photograph that used to be in all the shop-windows : Irving and Toole together; Toole evidently not quite comfortable in that public juxtaposition, but trying to look very dignified. And I remember another photograph, a large one, which I once saw in the window of a photographer somewhere near the northern end of the Edgware Road. It was gorgeously framed in the centre of the window, and evidently the pride of the devious artist who had made it. It represented a garden of Maida Vale-ish aspect, with Toole and Mr. Arthur Roberts standing in a small group of friends whose faces were not known to me. And how perfectly comfortable, in that juxtaposition, Toole looked ! I can see him now, and to this day I wonder what was the particular form of mystification that he and Mr. Roberts had just been playing on the local photographer, and were going to resume as soon as the sitting was over.

Who knows but that even in his last tragic years of waiting he used to plan new mystifications which could never be carried out? For it was a part of his tragedy that his mind did not cease to be

active. Though he could not, at the dinners and suppers which
he used to attend till even that melancholy distraction was denied
him, join in the general talk, and could but sit turning his eyes in
the direction of whoever happened at the moment to be talking,
his mind was working all the while. Now and again he would
make a motion with his hand, and the men nearest to him, bending forward, would hear, uttered laboriously in that fearful
whisper, some little comment that was always shrewd, often
witty, never (though it so well might have been) bitter.

MR. SHAW'S RODERICK HUDSON

November 24, 1906

When an artist takes a theme which has already been taken by
another and very different artist, comparison of the two works is
sure to amuse us, and will probably, too, instruct us, helping us to
realise the peculiarities of each man more clearly than before.

One of Mr. Henry James' earliest themes was a youth endowed
with artistic genius, but not endowed with moral sense. Roderick
Hudson, whom you doubtless remember—for who, having read
the book, could forget him?—went about "using" people quite
unscrupulously, taking everything, giving nothing except his
fascination, and caring not a jot how much distress he inflicted on
the people around him. Louis Dubedat, the central figure of
Mr. Shaw's new play, is, essentially, just such another as Roderick
Hudson. But Mr. Shaw is, essentially, not just such another as
Mr. Henry James. Indeed I cannot imagine two minds, or two
artistic methods, more divergent than the Shavian and the Jacobean. Mr. James must excuse my invention of this adjective. To
Mr. Shaw I need not apologise, for "Shavian" was invented by
himself. He was the first to feel the need of that adjective. He
has ever been conscious of himself as a peculiar, definite, detached
force—a light that must not be hidden under a bushel. Mr.
James, on the other hand, has never seemed to have that kind of
self-consciousness (a word which I use in no derogatory sense).

So far as he is conscious of self, he is eager only for self-effacement. He has used the "first person singular" very often in his stories; but only because he can observe his characters the more closely by playing some subordinate part in their midst. He is devoted, passionately, to his art—the art of portraying men and women as he sees them. He never judges men and women. Or rather, he never pronounces judgment. No industrious and intuitive reader of his books can have failed to deduce that he has a very strong moral sense. He hates selfishness. He loves honour—loves, indeed, a sense of honour so punctilious that its effects are apt to be rather exasperating to readers who are only averagely good. But he never lets his moral prejudices be prejudicial to his characters. He never tries to set in an unduly attractive light the things that he loves, or to blacken the things that he hates. The hand of the artist in him is held tightly over the mouth of the preacher. In Mr. Shaw, the preacher is ever vocal. Not that the artist in him is weak or idle : he manfully tries that all the characters shall have fair play. The preacher disapproves strongly of them, for the most part. They are all, with few exceptions, on the penitents' bench. But the artist insists that they shall all have their say, and a respectful hearing. And the ratiocinator (who is even stronger than the preacher in Mr. Shaw, and stronger far than the artist) insists that they shall all, severally, score—to the greater glory of G. B. S.

Louis Dubedat scores right and left. He is always scoring. He scores even under the shadow of death. And Mr. Shaw has, moreover, been as anxious to make his death-bed pathetic as was Dickens to make Little Nell's. And, where Dickens failed, Mr. Shaw has succeeded. The pathos here is real. I defy you not to be touched by it, while it lasts. But I defy you, when it is over, to mourn. Even if the curtain fell on Dubedat's dying breath, you would feel that his death was a good riddance. In point of fact, the curtain does not fall for some time. We hear the un-emotional comments of the doctors, varied by the very emotional comments of one of them. I could feel that the audience did not like this. And, though I have not, at the moment of writing, read any of the criticisms, I am sure that Mr. Shaw has been more or less violently attacked for lack of taste. Certainly the scene was rather painful. But if it was a true scene, what matter? And it *is*

443

true that doctors do not take death emotionally. The sentimental
platitudes uttered by one of the doctors in this scene would not
have been uttered by him in real life, for the sole benefit of his
colleagues. In that respect, the scene is untrue. But let no one
suggest that these platitudes, absurd though they are, are not very
like the kind of thing that would be said, at such a juncture, by a
rather stupid layman. Clever people, in the midst of great
emotion, say nothing; for they know that whatever they might say
would be inadequate. Stupid people rush into speech, speech not
one whit more ridiculous than this doctor's. No, Mr. Shaw was
not merely "playing for a laugh." He was trying to reproduce a
thing that exists in life. And his error was but in forgetting that
this man was a doctor addressing himself to his colleagues. There
was no "error of taste," such as, I am sure, he has been accused of.
Nor was there an error of art. For, as I have said, we do not, after
a moment, feel the slightest desire to mourn Dubedat.

And yet we have never ceased to mourn Roderick Hudson. He
was a selfish brute, but he cast his spell as surely over us readers as
he did over all the characters in the book. We, too, would have
gladly sacrificed ourselves to his convenience. We believed in
his genius. Those few things that he wrought—the Adam, the
Eve, the bust of his mother, and one or two others—were as real
to us and as fine as though we had beheld them with our own eyes.
And when Roderick Hudson died we thought of all those blocks
of marble from which beauty would never spring now. Mr. James
has a wonderful way of imagining and describing works of art. He
infects us with his own enthusiasm. The works of art are as real
to us as they are to him. Fortunately his books are not illustrated
with reproductions of some artist's notion of the masterpieces
described. Such illustrations, however admirable, would tend to
damp our enthusiasm. And, doubtless, one of the reasons why
we do not fervently believe in the genius of Louis Dubedat is that
we see his work. I do not say that they are not "able," these
sketches on the walls of his studio. Evidently, Dubedat could
have earned plenty of money as a "black and white man" on an
illustrated weekly paper. And the posthumous "one man show"
is a revelation of his versatility. Dubedat seems to have caught, in
his brief lifetime, the various styles of *all* the young lions of the
Carfax Gallery. Budding genius is always, I know, imitative;

444

but not so frantically imitative as all that. Nor was Dubedat exactly a budding genius. We are asked to accept him as a soon-to-be-recognised master. Of course, it is not Mr. Shaw's fault that the proper proofs are not forthcoming. But it certainly is a fault in Mr. Shaw that he wished proper proofs to forthcome. He ought to have known that even if actual masterpieces by one un-known man could have been collected by the property-master, we should yet have wondered whether Dubedat was so very remark-able after all. Masterpieces of painting must be left to an audience's imagination. And Mr. Shaw's infringement of so obvious a rule is the sign of a certain radical lack of sensitiveness in matters of art. Only by suggestion can these masterpieces be made real to us. And how can this suggestion best be made to us? Clearly, by the character and conversation of the artist himself as presented on the stage, and (in a lesser degree) by what is said of his work by other persons in the play.

The other persons in the play say a good deal about Dubedat's work. Mrs. Dubedat, especially, dwells on it. But a wife's evidence is no more admissible in the case of an artist than in the case of a man charged with murder. One of the doctors is a con-noisseur, and freely buys Dubedat's work. But the evidence of one connoisseur is not final. We examine Dubedat himself. He talks much, and well, about art. So do many quite bad painters. Indeed, it is generally the quite bad painters who are most fluent. Good painters think rather with their eyes and hands than with their brains, and thus have a difficulty in general conversation. If you coax them from silence, they will describe illuminatively, but they cannot ratiocinate: that is not their business. It is very much the business of Louis Dubedat. As I have said, he scores right and left. He has among strangers none of the shyness and the unreadiness of a man who can paint. And he "knocks off" brilliant sketches on the backs of menus with all the good-nature of a man who can't. In a word, we disbelieve in him as a genius. Only as a scamp is he real to us.

And his very scampishness is of a kind that would destroy any illusion we might have of him as a great painter. His is not the large, vague unscrupulousness of self-centred genius. It is the "slimness" of the confidence-trick man. When I said that Dubedat was "essentially" the same as Roderick Hudson, I meant, of course, that Mr. Shaw's intention had been the same as Mr. James'. But Mr. Shaw's deep-rooted disgust for the unmoral artist has prevented him, despite his constant efforts at fairness, from presenting this figure worthily. The ever-quick succession of petty impostures played by Dubedat is, of course, vastly amusing, but . . . why all these buts? Why have I been carping all this while about the central figure, instead of expressing the joy that the whole brilliant play gave me, and trying to communicate something of that joy to you? I evidently haven't yet learnt my business.

THE CAMPDEN WONDER

January 12, 1907

This sounds rather like a rose, but is something very different indeed. In Campden, in the seventeenth century, lived a certain Mrs. Perry, a widow with two sons. Neither of the sons was clever, but Richard, the younger, was good, and John, the elder, was bad. Richard earned higher wages than John, who spent the greater part of his time in drinking. The two quarrelled; and John determined to avenge himself for the taunts that had been thrown at him by Richard. Mr. Harrison, their master, had been missing for several days. Would it not, John asked himself, be a good thing to accuse himself, his mother, and Richard, of having murdered Mr. Harrison for gold? The more he thought the plan over, the better he liked it. And, in due course, the three were sent to the gallows. Just after they had been hanged, Mrs. Harrison arrived at the gaol to announce that her husband had come safely home.

Such, briefly, is the story which Mr. John Masefield tells us. And, on the whole, very well he tells it. The first of the three scenes is rather tedious, by reason of the manner of the quarrel between the brothers. "Ye're a drunken sot, John Perry." "No, I bain't." "Yes, you be." "Oh, I'm a drunken sot, am I?" "Yes, and you're a disgrace to Campden." "No, I bain't." "Yes, you be." "Oh, I'm a disgrace to Campden, am I?"

John says Richard has "crossed him" in his work. Richard denies that. John repeats it. Richard then calls him a drunken sot; and so on, round and round, interminably. Now, I dare say that the Gloucestershire peasants in the seventeenth century did not excel in the bright cut and thrust of controversy. I have no doubt that this scene between John and Richard is perfectly true to life—so far as it goes. For perfect truth, I dare say, it ought to go much further. But perfect truth to life is not art. And this scene, even so far as it goes, is very much too long. It is right that we should feel the dulness of these two peasant minds. But dulness is a thing which the artist should suggest. He ought not to drill it into us. Mr. Masefield ought to have started his play in the middle of the quarrel: "I tell's ee agen, John Perry, ye're a drunken sot," &c. My idea of the dialect may not be sound. But Mr. Masefield will perceive that dramatically I am right. For he has a very keen instinct for drama. The second scene—the scene of the confession—abounds in dramatic touches; and the third scene—the gaol scene—is so constructed that nothing is lacking to the full horror of the story; and this horror is intensified by various expedients, such as the mother's unfaltering tenderness for her son John, and as the ornate platitudes of the parson, and as the cheerfully querulous garrulity of Mrs. Harrison when she arrives and wonders where are the prisoners for whom she has brought the good news. Oh yes, the whole thing is decidedly harrowing.

Decidedly harrowing, also, is the sight of a man having a fit in the street. If that sort of incident were cleverly dramatised, it would be decidedly harrowing on the stage. Why doesn't clever Mr. Masefield proceed to dramatise it? I think I hear him say "Because it would be inartistic. Because it would be horror for horror's sake." And pray, what else is "The Campden Wonder"? I am not, as my readers know, squeamish. I have no patience with critics who, off-hand, condemn a play because the theme of it is painful—"morbid," as they used to call it. There is nothing necessarily morbid in what isn't cheerful. "Othello," for example, isn't morbid. Life, as a whole, isn't morbid, though it abounds in tragedy. I consider that one of the main faults of our modern stage is the dearth of tragedies. Why do our dramatists (Mr. Shaw excepted) so carefully eschew every tragic element in life? "Yes, why?" echoes Mr. Masefield. "And why not, therefore," (I told you he was clever) "be a little more cordial about 'The Campden Wonder'?" "Because," I reply, "it has not enough relation to life." Yet the things narrated in it actually happened? Oh yes, I remember being told the story some years ago, and remarking "How very curious!" Suppose that the actual facts had been pleasant instead of painful. Suppose that John Perry had one day received a message announcing that he was the rightful earl of the district, and his mother the dowager countess; and suppose that Richard Perry, on that same day, had discovered a gold-mine under his garden; and suppose that this access of general good fortune had so sobered John that he lived happily ever after in the bosom of his family. If that had been the story repeated to me, I should have said with equal fervour "How very curious!" But, had any one suggested that it would make a good play, I should have pointed out that it was really *too* curious for that purpose. Similarly, John Perry's determination to avenge himself on his brother by sending himself and his brother and his (quite unoffending) mother to the gallows is really *too* curious to be squared with the requirements of tragic art. John Perry is obviously not a responsible person; and, for the pivot of a tragedy, we (lacking the Greeks' belief in maleficent deities) must have human responsibility: no lunatic need apply. Conceivably, if "The Campden Wonder" were not a mere unrelated episode in three scenes, but a full-sized play, and if John Perry were not a half-witted drunkard . . . but no! if John Perry were but a normally bad human being, he would not, with however great a motive for vengeance, behave as he does here. "Normally!" laughs Mr. Masefield. And I admit that critics have often angrily flourished the word "normal" in the eyes of artists whose themes have merely been not commonplace. Though the greatest themes are the commonplace themes, certainly, I would not venture to hinder an artist from availing himself of strange themes. But, again, such themes must be normally strange. The sort of thing that could never have happened before, and could never happen again, is all very well as the subject of an anecdote in conversation; but art needs for its theme something that is, at least somewhere, rooted in life. Be the theme pleasant or unpleasant, and more especially if it be unpleasant, it must have also some measure of significance. "The Campden Wonder" means nothing. It is (if I may quote the striking words that I made Mr. Masefield use in a similar connexion) horror for horror's sake. I hope Mr. Masefield will soon find some theme worthy of his evident power for tragedy. Then I shall go and be harrowed with the greatest pleasure.

"THE PHILANDERER"

February 9, 1907

In the early 'nineties Ibsen began to flutter the London dove-cots, and every one was violently either an Ibsenite or an anti-Ibsenite, and much that was foolish was loudly said by each of the two sects. The New Woman appeared, springing (as she sup-posed) full-armed from the brain of Ibsen, who in later years un-kindly denied paternity; and she founded a club or two, amidst howls of obloquy. I was too young to be in the scrimmage, but its echoes penetrated to the place where I was being educated, and I remember hearing that a man named Bernard Shaw had written a satire on it—a play which, if produced, would restore general good-humour. The play never was produced, and I heard no more of it until, in the late 'nineties, Mr. Shaw, already much more than a name to me, published it among his "unpleasant" plays. As a satire, it seemed to me rather stale then: Ibsen had ceased to be a cause of silliness: Ibsenites and anti-Ibsenites had vanished, and the New Woman with them. Nor, on the other hand, had they been gone long enough for us to appreciate a reminder of them. Molière's satire on the précieuses ridicules must have seemed rather stale within a decade of its first per-formance. Mr. Gilbert's "Patience" would have seemed rather stale in 1890. But it was all right (so quickly does time fly) when I saw it performed four or five years ago. And doubtless "The Philanderer," as revived by Messrs. Vedrenne and Barker in 1920 or thenabouts, will be more mirth-provoking than it is at this moment.

It is a great pity that the royal family had not already in the early 'nineties discovered Mr. Shaw and thus drawn down on him the favour of the British public. How splendidly, by comparison, "The Philanderer," produced at the time when it was written, would have "gone"! How gaily these squibs would have snapped and sparkled, and these rockets have rushed into the empyrean, and with how sharp a lustre would have lingered in our memory the "set piece" of G. B. S. smiling sardonically through at us! Time has damped these fireworks. The rockets ascend, but not radiantly, and we are less dazzled by their flight than hurt by the downfall of the sticks. The sticks are very heavy—more like clubs than they ought to be. I think that even in the early 'nineties they would have somewhat marred the show. Even then they would have been rather a drag on the rockets, though we should not have been so sharply, as now we are, conscious of their impact on our heads. By his duality of equipment—his intense earnestness and his overwhelming high spirits—Mr. Shaw has often been discommoded in his work. It is just this duality that makes him so interesting a figure, and I would not that he were otherwise than the gods made him. But it cannot be denied that his plays, as works of art, are often marred by this duality. And none of his plays, I think, is marred more evidently than "The Philanderer."

Whether an artist be bent on pleasing or on preaching, or on both these functions, he should aim at unity of effect. There cannot, indeed, be any real effect without unity. There must, then, be unity of method. A play need not, of course, be wholly serious or wholly frivolous throughout. But either the seriousness must be evidently the main thing, with frivolity as a mere relief, or the seriousness must be a mere make-weight to the frivolity. Sometimes Mr. Shaw has contrived to work in accordance to this canon. But more often he loses control of the two sides to his nature, and the result, albeit delicious in itself, is not what he, as an artist, intended, and not what we, apart from our delight in him as a human being, can most thoroughly enjoy.

What did he, as an artist, intend "The Philanderer" to be? I doubt whether he ever made up his mind. After a lapse of years, finding himself compelled to label it, he labelled it "unpleasant," as I have already reminded you. "The scene with which it opens," he said in his preface, "the atmosphere in which it proceeds, and the marriage with which it ends, are, for the intellectually and artistically conscious classes in modern society, typical; and it will hardly be denied, I think, that they are unpleasant." It is one of the play's faults that we do not know how far the unpleasantness goes. What sort of a philanderer is Leonard Charteris? What was his relation to Julia Craven? It may have been one kind of relation, and it may have been the other. Nowhere in the play is there any definite information on this vital point. However, even supposing that there had been no actual "intrigue," the Charteris type is doubtless a harmful one, and to be deplored by sociologists. Mr. Shaw might have written a really edifying play around that type. Doubtless, this was his intention; but equally his intention was to write a light-hearted topical extravaganza. The result is a real person in fantastic surroundings which prevent us from believing in his reality, and which make the inherent unpleasantness of him seem a mere wanton intrusion of unpleasantness for its own sake. To a certain extent, indeed, even if the play were a serious one, Charteris would be more unpleasant than Mr. Shaw ought to have made him. He would not, in real life, have said to a woman whom he very much wished to please, and especially not to a woman of Grace Tranfield's kind, "you must marry some one else; and then I'll come and philander with you." He would very likely have *thought* it; but a certain grace and fastidiousness in speech are characteristic of the Charteris type. Barring one or two blots of this kind, however, Charteris is really well drawn, and in a more nominally "unpleasant" play would be thoroughly effective. As it is, Mr. Shaw's study of him is robbed of its force and point by Mr. Shaw's extraneous high spirits. Nothing but the unpleasantness (aggravated) remains. And furthermore, as I have suggested, this unpleasantness mars the prevailing fun. Some day in the far future, when Mr. Shaw finds his fertility beginning to fail, so that there will be time for him to dally with the past, he might well amuse himself by turning "The Philanderer" into two plays. The world will be ready, in that distant period, to enjoy fully a blithe satire on the foibles of the early 'nineties; and, of course, there will still be philanderers.

UNATTRACTIVE, UNDRAMATISED

February 23, 1907

Dramatists in our day have often been blamed for their neglect of the middle class as a material for their art. Their defence, I take it, would be a plea that the middle class is less interesting than the upper class. The middle class, they would say, is a struggling class; its units are preoccupied by various petty devices in the daily struggle for life, and have no time in which to be themselves, to develop themselves, to cultivate their intellects and their senses; and have, moreover, no time for just those things which go to the making of comedy and tragedy.

This defence seems, at first glance, rather plausible. If you walk, any morning or afternoon, through Westbourne Grove (say) or the High Street of Notting Hill, you will note a dreary uniformity, and an uniform dreariness, in the faces of the ladies who are "out shopping." What anxious, lack-lustre eyes, what tightly compressed mouths, what drab skins they have! And how inexpressive of any sense of life, of any self-respect even, is their shuffling gait! You feel that they are doing their duty, but doing it without the faintest satisfaction; and you feel that for anything beyond their round of petty tasks they have nothing at all left over. Many of them are accompanied by daughters; and these girls, for the most part, look as joyless as their mothers—less strained, of course, less anxious, but staring dismally forth into the future when they, too, (if they have the luck to marry) will have "responsibilities." They are prematurely old, these girls; and so are their mothers. If, again, you will travel westwards on the Oxford Street Tube, between the hours of five and seven, you will find that the fathers and sons returning from the City make on you just the same impression as do the mothers and daughters. Anxiety, dulness, and fatigue—no time left over for life; no capacity for any vital emotion of joy or grief. You will be somewhat consoled for sight of these spectres if you will betake yourself, at any hour of the day, to Mayfair or St. James'. There you will have a sense that life really is being lived, and that eyes and arms are opened bravely to all its possibilities. You will see people obviously thriving on life. The men are rubicund, keen-looking, and hold themselves erect, and walk with a swing. And how childishly happy look the women in the landaulettes—never more childishly happy than when they are assuming an air of languor. And how young they all look, how unlined! Not of one of them could you say that she is old. Some of them, of course, must be old according to the calendar. Some of them are accompanied by daughters; but, unless the landaulette happens to be blocked by the traffic, you will never be able to guess which is the mother, which the daughter, absurdly juvenile though the daughter always looks.

How do they manage it? Partly, doubtless, by never staying for more than five consecutive days in London, and by spending always a great deal of time in the open air, and by being careful of their diet. But I think the essence of their secret is in their freedom from small anxieties and inconveniences. Some of them, of course, are not rich proportionately to the display which they have to make. But at least their difficulties are not those petty and daily difficulties which, unless I am utterly mistaken, are the carvers of those wrinkles on the faces of the average man and woman in the middle class—the strainers of those features, the robbers of colour from those cheeks. The upper class does not wait for omnibuses at corners, calculating that a green omnibus will convey it to a point whence a red omnibus will deposit it within walking distance of its destination. For it, no scramble to get into the besieged vehicle, and no fumbling in pockets for the fare. For it no interviews with rate-collectors; no snappings of boot-laces, nor any lost collar-studs; and no desperate expedients to make old things look new. Butlers, valets, maids, tradesmen glad to extend unlimited credit, and many other faithful functionaries, are there to stand between the upper class and those horrors with which the middle class has to grapple unaided. You, reader, if you are, like me, a member of the middle class, living from hand to mouth, know how grim a thing that constant grapple is. Suppose that you are going abroad, or going to stay with friends in the country. You consult your pass-book, tremulously: yes, you will just have enough to buy the several necessary articles of personal adornment (necessary, for when did you ever find your wardrobe perfectly prepared for even your briefest excursion?)

and to take a return ticket (you have tremulously consulted the
A B C Guide), and to have a margin left over for personal expenses,
and for "tips"—"tips": how your heart sinks under that in-
auspicious word! More wrinkles, deeper wrinkles, I think,
have been carved by the calculation and bestowal of "tips" than
by any other agency. Assuredly, going away from London is no
joke for you. But suppose yourself nobly born. Suppose yourself, for example, a king, or a prince of the blood royal. Your
valet, or valets, without a word from you, will have packed much
more than everything that you could possibly need for whatsoever
personal emergency, whatsoever variation in climate. Your
secretary will have ordered the special train. Your equerry will
have ordered the brougham. The directors of the railway
company will have ordered the crimson carpet along which you,
without having yet exerted yourself in the slightest degree, will
have the slight exertion of passing to your own saloon carriage,
wherein a hearty meal will be served to you by your own footmen.
True, you will have to shake hands cordially with one or two of the
directors, as you pass, and smile graciously, and pause to ask an
intelligent question or two. But any Prince's any handshake is
construed as cordial, his any smile as gracious, his any question as
intelligent: you need not be alarmed. After your meal, while you
smoke one of your own cigars in preference to those provided by
the directors, you need fear no "smash": there is a pilot engine
for you. Smoothly, swiftly, your train rushes, with never a
pause, to its destination. The reporters who are assembled to
watch you "alight" will inform the nation that you "bore no
traces of the fatigue of the journey," and will marvel at you as a
prodigy of endurance, and will pay solemn tribute to your "in-
defatigability in the performance of public duty." Yet there is
not one of them but suffers in a day more wear and tear than you
suffer in the whole course of your illustrious and beneficent life,
Sir.

A traveller who is merely a member of the upper class has as
easy a time as a king or prince has. True, there is no red carpet
for him, and no pilot engine; but neither are there any directors to
be grasped by his hand, nor any reporters to make him ridiculous
in the eyes of people who can discriminate. I do not say that I
furiously envy these blest travellers. They know not the sense of

triumph and repose that comes to you and me when, after all that struggle and scramble, we find ourselves at length safely ensconced in the railway-carriage. They, who are always leaving London, cannot savour the full joy of escape. Providence is never altogether unjust, even in this world. We can always point to compensations. Still, it would be nicer not to deserve compensations. It would be nicer to have quite smooth, pink faces, and quite buoyant gaits, as the members of the upper class have. It would be nice to have as much physical vitality as they have—to have been so little exhausted as they have been.

An intense physical vitality, due to the absence of petty vexation, is the thing that chiefly distinguishes them from us. But are they correspondingly superior to us in spiritual vitality? Are we less capable than they in the matter of thought and of emotion? As I have suggested, we look as though we were. It is quite natural that our dramatists, being for the most part rather superficial persons, should suppose that we actually are. But, if our dramatists will condescend to make our acquaintance (or rather cease from trying to persuade themselves that they don't know us), they will find that we, too, the unmentioned by Debrett, the jaded in aspect, have brains and hearts. They will find that we, too, have a life of our own—quite an interesting, amusing, exciting life, a life quite rich in comedy and in tragedy. They will find that we, too, are capable of great joys and griefs, and that such things come our way quite often, really.

FANTASY IN DISTRESS

April 6, 1907

To Mr. W. J. Locke, whose new play, "The Palace of Puck," was produced last Tuesday at the Haymarket, my heart goes out in a gush of pity. Not that his play is unworthy of him; nor that it was received unkindly. It is (in itself) a most delightful thing. Also, the whole audience, throughout, seemed to be in raptures. Nevertheless, I was glad I was not Mr. Locke. Rapturously summoned to show himself, he bowed in a modest, deprecating way to the mimes on either side of him, and made a modest, deprecating gesture to the audience, thus trying to convey to it that really *he* had had very little to do with what it had just been enjoying so much—that what *he* had conceived and shaped was something totally different from what the mimes had made of it. His deportment was as urbane as could be; but inwardly, I wager, he was raging at the public's obtuseness in not having broken up the benches and asked for its money back. One little hope, perhaps, he clung to : surely the critics, men of trained judgment, versed in all the minutiæ not less of the art of acting than of dramaturgic art, had perceived and would in due course proclaim the true state of affairs. Ah, broken reeds! "It would be affectation to pretend that the author is not indebted to a considerable extent to his interpreters." This exquisite phrase, culled from one of last Wednesday's newspapers, is typical of what the reputed experts came out with. I suppose I shall be thought awfully affected when I declare that only to Mr. Esmond, among the four principal "interpreters," does Mr. Locke owe anything at all, and that, on the other hand, Mr. Frederick Kerr, Miss Marion Terry, and Miss Miriam Clements do urgently owe him something: a handsome apology, backed by a petition to Mr. Harrison to release them from their contracts and substitute for them people who can enter a little into the spirit of the play.

The play's genesis was evidently in a vision that once came to Mr. Locke—and what young artist has not been visited by the vision?—of some green French valley in which painters, poets, musicians, and grisettes dwell together under the roof of an enlightened patron, talking art and love, to an accompaniment of popping champagne corks. And what fun it would be, mused Mr. Locke, if there strayed into this earthly paradise a middle-aged husband and wife from one of the suburbs of London! A play might be made from that contrast. Not a play of fun merely: plenty of scope for sentiment : the prosaic couple gradually yielding to the magic of the place, each falling in love with one of the beautiful residents, and thus recapturing the secret which they, too, had once possessed, and finally falling with rapture into each other's arms. Fantastic? Of course. And Mr. Locke was careful not to break his butterfly—careful to keep it fluttering in

the air, and not to guide its poor little feet along the pavement.
He took good care that Mr. and Mrs. Podmore should be symbols,
not persons, and wafted them from Stoke-Tootington, a place not
on the map.   If they were presented as definite persons, and not
as exaggerated types of suburban life, then the story of them would
be merely a commonplace stagey perversion of probabilities; and
the earthly paradise, their background, brought through them to
the test of actuality, would be shorn of all its charm for us.   Mr.
Podmore must talk as no man ever talked: he must "disapprove"
of everything, however harmless; he must have become narrower,
pettier, stupider than any man ever was.   He must, also, not look
real.   Mutton-chop whiskers are no longer worn, but they still
thrive as a symbol (and as an inspiration to the soul of Mr. Frank
Richardson); and I am sure Mr. Locke would have liked Mr.
Podmore to wear them, and had even decided on the colour—
mouse colour.   Within five minutes of his introduction to Mr.
Kerr, he must, however, have perceived that here was a man with
whom the subject of whiskers could not be broached.   And I
daresay the rehearsals had not gone very far before Mr. Locke
perceived that here was a man who, without being born again,
could never enter into the spirit in which Mr. Podmore needs to be
played.   Mr. Kerr stands, as it were, firmly rooted on the steps
of Boodle's, and doggedly refuses to budge from his accustomed
pitch one inch in the direction of Stoke-Tootington.   His clothes,
his gait, his voice, everything about him, is as inexorably Boodleian
as it has ever been.   Even when, in the last act, he appears in fancy
dress, he is far from cutting the ridiculous figure that Mr. Locke
must have fondly conceived.   Mr. Podmore suddenly transformed
into the semblance of a beau of the eighteenth century!   Mr.
Locke must have laughed in anticipative sympathy with the roars
of laughter that would hail that situation.   As it was, Mr. Kerr
forfeited no tittle of his dignity, the audience respectfully admiring
his easy, natural demeanour: the clock had been put back more
than a century, but St. James' Street is not recent: Mr. Kerr was
still himself.   Quietly, authoritatively, from first to last, he walked
through, never for one instant demeaning himself by lightly
hinting to the audience that the part assigned to him was but the
incarnation of a comic abstraction.   Had he been playing in
realistic comedy, he could not have more steadily refused to "play

for the laugh.'' When Mr. Locke caused Mr. Podmore to find his daughter embracing an art-student, and to cry ''What is the meaning of this?'' he intended, of course, that all the horror of outraged Stoke-Tootington should be expressed in that cry, in those upraised hands. Mr. Kerr does not raise his voice, does not even take his hand out of his trouser-pocket, simply walks across the stage uttering the words in a stolid undertone. Even in real life a father would not be quite so phlegmatic. But it is obviously at realism that Mr. Kerr aims, here as throughout the play. ''Hang it all, no! I *won't* make an ass of myself!'' seems to be his motto. An admirable motto to live up to—except when one has undertaken to play an essentially ridiculous part in a fantastic entertainment. Mr. Kerr should not accept such parts. It is unfair to the author.

Mr. Podmore's wife is a good deal less ridiculous than he; and thus Miss Marion Terry's performance is a good deal less inept than Mr. Kerr's. But the main point about Mrs. Podmore is that she, like her husband, is a symbol of middle-aged suburbanism rejuvenated and illuminated by fresh experience. And Miss Marion Terry is from the outset as lively and picturesque and young and delicately mundane as ever I saw her; and thus the play at its turning-point stands still. Miss Miriam Clements, playing the artist's model who captivates Mr. Podmore, seems less like a mercurial siren in a fantasy than like an admirably well-behaved lady joining in a charade. She is altogether without ''abandon.'' Partly, perhaps, this is due to deficiency in technique. One is conscious of the process by which she puts her arms akimbo, and one sees her leaving them so till it occurs to her that she ought to be doing something with her hands, and then one sees her studiously putting her hands behind her back; and so on. But I think her rather formal ways are also, to a certain extent, intentional. She wishes to remind us that the Palace of Puck is a perfectly respectable place really. And this is by no means an inartistic impulse. For the realism of Mr. Kerr and Miss Terry has already made the Palace seem to us like a real place, to be judged by standards of actuality; and we know that in real life a house conducted on such lines would very soon be raided by the police; and so we are glad to know that there will be no evidence to secure Puck's conviction in court. It is well that our sense of impending doom—so alien from Mr. Locke's intention—should thus be banished. Puck himself could not be better played than by Mr. Esmond, who has caught exactly the spirit of Mr. Locke's fantasy, and is unafraid to express it with all his might. Mr. Ben Webster, also, as the musician who fascinates Mrs. Podmore, plays in a key of extravagant romanticism which is just right. But these two cannot undo the mischief wrought by the others. It is a pity. I could have told Mr. Harrison exactly what would happen to the play as cast by him. He evidently thought that nothing would matter so long as he engaged a number of expensive and popular mimes. And, in a sense, he was right. The public is enraptured, and the critics are quite well pleased. Only—poor Mr. Locke!

MISS ROBINS' "TRACT"

April 13, 1907

To be amused and touched, I constantly listen to the people who are preaching this and that in Hyde Park on Sunday afternoon. I cannot say that I ever come away with a sense that light has been let in on my darkness. I do not remember having heard from any of the holders-forth anything that was new without being nonsense, or true without being evident. But the odd stock of second-rate and second-hand and half-grasped ideas is usually set forth with skill. They are very fluent, these preachers, and have effective tricks of voice and gesture. They know their business; and it is because they not only know it but so obviously and whole-heartedly revel in it that I delight to stand under them. I am afraid they do not value my attendance; for I never interrupt them; and interruption is what they love most dearly. They have nimble wits, and can always trust themselves to score. Some of the interrupters, too, are well worth hearing. They have acquired in their own line almost as fine a technical skill as has the preacher in his. The duel is sometimes a long one; but it is always the preacher who vanquishes at last—partly, perhaps, because he looks down, while his antagonist looks up. See how his eyes

gleam and his face glows as he resumes the thread of his discourse,
lightly clutching, maybe, the lapels of his coat in the manner of
one well-known statesman, or thumping his left palm with his
right fist in the manner of another. If ever a man was happy, he
is; and none was ever more vain than he. Young or old, native
or alien, perched on a mere tub and minutely describing Heaven,
or on a solid little platform with "Clericalism: There Is The
Enemy" emblazoned in gold on a mahogany lectern, he is irresistible; and the only bitterness in my Sunday cup of joy is that I
cannot be in all the congregations simultaneously, so as to miss
nothing, and that Sunday comes but once a week. "Votes for
Women!" is being performed at the Court Theatre on Tuesdays,
Thursdays, and Fridays; and thus, for the present, the intervals
between Sunday and Sunday will not seem so long and barren to
me. I shall attend every performance for the sake of the play's
second act, which is a marvellously accurate reproduction of a
thing equivalent to what I have been describing. The scene is
laid in Trafalgar Square, and votes for women is the subject
preached on; but the spirit, the tone of mind, the mannerisms, of
the preachers are exactly those which I have studied near the
Marble Arch. True, I have never heard any preacher so actually
delightful as Miss Dorothy Minto; but she has caught exactly the
spirit of her part—the blithe spirit of the budding platformist.
She ought to be grateful to Miss Robins for a part so admirably
written; and Miss Robins ought to be grateful to her for perfection. Perfect, too, is Mr. Edmund Gwenn. For sheer humour
and vitality, in addition to its minute fidelity to the model, his
presentment of Mr. Walker, a popular artisan-orator, is a real
masterpiece in acting. Perfect is the rolling gait with which he
passes to and fro along the steps of the column, with his hands
thrust down in his pockets, and his chin thrust forward, and his
face cocked to one side and shining all over with the good-humour
that comes of absolute belief in oneself, and of the consciousness
that one is very magnetic—oh! I do assure you that Mr. Walker
magnetised the whole audience across the footlights, to say nothing
of the stage-crowd, whose very interruptions were a proof that he
was able to make them do exactly as he wished. Again and again
must I go to see Mr. Walker thriving on those interruptions. Miss
Robins has studied the mind of the crowd not less intently than

the mind of the popular orator; and Mr. Granville Barker has so drilled the crowd that its reality is overwhelming enough to be almost inartistic. The second act is thus a joy from first to last; and I do wish it could be so extended at each end that there would be no time for performing the first act and the third. If in those two acts Miss Robins had painted, after the manner of Mr. Bernard Shaw, an impartial and comedic picture of the ladies and gentlemen who are actively for and against female suffrage, the whole play would have been capital.

Miss Robins shows in her presentment of certain minor characters that she can extract plenty of fun from the feminist movement. Unfortunately, however, she is not "out for" fun. She is an ardent suffragist herself; and also an actress. As a suffragist, she wants to preach; and, as an actress, she wants to write thrilling parts, and to create thrilling situations. I don't mind being preached at, and I love being thrilled. But it does not follow that because an actress in her own person can thrill one (as Miss Robins, in plays written by other people, has often thrilled me) she can thrill one as a dramatist. Nor is a suffragist necessarily convincing by reason of her ardour. Indeed, her very ardour may be a stumbling-block to her, tripping up her determination to present her case with that firm cool grasp of logic, that rigid sense of justice, that good-humour, and that power of envisaging without personal bias every side to a question, which are among the prime glories of the daughters of Eve. Neither as dramatist does Miss Robins thrill me, nor as evangelist does she win me. I could hardly suppress a yawn when Mr. Geoffrey Stoner, the strong man of the Tory party, blenched and was for a moment transfixed at sight of Miss Vida Levering, of whom we already knew that ten years ago she ought to have been, but was not, married to some gentleman unknown. And I yawned outright when Stoner's fiancée, Miss Dunbarton, just before the curtain fell, learned through Stoner's knowledge of the name embroidered on a handkerchief that he had known Miss Levering in the past. In Trafalgar Square all was well. True, Miss Levering was on the steps of Nelson's Column, and Stoner and his fiancée were in the crowd; but the Court Theatre is not Drury Lane, and the principal persons of the play are not permitted to discuss their secrets loudly outside their own drawing-rooms.

Miss Levering, therefore, had to content herself with turning faint at the sight of Stoner in the midst of her indiscreetly modest confession that it would be a bad day for England if all women thought as she did of all men. My heart sank when, the curtain rising on a drawing-room in Eaton Square, I knew Stoner was about to be taxed with his guilt by Miss Dunbarton. Stoner cut an even poorer figure than I had expected. Surely, even in this distressing situation, the strong man of the Tory party would not so utterly lose his debating instinct as Stoner does. He would not think (until his fiancée scornfully undeceived him) that he was making a good point in declaring that he had practically forgotten the other lady's existence. He would not—let us, at least, for the Tory party's sake, hope he would not—be there merely to be trampled on and turned inside out by woman's superior intellect and eloquence; nor surely would he presently be driven, lamb-like, to offer marriage to a lady who had been his mistress ten years ago and had left him suddenly without giving him her address and had taken all possible pains to avoid him ever since. You see, Miss Robins does not make the strong man of the Tory party a villain: only weak, weak as in the time when he shrank from marrying against his father's will. The scorn with which Miss Levering rejects his offer I may safely leave to your imagination: you will have already foreseen it. What I defy you to have foreseen is this: Stoner, who has always scoffed at the suffragist movement, announcing his conversion to it, and vowing active and eternal fidelity to it, for no better reason than that he had once lived with a lady who ran away from him. Stay, there *is* another reason. Stoner's secretary has already informed him that the official wire-pullers anticipate the defeat of the party at the forthcoming elections unless Stoner "can manufacture some political dynamite." But Miss Robins lays no great stress on that bolstering reason. Indeed, I think she inserted the secretary's news not because she thought that philosophically a bolster was needed, but in order to give a tinge of opportunism to Stoner's conversion and thus get in an extra dig at male politicians in general. It was not enough that Stoner should do the right thing: Stoner must do it in the wrong way. Poor Stoner! I wonder whether any one of even our least gifted statesmen resembles him. Opportunistic, more or less, all statesmen are, and must be. But is any one of them so foolish as to be moved to turn a somersault over a great national problem by the reminder of a personal experience which has not the slightest bearing on the case? "I was seduced. I had not the vote. Therefore all women ought to have the vote" is a syllogism that evidently commends itself to Miss Levering, whom we must, therefore, alas, regret as a type of that incapacity for clear and impersonal thinking which some brutes have supposed to be characteristic of all women. Strange that Miss Robins, one of the cleverest of her sex, evidently takes Miss Levering quite seriously, presenting her not as the butt of a satirical comedy, but as the triumphant preacher in a didactic play! Is it possible that Miss Robins originally intended to make her play a satirical comedy? In that case, Stoner's offer of marriage, and his conversion to the cause, would—though still perhaps too farcically improbable for comedy—have been valuable, as helping to point the satire on the suffragists' argument that without the vote they can have no real influence. It is hard to believe that Miss Robins did not see that by making her two heroines so overwhelmingly influential she gave her whole case away. I think she *must* have treacherously intended to write a satirical comedy, and then have decided that a "tract," written apparently by a sympathiser with the cause, would be a deadlier mode of attack: suffragists might say of a clever satirical comedy that no man could have done it so well; whereas the "tract" designed by Miss Robins would be taken by anti-suffragists as an instance of women's incapacity for dealing seriously with public questions. I will not, by taking her play at its surface-value, give Miss Robins the chance of laughing at me as she must have laughed at the shrill suffragistic cheers which punctuated the first performance. I recognise on her shoulders the mantle of the late Mrs. Lynn Linton, a campaigner not less strenuous than she, but less subtle, less formidable.

MR. HAWTREY'S NEW BIRTH

May 4, 1907

No shock is more severe than the shock of seeing naked a face hirsute hitherto. The edifice of our knowledge of the man, knowledge which had seemed to be so stable, comes crumbling and crashing down about our ears. Always the fancy on which it had been founded is spiflicated by the fact. The chin that we had supposed to be so square, so strong, with a deep cleft in the middle, lo! tapers and recedes. Or the chin we had thought so pathetically weak is a replica of Napoleon's. The mouth of whose amiability and sensitiveness we had never harboured a doubt appears as the fissure in a rock. Or the mouth that we had imagined villainous is all a-quiver with good will. If the upper lip was evidently short, it is long; if long, short. Always the actuality turns our preconception inside out. We feel as though the whole face of nature had been changed; and we are appalled by the wanton daring of the man who has done the deed. Especially does the transformation appal us when the hair that has been shorn had a peculiar and striking quality of its own. I am sure that if the German Emperor, acting on one of his sudden impulses, shaved his moustache, the balance of Europe would be upset utterly. The fame of Mr. Charles Hawtrey is not, nor was his moustache, on so grand a scale as the Kaiser's. His fame is bounded by the silver sea. And his moustache was trimmed to a quite ordinary proportion and direction. But its very lack of obtrusiveness, its quiet, agreeable correctness, its urbanity and mundanity, its smoothness and silkiness, made it more than a mere appendage, made it an integral part of Mr. Hawtrey, made it a symbol of Hawtreyismus. And now it is gone. Have the hairs frizzled to nothingness in a barber's bonfire? Or were they rescued from annihilation by Mr. Clarkson, to be carefully reconstituted on a background of crêpe and presented to the nation? The nation demands an answer to these questions, or rather *will* demand the answer so soon as it recovers the breath which the sudden apocalypse of Mr. Hawtrey's whole face has taken away from it.

Meanwhile, there is one factor that somewhat relaxes the awful

strain of the situation. Usually, when a man has shaved the hair
from his face, our embarrassment is equalled, and reacted on, by
his own. He is a walking apology for not having asked our
permission. He is a walking entreaty that we will avert our eyes.
His behaviour is that of a leper. Not so Mr. Hawtrey's. At the
cue for his entrance, he bursts upon the scene with the radiance
of a man released from life-long servitude. Such a mood,
understand, has nothing to do with the part of John March,
Merchant Adventurer of London and Boston, A.D. 1773. On the
contrary, the minor characters of the play have prepared us to see
John March "in one of his black moods." Imagine Mr. Hawtrey
in a black mood! Imagine a man who for twenty-five years or so
has been compelled to impersonate invariably his own amenable,
sleek, quiet, fresh, sly, engaging self in his own perfect coats and
trousers, suddenly happening on the chance of impersonating a
morose New Englander of the eighteenth century! The sensation
of being actually born again could not, I fancy, be more bracing
and exhilarating. If ever a man was beaming with happiness, Mr.
Hawtrey was thus beaming when he made his entry. These
obvious radiations somewhat marred his presentment of John
March's black mood. But they helped to tide the audience over
its agony at the physical transformation—a transformation which
may be for better or worse: the time has not yet come when we
can calmly adjudicate that point: we only know that the transformation is complete and crushing. Towards the end of the first
act Mr. Hawtrey's joy in having something new to do ceased to
interfere with his power to do it satisfactorily ; for it was then that a
beauteous maiden arrived from the old world—a maiden whom
grim John March was to love at first sight, very rapturously.
(Never shall I forget the unction with which Mr. Hawtrey,
offering refreshment to the maiden, pronounced "China tea" as
"Chayny tay.") In the second act, too, for a time, all went well.
One of the minor characters primed us with the knowledge that
John March was walking up and down the adjacent room and
seeming "sort of inspired." And anon we saw Mr. Hawtrey
composing love-verses in the most convincing manner. But later
his own private high-spirits began to get in his way again. The
course of true love was not running smooth. John March believed
that Miss Perceval loved another. And here, alas, Mr. Hawtrey

found himself unable to purvey the requisite chagrin. But when the warrior awoke in John March, impelling him to hurl defiance at the minions of King George, then Mr. Hawtrey left nothing to be desired: no war-horse ever said "Ha, ha" with more ebullient gusto. And of course the love story had a happy ending, so that Mr. Hawtrey came off with flying colours at the last.

A REVIVAL OF "PRUNELLA"

May 11, 1907

"Prunella" does not wither. It is as delicately fresh a thing as ever. In despite of its fragility, it is one of the most "important" of modern English plays; for it is the most spontaneously poetic. It owes nothing to the tradition of poetic drama. It is a perfectly natural product of the time we live in. It comes not of a laudable determination to handle grand passions in the grand manner, but of an impulse to express something that was in the hearts of the authors—a wistful and melancholy little something, belonging to a time in which people, for all their outward strenuousness, are so frail, and so sick at heart. The something that the authors had to express was rather an emotion than an idea. There is nothing modern in the idea that youth wanes, and passion fades, and pleasure palls, and after the spring comes the autumn. What is modern is the sense that after all it doesn't much matter, alas, and can't, alas, be taken quite seriously. That is the sense which pervades "Prunella." We feel that in the character of Pierrot the authors have dramatised themselves, and us. Often as Pierrot has been presented on the stage, never, I think, has his nature been shown so thoroughly. However, it is not for its significance that "Prunella" is most highly to be valued, but rather for the mere story of it. The play is a succession of deliciously well invented scenes; and I know not which of these is the best. Prunella repeating her lessons in the prim garden, and hearing the distant sounds of the mummers' music; the coloured ribands thrown into the garden over the yew hedge, and the flight of Prunella's aunts into the house; and Prunella's own flight into the house after Pierrot has kissed her; Pierrot lounging in the moonlight while the baritone of his troupe sings the serenade for him to Prunella's window, and then taking the guitar and striking a right attitude before the shutters shall be parted; smug Scaramel holding the ladder down which Prunella is carried in Pierrot's arms; Prunella's bewilderment while the troupe of Pierrot dances round her, pelting her with roses and urging her out to life; and the terminal statue that utters words to her and makes music with its stone fiddle; and the old gardeners, roused from their sleep, coming to find the garden empty and the statue still fiddling; later, when it is autumn, Pierrot wandering into the garden, not remembering it—Pierrot all in black, with his followers all querulous, dishevelled, lame, but still trying to affect mirth; Pierrot recognising the window, and then remembering Prunella, and calling for moonlight and song, and bidding Scaramel prop up the ladder—all in vain; the homecoming of Prunella, and her meeting with Pierrot, and the way in which . . . no; the way in which Pierrot is converted from himself, and the play ends, seems to me the one fault in the play's scheme. It is a pretty notion that Pierrot should really love Prunella, and should prove his love by daring to touch her after she has told him that she is a phantom, and that if he touches her he too will die. But it is not a notion in key with the rest of the play. It is a dodge for securing a happy ending at the expense of truth to Pierrot's character. Either Prunella ought to be actually a phantom, and Pierrot to consent to touch her simply because he has lost even the melancholy joy that he once had in life, and because he is rather inquisitive of death; or Prunella ought to die in Pierrot's arms, and he to take a certain pleasure in the completeness of the romance, and in the arrangements for a prettily sombre funeral. There is for "Prunella" no possibility of a happy ending that shall be logical and congruous. The ending made by Mr. Laurence Housman and Mr. Granville Barker is not really a happy one; for we are sure that Pierrot, in his heart, was rather disappointed when, after touching Prunella, he found himself alive with a living girl in his arms. However, the play is in itself too exquisite a thing to be utterly marred for us by a wrong conclusion.

It is also too exquisite a thing to be utterly marred by faults of production. Nevertheless, the faults are annoying. The play is a fantasy, and, as such, should have a fantastic setting. The façade of the house in which Prunella lives is much too realistic. We ought not to be reminded of an actual little Georgian house of red brick. We ought to be given a symbol, a conventionalised synthesis, of all such houses. The cypress trees beyond the hedge ought to represent not actual, but ideal, cypresses. The hedge itself at the Court Theatre is less open to objection, because it is evidently a symbol for a hedge; but it is not a beautiful or ingenious symbol. It is a pity that Mr. Gordon Craig is not in England. He could have designed a setting lovely in itself and exactly in accord to the play's spirit. Mr. Charles Ricketts would also have laid us under obligations—for I suppose he would have stifled his first impulse to erect a tent over the Dutch garden. In default of him, why did not Mr. Housman himself design the scene? He has every qualification. And what a chance for his fancy to run riot in designing the costumes for Pierrot's revellers! The actual costumes, though bright in colour, are lamentably dull in conception. And the ballet which the revellers dance around Prunella at the play's crisis—a ballet that ought to have been weirdly delirious, after the fashion of the Brocken—is composed of the tritest and tamest figures imaginable. As a producer of realistic modern plays Mr. Granville Barker has no peer. But (if, as I suppose, he supervised the production of "Prunella") he is embarrassed by plays of fantasy (even when it is partly from his own brain that the fantasy has forthcome). Not as an actor is he thus embarrassed. His impersonation of Pierrot was flawlessly good, and our memory of it makes doubly hard the task of Mr. Graham Browne, who plays Pierrot in this revival. Evidently Mr. Graham Browne knows just how the part ought to be played; and he is helped, to a certain extent, by that quality of romanticism which often peeps out from his impersonations of quite prosaic parts. A romantic Pierrot is more than could be achieved by most of our younger actors. But a fantastic Pierrot is more than can be achieved by Mr. Graham Browne. He pirouettes and poses, but conscientiously. We feel all the time that Pierrot is a sterling person who for some reason—some reason which is, we are sure, a good one—has chosen to assume, for a while, an eccentric demeanour. In the last scene of the play—just when, as I have indicated, Pierrot ceases to be Pierrot—Mr. Graham Browne leaves nothing to be desired. At all other times his sentiment is much too full-blooded, much too sincere. As Scaramel, Mr. James Hearn masters the failing that so often mars his perform-ances: he manages not to over-act; and thus the very real fantasy of his conception of the part is most valuable to the general effect of the play. Prunella herself is played by Miss Dorothy Minto, who, among British ingénues, has no rival in the art of turning everything to favour and to prettiness. Some of our elder actresses would have got more than Miss Minto gets out of the pathetic scenes in the last act. But it is essential that Prunella should be in her 'teens. And Miss Minto's attempt at suggesting a broken heart is not such a poor attempt as to make us ungrateful for her perfection in the earlier scenes, where she is the child expectant and puzzled and happy.

READING PLAYS ALOUD

May 25, 1907

Much art is needed in this matter. In my time, I have heard many plays read, both by authors and by actors, but have heard few read well. I have grown to dread these readings. My heart sinks when with a gleaming eye the actor, or with an apologetic eye the author, fingering the first of those too, too numerous neat crisp type-written pages, seeks to explain to me the exact position of the doors and windows, and the exact nature of the high-backed settee whereon a person seated would be perfectly visible to the audience, but not necessarily so to any one on the stage. I nod intelligently, however; and the reader, reassured, clears his throat, says "Well then!" and begins. For a little while my attention does not wander from the dialogue; but ere long I begin to compare the number of pages that have been turned with the number of pages that have *not* been turned, and to work out little sums in rule of three, with an eye on the clock. Disheartening little sums! I presently cancel them, and let my mind dwell on things in general. But all the while my face wears an expression of animated receptivity—at least, I think so and hope so—and my occasional murmurs and ejaculations, though automatic, are never inappropriate, being, indeed, of a kind that might mean anything. In the pauses between the acts I find that the epithet "Capital!", uttered repeatedly in different tones, carries me through quite well; but when, at the conclusion of the play, I am asked for my valuable opinion on this or that point, my ingenuity is put to a test which is sometimes a trifle too hard for it; and I think I have seen more than once, in the course of my persistent declarations that I wouldn't have a word altered, a shade of suspicion come darkening the eyes of my questioner—suspicion which doubtless changes to certainty when the play, having been produced somewhere, is conscientiously slated in "The Saturday Review."

Once or twice (I hasten to say in self-defence) the difference between my oral and my written opinion has not been due to inattention. Once or twice I have heard a play really well read— read so well that I had to listen, and was enthralled, and had a genuine conviction that all was well with the play itself. A really good reader can make a play seem much better than it is. But I do not fancy that more than a very few of the many bad plays produced owe their production to this fact. For to read a play really well is the rarest of accomplishments. The ordinary dramatist reads shockingly. In the self-consciousness induced by his own work, and by the knowledge that he has no histrionic power, he takes refuge in that monotonous sing-song with which a poet utters a sonnet. The ordinary actor fails for an opposite reason. He is too histrionic. He throws himself so vividly and so violently into the manners and emotions of the various characters that all illusion flies from us. He cannot help acting as though he were on the stage. As he is reading in a room, and is dressed all the while like an ordinary citizen (or more or less like one) and not in an ever-changing sequence of costumes appropriate to the various persons of the play, his lack of restraint is quite fatal to his purpose. I well remember the reading of a play by a very virile old actor who assumed, whenever he was impersonating the heroine, a high falsetto voice. It is one of the few occasions on which I have found myself compelled to listen. Unfortunately the play was of a tragic character, so that the pent-up mirth which at last irresistibly burst forth, and would not cease till sheer exhaustion silenced me, caused rather grave offence to an artist for whom I had a profound respect.

Of course, that falsetto voice is an extreme instance; but the question is only of degree. More or less of absurdity is inevitable when the reader of a play forgets the difference between a room and a stage, and between himself and a "cast" in costume. His aim, which should be to make *us* forget that difference, can be achieved only by striking a mean between the inexpressiveness of the reader who is not an actor and the complete expressiveness to which an actor is naturally tempted. In a word, he must work by *suggestion*. There must be no violent changes of voice or face or manner. The characters and their doings must, if they are to illude us, be but indicated.

A PUBLISHED PLAY

August 17, 1907

I have just been reading Mr. Clyde Fitch's comedy, "The Truth," as issued by the Macmillans. I did not see it when it was first produced at the Comedy Theatre, but did see it, by social accident, some weeks later. I enjoyed it immensely. But afterwards, in cold blood, I wondered how much of my enjoyment might have been due to the fact that I had seen the play with no purpose of writing about it. For one who is accustomed to write about plays there must ever be a subtle alchemy in a play about which he is going to write nothing. He is like to mistake his joy of holiday for joy in a masterpiece of dramatic art. Strictly, he never does enjoy a play which he has to analyse. He may take a certain pleasure in the exercise of his faculties; but such pleasure is independent of the quality of his subject: his perception of faults is as pleasing to him as his perception of merits. He cannot surrender himself, as you can, to the story that the dramatist tells. He has to regard the story as a work of art, all the time, and is thus precluded from the rapture of illusion. This is unfortunate not only for him but also for his work. The best kind of criticism is, like poetry, "emotion remembered in tranquillity." A critic of the static arts, sculpture and painting, can purvey that kind of criticism. He goes to a gallery, happens on a masterpiece, drinks it in with his eyes, waves his arms about it, goes down on his knees to thank heaven for it, and presently rises and takes from his pocket his microscope and note-book. The masterpiece is still there, before his eyes. Had he not known that it would be so, he could not have afforded to indulge in those wholesome ecstasies. Them the dramatic critic must forgo because so soon as the curtain has fallen he is cut off from communion with the object of his criticism, and cannot investigate that object "as in itself it is." He might, of course, solve the difficulty by going to every play on the second as well as on the first night. But do not, I beg you, force this counsel of perfection on a class of men whose life is already quite arduous enough. After all, masterpieces are few; and so not much harm is done, not much fine criticism is lost, through the present system.

That I have not enjoyed reading "The Truth" so much as I enjoyed seeing it acted may be partly due to the fact that I have read it with the purpose of writing about it. But still more do I blame a lack in myself. I have not enough theatrical imagination to be able to enjoy reading modern plays. True, I can enjoy reading Mr. Shaw's plays. But the pleasure I derive from them is exactly proportionate to the quantity of what is not strictly dramatic in them. It is the philosophic expositions of Mr. Shaw himself that I read there with delight. The characters seem to me unreal, and there seems to be no dramatic development of any kind. You may remember—I recently reminded you of—the terrific "howler" I made when "Man and Superman" was first published. I announced that the characters were lifeless, and that the play (delightful for reading) had no fitness whatsoever for the stage. This is but one of many instances in which I have been hopelessly at sea; and I have finally determined never again to utter an opinion about the dramatic value of a play which I have not seen enacted. For me plays are somewhat like those "transferables" with which one used to play as a child. You remember the large sheet of shiny paper, printed all over with vague grey blurs; and how, when you had cut out one of the blurs, and dipped it in water, and pressed it violently down on some hard surface, you were rewarded with the sight of a bright yellow Swiss chalet on a yet brighter green mountain, or the Prince of Wales in scarlet and gold, or some other not less dazzling and inspiring apparition. One was never disappointed in a "transferable." It always came off, figuratively as well as literally. Plays do not, indeed, always come off thus. But they do resemble "transferables" in the sharpness with which their qualities (good or evil) appear when put to the test, and in the impossibility of knowing beforehand what those qualities will be. There have been periods when playwriting was an art which manifested itself as fully and pleasantly in books as in the theatre. But the present mode of playwriting is but to proffer certain choppy adumbrations, hints, vague and grey to all but the man who happens to possess in a high degree the gift of theatrical imagination. How rare that gift is we may gauge through the vast number of doomed plays produced by the theatrical managers, whose whole livelihood depends on their acquisition and cultivation of it. Thus I need not feel deeply humbled by not possessing it myself in a high degree. What worries me is that I am so destitute of it that even after I have seen a play performed I cannot, in reading that play, recapture aught of the emotion which it gave me. The close of the third act of "The Truth," for example, really moved me, in the theatre; but when I read "ROWLAND: Mrs. Warder's changed her mind. She's stopping here to-night. [*Putting his arms about her*.] BECKY: Father!"—why, then my eyes are as dry as though I were studying a railway time-table. Implicitly, a railway time-table is as romantic a thing as could be; and there may be people who, studying it, feel themselves whirling through space, this way and that, in a wild confusion of innumerable anxious or joyous journeys. But Mr. Bradshaw is not explicitly a romantic writer. He does but hint, drily, abruptly, at possibilities. And that is just what the modern playwright does.

Except in the scene which I have mentioned, "The Truth" is, of course, sheer comedy; and comedy can be appreciated more easily than pathos through the medium of a printed play. But, even so, my smiles over the book of "The Truth" were few in comparison with the laughs I had emitted in the theatre. Mr. Fitch can write witty lines that are amusing to read; but, for the most part, his comedy is of the kind that needs utterance on the stage—utterance by this or that character at this or that moment. He is essentially a man of the theatre. Nor has any one ever denied that of him. The objection that English critics have usually made to his work is that he is so essentially a man of the theatre that he is unscrupulous about reality. Some of his plays certainly have justified that charge. But in all of them have been evident a vitality and gay resourcefulness that set him high above the ruck of ordinary playwrights. And now, in "The Truth," he has shown that he can depict life as conscientiously and as accurately as though he were not steeped in theatrical lore. Becky Warder, fibster and "allumeuse," but an admirable creature, is one of the best-observed and best-presented characters in modern drama. Mr. Fitch has been blamed for shifting the scene of his play, after the third act, from New York to Baltimore (London to Brighton, in the English version), and for thus eliminating certain subsidiary characters from the last two acts. Such an objection is merely pedantic. The change of venue matters nothing so long as the play preserves its character and the idea is consistently worked out. Perhaps the best scene in the play is in the last act, when the unhappy Becky, to win back the husband whom her fibs have alienated, adopts a stratagem suggested by the parent from whom she has inherited her talent for fibbing. And not less ironic is the happy ending—Becky and her husband both believing that she will never tell fibs again.

THE BALLET AT THE EMPIRE

October 5, 1907

There is poetry in the idea of Covent Garden at dawn. That old piazza echoing with life and labour while all other places sleep! One likes to think of the freshness of the pearly and rosy dawn there—Aurora delighting, after the many square miles of chimney-pots she has just traversed, to linger in the fragrance of the multitudinous flowers and fruits that are heaped in that delicate oasis.

One likes to think that she has never yet got quite used to Covent Garden—that it is always by way of being for her a fresh rapture. And therefore one gives Covent Garden at dawn a wide berth, and tries hard to forget the occasions on which one has actually seen it. The actuality is something awful. Was ever elsewhere so much bad language as hurtles continuously from end to end of the piazza, above the din of horses' hoofs on the cobbles? And the masses of roses with dew on them, where are they? You look vainly for a single blossom. What inspiration can you draw from cabbages? What message have potatoes for your soul? The cobbles are slippery with scraps of rejected vegetables, and you must walk warily lest you fall—warily, too, lest you be kicked by one of the terrified horses, or be mixed up in one of the innumerable brawls. And all the while you are shivering, for even at midsummer the English dawn bites shrewdly, and you probably catch a cold as souvenir of a visit which you would far rather not be reminded of. Why are you not in bed? You pick your way out of the intimidating chaos, and hail a hansom.

Well, it is not the mission of ballet to hold the mirror up to nature. On the contrary, ballet's mission is to suppress and banish whatsoever in life does not pander to the senses, and to intensify by all possible devices the delightfulness of what is left over. In a ballet one looks to find embodied one's dream of an ideal state. On behalf of Mr. H. G. Wells I suggest to Mr. H. J. Hitchins that he should take Mr. Wells' "New Utopia" as the basis of the next ballet at the Empire. I do not feel that the world has thrilled with joy at Mr. Wells' vision of its future development. I myself was deeply depressed by that vision. But I fancy we might all be reconciled to it if it were presented to us in the form of a ballet, shimmering with the roseate hues which it evidently had for Mr. Wells' eyes. In his book the vision came out all drab; and thus, in this colour-loving world, the interval between us and the millennium is in no measure curtailed. Come, Mr. Hitchins: let a ballet pave the way to mankind's salvation. Mr. Wells might object to this procedure as savouring of trickery. But surely the end justifies the means. Even if the actual Utopia turns out to be a disappointment when it is established, just as an actual dawn at Covent Garden would be a blow to any one who had but seen it as depicted in the present ballet, mankind will not, with Mr. Wells' eye on it, dare revert to its ancient naughtiness. "The present ballet"? In my sociological ardour, I have strayed far from that. I was going to say how delightful it is to see the porters and costers of Covent Garden all turned to damsels, quite fresh and neat, smiling instead of frowning, all skipping and pirouetting in ordered ranks, while they pursue their Arcadian tasks, with never a curse on their pretty lips. The glow of dawn makes rosy the sky behind the chimney-pots, and yet there is no chill in the air around us. This is Covent Garden as it ought to be. Revellers, masked and unmasked, troop out from the Opera House, all of them gay, none of them haggard, all of them sober. Actual dawn in the piazza is especially unattractive when there are actual revellers to mingle with it. The English character was not formed for masquerade. No English crowd is so preternaturally gloomy as that which you find at a masked ball; nor can it be said that those units who seek to drown awkwardness in alcohol succeed in diffusing an air of gaiety: noise is not gaiety; and the mirth of these units rings more than ever hollow when it is prolonged into the cold grey unbecoming dawn without. If only the real thing could be like the thing at the Empire! Behold the merry demure face of Mlle Genée as she darts forth, at length, with fluttering hands and twinkling ankles, to meet the dawn. Surely she herself is the incarnation of dawn —the dawn that we read of in books, and dream of in bed with the curtains drawn to shut out the genuine article. It is mainly in virtue of this peculiar freshness in her that we set Mlle Genée so far above all other dancers. Others are clever, but have not the cleverness to hide it, and impress us with a sense of their responsibility to their art. Mlle Genée, for all the high formality of her steps, seems as artless as though she were but dancing for joy, with no one to look on. In a sense, indeed, she *is* spontaneous. So perfect is her mastery of her art that she can afford not to think of it in public, can afford to throw herself into the part she is playing. Alone among the dancers of this generation, she is an actress, and an actress so exquisite, so sensitive, that one might almost grudge her to ballet.

In ballet, one certainly grudges every moment when she is not on the stage. Mr. Hitchins has found an ingenious device for lulling us. He makes appeal to a sentiment almost as strong in us as our sentiment for Mlle Genée : to wit, our sentiment for our own past. The greater part of the new ballet is devoted to reminiscences of old comic operas. "La Grande Duchesse," "Madame Favart," "La Fille de Madame Angot," are things too antique to touch me. I was in the nursery when Offenbach and Lecocq were in their heyday ; and their music stirs but faint chords of memory in my breast. But, looking around, I saw the heads of my elders wagging in unison, and a strange light in their eyes, half-joyous, half-sad, as the old tunes were played, and the old scenes enacted. Just such a light, doubtless, shone from my own eyes (and was noted half-enviously, half-pityingly, by my juniors) when the turn came for "Dorothy." With the first bars of the hunting song, a wild confusion of little vague memories surged up to me, and swept me back, unresisting, into adolescence. And then "You are Queen of my Heart To-night" ! It was not Mr. Hayden Coffin whom this music conjured up, but a fellow-undergraduate who had hummed it, late one night, somewhat out of tune, on the terrace of an hotel in Lucerne. He had hummed it gazing up at a window on the third story, which he believed to be the bedroom-window of a young lady with whom he had fallen in love at first sight during table d'hôte. As he had not spoken to her, he hummed only under his breath ; nor was he quite sure that the window was hers. The adventure was not, you perceive, an exciting one. But it had touched my imagination, and I give it as one of many memories that sprang gladly, sadly in me as I listened to the old tunes. "Véronique," the last of the items in the ballet, is too recent to make me sentimental : for me it is a comic opera, and no more. But we live in so rapid an age that I daresay some of my juniors will find in "Véronique" a reminder, bitter-sweet, of the time when they, too, were young.

AT HIS MAJESTY'S THEATRE

October 12, 1907

"Jolly" is surely the right epithet for Mr. Oscar Asche's pro-duction of "As You Like It" ; and I think one might, without risk

of hyperbole, strengthen that epithet by the adverb "awfully."
Yes, it is an awfully jolly affair, compact of good will and hard
work and "go" and "snap" and "ginger." There is no shirking,
no fumbling. Sharp's the word, and there isn't a dull moment.
The whole thing is on a level with Mr. Asche's production of
"The Taming of the Shrew." But that play is not, one must
confess, on a level with "As You Like It." It is a capital farce,
straightforward, full-blooded. But it is not, does not set out to
be, a masterpiece of poetry. In "As You Like It" we have a
delicate fantasy into which Shakespeare has breathed the very soul
of spring. No other play is so fragrant, through and through, with
young lyrical beauty. It is less like a play than like a lyric that
has been miraculously prolonged to the length of a play without
losing its airiness and its enchantment. If butterflies were gregarious, one would liken "As You Like It" to a swarm of butterflies all a-wing. I think it is rather a play for the reader's imagination than for the spectator's eyes and ears. What actual Rosalind,
what actual Arden, could compete with the lady and the forest
conjured up for us by the music of Shakespeare's words? Ah, let
the butterflies hover in our imagination. Do not catch them for
us. But, if catch them you will, be very tender with them. Rub
off as little as you can of the bloom on their wings. As you are
strong, be merciful.

Mr. Asche is strong, and I am sure he has meant to be merciful.
Arden, as shown under his auspices, is a very beautiful place.
But it is not, like Shakespeare's Arden, an enchanted place. It is
"a lovely spot." One feels that it is mentioned by Baedeker, and
reproduced in colour on picture post-cards. I see the knicker-
bockered tourist buying a pack of these bright missives at the
village shop, and sending them off right and left to his best friends,
with stylographic inscriptions: "This is where I am," "Glorious
weather," "What's the matter with Arden?" and the like. I
think it a pity that Mr. Ricketts, who designed the scenery for
"Attila," was not recalled to insinuate something of fantasy and
mystery into the sterling naturalism of Mr. Harker's work. To
explain why I think so, let me submit an hypothesis. You are a
young man, desperately in love with a young woman. Circumstances force you to betake yourself to a forest. There you meet
the young woman in a suit of masculine clothes. But you have

not the faintest suspicion that it is she. You take her for a sympathetic gentleman, and confide to her the sorrow that is at your heart. You see her quite often, but never with an inkling of her identity. What think you of the hypothesis? You say it is a ludicrous one. Just so; and not less ludicrous seems the story of Rosalind and Orlando when it is enacted against a background that challenges, and successfully challenges, stark reality. Rosalind, we then feel, ought to be wearing a false beard and blue spectacles, and to be assuming a deep bass voice, in order to make the play verisimilar. Things have come to a pretty pass when we bother our heads about verisimilitude for such a dream as "As You Like It." As I have suggested, not the greatest genius in design could give us an Arden so good as the Arden dimly conceived by us when we read the play. But it would not be difficult to get an Arden better than Mr. Harker's. I am not one of those who think that the only possible backgrounds to poetic plays are of the highly-conventionalised type inaugurated by Mr. Craig and adapted by Mr. Ricketts. But assuredly Nature must not be slavishly reproduced, as by Mr. Harker it is.

Again, I am not one of those who would have dramatic expression, in poetic plays, utterly subordinated to the rhythm of the verse. I do not ask for monotonous chanting. But I think it essential that the rhythm of the verse should be recognisably preserved for us. And this can be done without any sacrifice of the verse's meaning. The greater part of "As You Like It" is in prose; and Shakespeare's prose has a rhythm as important, in its way, as the rhythm of his verse. To neither of these rhythms is enough importance attached by the players in "As You Like It." Perhaps if they were not munching apples quite so assiduously, the verse and the prose would stand a better chance. According to the modern doctor, apples are a splendidly wholesome diet, and I should not like the players to risk their health by abstaining. But I suggest that two-thirds or so of the fruit consumed on the stage might with advantage be consumed in the dressing-rooms. No doubt it is very natural that Jaques, for example, should be engaged on an apple while he describes the seven ages of man. No doubt the thoughts in that speech are not so profound that their thinker would have had to postpone his meal because of them. But I maintain that the speech is a beautifully written one, very vivid, quaint, and offering scope for great variety in enunciation. It ought to be given for all it is worth, and not in a series of grunts between mouthfuls. Was not Mr. Asche playing Frederick, some years ago, in the Benson company when Mr. Lyall Swete, as Jaques, enunciated the speech so tellingly? I have not forgotten Mr. Swete's performance, and I wonder that Mr. Asche can have managed to put it so completely out of his mind. Mr. Swete's personality was, of course, not incongruous with that of "Monsieur Melancholy"; and Mr. Asche's decidedly is. However sympathetically Mr. Asche might enter into the character, Nature would prevent him from seeming very like Jaques. Still, he need not seem so utterly dissimilar as he does. He has a natural dignity, dignity unlike that of Jaques, but still dignity. Why should he so carefully discard it throughout the play, to substitute the manner of a "boer carousing"? Mr. Ainley, as Orlando, is not undignified, but he seems thoroughly afraid of the beauty of his part. He avoids lyric rapture as though it were the plague. There is no nonsense about "the quotidian of love upon" *him*. One would say that his occupation in the forest was not to "hang odes on hawthornes and elegies on brambles," but to find some fellow to challenge his catch-as-catch-can championship. It is very natural that a handsome actor, who sailed into fame as Paolo, should be anxious to escape the snares of sugariness and mawkishness into which handsome actors are apt to slip. And it is quite true that Orlando was a manly person. But Orlando was very much in love, lyrically so. And so long as Mr. Ainley eschews lyric rapture, he will not be Orlando. Miss Lily Brayton, as Rosalind, pays more attention than any one else (except Mr. Brydone, as Adam) to the cadences of the verse and prose; and gives a very clever, mettlesome performance, somewhat lacking in softness. Mr. Courtice Pounds is amusingly unctuous, yet light, as Touchstone. And I suppose that if I were an Elizabethan in the cock-pit, Miss Caldwell's Audrey would keep me in fits of laughter. Being what I am, I wish she would tone her performance down: it is very much too wantonly ugly. Audrey was a slut, but a slut of the woodland, not of the gin-palace. Mr. Brydone plays Adam with real imagination, pathos, and sense of beauty.

MR. VEDRENNE

October 26, 1907

I do not remember exactly how many years ago, and at which of the suburban theatres, "The Devil's Disciple" was produced by Mr. Murray Carson. But I have clear recollection of a very happy evening—of two such evenings, indeed, for I could not resist a second visit. And last Tuesday evening I saw the same play at the Savoy Theatre. Yet I am not impatient to see it again. What is wrong with me? I am not blasé. Nor has the play grown old-fashioned. Reading it, I find it as fresh as ever—as witty a comedy, as vigorous a melodrama, as wayward and jolly an ebullition of Mr. Shaw's peculiar genius. Seeing it, I nearly slept. Mr. Granville Barker is the very last person of whom I should wish to speak lightly. I have a very keen admiration for him as playwright, and am at this moment angry at the prospect of not seeing "Waste" acted, and am disgusted by the wretched exhibition which nearly all the other managers have just been making of themselves in regard to the censorship. As a stage-manager and "producer" of modern plays, Mr. Barker has, in my eyes, no rival. At the Court Theatre, he laid me under a long series of obligations, which I shall never forget. How perfectly those plays were cast, and how well the mimes were made to act in unison! How meticulously were all the flats "jined," so that we were never conscious of the stage-management, and had only the smooth illusion of life! I find myself distracted between my sense of the fact that the production of "The Devil's Disciple" is a thoroughly bad one and my distaste for decrying anything done by Mr. Barker.

Luckily, Mr. Barker has, like Mr. Spenlow, a partner. Yes, hurrah, I am convinced that "The Devil's Disciple" was cast and stage-managed by Mr. Vedrenne alone.

The worst fault of the production is its general effect of dulness and lassitude; and this effect is undoubtedly due to the funereal and appalling slowness with which the author's words are delivered. English audiences may not be very quick-witted; but the meanings of dialogue can be caught well enough by us if they are expressively delivered. We do not need a snail's pace in delivery.

481

AROUND THEATRES

On the contrary, it does but cause our attention to wander. The
mimes in "The Devil's Disciple" are of various ages and schools,
and they act in various keys, with no effect of unity except in this
one particular: they have all agreed to emulate the snail. Mr.
Matheson Lang plays Richard Dudgeon, and is the one person in
the cast who has been rightly selected, and who seems to enter into
the spirit of his part. His performance is virile and intellectual,
and he gives us the very man that Dick Dudgeon was, in every
detail, except the all-important detail of pace. He talks as deliberately as his colleagues, and thus gives the impression of a
judicial slowness which cannot be reconciled with recklessness and
dare-devilry. Anthony Anderson, the parson, is a thoroughly live
character, and as such was played, in Mr. Carson's production, by
Mr. Macklin. Mr. Rann Kennedy reduces him to the level of a
dull melodramatic automaton. Stagey, too, is Miss Bateman as
Mrs. Dudgeon. Doubtless, Mrs. Dudgeon was a frightening
person, but her way of being terrific was not Sarah Siddons' way,
not the way of Miss Bateman, who seems to be ever clutching the
dagger in one hand and the bowl in the other. Miss Bateman is a
fine actress in high tragedy, but "The Devil's Disciple" is not
pitched in that key. Of course, no amount of suasion from Mr.
Vedrenne during rehearsals could have appreciably altered Miss
Bateman's inveterate method. But Mr. Vedrenne could, at least,
have saved this distinguished actress from making havoc of her
exit at the end of the first act. "My curse on you! My dying
curse!" says Mrs. Dudgeon to her son, "with her hand on her
heart," according to the stage directions, "as if she had received
her death-blow." Miss Bateman delivers this speech, not as the
parting shot of hatred and mean disappointment, but as the heart-
cry of a sweet, gentle, tortured lady who is nigh unto the valley of
the shadow. She makes, in fact, a direct appeal for sympathy—a
little sympathy to reward her for all the trouble she has been taking
to make our blood run cold. And she gets the sympathy, right
enough. This absurdity is all the more damaging to the play's
balance because, when Dick retorts "It will bring me luck. Ha,
ha, ha!" we see in him a monster of filial iniquity. Decidedly,
Mr. Vedrenne should have put his foot down. I did not notice
any point at which he could have improved Miss Wynne
Matthison's playing of Judith Anderson. He could not have made

her harmonise with the high tragedy of Miss Bateman, or with the conventional melodrama of Mr. Kennedy, or (such is the galli-maufry of manners) with the farcical clowning provided by certain other members of the cast. Miss Wynne Matthison is a wholly modern actress, and may be trusted never to force the note. The only trouble with her is that she cannot be trusted to strike the note. Judith Anderson is a highly emotional person, and that is just the kind of person whom Miss Wynne Matthison cannot sug-gest to us, and could not suggest to us if she were coached to eternity by a far more experienced stage-manager than Mr. Vedrenne. Chance after fine chance of implicit or explicit emo-tion she lets slip, throughout the play; and her evident earnestness, our knowledge that she is doing her best not ungracefully, is scant solace for Mr. Vedrenne's initial error in casting her for the part. I daresay that Miss Marjorie Day, who plays the part of the frightened child, Essie, is also doing her best, according to her lights. But these lights are dim. It was Mr. Vedrenne's business to illuminate the young lady. Essie is Cinderella translated into terms of reality; and Miss Day translates her industriously back into terms of Christmas pantomime. Her performance is well symbolised by her clothes—or rather by her costume. Essie was in rags. Miss Day wears a neat costume of brand-new bright brown cloth, with scollops round the hem to suggest abjection, in the traditional manner. And, when she comes on an errand to the parson's house, the prettiness of the confection is coquettishly accentuated by a cap of scarlet silk, so that she looks just as though she were going to a fancy-dress ball as Esmeralda. Surely Mr. Vedrenne, by the exercise of a little tact combined with firmness, might have prevented this charming spectacle. He could not have instilled into Mr. James Annand, as Christopher Dudgeon, that talent for imaginative comedy which delighted me in Mr. Wills' performance of the part. But he might have curbed the excesses in which Mr. Annand indulges at inopportune moments, dis-tracting the audience with violent by-play when important scenes are being enacted in the centre of the stage. To suppress that kind of zeal is surely one of the first, simplest and most sacred duties of a stage-manager. Mr. Kenyon Musgrave, as the Ser-geant, is another instance of Mr. Vedrenne's good-natured willing-ness to let mimes run wild in vengeance for having been cast for

small parts. The Sergeant has no business to roll his eyes and in-
flate his paunch comically when he calls for silence in the court-
room. The scene is in itself an intensely amusing one, and needs
no foisting-in of crude funniments. Major Swindon is quite a
real character, a brave and well-meaning gentleman, ridiculous
only because he is stupid. Mr. Arnold Lucy's comic make-up and
comic voice are quite inappropriate, therefore, and do much to
mar the intrinsic fun of the part. Mr. Vedrenne seeks to undo by
his acting what he omitted to undo as stage-manager. By playing
General Burgoyne in the faintest, saddest of minor keys, he seeks
to redress the balance displaced by Mr. Lucy as the Major. I am
aware that in the programme Mr. Barker is named as playing
General Burgoyne; and, as an odd coincidence with this printer's
error, Mr. Vedrenne's make-up and voice are such as might almost
lead one to mistake him for Mr. Barker, who, of course, would
never have dreamed of accepting a part so distinctly outside the
range of his own talent. General Burgoyne was a dashing soldier,
with a wit nourished on generous potations of port. He was not
the chaplain of his own regiment, as we should, if Mr. Vedrenne's
interpretation were all we had to go on, probably presume him to
have been. I have an ineffaceable memory of Mr. Luigi Lablache's
interpretation. What fulness, what elegant variety of lightness,
was there! I remember the picture he conjured up, and the roar of
laughter he won, when he spoke of "my friend Swindon in a black
cap." There was no picture, no laugh, when Mr. Vedrenne enunciated the words in the course of his plaintive monotone. There
was no laugh, there seemed to be no point, when the General,
inviting Dick to lunch after the scaffold scene, said "Bring Mrs.
Anderson, if she will be so good." The plaintive monotone was
fatal, throughout, to one of the most delicious parts ever written
in comedy. I have sometimes heard Mr. Granville Barker let his
voice degenerate into just such a monotone (though usually he is
alert and various). It is evidently from him that Mr. Vedrenne
has caught the trick. I do urge Mr. Vedrenne to abandon it.

"SARAH'S" MEMOIRS*

December 7, 1907

I wish I had read this book before I left London. In a very
small and simple village on the coast of Italy I find it over-exciting.
Gray and gentle are the olive-trees around me; and the Mediter-
ranean mildly laps the shore, with never a puff of wind for the
fishermen, whose mothers and wives and daughters sit plying their
bobbins all day long in the shade of the piazza. In mellow under-
tones they are gossiping, these women at their work, all day long,
and day after day. Gossiping of what, in this place where nothing
perceptibly happens? The stranger here loses his sense of life. A
trance softly envelops him. Imagine a somnambulist awakening to
find himself peering down into the crater of a volcano, and you will
realise how startling Mme Sarah Bernhardt's book has been to me.

Hers is a volcanic nature, as we know, and hers has been a volcanic career; and nothing of this volcanicism is lost in her description of it. It has been doubted whether she really wrote the book
herself. The vividness of the narration, the sure sense of what
was worth telling and what was not, the sharp, salt vivacity of the
style (which not even the slip-shod English of the translator can
obscure)—all these virtues have to some pedants seemed incompatible with authenticity. I admit that it is disquieting to find an
amateur plunging triumphantly into an art which we others, having
laboriously graduated in it, like to regard as a close concern of our
own. When Sarah threw her energies into the art of sculpture,
and acquitted herself very well, the professional sculptors were
very much surprised and vexed. A similar disquiet was produced
by her paintings. Let writers console themselves with the reflection that to Sarah all things are possible. There is no use in pretending that she did not write this book herself. Paris contains,
of course, many accomplished hacks who would gladly have done
the job for her, and would have done it quite nicely. But none of
them could have imparted to the book the peculiar fire and salt
that it has—the rushing spontaneity that stamps it, for every
discriminating reader, as Sarah's own.

* Memoirs of Sarah Bernhardt. London: Heinemann. 1907.

Her life may be said to have been an almost unbroken series of "scenes" from the moment when, at the age of three, she fell into the fire. "The screams of my foster-father, who could not move, brought in some neighbours. I was thrown, all smoking, into a large pail of fresh milk. . . . I have been told since that nothing was so painful to witness and yet so charming as my mother's despair." The average little girl would not resent being removed from a boarding school by an aunt. She would not "roll about on the ground, uttering the most heart-rending cries." But that is what little Sarah did; and "the struggle lasted two hours, and while I was being dressed I escaped twice into the garden and attempted to climb the trees and to throw myself into the pond. . . . I was so feverish that my life was said to be in danger." On another occasion she swallowed the contents of a large ink-pot, after her mother had made her take some medicine; and "I cried to mamma, 'It is you who have killed me!'" The desire for death—death as a means of scoring off some one, or as an emotional experience—was frequent both in her childhood and in her maturity. When she was appearing as "Zaïre," M. Perrin, her manager, offended her in some way, and she was "determined to faint, determined to vomit blood, determined to die, in order to enrage Perrin." An old governess, Mlle de Brabender, lay dying, and "her face lighted up at the supreme moment with such a holy look that I suddenly longed to die." Fainting was the next best thing to dying, and Sarah, throughout her early career, was continually fainting, with or without provocation. It is a wonder that so much emotional energy as she had to express in swoons, in floods of tears, in torrents of invective, did not utterly wear out her very frail body. Somehow her body fed and thrived on her spirit. The tragedian in her cured the invalid. Doubtless, if she had not been by nature a tragedian, and if all her outbursts of emotion had come straight from her human heart, she could not have survived. It is clear that even in her most terrific moments one half of her soul was in the position of spectator, applauding vigorously. This artistic detachment is curiously illustrated by the tone she takes about herself throughout her memoirs. The test of a good autobiography is the writer's power to envisage himself. Sarah envisages herself ever with perfect clearness and composure. She does not, in retrospect, applaud herself except when applause is deserved. She is never tired of laughing at herself with the utmost good humour, or of scolding herself with exemplary sternness. Of her sudden dash into Spain she says : "I had got it into my head that my Fate willed it, that I must obey my star, and a hundred other ideas, each one more foolish than the other." And such criticisms abound throughout the volume. It is very seldom that her sense of humour fails her, very seldom that she does not see herself from without as clearly as from within. She seems surprised that people were surprised at her sleeping in a coffin; and it still seems strange to her that a menagerie in a back-garden of Chester Square should excite unfavourable comment. Of this menagerie she gives an engaging description. "The cheetah, beside himself with joy, sprang like a tiger out of his cage, wild with liberty. He rushed at the trees and made straight for the dogs, who all four began to howl with terror. The parrot was excited, and uttered shrill cries; and the monkey, shaking his cage about, gnashed his teeth to distraction." Sarah's "uncontrollable laughter," mingled with that of Gustave Doré and other visitors, strengthened the symphony. M. Got called next day to remind Sarah of the dignity of the Comédie Française; whereupon she again had the cheetah released, with not less delectable results. Can we wonder that there were comments in the newspapers of both nations? Sarah can. "Injustice has always roused me to revolt, and injustice was certainly having its fling. I could not," says she, "do a thing that was not watched and blamed."

Now and again she pauses in her narrative to make remarks at large—to develop some theory of artistic criticism, or to handle some large social problem. And in these disquisitions she is always delightfully herself. She is a shrewd and trenchant critic of art, and in her ideas about humanity she is ever radiantly on the side of the angels, radiant with a love of mercy and a hatred of oppression. Capital punishment she abominates as "a relic of cowardly barbarism." "Every human being has a moment when his heart is easily touched, when the tears of grief will flow; and those tears may fecundate a generous thought which might lead to repentance. I would not for the whole world be one of those who condemn a man to death. And yet many of them are good, upright men, who when they return to their families are affectionate to their wives, and reprove their children for breaking a doll's head." That is the end of one paragraph. The next paragraph is : "I have seen four executions, one in London, one in Spain, and two in Paris." Was Sarah dragged to see them by force, as an awful punishment for lapses in the respect due to the dignity of the Comédie Française? She appears to have gone of her own accord. Indeed, she waited all night on the balcony of a first-floor flat in the Rue Merlin to see the execution of Vaillant, the anarchist, whom she had known personally and had liked. After the knife had fallen, she mingled with the crowd, and was "sick at heart and desperate. There was not a word of gratitude to this man, not a murmur of vengeance or revolt." She "felt inclined to cry out 'Brutes that you are! kneel down and kiss the stones that the blood of this poor madman has stained for your sakes, for you, because he believed in you!'" The wonder is that she did not actually cry these words out. Her reticence must have cost her a tremendous effort. Be sure that she really was horrified, at the time, by the crowd's indifference. Be sure that she really does altogether hate capital punishment. Be sure, too, that she had a genuine admiration for the character of the man whom she was at such pains to see slaughtered. You, gentle reader, might not care to visit an execution—especially not that of a personal friend. But then, you see, you are not a great tragedian. Emotion for emotion's sake is not the law of your being. It is because that is so immutably, so overwhelmingly, the law of Sarah's being that we have in Sarah—yes, even now, for all the tricks she plays with her art—the greatest of living tragedians. If ever I committed a murder, I should not at all resent her coming to my hanging. I should bow from the scaffold with all the deference due to the genius that has so often thrilled me beyond measure. And never has it thrilled me more than through this unusual medium, in this unusual place.

IN AN ITALIAN MUSIC HALL

December 21, 1907

Among the humbler and less obvious charms of an Italian city I would place high the music hall. I am not, of course, thinking of the big, cosmopolitan, embiographed and emballet'd affair in the principal street, but of the small and very racy one that you find after long gropings in the elder and poorer parts of the city. Outwardly, the tavern of your quest is as any other. No superscription proclaims it a temple of dance and song; no boards are out. But your ear catches through the window-pane the tinkle of a piano and the faint cadence of a voice; and in you go, trying to look as little like a "forestiere" as you can. A needless precaution, this; for Italians never stare, hardly indeed glance at you: the goodness of their manners is proof against any howsoever outlandish apparition. I do believe that if an archangel appeared in this tavern, they would merely make room for him. Not that there would be much room to make. Your first impression, as you enter, is of a black sea of sombreros, or should I say sombreri?—my local colour is lamentably faint where the language of the country is concerned. But room is made for you somehow, and in the smoke-thick and sombrero-thick atmosphere you await the moment when the one and overworked waiter can take the order which is the price you pay for admission. One and over-worked he is, but not abating in his wild rapidity the grave good-humour and dignity of his race. In the little tavern which I happen to remember most vividly among the very similar others—a tavern not far from the Bargello—the waiter is an exact replica of the portraits of Cavour, and, despite the agitating life he leads nightly, is so impressive and so gracious that the coffee he serves to you seems at the first sip quite palatable, and the monstrous blend of fire and sugar and water that accompanies it and is called "cognac" fails to poison you outright. One of the duties of this good man is to attend to the clock that hangs on the wall. To a casual eye, this clock might pass muster. It has an honest dial, and indeed does its best, and its best is indeed quite good until it indicates the half-hour. Thereafter, through some decay in its faculties, it can no more. Its minute-hand has climbed down nimbly and well, but cannot climb up. After the lapse of what he takes to be half-an-hour, the waiter borrows a walking-stick from one of the audience, and therewith pushes the minute-hand up and holds it in position while the clock strikes; after which, for another half-hour, all is well. When first I visited this tavern, a year ago, I imagined that the clock would presently be submitted to its maker and cured of its infirmity. I was delighted, this year, to find it in its old condition, tended by the same waiter in the same manner—a shining proof that romance lingers in a land where commercialism is now thought to reign unchallenged; and I felt a thrill of pride when, one evening, it was my own walking-stick that the waiter borrowed.

Do not think, though, that the clock is the only, or even the greatest, attraction of this tavern. Observe the intense seriousness of the man at the piano, and how strangely a cake-walk sounds when it is pliantly and floridly rendered in the manner of true Italian melody. It is a far cry from Tuscany to "Ga." A far cry, too, from our time to the cinquecento. The proscenium of the little stage is well of our time, with its card-board surface smeared over with the garish colours that the modern Italian loves. But the back-cloth, quaintly, is an evident copy from some canvas in the Pitti or Uffizi. Those two white colonnades tapering away on a pavement of white and black lozenges, with a little grove of cypresses beyond, were invented as the setting for an Annunciation or perhaps a Feast of Cana; and strange they seem to us, in this smoky tavern, as a setting for Signorina this and La that. Lest I should seem lacking in courtesy, I hasten to say that the actual names of these ladies are not known to me : the tavern does not run to a programme. But even if I knew the names, I should find it hard to differentiate for you the ladies. That is a part of their charm ; they have the appeal that comes of absolute yielding to a tradition, to a convention. They are as the figures on a frieze, these ladies; singly of no account, but irresistible in unison. This one's eyes may be a trifle brighter, that one's satinette a trifle shabbier, than another's. But all of them are very bright-eyed and shabby-frocked, and none is of less than middle age—I mean, of course, Italian middle age, between which and girlhood the interval is so tragically brief—and they all, all sing the same kind of song in just the same kind of way. If you happened to go to the cafés chantants of Paris three years ago, you will recognise all the tunes that these ladies sing. The tunes take just that time to get across the Italian Alps. And if you happen to know Italian, perhaps you will recognise the words as equally old friends. But I suspect they have been "diablement changés en route"; for they are delivered with an air of passionate yearning, or joy, or wrath, which is entirely in the manner of native grand opera, and in the very quaintest contrast with the familiar tinkle of the tune. I never weary of that contrast. And I never cease to wonder how the convention of the French café chantant has contrived to insinuate itself into these taverns of Italy. You never hear a French song hummed or whistled in the street. Most of the workmen and errand-boys who pass by are singing to themselves, with perfect seriousness and elaborate execution, with half-closed eyes and distended mouths, some scene from Verdi, or Rossini, or Puccini. Grand opera is as much in their bones as is the music hall in those of our own populace. How comes it that they sit nightly listening to alien music for which they have really no use? There they sit serried and solemn, never laughing; never beating time; seldom, and then but faintly, applauding. For three hours or so they sit thus. At length a curtain of striped cotton is drawn across the stage, in token that the singing is over. The three or four unencouraged nightingales presently appear from behind the scenes, one by one, women of the people, humbly dressed, chaperoned by elder women. They sit down and drink syrups. The men pay no heed to them, absorbed in the general conversation for which the drawing of the curtain was an apparently welcome signal. And in due time the waiter borrows a walking-stick, and the clock strikes midnight; and so home.

"ARMS AND THE MAN"

January 4, 1908

I do wish I had been in the Avenue Theatre on that night, fourteen years ago, when "Arms and the Man" was first produced. It would be amusing, as a gauge of the changes that time has wrought on me and on things in general, to compare my sensations on that night with my sensations at the Savoy Theatre last Monday. It is on young men, for the most part, that the revolutionary pins his faith. And that is the reason why so few revolutions succeed. The very people who are counted on as co-operators are the very last to co-operate. It is well known that schoolboys are always strictly conservative; but it is not so well known that their conservatism lingers in them for some time after they have left school. Quite young men do not think for themselves: they are dependent on what they have been told. They kneel ever at such altars as are already well illuminated. All the ardour of their youth goes to the worship of well-established gods. For unsanctified new forms, methods, ideas, they have no use. They regard that sort of thing as an impertinence, and are as down on it as the quite old men are. It is only in the interval between eld and youth, before the crabbedness of youth has had time to rest and pull itself together for its reappearance as the crabbedness of eld, that we are really capable of welcoming and understanding new things. I am quite sure that if I had been in the Avenue Theatre on that historic first night I should have been very indignant against the whole affair. In a sense, of course, I should have enjoyed it. I should have admitted that Mr. Shaw was very clever. But his gifts would have been the measure of my indignation: to think that such talent should be turned to such evil uses! I should have heartily agreed, next morning, with the elderly men who at that time monopolised dramatic criticism on the daily papers, that it was a very cheap joke to represent a soldier as shivering and whining after he had been for three days under fire, and as being in the habit of carrying chocolates into battle. I should have been revolted by Mr. Shaw's cynicism in making a young woman stoop to the telling of fibs—and she no villain-ess! Sergius Saranoff would have seemed to me "a hound," and I should have been ashamed of having been compelled to laugh at him instead of hissing him. The whole play would have seemed to me a disagreeable fantasy. If one must invent, I should have said, the invention must be of a beautiful kind; and I should have had some very severe things to say about jesting on such themes as war and love.

Since that time, and since the time when "Plays Pleasant and Unpleasant" were published, I have come to see that much of this seeming fantasy and flippancy was a mere striving after sober reality, and that the reason why it appeared fantastic was that it did not conform with certain conventions of the theatre which the majority of playgoers took as a necessary part of truth to life. Far be it from me to suggest that Mr. Shaw in "Arms and the Man" gives a wholly truthful picture of life in the Balkan States. There is a rich fantastic streak in Mr. Shaw, and it runs through all his work. What I mean is that he has given us more of the truth than we could have got from the average playwright who has no fantasy whatsoever. A platitude? It would have been a daring paradox fourteen years ago, and is worth enunciating as a measurement of the distance we have meanwhile covered. Mr. Shaw himself has covered some distance. Fourteen years ago he was not so far ahead in form, as he was in matter, of the average playwright. In form, indeed, he was merely abreast of the time. I should have had nothing to say, fourteen years ago, against the form of "Arms and the Man." How strange and rickety that form seems now! One studies with something of an antiquarian interest the elaborate intrigue that centres around the adventures of Major Petkoff's old coat. How ingenious, but to us how jejune nowadays, that intrigue is! And to think that this sort of thing was what all the dramatists used to labour at and to pride themselves on! Towards the end of the play, when Louka the servant becomes the affianced bride of Sergius Saranoff, we cudgel our wits to find some meaning in the strange conjunction. Does Mr. Shaw mean that the idealist must necessarily——? Peace, peace! There *is* no meaning. Saranoff has been thrown over by Raina, who is going to marry Bluntschli; and in the drama of the early 'nineties it would have been untidy, an offence against symmetry, not to mate Saranoff with somebody before the fall of the curtain. Louka is the only unmarried girl besides Raina, and so it is she who is requisitioned. There would have been "no questions asked" fourteen years ago. Certainly we have progressed. Nor has Mr. Shaw progressed merely in finding the proper form for expression of his peculiar qualities in drama. Those qualities themselves have much developed since he wrote "Arms and the Man." It is a brilliant thing, this play; but shrill in tone, and narrow in outlook, and shallow, as compared with the work of Mr. Shaw in his maturity.

ABOUT PANTOMIME

January 18, 1908

A slight drawback to the jollity of the pantomime season, year by year, is that nobody seems to like the pantomimes. I do not say that these productions are not lucrative. Many thousands of souls go to see them. But it is the rarest thing to be recommended by one of these souls to go and do likewise. And it is the commonest thing to hear complaints about this and that pantomime's dulness, vulgarity, incoherence, pointlessness, inordinate length, oppressive glitter, and so forth. As the malcontents do not take the obvious course of staying away from the pantomimes, it is perhaps not unreasonable to doubt the sincerity of their outcries, and to suspect that they take a real pleasure in alternations of music-hall "turns" and awfully expensive spectacles grafted on to a pretence of repeating the story of this or that nursery rhyme for the millionth time.

But a grievance is not necessarily the less genuine because it is unfelt by the people who utter it. And it is a very real pity that pantomime stays sprawling on its old low level, instead of rising towards the heights that are open to it. Pantomime, the one art-form that has been invented in England, an art-form specially adapted to English genius, is in itself surely as attractive as any art-form that the world has known; and it is amazing that no Englishman of genius has ever laid a finger on it. What possibilities could be more immense? To take a legend that you are fond of, or to invent a legend on your own account, and then to set it forth in poetry and prose, with the arts of music and dancing to adorn it, and with nothing to baulk you of any whim you may choose to indulge in by the way, any irrelevance whatsoever of time or space, so that you are free to celebrate or to satirise anything that is happening at this moment in your own city—off-hand, what chance could be less easy for the man of genius to resist? Strange that the chance should be left in the hands of hacks who can make no use of it! True, there is "Peter Pan." But Mr. Barrie's genius is not many-sided enough to produce a pantomime in the true sense of the word. Humour and fun and fantasy he has. But

494

poetry is needed, too; and Mr. Barrie's sentimentalism is not
poetry. Also, he has not at all that gift for which pantomime
affords such splendid scope—the gift of satire. Is there among us
no man who could supply all the needful qualities? I was amused,
the other day, by a leading article in "The Morning Post," deplor-
ing the present state of pantomime, and insisting that we ought to
have a pantomime that would be a national and immortal classic,
worthy to be compared with the works of Aristophanes. The way
we were to get it was not by taking any one illustrious person by
the scruff of the neck and maintaining our grip till he had produced
the requisite article, but by knocking the heads of various more or
less illustrious persons together. I forget the full list; but Mr.
Barrie, I remember, was to do the legend, and Mr. Rudyard Kipling the lyrics, while Mr. H. W. Lucy was to put in the satire!
Evidently the writer of this leading article was more accustomed to
deal with politics than with literature. He is betrayed by his naïf
notion that there is nothing in England worth satirising outside the
musty radius of the House of Commons, and by his not less naïf
notion that a good work of art can be produced very much as a
strong Ministry can be formed. Not even, as he doubtless knows,
does a Ministry of All the Talents make a composite success; and
much less hope is there, I assure him, for a pantomime composed
by a committee—even though the members happened, unlike the
persons named, to have something remotely in common.

Suppose Aristophanes were re-incarnated as an Englishman in
our midst, and were commissioned by Mr. Arthur Collins or another to pour forth all his gifts of poetry, wit, humour, foolery and
satire in the form of a pantomime. Undoubtedly, the production
would be a popular success, but the satire (which, after all, was
Aristophanes' strongest point) would all have to be cut out. There
we come to the reason why we are not likely ever to have a pantomime raised to its highest possibilities. In Athens there was an
audience for satire. Aristophanes could make a butt of this or
that thing in philosophy, in literature, in politics, in religion, with
the sure knowledge that none of his most delicate strokes would be
unappreciated. The Athenians had no newspapers to keep them
posted in the latest developments of philosophy, literature,
politics, religion. It might be supposed, therefore, that the satiric
dramatist would have an even surer chance of success now in

London than he had in unblest Athens. That supposition, however, would rest on ignorance of the fact that, whereas the average
Athenian thought and talked a good deal about philosophy, literature, politics, religion, and thus was able to see the point of Aristophanes' jokes, the average Londoner neither thinks nor talks about
such matters, and reads nothing in the newspapers except the
"disasters" and the "mysteries" and the "social doings" and the
accounts of cricket matches or football matches as the case may be.
It is for this reason that the attempts to popularise in London
something like the Parisian "revue" have been such dismal
failures. A few nights ago I was at the Coronet Theatre, where
"Humpty Dumpty" is being enacted. One of the comedians,
greatly daring, interpolated a joke about Mr. Bernard Shaw: he
expressed his delight in the prospect of going "where there is a
silent shore." He waited for the laugh; but not a titter rewarded
him; and the "principal boy," to help him out, said, "I'm shore I
don't know what you mean"—a remark which the quick-witted
Londoners received with roars of merriment. Topical allusions,
in London, must be aimed only at Mr. Winston Churchill, and at
one or two other public persons of whose existence the public has
a glimmering knowledge. For the rest, the jokes must be about
sausages, mothers-in-law, and the other few things which are fixed
by usage as being funny. Even if the British public had knowledge enough to understand satire on this or that aspect of the
more vital things in modern life, I doubt whether they would enjoy
it. Instinctively, they mistrust a satirist. Sir W. S. Gilbert's
libretti were popular partly through the accompanying music,
and partly because of their sheer fun. But, in so far as he was a
satirist, he was considered (as is Mr. Shaw to-day) rather inhuman.
The chances are, therefore, all against the ideal pantomime. But
the annual success of "Peter Pan" should encourage the managers
to aim at something above the present level. Why does not one
of them "approach" Mr. Chesterton, for example? I can imagine,
as the result, an admirable riot of fantasy and fun and poetry. And
there is Mr. Belloc. But he could hardly be trusted to keep satire
in leash.

Meanwhile, I suppose the production at the Coronet Theatre
must be regarded as a conscientious effort towards that higher level
at which I am pointing. But it is not the sort of effort which will

effect much. Not much can come of foisting touches of Barrie-ism into a quite ordinary pantomime. "Written with a thought for the little ones," says the programme, sweetly. And now and again there appears on the stage a girl, who, in the costume of Little Lord Fauntleroy, is supposed to be dreaming the whole thing. Also, the principal comic man, dressed as Queen Elizabeth, has to pull himself together and sing a serious song to a company of children in nightgowns—"God bless you, babies! Be babies as long as you can!" I do not suppose this plea for arrested develop-ment makes much impression on normal "little ones," in whom the unconscious act of growing is always accompanied by a conscious desire to be grown-up. I deplore it merely as an example of the maudlin and doddering futility of the modern pose towards children.

A MEMORABLE PERFORMANCE

February 15, 1908

Last week I wrote about a production of the sort that has a long run at a fashionable theatre. This week I write about a produc-tion of the converse sort. I trust that a few people, who care about the arts of drama and of acting, will have been moved by last week's article to avoid the theatre where a so fatuous play is being acted with complete lack of discipline by mimes who are mostly incompetent. And I hope that these few people may by this week's article be moved to visit an unfashionable theatre, Terry's, where a masterpiece, "Rosmersholm," is being played nobly. I might say "more than a few people," but for the fact that the day on which this article appears is the last of the days fixed for "Rosmersholm." On this day, however, there is to be a per-formance in the evening as well as in the afternoon. I strongly advise you to go to one or other of these performances—perhaps to both. Especially do I hope that these words may catch the eye of Mr. Frederick Harrison in time for him to visit Terry's, there to study the methods of his for-a-brief-while-brother-manager, Mr.

F. R. Pryor. With what evident care have the mimes been selected for the six characters in the play! And how evidently have they been controlled, with how true a sense of unity, by the stage-manager, Mr. Hubert Carter! It was not enough for Mr. Pryor that they should be well-known mimes. The fact that most of them are well known had probably no weight for him. The thing was to get the right mimes, and then to keep them acting rightly together. In such a play as "Rosmersholm," wherein all the characters have been meticulously thought out by their creator, and are all full and vital, it is possible even for bad or miscast mimes, under no control, to make individual successes—of a kind. But such successes do not constitute an interpretation of the play. This is a lesson which Mr. Harrison should set to heart, "not knowing in any wise the mind of Allah, not knowing in any wise his own soul, and what it shall some day suffer" in the form of a sudden impulse to produce a play that matters.

In "Rosmersholm" the characters are of two kinds. The play is curious as being the only one of Ibsen's in which the realistic method of his middle period and the poetic method of his first are mingled but not fused. His last period, of course, was the period of this fusion. In "Rosmersholm" there is merely the mingling. Mr. Edmund Gosse, in his critical biography of Ibsen (a fascinating book, of which I shall write so soon as I have an opportunity in these columns), objects to "Rosmersholm" as, for this reason, inartistic. For my part, I find the mingling so deft as to content me, and am unhampered in my enjoyment of either element in the play. But the duality is indisputable. On the one hand, we have a realistic presentment of the sort of thing that was happening anywhere in Norway during the early 'eighties. We see the sparks that were sent flying by the clash of liberalism with tradition. Shall the ex-Pastor openly range himself against the Rector, and have the news blazoned in the local paper?—and all that. On the other hand, we have the strange household of this ex-Pastor. Mr. Gosse, I think, exaggerates its strangeness. There is nothing impossible or essentially mystic in what goes on at Rosmersholm. It would be quite easy to state the story in terms of sheer realism, and not to strain any one's credulity. But such a statement would certainly be horrible, and not less certainly a breach of the good manners with which poetry should be approached. For it is a veil of poetry that Ibsen has woven around Rosmersholm. There is mystery in the air, and doom; here, where children never cry, and their elders never laugh, and death is heralded by the ghostly coming of white horses. And hither Ibsen conjured Rebecca from the North, almost as darkly as he was to conjure another lady from the sea. And the films of mist that cling about her do not obscure her, nor make her seem unreal, but do merely soften and magnify her outlines, giving to her something higher and more haunting than her reality—making her, in fact, a worthy centre of poetic tragedy. And while, gradually, in the strange way of which Ibsen was master, here a little and there a little, the tragedy that has been wrought by Rebecca is unfolded for us, and the tragedy that is in her is shown to us, and we are made to see with growing clearness the end appointed, it is always a sense of awe, not of horror, that is stirred in us.

Rosmer himself, of course, is the point at which the two elements in the play unite. He is a factor in the turmoil of his town, buzzed around by Rector Kroll, who stands for the old order, and by Mortensgard, the local editor, who stands for the new. On the other hand, he is the inmate of this strange house, and under the influence of this strange woman. Mr. Eille Norwood plays him with due attention to the balance. He suggests a queer strain somewhere in the ordinary good weak man that Rosmer is, and gives us a sense of tragedy impending. The only fault I have to find with him is that he utters his words too slowly—with a slowness greater than is required by tragedy impending. Mr. Edmund Gwenn offers the same fault to be found in an otherwise perfect little presentment of Mortensgard—a perfectly horrible incarnation of caution and malice. Mr. Charles Fulton takes Rector Kroll at the right pace, and gives an admirable performance, never losing sight of the fact that this prig and bigot is a fine fellow. As Madame Helseth, the old retainer at Rosmersholm, placed there by Ibsen as a chorus—a chorus all the more effective because of its little understanding—Miss Kate Bishop scores throughout by her quiet naturalness; and at the close of the play, when Rosmer and Rebecca have gone out to drown themselves, and she comes in and sees them through the window, she strikes the true note of tragedy. Reading the play, I had always thought this entry of Madam Helseth rather a superfluity and a bathos: why need we be assured of the happening of what we know to be happening? Ibsen, however, had a trifle more sense of the theatre than I have. Madam Helseth's broken words make the catastrophe doubly actual, doubly terrible and haunting. Mr. Hignett plays Ulric Brendel, the strange figure that Ibsen presently reproduced as Eilert Löv-borg. In the first act Mr. Hignett seems to me to miss some of the humour of the part, but he gives well, with touches of true pathos, the uncanny poetry of it in the last act. It is difficult to write about Miss Florence Kahn's impersonation of Rebecca; for it is never easy to analyse the merits of great acting. When first I saw Miss Annie Russell, two or three years ago, in "Major Barbara," I despaired of the effort to explain or describe the peculiar force of emotion eradiated by her. A very similar force is eradiated by this compatriot of hers. Rebecca is essentially a vessel for implicit, rather than a vehicle for explicit, emotion. She is a woman who has passed through tortures of the soul, and is now serene. At the beginning of the play the actress impersonating her must not let her serenity deceive us as to the past. And again, when Rebecca has to pass through yet greater tortures, and still, despite them, is calm and self-contained, the actress must not let her own restraint blind us to Rebecca's agony. The part is a very subtle and difficult one, a convoluted one, needing an intellect to grasp it, and extreme skill to express it. Such skill would not, however, suffice. Forthright emotion on the stage can often be expressed merely by artificial means. But secret emotion can be suggested only through a genuine emotion that is in the player. In the rare moments when Rebecca breaks through her reserve, Miss Kahn betrays the fact that she has a voice of great power and resonance, and a face that will eloquently express the soul. Throughout the rest of the play she never lets Rebecca obviously reveal herself. The suggestion of Rebecca's inward suffering, however, is not the less poignantly dramatic. There is not on the English stage any actress, except Miss Lena Ashwell, who could have made the scene of Rebecca's confession in the third act so moving, so thrilling, as it was made by Miss Kahn. In its appeal to the emotions, Miss Kahn's acting is not more remarkable than in its appeal to the sense of beauty. Throughout the play, not a tone is inharmonious, not a movement without grace. In this respect, her acting reminds me of Mrs. Campbell's. And with Mrs. Campbell she has this further point in common: her sacrifices to the graces are never sacrifices of nature. She is, with Mrs. Campbell, the most naturalistic of actresses; and when Rebecca is merely folding up her knitting, or giving an order to Madam Helseth, or doing nothing in particular, it is—or rather seems to be—just as a real woman in a real room would do such things. And yet, I know not how, one is kept mindful that Rebecca is something more than the lady residing at Rosmersholm. She never lacks the mystery that the poet left on her when he conjured her from the North. The poet's idea, the signification in her of something strange that has happened, and of something terrible that will happen, is never lost for us.

THE SICILIAN ENTERTAINMENT

February 22, 1908

As Sicily has been so good as to submit samples of her dramatic and histrionic manner, it were but decent in us to return the favour. Which of our West-end managers will grasp the chance of taking out his company to the land of Theocritus and Mr. Robert Hichens? It is mainly from these two writers that I had derived my notions of Sicily; and I was hardly prepared for the shock of the first-hand information offered to me at the Shaftesbury Theatre. I do not hesitate to prophesy that a display of English acting would create a not less profound impression in Sicily. I shall make a point of being there on the first night. Already I see the native audience gradually settling down under the influence of the overture—their savage breasts soothed by "The Lass of Richmond Hill," "Home Sweet Home," and "The Last Rose of Summer." Masculine fingers which, but a minute ago, in every part of the house, had been tightly gripped round hostile masculine throats, and feminine fingers which had been twitching epileptically under the stress of passion for this one or that of the combatants, will all relax and droop and be strangely still. A stillness as of death will reign throughout the auditorium during the performance of the play; not a movement will there be save when one or another of the hypnotised savages turns to his neighbour, to gape a mute inquiry as to who, what, are these strange, quiet, immobile figures across the foot-lights—figures either something more or something less than human. Next day, the critics (all of whom will pretend to know English) will rave about the quality of the acting, and will deplore that there isn't anything at all like it in Sicily. And the Sicilians, especially the "smart" ones and the intellectual ones (to whom new sensations especially appeal), will simply flock to see the outlandish troupe. Flushed with his success, the manager might then book a season in Lapland, where the effect of his production would be even more interesting to me, as being so exactly analogous to the effect of the Sicilians in London. Tier upon icy tier, I see the Lapps sitting huddled, swaddled, their dull faces partially visible under their hoods, a strange gleam discernible in their fishy eyes while the English leading lady is being made love to by the English leading gentleman. I think I hear, through their furry integuments, their poor hearts going pit-a-pat under the stress of this unimagined tornado of passion. The male Lapps will wonder whether the wild animal in the black coat is indeed a fellow-creature of their own; and the female Lapps will wish they were Englishwomen. The critics, next day, will extol the magnificence of the acting; and some of the more thoughtful among them will perhaps suggest a doubt as to whether the pleasure to be derived from the performance is in any true sense an artistic pleasure. I myself have no doubt that the Lapps' delight will be one merely of excitement, of curiosity. Those of them who happen to have lived long in England, and to whom the English modes of emotion are familiar, will doubtless be able to appreciate the art of the leading lady and gentleman aforesaid, and also to be dramatically illuded by the performance. But for the vast majority of Lapps such appreciation, such illusion, will be quite impossible. I am not one of the few English people who are conversant with Sicilian ways; and thus for me, as for the vast majority of people here, these strange players come into the category of entertainers, not of artists. A more exciting, a more amusing "show" than "Malia" I cannot imagine. I mention "Malia" because it is the only one of the Sicilian plays that I have seen. I should not care to see another. My curiosity has been gratified—highly gratified,

I assure you—and a second visit to the Shaftesbury would be rather an anti-climax. In the first act of "Malia" the strangeness of the performers is cleverly accentuated by the familiarity of the background. The scene is meant to be the garden of a Sicilian peasant, and there is a dash of local colour in the view of Etna on the back-cloth; but the actual garden, with the hollyhocks upstanding against the Georgian brick wall, and with a lattice window of some pre-Georgian period in the wall of the house itself, has evidently done service in many a vicarage idyll over here, and these hot, wild creatures of the south are the very last people we should expect to meet in it. Sada Yacco and her troupe would not have seemed nearly so incongruous; for they, who came to give us a rather similar thrill some years ago, had at least the air of belonging, like ourselves, to an ancient civilisation, whereas it is obvious that centuries of missionary labour would be needed to give a veneer of civilisation to these admirable Sicilians. Admirable they certainly are, in the strict sense of the word. To watch the Japanese players was a delight, because their every movement and posture was learnedly contrived in accordance to certain elaborate traditions of beauty. It is a delight to watch the Sicilians, by reason of their absolutely natural and untutored grace. See the peasant women swing by, lissom, erect, with baskets upon their heads. Observe the lightning freedom of their fingers when they gesticulate one to another, every finger doing some little eloquent duty of its own, emphasising or qualifying something or other— heaven knows what. Observe Signor Grasso dancing the sort of dance that the hornpipe would be if the British tar happened to be Sicilian. Throughout the play Signor Grasso's deportment is a model of dignity; but he has little to do, and perhaps his dignity does not stand the strain of having to do much: Signora Ferrau's certainly does not. So soon as she gets under way, which is soon, grace goes overboard. I have no right to doubt that she is a fine actress according to Sicilian standards, and that the capers she cuts and the noises she makes are, according to those standards, very significant and very beautiful. Nor do I suggest that those standards are less good than our own. I merely say that they are, in Lord Melbourne's phrase, "damned different." It is, I imagine, natural for a Sicilian girl to squeak and to squint when she is unhappy; to open her mouth and slap her teeth when she is praying to the Virgin; to throw herself upon a chair, fling out her legs, fling back her head, tickle her throat, and stay there panting, in the posture of a pugilist between the rounds, when she is nearly desperate; and to fling herself to the floor, foaming at the mouth, and arching and straightening her spine, when she is quite desperate. But to us these evolutions have not the meanings that are attached to them in Sicily. They do not illustrate any emotions for us, do not remind us of anything that might be seen outside Bedlam, do but make us smile or shudder according to our temperaments. Nor is it merely that they have no meaning for us. As performed by Signora Ferrau, they give us no visual pleasure—seem to us, indeed, the very negation of grace. Æsthetic judgments can never, of course, be absolute. Beauty is a matter of fashion—local fashion, temporal fashion. I once saw in a Bloomsbury boarding-house a governess who was in face and figure an exact re-incarnation of La Bella Simonetta. "Quite unfortunately plain" was the verdict of her fellow-boarders, and doubtless of the passengers in the omnibuses by which she travelled to and from her pupils. She may have cherished the sure knowledge that in her previous existence she had had a great prince for her lover, and a multitude of poets and painters to extol always her loveliness. Similarly, the women of Lapland, uniformly and "quite unfortunately" plain though they seem to us, are many of them very beautiful to Lapland's men. And the chances are that when one of our theatrical managers, fired by my idea, takes his company out for a season in Lapland, Lapland's men will not think the leading lady beautiful at all. No matter. Her method will seem to them as odd as does Signora Ferrau's to us; and with oddness they will be, as we are, content.

THE GRAND-GUIGNOL

March 28, 1908

The critics seem to have been disappointed by the performance at the Shaftesbury. A little previous reflection would have steeled them. The tourist, when he emerges, haggard with thrills, from

the tiny Théâtre du Grand-Guignol, falters a horrified admiration
for the acting—its quietness, its naturalness, by reason of which his
illusion has been absolute. Such a performance overwhelms him
with wonder. The mimes seem to him demons of genius, stage-
managed by the devil himself. Well, these mimes are very good,
and very well stage-managed. But the root of the great effect they
make is in the smallness of their stage and of their auditorium.
Set in a small frame, quite near to you, life-sized, they can carry
the conviction without any of the artifices necessary to mimes
working under the ordinary conditions. They do not have to raise
their voices. They do not have to exaggerate the expressions of
their faces. They need indulge in no large gestures. To carry
conviction across the footlights of an ordinary theatre, all these
tricks must be played ; and, naturally, the conviction carried cannot
be so strong. No symbol of life, however ingeniously fashioned,
can compete with life itself. To act well in the Grand-Guignol
postulates, of course, as much art as in any other theatre; but it
does not postulate those special artifices which are elsewhere
necessary. The effect of such artifices in the Grand-Guignol
would be instantly disastrous to illusion. Hardly less disastrous
must be the effect of their absence in the Shaftesbury Theatre.
On the night of my visit, I could see that the mimes realised the
necessity for a mode different from that in which they had been
trained. They were making efforts to act up to the size of their
surroundings. But the efforts were timid and spasmodic. With
the best will in the world, an artist cannot suddenly learn to do all
that he has been taught inveterately to leave undone. And thus
the general effect was of under-acting. And lost to us utterly were
the thrills, which in any case could not have been so violent as they
are in the small compass of the Grand-Guignol. I can imagine how
appalling must be, there, the effect of "Les Nuits du Hampton-
Club." The play is adapted from "The Suicide Club," and is far
more horrible than the original, because all the saving grace of fantasy
has been struck out. Not in the poetically impossible London of
Stevenson's invention, but in the prosaically impossible London of
the Parisian adapter's invention—in actual Paris, to all intents and
purposes—do we see those jaded gentlemen snatching an awful joy
in gambling with death. The whole thing is quite realistic, quite
"convincing," and at the Grand-Guignol must send shudders up

the spine. We should share fully there the "émotions violentes" of the actual gamblers. But at the Shaftesbury we merely look on. The agitation of the mimes is not simulated broadly enough to infect us. The scene goes tamely. Similarly is our blood not chilled by "Le Rouge est Mis." A jockey, dying from a "throw," is carried in to the surgeon's room near the course. The surgeon, and his assistant, and the jockey's employer, and the jockey's friends, are far more concerned about the result of the next race than about the soul that is passing. All the horror depends on our sense of the keenness of their pre-occupation, the extremity of their fever. Here again the acting was not laid on thick enough for the required effect. We were left to perform the task of imagining ourselves harrowed—harrowed yonder, in the Grand-Guignol.

Personally, I made no great effort to perform this task. I don't at all mind being harrowed incidentally. I am always ready to submit myself to the high thrill of tragedy, ancient or modern, and am always grateful to the giver. When horror is used as a means to an end, to illustrate some idea, to point some criticism of life, and so, in the end, to purge me through pity and awe, I am all for it. But horror for horror's sake offends me. I do not say that I always shun it: merely that I am rightly ashamed of yielding to it. Not all the repertory of the Grand-Guignol can be banned as horror for horror's sake. There are always the harmless farces; and even in the ugly episodes, which are the special feature of the repertory, there may sometimes be discerned, if not a reason, at least a flimsy excuse for their existence. Thus, among the plays enacted at the Shaftesbury, "Le Rouge est Mis" may be said to contain a criticism of life, cheap enough criticism indeed, but better than nothing. And a similar point may be stretched in favour of "Les Nuits du Hampton-Club." Gone are all the irony and charm and fun with which Stevenson turned horror into delight. Horror, doubtless, was the adapter's sole objective. But there is still a substratum of meaning. What ghost of meaning, however, can the keenest eye detect in such a play as "L'Angoisse" (which is the most typically Grand-Guignolesque thing in the programme)? There are three characters: a sculptor, his doctor, and a girl who is his model. He is conscious of something uncanny in the atmosphere of his studio. He believes it to be haunted. The doctor tells him he has been working too hard, and laughs at his hallucinations. During their conversation, the model falls into an epileptic trance. The doctor, to test her condition, drives a hat-pin through her arm. Presently, under his influence, she begins to have a vision of a thing that once occurred in the studio. She sees the previous tenant murdering his wife, and then concealing the corpse by building a column of plaster round it. The column still stands in the studio; and the two men, seizing hammer and chisel, duly reveal the corpse just before the fall of the curtain. And there you have a perfect example of horror for horror's sake. To the brain, to the heart, no appeal whatsoever: merely a gratuitous, unwholesome tampering with the nerves. I do not say that such a piece can have no claim to be regarded as art. "L'Angoisse" is, indeed, very cleverly constructed. Much care and skill have been used to produce the full effect. What a sorry prostitution of care and skill!

I have so often sneered at the British playgoer that it is a great pleasure to say something in honour of him. It does seem to me a matter for congratulation that native equivalents for such plays as "L'Angoisse" could not possibly become popular in London. And, as that sounds rather unctuous, I hasten to add that there is a very good lesson for London to learn from this visit of the Grand-Guignol. It is lamentable that we have no theatre for the production of short plays. Such a theatre (as tiny as possible) seems to me far more urgently desirable than the national theatre that we talk so much of. Why does nobody found it? The omens are all propitious. We live in an age remarkable for its lack of power to concentrate its mind for a long time on any one subject. It is because of this lack that the new journalism has swamped the old. It is mainly because of this lack that the music-halls are swamping the theatres. The one kind of theatre that need not fear the music-halls is the theatre that I suggest. There would be no difficulty about getting plays for it. To write a long play requires very much more technical skill than to write a short one. (The contrary theory is all humbug.) The only reason why the average writer with any sort of a dramatic idea almost invariably tries to spin that idea out through four acts is that a curtain-raiser does not—how should it?—fire his ambition. Given the certainty that good short plays would be worthily produced, he would turn his hand to short plays quickly enough. It is often asked, angrily, why none of our millionaires has enough imagination to endow a national theatre. I fancy that their coyness is due less to lack of imagination than to lack of prodigality. Even the dullest millionaire would like his name to go echoing gloriously down the ages; only, the price is rather a stiff one. On the other hand, if a millionaire would found a small theatre for short plays, the chances are that he would very soon be richer than ever. And though his praises would not perhaps be sung so lustily by the visitors to his theatre as they would have been sung, if he had founded a national theatre, by the far greater number of people who never set foot inside it, he would nevertheless have a very gratifying time indeed.

"GETTING MARRIED"

May 23, 1908

This play has, as Mr. Walkley suggests, some affinity to Plato's "Symposium." Well, after it has run its course at the Haymarket, Mr. Harrison and Messrs. Vedrenne and Barker might do worse than put up the Symposium. There is nothing arid about Plato. Always the persons of his dialogues are creatures of flesh and blood—presentable, actable creatures. I have no doubt that the Symposium, if it were carefully cast, would come out fairly well on the stage. But I do not fancy it would come out nearly so well there as it does in the study. Certainly, most of the people to whom it is not familiar would miss much of its savour. Some of them, as having exceptionally quick and retentive brains, might be able to do full justice to the progress of the dialectic, following it with never a stumble as it was unfolded by the mimes, and having a perfect grasp of it at the end of the performance. Such brains are rare. You and I, reader, in our respective studies, cannot dash through our Plato at the pace of spoken dialogue. Here and there we must linger and ponder, harking back to previous pages, doing exactly the things that cannot be done by people in a theatre. Certainly, the average member of the audience, never having devoted hours of leisure to Plato, would fail to appreciate the Sym-

posium fully. Very much in that position are you and I, on whom
Mr. Shaw's play has been sprung quite suddenly across the
Haymarket footlights.

Nay, our position is even worse. For between the method of
the Symposium and the method of "Getting Married" lies a vital
difference. Some days before the production of the play, I read
in the "Daily Telegraph" an interview with Mr. Shaw. It was
obviously written by himself, and thus its contents carried special
weight for me. I was convinced that the forthcoming play was
wrought in a high and astringent manner, with no concession to
the cheapness of popular taste; that it was on a plane with
Beethoven's Ninth Symphony; that the critics and the public
would, as G. B. S. prophesied, be very much bored and incensed.
The whole interview seemed to me excellent in point of tactics.
Critics of drama, like the critics of the other arts, are a nervous race
nowadays.   "Judex damnatur cum nocens absolvitur" is still
printed on the cover of the "Edinburgh Review," and you smile
indulgently at this quaint survival of the letter of truculence: the
spirit of truculence is so long since dead. The critics have been
so repeatedly found out. Time after time, their solemn judgments have been ignominiously reversed. The critic of to-day,
looking back, is confronted by a long line of gibbets from which
his predecessors are dangling, while the men whom they assailed
smile down on them from Olympus. It is the artist who has the
upper hand to-day. Let a publisher, a theatrical manager, and an
art-dealer go down to Colney Hatch, and severally secure the maddest novel, the maddest play, and the maddest daubs on the
premises. I prophesy that the critics will (if previously made to
expect great things) bow cautiously down as to a revelation of new
genius. All the more docile will they be when they are assured by
a very successful man, whom they were once rash enough to disparage, that his new work is on a level to which they cannot hope
to raise themselves. I myself was rash enough to prophesy that
"Man and Superman," though I had delighted in reading it,
would be quite ineffective on the stage. I still blush when I remember that pronouncement; and caution strongly inclines me to
take any new work of Mr. Shaw's at whatever valuation he may set
on it. Rashness, however, surges up from the positive conviction
within me that "Getting Married" has been over-rated by its

maker. It seems to me that Mr. Shaw has fallen short of the Beethoven plane through fear of doing the very thing which to readers of the "Daily Telegraph" he so loudly proclaimed himself unafraid of doing: that is, of boring us. Usually, his fun and his seriousness are inextricable one from another: you cannot see where one begins and the other ends. In "Getting Married" the fun does not seem integral: it seems to have been foisted in, for fear lest we should fidget. I conceive that what Mr. Shaw set out to do was to give us a conspectus of the typical tragedies and comedies caused by the marriage laws in twentieth-century England, through the mouths of certain typical characters taken straight from life, characters un-lifelike only in so far as they should all be (as, for the purpose of philosophic dialogue, they must be) abnormally introspective and ratiocinative. With this end in view, he drew up his list of characters: Mrs. Bridgenorth, a type of the normal, middle-aged woman who takes the conventional standpoint, and does not bother; her brother, the Bishop of Chelsea, a philosopher, who regards the present state of the marriage laws as irrational and impracticable, and holds that "until marriage be made human it cannot become divine"; his brother, General Bridgenorth, a confirmed sentimentalist; Lesbia Grantham, a spinster whom the General has adored for many years, and who would like to bear and rear children, but has a strong aversion from men, and cannot bear the thought of having a man permanently around her; Reginald Bridgenorth, who, having married a young girl, with unhappy results, goes in for a collusive divorce; Mr. St. John Hotchkiss, the young man whom, for natural reasons, this young wife wishes to marry (tenderly fond though she still is of Mr. Bridgenorth); Mrs. George Collins, another fond but dissatisfied wife, a woman of strongly amorous nature, casting a spell over Mr. Hotchkiss, who, for his part, is unwilling to offend against the marriage laws, though he regards them as monstrous; Edith Bridgenorth, a young girl who is engaged to be married, but is appalled by the prospect of surrendering all her own responsibility into the hands of her husband; Cecil Sykes, her betrothed, who is appalled, in his turn, by the prospect of taking that responsibility over; with several other characters to represent this and that phase of thought or feeling towards matrimony. I am sure that Mr. Shaw's original intention was to be no more frivolous than Plato would have been in his presentment of these characters. And I am sure that it was only because he was afraid of disappointing the public that he presently decided to make the characters funny. It would be funny to pitch the action on the morning appointed for Edith's wedding; the bridegroom, in due array, fresh from the perusal of a pamphlet by Mr. Belfort Bax, and agonised by the immediate prospect of the altar; and the bride, in dressing-jacket and petticoat, refusing to complete her toilet after having just read some other pamphlet. The General would be in full uniform for the occasion: a sure laugh there. And the local greengrocer would be present to act as butler—happy thought! let him be a re-incarnation of the delectable waiter in "You Never Can Tell." Let Mrs. Reginald Bridgenorth be solicitous as to whether her divorced husband is wearing his chest-protector; and let him have a catch-phrase about her future husband having "a face like a mushroom." Furthermore, let him have supplied evidence of cruelty for the divorce-court by knocking her down in a flower-bed. (In actual life the invariable device is "desertion"; but that would get no laugh.) Let the future husband have run away from a battle in the South African war, and have "The Celebrated Coward" printed on his visiting-cards. And let Mrs. St. John Hotchkiss be the wife of the mayor, so that she can be preceded by a beadle with a mace; and let her be the wife of a coal-dealer, who has supplied Hotchkiss with very bad coals; and let her have a very bad temper, so that she may try to "jab" the adoring Hotchkiss in the face with a chair, and also be found by the Bishop chasing him round the room with a poker. The Bishop, for some reason, is the one character whom Mr. Shaw has omitted to guy. He is presented as a quite possible person. I suppose it was in the fear that he might pall that Mr. Shaw attached to him a quite impossible chaplain, Rev. O. C. Soames, a sometime solicitor, who regards matrimony as a sin, like any other form of sexual union, against Heaven.

Well, this chaplain and the various other figures that I have described are certainly funny in themselves (though they are hardly on the level of fun that one expects from G. B. S.). In a high-spirited farce they would be very useful. But I protest they are destructive in a play which sets out to be, and of which the greater part *is*, a philosophic discussion of a serious theme. Far be it from me to suggest that such a discussion ought to be conducted in pompous gloom. There is no reason why it should not be amusing. Only, such fun as may occur in it must be merely fun arising from the ideas expressed, or from contrast between the characters of the (quite soberly presented) persons who are expressing themselves. If these persons are presented as figures of fun, how can we be in a mood to listen to them attentively, to take their opinions seriously—in a word, not to be bored by them? It is not we who are at fault, "John Bull's Other Island" was not less "a conversation" than Mr. Shaw's latest play. But there the talkers were recognisable, unguyed human beings, and accordingly we were in a mood to listen to the much that they had to say. We are not lost souls. We can take amusement under the guise of instruction. But Mr. Shaw must not expect us to take instruction under the guise of amusement.

There was an advantage for us in seeing the characters of "John Bull's Other Island" incarnate on the stage : their reality was intensified. It would be similarly an advantage for us to see Plato's Symposium acted. Nevertheless, for the reason given at the beginning of this article, the proper place for both those works is rather the study than the stage. Far more so is it for "Getting Married." Seeing the characters but faintly in the mind's eye, we shall be able to invest them with something of the reality that Mr. Shaw denied them, and to do full justice to the host of valuable ideas that he packed into them.

AN ADRAMATIST

June 6, 1908

We are, most of us, very dull creatures, very timid and tame. When Fate gives us the chance of behaving in a showy manner, of coming out as saints or scoundrels, we edge discreetly away, leaving the chance to others, who (ten to one) don't take it. Here and there, at some odd moment, a really exciting thing—such as the sudden inheritance of vast wealth, or being struck by lightning—

befalls some one of us, so that he, not in himself interesting, becomes an object of passing interest. But these benign occur-
rences are rare. As a rule, Fate doesn't help us out, and our lot is
humdrum, as befits our souls.

Dramatists used to ignore us. They used to fix their attention
on the rare spirits among us—the villainous or heroic spirits,
bitter spirits or sweet, spirits with a capacity for large and lovely or
unlovely manifestations. And such spirits they used to show to
us always in the thick of some "dramatic" crisis, so that the manifestations should be fully made. The naturalistic movement in
drama is a quite recent affair. It is but very recently that *we* have
been deemed worthy the playwright's notice; and we have not yet
got over our embarrassment: we shift nervously from foot to foot,
mumbling that no play with *us* for its material can be "dramatic."
With that epithet, I think, we beg the question. There is no
inherent reason why a play should be based on action—on drama.
The adramatic play, based on the typical humdrum of human life,
is as legitimate a thing, and may be as delightful a thing, as the
similarly-based novel to which now we are so well accustomed.

But the maker of that kind of play (as of that kind of novel) starts
under a rather heavy handicap. The relation of a playwright to his
audience is the same as the relation of any one to the friend whom
he button-holes, to tell him something, in a room. The playwright
wants to interest his audience, just as I want to interest my friend.
The more abnormal the matter of the communication, the likelier
is interest to be aroused. Let us, reader, take a homely hypothesis. I come rushing, one afternoon, into your room, and sink
breathless on a chair, gasping inarticulately, and holding my hand
to my side. You, alarmed at my condition, pour some brandy
into a glass, and "Drink this!" you say. I gulp it down, and presently regain composure enough to falter out what has happened.
"I have been," I begin, "motoring with the Smiths. I had
promised to go down with them to Broxbourne, to lunch with the
Browns. We started at eleven. Mrs. Smith was wearing a cap,
with a veil tied under her chin. Smith himself wore a cap, but
no veil. I remember—how it all comes back to me!—that, just as
I was getting into the car, Mrs. Smith said 'I do hope it won't
rain.'" Here I pause, staring into space. "Yes," you cry, "yes!
Go on!" "Soon before we were in sight of Broxbourne," I resume,

34

"we met a flock of sheep on the road. The chauffeur slowed down. The sheep huddled gradually aside, and one or two of them bleated. Not one of them was run over. After that, I have only a dim memory of what happened: I seem to remember that the Browns were perfectly well, and that we had our coffee in the garden. I remember nothing clearly till, on our way home, we came to a level crossing of the railway. Both the gates were open. The chauffeur, all the same, looked up and down the line. Then we passed across. And—and—here I am!"

Without accusing you of an unwholesome craving for the sensational, I take leave to fear that this story would disappoint you. On the other hand, if I told you quite another story, to the effect that, just as we were entering Broxbourne, we collided with a car which was coming full speed in the opposite direction, and that both cars leapt into the air, and collapsed in fragments, with every one instantly killed, except myself, who, miraculously saved, ran ahead to break the news to the Browns, and found Mr. Brown in the garden, standing on his head, and Mrs. Brown dressed as Marie Antoinette because (as she said) her children had whooping-cough —why then, I dare think, I should hold your attention, however halting and inadequate my way of unfolding the events.

Yet again, let us suppose that my day had been a quite ordinary one, such as I described in the paragraph before last. And let us suppose me to have a quite extraordinary sense of the superficial foibles of my fellow-creatures, and a quite extraordinary insight into their characters. Then, doubtless, I should be able to rivet you with my narration. The Smiths and the Browns would stand out revealed to you, not merely as themselves but as types of their class, and as types of all humanity. You would be stimulated, you would be entranced.

Bearing in mind these hypotheses, let us return to the theatre. It is evident the playwright who deals in heroes, villains, buffoons, queer people who are either doing or suffering either tremendous or funny things, has a very valuable advantage over the playwright who deals merely in humdrum you and me. The dramatist has his material as spring-board. The adramatist must be very much an athlete.

Is Mr. Maurice Baring such an one? His play, "The Grey Stocking," produced one afternoon last week at the New Royalty

Theatre, gives me the impression that he is very athletic by nature, but that he has not "trained" quite hard enough. His next play I shall probably enjoy more than I enjoyed this one (and that is saying much), not only because he is doubtless training hard for it at this moment, but also because I shall know just what to expect. I had not expected adramaturgy. I was on the look-out for things happening; and the fact that nothing happened rather bothered me. Adramaturgy is a recent thing, as I have said; and thus, unless we were forewarned that a play is adramatic, we are hardly in the right mood to receive it. We imagine, by force of habit, that a man who writes a play must have something sharply tragic or comic to reveal. We picture him very much as I have pictured myself rushing feverishly into your room to describe my day with the Smiths. And, if his story be in itself no more thrilling than mine was, there is a similar sense of disappointment. Mr. Baring ought to have given his play a more explicit title—"The Potterers," or something like that. For they are all of them potterers, these creatures of Mr. Baring's fancy. Mentally they are alert enough. They talk about all the fashionable topics, and talk well. Not that the play is "a conversation" à la G. B. S. After a while there are signs that the persons of the play are to be more than talkers at large, and that we are to see them under stress of particular emotion—see their souls at work. Lady Sybil Alston is married to a very religious man. A bore is always a rather dangerous person in a play: he is so apt to bore the audience. Mr. Baring is to be congratulated on having created a bore who really amuses us. Lady Sybil, not sharing our amusement, contracts a sentiment for an attractive foreigner who is staying in her house. Mrs. Willbrough has also contracted a sentiment for him. He has made love to her, and she is rather wounded when she finds that the hostess is the person he really cares for. However, she has a regular lover. With him she goes motoring. The other people in the house are rather uneasy when night falls and the couple has not returned. The couple does return, however, a little later. So *that* is all right. Also, it is all right about Lady Sybil and the foreigner. He does not care for her enough to elope with her. Nor does she care for him enough to elope with him; she prefers to remain with the tedious husband. Well, all this is very true to average life. But in a play where nothing comes of anything, and

where no one is an outwardly exciting person, we must be made
to know the characters very intimately: else we are in danger of
inanition. Mr. Baring gives us deliciously clever sketches of his
characters; but he does not give us the full, deep portraits that are
needed.

A DEPLORABLE AFFAIR

September 5, 1908

In the course of a theatrical season, the critic's proud spirit is
gradually subdued. Twaddling play succeeds twaddling play,
and, as the wearisome procession goes by, the critic's protests become fainter: he begins to acquiesce in what cannot, apparently,
be stopped. But when he comes back after a holiday, with a fresh
eye, with a soul invigorated by contact with real things and lovely
things and things that matter, and comes just in time to see the
same old procession starting placidly forth on the same old route,
then, oh then, it needs a very great effort in him to control his temper. Why should he try? I shall *not* try. All for art, and the
temper well lost, I say. How can Mr. Forbes-Robertson expect
me to be polite about his production at the St. James'? In the
provinces, recently, he produced a play by Mr. Henry James—a
play that was reported to be a great success. It would be a privilege to produce a play by Mr. Henry James, even though the play
failed utterly. In its failure, it would be more interesting, and
would bring higher esteem to its producer, than any number of
successful plays by second-rate men. Having produced Mr.
James' play with success, what does Mr. Forbes-Robertson do so
soon as he comes to London? Apparently in doubt whether Mr.
James be good enough for the metropolis, he gives us Mr. Jerome
Klapka Jerome. This tenth-rate writer has been, for many years,
prolific of his tenth-rate stuff. But I do not recall, in such stuff of
his as I have happened to sample, anything quite so vilely stupid
as "The Passing of the Third Floor Back." I do not for a moment
suppose that Mr. Forbes-Robertson likes it one whit more than I
do. And I wish his pusillanimity in prostituting his great gifts to

it were going to be duly punished. The most depressing aspect
of the whole matter is that the play is so evidently a great success.
The enthusiasm of a first-night audience is no sure gauge of success. Nor is the proverbial apathy of a second-night audience a
sure gauge of failure. It was on the second night that I saw "The
Passing of the Third Floor Back"; and greater enthusiasm have I
seldom seen in a theatre. And thus I am brought sharply up
against that doubt which so often confronts me: what can be hoped
of an art which must necessarily depend on the favour of the public
—of such a public, at least, as ours? Good work may, does sometimes, succeed. But never with the degree of success that befalls
twaddle and vulgarity unrelieved. Twaddle and vulgarity will
have always the upper hand.

The reformation of a bad person by a supernatural visitor is
a theme that has often been used. Mr. Jerome, remembering the
converted miser in "A Christmas Carol," and the converted egoist
in "A Message from Mars," and many a similar convert, was
struck by the bright idea that the effect would be just a dozen
times as great if there were a dozen converts. So he has turned a
supernatural visitor loose in a boarding-house inhabited by a round
dozen of variously bad people—"A Satyr," "A Snob," "A
Shrew," "A Painted Lady," "A Cheat," and so on. Now, supposing that these characters were life-like, or were amusing figments of the brain, and supposing that we saw them falling, little
by little, under the visitor's spell, till gradually we were aware that
they had been changed for the better, the play might be quite a
passable affair. But to compass that effect is very far beyond Mr.
Jerome's power. He has neither the natural talent nor the technical skill that the task requires. There is not a spark of verisimilitude in the whole dozen of characters. One and all, they are
unreal. Mr. Jerome shows no sign of having ever observed a
fellow-creature. His characters seem to be the result solely of a
study of novelettes in the penny weekly papers, supplemented by
a study of the works of Mr. Jerome K. Jerome. Take Major
Tompkins, and his wife and daughter, for example. Could anything be more trite and crude than their presentment? Major and
Mrs. Tompkins are anxious to sell their daughter for gold to an
elderly man. "His very touch," says the daughter, according to
custom, "is loathsome." The Major persists and says—what

else could a stage-major say?—"Damn your infernal impudence!"
The unnatural mother tries to persuade the unwilling daughter to
wear a more décolleté dress. The daughter, of course, loves a
young painter in a brown velveteen jacket; but she is weak and
worldly, and she is like to yield to the importunities of the elderly
man. The young painter—but no, I won't bore you by describing
the other characters: suffice it that they are all ground out of the
same old rusty machine that has served "The Family Herald" and
similar publications for so many weary years. Mr. Jerome's
humour, however, is his own, and he plasters it about with a liberal
hand. What could be more screamingly funny than the doings at
the outset? The landlady pours tea into the decanter which is
supposed to hold whisky, on the chance that the drunken boarder
won't notice the difference. Then she goes out, and the servant
drinks milk out of the jug and replenishes the jug with water.
Then *she* goes out, and the "Painted Lady" comes in and steals a
couple of fresh candles from the sconces on the piano and substitutes
a couple of candle ends. Then *she* goes out, and the Major comes
in and grabs the biscuits off the plate and drops them into his hat.
Then *he* goes out, and the "Cad" and the "Rogue" come in and
unlock the spirit-case with an illicit key and help themselves to
what they presently find is tea. He's inexhaustibly fertile in such
sequences is Mr. Jerome K. Jerome. When the "Passer-by"
knocks at the front-door, and is admitted with a limelight full on
his (alas, Mr. Forbes-Robertson's) classic countenance, the
sequences set in with an awful severity. The beneficent stranger
has one method for all evildoers, and he works it on every one in
turn, with precisely the same result. He praises the landlady for
her honesty; then the landlady is ashamed of her dishonesty and
becomes honest. He praises the Major for his sweet temper; then
the Major is ashamed of his bad temper, and becomes sweet-
tempered. He praises the "Painted Lady" for her modesty in
not thinking herself beautiful without paint; then the "Painted
Lady" is ashamed of her paint, and reappears paintless. He
praises—but again I won't bore you further. You have found the
monotony of the foregoing sentences oppressive enough. Picture
to yourselves the monotony of what they describe! For a period
of time that seemed like eternity, I had to sit knowing exactly what
was about to happen, and how it was about to happen, and knowing

that as soon as it had happened it would happen again. The art of dramaturgy, some one has said, is the art of preparation. In that case Klapka is assuredly the greatest dramatist the world has ever known. It is hard to reconcile this conclusion with the patent fact that he hasn't yet mastered the rudiments of his craft.

The third and last act of the play, like the second, consists of a sequence of interviews—next man, please!—between the visitor and the other (now wholly reformed) persons of the play. Steadily, he works through the list, distributing full measure of devastating platitudes, all the way. The last person on the list, the Major's daughter, says suddenly "Who are you?" The visitor spreads his arms, in the attitude of "The Light of the World." The Major's daughter falls on her knees in awe. When the visitor passes out through the front-door, a supernatural radiance bursts through the fan-light, flooding the stage; and then the curtain comes slowly down. Well, I suppose blasphemy pays.

"IMPRESSIONS OF HENRY IRVING"*

September 12, 1908

A very pleasant book, this, on a level far above the usual books about deceased actors. It is usually by some hack-journalist, who knew the deceased slightly, or by some pious understrapper who knew him too well, in too special a relationship, to have the faintest notion of what he roundly was like, that such memoirs are undertaken. Mr. Pollock has the prime advantage of being a man of letters; so that we can read with pleasure what he writes. And he has the corollary advantage of having met Irving on more or less equal terms. For many years there was an intimate friendship between the two men; nor was Mr. Pollock so spell-bound by Irving in private life that he could not detect, here and there, some little fault in this and that of Irving's performances on the stage, and point them out to Irving, who, like all men of active and creative mind, was always ready to learn from any one who had

* By W. H. Pollock. Longmans, Green and Co. 1908. 3s. 6d.

anything to teach him. Mr. Pollock's hero was, in some measure, also his comrade. And in the form of this book there is an appropriate free-and-easiness. Analyses of Irving's various conceptions, and descriptions of his "business" at such and such a moment, are mingled, in the haphazard way of table-talk, with reflections on the art of acting in general, and with anecdotes about the great man and his friends. There is a delightful glimpse of Mounet-Sully, about to start on a journey from London to the south coast, and being taught "some dozen complete English phrases" by Mr. Pollock and Robert Louis Stevenson. Why does that glimpse stand out so delightfully? There are a score of glimpses of Irving, not less vivid, not less amusing in themselves. Why does this one outstand? Because, I fear, "R. L. S." is in it. Him I never met; and not even he can have had a personality stranger or more magical than was Irving's as I so well remember it. And yet Stevenson is more real to me, means and matters more to me, than Irving. He worked in a durable medium. His work survives; and so he survives with it. Irving is but a memory, to be conjured forth from darkness. Mr. Pollock himself speaks of "the hard fate" of actors in all ages, and tries to console himself and them with "the fame, to take two instances, of Roscius and of Garrick." But, frankly, who cares twopence about either Garrick or Roscius? Suppose there were living at this moment some extremely old gentleman who had seen them both, and remembered both of them distinctly, should we—even the most stage-struck among us—be very keen to read that old gentleman's book of reminiscences? However great his skill in writing, he would not give us any clear or trustworthy vision, would not make us participate in his own enthusiasm. Mr. Pollock, very rightly, does not essay the impossible task of displaying Henry Irving's art to posterity. He writes solely for those who have seen Irving, taking all the essentials for granted, and pausing over just this and that incidental detail that may have escaped our notice, or may have been misunderstood. And already, despite the glow of his interest, these details have something of the dryness of archæology—the dryness that clings about things that are over and cannot be renewed. Despite Mr. Pollock's glow, I am conscious of a severe chill when he speaks of "the always charming Nelly Moore," "the always excellent acting of Mead," "Frl. Ulrich, then in the zenith of attraction and of dramatic subtlety and power," "Dettmer, who died all too young." Even had Dettmer lived just long enough for me to see him and to applaud him frantically, I should not now be very much interested in my recollection of him. But then, of course, I have not the advantage that Mr. Pollock has: the advantage of being a really ardent playgoer, to whom the theatre is a temple of high ecstasies. I can enjoy *a* theatre, when there is a good new play well-acted. "The" theatre means little to me; and its past, nothing.

It is only outside the theatre, in the contemplation of life at large, that I get *my* high ecstasies. And thus, since Irving was certainly one of the most remarkable personages of his day, the parts of Mr. Pollock's book that most interest me are those in which he tells us of Irving as he knew him in private life. Every one, even the least sensitive one, the most impervious one, who ever met Irving, must have in some measure felt the magnetism of the man. Mr. Pollock, as I have said, did not succumb so utterly that he could not be a useful friend, an adviser. Yet he succumbed rather too far to be now able to give us of Irving a portrait that we can accept as perfect. He was not, indeed, so magnetised that he did not ask Irving whether the guests for supper on the stage of the Lyceum, all crowded under a marquee, would not fare badly in case of fire. Irving soothed him by revealing to him "some" of the precautions, "which alone would have been enough to reassure the most timid. And," adds Mr. Pollock, ashamed, in retrospect, of his misgivings, "if the marquee itself had suddenly come crashing down I feel sure it would have been a case not of 'impavidum' but of 'impavidos ferient ruinae.' Irving's presence and demeanour would have reassured all who were tempted to panic, while his quiet commands would have brought order from chaos." I am afraid that I, suddenly buried under a heavy and inflammable sheet with a hundred other people, should have been one of "those who were tempted to panic" and that even the "presence and demeanour" of my host, similarly buried somewhere but issuing "quiet commands," would not have sufficed to make a man of me. Perhaps I should have felt all right if I had been, like Mr. Pollock, constantly in touch with Irving, and charged thoroughly with his magnetism. And then perhaps, too, I should, like Mr. Pollock, not dare to breathe on the legend that Irving was, in addition to his genius for

acting, a great scholar and a man of exceedingly fine taste in literature. Mr. Pollock must know, none better, how absolute a
legend this is; but he will not breathe on it. In "Much Ado
About Nothing" Irving "by an oversight fell upon employing an
entirely modern phrase" as an "aside" in one of the dialogues with
Beatrice. Some weeks later Mr. Pollock saw the play again, and
the offending "aside" was still in use. Then he spoke to Irving,
who was grateful for the hint. For "by an oversight" read "because he did not know better." Left to act for himself, Mr. Pollock was always bold enough to help Irving in matters of literature.
But he was, on one occasion at any rate, easily deflected by "a light,
meaning touch" on his arm from one of "the trusted and con-
fidential marshals" who guarded Irving's majesty. One evening
"Irving was sympathetically and generously enthusiastic over
Tennyson's work, and, referring to the beautiful lines beginning
'There was a little fair-hair'd Norman maid'—a speech which he
always delivered as one rapt in it—he expressed a strong doubt if
there was anything in Shakespeare to be preferred to it." Mr.
Pollock, "startled"—but was he really startled?—"by such a
delivery from such a source," was about to protest, when he felt the
aforesaid touch on the arm, and said nothing. I wonder if it was
Mr. Loveday, that faithful henchman, who administered the touch.
Irving was trying various sets of sledge-bells for "The Bells." He
"began to eliminate them one by one until one set was left for final
consideration. Then he listened more carefully than ever to that
set, and then he turned to Mr. Loveday, a very accomplished
musician, and said: 'Now, isn't that the right set?'—a question
which provoked an emphatic 'Not a doubt about it'"—an answer
which Mr. Pollock offers as a proof of Irving's omniscience, and
not as having the slightest element of comedy in it.

Irving had many faithful henchmen, of various grades. I think,
however, that Mr. Pollock goes rather too far in saying that he
inspired "a real affection in all—actors, supers, and stage-hands
alike, who ever worked with or under him." That he was much
loved by many people is quite true. It is a saying that would be
equally true of any man of genius. Whistler, for example, was
much loved by many people. But he was not, in the ordinary
sense of the word, "lovable." As a rule, he inspired fear rather
than love. I would not say that of Irving; though I would say

that in the love he inspired there was always a strong admixture of fear, and that in many cases the fear he inspired was (as a matter of common knowledge) not mitigated by love. In every man there is a mixture of kindness and unkindness. In Irving both these qualities existed in a very high degree; and the number of wonderfully kind things that he is known to have done is hardly greater than the number of wonderfully unkind things that he is known to have said. When Richard Mansfield was playing Hamlet in London, he told Irving, at supper, how awful the spiritual exigency of the part was to him, how he suffered all that Hamlet suffered, not only during the performance, but throughout all the hours of day and night. After Mansfield had dilated at tremendous length, and with tremendous force, on his sufferings, Irving removed his cigar from his lips, and said "I almost wonder you play the part, since you find it so—unwholesome." I quote that remark because it is so particularly good an example of the sardonic humour for which Irving was famous, and of which Mr. Pollock offers no example whatsoever. To ignore Irving's cruelty is to ignore a very salient part of him. Which quality predominated in him—cruelty or kindness? He was an actor, and, even more obviously than most actors, he acted a great deal in private life. How far were both his kindness and his cruelty exaggerated for effect? And, again, how far was his early Bohemian self merged and lost in his later Pontifical self? Did he actually become, at last, what he wished to seem? The people who knew him best are the people least likely to enlighten us in these problems. His magnetism, even through the pavement of Westminster Abbey, is still too strong on them.

"THE CORSICAN BROTHERS"

September 26, 1908

I had never seen this play, and had supposed it would appeal only to the antiquarian in me, and was surprised to find the simple playgoer in me really thrilled by it.

Not that it didn't delight me as a curiosity, too. In the sophisticated modern mode of dramatic exposition, derived by us from
Ibsen, our old friend "the confidant" has no place; and for that old
friend I have a sneaking kindness. He always touched me, with
his humility, his utter selflessness, his inexhaustible capacity for
framing apt questions and drinking in the answers with a look of
dog-like devotion. He never thrust himself forward, never was
there when he wasn't wanted, but, when he *was* wanted—and with
what sweet frequency he *was*!—instantly he turned up with a
string of his invaluable questions, and stood at 'tention to be tapped
on the chest by the hero, his hero, as often as need be, and never
moved a muscle of his devoted face lest our attention should be
distracted to himself. Each of the Corsican Brothers is a hero,
and to each of them is attached a confidant of the deepest dye.
Fabien dei Franchi owns M. le Baron de Montgiron. To Louis
dei Franchi belongs M. le Baron Martelli. To which nobleman
the palm? One might as well hope to discriminate the characters
of their twin masters. Enough that they are both perfect. When
the ghost of slain Louis appears to Fabien at the end of the play,
"Farewell, dear brother," says Fabien, "we shall meet again."
Fabien can afford to wait, I daresay, as being himself a living
souvenir of the departed. But how about poor M. le Baron Martelli? What is become of *him*? Let us hope Fabien takes him on
as joint-confidant with M. le Baron de Montgiron. But this would
be rather hard on Montgiron, that faithful soul. So let us hope
Martelli blows out his brains and goes to join Louis in heaven,
there to ask such questions as are necessary to the angels' understanding of who and what on earth Louis on earth was. . . . "Tell
me, Louis! When first, as a child, you felt within your breast
the chords of that mysterious affinity for your twin-brother which
you have just explained to me, was there vouchsafed to you a pre-
monition of your own untimely doom?" But no, I cannot hope to
imitate the manner of the dialogue in "The Corsican Brothers."
Such dialogue is a lost art—lost to all of us save Mr. Pinero alone.
"Be generous enough to call my carriage, and permit me to depart!" cries Mme Emilie de Lesparre to M. de Château Renaud.
The true Pinero touch there! But, whereas in Mr. Pinero's plays
this kind of lingo is vexatious, and we feel it our duty to try and
break Mr. Pinero of it, in "The Corsican Brothers" it has an

agreeable quaintness, the aroma of a past age—an age for which we are not responsible. Of course, human beings never talked like that; but that *was* how the dramatists used to write, thirty years or so ago; and we are interested and touched, even as by the costumes of the persons of the play. Mr. Martin Harvey is never perfunctory about the costumes in his productions. He always seems to have procured some good artist to design them. And in "The Corsican Brothers," so soon as the venue shifts from Corsica to Paris, we have a really good presentment of the fashions of 1830 —that most amusing of all periods. The scene of the Foyer de l'Opéra is a perfect realisation of Gavarni, with just that romantic pathos that Gavarni has for us. But come! I am writing as though I had not been thrilled by the play itself.

Melodramas about modern English life don't thrill me, because they don't illude me. But how should I be sceptical about anything in regard to Corsica and 1830? I could believe anything of the ladies and gentlemen in Gavarni's drawings. And as for Corsica, she is in herself notoriously melodramatic. Vendettas apart, did she not give us Napoleon? How should I reject the Franchi twins? Their mother, sweetly solicitous for their credibility, says twice in the course of the first act "In Corsica we are still in the sixteenth century." Never mind the sixteenth century, madam: Corsica's enough for me. And have no fear, madam, that I shall doubt the extraordinary powers of mutual telepathy said to be possessed by your two fine sons. When Sir Henry Irving produced the play, doubtless there were many who said that such powers could never have existed even in Corsica. In the middle-Victorian era telepathy was regarded as a silly superstition. In all ages, presumably, there have been cases of telepathic communication; but not till lately have they been scientifically investigated and collated and forced on us as solid facts—facts as solid as the Marconi rays. That Fabien in Corsica should know that Louis in Paris was in danger, and that Louis should thereafter appear to him at the moment of death, seems not at all strange to us; and all the greater, therefore—all the more personal—is the thrill we get when the murdered brother appears. The end of the first act—Fabien's decision to start forth and avenge Louis forthwith—left me in a state of lively speculation as to what would happen. Never having seen the play, I was not sure that

Fabien had not set out on a fool's errand. Telepathy is a tricky thing—might be so even between twins. Once I woke up in the middle of the night *knowing* that a friend of mine, many miles away, was in utmost distress. I could not go to sleep again, paced up and down my room, and, as soon as the telegraph office opened, I wired *Are you all right*. The answer was *Yes quite why*. I received it with mixed emotions. Usually, when I tell the story, I say that the answer was *Desperate will write*. I am, in fact, one of the people who bring discredit on psychical science. The strength of my belief goads me to the manufacture of proof for sceptics. I did not, of course, suspect that Fabien dei Franchi was a fellow-sinner in this respect. But it was quite possible that the apparition which he—and I, too, for that matter—had beheld, might be a mere hallucination, signifying nothing. And I reflected that it would be great fun if, on his arrival in Paris, he found his brother Louis perfectly well, thank you, and making desperate love to the lady of their twin hearts, Mme de Lesparre. But that was not to be. The second act (whose action is simultaneous with that of the first) shows that Louis is perfectly correct in his behaviour. He is merely trying to rescue Mme de Lesparre from the toils of M. de Château Renaud, who is "a destroyer of women" and the best fencer in Paris. Louis has never handled a foil; so that he would naturally have some presage of doom, to account for his obvious depression. In case he should cheer up, however, his father's ghost has risen to assure him that he will perish on the morrow—at ten minutes past nine, to be precise. I clutched faintly at the hope that perhaps the message would be falsified; but of course Louis perished punctually. A few days later, in the same glade of the same forest, we see M. de Château Renaud on his way to Switzerland. This time, it is *his* turn to have forebodings. He feels that some power is holding him for the avenger. His post-chaise has overturned, and, as he says with doubtful logic, "the post-chaise was not overturned because the postillion was drunk. The postillion was drunk because Fate had willed that the post-chaise should be overturned." Doubt his logic, but not his forebodings! Enter Fabien, with forebodings of triumph. They begin to fight; and, after the first bout, in case we should still make any mistake as to what is coming, M. de Château Renaud says good-bye to his second.

I do wish that just something in the play, here and there, were left to chance; or at any rate that the characters themselves were not quite so acutely presentimental. It is the fashion to say—I often say it myself—that without freewill there can be no drama. Certainly (with all deference to the Greeks) the persons of a play are by so much the less interesting when they are presented as puppets of destiny. Still less interesting are they when they are presented as puppets who know exactly which wire the showman is going to pull next. Therefore—but why theorise? The solid fact remains that "The Corsican Brothers" really thrilled me, even moved me. You might not think so, from my manner of writing about it; but I can't help my manner.

AGONISING SAMSON

December 19, 1908

For good downright boredom, mingled with acute irritation, commend me to the evening I spent last Tuesday in the theatre of Burlington House. The Milton Tercentenary has produced a fine crop of dulness and silliness, but nothing quite so silly and dull as this performance of "Samson Agonistes" under the auspices of the British Academy and under the direction of Mr. William Poel.

Let "Samson Agonistes" be read, by all means. (I wondered how many members of that academic audience had ever read a page of it.) It contains (along with many passages of arid prosiness, which may well be skipped) some passages of noble poetry, over which one may well linger. But even an ideal performance of it would be tedious; for there is in it no dramatic quality whatsoever: Milton was out to edify, not to thrill. In a play constructed exactly on the Greek model, the Chorus must, of course, be rich in moral platitudes. Milton's Chorus of Danites is rich in them beyond the dreams of avarice. And—here comes in the sting for us—so is Milton's Samson. "How counterfeit a coin they are who friends bear in their superscription (of the most I would be

understood :) in prosperous days they swarm, but in adverse withdraw their head, not to be found, though sought." These are not
the words of the Chorus. They are Samson's own, and a fair
sample of his abundance. Between him and the Chorus is kept
up a friendly rivalry in triteness. "My friends," he seems to say,
"you see me here betrayed, blinded, cast out, grounded, a mock
to my enemies. No matter! I can still take the lead in edifying
conversation. Yes! every cloud has a silver lining. It is a poor
heart that never rejoices. There are as good fish in the sea as ever
were caught" etc., etc. Even Dalila, the one dramatically
imagined person in the play, has a taste for copy-book headings;
and we feel that Samson enjoys her visit, brutal though his manner
to her is. What prevents him from being in the least a dramatic
figure is his sober acquiescence in what has befallen him. No
Prometheus he! No conflict in *his* bosom! He regards himself,
he points himself out to us, as an awful example. He had blurted
out to Dalila the secret which he ought to have kept to himself;
and for that indiscretion Jehovah has punished him, severely indeed, but not one whit too severely; and anyhow "these rags, this
grinding, is not yet so base as was that former servitude" to his
wife. He regrets that he is no longer able to serve his people
against the unrighteous Philistines; for himself he rebels not at all.
He does not even want to escape from his bondage. His father
comes, with a proposal to have him ransomed. That idea doesn't
at all appeal to Samson. "Let me here," says he, "as I deserve,
pay on my punishment, and expiate, if possible, my crime, shame-
ful garrulity." (Cf. "Mrs. Turner's Cautionary Tales in Verse,"
passim.) Dalila comes, trying to reawaken his passion for her.
In this scene there might easily have been a real conflict in Samson. Milton saw the opportunity. "Beauty, though injurious,"
says the Chorus, "hath strange power, after offence returning, to
regain love once possess'd, nor can be easily repulsed, without
much inward passion felt, and secret sting of amorous remorse."
But Milton wasn't going to be so unedifying as to *take* the opportunity, not he! and "Love-quarrels oft in pleasing concord end,"
remarks Samson drily, "not wedlock treachery endangering life."
It is only just towards the end of the play that a glimpse of drama
is vouchsafed to us, when Samson begins, at length, "to feel some
rousing motions" and decides that he will, after all, betake himself

to the temple of Dagon. But before that point was reached in the performance on Tuesday evening, I had betaken myself out of Burlington House, bored beyond endurance by the intrinsic dulness of the play, and beyond endurance exasperated by the series of gratuitous and grotesque blunders in the method of its production.

Against Mr. Poel's arrangement of the stage I have nothing to say. The tenebrous array of purple curtains that was so ludicrously wrong in his production of "The Bacchae" was not inappropriate here. (A lady sitting behind me remarked to her companion, before the play began, "Evidently this is going to be something in the Greek style." A great tribute, this, to Mr. Poel's educational influence.) Nor was I embarrassed by the hoop and the Medici collar that Dalila wore while the rest of the characters wore some sort of vaguely Phrygian attire. Such anomalies are dear to the mystic heart of Mr. Poel, and one makes shift to accept them for that reason. My quarrel with Mr. Poel is on larger issues. I take it that the first, the most important, task for a producer of this play is to find an actor who can be a passable Samson. The scope of the investigation is narrowed by the fact that only a man of great height and breadth can be Samson without making himself and the play that depends on him utterly ridiculous. The man must have a tremendous voice, too, and must be able to manage it with such skill, such power of variety in elocution, as is needed for the proper recital of many hundreds of lines in blank verse. I do not know of any man on the English stage who could be really successful as Samson, except Mr. Hubert Carter. He, perhaps, was not available for this occasion. But if it was impossible to find a likelier man than Mr. Ian Maclaren for the part, Mr. Poel ought to have asked leave of the British Academy to shelve the production altogether. Any one less like a blinded and brooding giant than Mr. Maclaren I cannot off-hand conceive. He has, certainly, a sense for verse, and his delivery of the long speeches was never monotonous in cadence. For the meaning of the verse, however, and for the character of Samson, he seemed to have no sense at all. Or perhaps the sense was in him, and he was simply unable to express it, by reason of the quality of his voice. A deep and resounding voice is even more important than great physical bulk. Mr. Maclaren has neither the one requisite nor the other. His voice is a baritone, a very pleasant baritone; and the sound of it was as inappropriate to Samson as were Mr. Maclaren's graceful attitudes. I think I strained a point in suggesting that this voice, and not lack of imagination, may account for the absurdity of Mr. Maclaren's performance. For the voice was used in a lingering and sentimental manner that cannot have been otherwise than intentional. I should like to see Mr. Maclaren as the Duke in "Twelfth Night." But I was sorry to see the Duke in "Twelfth Night" as Samson. Before I pass from the subject of Samson himself, I must speak a word or two about the youth who led him on to the stage. The stage-managing of this youth is a good example of the strange workings of Mr. Poel's mind. As if to emphasise the fact that Mr. Maclaren is not gigantic, the youth was stationed, throughout Samson's first long speech, on the step above him. And throughout all Samson's speeches, the youth stood close to him, but with his back turned to him (and presenting to the audience a strongly Semitic profile, in order to remind us, in Mr. Poel's freakish way, that Samson was a Jew and that Mr. Maclaren is a Gentile).

This immobile, averted, Semitic companion of the giant would in himself have sufficed to wreck even an ideal performance. But, as if to leave nothing to chance, Mr. Poel had contrived a yet more devastatingly ludicrous effect in the management of the Chorus. Samson appeared through an entrance at the side of the stage. One would have supposed that the Chorus would appear through this or some adjacent entrance. But trust Mr. Poel to have an ace up his sleeve! The theatre in Burlington House, as perhaps you know, is a semicircular one, with about twelve steep tiers of seats rising one above another. These tiers are divided by gangways, for people to pass down to their seats; and at the top of these gangways are the entrances to the theatre. After Samson's first speech our attention was attracted by a weird twittering noise at one of the entrances. The twitter developed into a murmur of feminine voices. Are the militant Suffragists upon us? we wondered, gazing up towards the door. A score of vaguely Phrygian figures came in view, and began to pick their way (very slowly, for fear of tripping up) down the steep gangway, ululating all the while, in our midst; and then the magnitude of Mr. Poel's inspiration dawned on us: here was the Chorus of the play! Of course, there could be no archaeological reason for this mode of entry. Aesthetically, of course, there could be no reason for it, since it must obviously destroy all aesthetic illusion, and send us all into paroxysms of internal laughter. So delighted was Mr. Poel at his joke that he repeated it till it grew just a little stale. Dalila came on by the door at the side of the stage, presumably because her hoop would have stuck in the gangway. But Manoa came down the gangway in fine style, and then up it again, as soon as his scene was over; and so did Harapha. Mr. Lionel Braham, who played the latter, is a man of truly gigantic proportions, and had assumed an incredibly fee-fi-fo-fum demeanour, so that Harapha's refusal to tackle Samson was one of the crowning absurdities of an absurd evening. The poor ladies of the Chorus, cramped and huddled together, failed to give the grace of audibility to the words they had to utter. But one of the two or three men of the Chorus seemed to be thoroughly enjoying his evening, and gave an elaborate character sketch of a rural dotard, somewhat in the manner of Mr. Chevalier.

MISS ELLEN TERRY'S BOOK

October 10, 1908

Once I went behind the scenes of the Lyceum after the first night of some play. (Reassure yourself, there was nothing indecorous in my going: I was not yet a dramatic critic.) Somewhere in the middle of the stage, but quite invisible and inaccessible by reason of the dense crowd of friends around him, stood Henry Irving. Everybody seemed to be standing on tip-toe, peering bright-eyed over heads, and everybody was talking at the top of his or her voice, and everybody's theme was composed of "Henry" and "Ellen" in about equal proportions. They all knew one another; and all, diverse though they were, were united in the bond of their hero-worship and heroine-worship. The crowd grew and grew, and though, according to Mr. Walter Pollock, Irving was always extraordinarily careful about every detail of his great hospitality, and foresaw every smallest requirement, there were no policemen to regulate us. Presently, having abandoned all hope of setting eyes on my host, I was consoled by a vision of Miss Terry. Accompanied by three or four of the ardent and picturesque young ladies who attach themselves to the suite of any very eminent actress, she was making her way down the narrow and crazy-looking wooden staircase that led from the dressing-rooms to the stage. Half-way, she paused suddenly and clasped her hands up in front of her as she gazed down at the sea of bobbing heads. The gesture betokened a mingling of rapture and fear—the emotion of a wood-nymph about to take her first plunge in the sea. Nor was it merely my sense of beauty that was stirred : the sense of history was stirred, too, in me, and I thought of the many other occasions on which Miss Terry must have descended this staircase to mingle with this adoring throng. Endlessly they unfurled themselves to me—the first nights, the hundredth nights, the last nights, on which she had beheld this sparkling sea outspread beneath her. And I wondered what, at this moment, was passing through her bonny brain. Was the whole thing as fresh as ever to her? Did she really, as her mien indicated, feel herself half-allured, half-terrified, by the prospect of a plunge into waters unknown? Or had she, after all these years, become habituated, as to the morning bath?

I think she felt just what she displayed. Of course, to any actor or actress, who has experience, emotion becomes a habit ; and a display of emotion by him or her is apt to be less significant than such display by us who are not called on to be emotional for our livelihood. But the emotion, though it be not fundamental, and be out of all proportion to its cause, and leave no trace when it is past, is not necessarily to be scouted as unfelt. Miss Terry, as her book* shows, has a great power of detachment ; and, had she not been born an actress, would have been—indeed, is, even so— a very good dramatic critic, and a very good critic of life. But it does not follow that her emotions, on or off the stage, are not all of them, at the moment of experience, perfectly genuine to her. And, actress though she is, it is clear from her book that she has more capacity for what I have called fundamental emotion than half-a-dozen ordinary women rolled into one. She is a woman—a very extraordinary woman—first, and an actress afterwards. I do not

* "The Story of My Life." By Ellen Terry. London : Hutchinson.

say she is not a born actress; merely that the born woman in her preponderates. This is not an original criticism of her. She makes it herself, more than once, in the course of her book. And throughout the book it is her insatiable love of life, rather than of the stage, that shines forth for us. When first she crossed the Atlantic, "the ship was laden with pig-iron, and she rolled and rolled and rolled. She could never roll too much for me! I have always been a splendid sailor, and I feel jolly at sea." One can well imagine that. But her jollity on land is quite enough to go on with. And there is in her retrospect a curious absence of that sadness which ordinary people feel when they think of what is past. Cares and sorrows she has had, but she looks back on them with the clear brow of one who was very well able to bear them. And her joys she records with the gusto that is possible only to a person who is just as joyous as ever. "I am afraid," she says—and this seems to be the only thing she *is* afraid of—"that I think as little of the future as I do of the past. The present for me!" Those last four words are a perfect summing-up of her nature, and might serve as a motto for all optimists. But it is by very reason of the delight she has always had in the passing moment that she writes so well about her past. It is because she saw things and felt things so vividly at the time that she can now make us partakers of her vision and emotion. Her emotional faculty has, as I suggested, been developed by the practice of her art; and just so must her visual faculty have been developed by communion with the painters and sculptors who clustered about her from the outset, seeking and finding inspiration, and giving such inspiration as they could in return. Her descriptions of people's appearances are always delightful—consisting usually of some image funnily far-fetched yet scrupulously exact. Of Mme Bernhardt she says "transparent as an azalea, only more so; like a cloud, only not so thick. Smoke from a burning paper describes her more nearly," and of another well-known lady "she reminded me, as always, of the reflection of something in water on a misty day," and of Irving in his last phase "he looked like some beautiful grey tree that I have seen in Savannah." Of Irving when she first knew him she says "there was a touch of exaggeration in his appearance—a dash of Werther, with a few flourishes of Jingle," and of William Terriss "sometimes he reminded me of a butcher-boy flashing past, whistling, on the high seat of his cart, or of Phaëton driving the chariot of the sun—pretty much the same thing, I imagine." The precision of these harlequin-leaps is positively Meredithian. And you can see that Miss Terry has been at pains here to give the exact literary expression to her thought. It is only rarely that she writes in that clean-cut manner. Her writing is for the most part frankly the writing of an amateur. But when an amateur happens, like Miss Terry, to be a born writer, the result is always charming, and one may well be thankful for the lack of professionalism. The average professional writer knows and cannot forget the easiest recipes for expressing this or that, and therefore expresses this or that exactly like all the other average professionals, and therefore expresses nothing of himself. Style is the expression of self. Every (gifted) beginner has style, and it is very rarely that when he has mastered the technique of writing his style comes out unscathed. Yet it is only after technique has been mastered that style can become beautiful in itself. Miss Terry might perhaps, if she gave her mind to it, become a really beautiful writer. The chances are that she would but lose that quality of freshness and life which makes her writing so adorable now.

COQUELIN'S DEATH

January 30, 1909

When a man dies quite suddenly in the fulness of his powers, we are apt to think that Fate has been unkind to him. This is a confusion of ideas. Who would not wish, just for his own sake, to die just such a death? The blow by which Fate strikes down a flourishing ordinary man is cruel only in its effect on those who were his friends. When a great man is stricken down untimely, then there is a vast number of people to be condoled with—people deprived, without warning, of a treasure that they had thought would be theirs to enjoy for many years. The death of Coquelin may without hyperbole be described as a blow to the whole educated world. And the blow falls most heavily on those who knew

534

the man himself, not merely because they lose in him a delightful friend or acquaintance, but because they were of all people the least prepared for his death. His air of soundness and robustness behind the footlights was as nothing to what it was in private life. Sixty-eight years old he was, according to the newspapers. It seems impossible. Time had pushed him into middle age, and then had grown tired of the exertion and left him standing there unmolested, privileged, a brilliant fixture. He had the toughness of the peasant, without the tasks that make the peasant grow old. His stout little legs seemed to be rooted in the soil. It was hard to believe that his father had been a baker. One would have said that a bakery was too artificial a place for the production of so earthy and windy a creature as Coquelin. "Intellectual" though he was, he had no "nerves" to trouble him. His brain found all the food it needed in his blood and muscle.

On the stage it was always with his brain alone that he made his effects. He had observed, and studied, and thought, and had thought out the exact means of expression. He never let emotion come between himself and his part—never trusted to imagination or inspiration. These, indeed, are qualities which he did not possess. They are incompatible with absence of "nerves." And it was, I suppose, because he could never surrender himself to a part, was always conscious master of it, that Sarah Bernhardt wrote of him in her memoirs that he was "plutôt grand acteur que grand artiste." Certainly, great emotional acting does demand the power of self-surrender—is a passive rather than an active business. Coquelin, in his writings and in his talk, was a sturdy champion of Diderot's paradox. And Coquelin, in the last act of "Cyrano de Bergerac," was a shining refutation of the truth of that paradox. All the paraphernalia of emotion were in that memorable passage of acting—were there most beautifully and authentically; but emotion itself wasn't there; and many a duffer could have moved us far more than Coquelin did. If Coquelin had been capable of the necessary self-surrender, he would not have been the unapproachable comedian that we loved and revered. It was because his fine brain was absolutely his master that he stood absolutely alone in his mastery of comedic art.

That he has died on the brink of what he believed would be his greatest triumph, and of what probably would have been his greatest triumph, will have seemed to many people an especially cruel fate for him to have suffered. There is no doubt that during the past seven years or so the prospect of "Chantecler" was the very pivot of his being. He had always had, very rightly, and very engagingly, an enormous self-esteem. But its centre of gravity seemed, in the past few years, to have shifted away from the past and present into the future—always the immediate future in which "cette admirable génie," Rostand, would complete and let go the MS. of "Chantecler." Years ago, a Frenchman whom I know, and who has a great talent for mimicry, gave me a general "sketch" of Coquelin saying stridently, with his sculptured elocution, "Moi, je ne parle jamais de moi; par-ce-que"—whereon followed a series of the most cogent and lucid reasons for Coquelin's avoidance of the topic. Like all the best satire, this satire was based on a sympathetic understanding of its butt. The mimicry could not have been so perfect if the mimic had not been truly fond of Coquelin. In later years he emended his "sketch": "Moi, je ne parle jamais de 'Chantecler'; par-ce-que"—. It was always mainly of "Chantecler" that Coquelin would talk to me whenever in recent years, and wherever, I had the honour of meeting him. And always it was in Dieppe (whither he went annually) that he talked with greatest unction and élan. Always an expansive man, he seemed to expand beyond measure in Dieppe. The manager of the Casino, M. Bloch, was an old and devoted admirer of him and his art, and always placed at his disposal a suite of rooms on the Casino's terrace. Year by year, Coquelin's first appearance on this terrace was a great occasion, semi-royal, but wholly human; a sight that did one's heart good. Splendid in a brand-new white yachting-cap and a pair of brand-new white shoes, and swinging in his hand a brand-new white umbrella, he came forth into the sunshine—sunshine than which he was more dazzling to the abonnés. "That's he!" or "That's him!" whispered the English ones. "Voilà la saison qui commence," murmured the French ones, with a smile that failed to conceal awe. And he, "la saison," was a picture of happiness, as he stood inaugurally there, with a plump thumb in the arm-hole of his waistcoat, and with his head thrown back at the well-known angle, snuffing the ozone through those great comedic nostrils. After he had stood awhile, he would make his progress along the terrace, flanked on either side by some friend or henchman for whose benefit he talked and talked, slowly, impressively, delightedly. "Moi, je ne parle jamais de 'Chantecler'; par-ce-que " . . . Now and again he would pause to salute or accost a passing friend, but always thereafter resumed the thread of his discourse. It was a pleasure to watch the splendid mobile mask that was his face; and the pleasure was greater when you yourself were elected as a companion—as a receiver of laws laid down by him in a voice that was like the twanging of a violoncello, and of theories elaborated in a penetrating whisper and with the cunningest of smiles. His manner alone would have sufficed for edification. But it was a strong and subtle brain, Coquelin's, and what he said was always as good as the way he said it. To converse with him might have been rather up-hill work. I fancy he was not a man to encourage interruptions. But I may be wrong. I was never tempted to interrupt; so well worth while was it to listen.

The last time I saw him, which was five months ago, he was fuller than ever of "Chantecler"—the beauties of it, the inspiring difficulties of it. He spoke especially of the scene in which he, as the cock, would call upon the sun to rise, and would address it, as it rose, in a speech of more than a hundred alexandrines. With tremendous relish he recited two or three score of these, but keeping his face absolutely expressionless, and keeping his hands behind his back. For there was the prime glorious difficulty: to hold the audience solely through the voice, since the face and hands would be hidden by the complete outfit of a cock. Once or twice he scraped the ground with his foot. That was the only gesture a cock would have. . . . His little eyes shone and danced with delight as he dilated on "le besoin d'achever l'impossible." He declared that Fate had been very good to him in giving him in his old age an absolutely new task, to make him young again. Rostand had all but finished now, at last—only a few more touches to be added by "cette admirable génie"! The piece would be produced in the autumn—oh yes, for certain.

I admit I was inwardly sceptical about that date. Coquelin himself, through his bitter experience of the coyness of "cette admirable génie," may have had doubts, too; but these he would not have admitted even to himself, dear sanguine soul! When autumn passed into winter, and still there was no imminence of "Chantecler," I was not surprised. But sooner or later, thought I, in this long-drawn contest between a nervous poet and a sanguine actor-burgess the victory would be to the sanguine actor-burgess. Sooner or later—and it turned out to be sooner. Last week I heard that the nervous poet had come out from the Pyrenees, with his wife, and his sons, and his sons' tutor, and his doctor, and his valet, and his chauffeur, and with "Chantecler" itself, and had made his entry into Paris. My heart was glad for Coquelin. I could imagine his look of triumph. I could imagine him throwing off his "grippe" in a twinkling. . . . Even now I can hardly imagine him dead—dead by such a master-stroke of irony. It seems impossible that Fate should not have spared him to drink the cup she had at last raised to his lips.

A terrible master-stroke, certainly. But terrible for us, not for the man stricken. He died without warning in the midst of his gladness; a death that is to be envied. And who knows that the cup raised to his lips was not a cup of bitterness? "Achever l'impossible"! Would even Coquelin have achieved it? He might have failed, even he. And that would have, figuratively, broken his heart. Perhaps it is well for him and us that he died as he did die, literally of heart-failure.

"THE FROGS" AT OXFORD

February 20, 1909

It has been my custom to tell the truth about the performances of the O.U.D.S. And, in so doing, I have paid the members a higher compliment, really, than they have received from my brethren, who have not thought it worth their while to utter anything but hasty and empty little eulogies. I doubt whether the members have always been properly grateful to me; but I will not depart from my custom of veracity. And, this year, truth compels me to congratulate them heartily on a great artistic success : a play performed with genuine spirit and conviction ; a performance infectious in its jollity. I was not able to be in Oxford on the first night, and it is but the dress-rehearsal that I have seen. Dress-rehearsals are not usually infectious in their jollity. The usual conditions reigned in the Oxford theatre on Tuesday evening—a dim auditorium, shrouded in grey sheets; here and there, dim figures seated, silhouettes of anxiety; now and again one of them darting up and scrambling over obstacles to confabulate in whispers with one of its fellows, and then either dashing out on some dark errand "behind" or relapsing into immobility. Maeterlinck's early plays would thrive well in this dim atmosphere of sporadic tension. Aristophanes demands bright lights, and a full audience of cheery irresponsibles. But he managed to do without them on Tuesday evening. Such was the gusto of the performers that, with nothing to carry the infection, I was kept rejoicing.

It was a joy indeed to see a Greek play treated not as a curiosity, but as a quite fresh and vital thing; to see it treated, in that respect, just as the Greeks treated it. I felt that now I did not regret the terrible hours I had spent in London at performances of Euripides. The memory of those very terrible hours gave a zest to my present pleasure. Metropolitan mimes are not, for the most part, on free and easy terms with Greek tragedy, and Professor Murray's translations are to them but a trifle less awe-inspiring and courage-destroying than the originals. Their effort to conceal stage-fright under a lugubrious pomposity is in itself so tragic that we lose all sense of the tragedy they are trying to enact. On the other hand, every undergraduate is familiar enough with "The Frogs"; it was a part of his curriculum at school, quite lately, and is one of the lines of least resistance in "Mods"; and he takes to it on the stage as a duck to the water. Aristophanes, moreover, is quite well-fitted to the modern theatre. As I have so often said, the tragic dramatists of Greece need always a theatre after the pattern of that for which they wrote. But space and air are not requisite to Aristophanes' not-elemental spirit. Indeed, I think that beneath the sky a great deal of his fun must have evaporated, and many of his shafts have missed their mark. He is the most intimate of satirists, and his place is indoors. The interior of a modern theatre for him seems not a bit anachronistic; for who more modern than he? True, he is, above all things, rollicking, whereas the satirists of our own day are evidently sad at heart even when they are kicking up their heels. They are depressed by the mockeries they mock at, and their knowledge of history has taught them that ridicule never kills. Aristophanes, on the other hand, always lustily rejoices in his objective, and goes for it in the manner of a man certain that he is going to victory. And yet the effect of him is as of a man born into our own time. Ridicule never kills: it dies, and an early death at that. The lampoons of the last generation, how grisly they are to us! But, wherever a high state of civilisation is, at whatever date, there is Aristophanes in the midst of it, alive and kicking, as fresh as paint, and perfectly apposite all round. No scholar of any nation will ever make a standard translation of him. For, while the vernacular changes, and the idioms of ten years ago are not our idioms, Aristophanes is always sharply contemporaneous, and only through the slang of the moment can his dialogue be given as it deserves. Professor Gilbert Murray's translation, which is printed with the text of the acting edition of "The Frogs," has not perhaps the full virtue that is to be found in his translations of Euripides. It seems to me, reading between the lines, to come less from a spontaneous impulse than from a desire to achieve a tour de force. As a *tour de force* it is amazingly good, in its thorough command of early-twentieth-century colloquialism. And the performance of the original by the O.U.D.S. is just as thoroughly and rightly modern.

MR. HENRY JAMES' PLAY

February 27, 1909

From Jerome to James—from "The Passing of the Third-Floor Back" to "The High Bid"—it is rather a long way for an actor to travel, is it not? And yet my first impression of Mr. Forbes-Robertson, at the Afternoon Theatre, was that he had walked literally out of the one play into the other. The last I had seen of him was his back, graciously bowed, as he passed slowly out of the front-door of the Bloomsbury lodging-house, with a momentary illumination in the fanlight to show that "The Stranger" was more or less divine. And now it seemed as if the stage had just been swung round on a pivot: here was the front of "The Stranger";

the tender, grave, gently radiant front; emerging, however, not into Gower Street, but into the hall of a great old house in the country. Knowing that the central man in Mr. James' play, besides having served in the Army, was an active worker in East-end settlements, and not a mere aimless rambler in Jeromian platitudes, I rather feared that he had not found an ideal representative—that he had found too idealistic a representative—in Mr. Forbes-Robertson. But my misgiving soon vanished. The actor soon threw off the sublimity of mien that was needed to make Mr. Jerome's sort of thing pass muster, and showed that for the interpretation of Mr. James' sort of thing he was exquisitely equipped. "What are you exactly?" asks Captain Yule of the aged and shabby butler who is in charge of the house; "I mean, to whom do you beautifully *belong*?" There, in those six last words, is quintessence of Mr. James; and the sound of them sent innumerable little vibrations through the heart of every good Jacobite in the audience. Mr. Walkley, properly vibrant, treasured the words up to be the refrain of a criticism for which all we fellow-Jacobites of his are grateful to him. The words could not have been more perfectly uttered than they were by Mr. Forbes-Robertson. We realised at once to whom *he* beautifully belongs. It is to Mr. Henry James. Mr. Walkley, I notice, places the word "beautifully" between two parenthetic dashes; and certainly this way of notation gives the true cadence better than the way that I have used—the way that Mr. James himself would use; but it is still very far from the perfection of Mr. Forbes-Robertson's rendering of the words. "To whom do you—beautifully *belong*?" is nearer. But how crude a medium print is—or even hand-writing—for expression of what such a face and voice as Mr. Forbes-Robertson's can express! In his eyes, as he surveyed the old butler, and in his smile, and in the groping hesitancy before the adverb was found, and in the sinking of the tone at the verb, there was a whole world of good feeling, good manners, and humour. It was love seeing the fun of the thing. It was irony kneeling in awe. It was an authentic part of the soul of Mr. James.

When I think of Mr. James' books, and try to evaluate the immense delight I have had in that immense array of volumes, it seems to me that in my glow of gratitude the thing I am most of all grateful for is not the quality of the work itself, but the quality

of the man revealed through that work. Greater than all my
aesthetic delight in the books is my moral regard for the author.
This confession, if it chance to meet his eye, may startle him. He
was not in Paris in the early 'seventies for nothing. His "form"
in fiction rigidly forbids self-assertion. Not his to button-hole
us and tell us what he thinks of his characters. We must find out
about them for ourselves. No philosophics will be expounded to
us, no morals pointed for us. The author, as at the Afternoon
Theatre the other day, "is not in the house." Well, this is a
"form" like another. It is not, as it was thought to be, final, inevitable; it is already going out of fashion. Certainly, if illusion
of reality were the sole aim of fiction, this "form" would be the
only right one. Reality flies out of the window when the author
comes in at the door. Nevertheless, even the most retiring author
must, in the nature of things, be somewhere concealed on
the premises; and you will find him if you look for him. Mr.
James is devious—say, in a cupboard in the basement. But rout
him out: the "find" is its own reward, and an ample one.
"E. A. B." of the "Daily News" pronounces that Mr. James,
whose books he has read, is "a clever man"—a remark that gives
me somewhat the impulse that Charles Lamb had in regard to a
gentleman who had fired off precisely that remark about Shakespeare. How much more than clever Mr. James is, how many
qualities unrelated to cleverness are in him, is measured for us by
the fatuous inadequacy of this remark from a man who is, as
"E. A. B." is, himself a very clever man. "Subtle," adds
"E. A. B.", as a make-weight. It is the Gradus epithet for Mr.
James, and saves time. But I am sorry for any one who, having
read even but one or two of Mr. James' earliest short stories, could
find no other epithets to affix. And you need search heart and
brain for epithets to describe the later James—the James who has
patiently evolved a method of fiction entirely new, entirely his own,
a method that will probably perish with him, since none but he,
one thinks, could handle it; that amazing method by which a novel
competes not with other novels, but with life itself; making people
known to us as we grow to know them in real life, by hints, by
glimpses, here a little and there a little, leaving us always guessing
and wondering, till, in the fulness of time, all these scraps of revelation gradually resolve themselves into one large and luminous whole,

just as in real life. To read (say) "The Golden Bowl" or "The Wings of the Dove" is like taking a long walk uphill, panting and perspiring and almost of a mind to turn back, until, when you look back and down, the country is magically expanded beneath your gaze, as you never saw it yet; so that you toil on gladly up the heights, for the larger prospects that will be waiting for you. I admit, you must be in good training. People often say "Oh, what a pity it is that dear Henry James won't write the sort of books he *used* to write. Do you remember 'The Portrait of a Lady'?" etc., etc. I always hint to these people, as politely as possible, that an artist's business is not to keep pace with his admirers, and that their business is to keep pace, if possible, with *him*; and that, if they faint by the way, they will be safer in blaming themselves than in blaming *him*. Mr. James, that very conscious and devoted artist, may be trusted, he especially, to have followed the right line of progress—to have got the logical development of his own peculiar gifts. I know no fictionist so evidently steeped as he is in the passion for literature as a fine art—none who has taken for his theme writers and writing so often, and with such insight. "The Pattern in the Carpet," "The Aspern Papers," "The Death of the Lion," "The Middle Years," "The Lesson of the Master"—where is the literary passion and conscience drawn for us so lovingly, and analysed so cunningly, as in these grand short stories by this master? That his sense of beauty is not confined to the manifestations of art in letters, that he has a passionate eye for what is fine in the arts of sculpture and painting and architecture, and for what is fine in Nature, is very manifest to all readers of him in his early and middle periods. And sometimes I cannot help regretting that in his present period he vouchsafes us none of those extraordinarily sensitive visual impressions that were so integral a feature of his tales. Gradually, austerely, they have been banished, these impressions of his, by force of that greater passion of insight into the souls of men and women. I had nearly written of "ladies and gentlemen." For it is very true that Mr. James does not deal with raw humanity, primitive emotions and so on. Civilisation, and a high state of it at that, is the indispensable milieu for him; and just when the primitive emotions surge up in the complex bosoms of his creatures, to cause an explosion, Mr. James escapes with us under his wing, and does not lead us back until the crisis is over—until the results, the to him so much more interesting results, may be quietly examined. I suppose it is by reason of his avoidance of emotional crisis even in the most complex bosoms, that Mr. James has so often been charged with lack of human feeling. Well, there are all sorts of human feelings; they aren't all summed up in "Antony and Cleopatra," there is plenty of them left over; and Mr. James' characters are made to display a very full share. The feeling that they display most constantly is the feeling for right and wrong, for what is noble in conduct and what ignoble. It is by this that they are especially pre-occupied, whether or not their conduct be—it usually is—thereby conditioned. The passion of conscience, a sort of lyrical conscience, conscience raised to the pitch of ecstasy, both in great matters and in small, is what is so common among Mr. James' characters that one might almost take it as a common denominator. When you find the creatures of a creative artist animated thus by one recurring motive, you need not be a skilled detective to "spot" the main characteristic of that artist as man. Despite his resolute self-suppression for his "form's" sake, Mr. Henry James, through his books, stands out as clearly to me as any preacher I have seen perched up in a pulpit. And I do not happen to have heard any preacher in whom was a moral fervour so great as (with all its restraint) is Mr. James' fervour, or one whose outlook on the world seemed to me so fine and touching and inspiring, so full of reverence for noble things and horror of things ignoble—a horror and a reverence that are never obscured for me by the irony that is so often Mr. James' way of writing. More perfectly, perhaps, than in any other work of his do we find expressed in that dear masterpiece "The Altar of the Dead" the—but I am coming to the end of my "space," and have done so very little to justify the title of my article.

My excuse must be that of all that I love in Mr. James' mind so very little can be translated into the sphere of drama. I well remember reading "The High Bid" in the volume entitled "The Two Magics"; and it was clear to me that the story had been conceived (and perhaps written) as a play and then wrought into narrative form. The arrangement of entrances and exits was proof enough of that. But further proof was in the trite conventionality of the story—precisely the sort of story that a true man of letters would select for a venture in dramaturgy, muttering, "I suppose this is the sort of thing they understand." Needless to say, the workmanship was exquisite; and the characters, though essentially puppets, moved with a lively grace and distinction, a bright reality of surface, so that you half forgot they were unreal. What I say of the story is equally true of the play. I have spoken already of the delight it is to hear Mr. James' dialogue from the lips of Mr. Forbes-Robertson, who is not merely Captain Yule but a figure that evokes innumerable cherished memories of Mr. James' books at large—the very spirit of Jacobeanism. Mr. Ian Forbes-Robertson is fine as the old butler. And Miss Gertrude Elliott's vivacity and touching grace are just what are needed for Mrs. Gracedew. "The High Bid" is not the only story that bears traces of having been conceived by Mr. James as a play; and I hope Mr. Forbes-Robertson will soon claim the one or two others. For, little though Mr. James can on the stage give us of his great art, even that little has a quality which no other man can give us; an inalienable magic.

A TOUCHING DOCUMENT

April 10, 1909

I will not forget to take away with me, for Easter, the Report of the Shakespeare Memorial Executive Committee. It has been in my possession for the past fortnight or so. But I am not tired of it yet.

Strong in every man, as in every child, is the instinct for fantastic building. The child builds with sand, or with wooden bricks, peopling the rude and fugitive edifices with the creatures of his imagination, and furnishing them throughout with such luxuries as are dear to a child's heart. If, when he grows up, he become a philosopher, or remain a poet, his manner of building will be but little changed. From the dull chaos of things as they are he will be seeking sanctuary in some little private and personal Utopia, where every law is exquisitely just and unquestioningly obeyed; or you will find him lolling at ruined casements of his own design, his eye roving over some kind or another of faëry lands forlorn. If he happen to be just the average practical citizen, he will charm his leisure by constructing in minute and business-like detail some ideal organisation that might possibly, some fine day, be established on the plane of actuality. Being (as neither the philosopher nor the poet is) gregarious, he will prefer not to work alone. He will be happiest on a committee. To move a resolution, to beg to second an amendment, to rise to a point of order, to say "ipso facto" and "ex officio" and "ad hoc," to cry "Hear, Hear" or "Oh, oh," to move that a sub-committee be appointed to consider such and such a matter, to serve on that sub-committee, to call an extraordinary general meeting—all these are functions very dear to the heart of the average man. Why they should be so, I cannot conceive; I merely state the fact. When this dear flummery is combined with the revolving of his pet ideal, then the average man feels that his cup of joy is brimming over.

I should not like to be a constant attendant at the meetings of the Shakespeare Memorial Executive Committee. That way, for me, madness would lie. But this Report, the garnered fruit of those deliberations, does make glad my heart. In every line I can see what joy has gone to the making of it. True, among the signatories there is a sprinkling of literary artists and of actors; and they, I conceive, have not been partakers of the general rapture. But most of the signatories are just average practical citizens with a soft corner in the heart for the notion of a National Theatre, and with a passion for serving on committees. And they have been having the time of their lives. Oh wooden bricks! Oh sand! Oh permanence of the imaginative faculty! Oh fuss! Oh pomp! No detail of organisation has not been considered, no possibility has not been foreseen and weighed. Nothing could be more thorough if everything were not in the air and likely to remain there. One cannot be too careful. Does it ever occur to you, reader, when you are weaving a castle in the air, that some unscrupulous person or persons might come and oust you from the woven premises? Be warned in time. Aërially safe-guard yourself, before it is too late. The dear gentlemen of the Executive Committee are "of opinion that in order to provide for the legal ownership of the Theatre and of the Endowment Fund, steps should be taken for the incorporation of the Governing Body, either by Royal Charter (should His Majesty in Council be pleased to approve of the grant of such a Charter), or by License of the Board of Trade under Sec. 23 of the Companies Act, 1867 (30 and 31 Vic. c. 131)." Can you not hear the dear gentlemen rolling that phrase "His Majesty in Council" over their tongues, slowly? And then the sweet alternative, "License of the Board of Trade under Sec. 23." . . . You can see in the eyes of those dear gentlemen a rapt, veiled look, as at the sound of viols and dulcimers . . . . . . "Companies Act, 1867" . . . "If music be the food of love, play on," they murmur; "give us excess of it that, surfeiting, the appetite may sicken, and so die" . . . "30 and 31 Vic. c. 131." And the music grows more and more voluptuous. There are to be "Five Governors appointed by the Crown" and six by the elder Universities, and one by the Royal Academy, and another by the British Academy. These are to serve for five years. But certain other Governors, such as they who are to be nominated by the London County Council, and by the Corporation of London, and by the Municipalities of Manchester, Birmingham, Liverpool, Leeds, Bristol, Edinburgh, Glasgow, and Dublin, are to serve not a moment longer than three years. I know not why this distinction has been made, but I can well imagine the joyousness of the long and subtle debate that preceded it. India, it seems, is not to be allowed to nominate a Governor. Only the self-governing Colonies are to have a look-in. The President of the Board of Education is to be an ex-officio Governor. So is the Ambassador of the United States. So are various other seemingly irrelevant worthies. The Commander-in-Chief, the Chairman of the Thames Conservancy Board, the Astronomer Royal, and the Senior Magistrate at Bow Street Police Court, have, for some reason, not been included in the list. Let them not feel hurt. Let them not feel that the Committee did not think them likely to be just as useful as the others to the cause of dramatic art. I take it that the reason for their exclusion was simply in the Committee's fear that an unlimited indulgence in the ecstasies of imagination would bring satiety in its wake. And, after all, there is still a chance that the list of Governors will be extended. The Committee does not definitely commit itself on all points of policy. It considers, for example, "that should any Governor, appointed for a stated time, die or resign during his term of office, or should any of the above-mentioned bodies waive its right of nomination, or should any ex-officio Governor decline to serve, the vacancy so created might be filled by co-option." "Might," you observe, not "shall." Evidently there was a strong anti-co-option clique in the Committee, and a compromise was the only way out. Oh sand and wooden bricks! Oh energy and subtlety and pomposity and triviality! The Report goes on, from clause to clause, in an ascending scale of unconscious humour; and the names of the signatories—with the Lord Mayor first, then some peers, and then the commoners in alphabetical order—are not an anti-climax.

Let us strain our imaginations a little. Let us suppose that all this solemn enjoyment is destined to be remembered not as an end in itself, but as a prelude to the actual establishment of a National Theatre. Let us suppose that the necessary £500,000 forthcomes. What sort of a theatre would be the result? All institutions, howsoever cheerful the auspices under which they are started, tend to become, in course of years, stodgy. This National Theatre would be stodgy at the outset—so stodgy that I don't suppose it would tend to become, in course of years, stodgier. What of vitality, what of any real interest, could be vouchsafed us in a theatre governed by a standing committee appointed by these Governors from amongst their own ranks? Imagine the dulness, the deadness that would result from the various highly-respectable compromises between the minds of these various highly-respectable Governors. The Governors, I have no doubt, would enjoy their dabblings, just as this Committee has enjoyed its. But £500,000 is a tall price to pay for their fun. The fun would not filter through to the community. In one way and another, we get all the performances of Shakespeare that we need; and as for "revivals of whatever else is vital in English classical drama," what else really is vital? "The School for Scandal" and "She Stoops to Conquer" live by reason of the public's desire to see this and that mime in this and that celebrated part. But who, really and truly, in his heart of hearts, wants to see a performance of a play by Ben Jonson or any other Elizabethan or Jacobean, or by Congreve or any other Restorationist? These plays are interesting curiosities, and many of them may be read with enjoyment. But, as plays, they are dead utterly; and a theatrical production of any of them is a mere rattling of dry bones. Again, what "recent plays of great merit" have been "falling into oblivion"? And when, as so very often happens, we see a revival of a play which we admired (say) five years ago, are we not invariably appalled by the shabbiness that has come over it, and puzzled to account for our old admiration? "To produce new plays and to further the development of the modern drama"— ah! there is a thing worth doing; a thing that ought undoubtedly to be done. But I am not—and I hope no one is—quite such a fool as to suppose that new young dramatists, with new young ideas and methods in their heads, are going to get any help from an institution governed by a great number of highly-respectable gentlemen desperately afraid of making a mistake and so lowering the prestige of their precious institution. What is needed, of course, "to further the development of the modern drama" is a quite small theatre, decently endowed, with one enlightened despot to govern it. The Court Theatre, for example; and, for example, Mr. Granville Barker. Of course, he could not do all the work singlehanded. He would have to have a committee working under him. But the less eminent were that committee, the better it would be for that theatre. After a long and tedious debate in my own breast, I recommend that the committee be composed of six policemen, selected in annual rotation from six of the divisions of the Metropolitan Police Force, each selection being made by the Divisional Inspector in co-operation with two Sergeants, such Sergeants to have held their rank for a period of not less than three years, and such selections being subject to the veto of the Chief Commissioner, if such veto be upheld by the Home Secretary; and furthermore . . . but no! I take an exquisite pleasure in reading that sort of thing, but I won't waste time in writing it. I will leave my idea undeveloped—just a bright and promising idea, that may take root in the mind of some bright and promising rich man. I don't advise any one, however rich, to subscribe so much as a shilling to the National Shakespeare Theatre. All the shillings that can be spared should go in the direction of a small theatre without any flummery about it, and with some such person as Mr. Granville Barker at the head of it. That theatre would be of real use. The most that can be said of the National affair is that it would do no harm.

I don't want to be unkind to the committee of the National

affair. I shall be very glad, for their sakes, if their scheme is realised after mine has been realised. But I object to their useless scheme as an obstacle to my useful one. I ask them to be so good as to drop it for the present. After all, they have drawn up, with infinite labour and delight, their monumentally ridiculous Report. What more do they want?

MADEMOISELLE PANDORE

May 29, 1909

In the court of Le Roi Soleil dwelt a certain Mademoiselle Pandore, hardly less powerful, in her way, than the reigning favourite; and even more artificial; and far more lasting. Favourites reigned and were sent packing. But Mademoiselle Pandore queened it year after year, and was unquestionable law to all the ladies around. She was life-sized, and stood upright in the centre of a room specially set aside for her. She was made of painted card-board; and her clothes, which could be taken off, were of the same lowly material, but were always of the latest fashion—the one and only authentic fashion, the fashion with which all ladies, young and old, must conform. Whenever the King, in his wisdom, decided that corsages should be lengthened or paniers be made more ample, or coiffings and mantillas be exalted, or jewels and flowers and "mouches" be worn thus and thus, his decree was illustrated on the person of Mademoiselle Pandore, into whose presence all the ladies of the court came forthwith, attended by their maids and their modistes, to take humble and careful note of the change appointed. It was from Paris, even in those days, that fashion radiated. The action of the rays was slow, but sure. And thus Mademoiselle Pandore made her influence felt in all the courts of Europe. She survived the death of her master—survived Louis XV, too, and all his favourites, and fell only when the head of Marie Antoinette fell from the block. It is not known what became of her. Perhaps the sans-culottes tore her limb from cardboard limb. Last Monday afternoon, on a platform in a room at

Princes Restaurant, a re-creation of her was presented to a large assembly by Mr. John Abbot, an erudite Bostonian, who seemed to know all about her. You must be an American if you want to be filled through and through, in every fibre, with an intense sentiment for the past of Europe. You must have had President Roosevelt bawling moral platitudes at you for many years from the roof of the White House, if you would savour fully the rapture there is in contemplation of the sublime futilities of the gospel according to Le Roi Soleil. But for his evident sense of humour, I doubt whether Mr. Abbot would have been able to address his audience at all: he could only have serenaded Mademoiselle Pandore on a viol of the period, with large American tears coursing down his either cheek. As it was, appreciating as much the absurdity as the charm of his subject-matter, he gave a delightful lecture. He had made the doll with his own hands, and had painted the various costumes and their accessories with a skill equal to his curious knowledge; and every time he showed her in a fresh costume, or with some modification of the costume she was wearing, he cast for us a succession of admirable little side-lights on the manners of the time—manners that were partly reflected by the costumes, partly conditioned by them.

Nowadays, fashion is inseparable from caprice. The engines of science have made the whole world restless. People are not satisfied with this or that: they want the other, and are always seeing that they get it—get it instantly, in some extreme form. But there was no restlessness, no caprice, in the fashions that were set by Mademoiselle Pandore. The thing that most struck me among the many things to be deduced from Mr. Abbot's survey was the slowness with which in the great era of frivolity one fashion was evolved from another. Essentially, costume never changed; it merely developed. For more than a decade the general aspect might be left exactly as it was, only the details being modified or accentuated, or new details introduced. But always these new details were truly novel—true inventions. Nowadays, the designer of dresses, though always agog for novelty, can invent nothing. Like the architect, or the designer of furniture or pottery or any other visual object, he can but hark back to this or that period. His nearest approach to the effect of originality is made by combining two or more periods of the past. Inventiveness in

design is a faculty which, for the present, has been lost. Mode
follows on the heels of mode, perspiringly; and in a very short
space of time women are made to don the modes of half-a-dozen
long periods; but never the mode of their own period: there is no
such thing. In the days of Mademoiselle Pandore, women of
fashion were dressed as no women in history—except, more or less,
their mothers and grandmothers—had yet been dressed. They
were content with that privilege, content with the little subsidiary
changes that were vouchsafed from time to time. They never
rebelled against Mademoiselle Pandore. Nor, for that matter, do
they ever rebel against the Parisian mannequins who illustrate the
will of the Parisian modistes exactly as Mademoiselle Pandore
illustrated the King's. Why don't they rebel? It is well to obey
a king—especially if he be a wise one. But what allegiance do
women owe to modistes whose one aim is to get the utmost amount
of money out of them by changing the fashion as often as possible?
I suppose women obey the modistes by force of that inward restlessness of which I have spoken. It is a great pity. The fashion
may happen to be, as it happens to be at the moment of writing, a
fairly rational and becoming fashion, on the whole. (Belike this
fashion will have been superseded before this article is printed.)
But no fashion is rational and becoming for all women. The present fashion is fatal to the appearance of many women. It is a pity
that they should all adopt it. For every woman there is some one
particular mode of dress that suits her best—some one right mode
for her. Having discovered by constant thought and experiment
what that mode is, she ought to adhere to it ever after, making only
such differences in accessories as will prevent monotony without
changing the essential form. The one plausible defence of
fashion-following that I have ever heard is that the effect of uniformity has a charm of its own. Any one figure in the Parthenon
frieze is beautiful, but not nearly so beautiful as the effect produced by the multiplicity of similar figures. Any one hospital
nurse may be plain, but a group of hospital nurses is always a pretty
sight. But we must remember that the draperies of the figures on
the Parthenon frieze are lovely in themselves, and that the costume
of a hospital nurse is in itself prettier than nine out of ten of the
costumes evolved in blind haste by the Parisian modistes. A procession of fashionable ladies, at any average moment of fashion, is

only less unsatisfactory to the eye than a single fashionable lady. And, after all, it is not woman's mission to form a pattern. It is the duty of every woman to be herself, and to make the very best of herself, in surface not less than in soul. Some women are claiming the right to vote, on the ground that they are perfectly well able to think for themselves. Well, one cannot see into a woman's brain, but one can see what she has got on. And her power of thinking for herself would be taken the more readily on trust if she proved that she could dress for herself.

Meanwhile, if fashion there must be, I wish the dominion of Mademoiselle Pandore could be reconstituted. For many years, the lady who is now queen in England has dressed, with but few modulations, in a fashion of her own. It is a fashion that would be disastrous to the appearance of many women. But it would be not half so disastrous as is the great majority of the innumerable fashions which these women now follow in the course of a very few years. The influence of English royalty to-day is potentially not less strong than the influence of French royalty in bygone times. It needs but to be exerted. I advise Mr. Abbot to offer his doll to Queen Alexandra, with an humble petition that she insist that all the ladies of her court shall dress exactly according to this doll's costume as designed, and from time to time modified or amplified in this or that detail, by herself.

MIDDLE-CLASS LIFE FROM WITHOUT

July 10, 1909

I have often urged our dramatists to give the aristocracy a rest, and write plays about the class to which they themselves belong. An intimate and complete study of Mrs. Brown is of more account than the presentment of the Duchess of Hampshire as she is vaguely and respectfully supposed to be. In real life, doubtless, and as woman to woman, Mrs. Brown is at a disadvantage. Where is her tiara? Where are her electric and other cars? Her house has no courtyard, and on the inner walls hang no portraits of her husband's forbears by master hands. And, as against a battalion of powdered footmen, what is a house-parlourmaid? Mr. Robinson, Mr. Jones, and the other callers at Mrs. Brown's—how far less obviously exciting they are than the statesmen, the sportsmen, the diplomats, and the few carefully-selected millionaires, who surround Her Grace! I don't pretend not to be dazzled, even in this outer darkness, by the thought of them; and, if I were a dramatist, I daresay my plays would be exclusively about that exclusive world. Dazzled, blinded, I should trust inspiration to guide my reverent pen aright. The chances are that my confidence would be misplaced. Certainly, the average play about the aristocracy leaves me unconvinced of its truth. It *may* be all right, but I feel that it somehow isn't. That is why I have often wished that some aristocrat, or somebody whose life has been spent mainly among the aristocracy, would find time to write a play. For aught it might lack of technical merit, "connaissance de cause" would amply compensate us. My heart began to beat quickly, therefore, and my pulse throbbed, and my temperature rose, when I heard that Mrs. George Cornwallis-West had written a play. We know that for many years she has been in the midst of the beau monde. She was the wife of one distinguished politician, and is the mother of a second. Also, her foreign birth must have tended to prevent her taking her environment as a matter of course—must have kept her keenly alert and watchful, sensitive to impressions. Here, then, thought I, will be the play I have long looked for. Alas, I reckoned without the law of human discontent. The Olympian gods, whom struggling mortals envied their luminous repose, looked down and contemplated and were amused. But the Olympian mortals, whom we of the middle class envy, are envious of us. There is a magnificence about all things unknown. It is ever sweet to escape from one's own familiar knowledge, and let fancy go flying where it listeth. Strawberry-leaves and stars-and-garters, whispered secrets of high policy, all the paraphernalia that are so dear to the brooding heart of you and me, are as dust and sand to Mrs. Cornwallis-West. She swishes them aside and makes a bee-line for our abject selves.

Well, it is a proud moment for us. But we do wish, in the interest of dramatic art, and for general enlightenment, that "His Borrowed Plumes" had been a play about the sort of people the author really knows, and not about the sort of people she fondly imagines. At the very outset her ignorance betrays her. It was convenient to her purpose that she should get all her characters staying together under one roof. But here she was confronted by a grave difficulty. She remembered having heard or read somewhere that middle-class people don't have big country-houses in which to entertain their friends. "What," she wondered, "does a lady of the middle class do when she wishes to have a big house-party?" After prolonged thought, and after fruitless search under "M" and "C" in the Encyclopædia Britannica, it occurred to her that middle-class house-parties are probably given in river-side hotels hired for the purpose. To make sure, she telephoned to some of her friends, who one and all assured her that it sounded likely enough. To us, however, the notion is more than a mild surprise, and strikes a key-note of fantasy that prepares us for surprises in store. The middle-class hostess, Mrs. Sumner by name, is a distinguished novelist. It is always rather difficult to believe any one of the characters in a play is really a great writer or painter, or excels in any other kind of art—except, possibly, in the art of acting. In reading a book, if the author has (as Mr. Henry James so pre-eminently has) an insight into the minds of creative artists, we can believe in the artistic achievements of this or that character: we can believe in the masterpieces that are hinted at. But when we see a well-known actor dabbing at a canvas on an easel, or complacently fingering a sheaf of MS., we do but smile. The dramatist may have a keen insight into the soul of a painter or writer; but we cannot be illuded by the actual presentment on the stage. I am afraid that not even in reading the script of "His Borrowed Plumes" should I be able to believe in Mrs. Sumner as a distinguished novelist. As a woman she is brave, affectionate, pure, self-sacrificing, what you will: a perfect "heroine," of a mould far more nobly heroinic, indeed, than is ever found in a member of the middle class; but at no point can a trace of the literary artist be detected in her. True, she does show something of the artist's pride and aloofness when Mr. Delaine, K.C., asks her to tell him the plot of her forthcoming book. She says she prefers to keep such things to herself. But she instantly relents when he asks her to show him the MS. "as a mark of confidence." This somewhat sinister phrase had prepared me, as a man of the

world, to see Delaine instantly decamp with the lady's property.
I wronged him. He merely adjusted a pince-nez, and, fifteen
seconds later, having turned the pages with lightning rapidity,
pronounced Mrs. Sumner's latest work to be her strongest, and
predicted that it would be her greatest success. Whether his
literary judgment was as sure as his rapidity in mastering a brief,
is a point which will never be cleared up. Fate, in her wisdom or
her folly, ordained that the MS. should never be given to the
world. One of the members of Mrs. Sumner's house-party was
an adventuress, Mrs. Cranfield by name, a very wicked woman,
but one to whom much might be forgiven because she was such an
arrant fool. Mrs. Cornwallis-West may have met an adventuress
or two in her time; and I daresay that adventuresses, when they
come among the aristocracy, lose their heads and carry on in the
strangest fashion. But Mrs. Cornwallis-West may take it from
me that any adventuress who behaved among the middle class as
Mrs. Cranfield behaves would presently find herself in a lunatic
asylum. What other place would be fit to receive a lady who, sitting with a gentleman in the hall of a river-side hotel just after the
other guests had gone to bed, and hearing this gentleman's wife
approach, insisted on being shut into his bedroom, with a view
to preserving her good name? Yet this is not the full measure of
poor Mrs. Cranfield's madness. Major Sumner, whom she
adores, is, like his wife, a writer. Only, his work does not amount
to much. Mrs. Cranfield is struck by what seems to her a happy
thought. Why not steal the type-written scenario of Mrs. Sumner's book, read it carefully to herself, and then suggest it to the
Major as the scenario for a play? Of course she will be presently
found out, and her beloved will spurn her from him, and there will
be the deuce to pay all round. But what of that? The adventuress nabs the scenario, and the Major writes the play. You
would not expect that a cape-and-sword romance, written at
second hand by a very mediocre writer who had never essayed a
play before, would be accepted for production at the National
Theatre. Mrs. Cornwallis-West, peering into the future, is convinced that such a thing might be. As she is an active supporter of
the schemes for a National Theatre, this conviction of hers is the
more surprising. It is only fair to the Major to say that he himself
is very much surprised. That he does not, however, describe the

play to his wife until it has been accepted, is a lamentable proof of the distance he has drifted away from her. As soon as he does begin to tell her all about it, she sees what has happened. Rather than humiliate him, she holds her counsel and burns her MS. But she is not above a good strong scene with Mrs. Cranfield in private. Trust Mrs. Cranfield to have been fool enough to write blackmailing letters to a Frenchman, on the strength of which documents a confession is wrung from her by the K.C. And trust the Major to tell the enraptured first-night audience, in a soldierly and a gentlemanly fashion, that the author of the play is none other than his wife.

Now, from the standpoint of the average simple playgoer, "His Borrowed Plumes" is a very good entertainment. From the standpoint of the purely technical critic, it is a very good piece of work : a story conceived and set forth clearly, without halting, with a thorough grasp of dramatic form. From the standpoint of a critic who desires an illusion of real life, it does not pass muster. The characters have been sacrificed to the story. Now and again, as in the scene between the two jealous women, the characters emerge and are natural, real, and moving. There is much that rings true in the relations of Mrs. Cranfield and the Major. But, for the rest, Mrs. Cornwallis-West has let herself be led into the temptation that awaits every one who essays dramaturgy for the first time —the temptation to write not as a seer of life, but as a playgoer who knows all about the theatre. I conjure her not to bother, henceforth, about what she thinks is needed to make a good play, but rather to let her characters do just as they would in real life. Having, as she evidently has, an instinct for dramatic form, she need not fear for the result of this process. But of course she must select her characters from the milieu that she knows. They must be the kind of people on whose behaviour she can regard herself as an authority. I daresay she thought that the strange things which happen in "His Borrowed Plumes" were really not less usual in the middle class than in the theatre. That is a notion which she must banish for ever from her mind.

AT THE GAIETY

October 30, 1909

I am elderly enough to have seen two or three of the old Gaiety burlesques, though I am young enough not to weep bitterly over the reminiscence—young enough not to feel that the Gaiety, as it is to-day, insults my heart. To me, indeed, the place's main charm seems to be in its abiding likeness to what it was in the dim past. What though "the Sacred Lamp" has been snuffed out, and the arc-lamp of musical comedy installed? What though the old walls have fallen, and others have arisen on their site? The spell has not been broken. The old traditions still linger. The spirit, the "note," is as it always was. The temple stands true to its name, and true to that special and peculiar sort of gaiety with which we have always associated it. What though the master-pieces of literature and drama be guyed no more there? Gone are the rhymed couplets, and the puns, and other things that are sweet in retrospect: what matter? These were but the trappings and gauds that the Muse was decked in. Soul and body, she is her same old self.

It is easy to recognise, hard to define, the "note" of the Gaiety. One reason why the place is irresistible is that nowhere else do we feel that we are so far away, and so harmlessly and elegantly far away, from the realities of life. We are translated into a sphere where the dwellers have nothing whatever to think about, and would be incapable of thought if there were need for it. Nothing jars there. All the people (except the ladies of the chorus, whose languor is part of the fun) are in the highest spirits, with no chance of a re-action, yet never in the extravagance of their joy do they become loud, or infringe the by-laws of deportment: they are all graceful and tuneful. They are all of them refined, though not in the least like "ladies" and "gentlemen" in actual life. They have a school, a higher school, of their own. Some of them are sup-posed to impersonate the aristocracy, others the proletariat; but in point of refinement there is nothing to choose between them: never a crude word or gesture. And all classes mingle on the easiest of terms. Every one wants every one else to have a good time, and tries to make everything easy and simple all round. This good time, as I need hardly say, is of a wholly sexual order. And yet every one, from the highest to the lowest, is thoroughly "good." The most attractive of the men do no harm to the ladies who love them at first sight. Not less instantaneous than theirs are the conquests made by the most unattractive men. A homuncule, made up to look as absurd as possible, has only to come by and wink at the bevy of lovely ladies to whom he is a perfect stranger, when behold! their arms are about his neck, their eyes devour him, they languish and coo over him, and will follow him to the world's end in deference to his wish for a good time. But be sure he will take no vile advantage. Absurd though he looks, he has his code of honour, like the rest, and never outsteps the bounds of that innocent libertinism which is the rule of Gaiety-land. Evil here is as remote as what we call propriety; and goodness and a good time go hand in hand. Gaiety-land is the Mohammedan paradise, reorganised on a perfectly respectable basis. Emotion is not more alien from its inhabitants than thought. True, there is always a thread of humdrum human love-story woven into the fabric of these plays. In "Our Miss Gibbs" there appears now and again a young man, with a Guards' riband round his straw hat, saying, in reference to Miss Gibbs, "I love her, and want to make her mine," quite soulfully. But who heeds him, or cares twopence whether the marriage will take place? In so far as we notice him at all, we do but deplore that any one so cloddish should have strayed into this ethereal domain.

The fact that in these plays (being what they are, an appeal to our eyes and to our sense of fun) there is no hint of love except "pour le bon motif," is what most of all bewilders Frenchmen when they visit the Gaiety. They cannot understand how an entertainment of this kind can be kept going without more or less explicit ribaldry; and, when they return to their own shores, it is always the Gaiety that abides in their memory as the most amazing of all our amazing institutions. Also, they never can get over their surprise at the lightness, the vivacity, the exquisite technical accomplishment, of the chief performers. These qualities they had deemed to be inalienably Parisian. And certainly nowhere in London are they to be found in such high degree as at the Gaiety. They are in the air there—have been so since the time of Nellie

Farren and Fred Leslie and Kate Vaughan. They are a tradition, handed down through James Lonnen and Lettie Lind. They admirably survive in Miss Gertie Millar, Mr. Edmund Payne, and Mr. George Grossmith. Miss Millar, though her charm is so distinctly original, is not, certainly, a born comedian; but she has achieved an exquisite style in comedy, of a kind precisely fitted to the tasks laid on it; and this, with her charm, is all-sufficient. One cannot imagine her at any theatre but the Gaiety, nor imagine the Gaiety without her. Mr. George Grossmith has brought his innate comedianship to a fine point now; and his singing and dancing are perfect of their kind. I am told that the song "Yip-i-addy-i-yay" was imported from America; it may have been; but as rendered by Mr. Grossmith it becomes a pure symbol of the very spirit of the Gaiety; monumental, in its airy way; banality raised to the sublime. Mr. Edmund Payne, by temperament and physique, belongs rather to the music-halls (where he would certainly have outshone all but Dan Leno). But he, too, has schooled himself in the traditions of the Gaiety, and is a worthy *sociétaire*. All the minor parts in "Our Miss Gibbs" are played by people who have been carefully trained to produce the traditional effects. But, as always, the surpassing delight is the chorus. The look of cold surprise that overspreads the lovely faces of these ladies whenever they saunter on to the stage and, as it would seem, behold us for the first time, making us feel that we have taken rather a liberty in being there; the faintly cordial look that appears for the fraction of an instant in the eyes of one of them who happens to see a friend among us—a mere glance, but enough to make us all turn with servile gaze in the direction of the recipient; the splendid nonchalance of these queens, all so proud, so fatigued, all seeming to wonder why they were born, and born so beautiful. . . . I remember that when "The Belle of New York" was first produced in London every one prophesied that the example of that bright, hard-working, athletic American chorus would revolutionise the method of the chorus at the Gaiety. For a while, I think, there was a slight change—a slight semblance of modest effort. But the old local tradition soon resumed its sway, and will never be overthrown; and all the Tory in me rejoices.

MR. SHAW'S "DEBATE"

February 26, 1910

Very queer was its effect on me. As the evening wore on, the footlights receded, the audience vanished from around me, and though, far away, there the stage still was, with people talking on it, and with me over-hearing them quite distinctly, I felt nevertheless that it was Sunday morning, and that I was walking along Praed Street, with a keen and unremitting north-east wind against my face. Keenly, unremittingly, from the road unswept in deference to the Sabbath, the wind drove into my eyes and mouth and ears dry particles of refuse. Bits of trampled paper careered wildly past me along the gutters. Orange peel and wisps of straw danced unholy measure. For all the wind's violence, there was a faint odour of staleness everywhere. I pressed on, wondering if the wind would ever drop, wondering that it had not yet blown all the dust and other remnants past me. But these seemed to be un-ending, and the wind permanent. It was with intense relief that I espied a hansom, and jumped in. . . . Only as I was driving away from the Duke of York's Theatre did I realise that all this was a parable, and not a fact. . . . The keen and unremitting north-east wind is, of course, symbolic of Mr. Shaw's brain. The dust and other remnants stand for the staleness of the characters and the ideas which Mr. Shaw here fragmentarily reproduces from his past work (in which they were so fresh). And Praed Street on Sunday morning is my hint of the cheerlessness of that resurrection, and of its distressing unloveliness. Still the parable is not complete. It does not include the unreality, the remoteness from human truth, that pervades the whole "debate." Let the fact that I never have been in Praed Street on Sunday morning stand for that.

There never was any reality in Mr. Shaw's typical young men and women. (I except Anne Whitfield, in whom—though she was certainly not, as Mr. Shaw claimed, "Everywoman"—there was humanity enough.) Mr. Shaw has often explained that the critics' scepticism is because they are steeped in the conventions of the theatre and can't recognise a real thing when they see it. Well, speaking for myself, I deny that charge. The "ingénue" and "juvenile lead" of old-fashioned commercial drama have never imposed on me. They never have seemed to me to resemble the actual young women and young men whom I have known. I see them as figments. And in that respect they do very closely resemble the young men and women of Mr. Shaw. The difference is that they are pretty figments. Mr. Shaw's are ugly. If a man invents, we prefer the result to be something better than life. We cannot understand a man taking the pains to invent something worse. In point of fact, a man never does consciously set himself that task. What he invents—however much worse it be than life —is either what he (by obliquity of vision) supposes life to be, or else what he would like it to be. Mr. Shaw's young men and women are the more distressing by reason of the fear lurking in us that—Impossible! Mr. Shaw is as distressed by his puppets as we are, and only by his righteous indignation against what he takes to be mankind is he enabled to go on with the task of fashioning them. When they were brand-new to us, their ugliness was atoned for by their brand-newness, and by the force and brilliancy with which they were presented. But now that we know them so well, and now that their creator just trots them perfunctorily out as figures in a debate that occasionally drifts into harlequinade and "knock-about," these alternately impudent and whining young men, and these invariably priggish and hectoring young women, all of them as destitute of hearts as they are of manners, and all of them endowed with an equal measure of chilly sensuality, evoke in us a rather strong desire to see no more of them. Some comfort we take in our certainty that we shan't, at any rate, run up against them in the actual world. We are safe, for example, from meeting there Bentley Summerhays (son of Lord Summerhays), the first of the characters to confront us in "Misalliance." He is Mr. Shaw's notion of an intellectual but neurotic youth. His intellectuality consists in being rude to elder people; and the exact manner of his rudeness may be gauged from a typical remark to the man whose daughter he wishes to marry: "You're very full of beef to-day, aren't you, old boy?" Such is not the manner of any intellectual but neurotic youths whom I have met. But, as he showed in his portrayal of the poet in "Candida," and of the painter in "The Doctor's Dilemma," and of numerous other characters, Mr. Shaw cannot believe that young people, of what type soever, are not always making themselves offensive. Let it be granted that many young men are physically cowards. They are then all the more loth to give offence to people stronger than themselves. They do not, when they are left alone with such people, proceed to insult them till the moment comes for dodging behind the furniture and throwing themselves upon the carpet and shrieking for their sweethearts to come to the rescue. This, however, is what Bentley Summerhays does; and such, according to Mr. Shaw, is life; and any one who doubts it is "incorrigibly romantic." Let it be granted, again, that many young women find their homes and their inexperience irksome, and are restless and inquisitive. These young women don't, like Hypatia Tarleton (beloved of Bentley Summerhays), prate to the family circle about their desire for "adventures." Hypatia's father is master of a large emporium, and she suggests to him that shop-girls often have "adventures," and feels, as perhaps her creator feels, that she has scored. Of course she scores, in the approved Shavian fashion, off the man whom, also in that fashion, she desires to trap into matrimony. "What," she asks him, "are you going to do?" "Bolt," he replies; and bolt through the window he does, pursued, in the approved Shavian fashion, by Hypatia. When she returns she has been kissed. The man tells her father that he will marry her if the settlements are handsome enough. The father consents; and there is the end of *that* little idyll. Not very life-like, is it? Nor a pleasing invention? The father, speaking of the young people of this generation, complains that they are all of them "hard and coarse, shallow and dirty-minded." So far as Mr. Shaw's young people are concerned, this is true. So far: no further.

I have said that these characters are perfunctory. Throughout the play, indeed, I had the impression that Mr. Shaw had not done his best—that the work had been thrown off in intervals snatched from lecturing and speech-making and organising this or that. I wished he would have more conscience in organising his own art. I do not mean to decry his present fashion of writing "debates" for the stage instead of plays. But a debate, to stand the test of the theatre, must be treated as an art-form. It must have some central point, and it must be progressive; must be about something, and lead to something. "Misalliance" is about anything and everything that has chanced to come into Mr. Shaw's head. It never progresses, it doesn't even revolve, it merely sprawls. Throughout the evening we are clutching at loose ends, all of which come off (though not in the slang sense); and we very soon grow weary of the pastime. So careless of his effects has Mr. Shaw been that he repeats not merely from his previous plays, but from within the play itself. Thus, after Summerhays has whined in fear of physical violence from one man, there is a City clerk who whines in fear of physical violence from another. And in the end we have Summerhays whining and collapsing once more. Intensely tedious, too, is the fun made out of the difficulty of pronouncing the name of the female Russian acrobat who is introduced to reinforce Miss Tarleton as a proof of the Shavian doctrine that men are no match for women. Of course, there are many delightful lines, such as "I believe in morality. You just draw a line, and make other people toe it; that's morality." And there are lines that have that quality of quaint surprise which Mr. Shaw understands so well; as when John Tarleton says to the bank-clerk, his illegitimate son, who has come to shoot him and stands with levelled revolver, "I suppose you are out of work?" and the reply is "Oh, no. This is just my Saturday afternoon." But the fun of this scene is of a jarring kind. A few years ago, an eminent tradesman was shot dead by an hysterical young man who was his illegitimate son. The murderer then shot himself, but was nursed back to health with a view to the gallows. Public sentiment then stepped in, saying, "Don't rob us of this young life! Wouldn't twenty-five years' penal servitude meet the case?" So again the murderer was baulked of extinction, and, since he has been in prison, has made two other determined but unsuccessful attempts at suicide. One cannot imagine a more horrible story than this. It is too horrible to be a proper theme even for tragedy. Yet Mr. Shaw has sought to enliven his debate by presenting a farcical Whiteley and a farcical Rayner. Mr. Shaw is the most humane of men. And I take this scene in his play as a further proof of sheer carelessness. He must have just thrown it in without thinking.

To condemn a work of Mr. Shaw's is for me a new and disagreeable sensation. I wonder if the fault is really all his. It is a mistake to suppose that in the things of the mind we are less apt to be inconsistent than in other matters. We know that a man may love a woman sincerely, and yet for no apparent reason, gradually or suddenly, cease to love her. Not less in his opinions about art is he at the mercy of inscrutable change. He may love this or that work, and then, without being able to give any satisfactory reason to himself, grow cold. Can it be that I . . . no! I have given very satisfactory reasons why I don't like "Misalliance" . . . Praed Street, Sunday morning, and a not bracing, a blighting, wind.

"JUSTICE"

March 5, 1910

We are getting on. Time was when our drama was so utterly divorced from life that the critics never dreamed of condemning a play for artificiality. It is but a few years since they acquired the habit of judging plays in relation to life. And now (so fast has our drama been moving) they are beginning to decry plays on the ground that they are indistinguishable from life. Well, I am not going to join in the doubts expressed by so many critics whether "Justice," in the repertory at the Duke of York's, be proper art. "Cinematographic" they call it. So it is, in a sense. We really do, in seeing it, have the sensation of seeing reproduced exactly things that have happened in actual life. Or rather, we feel that we are seeing these things actually happen. If the cinematograph were chromatic and stereoscopic, and free from vibration, and gramophonic into the bargain, Mr. Galsworthy might—no, even then, as I shall presently show, he would not have a dangerous rival. In the first act of "Justice" we do not feel that we are seeing an accurate presentment of the humdrum of a lawyer's office: we are *in* a lawyer's office. The curtain rises on the second act; and presently we have forgotten the foot-lights, and are *in* a court of law. At a crucial moment in the cross-examination of a witness, somebody at the reporters' table drops a heavy book on the floor. An angry murmur of "Sh!" runs round the court, and we ourselves have joined in it. The jury retires to consider its verdict, and instantly throughout the court there is a buzz of conversation

—aye, and throughout the auditorium, too : we are all of us, as it were, honorary "supers." In the third act, we arrive at a prison. Gloomily producing a special pass signed "John Galsworthy," we are shown over the interior. We interview the governor, the chaplain, the doctor. Through the wire-blind of the governor's office we have, all the while, a blurred glimpse of certain automata, quickly-revolving—the convicts at exercise. Some of these men we see presently at closer quarters in their cells. We are haunted by it all afterwards as by an actual experience, not as by a tragic play. And part of this effect is due, of course, to the excellence of the stage-management and of the acting. But of what avail would these things be if the play itself were not true to life ? At the game of producing an absolute illusion of reality a dramatist is heavily handicapped in competition with the cinematograph, undeveloped though that machine still is. What the cinematograph presents to us has happened, is ready-made. What the dramatist presents to us has not happened, has to be specially concocted. Only by constant observation of the surface of things, and by the intuitive sympathy with the soul of things, and then by a laborious process of selection and rejection, can the dramatist evoke in us that absolute illusion. For him there are no happy accidents. Every character must be an amalgam of many actual persons seen from without and within ; and every incident must be relevant to these characters, and to the story told through them, and to the idea or ideas through them expressed. Especially such a play as "Justice," which is the vehicle for criticism of certain conditions of modern life, would be of no value whatsoever if the characters were not types, and if the story were not typical. I think that in "Justice," as in "Strife," it is because Mr. Galsworthy so carefully eschews any show of sympathy with one character, or of antipathy against another, that the charge of cinematography is preferred against him. In showing us a young criminal caught in the toils of law, he shows us no hero, but a rather uninteresting youth with a tendency to hysteria, who does not, when he is confronted with the cheque that he has forged, hesitate to let suspicion fall on an innocent colleague. There is nothing brutal or vindictive about the young man's employer : he lets the law take its course, but does so as a matter of principle, and reluctantly. In court, the counsel for the prosecution does not go beyond this duty ; and the judge's summing-up is perfectly fair; and the sentence which he passes is according to his sense of duty to the commonweal. The governor of the prison is a very humane and sympathetic man. The chaplain is nothing worse than a prig. The doctor is not only conscientious but intelligent. Mr. Galsworthy never takes an unfair advantage. He dispenses with many quite fair advantages. Is this because he is merely a detached and dispassionate observer of life? The reason is the very contrary. It is because he is fulfilled with pity for the victims of a thing he vehemently hates, and because he is consumed with an anxiety to infect his fellow-men with this hatred and this pity, that he strives so unremittingly to be quite impartial. He knows that a suspicion of special pleading would jeopardise his case. He is determined to give us no chance of soothing our nerves by saying to him "Oh yes, no doubt there is a lot in what you say, but you have let your feelings—which do you great credit—run away with you." He doesn't mind losing the credit for having fine feelings and being regarded as merely a cold-hearted person who just wants to frighten and depress us, so long as he does succeed in his object of frightening and depressing us. He wants us to have to say "This is life"; and if we then round on him, saying "And you're a blooming cinematograph! Yah!" he takes our outburst as rather a compliment than otherwise. He sees that his object is achieved. That we should recognise the passion and the artistry in him is a matter of less importance.

In some of his works he does certainly lay himself open to a (very superficial) charge of inhumanity. In "Strife" he showed us a conflict, and in "Fraternity" a contrast, between the poor and the rich; and the implicit moral of the play was that this conflict would be for ever. If things are irremediable, why, it might be asked, harrow us about them? To which, I take it, Mr. Galsworthy's answer would be that to recognise the sadness of things is a duty we owe to honesty, and is good for our souls. In "Justice," however, there is no fundamental pessimism. Mr. Galsworthy sees that our criminal law and our penal system are clumsy, mechanical, mischievous. But he sees them as things not beyond redemption. A little spurring of the scientific intelligence in us and of our common humanity is all that is needed to induce reform. Perfect justice there can never be, of course; but the folly and barbarism of our present method—which is far less barbarous and foolish now than it used to be—can be amended. Already it is a universal axiom that society's duty to the criminal lies not in avenging itself on him but in reforming him. Let practice be adjusted to theory. At present our practice is mainly in accord with a theory discredited. The method of solitary confinement, for example, is good merely as a torture. And it is against this particular part of our penal system that Mr. Galsworthy directs his strongest shafts. No one, nowadays, has a word in defence of solitary confinement. And I shall be surprised if Mr. Galsworthy has not delivered its death-blow. The cell-scene in the third act is, for purposes of horror, more effective than tomes of written words, however pungent. When the curtain falls, the auditorium is as silent as the very prison whose silence the convict has just broken by hammering with his fists against his door; and not even when, a moment later, the curtain rises, and we see Mr. Dennis Eadie cheerfully bowing his acknowledgments to us, is the horror undone. Cheerfully? No, I am very sure that Mr. Eadie is too fine an artist not to shudder at this rising of the curtain—this bland, idiotic attempt, on the part of the management, to undo the horror.

"THE MADRAS HOUSE"

March 19, 1910

Two or three weeks ago, when I was depreciating Mr. Shaw's "Misalliance," I was careful not to say anything against his preference of a "debate" to a play in the ordinary sense of the word. But (if I remember rightly) I pleaded that a debate, to be effective on the stage, must have some sort of unity. In art you cannot do without form. Nor, for that matter, can you very well do without it in life. Suppose the debates in the House of Commons were conducted in the manner of Mr. Shaw's. Suppose that Mr. Lowther had been deposed from his chair, and that G. B. S. reigned in his stead. There would be no calling to order. Every member would be allowed to talk of whatever thing were uppermost in his head, without relevance to the set topic. Nay, there would be no set topic. Mr. Speaker would regard set topics as an old-fashioned method of crippling and sterilising the senate. Consequently, there could be no "winding-up" of the debate from the two front benches, and no "division." The debate would go on and on, the members revelling in their freedom, until Mr. Shaw, prevented by his office from talking himself, and bound by the same token to sit and listen with an air of polite interest, gradually pined away at his post and died there. There would be a certain poetic justice in that sombre conclusion to the proceedings. But the strangers in the gallery, as they filed out with bowed heads and noiseless footsteps, would not have for consolation the feeling that they had attended a memorable and useful debate.

On the other hand, any one who leaves the Duke of York's Theatre after the third act of "The Madras House" will feel that he has derived an immense amount of amusement and instruction. For here is a debate that has unity. Mr. Granville Barker sticks to his theme. We know where we are. A steady flame burns for us, in place of mere showers of disappearing sparks. In the fourth act the flame still burns, but only in its socket, and dimly. The debate has gone on long enough, and what Mr. Barker has left over to the last is in itself of inferior interest. Thus your gratitude to him is like to be mitigated unless you depart immediately after the magnificent third act. Take this advice. I wish there had been somebody to advise *me*.

The unifying principle of the play is that the theme throughout is the present and future of woman—woman regarded from various standpoints, moral, æsthetic, economic, and so on. There is no lack of men in the play, all of them sharply-differentiated types, but the main reason for their existence is not in the presentment of them as types, but in their typical contributions to the discussion of the theme. They are far out-numbered by the women. Some of these are elaborate studies, and with any amount to say for themselves; whilst others, such as the five unmarried daughters in the suburban home, and the three "mannequins" in the drapery shop, are as the chemicals which in certain experiments do but "act by their presence"—inobtrusive figures, yet philosophically significant, needed by the theme. Nor is it merely in theme that this debate coheres. Its manner is one throughout. In

38

"Misalliance" Mr. Shaw constantly changes his manner for fear of boring us; as when he introduces an acrobat on an aeroplane. He makes his characters mostly comic in order to compensate us for the serious views they are to express. This is a manœuvre that defeats itself. We can listen with pleasure to the jests of serious people. (That is one of the reasons why Mr. Shaw achieved his great popularity.) But we cannot take clowns seriously. A clown straddling about with a red-hot poker is all very well, in his way. But the clown at the lectern won't do at all. There is nothing specifically funny about the characters in "The Madras House." They are all a trifle exaggerated and simplified, so that their typical qualities be brought out and carried across the footlights. But this process is used no further than the art of the theatre rightly demands it. Every character in the play is a true study, made by a man with a lust for accurate observation, and with an immense talent for sympathy. Yes, perhaps it is not so much sympathy that Mr. Barker has as an immense talent for it. He is sympathetic through sheer force of intellect. So would Mr. Shaw be if he could (or, let us say, if he chose to) observe men and women accurately instead of inventing in some dark corner of his soul men and women with whom not all the concentrated forces of his intellect can make him sympathise. In "The Madras House" there is only one character that does not stand forth vital and salient; and this is the character of Philip Madras, the wise and good young man who is always in the right—always perspicacious, unselfish, and charitable by virtue of being himself so shadowy and cold. It is a note that pervades modern drama, this doctrine that human beings are always hopelessly in the wrong, and that only the inhuman ones can hope to be in the right. I don't say it is a false doctrine; but it certainly is a lugubrious one. And we must be pardoned for a certain measure of impatience with Philip Madras. Repressing our impulse to call him an impostor, and hailing him reverently as pope, we can't, even so, stand him— whether we feel we are in the right with him or in the wrong with the others.

And unluckily it is on him that the last act of the play mainly depends. We have already had many glimpses of his perspicacity, unselfishness, and charitableness; glimpses only. But now, so soon as the other characters, with the exception of Mrs. Philip, have taken leave of us, he asserts himself at great length. It is a very long, very quiet conversation that he has with his wife; and the upshot of it is that the one chance for a man who hopes in this chaotic and evil world to preserve his self-respect, the one chance for him not to be crushed under the collapsing edifices of our jerry-built civilisation, is that he become a member of the London County Council. Slipped somewhere into the middle of the play, this discourse might be interesting enough, but it is not nearly interesting enough to be otherwise than a tedious anti-climax to the tensity of the first three acts. The first act is tense as a pre-paration, and as a picture—a picture of prosperous suburban life, a picture of Sunday afternoon in a large new drawing-room that commands a view of the Crystal Palace. Not all the drawings of Charles Keene could give us a firmer impression than Mr. Barker here gives us of typical middle-class life. It is as though we our-selves had spent Sunday afternoon in the bosom of the Huxtable family—nay, innumerable Sunday afternoons in the bosom of in-numerable families like them. It is a stupendous synthesis. In the second act the venue is changed; we are away from the Misses Huxtable (though they haunt us), and from Mrs. Madras, the long-ago-deserted of Mr. Madras. There has been (as indicated in the first act) a scandal in the drapery shop of which Mr. Hux-table is chief proprietor. One of the female staff has been seduced. Mr. Huxtable has failed to handle the matter satisfactorily to him-self: he has heard his voice "saying things" in which he didn't believe, though he believed on principle that they were the correct things to say. So now Mr. Philip Madras has been left to deal with the matter. On the one hand is Miss Chancellor, the over-seer of the establishment, who holds the bitter conventional view. On the other, Mrs. Brigstock, wife of an employee who "lives in" —an excitable woman, who believes that she has cause for jealousy. Both women are admirably presented. But the principal study is that of Miss Yates, the delinquent—a capable young person, who does not in the least regret what she has done, and is, on the con-trary, glad and proud of it, though her spiritual revolt does not preclude passing doubts—"I suppose I am bad. Perhaps I de-serve to 'go under.' I don't know!" From this particular study the play opens to general issues. The third act ranges at large over the whole position of woman in modern life. The discussion

is carried on mainly by Constantine Madras (a convert to Moham-
medanism) and Mr. Eustace Perrin State (a deeply sentimental
American "hustler," with all the leisureliness of his kind; altogether the truest presentment of an American ever made by an
Englishman, and acted with quite uncanny realism by Mr. Arthur
Whitby). It is impossible to give any idea of the breadth and
brilliancy of this scene. There is deeper and nimbler thought in
it, and richer humour, than in any scene known to me in modern
drama. I am impatient to possess it in a book. By this I do not
mean that it has not on the stage certain qualities that it would lose
in a library. It is thoroughly dramatic, by the contrast of the
characters of the talkers; and the talkers are vivid characters who
gain by being presented in actual flesh and blood. But their talk
is too good for us not to want it in a form that can be held captive.

In praising "The Madras House" so highly after my disparagement of "Misalliance," I ought, in decency, not to forget how
much Mr. Barker owes to Mr. Shaw. He was not, of course,
created by Mr. Shaw; but deeply influenced he was and is. I hope
he will now repay the debt by deeply influencing Mr. Shaw. Then
I shall be as happy as the day is long.

"A FASHIONABLE TRAGEDIAN"

April 2, 1910

If I had never read "Othello," nor ever seen it played, my visit
to the Lyric Theatre last Wednesday evening would not have
helped me towards appreciation of that masterpiece in tragic art.
"Othello" is one thing; "Otello (Tragedia in Cinque Atti di W.
Shakespeare)" is another; at least, for me. The Italian version
may be quite worthy of the original. For aught I know, the translator—so far from being the usual "tradditore"—may have intensified the beauty and dignity of thought and language, and the
fineness of characterisation, brought by "W. Shakespeare" to
bear on the Italian novel which gave him the scheme of the play.
Unluckily, I don't understand Italian—not even when it is spoken

by Sicilians. (I wish I were any one of my colleagues in dramatic criticism.) Hoping that perhaps intuition might come to rescue my lack of learning, I listened to "Otello" with both ears pricked up unremittingly. My reward, at the end of the evening, was in having caught from time to time the words "io," "Otello," "basta," "tradditore," and "non," quite distinctly, and with a very shrewd guess at their meaning. I do not pretend I was not rather proud of this. "I was able to say grace for the temperate meal the gods had spread for me in the wilderness of my withered hopes." But there the wilderness was. The five words or so that I had understood—what were they as compared with the immensely copious vocabulary which Shakespeare used with such fine discrimination? Stripped of Shakespeare's language, and preserving (for me) merely the action and structure of "Othello" (the action syncopated, and the structure hacked about, to suit the modern Italian taste, which I have no reason to suppose better in drama than it is in architecture, painting, and other arts), "Otello" seemed to me no better than a dismal throwback to the form which Shakespeare had transmuted. It came out as a tedious tale about a brave and good but incredibly stupid soldier who, by the machinations of a not very clever villain of the deepest dye, smothered his wife with a bed-pillow and presently cut his own throat. It came out as the sort of thing which, ruthlessly abbreviated, and transposed into modern life, would do very well at the Grand-Guignol. It did not come out as anything nearly related to a work of tragic art.

Is that a frown I can see on your brow, fashionable reader? a gleam of gathering wrath in your fine eyes? Have you been wondering why I did not begin this article with a wild whoop to the greater glory of Giovanni Grasso? And now is there surging in your breast—that once mild breast, now grown seemingly so fierce through your choice of so fierce an idol—a horrible suspicion that the whoop is not going to be uttered by me at all? I see your fingers twitching convulsively around the long Sicilian dagger which you bought in Wardour Street soon after Signor Grasso first appeared in London, two or three years ago. You glower fixedly at me, making very odd noises in your throat. O spare me, Sir, spare me! In the title-rôle Grasso was, of course, absolutely superb; not only did he look the part marvellously well,

but by temperament and method he is absolutely fitted to play it.
—But no, taking my courage in both hands, and relying on the
chance that you are quite a mild person really (nay, taking your
hankering after savagery to be an indication that you are very mild
indeed), I confess that the foregoing sentence is not my own. I
copied it out of the current number of a popular weekly newspaper.
To me, when I went to the Lyric Theatre, it was *not* a matter of
course that Grasso would be absolutely superb. I am somehow
not at the mercy of those gusts of hysteria which from time to time
sweep over London. I was glad, but not mad, when Mafeking
was relieved. And when Grasso on his first visit made London
crazy I was as little impelled to acclaim him thereby the greatest
of actors as I had been to acclaim Baden-Powell the greatest of
soldiers. "Malia," the only play in which I saw him, was a play
in which he had little chance of acting. I wrote here that he was
distinguished in bearing, and that he might be, for aught I knew, a
tragedian ; but I refused to confound with great tragic acting the
contortions of Aguglia, who was at that time the leading lady, and
on whom lay the whole burden of "Malia." When this article
appeared, many of my most intimate acquaintances behaved quite
coldly to me. They were disappointed in me. They had known
that I had faults, but that blasphemy was one of these had never
occurred to them. A little while, and the matter blew over, the
wound was healed. On my way to the Lyric Theatre last Wednesday I was hoping the wound would not be re-opened. Such
prejudice as I had was all in favour of Signor Grasso. Othello
himself was not a more unwilling executioner than I am. "It is
the cause, it is the cause, my soul!"

Othello was certainly a great animal ; but not less certainly he was
also a great gentleman—a knight, in whom simplicity was the
reflection of a spirit noble and high. The animal side of his nature
has been no more than suggested by such English actors as I have
seen in the part. Signor Grasso certainly gives us the great
animal for all it is worth ; but in itself it is not, in relation to tragic
art, worth very much. Only when it exists as a part of the great
gentleman can the true Othello be shown to us. By Grasso the
great gentleman is not (except in the scene of the council chamber)
suggested. Physically, Grasso is greater than when he first visited
England. He has—not to put too fine a point on it—grown rather

stout. And this development, together with an odd mannerism in walking—a careful planting of the feet and swaying of the elbows, supposed by our music-hall comedians to be characteristic of our costermongers—undoes that distinction of bearing which he signally had in "Malia." In the scene of the council chamber, where he stood quite still, draped in a white cloak, all was well. Spiritually not less than physically he suggested the Moor of Shakespeare, speaking his lines with the massive reserve appropriate to their meaning. And only when Desdemona appeared, and he, instead of merely not looking at her, shut his eyes tight and kept them so, in the manner of a child at hide-and-seek, did I begin to suspect that so soon as Othello was no longer on his best behaviour before the Doge he would be just a Sicilian "handful," splendid in point of vitality, no doubt, but nowhere on the plane of tragic significance. As I have said, I was unable to understand the words of the play; and it is possible that Signor Grasso's interpretation of them was as good as they deserved. But to regard him as from the English standpoint a passable Othello—let alone a "superb" one—is possible only to people who cannot distinguish tragedy from "knock-about." I don't disparage the latter art. All honour to Signor Grasso that when he threw Signor Campagno down on the stage, and stamped on him, it really did seem as though every bone in Signor Campagno's body must have been broken. But let not the public suppose that the thrills it derives from the stupendous and unlovely roarings and rampings and gruntings of Signor Grasso throughout the play are the thrills that we derive from the contemplation of tragedy. The public, not to be outdone by its hero, roars stupendously when this Othello, having bared his throat and gashed it slowly across with his knife, drags himself to the foot of Desdemona's bed and proceeds to "gargle" realistically. But let not the public suppose that its delight in sheer physical horror has anything to do with those emotions of pity and awe which are the tragedian's target. Strength Signor Grasso has. Dignity, a sense of beauty, intellect, he may have; but there is no sign of them. Let us admire his strength. For the good of the theatrical profession, let us urge him to remain among us, another Eugen Sandow, willing to impart his secret to those who have need of it. But let us not make fools of ourselves about his alleged Othello.

HABIT

April 16, 1910

Some writers have a dread of platitudes. I have not. What is a platitude but an expression of the wisdom of the ages, the synopsis of a theory that was long ago propounded, tested, established, never subverted? Truth, of course, is a delicate and many-sided affair. For every platitude there is at least one other platitude to dilute and qualify it. Thus, when we speak of ourselves as "creatures of habit," let us not forget to throw in something about "the charm of novelty." And never let our love of novelty break us of our wholesome habit of platitudinising. It is good fun to say quite a new thing—marred though the fun is by the certainty that our message has been delivered by forerunners, and forgotten by mankind, times out of number. To utter a quite old thing, to be the mouthpiece of sanctified and indisputable lore, is, or ought to be, an august gratification. When next you find a platitude on the tip of your tongue, do not slur it out apologetically. Examine it, test it, for the first time, maybe, with a fresh eye; steep yourself in the truth of it: rejoicing, you will then roll it off your tongue, the manner it deserves.

"We are creatures of habit," for example. Perhaps you have never realised how deep this saying cuts. You are aware (though all due allowance be made for "the charm of novelty") that the oftener you do a thing that you like doing, the more you like doing it. I do not know what morning paper you read at breakfast; but certainly, if you have read that particular paper every morning for many years, it has acquired a hold on you that none of its contemporaries could now relax. I do not know what is your method of reading it. My own newspaper I approach always through its outskirts, lightly lingering over the reviews of books on the one hand, and the law reports on the other, all the while listening to, but not obeying, the insistent call of the central page, which may or may not contain some tremendous piece of news to stir the very depths of my soul. Such is my procedure. Yours may be to envisage straightway the central page. Yours may be the better. There is no reason why I should not have acquired it in the first instance. But, if it were forced on me now, all the magic of my morning would be stripped away. The tobacco you smoke after breakfast may be better than mine. But, thank you, I prefer my own. The brand has deteriorated in quality since first I began to smoke it. But, while life lasts, allegiance will not waver. I know not which seat at which luncheon table in your club is preferred by you. Probably you could not justify your preference. Probably you would be puzzled to account for the various preferences that spangle your daily life. They are not of reason, but of habit. Opening the morning paper, lighting one's tobacco after breakfast, sitting down to luncheon—all these are pleasant functions. It is no wonder that the oftener we perform them, the higher we rate them, the closer we cling to them. Habit's signal triumph is in the power to endear to us even such things as are in themselves repellent.

I cull, at random, one simple illustration from the diary of my own days. What is more repellent than an oil-stove? Two or three years ago, in mid-winter, I went to spend a week in an ancient rustic inn. The proprietor conducted me to my bedroom. This was nobly panelled and had an ample Jacobean grate and hearth, to which I pointed admiringly, saying I should like the fire lit at once. The proprietor was very sorry: the chimney-pot had been blown off, and if the fire were lit the room would be full of smoke. He hoped the damage could be repaired to-morrow or next day; and meanwhile he would bring me a small stove which gave out ample heat. This instrument—a sort of upstanding cylinder, freshly black-leaded—was promptly installed. It was a thing of mean, incongruous, and sinister aspect. It might have been a patent hive for black-beetles. Certain little bits of red and green glass inlaid in the top of it, for the purpose of cheeriness, especially annoyed me. It gave out very little heat. It filled the room with an unctuous, cloying odour. I hated and despised it. And yet, when, four days later, I came in from a long walk, and found, in the stove's stead, a beautiful big fire roaring in the grate, somehow I was stricken with a sense of loss. I had grown used to the little stove. It had had its faults. But which of us is perfect? It had done its best. So far as in it lay, it had served me well. And now it was gone. And it had never had one kind look from me. I realised, too late, the habit that had endeared it to me.

At the risk of being thought egoistic, I cull from the diary of my days another instance of habit's alchemy. Twelve long years, all but a short month or two, have elapsed since I became a dramatic critic. I had no desire to become one. "G. B. S." had just stepped aside : I found myself in his place, blinking. Had I been told that I was destined to write about plays for twelve weeks, I should have shuddered. Had I been told that I was destined to write about them for twelve years, I should have expired on the spot, neatly falsifying the prediction. But Fate weaves in darkness (which perhaps is why she weaves so badly), and it was not long before I acquired a vivid interest in the thing that, unbeknown to me, was going to take up so much of my time on this planet. Not that my pen ever ran away with me. I do not recall that I have once sat down eager to write, or that I have once written with ease and delight. But the cause of this lack was not in the nature of my theme. It was in myself. Writing has always been uphill work to me, mainly because I am cursed with an acute literary conscience. To seem to write with ease and delight is one of the duties which a writer owes to his readers, to his art. And to contrive that effect involves very great skill and care : it is a matter of technique, a matter of construction partly, and partly of choice of words and cadences. There may be—I have never met one— writers who enjoy the act of writing ; but without that technique their enjoyment will not be manifest. I may often have failed in my articles here, to disguise labour. But the effort to disguise it has always been loyally made. And thus it is that Thursday, the day chosen by me (as being the latest possible one) for writing my article, has for twelve years been regarded by me as the least pleasant day of the week. On Wednesday I have had always a certain sense of oppression, of misgiving, even of dread. On Friday—the danger past, the sun shining, my feet dancing ! And yet (such is habit, and so subtle a thing the human organism), whenever I have let pass a Thursday I have felt uncomfortable, unsatisfied, throughout the day. Even during my annual holiday, away from England, when I have kept no count of the days of the week, I have always recognised Thursday by the vague feeling of inanition in me, of impatience—the sort of feeling a clock may have when it has not been wound up. And I am wondering now, as I write, just how I shall feel next Thursday, and on the Thursdays to come.

HABIT

Last week Mr. Runciman wrote in this Review suggesting that we two should retire to a desert island and stay there until the respective vogues of Dr. Strauss and Signor Grasso had blown over. Very well: what island shall we go to? and what boat shall we sail by? I am quite ready. But I fear my comrade's is too belligerent a nature to tear itself away from the thick of the hurly-burly. I myself am not such a peace-at-any-price man as to be frightened away by Signor Grasso. Let no one suppose that the retreat I beat is not a dignified one. For some weeks I have been meaning to beat it; and now the hour happens to have come. And the reason for my resolve is not in any feeling that I have said all that is in me to say about drama and acting. The reason is in a feeling that twelve years is a rather long time for any man to devote to the consideration of those two arts. So farewell, my readers! And farewell, my Thursdays!

Is love of my readers as strong in me as hatred of my Thursdays? It is not half so strong. I feel extraordinarily light and gay in writing this farewell—at least, I shall so soon as I have finished it. And yet (to return to the actual theme of my essay) habit is mighty; and habit, which made me mourn in retrospect that abhorred oil-stove, may yet make me envy my successor here. And you, by the same token, will miss me a little, for a little while? Ah, you don't know who my successor is.

INDEX OF PLAYS (AND BOOKS)
CRITICISED

INDEX

INDEX